Irish Examiner
100 YEARS OF NEWS

Irish Examiner
100 YEARS OF NEWS

Edited by DES O'DRISCOLL

Gill & Macmillan
in association with the *Irish Examiner*

Gill & Macmillan Ltd
Hume Avenue
Park West
Dublin 12
with associated companies throughout the world
www.gillmacmillan.ie

0 7171 3913 1

Design and Layout by Designit
Index compiled by Julitta Clancy
Printed by Butler & Tanner, Frome

The paper used in this book is made from the wood pulp of managed forests. For every tree felled, at least one tree is planted, thereby renewing natural resources.

A catalogue record is available for this book from the British Library.

1 3 5 4 2

Introduction

The *Irish Examiner – 100 Years of News* is the first book of its kind in Ireland. Commissioned to commemorate Cork 2005: European Capital of Culture, it takes a look at how the only Irish daily broadsheet newspaper published outside Dublin has presented the magnificently varied elements of life in this country and beyond, between 1905 and 2005.

Stories from each year are presented as they were originally written, along with pictures from our archives and reproductions of actual newspaper pages, to present a unique flavour of the era.

While the book obviously contains a huge amount of historical information, it is categorically not a history book, and should not be viewed as such. Reports and photographs are presented as they appeared and are therefore devoid of historical perspective. Similarly, the selection of material has not been informed by a desire to produce a book of the most important events between 1905 and 2005. If it were, the furore over Jayne Mansfield's visit to Tralee in 1967 would hardly have made it onto page 120 ahead of other more significant national and international events of that year. No, the selection of material has been informed by a desire that the book entertains as well as informs; so worthy historical perspective has had to take a metaphorical back seat.

Major figures such as Michael Collins, John F Kennedy and Osama Bin Laden feature, of course, but so do stories such as the conflict between broadcaster Gay Byrne and the church in the 1960s, the 'horsenapping' of Shergar, and the mystery over who shot JR Ewing, which kept the nation enthralled in the glum 1980s. As such, the book provides a fascinating insight into the actual issues that people were talking about at the time.

Obviously, for a sports-mad nation, sports have been a major component of the newspaper over the decades, so the book revisits memorable occasions such as the débâcle of Saipan in 2002, the unprecedented national celebration during that incomparable summer of Italia '90, the magical artistry of Christy Ring, Stephen Roche's Tour de France victory, numerous great GAA encounters and vintage occasions, and Ireland's first Grand Slam in rugby.

For much of the last century, the newspaper's front pages were devoid of photographs, carried little news and were largely devoted to advertisements. This was common to all newspapers of the time, so the 'front pages' reproduced here for several decades have been reconstructed from different elements of the newspaper, using the revolutionary concept of bringing news stories, photographs and advertisements together on Page 1!

While the *Irish Examiner* began life as the *Cork Examiner* in 1841 – which makes it Ireland's oldest daily newspaper – coverage here of the hundred years since 1905 pays tribute to the paper's southern home city in the year when it carries the mantle of Europe's Capital of Culture, the first Irish city to do so. After 140 years of being published as the *Cork Examiner*, the title changed to the *Examiner* during an expansionist move in 1996 and became the *Irish Examiner* in 2000 as the newspaper's national audience continued to grow.

The paper has held an important place in its home city's culture since its inception, and its base there has often given it special access to numerous stories of national and international importance – from staff photographer Tom Barker's last photographs on the deck of the *Titanic* (complete with deckchairs) before it set off on its ill-fated journey from Queenstown (known today as Cobh, of course), to the award-winning coverage of the Air India disaster in 1985, to exclusive insights into Ireland's most prominent sporting personality of recent times, Roy Keane.

In an age of instant international communication through the internet, it is interesting to note that the newspaper's location in Cork frequently allowed it exclusive European access to world news in the late 19th and early 20th centuries. Before the laying of a telegraph cable between Ireland and America, news from the New World would first reach the Old World when the trans-Atlantic liners docked in Europe. And because Queenstown was the first port of call, reporters from the then *Cork Examiner*, who would row out to meet the liners, would often have important international stories before the major European newspapers, such as *The Times* of London.

One such reporter was Thomas Crosbie, who was an invaluable aide to the newspaper's founder and owner, John Francis Maguire. Crosbie was a hard-working and enterprising young man who would diligently source the trans-Atlantic liners for news, which he would subsequently relay to the London *Times*, for whom he was an invaluable 'stringer'. (So invaluable that he was offered a well-paid staff job, only for the offer to be withdrawn when the people at *The Times* made the appalling discovery that he was a Catholic!)

That was prior to the 100-year ambit of this book, but it helps set the unique context in which the newspaper has operated from its very beginnings. Initially it was an evening broadsheet, with a small circulation in the southern capital; today, while still proud of its Cork and Munster heritage, it enjoys a respected national platform and provides a vibrant and challenging daily alternative to the Dublin-based print and broadcast media.

Tim Vaughan
Editor, *Irish Examiner*, 2005

Editor's Acknowledgments

Firstly, thanks to Lillian Caverly and Joe Healy for all their work on processing the photographs; to Fintan Lane for his excellent research and Eddie Butt for his design suggestions. Also, at the *Irish Examiner*, thanks to all those who made suggestions and contributions, including Margaret Von Mensenkampff, Des Quinn, Declan Ryan, John O'Donovan, Tim O'Brien, Anne Kearney, Donal Musgrave, Paul McCarthy, Liam Moher, Pat Maloney, Mairéad Maher, Catherine Lougheed, Pat Good, Suzanne Crosbie, Kieran Bohane and Paddy Barker. In addition, thanks to Kieran Burke at the Cork City Library and Donal Ó Drisceoil at University College, Cork and thanks to Krish Naidoo and Helen McDonnell.

Among the books that provided invaluable background information were: *20th Century Ireland* by Dermot Keogh; *The Newspaper Book* by Hugh Oram; *The Irish Times Book of the Century* edited by Fintan O'Toole; *An Outline of Modern Irish History* by ME Collins; *Censorship in Ireland 1939–45* by Donal Ó Drisceoil and Longman's *The Chronicle of the 20th Century*.

Picture Credits

The *Examiner* was the first newspaper in Ireland to employ a full-time photographer and has also retained its superb collection of glass plates and other photo negatives through the decades. Not all of these photographs are credited to specific photographers, so I would like to acknowledge the work of Tom Barker Snr, John O'Keefe, Tommy O'Brien, Tom Barker, Louis McMonagle, Michael O'Kelly, Roy Hammond, Cyril Perrott, Sean Horgan, Michael Minihane, Richard Mills, Donal Sheehan, Michael Olney, Des Barry, Denis Scannell, Denis Minihane, Eddie O'Hare, Maurice O'Mahony, Paddy Barker, Dan Linehan, Norma Cuddihy, Dennis Scannell, Pat Good, Brian Lougheed, Billy Higgins, Gavin Brown, John O'Keeffe and Kieran Clancy.

1905

In 1905, Ireland was a relatively integrated part of the British Empire. Home Rule was being pushed by MPs in Westminster, and Arthur Griffith was in the process of launching Sinn Féin, but the Irish at the time were more peaceful than in other colonies, such as Tibet and Zululand.

Landlords were still powerful, but a major transfer of land to the ownership of the tenants was well underway and a huge class of small farmers was being created.

Industry was mainly comprised of flour mills, textiles and the manufacture of alcohol in the southern counties, while shipbuilding and linen helped make Belfast the industrial capital of the island.

Women couldn't vote and there were still plenty of people alive who had experienced the famine. Extreme poverty was common in both the cites and rural areas, though there was also a sizeable middle class which had helped foster the 'Irish Renaissance' of which the Abbey Theatre was a major part.

The Wright brothers had made their first flight barely one year earlier in America, and the sea played a central part in many Irish people's lives. The *Examiner* at the time carried daily accounts of liner and cargo traffic, as well as shipwrecks and drownings. Rather than being on the periphery of Europe, the island was at a very strategic location on the transatlantic travel and trade routes.

Events involving Russia dominated the international news for the year. The Czar's state was engaged in a bloody war with Japan, and domestic strife increased when Cossacks killed hundreds of people in St Petersburg on Bloody Sunday.

Terrible carnage in Russia

Monday, January 23

St Petersburg - The city has been plunged into a state of open revolution. The trouble began at 11 o'clock when the military tried to turn back some of the thousands of Putiloff strikers at one of the bridges.

The Cossacks at first used their knouts, then the flat of their sabres; finally they fired. The strikers in the front ranks fell on their knees and implored the Cossacks to let them pass, protesting that they had no hostile intentions. They refused, however, to be intimidated by blank cartridges, and orders were given to load with ball. The passions of the mob broke loose like a bursting dam. The people, seeing the dead and dying carried away in all directions and the snow on the streets and pavements soaked with blood, cried aloud for vengeance. Meanwhile at the Palace, the order was given to open fire also. Men, women and children fell at each volley and were carried away in ambulances, sledges and carts.

Trams on Patrick's Street, Cork.

Enthusiastic welcome of eviction defenders

Friday, June 23

The proceedings in the city in honour of the release of the 21 defenders of Fort Murphy, who were imprisoned three months ago in connection with the now famous Watergrasshill eviction, supplied an eloquent and stirring tribute of appreciation from the Nationalists of the city of the brave and sturdy stand made on that occasion against landlordism.

About one o'clock a procession was formed, and headed by a green banner. Along the route to Annascarthy bridge not a house or cottage but bore evidence of the people's appreciation of the occasion.

The lengthy train of brakes, cars and horsemen swept triumphantly on until the village of Watergrasshill was reached and here they were received with the wildest enthusiasm. With the exception of the local barracks, every house in the village sported laurels and bunting in profusion whilst two large festoons of greenery, one bearing the words 'Céad Míle Fáilte' and the other 'Remember Fort Murphy', spanned the street.

NEWS BRIEFS

Mar Maryland, USA - Most interesting sequels are coming to light of the death of Edward McKenna, native of Ireland, octogenarian fruit gardener and expert fruit grower. In his home 3,700 dollars were found behind pictures of the Crucifixion and of Pope Leo XXIII. (18)

The strange case of two women - mother and daughter - who have been lying in a comatose condition in the Presbyterian Hospital for a fortnight is interesting to the entire medical faculty of New York. It was at first thought that the women were suffering from gas poisoning, but after a consultation today the doctors decided that they had hypnotised each other. (24)

Sept The death was announced of Dr Thomas John Barnardo, the Irish philanthropist who had set up schools and other institutions for destitute children.(21)

1906

The sizeable Irish population in San Francisco ensured a significant amount of interest in Ireland when the city was hit by a devastating earthquake in April.

Several Irish people won medals at the Olympics in Athens, but they weren't officially representing Ireland. When the Union Jack was hoisted at the long jump medals ceremony, silver-winning Peter O'Connor from Wicklow scaled the flagpole, ripped down the offending ensign and waved a green flag in its place while fellow jumper, Con Leahy from Charleville, stood guard at the base of the pole.

In politics, a general election brought a Liberal victory which would herald the beginnings of the welfare state, while the Irish Party under William O'Brien was the main representative of constitutional nationalism in Westminster. The more militant tradition saw the continued growth of the IRB and Sinn Féin.

The year was bookended by terrible weather which caused several shipwrecks and many casualties.

San Francisco in ruins

Friday, April 30

The earthquake disaster in the States is even more terrible than the first reports made it appear. San Francisco is still burning. Over 5,000 lives have been lost, and 200,000 people are homeless. The Irish quarter is in ruins.

Messages of sympathy have been sent from Mr John Redmond MP on behalf of the Irish Party, and the Lord Mayor of Dublin.

Mr Anthony, a business man, gives the following vivid description of the disaster. He was sleeping in the Ramona Hotel when at six o'clock he was awakened suddenly by the first shock, and leapt hurriedly out of bed. He saw a score or more of people killed. Women became hysterical and prayed in the streets, while the men sat on the kerbstones in an apparently dazed condition. The whole earth seemed to heave and fall.

Skibbereen – The appalling catastrophe reported in this day's *Examiner* caused feelings of gloom and widespread apprehension in this town and district. Several hundred people from West Cork have made homes in the 'Golden Gate of the West', and the intelligence of the havoc caused by the earthquake and fire came on the people here this morning in the nature of a shock. Large numbers of families from the district have sons and daughters, relatives and friends, in the stricken city.

Picking raspberries at a farm on the banks of the River Lee, Cork.

Celtic struck by a wave

Tuesday, January 2

The White Star liner *Celtic* was struck by a mighty wave on Christmas night. Portions of the great bulwarks were ripped off and swept away, 50 rivets, one and a half inches thick, being drawn out like carpet tacks. An iron door, weighing four tons, was torn from its hinges, and flung 50 feet away.

Fifteen women were gathered around a Christmas tree in the second saloon. They were flung to the floor by the shock and many of them fainted from terror. A group stood round the piano in the music saloon. One man, who was playing 'Sing me to Sleep', was flung from his seat and stunned. Another took his place and, while the water swept the decks above, stayed the panic by shouting the words of an old English song.

Man cuts throat in Dublin

Friday, January 5

In the presence of numerous passers-by a middle-aged man, named William Jameson, took out a razor and drew it across his throat, inflicting an ugly wound. He then threw the razor under the seat on which he was sitting at the time and ran along Stephen's Green and Grafton Street, with blood flowing freely from his throat. He caused a sensation in the crowded thoroughfare, and his appearance soon attracted the attention of a police constable who pursued and captured him. The injured man was taken to Mercer's Hospital where he was attended.

NEWS BRIEFS

Jan The last gale, whenever it blows, is always said to be the worst, but if ever the storm which is raging since three o'clock yesterday has been equalled, it must tax the memory of the eldest to say when. (1)

The Queenstown route for American mail purposes was fairly dealt with during the past month, inasmuch as 25,000 bags of mail matter, to and from America, passed through the Queenstown Railway Station. (5)

Oct At a sitting of the Royal Commission into the Congested Districts Board held at Burtonport, Co Donegal, the high percentage of illiteracy in the area was attributed to the fact that children had to be hired out for economic purposes. One witness said the average age at which children were hired was nine years, but he also knew of a case where a four-year-old had been hired out. (12)

1907

Guglielmo Marconi had strong links with Ireland even before he opened the world's first point-to-point wireless telegraphy station at Clifden in October. The great inventor's mother was Irish and he was married to Beatrice O'Brien from the aristocratic family based at Dromoland Castle, Co Clare.

As the report below shows, the opening of the Clifden facility was of huge significance as it made the County Galway station the main point for communications between North America and Europe.

In Dublin, JM Synge sparked disturbances when his new play didn't fit with the idealised version of Ireland being promoted by the Gaelic League.

Wireless system opens in Clifden

Friday, October 18

If there is a limit to man's inventive genius the time is not yet, nor can we read it in the dim mists of the future. Expert brains are at present at work on some of the most momentous inventions of the age. These for the most part are in the elementary stages of their progress, but one - and that perhaps the most remarkable in the world's history - has today reached the high pinnacle of complete fruition.

A permanent and apparently flawless system of communication by means of wireless telegraphy has been opened between the Marconigram Stations at Port Morien, Nova Scotia, and Clifden, County Galway.

Whilst the problem of man's flight in the air still remains, to put it mildly, imperfected, this other mighty aerial problem has been solved by the ingenuity of a man who, we are proud to know, is bounded by several links with the Green Isle. Today must be written down as a big red letter day in the history of the scientific world.

The controlling mechanism enables an ordinary Morse telegraph instrument to be brought into use, and the operator can be seen tapping the key of this instrument on a table before him in a conventional manner. The mere pressure of the fingers on the key is enough to send 20,000 volts of electricity flying up into the connection room overhead, where a series of flashes and peculiar noises accompany the completion of the electric circuit.

The Marconi Station at Clifden.

Public houses close early

Monday, January 7

On Saturday night by the operation of the new Licensing Act the public houses in Cork closed at 10 o'clock, and brief though the curtailment of the drinking hours was, its salutary effects were plainly visible.

Anybody who walked the streets at 11 o'clock could not fail to be impressed by the change. The Saturday night of the past with its knots and groups of evicted ones standing outside public house doors arguing or articulating with that precious disregard for coherency and logic, was but a thing of the memory and instead there was a quietness and an orderliness.

Uproar at Abbey over Synge's *Playboy*

Tuesday, January 29

There were uproarious scenes tonight at the performance of Mr Synge's play *The Playboy of the Western World* at the Abbey Theatre. The play deals rather unfavourably with Irish character, the central figure being a rough customer who has nearly murdered his own father and who on account of this great feat is beloved by several women.

The first performance on Saturday evening passed off in comparative quiet, but after the unfavourable notices in the Press a number of Gaelic Leaguers turned up to express their feelings upon it. Shortly after its opening, hisses, groans and disorder broke out. There was stamping of feet and beating of sticks, and the din was terrific.

Mr Fay, who took the principal part, essayed to get a hearing. He was understood to say that he was a Mayo man himself and that no insult was intended to his county.

The police were called in and they entered amid loud groans and took up their positions in the pit.

At the end of each act the players bowed their acknowledgments ironically, and the uproar was thereby increased. The performance was brought to a conclusion in this disorder.

NEWS BRIEFS

Jan Seventy-five stands were in operation at Ireland's first ever motor show at the Showgrounds, Ballsbridge, Dublin. Among those praised at the opening of the show was a Mr Burke of Clonmel for the motors that he manufactured. (7)

Nov The Cunard liner *Lusitania* set a new record for the crossing of the Atlantic when she took 4 days, 19 hours and 52 minutes to go from the Daunt's Rock lighthouse off Ireland to New York. (11)

1908

Pressure to allow women to vote gained momentum during the year with an estimated 200,000 people demonstrating on the issue in London in June. When leading suffragettes Emmeline Pankhurst and her daughter Christobel were imprisoned in October, they demanded political status.

Labour unrest also hit the news when James Larkin led the dockers in both Dublin and Cork in a number of strikes for better working conditions. A new system of grants to local authorities to provide public housing was another boost to the lower classes.

Southern Italy and Sicily were devastated by a huge earthquake and subsequent tidal waves that killed up to 200,000 people. In Detroit, the first Model T rolled off the innovative assembly line designed by Henry Ford.

Italian catastrophe

Wednesday, December 30

The earthquake in Italy proves to be one of the most appalling disasters in the history of the world. The city of Messina in Sicily has been almost wholly destroyed, and here alone over 50,000 persons have lost their lives. Many adjoining towns and villages in Sicily and the adjoining mainland of Calabria have been laid in ruins, and the total deathroll will, it is thought, reach 100,000.

Some who were not killed in the earthquake went mad with grief and terror, and ran among the flaming ruins. At Riposto the sea receded a considerable distance, and then rushed back with terrible force, sweeping all before it for 300 yards inland. Bodies horribly mutilated and clothed only in undergarments or night clothes were to be seen scattered about on all sides, while here and there the writhing limbs of persons vainly trying to extricate themselves from the wreckage, the muffled cries of the helpless victims appealing for help and the groans of the dying added to the horrors of the situation.

The RIC on the march.

Wright sets flight record

Wednesday, September 23

Paris – It was amid scenes of tremendous enthusiasm that Mr Wilbur Wright last night completed his marvellous flight of an hour and a half, breaking all records and winning £200. The performance was a stirring and grandiose spectacle, taking place during a glorious sunset, and only terminating owing to the blackness of the night during which for some time the machine continued to flit to obscurity like some weird bird. So dark was it that a lamp had to be placed in the field to show the aviator where to alight.

NEWS BRIEFS

Feb Thirty-five terrorists were arrested yesterday in various parts of St Petersburg. Documents show that the police have laid hands on a gang which intended to perpetrate a series of outrages on highly placed personages. (22)

Aug Kentucky – Four Negroes were taken out of gaol here last night and hanged on a tree at the edge of town. The mob, comprised of about 50 persons, fired no shots and the inhabitants knew nothing of the affair until daylight revealed the dangling bodies. (2)

Oct Dublin – A further case of typhoid in the Clontarf area was reported to the Public Health authorities today. It occurred in a home not previously affected. Sir Charles Cameron spent the day in a further examination of the locality in which the disease prevails. (19)

Letter to the editor

Tuesday, October 13

The Suffragettes and the Government

Sir – Your valuable columns have recently been very much occupied by reports on the above subject. I beg to submit that the solution of the difficulty is indeed a very simple one. Let the Government grant a female franchise.

In the Commonwealth of Australia and in the Dominion of New Zealand women folk enjoy the Parliamentary franchise, and why should their sisters in the home countries be denied a like privilege? It cannot be denied that on many questions of domestic economy and hygienic science in general women are better and more reliable authorities than men. Why, therefore, deprive them of the right to express their opinions through the medium of the ballot box?

In Australia, when it was first contemplated to give a Parliamentary vote to women, some of the crusted old Tories held up their hands in holy horror at the impending desolation. The women, however, got the franchise and from there has come no cataclysm of woe. By all means, then, let the suffragettes continue to knock at the Parliamentary door until they are admitted to the right of the franchise. – Yours faithfully, Jeremiah J Doyle, Bishop of Lismore

1909

With serious poverty on both sides of the Irish Sea, the introduction of the Old Age Pension helped relieve some of the suffering of the older population. Around 160,000 Irish people over the age of 70 had applied for the four shillings a week which had its inaugural payment on the first day of the year.

Breach of promise cases, in which one party in an engagement decided not to go ahead with the marriage, often ended up in court and were regularly reported in the *Examiner*. In one case, a Miss Keegan, the plaintiff, was described as "a pale and rather interesting lady, dressed in deep mourning". Defendant Chevalier Bergin laughed off the suggestion that there was an engagement, blaming the situation on the fact that Keegan was "continually reading novels".

It was a good year for polar exploration when Kildare-born Ernest Shackleton led an expedition that got closer than anyone ever had to the South Pole, a distance of 97 miles.

At the other end of the earth, controversy raged as two American explorers claimed they had been the first to reach the North Pole. Eventually Frederick Cook was disgraced when his Eskimo guides said he had lied about his journey and the National Geographic Society recognised the feat of Robert Peary.

Disastrous bog slide

Wednesday, January 20

A visit to the scene of the deplorable bog slide near Ballygar, Co Galway, confirms the fear that the quantity of bog displaced and the loss to small farmers in the vicinity would be much greater than was at first expected. Mrs McDonnell's body has not yet been recovered.

The bog moved again this morning at the rate of about five miles an hour. Farmers whose holdings lie in the course of this second movement became greatly alarmed, and immediately set about clearing out their stock and furniture. Laden carts filled the roadways in a scramble to reach a place of safety.

Over 100 acres of land which yesterday was under grass is today covered by 12 feet of bog.

A Home Rule rally on O'Connell Street, Dublin.

Death of Mr JM Synge

Wednesday, March 3

I regret to announce the death today in a Dublin hospital of Mr JM Synge, the dramatic author and writer. Mr Synge was not known to the Irish public till a few years ago, when he associated himself with Lady Gregory and Mr Yeats in the management of the Abbey Theatre and contributed several plays to their repertoire. One of these, *Riders to the Sea*, is a very poignant and intense tragedy, which has been greatly appreciated, not only in Ireland, but also in England and Scotland. The other, *The Playboy of the Western World*, it will be remembered, was received at the Abbey Theatre with great opposition. It has not since been given on those boards, but was presented afterwards in several cities on the other side of the Channel.

NEWS BRIEFS

Jan Palermo – A grim message reaches here this morning to the effect that clouds of crows have descended in the earthquake-stricken districts, having crossed the Mediterranean from Africa in response to a mysterious intuition of the disaster. In Messina the rescuers frequently encounter processions of naked persons bearing images of the saints which have been broken and mutilated by the earthquake. Dealing with these frenzied survivors is very difficult. (1)

Thousands of men and a number of bands arrived in Thurles, Co Tipperary, to parade in support of a number of local farmers involved in court disputes with local landlords Sir John Cardon, Lieut-Col Fitzgibbon Trant and Mr Charles Clarke. Rents had been withheld from Cardon and Trant, while Clarke's mansion had been vandalised by a mob of farmers. The judge ruled in favour of all three landlords. (20)

Aug A controversy ensued when the Abbey Theatre planned to stage George Bernard Shaw's *The Showing Up of Blanco Posnet*, a play which had been banned by the censor in England for being blasphemous. Shaw reluctantly agreed to a number of changes to the script so that it could be produced in Ireland, but nobody in Britain saw it for another 12 years. The *Examiner* published a letter from Shaw to Yeats in which the censored playwright remarked sarcastically: "In point of consideration for the religious beliefs of the Irish people the play compares very favourably indeed with the Coronation Oath." (24)

1910

The death of King Edward VII was to be the last time the death of a member of the British royal family would have such an impact in Ireland until the passing of Princess Diana in 1997.
In domestic politics, John Redmond's Irish Party had pushed Home Rule back on the agenda in Britain by winning enough seats in January's election to hold the balance of power that kept the Liberals in government. *Examiner* Editor-in-chief George Crosbie had been an election candidate for Redmond's party, and the paper's leanings in this regard are obvious in the report of the party leaders' visit to Cork.

Irish leaders in Cork

Monday, May 23

Messrs Redmond, Dillon and Devlin on arriving in Cork on Saturday night were accorded an enthusiastic welcome. A great crowd met them at the railway station, and they were escorted to the Victoria Hotel by a procession with bands and nearly a thousand torch bearers.
The Nationalist leaders delivered speeches in which they declared that their reception was the greatest demonstration in support of the Irish Party that had yet been held in Ireland.
Shortly after 12pm yesterday deputations began to arrive at the Victoria Hotel. While these proceedings were in progress, contingents were arriving at the various city stations.
On the South Mall and in Patrick Street the factionists came into collision with some of the supporters of the Irish Party. A number of exciting incidents were witnessed, and several persons had to be treated at the infirmaries. Elaborate police arrangements prevented any disturbance, and when the Nationalists formed up in Patrick Street at about two o'clock, a scene of tremendous enthusiasm was enacted. The demonstration was an unqualified success, and was one of the greatest, most orderly and most enthusiastic ever held in the ancient Borough of Cork.

John Redmond addressing a Home Rule meeting.

King's death

Monday, May 8

Clonmel, Saturday: The news of the death of King Edward was received in Clonmel and throughout Tipperary this morning with profound regret. It came, indeed, as a shock to everybody, for the sad event was wholly unexpected.
At eight o'clock this morning the wires brought the brief and ominous message, and the daily newspapers, arriving a few hours later, were eagerly bought up. It was easy to see that the people recognised that in King Edward had passed away not only a wise, sagacious and kindly sovereign, and a good sportsman, but a true friend to Ireland. Everywhere the dead monarch was spoken of in kindly terms. Women in the market place on learning the melancholy intelligence were heard making such exclamations as: "Ah, the poor gentleman. The best King for Ireland we ever had."
The simple pathos of these expressions shows how thoroughly the King had won his way to the hearts of the Irish people.

NEWS BRIEFS

June The Catholic hierarchy protests against the mixing of boys and girls in schools. "Apart altogether from moral considerations, we believe that the mixing of boys and girls in the same school is injurious to the delicacy of feeling, reserve and modesty of demeanour which should characterise young girls." (21)

July One of the most significant sporting events ever held sees the world's first black heavyweight boxing champion Jack Johnson defeat the white Jim Jeffries in Nevada. Johnson's win was greeted with joy by America's black population, but race riots following the fight left many dead. Stakeholder for the fight was 'Big Tim' Sullivan, the son of Kerry emigrants. Sullivan had visited his parents' birthplace a month earlier and had been interviewed by the *Examiner* at Queenstown. The first person to congratulate the 'conquering negro' after the fight was John L Sullivan, another second generation Irish fighter who was the last of the bare knuckle champions. (4)

Dec Up to 350 miners are reported killed in an explosion at the Hulton Colliery, near Bolton in England. (22)

Ulster earthquake

Friday, May 27

A Newtownards telegram states that the usually quiet town was thrown into a state of great excitement yesterday afternoon, when a number of violent earthquake tremors, in all about a dozen, were felt.
The shocks, while they lasted, were particularly severe, the houses being shaken to their foundations, open doors banged and delph rattled on the shelves. The inhabitants passed into the streets, and the phenomenon was the subject of general comment.
A peculiar underground rumbling noise, reminiscent of distant thunder, could be distinctly heard. A peculiar incident during the noise was that the dogs belonging to some of the people crept in apparent terror to their kennels.

CITY EDITION

The Cork Examiner.

NO. 17,698 SATURDAY MORNING, MAY 7, 1910 PRICE—ONE PENNY

KING EDWARD DEAD.

HIS LAST MOMENTS.

FAMILY AT BEDSIDE.

SCENES AT PALACE

QUEEN ALEXANDRA'S GRIEF

SENSATION IN LONDON

THE LAST BULLETINS

SKETCH OF HIS CAREER

MESSAGE FROM NEW KING

PARLIAMENT TO MEET

NEW KING'S TITLE

King Edward VII. died at midnight. The news of his Majesty's death was sent out about two hours after a statement had been made at Buckingham Palace that no further bulletin would be issued during the night. It was known that the Royal family had been summoned to the bedside, and that many of them were in tears, but the end was not expected so soon. King Edward, who ascended the throne in January, 1901, was 68 years of age. He is succeeded by his son George, Prince of Wales.

The Cork Examiner.

SATURDAY MORNING, MAY 7, 1910.

THE WEATHER.

(From the Meteorological Office).

The following is the forecast for to-day:—North-Westerly winds, strong, changeable in places; squally; showers of hail or sleet; locally cool.

On the judges who are trying the East Dorset Election petition rising for the day last evening, Mr. Pickens, K.C., intimated that he hoped and expected to conclude the case of the petitioner to-day. Great progress was made with the petition, evidence being given in respect to the alleged bribery, creat-

OFFICIAL ANNOUNCEMENT

The Press Association was officially informed early this morning the following is the official bulletin in which the death of his Majesty was announced to the Secretary of State for the Home Department:—

May 6th, 1910, 11.50 p.m.

His Majesty the King breathed his last at 11.45 p.m. in the presence of her Majesty Queen Alexandra, the Prince and Princess of Wales, the Princess Royal, and the Duke of Fife, Princess Victoria Princess Louise, Duchess of Argyll.

(Signed),
F. Laking.
J. Reid.
R. Douglas Powell.
J. Bertram Dawson.

The Press Association adds that the news of the King's death was received outside the gates of Buckingham Palace at 12.15, immediately after the departure of the Princess of Wales. The news was received in silence, and a considerable time elapsed before the crowd could be brought to understand that their esteemed Monarch had passed away. For a considerable time they remained in the vicinity of the Palace waiting for the official intimation to be publicly posted.

TELEGRAM FROM THE NEW KING.

London, Friday Midnight.

The Press Association says the Lord Mayor of London to-night received the following telegram from the new King:—

Buckingham Palace.

To the Lord Mayor, Mansion House.

I am deeply grieved to inform you that my beloved father, the King, passed away peacefully at a quarter to 12 to-night.—George.

THE HOME SECRETARY'S ANNOUNCEMENT.

London, Saturday Morning.

The Press Association says:—The Lord Mayor of London early this morning received the following communication from the Home Secretary:—"Home Office, Whitehall, May 6th, 1910. My Lord—It is my painful duty to inform your lordship of the death of our most gracious Sovereign King Edward. This melancholy event took place at Buckingham Palace at 11.45 to-night. I have to request your lordship to give directions for tolling the great bell of St. Paul's Cathedral. I have the honour to be, my lord, your lordship's obedient servant,

"Winston L. Churchill."

TO-DAY'S PRIVY COUNCIL.

ALLEGIANCE TO NEW KING.

GEORGE V.

London, Saturday Morning.

The Central News says—Almost simultaneously with the announcement a special messenger was despatched to the Mansion House bearing a note signed by the Prince of Wales conveying the news to the Lord Mayor. Some time afterwards the Lord Chamberlain proceeded to his office, where he was soon deeply engaged with the officials of the department in making the important and indispensable arrangements which follow upon the demise of the Sovereign.

Kingdom of Great Britain and Ireland, defender of the faith, Emperor of India, to whom we do acknowledge all faith and constant obedience with all hearty and humble affection, beseeching God, by whom Kings and Queens do reign, to bless the royal Prince George the Fifth with long and happy years to reign over us." Thereafter his Majesty will address the Council, and will promise to reign as a constitutional Sovereign.

PARLIAMENT TO MEET.

MINISTERS SENT FOR.

London, Saturday Morning

The Press Association says—On the demise of the Crown it is the duty of the members of Parliament, as soon as the news reaches them, to instantly repair to Westminster, and as soon as the Speaker or his authorised deputy takes the chair, the House of Commons is competent to act. No summons of any kind is needed or is accustomed to be sent officially to individual members. In the same way, the members of the House of Lords are required at once to meet.

Mr Lowther, the Speaker of the House of Commons, is at present on a visit to his brother, the British Ambassador at Constantinople, but he has been communicated with, and is expected back in London in two or three days.

Mr Asquith and Mr Lloyd George have already started for home. Mr. Balfour and Mr Wyndham have been staying at Salisbury. Sir Edward Grey is also within easy reach of London, and Mr Buxton and Mr Burns have not left town. Thus, in spite of the startling suddenness of the termination of the King's illness, occurring during a break in the ardnous labours of many months, when most members were intent only on holiday-making, it will be possible with a minimum of delay to proceed in both Houses with the business necessary on such an occasion.

The Lord Chancellor in the House of Lords, and the Speaker in the House of Commons, rising, take the oath of allegiance, and all other members are sworn in as at the opening of a new Parliament. This ceremony usually occupies three days. When the swearing in is complete, it is customary for the King to send a message to his Parliament, and humble addresses are voted in reply, sympathising with his Majesty's sorrow, and assuring him of the most loyal attachment to the Throne. It is probable that after this duty is performed, Parliament will adjourn, and most likely the date for its re-assembling is May 26th the day fixed when members separated for the spring holiday.

DAY OF GRAVE ANXIETY

(Press Association Telegram).

London, Friday Night.

The Press Association telegraphs—To the great majority of the King's subjects the news of his Majesty's grave illness came as a great shock. The notices in the morning papers supplied to many the first intimation, and it was hoped that his Majesty would speedily throw off the attack of bronchitis. It was soon seen, however, that there was ample occasion for public anxiety and alarm. Two of his Majesty's physicians, Sir James Reid and Sir Francis Laking, remained all through the night within easy call of the King's apartment.

A quiet night passed by. The Royal patient had given the impression that he was making good progress, and to some early enquirers, notably Mrs. Asquith and Lord Rothschild, this news was given. It is understood that the Queen and the members of the Royal family generally all looked for a more favourable bulletin, and great, therefore, was the consternation caused when it was found that the first official report was distinctly unfavourable. Dr. Bertrand Dawson and Dr. St. Clair Thompson joined Sir F. Laking and Sir J. Reid at the Palace at about 10 o'clock, and the fact that one of them is a well-known throat specialist

Page recreated

1911

The *Examiner* reporter at Queenstown claims to have noticed a shift in the mood of people leaving Ireland.

A taste of the industrial strife ahead came with a series of strikes led by Jim Larkin and a major railway dispute, while William Martin Murphy formed the Employers Federation to fight the unions.

Ireland was just one region experiencing trouble between workers and employers, with major strikes across Europe and troops in Britain shooting several people in the attempt to quell unrest there.

The visit of recently-crowned King George V and Queen Mary brought many people to the streets of Dublin and a special train from Cork carried 1,000 people for the occasion. However, not everybody was happy about the visit and a near-riot ensued in Irishtown, Limerick, when the owner of a lodging-house flew a Union Jack in tribute to the royals.

By now the *Examiner* was using a single telegraph line to bring in copy from external sources at 50 words per minute.

Irish emigration

Thursday, November 30

Our Queenstown Correspondent writes: Once again the annual exodus from Ireland to America has begun, and with it comes the question, will this ever end?

No doubt the emigration statistics of late years form a marked contrast to those of even a decade ago, but still the numbers are too large for an already depopulated country.

By the White Star, Cunard and American Line steamships which left Queenstown during the past week, over 600 persons left for America from here.

Among the awful horde which find their way to America today the immigration officials tell us that the Irish stand out prominently as being the most acceptable, the cleanest, most intelligent and most useful of all that seek the sheltering Government of the States to aid them in their new venture.

The days are gone forever of the abnormally high wage. The Italian can afford to, and does, successfully oust people of our race from employment by working at a lower wage.

Judging by appearances, the emigrant of today is gay and blithesome, and anything but broken-hearted at the farewell. The truth is that the feelings of people have undergone a remarkable change.

Time was when the saddest scenes that one could well witness were on the wharves at Queenstown during the emigration hours, but today mirth and music take the place of tears and sadness so manifest formerly.

A political meeting in Glenville, Co Kerry.

Women's Franchise League

Saturday, September 28

Under the auspices of the Munster Women's Franchise League a lecture on 'Woman Suffrage in Australia' was delivered in the Imperial Hotel by Miss Vida Goldstein.

Miss Day, hon sec of the League, explained its objects. All they asked for was that the Parliamentary franchise would be given to women on the same terms as it was or as it might be given to men.

That was not an unreasonable demand seeing that women paid rates and taxes equally with the men.

They were not asking for votes for rich women alone. They were asking them for the poor woman who could not help herself, the unfortunate city workers, hundreds and hundreds of whom lived with their families in one small room earning ¾d per hour, and sometimes making children of two years of age help them in their work.

NEWS BRIEFS

April The tramp nuisance reached its high water mark in Carrick-on-Suir last week. On Thursday, Friday and Saturday evenings an average of about 200 male and female tramps swept down on the town, coming, it is believed, from races in the districts around. They slept in forges and out-houses around. In Carrick-on-Suir over 100 of them visited the workhouse at night. At the workhouse some of them threatened to pull down the house if they were not supplied with soup and tea. Some of them were sent to gaol at a special court on Friday and Saturday. (3)

Dec A meeting of the Association for the Opposing of the Granting of Suffrage to Women was held tonight at the Mansion House. A number of suffragettes attended, and punctuated the speeches with interruptions and hostile shouts. The proceedings were very protracted and, towards the close, rather confused. (7)

YOU CAN ALWAYS TELL
WOODFORD, BOURNE & CO.'S
DELICIOUS TEA 2/- DELICIOUS TEA
By the Special Flavour.
For Breakfast—Refreshing.
For Afternoon—Delicious 6301

The Cork Examiner.

CITY EDITION

WOODFORD'S
MATURED WHISKIES.
CORK (7 Years Old) Per Gallon 21/-
DUBLIN (8 Years Old) do. ... 22/6
'EXTRA' J. J.&Sons (Brown Label) 25/6
SCOTCH Choicest (8 Yrs Old) 23/6
BONDED AND MATURED IN OUR OWN
BONDED STORES AT NILE ST., CORK.
WOODFORD BOURNE & CO. LTD.
CORK. 6301

NO. 18,062 MONDAY MORNING, JULY 10, 1911 PRICE—ONE PENNY

THE KING'S VISIT TO DUBLIN.

The Arrival of the Procession at Leeson Street Bridge, the confine of the civic authority, where, when a civil welcome was extended the keys of the city were handed over to the Royal visitor. It was not done on this occasion. (Photo by Keogh Bros, Dublin.)

SCENE AT LEESON STREET BRIDGE

(Photo by Topical Press, Lo

HENLEY REGATTA.

THE LATE MR. EATON, J.P.

TIPPERARY GUARDIANS' ACTION.

At the meeting of the Tipperary Guardians on Saturday, the Chairman, Mr. Thomas Dwyer referred to the death of Mr. W. Eaton, J.P., who was very much respected and good to the poor around Tipperary.

Clerk—He was a very good, charitable, and respected member of the community. He took

LATE MR. WM. EATON, J.P., TIPPERARY.
Photo by Elliot and Fry, London.)

an interest in everything that was for the general good, regardless of sect or politics.

The Chairman proposed the following resolution:—"That we desire to place on record an expression of our deep regret on the occasion of the death of Mr. William Eaton, J.P., Sandymount, which took place during the week, he being an honoured member of the community, charitable and well-disposed in everything tending to the welfare of the country, and a generous friend to the poor. We hereby tender to his afflicted widow our heartfelt sympathy in her bereavement, and we direct our clerk to convey the foregoing to that lady."

Mr. W. O'Neill seconded.

Mr. Stapleton—He was well worthy of it.

Mr. Kirby—He was a perfect gentleman, and Tipperary can ill afford to lose his equals.

The resolution was passed in silence.

NORTH WEST HAM ELECTION

A CHALLENGE LINE

AT

8/11-

Ladies' Patent Goloshed Laced Shoes, Cuban Heels, Suede, dull Kid, or Self Tops. Also

LADIES' TENNIS SHOES

COMPLETE VARIETY FROM

5/11 TO 10/6.

THE LONDON HOUSE, LIMITED,
14 & 15, PATRICK-ST., CORK.
Telephone—362. 6304

ALLMAN'S
STOCKTAKING SALE, THIS DAY.

HIGH CLASS GOODS, at Reduced Prices, in SAMPLE UNDERCLOTHING, CORSETS, BLOUSES, AND COSTUMES.

BARGAINS IN

HOSIERY, GLOVES, PARASOLS, UMBRELLAS, SILK SHAWLS, MEN'S SHIRTS, TIES, BRACES, STRAW HATS, CAPS, AND HANDKERCHIEFS.

1 & 2, WINTHROP STREET.
6305

NOW READY.

UNIVERSITY COLLEGE REGULATIONS, 1911-'12.
PRICE 3d PER POST, 4½d.
To be had of the Publishers—
PURCELL AND COMPANY,
124. PATRICK-ST., CORK.
Or
W. and T. EVANS, 11 PATRICK ST, CORK.
6306

FERMOY.

PURE POT STILL WHISKIES

	Per Gal.
Midleton 7 Years Old	21s.
Midleton 8 Years Old	22s.
John Jameson and Sons' 8 Years Old	25s.
John Jameson and Sons' 12 Years Old	27s.
John Power and Sons' 10 Years Old	24s.
Finest Old Dublin. Lombard's Speciality, 10 Years Old	23s.
Gilbey's Castle Grand	24s.
Do. J. J. and S. Liqueur, 12 Years Old	30s.
Do. Old Scotch (Islay)	23s.

JAMES LOMBARD.

BANKS.

£10 TO £5,000

ADVANCED by Private Lender on Simple Promissory Notes. No Bills of Sale taken, and absolute Privacy guaranteed. First letter of application receives prompt attention, and intending borrowers are waited upon by a representative who is empowered to complete transactions on terms mutually arranged. NO CHARGE BEING MADE UNLESS BUSINESS ACTUALLY COMPLETED. Special Quotations for short Loans. Write in confidence to C. WELLS, 31 Exchequer Street, Dublin. Head Office: Corridor Chambers, Leicester. 6360

IMPORTANT TO FARMERS AND OTHERS.

CITY AND COUNTY LOAN AND DISCOUNT BANK,
O'CONNELL STREET, WATERFORD.

MAKES Cash Advances from £10 upwards on approved Personal Security without publicity. The amount borrowed can be repaid by instalments, or as may be arranged. They are the Best and most reliable Financiers that advance on Private Security.

Apply for terms as above. 6361

LOANS BY POST.

FROM £20 to £1,000, to Noblemen, Ladies and Gentlemen, and all others, in any part of Great Britain and Ireland, on their own Signature, without Sureties. No Fees. Easy Repayment. Apply personally or by letter to J. C. WALSHE, Manager.

STANDARD PRIVATE BANK OF IRELAND
15 ANGLESEA ST. (off Dame st.), DUBLIN.
No connection with any other so-called Bank.

MONEY LENT! MONEY LENT!
MONEY LENT.

FROM £10 upwards may be obtained at the SOUTH MALL LOAN AND DISCOUNT BANK, 85 SOUTH MALL, CORK.

Loans also granted on Life and Endowment Policies, leases, and all other suitable security.

Please Note Address—

THE MANAGER,
LOAN & DISCOUNT BANK
85, SOUTH MALL CORK.
6307

MONEY LENT!
MONEY!

THE CITY AND COUNTY ADVANCE BANK,
23 MARLBORO' STREET, CORK.
Established 1885.

LOANS advanced daily from £10 upwards to FARMERS and others on their own Signature, privately, with or without BAILS, to be repaid by instalments.

Prospectus free on application to
D. COWAN. 6320

Money Lent at 2/6 in the £
FROM £5 TO £500.

CASH ADVANCES made Daily in Town or Country, to all responsible Householders, Shopkeepers, Farmers, and others, on approved note of hand. Repayments by weekly or monthly instalments. Special terms to farmers. Applications attended to immediately.

Call or write to

THE LOAN BANK,
81a SOUTH MALL (Next County Club),
Entrance, Crane Lane 6362

12 PRIZE MEDALS AWARDED
MULLINS AND SONS,
CARRIAGE BUILDERS, CORK.

INVITE the Attention of INTENDING PURCHASERS to their LARGE STOCK of CARRIAGES, TRAPS, and JAUNTING CARS.

M. and S. Employ the LARGEST STAFF in Ireland; hold the LARGEST STOCK of Seasoned Woods, and PERSONALLY SUPERINTEND all Work Done, thus Securing EXCELLENCE in QUALITY and PUNCTUALITY IN DESPATCH.

WORKS AND SHOWROOMS........WARREN'S PLACE.
MOTOR GARAGE..........................SOUTH MALL.
ESTABLISHED 1843. 6327

COOLEST CLOTHING
PURE IRISH LINEN MESH UNDERWEAR.
NEGLIGE SHIRTS, PANAMA HATS.
WHITES FOR TENNIS AND CRICKET.
FITZGERALD,
THE FAMOUS SHIRTMAKER,
44, PATRICK STREET, CORK. 140, CHEAPSIDE, LONDON 6334

COAL! COAL! COAL!

PRESENT PRICES, PER TON, OF
CITY OF CORK STEAM PACKET COMPANY'S
COALS DELIVERED IN CITY AND SUBURBS:—

Best LYDNEY or STAFFORDSHIRE ORRELL RANGE COAL	23/-
BEST LANCASHIRE RANGE COAL	22/-
SPECIAL "MADOK" RANGE COAL	21/-
Large Screened Coals of above Qualities 1/- Per Ton Extra	
BEST SCREENED NUT COAL	20/-

ORDERS RECEIVED AT PENROSE QUAY AND ALBERT QUAY.
Telephones:—Penrose Quay, 105; Albert Quay, 707. Telegrams:—Packet, Cork.
Country Orders put on Rail at shortest notice. Specially low quotations for wagon lots.
CITY OF CORK STEAM PACKET COMPANY, LTD.

Page recreated

1912

The fact that the *Titanic* was built in Belfast and its final port of call was Queenstown, where an *Examiner* photographer took some of the last pictures of the ill-fated liner, gave news of the disaster a special resonance in Ireland.

However, the most significant link with the ship was that almost 200 of the people on board were Irish. Unfortunately, most of them would go down with the ship as the class distinction in deciding who had access to the lifeboats meant that the Irish passengers, who were mostly in Third Class, were well down the pecking order.

Sorrow in the city

Wednesday, April 17

The loss of the *Titanic* with so many of her passengers has created feeling of deep sorrow in Cork. Many residents of Cork city and county were passengers on the doomed ship. Relatives of those passengers called at the offices of the *Evening Echo* during the day, and their distress at not being able to obtain favourable news regarding their friends was indeed acute. One gentleman whose sister went to America against the wishes of her people, showed deep anguish on not being able to obtain assuring news. The list of the rescued is anxiously awaited by grief-stricken friends.

Titanic survivor's story

Saturday, April 20

The following account of the disaster is given by Mr Beesley of London:

On Sunday evening I had been in my berth about 10 minutes when at a quarter past 10 I felt a slight jar. The engines however stopped immediately afterwards. We saw through the smoking room window that a game of cards was going on and I went in to ask if they knew anything. They had noticed the jar a little more and looking through the window had seen a huge iceberg go by close to the side of the boat. The game of cards was resumed and without any thought of disaster I retired to my cabin.

A little later hearing people going upstairs I went out again. Going up on the deck again I saw what was an unmistakable list downwards from the stern to the bows. I went down to my cabin where I put on some warmer clothing. As I dressed I heard the order shouted, "All the passengers on deck with lifebelts on." There was a total absence of panic or expression of alarm. I suppose this must be accounted for by the exceeding calmness of the night and the absence of any signs of an accident.

Gift of the gab: Winston Churchill on a visit to Blarney Castle.

Presently we heard the order, "All men stand back away from the boats; all ladies retire to the next deck below." The boats were then swung out and lowered from A deck. When they were level with B deck, where all the women were collected, the women got in quietly with the exception of some, who refused to leave their husbands. In some cases they were torn from their husbands and pushed into the boats.

Presently the boats near me were lowered with much creaking as the new ropes slipped through the pulleys. When they were afloat and had their oars at work the condition of the rapidly sinking liner was much more apparent. In common prudence the sailors saw that they could do nothing but row from the sinking ship.

In the distance the *Titanic* looked enormous. Every porthole and saloon were blazing with light. It was impossible to think that anything could be wrong with such a leviathan were it not for that ominous tilt downward in the bows where the water was by now up to the lowest row of portholes.

At about two o'clock we observed her settling very rapidly, with the bows and the bridge completely under water. She slowly tilted straight to end with stern vertically upwards. As she did so the lights in the cabins and the saloons died out. At the same time the machinery roared down through the vessel with a groaning rattle that could have been heard for miles.

To our amazement she remained in that upright position for a time which I estimated as five minutes. Then with a quick slanting dive she disappeared beneath the waters. Then there fell on our ears the most appalling noise that human beings ever heard, the cries of hundreds of our fellow beings struggling in the icy waters crying for help.

The Cork Examiner.

NO. 18,302 [illegible] TUESDAY MORNING APRIL 16, 1912 PRICE—ONE PENNY

APPALLING DISASTER

TITANIC LOST

COLLIDES WITH ICEBERG.

2,358 ON BOARD.

ONLY 675 SAVED

187 IRISH PASSENGERS

MEAGRE DETAILS

CONFLICTING MESSAGES

News received shortly before going to Press makes it only too probable that one of the most appalling disasters in the history of the sea has to be recorded.

The White Star Liner Titanic, the largest in the world, which left Queenstown on Thursday with 2,358 souls on board, was in collision on Sunday night with an iceberg off Newfoundland.

It was at first reported that the liner had sunk. Later it was declared that her watertight compartments held so well that she was able to make for Halifax, accompanied by several liners whose aid she had summoned by wireless telegraphy.

All the passengers were believed to be safe.

Mr. and Mrs. Phillips, of Farncombe, Godalming, parents of the wireless telegraphing operator on the Titanic, last night received the following message from their son:—"Making slowly for Halifax; practically unsinkable. Don't worry."

Unhappily, in the early hours of this morning cables from Reuter's Agency stated that the liner had sunk, and that only 675 were saved. As she had 2,358 on board at Queenstown, the death-roll must be nearly 1,700, unless by some happy chance some steamer may have picked up more survivors. 187 of the passengers [illegible]

New York, Monday.

A telegram received here from Montreal says the liner Virginian reports, in wireless communication, that the liner Titanic, which is reported to have been in collision with an iceberg, has requested assistance. The Virginian is hastening to her aid.

New York, Monday, 3.45 a.m.

A telegram from Cape Race at 10.25 on Sunday evening says:—"Titanic reported she had struck an iceberg. The steamer said that immediate assistance was required. Half an hour afterwards another message was received saying that the Titanic was sinking by the head, and that the women were being taken off in lifeboats."

New York, Monday, later.

A telegram from Cape Race says:—The wireless telegraph operator on board the Titanic reported the weather calm and clear, the position of the liner being then 41.46 north, 50.14 west. The Virginian at midnight was 170 miles west of the Titanic, and is expected to reach her at 10 o'clock this morning. The Olympic at midnight was in 40.32 north latitude, 61.18 west longitude. She is also in direct communication with the Titanic and is hastening to her aid.

New York, 3.30 a.m.

The liner Baltic has also reported herself within 200 miles of the Titanic, and says she is speeding to her help. The last signals from the Titanic came at 12.27 this morning. The Virginian's operator says that these were blurred and ended abruptly.—Reuter.

London, Monday.

The White Star liner Titanic, which Reuter states is sinking in mid-Atlantic, as a result of a collision with an iceberg, left Southampton last Wednesday on her maiden voyage to New York.

The Titanic is the largest vessel afloat, having a tonnage of 46,382, or 1,004 more than the Olympic. She had a length of 882 feet, with 92 feet beam, and was luxuriously fitted up with especial regard to the requirements of wealthy Americans.

When she left Southampton the Titanic had on board 1,[illegible] passengers, including 3[illegible] first-class, but the number was greatly increased at Cherbourg, where she called to pick up the French travellers. In addition she carried a crew of 650.

In design and construction the Titanic was similar to her sister ship the Olympic, and it is a tragic coincidence that both met with misfortune.

The Olympic, it will be remembered, was in collision with the cruiser Hawke soon after leaving port, and sustained such damage that she had to be placed again in the hands of her builders, and such misfortune as has now befallen the Titanic will cause widespread regret, the vessel in the estimation of those who were privileged to view her being another triumph in British shipping and shipbuilding in every detail.

The latest addition to the White Star Line left nothing to be desired, and it was stated at Southampton that she had cost considerably over a million to build and fit out. The luxury to be found aboard the Titanic may be gathered from an official account. Speaking of the breakfast dining-room, it is pointed out that the decorations are reminiscent of the early Jacobean times, but instead of the sombre oak of the sixteenth and seventeenth centuries, it is painted a soft rich white. The furniture is also designed to harmonise with its surroundings, and over 550 passengers can dine at the same time. A feature of the room is the arrangement of recessed bays, where family and other parties can dine together in semi-privacy.

The Titanic is under the command of Commander Edward J. Smith, who had been transferred from the Olympic.

Among the passengers on board are:—Col. and Mrs. J. J. Astor, Major A. W. Butt, President Taft's Aide-de-Camp; Mr. B. Guggenheim, of the well-known banking family; Mr. C. M. Hays, President of the Grand Trunk Railway, Mrs. Hays, and Miss Hays; Mr. Ismay, of the White Star Line; Countess of Rothes, Mr. W. T. Stead, Mr. Clarence Moore, and Mr. Isidor Straus. There are 318 first-class passengers on board.

NUMBER OF PASSENGERS.

The number of passengers on the Titanic when she left Queenstown, including the Cherbourg passengers, was: First class, 330; second class, [illegible]; third class, 700, with a crew and stewards numbering 903, or a total on board of 2,358. The mail was 3,418 sacks.

MESSAGE FROM WHITE STAR COMPANY.

New York, Monday, 8 a.m.

Up to this hour the officials of the White Star Line have not received a word regarding the reported accident to the Titanic.

The Company have issued the following statement:—"Twelve hours have passed since the collision of the Titanic is reported to have taken place. We have heard nothing of an accident. It is very strange that the Titanic's sister ship Olympic, which has wireless installation of sufficient strength to send a message across the Atlantic, should have sent us nothing. The Olympic should be alongside the Titanic at two this afternoon.—Reuter.

OTHER LINERS' PERIL.

New York, Monday.

The liners Cymric and Niagara also encountered icebergs. The former had a perilous time threading her way through. The Niagara was less lucky, and had two holes knocked in her bottom and several plates bent. The ice was encountered on the west bound track off the Grand Banks.—Reuter.

THE TITANIC'S PASSENGERS

New York, Monday, 11.30 a.m.

The transfer of the passengers from the Titanic is now being carried out. Twenty boat loads have already been taken on board the Carpathia.—Reuter.

BOATS PICKED UP.

LINERS STANDING BY.

London, Monday Night.

The Press Association's Liverpool correspondent telegraphs:—The following cablegram was received to-night at the White Star Line from their New York offices:—"Captain Haddock, of the Olympic, wires the Parisian reports the Carpathia to be in attendance on the Titanic and has picked up twenty boats of passengers. The Baltic is returning to give assistance. Position not given."

It is reported that all the passengers are saved, and that the Virginian is towing the Titanic towards Nova Scotia.

The report is also confirmed that the Virginian, Parisian and Carpathia are in attendance on the Titanic.

WIRELESS OPERATOR.

MESSAGE TO PARENTS.

London, Monday Night.

The wireless operator on the Titanic is Mr. Jack Phillips, son of Mr. and Mrs. G. A. Phillips, of Farncombe, Godalming, Surrey. He is 25 years of age, and served as a telegraphist in Godalming Post Office, afterwards joining the Marconi School at Liverpool. His first wireless appointment was on the Teutonic, after which he was appointed to the Mauretania, Lusitania, and Oceanic, from which last he was transferred to the Titanic for her maiden trip. His parents received a message from him to-night as follows:—"Making slowly for Halifax; practically unsinkable, don't worry."

RACE FOR LAND.

New York, Monday.

An official message received here via the cable ship Minia off Cape Race says that the steamers are towing the Titanic and endeavouring to get her into the shoal water near Cape Race for the purpose of beaching her.

A message from Halifax states that the Government Marine Agency has received a wireless message to the effect that the Titanic is sinking.

Mr. Franklin, Vice-President of the International Mercantile Marine, at one o'clock this afternoon gave out the following message received from the Boston office of the White Star Line (Allan Line, Montreal, confirms the report):—"Virginian, Parisian, Carpathia, in attendance, standing by Titanic." In order to refute the unconfirmed report that the Titanic had sunk, "I don't believe it possible," said Mr. Franklin.—Reuter.

4.30 p.m.

Mr. Franklin said that at 4 o'clock he had definite information that all the passengers had been transferred from the Titanic; he had, however, received nothing indicating the extent of the damage sustained by the liner.—Reuter.

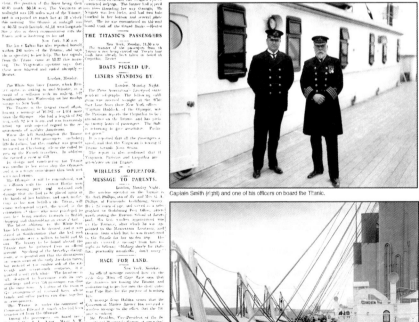

The Titanic anchored off Roches Point, Cork.

Captain Smith (right) and one of his officers on board the Titanic.

Passengers stroll past the lifeboats during the ship's stay at Queenstown

HOME RULE BILL.

DEBATE RESUMED.

MR. BALFOUR'S ATTACK.

MR. SAMUEL'S REPLY.

FINANCIAL PROVISIONS.

MINISTERS' EXPLANATIONS.

IRELAND'S POSITION.

SPEECH BY MR. DILLON.

[illegible]

Page recreated

1913

This was a year of struggle on many fronts: workers against employers, nationalists against unionists and women against the laws which denied them a vote. In Dublin, the lockout was the most significant event of major industrial unrest in several parts of the country.

Extreme poverty was already manifest in the capital, with thousands of people living in one-room tenements. Many workers were joining unions and seeking an improvement in their conditions and, after prolonged tensions, 400 employers agreed to lock out all union members.

Major rioting resulted in several deaths and the *Examiner* was among those who questioned the police response to the situation as heavy-handed and defended the workers' right to strike.

Home Rule took a step closer when the House of Lords defeated the bill for the last time. Under parliamentary rules it would become law in 1914.

At the Epsom derby a suffragette ran in front of the King's horse. She died a few days later as a result of injuries sustained.

Allegations against the police

Monday, August 11

Extraordinary allegations against the police in the course of baton charges in Moss Street and Townsend Street on Sunday night were made to our representative this afternoon. He was shown shattered windows, broken furniture and persons seriously injured, and told that all was the result of the indiscriminate batoning of innocent people by police strongly under the influence of drink.

Mrs Andrews, a respectable looking woman, who resides in 8 Moss Street, told a harrowing story: "My husband, a labourer," she said, "and my son, Christie, were in our room on Saturday night when the police broke in. They were all DMP men. No one in the house had done anything to provoke the police. When I saw the police coming in – there were 14 or 15 of them – I said, 'No one in the house ever meddled with you.' They had the batons swinging in their hands, and they were roaring like wolves".

"They attacked my husband with batons but made no charge against him or arrested him. I cried for mercy. They had batons over me, and my son, Christie, cried out, 'Don't strike my mother.' As soon as he said that they attacked him. Another policeman dragged me out of the room and thought to throw me downstairs, but I caught hold of the banisters."

Killorglin, Co Kerry, during the Puck Fair.

NEWS BRIEFS

Sept An estimated 20,000 people gathered in Dublin to welcome a relief ship carrying food sent by union members in the UK. (29)

Nov The Dublin Housing Inquiry is told by Sir Joseph Downes that he knew of a house, albeit large, where 88 people lived. Fr Monaghan told of another house with 107 people in it and only two water closets to meet all sanitary necessities. (28)

Amazing incident at the Derby

Thursday, June 5

The great racing carnival at Epsom and the race for the Derby this afternoon were marred by two sensational incidents which had the result of depriving Craganour, the winning favourite of the race, and of putting the King's horse, Anmer, out of the running.

The horses were making for Tottenham corner when a woman, believed to be a suffragist, broke away from the crowd at the rails, and dashing across the course placed herself in front of the King's horse, Anmer, holding both her hands above her head. The rider of Anmer being unable to avoid her, the woman was knocked down and seriously injured. Anmer, as the result of the collision, turned a complete somersault and fell upon his jockey. The latter was badly hurt but his mount escaped serious injury and quickly regained his feet.

The King and Queen witnessed the race from the grandstand, and immediately after the accident His Majesty despatched a messenger to ascertain the extent of his jockey's injuries.

The woman knocked down by Anmer was Miss Emily Wilding Davison, a well known suffragist who had been sentenced on several occasions for acts of militancy.

CITY EDITION

The Cork Examiner.

NO. 18,822 TUESDAY MORNING, SEPTEMBER 2, 1913. PRICE—ONE PENNY

Registered for transmission at newspaper rate of postage in the United Kingdom, and at magazine rate to Canada and Newfoundland.

AMERICAN NEWS.

LORD HALDANE'S TOUR.

ARRIVAL AT MONTREAL.

THE THAW CASE.

A SURPRISE MOVE.

(From our Correspondents—Copyright.)

New York, Sunday.

After a hurried motor tour of the commercial districts of New York Lord Haldane and his party boarded Mr J. P. Morgan's yacht Corsair, for the trip up the Hudson to the West Point Military Academy. The party, which had been reinforced by Mr. Morgan, his sister, Mrs. Satterlee, Lord and Lady Strathcona, and Judge Alton Parker and his wife, were received at West Point with full military honours. A squadron of cadet cavalry in their smart blue and white uniform escorted the party from the landing stage to the Review Ground, where the infantry battalion was drawn up for inspection. Colonel Townsley, Commandant of the Academy, and his officers, accompanied by Lord Haldane and most of the distinguished visitors, then carefully inspected the ranks, and the Lord Chancellor expressed his admiration of the smartness displayed by this crack corps of embryo officers. Lord Haldane declared that he had studied West Point from a distance while he was Secretary for War, but that he was surprised and delighted by the reality. The party afterwards lunched with Colonel Townsley, and then took a special train to Albany. There a hustling sight-seeing tour had been arranged for them, and in the evening they were the guests at dinner of Mr. Charles Doherty, Canadian Minister of Justice, and Chief Justice M'Cullen, of the New York State Court of Appeals. At midnight the whole party left Albany for Montreal. Lord Haldane and his companions have nothing but delighted commendation for the manner in which they have been received everywhere, and on their part Americans are loud in praise of England's affable Lord Chancellor.

Montreal, Sunday.

Lord Haldane's party, escorted by Mr. Charles Doherty, Dominion Minister of Justice, the Quebec Premier, Sir Lomer Gouin, and Lady Gouin arrived here this morning from Albany, and the day was spent very quietly at their hotel. This afternoon Lord Haldane took tea with the members of the Montreal Bench, and to-night he and his party are the guests at dinner of Mr. Frank Kellogg, President of the American Bar Association. To-morrow morning Mr. Borden, the Dominion Premier, will officially welcome the members of the Bar Association, and at three o'clock Lord Haldane delivers his address on "The Higher Nationality" in the Empress Theatre. Afterwards honorary degrees will be conferred on the Lord Chancellor and other distinguished jurists at McGill University.

Montreal, Sunday.

Harry Thaw is to be brought into court at Sherbrooke on Tuesday on another Habeas Corpus application. This time it is the New York State lawyers who have been granted a writ, for Mr Jerome, who is leading the Americans, made a surprise move in the absence of Thaw's lawyers, who were in Montreal trying to arrange the release of their client on bail, and appealed to Justice Hutchinson, of the Superior Court, for the release of the prisoner. Mr. Boudrey, Chief of the Police at Coaticooke, who arrested Thaw, made the application on the grounds that Thaw was erroneously committed to prison, and that he desired the prisoner's release in order to "redress any wrong that the petitioner may have done to the said Harry K. Thaw." Mr. Greenshield, one of Thaw's counsel, rushed back to Sherbrooke by special train, but he arrived too late to contest the point, and according to Mr. Jerome, "Thaw is as good as in Matteawan now." Should Thaw be released on Tuesday he will immediately be seized by the Immigration officers and deported. The prisoner was furious when he heard of yesterday's decision, and immediately sat down and wrote a slashing attack on Mr. Jerome for publication in the newspapers. Mr. Jerome conducted the prosecution in New York when Thaw was tried for the murder of Stanford White, and the prisoner regards him as his arch-enemy.

DUBLIN STRIKE.

FATAL RIOTING.

TWO DEAD; HUNDREDS INJURED

HOSPITALS OVERCROWDED.

MILITARY CALLED OUT.

LARKIN'S ARREST.

LABOUR LEADERS CHARGED

Serious rioting occurred in Dublin on Saturday as the result of the tramway strike. The police had proclaimed the strikers' meeting called for yesterday in O'Connell St., but Mr James Larkin announced his intention to hold the gathering. A warrant was obtained for his arrest and that of the other labour leaders. The police were unable to apprehend Larkin on Saturday, but arrested Councillor Partridge and Mr. James Connolly, of Belfast, who were later ordered to find sureties to keep the peace. Partridge gave bail, but Connolly declined, and was sentenced to three months' imprisonment. At seven o'clock on Saturday night, rioting commenced with an attack on the tramcars, and continued until midnight. The police were repeatedly assailed with volleys of stones and broken bottles, and retaliated with baton charges. As a result, over two hundred people and thirty policemen were treated for injuries in the city hospitals, and one man named Nolan succumbed to his injuries. To-day another man named Moore is in a critical condition. The injured included men, women, and children. Last evening's meeting was abandoned by the Strike Committee, and a procession was arranged instead. Shortly after one o'clock, Mr. Larkin made a dramatic appearance on the balcony of the Imperial Hotel, and addressing the crowd below said he had promised to appear that day. He was immediately arrested. Portion of the people raised cheers for Larkin, and the police made a baton charge. Many persons were injured. Over fifty arrests have been made. Most of the injured were treated for scalp wounds.

The Press Association's Dublin correspondent, telegraphing at midnight says—It is reported a second man has succumbed to injuries received on Saturday night. The name of the deceased has not yet been ascertained. The military were called out to assist the police in Inchicore, where rioting has been proceeding since sundown, and tram lines have been torn up. Lines were also torn up in Fairview district. Batton charges continued in outlying districts up to 10 o'clock, but the principal thoroughfares were then quiet. In the outlying districts rioting continued at 11 o'clock.

The Lord Mayor of Dublin says he will immediately move for an inquiry into the action of the police in battoning the people in the streets.

Some hundreds of people were treated at the city hospitals, which had to refuse serious cases.

(Press Association Telegram.)

Dublin, Sunday Night.

The Press Association's Dublin correspondent says—The week-end has witnessed a serious development of the labour disputes in the city surrounding the tramway strike. The Irish Transport Workers Union, of which Mr James Larkin, who had been conducting the strike, is general secretary, arranged for a mass meeting to be held in O'Connell street this afternoon. The meeting was proclaimed by Mr Swifte, the Divisional Magistrate, but Larkin and his fellow-leaders announced their intention of holding the meeting despite this prohibition, and the first named publicly burned the magisterial proclamation.

A warrant was issued on Saturday for the arrest of Larkin and other leaders, but in Larkin's case the police were unable to execute it. He had announced his intention of attending the meeting to-day, "dead or alive," and there was a dramatic possibility of his turning up despite the efforts of the police to apprehend him.

of police was on duty in the vicinity, reinforcements had to be telephoned for. Upon their arrival, they were received with derisive cheers by the crowd, and Superintendent Kiernan ordered his men to charge. In the subsequent melee, several women and a number of boys and girls sustained injuries. In Abbey-street, where the offices of the "Irish Independent" are situated, a force of about fifty police made a charge, and a number of persons sustained injuries.

During the disturbances, and for some hours afterwards, a continuous procession of ambulances was going to the city hospitals. Most of the cases were treated at the Jervis-street Hospital, where the total numbered over one hundred. A large staff of doctors and nurses were kept busy dressing cuts and scalp wounds but only three cases were detained. At Sir Patrick Dunn's Hospital the staff was also kept treating cases, but only one man was detained.

LEADERS IN COURT.

In the Police Court on Saturday, William P. Partridge, Trade Union Organiser, and James Connolly, of Belfast, were charged with having made use of language calculated to incite others to breaches of the law.

The police stated that they had not been able to execute the warrant against Mr. Larkin.

1914

The outbreak of World War I was greeted with optimism and cheeriness in some quarters. In London, crowds poured on to the streets cheering and singing the national anthem.

Ireland's nationalist leader Redmond pledged the support of the Irish Volunteers to the government and the *Examiner* wholeheartedly supported Redmond's position. "Every sensible man in Ireland will agree with the proposal which the Irish leader has made," stated an editorial on the matter.

While plans for a Home Rule bill were suspended until after the conflict, Redmond also called on the Volunteers to join the British army to fight in the war. Over 10,000 members left the organisation because of this call, but more than twice as many heeded his call and went off to war.

By the end of the year, 100,000 people, including many Irish, had already been killed on the British side, but the pro-war stance of the media, as well as the strict censorship regulations, meant it took some time for the public to become aware of the horrors that were unfolding in the trenches.

Xmas in the trenches

Saturday, December 26

The thoughts of all English people today have been with our soldiers in the field. Our men out here have, for their part, had no thought for anything but home. I have always been struck, and never more so than during this Christmastide, with the large-hearted, tolerant attitude, our men have unconsciously adopted towards the individual German soldier. "We only want to meet him and beat him on a purely sporting basis," said a non-commissioned officer to me, and so saying epitomized the creed of his comrades in the field.

Malice finds no place at all in the British military equipment, and that is why a season consecrated to goodwill and fellowship finds the hand and heart of the British soldier in sympathy with the Christmas spirit.

Last night Christmas carols were sung in the British trenches. 'Tipperary' was for once in a way ignored. In one instance at least British and German soldiers sang a hymn together.

But no sooner had the carol ended than the cynical Teutonic touch was introduced by a shower of bullets from the enemy's trenches.

The Christmas cards which King George and Queen Mary sent to every man made a cheery opening for the day, and the Royal message, "May God protect you, and bring you home safe," reproduced in facsimile from the King's handwriting, in conjunction with a Christmas greeting, roused lusty cheers.

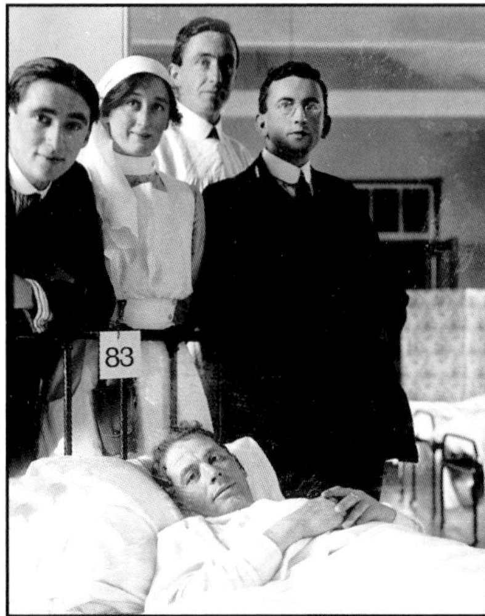

Hospital staff and visitors stand by the bed of a wounded soldier in Cork.

RIC volunteers leave today

Tuesday, December 15

The Cork city and county contingents of the Royal Irish Constabulary volunteers for the Irish Guards will leave Glanmire Terminus today by the 12.45 train.

The men, who are physically magnificent types of Irish manhood, will be sure to give a splendid account of themselves, not alone as regards knowledge and discipline, but in the field of battle, where several of their comrades have behaved with conspicuous gallantry and courage.

The scene presented on the march through the city and at the railway station will be very impressive in its character, and the constabulary men, who will leave to do duty in the battle line, will carry away the best wishes of the people of Cork.

NEWS BRIEFS

Mar Brigadier-General Gough and some 70 officers of the Third Cavalry Brigade, stationed at the Curragh and Dublin, decided to hand in their papers rather than serve against the Ulster disturbers. (28)

Oct Clare beat Laois in the All-Ireland hurling final, 5-1 to 1-0. The Clare team was trained by Jim O'Hehir, whose son Micheál would later become a renowned sports commentator on RTÉ. The Banner County wouldn't win another championship until 1995. (18)

From a wedding to a wake

Tuesday, August 4

Intelligence has reached Tralee of a peculiarly painful tragedy which has occurred in the neighbourhood of Castlemaine. A marriage was celebrated at which a young man named Flynn acted as best man for his brother.

On returning to the bride's house the party was seated at dinner, when the best man, after partaking of the first piece of meat, fell in a choking fit and died a few minutes after in the arms of his brother, the bridegroom.

The piece of meat had got stuck in the unfortunate man's throat, and he was suffocated before any assistance could be rendered.

Needless to say, the wedding festivities were quickly terminated and a wake followed on the deceased young man.

The Royal Munster Fusiliers march through Cork before they leave for war.

Soldiers wave goodbye as they leave the station in Cork.

1915

The Cunard-owned *Lusitania* had been a frequent visitor to Queenstown, picking up passengers and mail for its trans-Atlantic journey. On its final voyage, the ship had been heading for Liverpool on the last leg of its journey from New York.

About 1,400 people died when the ship was torpedoed by a German submarine.

A few days before the ship sailed, the *Examiner* had printed a story revealing that individuals on the *Lusitania's* passenger list had received telegrams warning them not to travel on the liner and that the German Embassy in Washington had placed advertisements stating that any ships flying the British flag would be targeted. Many of those lucky enough to make it to Queenstown told of the calmness of the evacuation.

Among the *Examiner* pictures of the survivors is an unnamed fireman who was either very lucky or extremely unlucky, depending on perspective. He said he had previously been a hand on the *Titanic* during its ill-fated voyage in 1912 and also had served on the *Empress of Ireland* when it was wrecked in Canada in 1914.

Among the prominent Irish passengers to go down with the *Lusitania* was Hugh Lane, the art collector whose gallery in Dublin still hosts one of Ireland's most important collections.

Another prominent Irishman to die that year was the former Fenian leader O'Donovan Rossa. Pádraig Pearse's famous graveside oration went unreported, probably because it would not have been allowed under censorship regulations.

Meanwhile the war raged on, with chlorine gas being used as a weapon at Ypres and many soldiers on the British side, with just wet rags to protect themselves, were left poisoned or blinded.

Lusitania disaster described – thrilling interviews

Saturday, May 8

Monsieur Samuel Abramowitz of Paris, who spoke a mixture of English and French, said to an *Examiner* reporter: "I heard a 'crack' and I see all these wooden chips go into the air, and the ship is gone to starboard. When we got the second torpedo the ship started to go with her nose in the water and listed to starboard. What followed was a picture nobody could believe with his eyes. All the crew did their duty. The captain started to calm the people; but the time was so short that the *Lusitania* went to the bottom, and all those women, children and men went down with her. All those people with their eyes to God and looking at death were swallowed up by the sea."

Helen Smith, a little girl of six years, was a very pathetic person, but in herself most happy in that she was at Queenstown. For she with her parents was coming from New York to Liverpool on a visit to her grandmother. She is a charming little girl, and her confidence that her mamma and her dada were going to join her in the Rob Roy Hotel excited only the deepest sympathy – for it was reported they are both drowned.

A gathering of the Volunteers in the Phoenix Park, Dublin.

O'Donovan Rossa buried in Dublin

Monday, August 2

Every district throughout the length and breath of Ireland paid its tribute of respect to the memory of O'Donovan Rossa in Dublin yesterday afternoon.

Though the policy in which O'Donovan Rossa was such a prominent figure is not one that will appeal to Irishmen of the present day, it must be stated that the people connected with the Fenian movement were animated with feelings of the purest patriotism and to achieve the noble and worthy object they had in view – the freedom of their country – they made many brave and even terrible sacrifices. In that movement Mr Jeremiah O'Donovan Rossa was a leading and active worker, and his demise has recalled to every Irishman stirring times in the history of his country. It was a funeral of most representative and imposing dimensions. It occupied one hour and five minutes to pass a given point.

NEWS BRIEFS

Jan German professor Kuno Meyer is removed from the list of Freemen of Cork for a speech he had made in New York against the British Empire. Meyer, who was also a Freeman of Dublin and several other towns, had been originally granted the honour because of his work promoting the Irish language. (9)

April To the north of Ypres the Germans, by employing a large quantity of asphyxiating bombs, the effect of which was felt a distance of two kilometres behind Allied lines, succeeded in forcing them to retire. (24)

The Cork Examiner.

NO. 19,346 — SATURDAY MORNING MAY 8, 1915. — PRICE—ONE PENNY

Registered for transmission at newspaper rate of postage to the United Kingdom, and at Magazine Rate to Canada and Newfoundland.

HUNS AWFUL CRIME.

LUSITANIA TORPEDOED OFF CORK HARBOUR WITHOUT WARNING.

NEARLY 1,500 DROWNED

SINKS IN TWENTY MINUTES.

APPALLING SPECTACLE.

RUSH TO RESCUE.

SAVING SURVIVORS.

QUEENSTOWN SCENES.

THRILLING INTERVIEWS.

Survivors from the Lusitania at Queenstown.

One of the most appalling crimes in history was perpetrated on the Cork Coast yesterday.

About two o'clock in the afternoon, in beautiful weather, the Cunarder Lusitania, which left New York last Saturday, was passing the Cork Coast on her way to Liverpool.

When a few miles off the Old Head of Kinsale, while the passengers were at lunch, a torpedo was fired from a submarine. No warning whatever was given.

The great liner was struck near the second funnel, and at once began to sink by the head.

A second, and, some say a third, torpedo, struck the ship. In a very few moments the liner began to fall over on the side, rendering the lowering of many of the boats impossible.

In about twenty minutes from the time of the first torpedo having struck her, the Lusitania had disappeared beneath the waters. Interviews full of the most thrilling details appear with the survivors.

A large number were brought to Queenstown, while a few, with some dead bodies, arrived at Kinsale. A number of others are said to be on trawlers and steamers that had not reported themselves up to last night.

Until it is known how many these will add to the list of saved, reliable figures cannot be given.

But last night the calculation was made that the death-roll can not be much less than that of the Titanic—about 1,5?? souls

It was stated from Queenstown early this morning that the captain is amongst the saved.

Yesterday's French despatch announced that in the evening of the 6th the Germans delivered a futile attack at Bagatelle, in the Argonne. To the north of Ypres and elsewhere there had been violent artillery duels.

A well-known German military expert, Major Moraht, warns the German people not to base extravagant hopes on the claims of victory against the Russians.

In Ypres district, he points out, that the British are in a position of great strength. There was no question of breaking through or achieving any decisive success at an early date.

He pooh-poohs recent German claims of important successes, and ridicules the rumours of dissension among the Allies.

The news of the torpedoing of the Lusitania created consternation amongst all classes in the South of Ireland, and though German methods of warfare on land and sea had prepared the public mind for surprises, still it was scarcely regarded as conceivable that German brutality should take such a colossal and fiendish shape as to murder hundreds of people who had taken no part in the war, and who came from a country which has never wearied of proclaiming its neutrality. Never in the world's history has such an appallingly callous and senseless sacrifice of human life been made—never have victims been immolated so brutally to satisfy a tyrant's greed for world power. The instinctive feeling amongst civilised people which recognises the right of women and children to protection in times of peril, seemed to preclude the possibility that Prussian methods of warfare would include the destruction of mothers and babes, who were not Germany's foes, and who owed allegiance only to the Stars and Stripes. Yet all these views were dissipated and shattered when it became known that the Lusitania had been sunk by a German submarine, and the feeling of amazement that followed the realisation of such brutality was succeeded by the overwhelming desire that a country which could perpetrate such a crime in cold blood should be humbled before the world and made to taste the bitterness of defeat.

(From our Reporters).

When it became known that the liner had sunk, sensation prevailed in Queenstown. Persons of all classes anxiously sought for the latest news, and not many there were who had near relatives on board. Therefore, the tension that the news created may be readily imagined. People excitedly inquired of the Cunard Office as to the fate of their friends, and the laconic answers to their questions brought but little consolation.

There was no case to the state that was naturally created, and consequently it was not surprising to see the general rush to the Cunard wharf as the first boat conveying the rescued berthed. The most stringent regulations were enforced by the authorities to prevent any congestion that may hinder the facilities for the removal of the rescued to hotels.

Therefore, it was difficult to obtain any ideas as to the exact toll that the German brutality had exacted. It was, however, subsequently ascertained that the total on board—passengers and crew—was 2,150—made up as follows:—290 first, 600 second, 360 third, and the remainder crew. Of these, only between 500 and 700 have been saved, and this leaves about 1,400 lost.

As the survivors were landed, the scene was most pathetic. Many there were borne on stretchers, some of whom were dead; others limped between naval men, and more still walked between the lines of people, who cheered them, without coats or any comfortable apparel.

It was really a most pathetic sight, and excited the most profound sympathy of the crowd of people who watched their removal to hotels and other places of comfort.

There were many conjectures as to the number saved, but this much is positively ascertained from those who arrived at Queenstown. The Stormcock was the first vessel with survivors to arrive. She had on board about 150, and most of the passengers which she landed presented very sad sights. Not one of them had any substantial garments on them, and the majority of the men were without their coats, and carried lifebelts. Their appearance was certainly dejected, but as nothing compared to the women, who, without hats, cloaks, or wraps, and with hair tossed by the waves, looked ruffled and miserable.

Those of the complement on board, who had escaped without injury, were cheerful, and under their extreme trial bore up well. The procession was sad, and, indeed, pathetic. The crowd cheered with an intense sympathy, but this, the message of the welcome of the townspeople, seemed only to accentuate the unhappy condition of people, who, in the best of spirits, set out to cross the Atlantic on board the Lusitania last Saturday.

The real awfulness of the happening was foreshadowed in the dejected appearance of all who traversed the Cunard wharf from the Stormcock, which brought 150, the Brock with about 100, and another trawler with an equal number. In computing the number saved it must be reckoned that two schooners also assisted in the work of rescue, and made for the English Coast. In this way the conclusion is arrived at by many of those on board that between 500 and 700 have been rescued.

It is reported that Mr. Vanderbilt was among those who were drowned. But this is at present only a matter of conjecture.

The pitiable plight of those who landed at Queenstown was very evident, because many of them had been for hours in the water, and most of them had to endure the hardships of being tossed about in the ocean in small boats. Some of the men were not half dressed, and others had to be satisfied with the covering of a rug.

The women folk presented a most pathetic sight. Their hair was dishevelled, they sobbed bitterly, and their clothing was indeed very scanty in many cases, while in more than one case the kindness of a sailor in giving them his overalls or pants and vest constituted their attire.

Then there was the careless joy of the little ones—and there were many children on board. Their laughter and intense excitement to babble over all that had happened, heightened the awful sadness of the picture of so many hundreds of human beings walking in processional order to a place of shelter—they had lost all they possessed. From this fact may be gathered their hurried exit from the doomed liner. For be it remembered that the magnificent liner was torpedoed about two o'clock in the day. The passengers were partaking of luncheon when the loud crash of the torpedo was heard on her starboard side. There was an immediate confusion. The bells rang to lower the boats, but that sound had only died away when yet another torpedo struck her and passed right through. She listed to starboard, and her bows dipped. The boats were being lowered, but only about twelve got clear; and within fifteen minutes the liner had fallen right over and sank.

There was no time to regulate matters, and it is natural to assume that panic prevailed, for within a short quarter of an hour over two thousand souls had death staring them in the face. It was a case of every man for himself, but taking the proportion of women and children landed at Queenstown, it is also reasonable to believe that there was the utmost gallantry exhibited.

It is a sad story, but a short one. The Lusitania was gone; it remained for those on board to save themselves. Fortunately the sea was calm, and those who were safely lowered in the boats had reason to thank the mercy of Providence. Yet, again, others who disregarded the boats but took on life-belts and plunged into the ocean were given an excellent chance to save their lives. They struggled hardly for what seemed an interminable time, and ultimately reached the comparative safety of a boat. Many clung to spars, and others there were who reached upturned boats, which they eventually righted, and not alone rescued themselves, but by pulling around for some time were afforded the opportunity of taking others out of their unhappy plight.

Their disconcerting state may be easily imagined, as also the joy with which they hailed the hoving in sight of the rescue tugs Stormcock, Warrior, Flying Fox, and some trawlers. The work of rescue was a matter of not a little difficulty, and considering the distance to her—about 30 miles from Queenstown—it is gratifying that the ships which left Cork Harbour to give assistance were able to accomplish so much. Their arrival back in port with their passengers was hailed with much satisfaction. The injuries to many may be accounted for by their difficulty in getting clear of the sinking liner or by wreckage falling on them.

In view of the fact that the rumour has gained currency that the captain of the Lusitania, Capt. Turner, fired on the submarine when called on to stop, it is imperative to state that our representative learned on the authority of a steward of the liner that she was not armed. Therefore, it is obvious that there is no truth in the rumour, which evidently was made to justify the barbarity of the Germans in torpedoing, without warning, a Transatlantic liner, and not alone firing on her once, but twice to make sure that she would go to the bottom with her human freight and large mail. It is authoritatively stated that she was fired on without warning; and thus with absolute callousness were over two thousand souls left to the mercy of the waves, and to find the easiest way from a watery grave by the abominable act of the Germans, whose desperation appears to have driven them mad.

DISASTER DESCRIBED.

THRILLING INTERVIEWS.

CANADIAN JOURNALIST'S STORY.

Mr. Ernest Cooper, a journalist, belonging to Toronto, Canada, was on board the Lusitania. He was travelling across with his editor, and for the purpose, as he put it, of getting first-hand war copy.

In the course of a conversation with an "Examiner" representative Mr. Cooper said for some days before the catastrophe everybody on board seemed to be talking about the chances of the Lusitania getting torpedoed. There was a good deal of chaffing amongst the passengers, but everyone was in the best of spirits, and had complete confidence in the liner. Those who spoke so lightly about the prospects of falling in with German submarines never dreamt that they were so near death. Approaching the Irish coast a sharp look-out was kept by the crew, and it appears the boats were made ready for launching at a moment's notice.

"I was standing aft," said Mr. Cooper, "near the entrance to the smoking saloon, chatting with a friend, when I thought I saw what was the conning tower of a submarine about a thousand yards distant. I called my

Page recreated

1916

The Easter Rising began on Monday, April 24, but a suppression of news meant that only minor reports were published in the *Examiner* until the insurrectionists were almost completely defeated.

Reports in the aftermath of the Rising carried concerns among the legal profession in the UK that, by trying the rebel leaders through court martial, they would be denied certain rights that they would be entitled to in a civilian court.

The *Examiner* was one of the constitutional Nationalist voices that saw the Rising as misguided and urged restraint in how the rebels should be punished. These calls weren't heeded and, in a massive miscalculation, the speedy execution of the rebel leaders turned the tide of public support in favour of the rebels.

More poor military planning was in evidence in the Somme offensive in July. The gap between the version of events allowed in the newspapers and what was actually going on at the Western Front is apparent from reports of the assault on heavily defended German positions. Overall it was an absolute disaster, which left 650,000 dead on the British side alone.

Dublin up in smoke

Monday, May 1

Dublin, Thursday: The rebels are fighting with the courage of despair and recklessly they have taken little precaution to prevent risk to the civilian population.

The city today presented a remarkable spectacle. Under martial law, the military has taken charge of the town, and hardly a civilian was to be seen in the thoroughfares. For three and a half days Dublin has been held in the throes of warfare. Great buildings have been set on fire with dense smoke hanging like a black roll in the sky. A Sinn Féin gun was discharged, and then came an instant reply from the loyal rifle, and then a short lull after which the practice was repeated. At intervals came the sounds of machine gun fire. So the dreary day passed on.

Yesterday the military authorities had completed their line round the rebels where the outbreak occurred, and fully established their ascendancy over their adversaries.

The rebels had in their possession practically the whole of Sackville Street, which was heavily barricaded. They were also in possession of their outreached position in St Stephen's Green.

Dubliners pass by the GPO in the aftermath of the Easter Rising.

Shops looted

Monday, May 1

Consternation seized the peaceful citizens. They were unarmed, and what could they do against thousands of armed and desperate men who had suddenly raised the standard of rebellion? Men and women broke into shops and looted their contents.

Here would be seen a man with an armful of boots, carefully selecting the proper fit as he sat on the pavement. Women could be seen in jewellers' shops making a selection of rings and brooches. Children did not forget the opportunity to get unlimited sweets for nothing.

Mr FH Mullin of Reading left Dublin on Friday evening. He told the following story: "In Sackville Street shops have been burnt and looted. Gold watches were going for half a crown apiece, and it was a common sight to see the womenfolk of the rebels trying on the latest thing in hats in public."

Western blow on 25-mile front

Monday, July 3

(Philip Gibbs, with the British Armies in the field): The great attack which was launched today against the German lines on a twenty-mile front began satisfactorily. It is not yet a victory, for victory comes at the end of a battle and this is only the beginning. But our troops fighting with splendid valour have swept across the enemy's front trenches along a great part of the line of attack, and have captured villages and strongholds which the Germans have long held against us.

They are fighting their way forward not easily but doggedly. Many hundreds of the men are prisoners in our hands. His dead lie thick in the track of our regiments. And so after the first day of the battle we may say with thankfulness all goes well. It is a good day for England and France. It is a day of promise in this war, in which the blood of brave men is poured out upon the sodden fields of Europe.

Last night Paris reported that north of the Somme fighting continued all day in their favour. Thanks to the effective artillery preparation, thanks also to the dash of their infantry, their losses have been very slight.

CITY EDITION

The Cork Examiner.

NO. 19,652 | MONDAY MORNING MAY 1, 1916 | PRICE—ONE PENNY

Registered for transmission as newspaper rate of postage in the United Kingdom, and at Magazine Rate to Canada and Newfoundland.

DUBLIN.

DETAILS AT LAST.

AMAZING SCENES.

LEADERS AND SURRENDER

OFFICIAL ANNOUNCEMENT.

POST OFFICE DESTROYED.

On Saturday night we were officially informed that a document had been signed by Mr. Pearse, the leader of the Volunteers, stating that in order to prevent the further slaughter of unarmed people and in the hope of saving the lives of their followers, now surrounded and hopelessly outnumbered, the members of the Provisional Government present at Headquarters have agreed to an unconditional surrender.

Last night it was officially added that Mr. James Connolly, the Larkenite leader, unconditionally surrendered to the General Officer Commanding-in-Chief in Ireland. The leaders, anxious to avoid further bloodshed, have signed a notice to other leaders and their parties both in Dublin and in the country calling on them to surrender as their cause is hopeless. A large number of men surrendered, and it is expected that others followed during the course of the day.

It was also stated that emissaries have come in from the Sinn Fein party at and about Ashbourne and Swords and from Wexford to verify the fact of the above surrender with a view to their immediate surrender.

Earlier in the day it was officially announced that the Dublin Post Office and other buildings were destroyed by fire. The troops surround the rioters' strongholds. The remainder of Ireland is generally satisfactory.

At midnight a Viceregal communique stated that Pearse had surrendered, and the great bulk of his supporters in Dublin and throughout the country have done likewise. Only a few detached bodies have not yet made their submission, and these are being effectively dealt with, the despatch said.

Details of the events in Dublin from journalists who accompanied Mr. Birrell appear to-day.

It is officially announced from the Tigris that General Townshend has been compelled by final exhaustion of supplies to surrender. Before doing so guns and ammunition were destroyed. 2,970 British troops and 6,000 Indian troops constituted the force.

H.M.S. Russell struck a mine in the Mediterranean and sunk. About 124 officers and men missing. The Russell was a battleship of the "A" class, completed in 1904. Her tonnage was 14,000, and her ordinary complement 750 men.

A German submarine was sunk off the east coast. One officer and seventeen men surrendered.

Sir D. Haig reports that near Loos the gallant fighting of the 16th Irish Division broke up a German attack delivered under cover of gas.

A French expert, writing on the subject of the loss of the British battleship Russell, says that what will console the British Navy is the certainty that since the capture of the U26 at Havre the two fleets have destroyed or captured several more German submarines both in the Mediterranean and in the North Sea.

The French officially report that two attacks made by the Germans on the right bank of the Meuse were repulsed.

DUBLIN SCENES.

The O'Connell Statue in O'Connell Street, showing the Dublin Bread Company's great tea rooms and other premises at the corner of O'Connell street. (N.I.)

MR. AUGUSTINE [illegible], who has resigned his position as Chief Secretary for Ireland.

Examining passengers' passports on a Liffey bridge. Carts, etc., as barriers placed by the rebels not yet removed. Law Courts on the left at back. (N.I.)

Page recreated

1917

America's entry into the war in April was a great boost for the Allies. However, in the United States itself, among the main voices opposing the move was a large body of Irish-American opinion which didn't want to support the British.

While Britain gained one ally in 1917, it lost another when the Bolsheviks took over in Russia. *Examiner* editorials after the October revolution were much more concerned about Lenin's plans to remove Russia from the conflict, rather than expressing any of the 'godless Communist' fears that would follow later.

By now, several columns of the *Examiner* would regularly be filled with lists of dead officers, many of whom were from the Irish regiments.

One group of men who did come home were those who had been imprisoned after the Easter Rising. Their unconditional release helped rejuvenate Sinn Féin and, at the Árd Fheis in October, recently-elected MP for East Clare, Éamon de Valera, was made president of the organisation.

Meanwhile, Michael Collins was in the process of reorganising the IRB into a more effective military force.

In fashion, as can be seen from the advertisement on the opposite page, Ireland's well-to-do ladies had a range of exotic animal furs on offer to keep them warm in winter.

Huge welcome for de Valera

Tuesday, June 19

The city wore a holiday appearance yesterday, deriving its extra animation from the crowds of young men and women who gathered to greet the released Irish prisoners. Sinn Féin colours were to be seen everywhere and young girls in green costumes were numerous.

All prisoners except the Countess Markievicz arrived at Holyhead by special train yesterday morning. The prisoners were in the charge of Mr de Valera. They were in fair health but looked haggard, and wore stubby beards. On alighting from the train they sang 'The Soldiers Song', formed up and joined the Kingstown boat before the ordinary passengers. They declined to make any statement.

On the boat, so accustomed had they become to the ways of prison life, that the released prisoners walked around the decks in the same manner as they exercised in the prison yards. De Valera was dressed in a grey suit and appeared very pale; whilst W Cosgrave was very thin and looked in delicate health. Thomas Ashe was very strong looking.

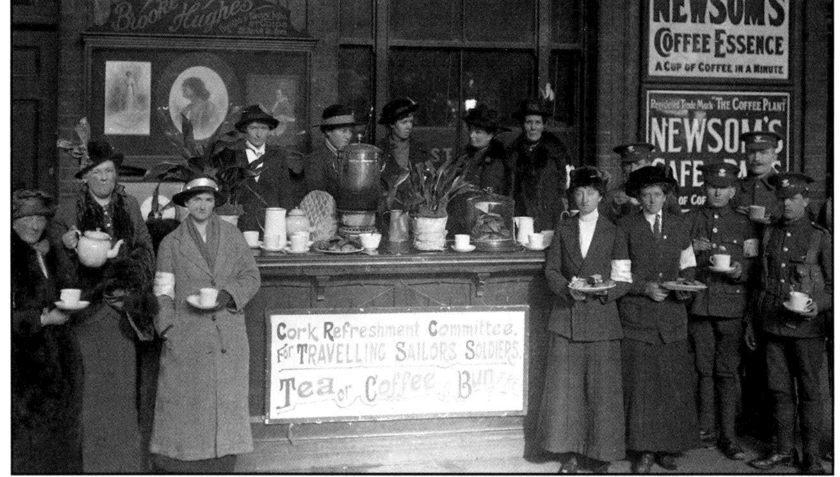

Refreshment rooms in Cork for members of the armed forces.

NEWS BRIEFS

Mar On the same hundred yards or so of the Dublin quays yesterday, the interesting spectacle was witnessed of an extensive and numerous collection of Irish draught horses drawn up in a more or less orderly queue and awaiting the opening of the gangways leading to outward-bound steamers. Virtually side by side with these horses leaving Ireland was another line – of puffing field tractors, which now take the place of the exiled equines and 'come in' as regularly as the deposed agricultural animals 'go out'. (28)

On footpaths people should keep to the right. But for the one person who follows this rule at least five are apparently unaware of its existence. Even in Dublin everybody does not keep to the right on the footpath. In Cork notices have been put up on the principal streets directing people to "keep to the right", but so far no great improvement is observable, and no little confusion occurs where the streets are crowded. (28)

The number of deaths from measles in Dublin last week was double that of the previous week, being 16. Not withstanding the recommendation to have the infant schools closed during the epidemic, some of them still remain open, thus helping to spread the disease. (29)

Oct Mr John Dinan, Managing Director of Messrs Eustace and Co, Cork, has received a telegram from the King commiserating with him on the death of his three sons at the Front. (16)

The Cork Examiner.

NO. 20,093 FRIDAY MORNING, SEPTEMBER 28, 1917 PRICE—ONE PENNY

Registered for transmission at newspaper rate of postage in the United Kingdom, and at Magazine Rate to Canada and Newfoundland

OUR BUYER

HAS RETURNED FROM THE LONDON MARKETS WITH A VERY PRETTY SELECTION OF

LAMP, CANDLE, & ELECTRIC LIGHT SHADES.

ALSO A CHOICE SELECTION OF

PHOTO FRAMES AND LADY'S VANITY BAGS,

ANTIMONY AND SILVER WARE.

ARTIFICIAL FLOWERS FOR TABLE DECORATION, including a

LARGE VARIETY OF FANCY GOODS

THE LONDON HOUSE,
LTD.,
14 & 15, PATRICK STREET,
CORK.
Tel.—562. 5

F. ALLMAN & CO.

Reliable Underclothing
— AT —
A MODERATE PRICE.

NEW GOODS NOW ON SHOW.

1 & 2 WINTHROP STREET.
CORK 0

PRE-WAR PRICES

DISH PAPERS.
ASSORTED SIZES. 1/- PER BOX.

PHOTO FRAMES
IN GREAT VARIETY.

FANCY CLOCKS—a large number to select from.

PURCELL AND COMPANY.
124 PATRICK STREET, CORK. 7

BOLSTER'S

Breakfast Tea
IS UNRIVALLED.

BOLSTER'S,
79, Patrick St., Cork. 13

NAT ROSS

THE BEST
FURNITURE REMOVER

ST. PATRICK'S BRIDGE.
6724

— FOR —

CASH ADVANCES, FROM £5 UPWARDS

THE CITY AND COUNTRY LOAN CO., LTD., is the best and most reliable. For terms and particulars apply 12 O'CONNELL STREET, WATERFORD. 24

Refreshments ! Refreshments

THE CAFE

DRAWBRIDGE STREET, CORK.
(Near the Mathew Statue).

DINNERS, TEA AND COFFEE, MILK, MINERALS, ETC.

WOULD YOU BE WELL ?

The question may seem to be needless. Every sensible person would of course reply in the affirmative. Yet—strange as it may appear there are numberless people who require to be reminded to take care of their health! How many are there for example who are apt to treat lightly such an ailment as indigestion? They need to remember that numerous forms of ill-health can be traced, directly or indirectly, to defective digestion and the consequent imperfect assimilation of food. To anyone who is threatened with attacks of a dyspeptic nature this question: "Would you be well?" should arrest attention. They will act wisely who

THEN TAKE

the necessary steps to remove the trouble. A medicine to be recommended in the early stages of digestive troubles is that popular preparation known as Beecham's Pills. This is a remedy which has brought an immense amount of benefit to an enormous number of people. Three successive generations of men and women have experienced the beneficial effects of this unrivalled stomach and liver medicine. Would you be well? Would you feel and look well? Then take

BEECHAM'S PILLS

THE MODERN

MILLINERY, MANTLE, and FUR WAREHOUSE.

LYNX SET .... 35/6. SKUNK SET .... 9 GNS.

AUSTRALIAN OPOSSUM COAT, Skunk Trimmed. 20 GNS.
SIMILAR STYLE, Coney Trimmed Opossum .... 12 GNS.
„ „ Poney Fur Trimmed .... 10 GNS.

BLACK MUSQUASH COAT, Skunk Collar. 25 GNS.
Similar Style, SQUIRREL COAT .... 16 GNS.
NATURAL FLANK MUSQUASH .... 12 GNS.

FUR COATS.

A large Select Stock. Latest Shapes. Beautifully selected skins in Silver Flank, Natural and Black Musquash, Pony Skin, Coney, Wallaby, Squirrel, Opossum, etc., etc.

FURS & FUR SETS

Choice and Extensive Selection. All the Leading Shapes in Skunk, Skunk Opossum, Black, Natural, Blue, White and Red Fox, American and Australian Opossum, Fitch, Black and Brown Bear, etc., etc.

COSTUMES.

Smart New Plaid, Cheviot and Velour Models.

GOWNS.

New Bodice Gown, in Georgette, Ninon, Crepe-de-Chine, etc.

COATS.

Velour, Fleecy and Blanket, Plain, Fur-lined and Fur-trimmed Trench Coats. Large Selection.

MILLINERY.

Charming Dainty Models. Latest ideas in Hatters' Plush Munchon, Velours and Velvet. New Suede and Velvet Stitched Caps in all the Newest Colourings.

BEAR SET .... £3 19 6. SKUNK OPOSSUM, £5 15 6 FITCH SET .... 6 GNS.

10 & 13, GRAND PARADE, CORK.

MONEY.

£10 TO £5,000

ADVANCED by Private Tender on simple Promissory Note. No Bills of Sale taken, and absolute Privacy Guaranteed. First letter of application receives prompt attention, and intending borrowers are waited upon by a representative, who is empowered to complete transaction on terms mutually arranged—NO CHARGE BEING MADE UNLESS BUSINESS ACTUALLY COMPLETED. Special Quotations for Short Loans. Write in confidence to C. WELLS, 21 Exchequer Street, Dublin. 30

IMPORTANT TO FARMERS.

THE MUNSTER PRIVATE LOAN AND DISCOUNT OFFICES, LTD., 6, Sullivan's Quay, Cork, makes Cash Advances from £10 upwards, on approval personal security, on their own Promissory Note; also on Life and Endowment Policies. Before going elsewhere, kindly inspect our terms. All information can be had by writing or calling to above address. 29

EXTRAORDINARY OFFER.

A LARGE AMOUNT to lend in sums from £20 upwards on note of hand alone. Special low rates to all approved applicants and those dealing with other lenders can have their loans paid off or in-

"THE EXAMINER"

SMALL PREPAID ADVERTISEMENTS.
24 WORDS SIXPENCE.

BUSINESS NOTICES.

O'SULLIVAN'S celebrated Smoking Mixtures, best roll tobacco, bar and cut plug; large selection of cigars and cigarettes; the trade, hotels, clubs, supplied at moderate prices.—New York House. 863

EMBROIDERED Linen Blouse Fronts—Three for 5s 6d, assorted designs; fine white linen supplied to match, 36in wide, 1s 4d yd. Send for monthly Bargain Catalogue, free. Hutton's, 170, Larne, Ireland. 0567

BLAIR'S Tonic Blood Purifier is the best of all, as it makes pure rich blood, cleansing it from all impurities, and invigorating the system, price 1s 6d, by post 1s 10d. John Blair and Son, Chemists, 7 St. Patrick St. 263

MEDICINES sent to all parts of the country. Prescriptions carefully made up and forwarded by post without delay. Lowest prices. John Blair and Sons, Chemists, 7, St. Patrick Street, Cork. 42

THRESHING machine owners who require endless belts in Balata or leather; also machinery oils, galvanized pipes and fittings, steam jointings, etc., should send a postcard for price and particulars to Daniel R. Baker, mechanical and electrical engineers' supply store, Metropole Buildings, King St., Cork (two doors from Metropole Laundry). 898

TOMBSTONES, Crosses, and Memorials of

BUSINESS NOTICES.

BLASTING Explosives—Full strength Gelignite, standard quality, 50 per cent N.G. Gelignite (second quality); warming pans, detonators, safety fuses; special nippers, etc. T. W. Murray and Co., Cork, wholesale agents for Curtiss and Harvey, Ltd., London and Ballincollig. Note—Instructions for use of explosives in cold weather on application. 003

INCOME Tax—Relief and refunds got by Thomas Sweeney, Recovery Agent, Patrick St., Fermoy. 898

POTATOES! Potatoes! Potatoes—Farmers' Supply Stores, John St, Cork, beg to intimate to their numerous clients that they are receiving daily large supplies of best table potatoes; all orders will be promptly executed; 'phone 438; wires, Supply, Cork. 748

GRAMOPHONE Records—Double-sided Zonophone and Royal, 2s; 200 needles, loud tone, 1s; violin strings from 6d; oxygen gas, etc. W. V. Morris, 34, Grand Parade. 'Phone 392. Telegrams, "Limelight," Cork. 57

LAMPS, Lamps—Table, floor and suspension lamps, wick and chimneys, cart, van and carriage lamps (as approved by County Council). Large stocks; inspection invited. Haughton's (the Cork Timber and Iron Co., Ltd), 15 and 16 North Main St., Cork. 'Phone 851 (3 lines). 018

HIGH-CLASS ladies' and gents' hairdressers—Scalp and face vibro electric massage. Transformation wigs and ornamental hair of every description manufactured on scientific principles. Marcel and water wavers; combings made up at 1s per oz; orders promptly attended. Note address: 15 Patrick St. (over Wolfe's), next to

FINANCIAL.

£2, £3, £4, £5, £10, £20, to £200 advanced daily to all responsible borrowers, to be repaid by easy instalments; distance no object; no fees. Apply the Manager, King St., Queenstown. 377

ESTABLISHED since 1821—Estate and Discount Co., 6 Paul St., Cork—Loans granted on special terms, on leases, scrip or shares, life or endowment policies. 385

BUILDERS' MATERIALS.

ARTISTIC mantelpieces, fire grates, etc; hearths, fenders and kerbs, kitchen ranges, cooking appliances, locks, scales; large stock to select from. Haughton's, North Main St., Cork. 018

BEAVER board panelling dispenses with laths, plaster, and wall-paper; made of pure wood fibre; ideal finishing for walls and ceilings. Sole distributors for Munster and the South of Ireland—The Cork Timber and Iron Co., Ltd. (Telegrams: "Haughton, Cork"). 018

PLUMBERS' Requisites—Enamelled baths, lavatory basins, glazed sinks, sheet lead, lead piping, sewer pipes, and connections. Haughton's, 15 and 16 North Main St., Cork. 018

MOTORS AND CYCLES.

CYCLES and motor cycles—New stock just received. Place your orders now to avoid disappointment; old machines taken in part payment. J. T. Mulligan and Co., King St., Cork. 62

THANKSGIVING.

THANKSGIVING to the Sacred Heart, Our Lady of Lourdes, St. Joseph, St. Anthony, St. Theresa, Little Nellie, Holy Souls for favours received; publication delayed.—A.L. 144

IN thanksgiving to the Holy Family, Holy Souls, and Jesus in the Blessed Sacrament for favours received and others asked.—Heart-broken Kerry. 885

IN grateful thanks to the Sacred Heart, Blessed Virgin, St. Joseph, and the Little Flower of Jesus for a favour received by a poor woman. 5

MOST grateful thanks to Little King, Our Lady, and the Holy Souls for favours obtained; more wanted.—E. de M. 10

GRATEFUL thanksgiving to Our Lady of Lourdes, Mother of Perpetual Succour, Sacred Heart, Little Flower, Saints Joseph, Benedict, St. Anthony, and Poor Souls.—E. de M. 143

PROVISIONS.

TO Farmers—If you want to get best value at lowest price in Lunham's and Denny's pigs' heads, best green and smoked Irish bacon, finest ling and cod fish; best Cork-milled flour, meal, bran, etc., apply to Dorgan's, Coburg St. (a few doors from King St.), Cork. 601

PIGS' Heads! Pigs' Heads!—Finest Irish, 80s cwt; American bacon, hams, shoulders, dripping, lard, Irish cheddar cheese, dried ling, codfish, red and pickled herrings, all at lowest wholesale prices. Hayes Bros. and Co., Cork. 282

1918

By the time moves came to introduce conscription in Ireland, attitudes towards the war had changed considerably since the outbreak four years previously.

Irish casualties during the conflict were well on their way to the eventual total of 30,000 and the thousands of wounded returning from the battlefields helped ensure that no amount of press censorship could hide the awfulness and pointlessness of the war.

The aftermath of the Easter Rising had also hardened attitudes towards Britain and a plan to introduce conscription in Ireland found a united front of Nationalist opinion ready to campaign against the move.

Trade unions organised a one-day strike and both the Catholic hierarchy and Sinn Féin were at the forefront of resistance to conscription. Ultimately, British gains on the battlefield meant that the issue was never forced in Ireland.

Even with the huge Irish death toll already sustained during the war, the deaths of 500 people on the MV *Leinster*, a passenger ship torpedoed an hour out of Dún Laoghaire, had a huge impact, causing widespread mourning and the cancellation of sports events.

The latter part of the year at last brought some room for optimism, with the end of the war and the first general election since 1910. It was the first election where women could vote and Ireland returned the only woman MP when Constance Markievicz was elected for Sinn Féin in Dublin. De Valera's party had campaigned on a promise to declare a republic if elected and emerged as the biggest political force on the island.

An influenza epidemic swept across the world during the latter part of the year, resulting in an estimated 21 million deaths.

End of War

Tuesday, November 12

There was no hiding the great feeling of relief with which the news of the cessation of hostilities was received in Cork yesterday. All through the previous 48 hours the one great question on the lips of the people was "Has the armistice been signed?" Sunday night it was everywhere asked and yesterday it was answered. From early morning people foregathered around the city newspaper offices, the post office, at all points where speedy word might be expected to arrive.

Even though it was expected, the news spread like wildfire. "The war was over, slaughter was at an end" was the universal thought but there were thousands of homes in Cork to which it brought the great relief of the assurance of the safety of their loved ones on active service, wounded once, many times, or not at all, but still alive. Already visions of the homecoming chased themselves through the relieved but excited brains of mothers, sisters and wives.

A soldier crouches in his trench on the Western Front.

Anti-conscription pledge

Monday, April 22

Cork – Yesterday, the day appointed by resolution of the Irish Hierarchy at the meeting in Maynooth last Thursday, Masses of Intercession "to avert the scourge of conscription with which Ireland is threatened" were celebrated at a stated time in the several churches throughout the city.

The second step on the path of duty for the people outlined by the Bishops was taken outside the churches after all the Masses.

This pledge was: "Denying the right of the British Government to enforce compulsory service in this country, we pledge ourselves solemnly to one another to resist conscription by the most effective means at our disposal." The scenes so witnessed were truly remarkable, as the priest, having just left the Altar at which he had offered up the Holy Sacrifice of the Mass, removed his vestments and came outside the church wearing his alb and stole.

He stood on a pedestal, and bidding the thousands of men to remove their hats and lift their right hand, the priest, with his hand so uplifted read out the pledge, the words repeated by the vast crowds echoing through the streets or dying away over space and hills.

NEWS BRIEFS

Oct Cork – The callous inhumanity that sent to a watery grave so many hundreds of innocent people, men, women, and children, has excited widespread horror throughout the city. The grief that the sinking of the Royal mail steamer *Leinster* has brought into many homesteads in the city and the South is intense. (12)

Nov Limerick – Since last Friday there has been a recurrence of the influenza epidemic in the city. The number of deaths on Saturday has been considerable and on Sunday the interments to Mount St Lawrence were unusually high. (12)

Women sort tobacco leaves at Lambkins factory in Cork.

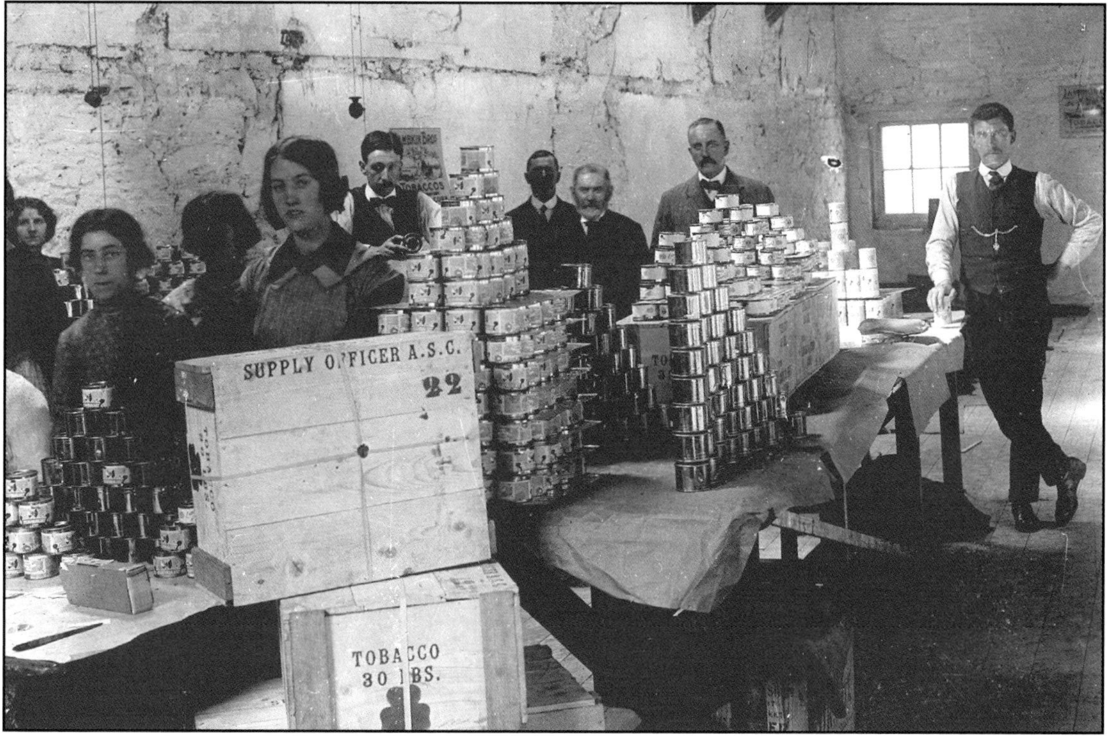

Tins of tobacco ready to be sent to the troops.

1919

The end of World War I did not mean that newspapers would now be filled with more peaceful news. On the same day that the first Dáil met, the first incident of the War of Independence took place when two policemen were killed in Tipperary.

For that first Dáil sitting, Sinn Féin was the only party that showed up and the fact that over half their TDs were in prison meant a house of only 27 people.

The new administration attempted to function as close to a government as possible under the circumstances while, on the military side, the Volunteers became the army of the Irish republic – the IRA.

In Limerick a major strike followed the imposition of military rule and the city was brought to a virtual standstill.

A soviet was declared that even used its own currency and, for a short time, proved to be quite an effective challenge to British rule in the city.

However, neither the trade union leadership nor Sinn Féin were up for such a fight and, after twelve days, opposition from the Catholic Church and employers helped bring the strike to an end.

Some relief from all this introspection was provided in June when British airmen John Alcock and Arthur Brown became the first people to fly non-stop across the Atlantic.

Dáil Éireann's first sitting

Wednesday, January 22

Within recent years no such interest has been centred in any function in the capital of Ireland as that associated with the Sinn Féin Constituent Assembly, which commenced its deliberations in the Mansion house this afternoon.

For some time past the opening sitting of Dáil Éireann (to give the function its Irish title) has attracted a considerable amount of publicity, and all forms of rumours or speculation have been circulated with regard to it.

A large crowd formed on the footpaths and sidewalks in the precincts of the Mansion House and occupied their time in watching the arrival of the Republican representatives, and extending to each a hearty welcome.

There was no delay in proceeding with the business, which was conducted in the Irish language.

The Chairman said they were met to do important work, the most important work that had been done in Ireland since foreigners landed in that country (cheers).

A British submarine passing Queenstown.

Limerick strike continues

Tuesday, April 22

Yesterday being Easter Monday and a long established holiday was, despite strike conditions and necessary limitations, observed with customary honours.

Some people may not be over-enthusiastic as to the methods which they pursue, but however that may be, their action has received general support, and from their point of view, scored success largely all through the city. Their establishment of milk and food depots has done great good and service, more especially to the poorer sections of the population, which the suddenness of the strike in a way caught napping.

It has improved the supply all round, lowered prices substantially, and afforded consumers an easy way of meeting and procuring their requirements.

As to the food supply depots, it is gratifying to learn that sympathisers from outside are sending in articles free of charge for distribution among the needy.

The strike committee are receiving their purpose-issued strike money notes for one shilling to 10 shillings each. On the outside border are printed the words: "General strike against British militarism, Limerick, April 1919".

In Limerick yesterday food supplies were received from many quarters. By proclamation of the Strike Committee, though it was a Bank Holiday, milk supply depots, bread shops and chemists opened.

NEWS BRIEFS

Jan The Catholic Church expresses its opposition to prohibition in America. Cardinal Gibbons declares: "Absolute prohibition will prevent 20,000 Catholic clergymen in the United States offering the daily sacrament of the Mass. Individual liberty of worship is thus restricted." (22)

Two policemen were shot dead by masked men while escorting a quantity of gelignite from Tipperary to Soloheadbeg Quarry, a distance of three miles from Tipperary. The affair has caused a great sensation in the district. (22)

April The high prices and scarcity of whiskey has led to the resumption of poteen manufacture on an extensive scale in many Irish districts. (16)

June German delegates at the post-war peace conference express their unhappiness at the terms imposed on them. They warn: "A permanent peace can never be established upon the oppression and enslavement of a great nation."(16)

CITY EDITION

The Cork Examiner.

NO. 20,628 MONDAY MORNING, JUNE 16, 1919. PRICE—THREE HALFPENCE.

Registered for transmission at newspaper rate of postage in the United Kingdom, and at Magazine Rate to Canada and Newfoundland.

ATLANTIC FLOWN.

PLANE LANDS NEAR GALWAY

16 HOUR FLIGHT.

TROUBLE IN ENGLISH TROOP CAMPS

COAL COMMISSION SENSATION

FRENCH STRIKE CRISIS.

The Atlantic has been successfully flown from St John's. Capt. Alcock with Mr. Brown as navigator, at 9.40 yesterday at Clifden, Galway, after a 16 hours' flight. The landing was difficult, owing to boggy ground, and both airmen were badly shaken and the machine injured. They were tired, Capt. Alcock said, of being alone in the fog. Sometimes they discovered they were flying upside down. Capt. Alcock contemplates flying on to Hendon.

It is believed that the Allies' reply to the German counter-proposals will be given to-day. Five days will, it is said, be the period of grace to sign. or reject. French newspapers express the fear that the Allied reply makes important concessions, including the suppression of the economic restrictions on Germany, and the speedy admission of Germany to the League of Nations.

At Macroom Judge Hynes awarded £800 compensation to Constable Butler and £500 to Constable James Bennet, both of whom were attacked on the night of the 7th July last, while returning from a proclaimed Feis in the vicinity of Ballyvourney to their station at Ballingeary.

In Cork yesterday, Blackrock hurlers beat Redmonds by 7 goals to 2 goals and a point.

A man died in the South Infirmary on Saturday night from injuries received some hours before, by falling from a swing boat on the Marina.

Canadian troops at the Witley (Surrey) Camp demonstrated on Saturday night against delays in repatriation. Some buildings were destroyed by fire.

At the Coal Commission on Saturday it was alleged that at a meeting addressed by Mr. Duncan Graham, M.P., one of the miners' secretaries in Scotland, he advised his hearers not to exert themselves, but to do as little as possible and see that they got as much money as possible for it.

Following the proclamation of Kilmallock Feis baton charges took place in the town. Many persons were injured.

French Miners strike to-day, but Clemenceau settled the trouble with the transport workers.

Big military forces have been searching the Glen of Aherlow and adjoining districts. It is said they were seeking a man wounded in the Knocklong affray.

Onlookers view the plane in Clifden, Co Galway.

BUSINESS NOTICES.

BLASTING Explosives.—Curtis's and Harvey's world-renowned explosives. Magazine's: Ballincollig, County Cork. Gelignite, Blasting Powder, Safety Fuses, detonators, warming pans, special nippers, electric fuses, etc. T. W. Murray and Co., Patrick street, Cork, wholesale agents for South of Ireland. 603

GUN Cartridges—Loaded best smokeless powder No 5 or 6 shot can be supplied on receipt of the necessary permits. T. W. Murray and Co., Cartridge Loaders, 87 Patrick street, Cork.

HEMSTITCHED Sheets.—Snow-white hemstitched cotton sheets, superior quality, 2 by 3 yds, 25s; 2¼ by 3 yds, 28s; 2½ by 3 yds, 31s per pair. Hutton's, 170, Larne, Ireland. 13

THE Sawmills, Carriage and General Works of the late E. McSweeney, Crookstown, are carrying on business as usual. Orders promptly attended to. Funeral undertaking added. 735

SPECIAL line of cream laid envelopes, 25 for 4d, 100 for 1s 3d, postage 6d extra. Eagle Stationery Warehouse, South Mall, Cork. 522

MOTHIDIE, the king of insect powders, kills all insects, 1s 2d per tin, post free 1s 4d. Rohu and Sons, 72 Grand Parade. 524

MALACCA canes for chimney and drain brushes, 1s, 6d; whips and hurling balls from our tanned leather; all prices.—McNally, 7, Bowling Green street, Cork. 531

552

SMOKERS—The up-to-date house for smokers. T. Barrett and Son, 10, Cook St., Cork. 694

NOTICE—Bazaars, galas and fetes attended with juvenile hobby horses, swings, houp las, and numerous side shows; terms most moderate. Apply F. Tierney, 15 Winthrop street, Cork. 329

MEDICINES sent to all parts of the country. Prescriptions carefully made up and forwarded by post without delay. John Blair and Sons, Chemists, 7, St. Patrick street, Cork. 47

BLAIR'S Tonic Blood Purifier is the best of all, as it cleanses the blood from heat and all impurities, and invigorates the system. Price 1s 8d, by post 2s 0d. John Blair and Sons, Chemists, 7, Patrick St.

LONG Oilskin Coats, 11s 6d; heavy fawn cycling capes, 8s; navy canvas leggings, 3s 6d; navy wool blankets, 16s 5d; base drum, 73s. Lawlor's, Fownes' St., Dublin. 355

INCOME Tax.—Finance Act, 1918.—Farmers assessed and desiring exemption, should apply at once, Patrick Cronin, Tax Adjustment Office, Charleville. 937

SUIT lengths at very lowest prices. Patterns post free. Minson (Dept E.), 17 Swaine street, Bradford, Yorks. 205

DRESS and Costume lengths, at very lowest prices, patterns free. Minson (Dept. E.),

WANTED.

WILLIAM Kinmonth and Sons, Cork, want fowls, ducklings, chickens, in large quantities; high prices paid. Cash returned daily. Crates supplied. Established 1850. 660

WILLIAM Kinmonth and Sons, Cork, want large consignments of clean, new-laid eggs; highest prices paid. Egg merchants, Woods St., Cork. Established 1850. 659

WILLIAM Kinmonth and Sons, Cork, want feathers of all kinds. Send postal samples.

WILLIAM Kinmonth and Sons, Salmon Factors, Woods street, Cork, want large quantities of salmon and trout during the season; highest prices paid. Established 1850. Ref: Munster and Leinster Bank. Telephone, 413.

J. TWOHIG wants any quantity of old fowl, ducks, geese and turkeys; highest prices paid. Crates sent to nearest station. Stores: 7 and 8, Lough- road, Cork. References: National Bank. 681

T. O'SHEA and Son, Merchant St., Cork, want consignments of large, clean, fresh eggs in large quantities; highest prices paid. Bankers: Provincial Bank of Ireland, Ltd., Cork.

JAM Pots.—Orders booked for 50,000 gross; dealers' prices quoted privately on application; highest prices paid for mixed or sorted rags and tailors' clippings. Goldberg, 15 Adelaide street, Cork. 110

HIGHEST price paid for rags, old iron, metal, copper, brass, lead, zinc, horse and cow hair, tailors' and dressmakers' clippings. S. Sherling, iron and metal merchant, 25 Kyrl's quay, and 33 Maylor street. 768

WE are buyers of old gold, jewellery, emeralds, diamonds, pearls, etc., for highest cash prices; post parcels receive prompt attention. Wm. Egan and Son, Ltd., Jewellers, Patrick street, Cork. 70

J. HARRINGTON, 13, Great George's street, Cork, wants fowls, chickens, etc; also new-laid eggs; highest prices paid. Cash returned daily. Reference: Ulster Bank, Cork. 620

CLIPPINGS—Tailors' and dressmakers' clippings, mixed rags, feathers, curled hair; highest prices paid. Mednitc, 23 Tuckey street. 174

WE pay higher prices than any other merchants for brass, copper, lead, zinc, iron and metal, waste rubber, tailors' and dressmakers' clippings, and rags. Sayers and Co., Lavitt's quay. 196

TO Dealers Only—Jam Pots! Jam Pots!—We pay 2s 1d per dozen 2lb pots; 1s 7d for 1lb pots per dozen. We also buy all sorts of bottles. Sayers and Co., Lavitt's quay. 195

EGGS! Eggs! Eggs!—John G. Marsh, Wholesale Provision Merchant, Whitechurch, Cardiff, is a buyer of fresh, clean eggs, for cash, or will accept on consignment; best prices given. Bankers: Messrs. National Bank, Ltd.,

FARM—GARDEN—POULTRY.

MOWERS—We are now booking orders for Pierce's Irish-made "Victor" Mowers, the machines with world-renowned record, guaranteed second to none, and superior to most imported machines. Farmers, be practical, buy the "Pierce," and save money and trouble in harvesting your crops. Sole Cork agents—Lucey and O'Connell, Mulgrave road.

ANTIRRHINUMS (leading varieties), Calceolarias, Lobelia, Sweet Pea., Stocks, Asters, Mimulus, Dianthus, and all other varieties of bedding plants. Tomato, Cucumber and Vegetable Marrows, at moderate prices. M. Kirwan, Skahabeg Nurseries, Douglas road, Cork. 430

ASTERS (latest novelty), America's finest strain; Giant "Grego," branching varieties (to colour), colossal flowers like huge Chrysanthemums, 12 to 15 blooms per plant. First time offered in Ireland, 1s 6d per doz, cash with order, postage 6d extra. M. Kirwan, Skahabeg Nurseries, Douglas road, Cork. Price list post free. 431

CELERY—Strong Stocky, well grown stuff, 3s per 100; 25s per 1,000; postage extra.—Skahabeg Nurseries, Cork. 556

MOWING Machines—The world-famed Albion and Massey-Harris mowers; every machine guaranteed. Agents, McBride and Sons, Ltd., Merchants quay, Cork. 180

MOWERS! Mowers! Mowers!—Come and see our stock and ask prices from McBride and Sons, Ltd., Merchants quay, Cork. Repairs a speciality. 181

POTATO Blight Preventative.—Spraying powder, prepared for immediate use, also bluestone and washing soda, at lowest prices. Browne, Thompson and Co., Seedsmen, Cork. 204

TURNIP seed from finest selected stocks—"Best of All" and "Conqueror" Swedes, Yellow Flesh and White Flesh turnips. Harris and Beale, Grand Parade, Cork.

BRADSHAW—Tomato plants, all the finest varieties; also open plants, at 2s 3d per doz; all prices; pots, post free; celery, white, red and pink, at 3s per 100; 50, 1s 9d, free.

BRADSHAW, Artane, Dublin—Cauliflower, Early London, at 4s 6d 100; sprouts, 2s 6d; onions, 2s; cabbage, 1s 6d; all per 100; thyme, mint, parsley, and red cabbage, 6d per doz.

BRADSHAW, Artane Dublin—Over 100,000 Stocks, Asters, Antirrhinums, and Pansies to offer at 1s per doz., post paid. Please ask for my price list, free.

BRADSHAW, Artane, Dublin—Violas, I hold the premier collection in Ireland; 48 distinct varieties to select from, at 2s 9d per doz, free; get my Viola list, free.

BEE hives bar frame, C.D.B. and cottagers; wax foundation, sections, feeders,

ATLANTIC FLIGHT.

VICKERS-VIMY STARTS.

St. John's, Saturday.—The Vickers Vimy machine started at 4.13 Greenwich time.—Reuter.

St. John's, Saturday, 4.20.—When the Vickers Vimy aeroplane, piloted by Capt. John Alcock, with Lieut. Arthur Brown as navigator, started on the Atlantic flight at 4.13 this afternoon the machine had a heavy pull at first to gain her altitude, owing to the heavy load, but continued to climb slowly as she sped westward towards Conception Bay, barely missing houses, trees and hills as she went. In Conception Bay she swung around. With a following breeze she climbed gradually to a greater height, and returned over the ground north of the aerodrome.

The aeroplane left the Coast line by the signal station overlooking the harbour, at a height of about a thousand feet. She has now passed out of sight, heading direct for Ireland.—Reuter.

St. John's, Saturday (later).—The Vickers Vimy aeroplane has now been gone for three hours, and no wireless report regarding its progress has yet been received. The steamer Digby has sent a wireless message stating that she is in a dense fog, and is unable to see anything, nor has she received any news by wireless of the machine.—Reuter.

Page recreated

1920

What had been a series of attacks on the security forces in 1919 had evolved into full-scale guerrilla warfare by the end of 1920. Much of the activity was in the *Examiner's* Munster catchment area, and most of the province was placed under martial law.

With recruitment to the RIC at a standstill, the introduction of the 'Black and Tans' further increased resentment of British rule. This infamous force joined with the Auxiliaries in a burning and looting rampage in Cork city in December.

While nobody reading the *Examiner* reports would have been in any doubt as to who was responsible, the paper never actually states that it was the British forces, presumably because of military restrictions.

Cork also lost two Lord Mayors in the troubles – Tomás MacCurtain was shot at home by men widely suspected to be from the security forces, while Terence MacSwiney died in Brixton prison after a 74-day hunger-strike in pursuit of political status.

Ten persons shot dead at Croke Park

Monday, November 22

Terrible scenes took place during the Tipperary and Dublin match at Jones's road today. At about 3.30pm twelve lorries containing armed forces of the Crown drove down on the grounds.

Shots at first seemed to be fired in the air, but subsequently shots were discharged into the crowd. The armed forces, according to many present, gave no warning to the spectators to disperse, beyond the preliminary volley fired into the air.

During the stampede that followed men, women and children rushed wildly for shelter. Michael Hogan, the well-known Tipperary player, was shot through the mouth and died instantly. Many people were injured in the stampede.

Pathetic scenes were witnessed in the grounds when, prior to the arrival of the ambulance, small crowds gathered around Hogan's body and recited the Rosary.

He was a ghastly spectacle as he lay there on the ground in his player's costume, decorated by a green and gold sash.

A priest who was present found poor Hogan lying in a pool of blood, his feet stretched out in the playing pitch, and blood oozing from his left side.

Part of the first group of Auxiliaries to arrive in Cork.

Night of terror

Monday, December 13

Cork has never experienced such a night of horror as that of Saturday. The residents in every part of the city were terrified by the rifle and revolver firing, bomb explosions, extensive outbreaks of fire, the breaking and smashing of windows and business premises and crashing of walls of buildings.

Ten o'clock had only arrived when a serious conflagration broke out in the fine business premises of Messrs A Grant and Co at Patrick Street. The flames raged with great intensity and within an hour the building was reduced to ruins.

During the outbreak, the smashing of glass and breaking of shutters on premises in different parts of the city resounded through the air, and intensified the consternation of the residents in the flat of the city.

With remarkable suddenness the extensive and valuable premises of Messrs Cash and Co and the Munster Arcade burst into flame. These were two terrible outbreaks and as the flames shot towards the sky they could be seen for many miles beyond the city.

When dawn came an appalling spectacle presented itself. It was a terrifying spectacle. Fine buildings with highly valuable stock had been wiped out, and thousands of people had been rendered idle.

Amazing scenes in Templemore

Monday, November 1

The residents of Templemore tell of weird happenings on Friday night when between 30 and 40 uniformed men raided the town, broke into and fired three shops and smashed the windows of 50 other shops and houses.

The raiders first of all broke into two spirit groceries, which they looted and then set on fire. Forgarty's drapery shop was next broken into, and the raiders arrayed themselves in women's blouses, lingerie skirts and other apparel.

They then went to a jewellery and musical instrument shop. The men, in their strange get-up, took alarm clocks, mandolins and guitars.

The raiders went on to a side street where a woman was being waked. They frightened the people assembled, and played mandolins around the corpse.

They entered a house where a woman lay dangerously ill and sang ribald songs.

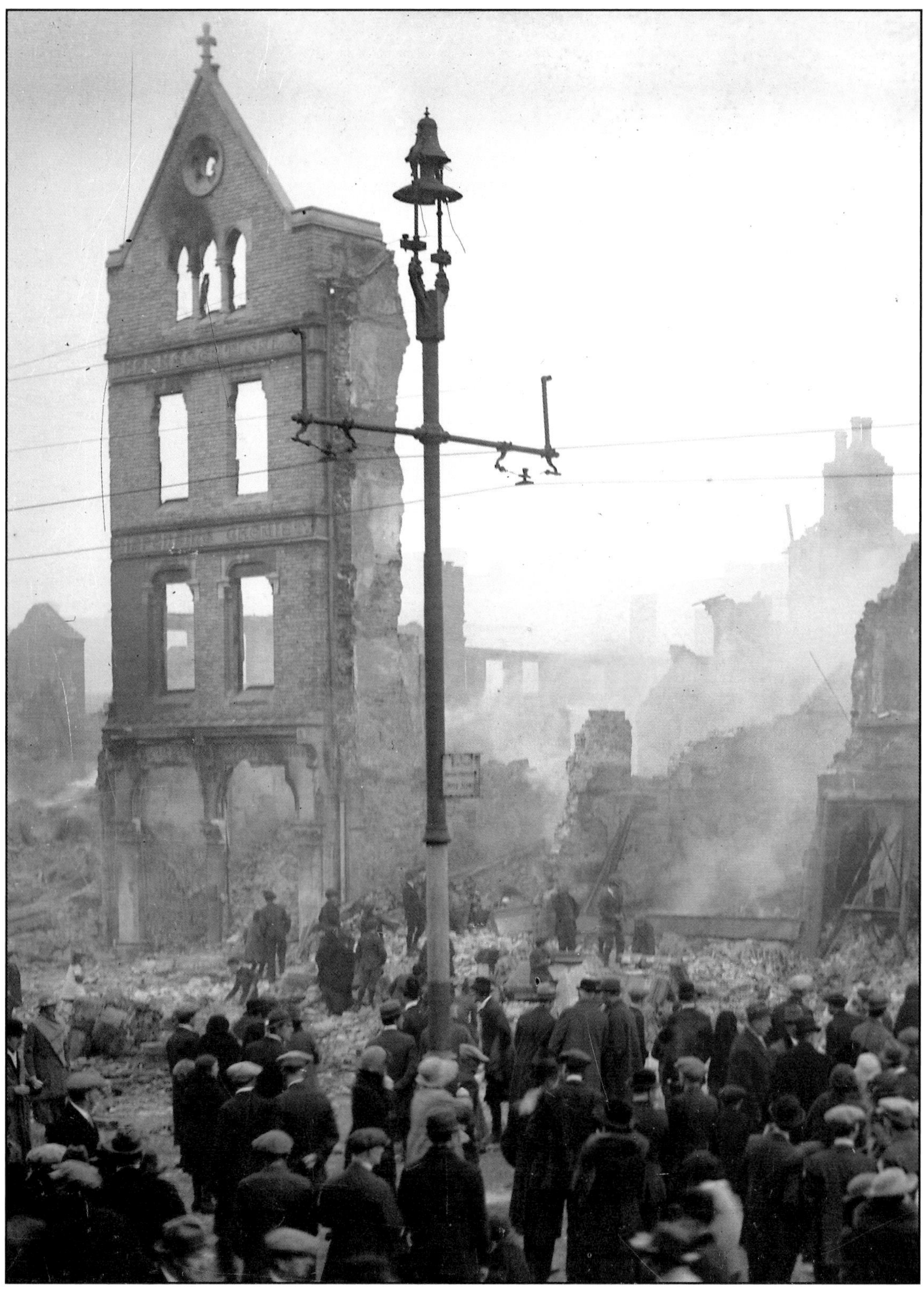

Citizens of Cork view the destruction caused by the rampage of British troops.

1921

While the War of Independence continued to be a rich source of stories for the *Examiner*, among the problems that the paper encountered were visits from the British forces demanding that official versions of incidents be published. Reporters were threatened and even arrested. The first half of the year saw an intensification of the war with around 300 soldiers killed and more than twice that on the Irish side, including many civilians.

Despite the success of the Third West Cork Flying Column at Crossbarry, where at least 39 British were killed, the IRA was finding it increasingly difficult to operate and martial law had been extended to other parts of the country.

A general election further increased Sinn Féin's position as the biggest party in the south of Ireland and de Valera negotiated a truce with the British in July. For the public, it brought a welcome respite from the violence.

The latter part of the year was taken up with negotiations between the two sides on a treaty. British proposals of almost complete independence for the south, albeit within the new concept of a 'Commonwealth', with a Boundary Commission to sort the status of the northern counties, were to open up bitter divisions in Sinn Féin.

In the science world, Albert Einstein won the Nobel Prize for physics and the discovery of insulin helped prolong the life of diabetics.

Truce brings rejoicing

Wednesday, December 7

"Too good to be true!" was the expression of one man early yesterday on hearing the news that an agreement had been reached between the Irish and British plenipotentiaries, but his doubts as to the truth of the statement were quickly dispelled when he read the *Examiner*, and there remained only a feeling of relief and joy.

The general public experienced much the same sensation. The signing of the truce last July was celebrated every night for weeks after in all parts of the country. But the people were not at liberty to give full vent to their feelings at that time.

Today is different. An agreement has been reached and the public, realising that the movement towards a final settlement has progressed further in 1921 than ever before in the history of the seven centuries' dispute, are full of rejoicings.

The season, too, is appropriate. People were preparing to enjoy the first peaceful Christmas for some years.

If arrangements can be made to have the prisoners released within the next fortnight, Christmas 1921 will indeed be a happy Christmas in Munster and in Ireland.

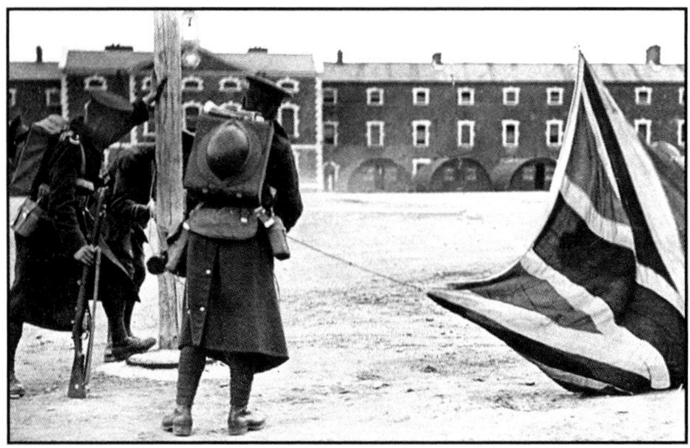

The Union Jack is lowered for the last time at Victoria (now Collins) Barracks, Cork, as British troops prepare to leave.

Big encounter at Crossbarry

Monday, March 21

Saturday – Early this morning, eight lorries proceeded from Bandon towards Crossbarry and dropped a number of soldiers in the vicinity. Later on, another party of military came from Bandon and were ambushed.

Constable Kenward, the driver of one lorry, was shot dead immediately, his head being practically blown off. A battle then ensued, and while it was in progress, the original party of soldiers endeavoured to encircle the attackers.

The battle lasted about three hours. Three lorries were burned and a quantity of arms and ammunition taken by the attackers. The dead of the Crown forces were brought to Bandon military barracks, as well as four dead civilians stated to belong to the attacking party.

News of the encounter reached Cork on Saturday afternoon. Vague rumours as to the actual occurrence quickly spread about the town, and from the information to hand, it was obvious that an unusually big encounter had taken place, and that the casualties were heavy.

Following the ambush there was intense military and police activity in the district. Houses, or at least hay, straw and other farm produce are reported to have been burned to the ground.

NEWS BRIEFS

Mar The Central Hall, Westminster, was crowded when a women's protest meeting regarding the condition of Ireland was held. Lady Sykes alleged that the auxiliary forces had committed excesses. Members of the platoon who, she contended, were guilty of the burning of Cork went about with half a cork in their caps as a boast of their deeds. (19)

Nov Riots broke out in Bombay during the visit of the Prince of Wales as Mahatma Gandhi set a bonfire of foreign cloth to object to British imports. (17)

CITY EDITION.

TEA
DELIVERED TO YOUR HOME BY PARCEL POST
Specially Good Quality.
WOODFORD, BOURNE AND CO., LTD., CORK AND LIMERICK

The Cork Examiner.

OLD MATURED WHISKIES
WOODFORD, BOURNE AND CO., LTD. CORK AND LIMERICK

NO. 21,398 THURSDAY MORNING, DECEMBER 8, 1921 PRICE--TWOPENCE.

Registered for transmission at Newspaper Rate of postage in the United Kingdom, and at Magazine Rate in Canada and Newfoundland.

IRISH PEACE

INTERNEES TO BE FREED.

RELEASE ORDERED YESTERDAY.

SOUTHERN UNIONIST INTEREST

MR. A. GRIFFITH'S IMPORTANT LETTER

IRISH DELEGATES RETURN.

THRILLING EUSTON SCENE.

NORTH AND THE TREATY.

CORRESPONDENTS' SPECULATIONS.

CRAIG'S STATEMENT.

R.I.C. AND SETTLEMENT.

IRISH RAILWAY CRISIS DEVELOPS.

CORKMEN RESUME.

It is officially announced that in view of the Irish agreement, all Irish internees are to be released forthwith.

At a meeting of the Privy Council, attended by King George an a large number of Ministers, a Royal Proclamation was signed calling Parliament together for Wednesday next to ratify the Irish Treaty.

Sir James Craig, in the Northern Commons, stated that after the meeting of the Government supporters to-day, if his colleagues desired it he would himself cross over to London to discuss the proposals. He made an emphatic protest against the speech of the Lord Chanceller, and warned Imperial Ministers against irritating Ulster loyalists.

A full meeting of the Dail Cabinet will be held to-day.

An arbitration in the Cork railway troubles starts to day. In the meantime the men return to work.

Mr. Arthur Griffith writes to Mr. George saying that he has agreed with representatives of the Southern Unionists that steps will be taken to give them full representation in both Irish Houses. Ireland looks for the co-operation of Unionists, in common with all other sections of the Irish Nation, in the making of an Irish Free State.

The Press Association says that a week or ten days will be sufficient for the passing of the Irish agreement resolution through the English Parliament. Parliament will then, it is expected, adjourn till after Christmas, when the Bill establishing an Irish Free State will be introduced. This Bill is already being drafted.

The R.I.C. ask assurances that the unanimous demand for the disbandment of the force on the terms, admitted by the Chief Secretary to be just and reasonable, be at once acceded to.

Mr. Arthur Griffith says the Irish settlement puts Ireland's future in her own hands. In short, they had won liberty after the struggle of centuries.

In the Canadian General Elections the Liberals appear to be sure of a large majority. Mr. Meighen, Prime Minister, has been defeated.

In the Dublin and London Stock Exchanges the tone continued strong. In Dublin, Railways and Guinness were features. In London, Gilt-edged Securities, Home Rails, and Mexican Eagles were bought. Marks, 850. Dollars, 4.08.

The General Council of the Trade Union Congress and the Executive of the Labour Party welcomed the conclusion of an agreement between the British Government and Irish representatives. They expressed the hope that Northern Ireland would adopt the agreement, and that the Government would crown their achievement by immediately declaring a general amnesty, and releasing all the Irish political prisoners.

Developments in the Irish railway crisis are threatened. An All-Ireland Delegates' Conference is summoned for next Sunday with the object of taking measures to defeat the Carrigan award.

Speaking at Paisley last night, Mr Asquith said that, as a whole, the settlement seemed to proceed on large and liberal lines of equity and policy. The Irish aspiration of a united Ireland was not permanently prejudiced by the Treaty.

Mr. Lloyd George is not going to Washington. He declares that the signature of the agreement is due as much to Irish as British statesmanship.

A MEMORABLE CEREMONY

PRESIDENT DE VALERA PLACING HIS NAME ON THE ROLL OF FREEMEN OF LIMERICK.

IRISH CONFERENCE FIGURES

MR. ARTHUR GRIFFITH.

MR. DESMOND FITZGERALD.

MR LLOYD GEORGE.

LORD BIRKENHEAD.

MR. MICHAEL COLLINS.

MR. E. J. DUGGAN,

(Lafayette, Dublin
MR. AUSTEN CHAMBERLAIN.

MR. WINSTON CHURCHILL.

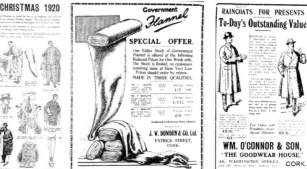

Page recreated

1922

What should have been a joyous year for Ireland with independence for 26 of the island's 32 counties instead turned to tragedy as disagreements over the treaty led to a civil war.

The most famous casualty of this bitter campaign was Michael Collins, 32, the man who had led the IRA through the War of Independence and who famously predicted he was signing his own death warrant when he put his name to the treaty.

The *Examiner*, which had itself been pro-treaty, was forced into a direct role in the civil war when Cork city became the headquarters of the republican forces.

The paper's premises were taken over for much of the summer by the rebels and a censor's office established in the building to oversee the news and to include a section of republican propaganda.

When the pro-treaty forces made their breakthrough up the River Lee, the rebels set about wrecking the *Examiner's* linotype machines and printing press before they retreated to West Cork.

Meanwhile, the year was also a particularly bloody one in the North with over 200 people killed – most of them Catholics – and thousands driven from their homes and jobs.

Michael Collins killed in ambush

Thursday, August 24

An appalling catastrophe has befallen the Irish people. The nation was plunged into grief yesterday morning when the almost incredible fact became known that General Michael Collins was dead. Though generally disbelieved at first, the news was but too true.

Cork was at once plunged into mourning. All the business establishments ceased work for the day and all the trams stopped running.

General Collins was shot dead by ambushers at Bealnablath, a spot situated between Cork and Macroom. The party were proceeding to Bandon by by-roads, accompanied by a whippet armoured car, when they were attacked by a large party of Irregulars.

An hour's fierce fighting ensued. The Irregulars lost heavily, but just before the attack was beaten off, General Collins was shot through the head and in a short time died.

In a feeble voice he asked for Major General Dalton and this officer and General Seán O'Connell went to the dying hero, says our reporter. They whispered a few prayers, reciting the Act of Contrition. The Commander-in-Chief's last words when he lay dying on the roadside were: "Forgive them." The body was removed – under fire – to the armoured car and brought to Shanakiel Hospital.

Free State troops with an unidentified woman soon after they had taken Cork city from the republicans.

"Examiner" Publications and the Censorship.

The Editor of the "Examiner" and kindred publications desires his readers to understand that all matter appearing under the headings "Republican Army—Official Bulletin" and "Republican Publicity Department" is not under his control, and he is not responsible for any statements appearing therein.

The disclaimer notice which republican forces, who had taken over the* Examiner*, allowed the newspaper to publish alongside their propaganda.

Burial of beloved Chief

Tuesday, August 29

The Nation today paid its last tribute to the dead soldier Chief. Never in living memory have such crowds thronged the streets of Dublin. They came to honour a leader who had dedicated his life to the service of his country, and they came also to proclaim that the work which was not given him to finish shall be carried to a triumphant conclusion.

Never has Dublin witnessed such a wonderful manifestation of grief and mourning as was seen in the streets today. Not alone did the population of the city, but representatives from all parts of the country, turned out to pay the last tribute to Michael Collins.

The cortège itself was of immense proportions, and extended between five and six miles. It is stated to have assumed proportions even larger than that of Parnell's funeral.

At the head of the coffin was placed a single lily, the tribute to the dead chief by his fiancée, Miss Kiernan.

Free State soldiers after their arrival in Cork.

Michael Collins (left) at St Francis Church, Broad Lane, Cork.

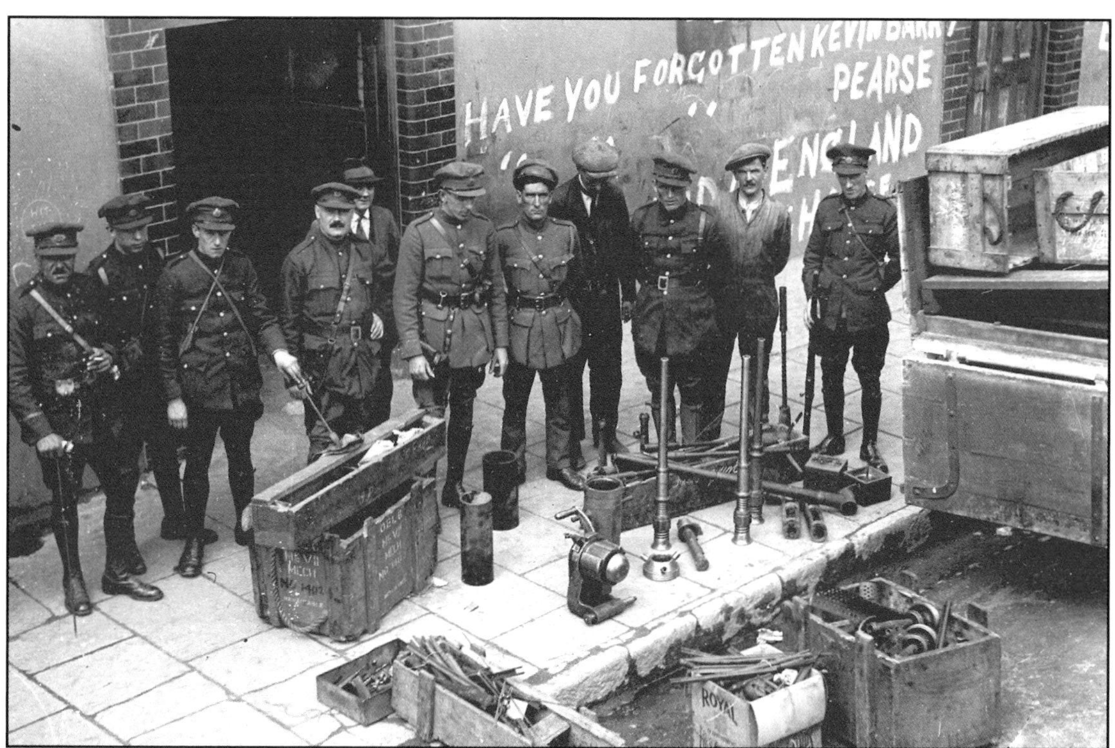

Graffiti taunts Free State troops as they unload unidentified machinery in Cork.

1923

The death of republican leader Liam Lynch in April hastened the end of the Civil War. Before the fighting finished, one of the worst atrocities of the campaign came at Ballyseedy Bridge, Co Kerry, when nine republicans were tied around a landmine, which was then blown up.

One of the group was miraculously blown clear and lived to rubbish the troops' claim that the men were killed accidentally. The *Examiner* was careful to point out that its report of the event was the official version of what happened.

The Ballyseedy incident came around the same time as some of the fiercest fighting of the war took place in Kerry and several hundred state troops and republican irregulars battled in the mountains near Caherciveen.

The eventual cessation of hostilities paved the way for a general election which allowed the newly-formed Cumann na nGaedheal with William T Cosgrave, Michael Collins' successor, to form a minority government.

The business of nation-building could begin, with economic policy largely based around agriculture. One of the measures introduced was the compulsory purchase of land still owned by landlords.

In international news, the name Hitler made an early appearance in the *Examiner* in November when the hitherto unknown leader of an extreme nationalist group was involved in an attempted *putsch* in Munich. Feelings in Germany had been running high following France's occupation of the Rhineland.

Prisoners killed in Ballyseedy

Tuesday, March 8

The Army Headquarters issued the following official report tonight: A party of troops proceeding to Killorglin last night came across a barricade of stones built on the roadway at Ballyseedy bridge. The troops returned to Tralee, and brought out a number of prisoners to remove the obstruction.

While engaged in this work, a trigger mine, which was concealed in the structure, exploded, wounding Captain Edward Breslin, Lieut Joseph Murtage, and Sergeant Ennis, and killing eight of the prisoners.

Lieut Joseph Murtage and Sergeant Ennis were seriously wounded. On the Countesses bridge the troops found a barricade similar to that at Ballyseedy bridge erected across the roadway. While the obstruction was being removed, a trigger mine exploded, wounding two of the troops and killing four irregular prisoners who had been engaged removing the barricade.

Priest's housekeeper's hair cut off

Saturday, April 28

A shocking occurrence is reported from Cloghduv, Crookstown, Co Cork. Two men entered the residence of the Rev Father Murphy. In the kitchen at the time was the priest's housekeeper, a woman of advanced years.

At the point of a revolver she was ordered out of the house. The old lady was then placed on a car and carried away a captive to an unoccupied lodge. Here one of her captors cut off her hair. She was told never to return to Cloghduv, but to go home, that is to the neighbourhood of Ballincollig.

The reason for the outrage committed on the woman is not quite clear, but it is understood that the allegation had been made that she had given information to Rev Canon Tracy, PP Cookstown, as to the movements of irregulars.

Soldiers and civilians cross the bridge between Rochestown and Blackrock in Cork. The bridge was under repair after being blown up in the Civil War.

Quiet election polling

Tuesday, August 28

Commenting on events in Dublin, the special correspondent of the Press Association wires: The election was the dullest of affairs. There was no excitement, no life, no laughter. There appeared to be little interest and except in two or three cases there were no queues outside any of the polling stations.

The only sign of life at some of the polling booths in the morning was the presence of one or two National soldiers, nursing rifles and smoking cigarettes.

Penalties laid down were considered much too severe for a man to risk being caught trying to pose as John James O'Reilly, deceased. One has not, as on other occasions, met respectable citizens who boasted of having voted 17 times.

NEWS BRIEFS

Mar The 1921 All-Ireland hurling final, which had been postponed due to the war, was played at Croke Park between Dublin and Limerick. The Munster men became the first ever team to receive the MacCarthy Cup when they overcame the Dubliners by 8-5 to 3-2. (4)

May Thousands turned out in the streets of Dublin tonight to see James Larkin pass through on his return from America. Outside Westland Row station a procession was formed, and accompanied Larkin to Liberty Hall, where he addressed a big gathering. (1)

The Cork Examiner.

No. 21,650 TUESDAY MORNING MAY 29, 1923 PRICE—TWOPENCE

Registered for transmission at Newspaper Rate of postage in Ireland and Great Britain, and at Magazine Rate to Canada and Newfoundland.

IRISH UNITY.

Home Minister's Speech.

GEN. MULCAHY AND ARMY'S TASK.

(From Our Correspondent.)

Dublin, Monday—Mr. Ernest Blythe, Minister for Local Government, speaking to-night at a meeting of Cumann na nGaedheal, said the outstanding big questions which should be dealt with by people who thought along the lines the present Government thought along. They had the great question of the Boundary, and of doing something to secure national unity (applause). The present Government, or a Government similar to it, would be able to deal with that question—keeping the national view point to the fore—and it seemed to him that the Boundary situation was one of the strongest reasons for returning to the Dail a majority which would be a National Party, whatever name they called it (hear, hear). That question was a very big question, indeed. If they secured national unity it would mean that in effect all the hopes with which they started out in this struggle had been realised (applause). From the point of view of the Boundary, it was most important that they did not have in the Dail a party representing some economic group dealing with the Boundary question from the point of view of getting the greatest political capital out of it, or trying to avoid losing political prestige by it. This question would want to be dealt with by a Government which would face the situation; which would be prepared to do anything that may be necessary to be done; which would not care greatly whether that was a matter that would give it an advantage over say the Labour Party or over the Farmers' Party, but which would think of it solely form the point of view of the national interests and as the means of unifying this country as one State and one nation (applause).

Mr. Kevin O'Higgins, Minister for Home Affairs, who also addressed the meeting, said there were many areas in the country which owing to organisation during the truce and so on the I. R. A. became practically little short of a regular army, and that when the time of the crisis arrived the unit there had as much and as little choice perhaps as the unit in any army when the drums began to beat (hear, hear). He had very little doubt that in Kerry and in Cork men were out fighting the Government in the last ten months, who in their inmost hearts believed that Mr. Collins, who had done many big and brave things for this country, never did a bigger or a braver or a more selfless thing than he did on the night when he took pen in hand and signed the Treaty (applause). He believed that men went out against the Government who felt that way, and, while one could not exactly admire that, it had to be remembered, and if he had felt throughout the last ten months any bitterness it was reserved for those who, with a very clear mental picture of the state of affairs that they were going to bring about, pressed the button (applause). Further than that, if there was any bitterness it was impersonal, and those with whom he had worked would probably say that it was not increased by any personal sorrow or persecution that he had himself.

There would be an election probable within the next four or five months. They wer asking the people to realise that it would have been easier for the Government to have left undone the stern things, the things that to people who thought superficially were unpopular. They had to do many things within the last year that were most unpopular—even amongst themselves—things that not one of them had done out of sheer zeal for blood-letting—because he did not think there was any bloodthirsty person among either the Executive Council or the Army Council (applause). But they had done these things because they believed that they were necessary, and they had no apologies to offer to any one for the doing of them.

But if those who differed from them over hte last year were prepared to help in any way, they would be very glad to forget those things and to forget the necessity that gave use to them. They would ask the people at the coming elections for an endorsement of that which they had thought it necessary to do.

General Mulcahy, Minister for Defence, who also spoke, said they knew that as far as having from a military point of view to put an end to what had so unfortunately taken place in the country, that task was finished (applause) and they knew that among a very large number of people on both sides of the conflict that situation was finished with very little bitterness compared with the bitterness that might have been expected to have been there (applause). They learned from that day's papers that those responsible for the development of the continuance of the destruction and fighting had ordered their followers to dump their arms (applause).

END OF WAR.

ORDERS FROM IRREGULAR CHIEFS.

ARMS TO BE LAID ASIDE.

CAPTURED DOCUMENTS ISSUED.

Mr. De Valera, in a message addressed to the soldiers of Liberty, Legion of the Rearguard, declares the Republic can no longer successfully be defended by arms, and describes the laying aside of arms as an act of exalted patriotism.

Other means, he says, must be sought to defend the nations rights.

Mr. Frank Aiken, Chief of Staff, states arms are to be dumped. The foreign and domestic enemies of the Republic have for the moment prevailed.

(From Our Reporter.)

Dublin, Monday Evening.—The Government Publicity Department issues the following this evening:—

The following documents, signed by Mr. De Valera and Mr. F. Aiken respectively, were captured on the 25th inst. in the possession of an irregular leader:—

"Order of the day to all ranks from the President:

"Soldiers of Liberty, Legion of the Rearguard.—The Republic can no longer be defended successfully by your arms. Further sacrifices on your part would now be vain, and continuance of the struggle in arms unwise in the National interest. Military victory must be allowed to rest for the moment with those who have destroyed the Republic. Other means must be sought to safeguard the Nation's right.

"Do not let sorrow overwhelm you. Your efforts and the sacrifices of your dead comrades in this forlorn hope will surely bear fruit. You have saved the Nation's honour and kept open the road to independence. Laying aside your arms now is an act of patriotism as exalted and as pure as your valour in taking them up.

"Seven years of intense efforts have exhausted our people. Their sacrifices and their sorrows have been many. If they have turned away and have not given you the active support which alone could bring you victory in this last year it is because they are weary and need a rest. Give them a little time and you will yet see them recover and rally again to the standard. They will then quickly discover who have been selfish and who have spoken truth and who falsehood. When they are ready you will be, and your will be once more, as of old, with the vanguard.

"The sufferings which you must now face unarmed you will bear in a manner worthy of men who were ready to give their lives for their cause. The thought that you have stood to suffer for your devotion will lighten your present sorrow, and what you endure will keep you in communion with your dead comrades who gave their lives and all these lives promised for Ireland.

"May God guard every one of you and give to our country in all times of need sons who will love her as dearly and devotedly as you.

"(Signed) EAMON DE VALERA."

"To all ranks:

"Comrades.—The arms with which we have fought the enemies of our country are to be dumped. The foreign and domestic enemies of the Republic have for the moment prevailed. But our enemies have not won. Neither tortures nor firing squads nor a slavish Press can crush the desire for independence out of the hearts of those who fought for the Republic, or out of the hearts of our people.

"Our enemies have demanded our arms. Our answer is: We took up arms to free our country and will keep them until we see an honourable way of reaching our objective without arms.

"There is a trying time ahead for the faithful soldiers of Ireland, but the willing sacrifices of our dead comrades will give us the courage to face it in the knowledge that these sacrifices have insured the ultimate victory of our cause. Their examples and their prayers will help us to be, like them, faithful to our idea's unto death.

"(Signed) FRANK AIKEN,

"Chief-of-Staff."

DAIL AND PEACE

Question Of The Prisoners.

The Land Legislation.

(From our Reporter.)

Dublin, Monday.—The captured letters issued by the Government Publicity Department this evening were published in special editions of the papers here and created rather a sensation. The immediate impression was one of general satisfaction that armed opposition to the Government of the country had been definitely ordered to cease. The feeling of relief however would, it was easy to discern, be more genuinely gratifying if it were possible to have it embodied in a declaration of peace. Such a development may readily follow, for the momentous issues involved demand an attention that it is anticipated will be voiced in the Dail to-morrow.

In President Cosgrave's visit to Kilkenny there was convincing evidence of a return to normal condition, and in his reference to the burning desire for peace there is great hope that that end will quickly ensue.

One factor of the situation now existing, agitating critical students of the entire position is in regard to the thousands of prisoners. Their release, it is maintained, is dependent on some set form of a declared peace, and that that should come is suggested in the terms of the published letters. That it should come is ardently hoped, particularly in view of the immediate legislation formulated by the Present Ministry for the future prosperity and welfare of the country.

This is especially indicated at to-day's meeting of the Dail when the Minister of Agriculture asked leave of the House to introduce a land Bill. The measure received a cordial endorsement from all sections of the House, and is one of historic and far reaching importance. It is a Bill for the completion of land purchase and the establishment of peasant proprietorship in the Free State.

The Bill deals with 70,000 unpurchased tenants, representing a rent-roll of between £8,000,000 and £10,000,000 annually. Its operations are estimated to cost £25,000,000, and powers are sought compulsorily to acquire land anywhere for the purpose of relieving congestion. All untenanted lands in the congested areas will first be acquired automatically. Provision is made for tenants evicted since 1881, and powers taken to sell lands where available to sons of tenants, to labourers, and other suitable persons. Arrears of rent due up to the first gale day of 1920 shall not be payable, and arrears from that date are subject to 25 per cent reduction.

The scheme brings the purchase price approximately to fifteen years purchase. Tenants whose rents were fixed before 1911 will pay annuities representing 35 per cent reduction of rents. Those who went into court after 1911 will pay annuities representing 30 per cent reduction. Payments will be in bonds bearing half per cent and sinking fund. The Government will contribute 10 per cent to purchase relief of tenants.

At to-morrow's sitting another measure of equally great importance will be introduced by the Minister of Home Affairs, viz., the Increase of Rent and Mortgage Restriction Bill. In even these two legislative proposals there is sufficient to emphasise the constructive enactments that should engage a native Parliament in a country with stable conditions to bring prosperity and contentment to its citizens, who have reasonably grown apathetic because of the tragic events.

The Cork Examiner.

TUESDAY, MAY 29, 1923.

WEATHER FORECAST.

(From the Meteorological Office).

The following is the forecast for to-day—Wind north-east or north; moderate or fresh; mainly fine; day temperature rising somewhat, but risk of night frost.

HIGH WATER.

(New Time).

	Morn.		Evg.
Cork	5.24	...	5.46
Cobh	5.21	...	5.43
Kinsale	5. 7	...	5.29
Youghal	5.25	...	5.47
Ballycotton	5.16	...	5.38
Courtmacsherry	5. 1	...	5.23
Baltimore	4.51	...	5.13
Waterford	5.38	...	6. 0
Limerick	6.39	...	7. 1

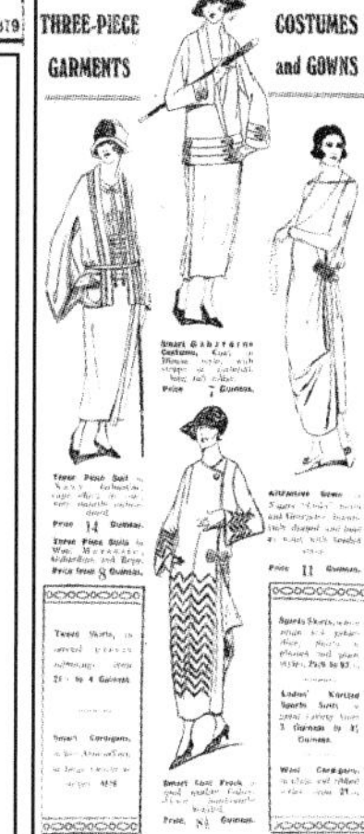

Page recreated

1924

While the Irish army did take out large newspaper advertisements looking for new recruits, its demobilisation of some sections was one of the resentments which fuelled a mini-mutiny in March. Officers were arrested, Garda chief Eoin O'Duffy was made head of the army and some skilful political manoeuvring prevented the situation from getting out of hand.

In sports, the state entered its first ever team in the Olympic Games at Paris. The soccer team were the first to represent the state at a major tournament and both Jack Yeats and Oliver St John Gogarty received medals in the artistic competitions which were then part of the Olympics. In terms of media attention, the event was overshadowed by the first modern revival of our very own Tailteann Games.

Ancient Ireland's version of the Olympics featured sports such as hurling and tug-of-war and the revival was expected to act as a kind of unifying event for the scattered Gael.

Tutankhamen's sarcophagus opened

Wednesday, February 13

The secret of the tomb at Luxor, on which the interest of the world has been turned for such a long period, was partially revealed yesterday when the lid of the sarcophagus was opened.

As the lid gradually rose, and the light shone into the sarcophagus, a sight met our eyes that at first somewhat puzzled us. The contents were completely covered by a linen shroud, somewhat discoloured but still in a perfect state of preservation.

This linen covering, which was obviously placed there for protective purposes, almost completely covered a coffin of which six inches of the richly gilt head could be seen, while a glint of what looked like golden objects appeared through the fabric. Mr Howard Carter began carefully to roll the shroud back towards the foot of the coffin. It was the head that drew everyone's attention and admiration. The face was one solid piece of gold, with eyes of crystal, and on the forehead an uraeus (sacred serpent) and a vulture of gold encircling the latter being a 'crown of justification', made of olive leaves.

There before us, a product of the splendid age to which he belonged, lay the coffin of a king whose name has been on everyone's lips for the past year, and the romantic circumstances of the discovery of his tomb will cause him to be remembered when most other episodes have passed from public memory.

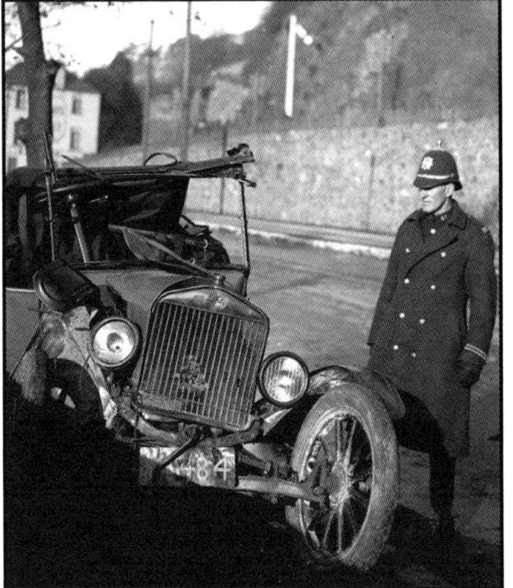

A policeman inspects a Ford Model T after it collided with a tram at Tivoli, Cork.

Tailteann Games begin

Monday, August 4

Saturday – Aonach Tailteann opened today, and there was abundant evidence that the sustained enthusiasm in organising the historic fête had been well compensated. The city had put on garlands of flowers and monuments were festooned with shrubs. The streets were never so animated as they never looked so gay.

With such pleasantness permeating the city it is hard to conceive of the sad consequences of the grip of an expansive strike or to permit any promptings of anxiety over the delicate position of the political situation on the Boundary issue. The latter caused the absence of President Cosgrave, the former has its disturbances of trade and business.

The scene at Croke Park was not alone memorable but inspiring. For some hours before 3 o'clock, aeroplanes of the State flew at all degrees of altitudes. Suddenly these craft disappeared, a short silence, and then a salvo of guns. Aonach Tailteann was opened formally, and at once the 'Ode of Welcome' was sung with fervour by a well-trained choir of many hundreds.

NEWS BRIEFS

Jan The Soviet Delegation in London received official news today of the death of Lenin, which occurred yesterday. It is stated that the Soviet Government will continue the work of Lenin. "It stands firm at its post, watchful over the conquest of the proletarian revolution." (23)

Aug Berlin – coincident with the tenth anniversary of the outbreak of World War I, General Fretherr von Schoenarch has issued a book entitled *The War of 1930*, in which he describes how the third Franco-German war will arise. General Schoenarch described how in 1930 England and Japan will wage war, and Russia will attack Poland, giving the rest of Europe a chance to engage in their own bloodshed. (7)

The Cork Examiner.

NO. 22,159. MONDAY MORNING, MAY 26, 1924. PRICE---TWOPENCE.

Registered for transmission at Newspaper Rate of Postage in Ireland and Great Britain, and at Magazine Rate to Canada and Newfoundland.

Page recreated

1925

A consistent source of worry for the Catholic hierarchy was the behaviour of an otherwise fairly-acquiescent populace when they went to dances. No licenses were needed for such events and in an era without too many other leisure pursuits, dancing was extremely popular in both rural and urban areas.

"It was bad enough that people danced with members of the opposite sex, but the added vice of alcohol paved the way for the wholesale destruction of the virtue of Irish girls," said a statement from the hierarchy.

On the subject of divorce, President Cosgrave sought the bishops' advice on the matter and legislated accordingly. Divorce had been available before independence, but would now be prohibited in the state until 1995.

In international rugby, the first ever sending off took place when a New Zealand player kicked an Englishman on the ground at Twickenham, while the art world saw the opening of the first Surrealist exhibition in Paris.

Banshee noises heard

Monday, June 29

For some weeks past there has been growing speculation in the Frankfield-Douglas area of Cork as to the origin of certain weird sounds which are audible almost nightly in that area.

They were first heard about three weeks ago and when it became rumoured that sounds resembling moaning and wailing had been heard, the usual fanciful ghost stories were quickly spread.

Some have already christened the unexplained noises 'the banshee' but others are convinced that the cause of the disturbance is some strange bird that has paid a visit to Cork.

The sounds are usually heard about one o'clock in the morning, and cause a good deal of misgiving to people of a nervous temperament.

Another theory which has been advanced is that the moaning is done by some human being, though the motive is not clear.

One of the night audience, describing the noise, says it is weird and melancholy, rising into a sort of whistle or screech.

He went out with a gun one night last week, but the bird or banshee was not on duty on the occasion. He regards this as evidence that the Frankfield visitor exercises a certain kind of primitive discretion.

Hats off to Archbishop Daniel Mannix of Melbourne on his return to Cork. The Charleville-born clergyman had led opposition to conscription in Australia during World War I and had also spoken out against British policies in Ireland.

NEWS BRIEFS

Feb A very important decision was taken in the Dáil, when a motion was passed to prevent the introduction of Bills of Divorce, with the right to re-marry. Deputy Prof Thrift argued against the proposal, alleging it would deprive a section of the community of freedom of conscience on religious matters. (12)

July The ringing of church bells, the blowing of trumpets from the spires of churches, the sounding of sirens and the rejoicing of the population in the streets greeted the end of the French and Belgian occupation of the Ruhr at midnight last night. The streets were thronged with enthusiastic crowds singing patriotic songs and repeating over and over again, 'Deutschland Uber Alles'. (22)

Oct A dispute between the German firm Siemens and Irish workers employed on the Shannon scheme leads to an attack on four German clerical staff in Limerick. The men were set upon by a group carrying clubs and knives as they walked from O'Connell Street to their accommodation. Though battered and bruised, their injuries were not serious. (7)

Dancing and vice

Wednesday, October 7

The Irish Catholic Hierarchy at their meeting in Maynooth today adopted a statement of entreaty, advice and instruction, lest the name which the chivalrous honour of Irish boys and the Christian reserve of Irish maidens made for the country should be lost.

"Purity and Faith", it says, "go together, and both virtues are in danger, the former more directly than the latter. The danger comes from pictures, papers and drink."

The statement condemns improper company, and refers to the dancing hall as the worst fermenter of the evil. These halls brought girls now and then to shame, and obliged retirement to institutions, or to the dens of great cities.

"Imported dances of an evil kind," say their lordships, "the surroundings of the dancing hall, withdrawal from the hall for intervals and the backways home have been the destruction of virtue in every part of Ireland. The dancing of dubious dances on Sunday, more particularly by persons dazed with drink, amounts to woeful desecration of the Lord's Day."

The Cork Examiner.

NO. 22,456. FRIDAY MORNING, DECEMBER 4, 1925. PRICE---TWOPENCE.

Registered for transmission at Newspaper Rate of Postage in Ireland and Great Britain, and at Magazine Rate to Canada and Newfoundland.

BOUNDARY CRISIS OVER.

SETTLEMENT REACHED AT LONDON CONFERENCE.

TREATY TO BE ALTERED.

FREE STATE LIABILITY FOR WAR DEBT CANCELLED

EXISITING BORDER TO STAND.

BRITISH PREMIER OUTLINES NEW TRIPLE PACT.

The Boundary Crisis, which has been the subject of prolonged and anxious conferences in London, ended yesterday, when an agreement was reached between the Free State, Britain and Northern Ireland.

The terms of the new Pact were announced in the House of Commons by Mr. Baldwin, who said legislation would be immediately necessary for the purpose. The Free State delegates returned to Dublin last night.

Under the new arrangement the responsibility of the Free State, under Article Five of the Treaty, to pay portion of the British War Debt is cancelled. In return the Free State accepts responsibility for the payment of that portion of the malicious injury claims arising out of the Anglo-Irish war which, under the Treaty, was payable by Britain.

The boundary line between the Six Counties and the Free State is to remain as at present existing. The British powers in the Act of 1920 regarding the Council of Ireland are transferred to the Government of Northern Ireland, and these powers are to be used for the purpose of conference between the two Irish Governments on matters of common concern.

The Free State undertakes to pay a 10 per cent increase on all compensation awards made in respect of malicious damage to property between July, 1921, and May, 1923, and to provide for such payment by the issue of 5 per cent bonds.

President Cosgrave, in an interview, stated that the result reached was, in his opinion, the only solution of a very difficult situation. He was convinced it would tend surely and speedily towards the political unity of all Ireland.

The agreement was signed last night by representatives of the three Governments, and will come into force as soon as the necessary legislation has been passed.

Mr. Churchill, in a statement on the subject, intimated that the report of the Boundary Commission, which had now been superseded by the new agreement, would not be published for the present. He paid a tribute to the work of the Commission members, and ascribed to their labours the happy situation which had come about.

An animated debate took place in the Dail on a suggestion that there should be an adjournment until Tuesday next. Several members asked for information regarding the London negotiations. The Minister for Industry and Commerce said that the Executive Council had the right to explore the paths of peace, and that was all that had been done; while the Minister for Agriculture said that when the deputies were faced with the recommendations of the Executive Council they should, if they had strong convictions against them, take the consequences of their convictions and not wash their hands like Pontius Pilate.

The Minister for External Affairs said that if there was going to be a change in the Constitution or the Treaty—which could not be done by a stroke of the pen—the country and the deputies would have ample time to discuss the matter.

Page recreated

1926

Cinema was becoming an increasingly popular leisure pursuit for people in Ireland, and an assistant projectionist at the Assembly Rooms in Cork decided to take advantage of the premises' closure on Sundays by showing a cowboy film and a comedy in Dromcollogher, Co Limerick.

The highly flammable celluloid came into contact with a candle and the flames soon cut people off from the only exit.

Ireland got its first radio station with Dublin-based 2RN, but listeners on their valve radios in Munster complained about the poor reception. Stations in Britain were still providing a clearer signal.

Mandatory schooling was introduced for those aged 6–14, though the vast majority of children were only educated as far as primary school level.

Mussolini shot by Irish woman

Thursday, April 8

Rome – An attack was made on Mussolini today, an elderly woman firing at him with a revolver. He was slightly wounded in the nose. Signor Mussolini remained perfectly calm, and with the greatest *sangfroid*, immediately gave directions with a view to preventing any disturbance of public order. The woman, who was with difficulty rescued from the incensed crowd, was taken to a women's prison.

Signor Mussolini's assailant told the police her name was Violet Gibson, and that she was aged 62, of Irish nationality. She is sister to the present Lord Ashbourne, who was a former President of the Gaelic League in London. He usually wears the Irish kilts.

When Lord Ashbourne was informed of the affair he hastened to Rome. "The poor dear," he added, "has been ill all her life, and at times she was much depressed and very nervous."

The report of the attempt spread like wildfire, and caused intense emotion throughout Rome. As a sign of the immense relief felt at Signor Mussolini's escape, flags were flown everywhere, and the city suddenly took on the aspect of a great celebration, the tricolour waving brightly in the hot sunshine.

Uproar at O'Casey play

Friday, February 12

Scenes of wild excitement were witnessed tonight at the Abbey Theatre, during the performance of Mr Sean O'Casey's play, *The Plough and the Stars*, which has been running since Monday night.

The play was in progress for some time when protests, which first took the form of organised booing and hissing, broke out almost simultaneously from various parts of the gallery and pit.

Mrs Sheehy-Skeffington said in a loud voice: "We have not come here as rowdies, we came here to make a protest against the defamation of the men of Easter Week."

A young woman, jumping on the stage, got into handgrips with two of the female players, and a couple of the male actors pushed the intruder out.

A young man vaulted on to the stage and was attacked by the players. When a further attempt was made to resume the performance a renewed outburst put it out of the question. Mr WB Yeats arose excitedly and amidst the din was heard to say: "This is a disgrace to the nation."

Mr Yeats at one time rushed hatless into the streets, apparently looking for the police, and excitement continued to some extent till the building closed for the night.

NEWS BRIEFS

Mar The first ever senior soccer international for the Free State ended in a 3-0 defeat by Italy in Turin. (22)

May The Fianna Fáil (Republican) Party was launched in Dublin with a public meeting at the La Scala Theatre. The principal speaker was Mr de Valera. (17)

Nov George Bernard Shaw was awarded the Nobel Prize for Literature. (11)

Baboon's attack

Wednesday, June 2

Miss Lizzy Duffy, an equestrienne in Duffy's circus, was severely mauled in Clonakilty today by a baboon monkey. The incident, which created the wildest excitement, occurred before the midday performance.

Miss Duffy was feeding a pet goat in a cage, which in a second compartment contained a ferocious Arabian monkey, 3ft 6in in height.

Her right forearm was almost cut clean to the bone by the savage brute's tusks, while other injuries equally bad marked her body and limbs.

She was making a plucky and desperate fight for her life when Mr John Duffy arrived. He quickly procured an iron bar, with which he stunned the infuriated brute, and the lady was removed from the scene of her thrilling life struggle in a fainting condition.

The Cork Examiner.

NO. 22,691. TUESDAY MORNING, SEPTEMBER 7, 1926. PRICE---TWOPENCE.

Registered for transmission at Newspaper Rate of Postage in Ireland and Great Britain, and at Magazine Rate to Canada and Newfoundland.

IRISH CINEMA TRAGEDY

SHOCKING HOLOCAUST IN COUNTY LIMERICK.

OVER FIFTY LIVES LOST.

Appalling And Heart-Rending Scenes.

LIST OF VICTIMS.

Messages From President Cosgrave And The Bishop Of Limerick.

A terrible **disaster, involving the loss of at least fifty lives,** occurred at a **cinema fire at Dromcollogher** on Sunday night.

Owing to the **ignition of a film** near the only exit from the hall a devastating fire broke out, and in the panic that followed an appalling **casualty toll was enacted.**

The latest estimates say that out of an attendance of 150 persons, 50 have perished in the flames, and ten are in hospital. One died in the Croom Co. Hospital after admission.

The inquest was formally opened and adjourned.

Messages of sympathy have been received from many sources, including President Cosgrave and His Lordship, Most Rev. Dr. Keane, Bishop of the Diocese.

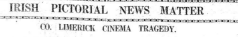

IRISH PICTORIAL NEWS MATTER

CO. LIMERICK CINEMA TRAGEDY.

Photo shows some of the relatives and friends of the victims at the scene of the Dromcollogher Cinema Tragedy which occurred on Sunday night, and in which fifty people lost their lives.

The interior of the building, in the right-hand top corner of which were deposited the charred remains of the victims.

Page recreated

1927

The bitterness of the Civil War continued well into the decade and claimed the life of government minister Kevin O'Higgins who was shot as he walked to Mass. As a cabinet member during the war, O'Higgins was particularly hated by republicans for some of the actions of the Free State government.

The assassination came a few days after a drama in the Dáil caused by the refusal of Fianna Fáil deputies to take the oath of allegiance to the British king that was still part of parliamentary procedure. De Valera's party agreed to take the oath later in the year.

In international news, Charles Lindbergh became the first person to fly solo across the Atlantic.

In cinema, Al Jolson starred in *The Jazz Singer*, the first 'talkie'.

No fireworks in Dublin

Friday, June 24

As so often happens when exciting events are anticipated, today's proceedings at the opening of the new Dáil passed off quite peaceably in comparison with the expectations that had been aroused. This is true of the happenings both inside and outside the debating chamber.

Mr de Valera and his colleagues duly turned up, having marched from the party headquarters in company with a large crowd of their supporters. The latter were stopped at the bottom of Kildare street, but the deputies were allowed through to Leinster House, where they were courteously received by Colonel Brennan, the superintendent of the building, and ushered into a committee room immediately inside the entrance. Beyond this they did not get, for when after refusing to take the oath rendered to them by the clerk, they left the room in a batch and endeavoured to advance to the debating chamber their progress was barred by Colonel Brennan, supported by a couple of superintendents and other members of the Civic Guards.

Students from University College Cork provide a curious sight during rag week, as they parade through the streets.

Ghastly exhibits

Monday, May 23

Dublin – A van bearing anti-vivisection posters and exhibits is attracting groups wherever it is pulled up. The posters are intended to illustrate the cruelty to which animals are subjected by experimentalists, and the men of science are rebuked by Cicero's phrase, "No cruelty is useful."

The exhibits are gruesome – a stuffed cat and some other animal trussed up for operation. It should not be necessary to enforce the argument so violently. Some years ago the van would have been in danger of attack by students, but the wiser and more scientific course of allowing the propagandists to have their say, no matter how challenging it is, is now being followed.

Wonderful reception for Lindbergh

Monday, May 23

Almost indescribable scenes attended Capt Lindbergh's arrival at Le Bourget from New York last night. So enthusiastic were Parisiens that there was a veritable exodus in the direction of the aerodrome, and by eight o'clock it was surrounded by an enormous human barrier containing, it is estimated, 150,000 people.

When darkness descended on the scene, rockets were sent up; then the beacons were brought into action. Suddenly at 10.15 the faint whirr of an engine was heard in the distance. The sound grew clearer though nothing could be seen. Then at last, amid a great wave of emotion, Capt Lindbergh's machine appeared in the light of the beacons, flying at a height of 500 feet.

Wheeling over the heads of the vast crowd, he landed gently in front of the battery of flares. There was a mad rush for the spot where he had come down. So irresistible was the movement that the police and troops were powerless, the iron barriers gave way, people shouted and wept for joy, some of them sang the American National Anthem.

NEWS BRIEFS

July Countess Markievicz died at Sir Patrick Dunn's hospital at 1.25am this morning. The Countess was a member of a well-known landowning family, the Gore Booths of County Sligo. She was one of the leaders of the Dublin rebellion in Easter, 1916, and was the first woman MP elected to the British Parliament. (16)

For the fourth day in succession Cork experienced abnormal heat again yesterday. Quite a large number of businessmen were to be seen wearing tennis shirts and other unconventional apparel. The summery frocks on women imparted many touches of colour and bathing places in and near the city were fully patronised all day. (19)

The Cork Examiner.

NO. 22,953. MONDAY MORNING, JULY 11, 1927. PRICE---TWOPENCE.

Registered for transmission at Newspaper Rate of Postage in Ireland and Great Britain, and at Magazine Rate to Canada and Newfoundland.

MR. KEVIN O'HIGGINS DEAD

FATALLY SHOT BY PARTY OF ARMED MEN.

ATTACKED GOING TO MASS.

FOUND IN ROADWAY IN POOL OF BLOOD.

HEART-RENDING DETAILS.

PRESIDENT COSGRAVE'S MESSAGE TO THE NATION.

Mr. Kevin O'Higgins, Vice-President of the Free State and Minister for Justice and for External Affairs, was attacked and fatally shot by a party of men at Booterstown, Co. Dublin, yesterday.

The Minister was on his way to 12 o'clock Mass at the time. The attackers, seven in number, drove up in a car, and then walking past Mr. O'Higgins, suddenly turned and fired with revolvers. The Minister essayed to run after the first volley, but further shots struck him and he collapsed.

He was found bleeding on the roadway by Dr. Beckett, a resident in the locality, who was returning from church at the time. Other medical assistance was procured, but Mr. O'Higgins succumbed to his terrible wounds at 5 o'clock.

Following the shooting, military and police activity of a most extensive nature took place, all motor cars being held up and searched over a wide radius. No arrests were reported up to a late hour last night.

A meeting of the Executive Council was held last evening, after which President Cosgrave issued a message to the people. Paying a tribute to the work of the deceased Minister, Mr. Cosgrave says the assassin's bullet will not terrorise the people in this hour of national mourning. Other men, he says, will tread the path blazed by Griffith, Collins and O'Higgins.

The terrible occurrence has caused a painful and profound sensation throughout the country, where the dead Minister was everywhere recognised as a brilliant administrator, an efficient and fearless leader, and a man whose services to the country ever since 1916 have been of the most devoted and invaluable kind.

Dublin, Sunday.

Mr. Kevin O'Higgins, Minister for Justice, and Vice-President of the Executive Council of the Irish Free State, was fired at and fatally wounded near his residence, in Blackrock, Co. Dublin, this morning.

That the attack was an organised and well planned affair is obvious from the fact that several men in a motor car took part.

Mr. O'Higgins with whom Mr. P. Hogan (the Minister for Agriculture) resides, has his residence on Cross Avenue, Booterstown, and was on his way to Mass when he was shot.

It was his usual custom to attend an earlier Mass at Booterstown with Mrs. O'Higgins and Mr. Hogan. This morning, however, the two latter attended the earlier Mass, and the Minister for Justice was alone when attacked.

He was only a short distance from his own house just at the junction of Cross Avenue and Booterstown Avenue when a grey motor car that had apparently been waiting in the vicinity, drove smartly from the direction of Dublin towards him.

On coming level with Mr. O'Higgins, the car slowed down, and when almost at a dead stop beside him first attracted his attention.

There were a number of men in the car, all apparently young, and without a word these opened fire.

A regular volley of bullets whizzed about him, and he was struck by several about the body.

The Minister made a dash for the shelter of a neighbouring gateway, but before he could get cover several more shots were fired, one catching him in the head.

Mr. O'Higgins at once collapsed on the footpath, and with some parting shots the car drove off.

The sound of the shots had alarmed the neighbourhood, but as there was nobody in the street in the immediate vicinity, the Minister lay for a few minutes bleeding profusely in the street.

When he was discovered messengers were immediately despatched for priest and doctor. Dr Bennett, a local resident, who was returning from Church service, hurried to the scene, and after rendering such aid as was possible, had Mr. Higgins removed to his home.

The Minister was in a semi-conscious condition, and was suffering from several wounds in the body, and one on the head. In all, apparently, seven bullets had taken effect.

Surgical experts were immediately summoned, but despite their utmost efforts, the Minister died from his wounds at 5 o'clock.

THE ASSAILANTS.

The number of men in the motor car is variously estimated by those who observed the car before and after the occurrence, at between four and seven. The number of shots fired would indicate that there were at least four revolvers simultaneously in action, as there are evidences at the scene of the shooting of many bullets having missed the Minister.

So far as can be ascertained, Mr. O'Higgins himself was unable to give any account of the number or appearance of his assailants, who apparently were able to get clear away from the district before the alarm was raised.

It would seem that they had arrived in the district from the Dublin direction, and it is said that the motor car was seen in the district a considerable time before the attack took place.

Owing to the number of intersecting roads within easy distance, the fact that the attackers drove off in the direction of Blackrock is regarded as offering no clue to their destination.

Immediately that [illegible] of the occurrence was conveyed to the authorities, police and military became active. Orders were despatched over a wide area instructing that all motor cars should be held up and their occupants [illegible] questioned. In Dublin city these operations were carried out by the police, and the holding-up of passing motor cars was the first indication the people had of the occurrence. Throughout County Dublin and Wicklow similar holds-up and searches went on simultaneously, but up to the present apparently without result.

No arrests have been made, and the location of the assailants and their grey motor car remains a mystery.

These search operations began within 20 minutes of the shooting, but despite these prompt measures it would appear that the plans for the attack were so well laid that practically all traces of the attackers had disappeared.

ANOTHER ACCOUNT.

Seven Attackers Fire On Minister.

Our special representative, wiring last night, said:—

Shortly before noon to-day Mr. Kevin O'Higgins, Vice-President of the Executive Council, Minister for Justice, and Minister for External Affairs, was shot at, and died at 5 o'clock from two severe wounds which he received. When the news of the affair spread it created the utmost sensation, and that in a country where the cause of such excited interest unfortunately grew too common.

The salient features of the occurrence are that Mr. O'Higgins was on his way to divine service at Booterstown Church, which is but a short distance from his home. He was alone, and without, as usual, the company of his wife. The exact location of the shooting is quiet and secluded, and there was nothing to arouse any suspicion of lurking death in the mind of Mr. O'Higgins as he walked briskly along. He just reached the junction of Cross Avenue and Booterstown Avenue when two men pressed on to him from behind and fired several shots into his back.

In the first impulse the Minister essayed to run across the rather narrow roadway to the meagre shelter of a gateway. But a few hurried steps, and he fell to the ground unconscious. In the quickly passing seconds more shots rang out, and one of the bullets hit him in the back of the head. The noise of the rapid shots was distinctly heard on the main road from which Booterstown Avenue leads to the parallel road, giving the direct route to Bray—the Stillorgan road. There was no great attention, however, attracted, and Mr. O'Higgins must have been lying in his unconscious state with blood flowing profusely from the head wound, and oozing from the wounds in his back.

This was the appalling sight that confronted Dr. Bennett, of Merrion Avenue, when returning from his Church. About the same time the policeman on point duty on the main road had hurried on to Booterstown Avenue in the direction of the shooting. Finding Dr. Bennett in attendance the constable immediately returned to procure an ambulance and within ten minutes Mr. O'Higgins was brought to his house, where Dr. Bennett was joined by Dr. Dale and Dr. O'Reilly.

SEVEN MEN IN ATTACK.

The assailants of Mr. O'Higgins are estimated to number from four to seven. There is great difficulty to get the exact story, for Cross Avenue is a quiet thoroughfare with few residences, while Booterstown Avenue, if more populated, is still very quiet and very suburban. About seven men, it is related, drove along Booterstown Avenue shortly after eleven o'clock this morning in a grey coloured motor car. When it passed the intersection of Cross Avenue it pulled up, and two men left the car, walking back in a careful manner.

"LITTERED WITH BULLETS."

Approaching the entrance to Cross Avenue they walked it down. Towards them Mr. O'Higgins was walking. The passing in the roadway had scarcely happened when shots were fired at close range, and pierced the back of Mr. O'Higgins, injuring the spine. At least seven shots entered the body, which, as one of the medical men said, "is littered with bullets." Mr. O'Higgins essayed to escape his assailants by an effort to run to the shelter of a gateway in Booterstown Avenue. As he did so shots were again fired, and one of them, if not more, pierced the back of his head as he fell.

The medical men at once appreciated that the deadly nature of the wounds gave no hope for recovery, and for a short five hours Mr. O'Higgins lingered on.

SHOTS INTO BODY.

Further Details Of The Attack.

A Special Correspondent wires:—That the attack was the result of previous arrangement is indicated by the fact that Mr. O'Higgins' assailants were apparently lying in wait for him a short distance from his house. He had proceeded about three hundred yards from his residence when he was approached by three men who spoke to him. Mr. O'Higgins, becoming suspicious, ran across the roadway in the direction of a gateway in an endeavour to gain the shelter of the surrounding wall. Immediately he crossed the road fire was opened on him with revolvers, and he fell beside the gate, practically riddled with bullets. The scene of the occurrence is a comparatively quiet spot. Mr. O'Higgins' residence is some 300 yards away on Cross Avenue, at right angles to which runs the Stillorgan road and Booterstown Avenue. From the junction of the two roads the Church, which was Mr. O'Higgins' objective, is about 100 yards down Booterstown Avenue.

Mr. O'Higgins, shortly before 12 o'clock, left his house, "Dunamase," and walked slowly in the direction of the Stillorgan road. He was alone, as his wife had already attended the 10 o'clock Mass with Mr. P. Hogan, Minister for Agriculture, who also lives in "Dunamase." On reaching the corner of Booterstown Avenue and Cross Avenue, it is stated three men approached and addressed him. Mr. O'Higgins, becoming suspicious of the menacing attitude of the men, commenced to run across to the opposite side of the road in the direction of the gateway of "Sans Souci," the residence of a local doctor. This action on the part of Mr. O'Higgins was the signal for a volley of revolver shots from the three men at the corner.

Using parabellum revolvers, the men directed a fusilade of shots in Mr. O'Higgins' direction. He by this time had reached the footpath on the opposite side. The range being nearly point blank, the Minister was an easy target for his attackers, and on reaching the pathway he was hit in the back of the head, and fell at the foot of a lamp-post a few feet from the gateway. The men then crossed the road, and, it is stated, fired several shots into Mr. O'Higgins' body as he lay on the path.

Having completed their work they ran a short distance up the Stillorgan road, where a Morris Cowley car was drawn up at the road-side, and, entering it, they drove rapidly away. It is also stated that two men on their way to Mass were eyewitnesses of the attack. They are alleged, on observing the action of the men, to have stood with their backs to the wall and with their hands up. No attention, however, was paid to them by Mr. O'Higgins' attackers.

Mr. O'Higgins was wounded in seven places. Four bullets entered his body, two passed through his neck, and one struck his head. Bleeding profusely from his many wounds, Mr. O'Higgins lay on the footpath for several minutes until the arrival of Dr. Beckett, of Merrion Avenue, who was returning from the Protestant church at Booterstown. Observing the condition of the wounded Minister, he immediately attended to him pending his being taken to his home.

In "Dunamase" the shots were heard by Mr. Hogan, the Minister for Agriculture, and Mr. McGilligan, Minister for Commerce—who had an appointment with Mr. Hogan—and Mrs. O'Higgins, who became alarmed at the firing. The two Ministers quickly reached the scene, and, with Dr. Beckett, conveyed Mr. O'Higgins to his home. He at no time lost consciousness despite the wound in his head, and was able to give a description of the attack.

Nearly five hours after the occurrence Mr O'Higgins succumbed to his injuries.

SKETCH OF DEAD MINISTER'S CAREER.

The late Mr. O'Higgins was born on June 7th, 1892, being a son of the late Dr. Thos. F. O'Higgins, Stradbally. His mother was a daughter of the late T. D. Sullivan. He was educated at Knockbeg College, Carlow, and at Clongoweswood, and at the National University, Dublin, where he secured B.A. and LL.B. Degrees.

In 1918, when a student for the solicitor's profession he joined the Sinn Fein movement and took part in many of the electoral struggles during the historic election of 1918. He spent a term of imprisonment for a speech delivered during the anti-conscription campaign, and was returned by an overwhelming majority in Leix as a Sinn Fein candidate.

In 1920, when President Cosgrave was arrested, Mr. O'Higgins, who had been on the run for some time, took his place as Minister for Local Government. In the election of 1921 he was again elected for Leix-Offaly. A supporter of the Treaty in the Dail debates and following the Pact Election in 1922 he was appointed Minister for Home Affairs. In subsequent Cabinets he was Minister for Justice, and passed several Acts which are of outstanding importance in the life of the Free State, including the Liquor Bill. He was called to the Bar a few years ago.

He took a strong line during the crisis following the resignation of Mr. John McNeill in connection with the boundary question, and it was largely due to his exertions that the Government was able to present a united front to the nation. He passed into law the Licensing Act, 1926-27, which followed largely upon the recommendations of the Liquor Commission set up a few years previous, and during the passage of this Act displayed characteristic courage, facing, as he did some of the largest vested interests in the country.

Following the recent general election he took up the dual office of Minister for Justice and Minister for External Affairs, and had returned from Geneva on Friday to learn of the death of his aunt, the wife of the Governor General.

ACTIVITY IN CORK.

In the Cork area great activity was displayed by the Civic Guards and detective forces when the news of the attack on Mr. O'Higgins reached the city. Close watch was kept on trains, and around the city motor cars were held up, and the drivers interrogated. Up to a late hour last night, however, no arrests had been made.

LOSS TO THE NATION.

If sensation ensued at the news of the shooting it was as nothing to the shattering shock of the news issued a few minutes before five o'clock of his death. It is but the merest truth to say that Mr. O'Higgins was the most brilliant member of the Executive Council and the Government of the Free State. His untimely and tragic death evokes much more than the sense of sympathy. The President and the members of the Executive Council and Government party lose an able and sincere colleague, while every member of the Dail will readily pay tribute to his outspoken manner and manifest belief in the causes he espoused. There was also the winning trait of utmost courtesy, and the desire to seek values on the varying points of view expressed. These were qualities that made Mr. O'Higgins at once admired and respected. And these are qualities that even his bitterest political opponents freely admitted, and the regret over his sad death will be shared by them.

LATE MR. KEVIN O'HIGGINS. (Lafayette, Dublin).

"I FORGIVE THEM."

Pathetic Details Of Terrible Tragedy.

"I forgive them." These were the last words whispered to the Very Rev. Canon Breen, Booterstown, who was quickly summoned to the aid of Mr. O'Higgins as he lay full length on the pathway in Booterstown Avenue, less than 100 yards away from the church at which he was going to assist at 12 o'clock Mass.

Canon Breen having administered conditional Absolution within 10 minutes, Mr. O'Higgins was being conveyed in an ambulance back to his home, there to be received by his youthful and loving wife—who was distracted with grief—Mr. P. Hogan, Minister for Agriculture, and a few other intimate friends.

Dunamase, the residence, is midway in Cross Avenue, which is a semi-circular detour giving access to Blackrock at one end and the little village of Booterstown at the other. It is a thoroughfare of substantial houses with spacious grounds and fairly well wooded. The traffic at any time would be very quiet, but on Sunday mornings would have some passers-by on their way to church.

"YOUR TIME HAS COME."

Mr. O'Higgins set out about ten minutes to twelve, and there accompanied him one of a bodyguard. This man, it is said, was asked to return to the house by Mr. O'Higgins for a message, so that he continued along to turn into Booterstown Avenue, which faces a residence, Sans Souci, with big sweeping access gates opening to a wide avenue. The turn to the Catholic Church is to the right, and just as this was reached two men—some say three—approached Mr. O'Higgins, and, saying to him: "Your time has come," levelled revolvers at him. He at once made for the shelter that would offer at Sans Souci, but the gates were closed. However, before he had got across the narrow roadway shots rang out. The first hit him in the left hand, then two fired lodged in the back, near the spine. Mr. O'Higgins fell as some five or six other shots were fired, and these took effect, one in the head, two in the neck, and three in the body, one of which was over the heart.

"MY LIFE FOR IRELAND."

The assailants walked to a waiting motor and quickly left the scene of their deadly assault. It is said their car proceeded down to Booterstown, and if that was so they passed the Civic Guard Barracks at the end of the road. More probably they made out the other way, on the Stillorgan road, and could then direct themselves off to Bray or back into the city, via Donnybrook. There were two young women walking immediately in front of Mr. O'Higgins as he came up Cross Avenue, and they, too, were going to the Church. The shooting alarmed them, and they ran, and the first to come on the prostrate form of Mr. O'Higgins was a small boy.

Professor McNeill, who lives in Booterstown Avenue, was the second person to arrive, and then Dr. Beckett. Everything possible was done to assuage Mr. O'Higgins, who bore up bravely, but who answered every weak but good-natured encouragement with a wan smile and the oft repeated words: "I am done, but I give my life for Ireland."

AT SCENE OF TRAGEDY.

Word of the tragic event reached the several police stations about 12.30, and at once every available man was put on point duty to intercept passing vehicles, and question the drivers and passengers, and examine their cars. This was the first hint to the public generally that something unusual had happened. There was, however, a very slow disposition to associate the police activities with anything more serious than a surprise quest for motor and driver licences. It was about an hour before people got to learn of the attempt on the life of Mr. O'Higgins, and the news was received with a feeling approaching consternation. During the afternoon and evening large numbers visited the scene. There were faint bloodstains on the pavement and here and there the "dashed" wall showed bullet grazes. All these spent tokens of the tragedy were examined with a sympathetic interest, and there were here and there groups trying to construct the sad drama of which no more than two or three persons had been alarmed witnesses. There were many callers at Dunamase to convey their condolences. These included President Cosgrave and the other Ministers of State.

CONSCIOUS TO THE END.

Interview With An Eye-witness.

The Press Association Dunleary correspondent says:—Mr. O'Higgins had arrived at the corner of Cross Avenue, a broad road with villas only on one side, when three men at a short distance opened fire on him with "Peter the Painter" pistols. He was struck by several bullets and collapsed, and more shots, it is stated, were fired into his body as he lay on the ground. The only person near was a woman.

In an interview with the Press Association representative she said:—"I saw a new Morris motor car standing at the opposite corner. There were two men seated in it and one standing in the road. As Mr. O'Higgins came to the corner they all came towards him and then I heard shots. I looked round and saw Mr. O'Higgins lying on the footpath and the three men running to their car. The car quickly disappeared."

Professor McNeill, formerly Minister of Education, and two Civic Guards came up a moment later, and a priest and doctor were sent for. Blood was streaming from Mr. O'Higgins's chest and neck. After the first shock he spoke to the Civic Guard sergeant, "I forgive them all."

In reply to a question he said, "I forgive them all."

The priest arrived, and kneeling down in the stream of blood ministered to him.

A man named Fleming, a neighbour, also arrived, and was shortly afterwards followed by Mr. Hogan, Minister for Agriculture. Mr. O'Higgins said he was dying, and in perfectly coherent terms expressed his last wishes in regard to his family and his property. By this time, twenty minutes after the shooting, a doctor, who had been fetched from a church near by, arrived and had the Minister removed to his home.

SHOT SEVEN OR EIGHT TIMES.

On medical examination it was found that Mr. O'Higgins had been shot seven or eight times. A bullet had entered in front of the right ear, and four bullets had gone right through his neck. He never lost consciousness, and spoke to everyone admitted to him. Mrs. O'Higgins saw him, and he asked after the children, who were out with the nurse.

"I DIE FOR MY COUNTRY."

To those about him he said—"I am dying at peace with my enemies. I die for my country. I go to join Michael Collins." Despite the number of wounds, such was his vitality, that the majority of his friends about his bed seemed to have suffered more from shock than the wounded man. Mr. O'Higgins told them that he felt little pain.

(CONTINUED ON PAGE EIGHT.)

"EVEN UNTO DEATH."

President's Tribute To Mr. O'Higgins.

MESSAGE TO THE NATION.

Dublin, Sunday.—There was a special meeting of the Executive Council at which President Cosgrave presided, this evening, at 5.30. It lasted nearly three hours, and important discussions took place. President Cosgrave to-night issued the following message:—

"Kevin O'Higgins was shot this morning on his way to Mass. The Vice-President of the Executive Council, the second Minister of the State has been struck down by the hand of an assassin.

"In this hour of National loss and of National mourning, mindful of the steadfast and heroic figure who has been sacrificed, the Irish people will not falter.

"O'Higgins in his dauntless courage and unflinching determination has trodden the path blazed by Griffith and Collins even unto death. Another great defender of the Nation has passed away.

"The Irish people may rest assured that the assassin's bullet will not succeed in terrorising this country. There are, and will be, men enheartened by the noble example of the late Vice-President, and—profiting by his labours—ready to step into his place and to maintain his high tradition of devotion to the welfare and safety of the Nation.

"LIAM T. MacCOSGAIR,
"10th July, 1927."

WIDESPREAD MOURNING

Arrangements For State Funeral.

Dublin, Sunday Night.—All the public buildings in Dublin and district have for the last few days their flags flying at half mast in sympathy with the Governor General, Mr. Healy, on the death of his wife. These visible condolences are now extended to the wife and family of Mr. O'Higgins, who is his nephew.

The Dublin Broadcasting Station to-night closed down as a mark of respect.

An inquest on Mr. O'Higgins will be held to-morrow, when one of the few witnesses to be examined will be his old colleague, Professor Eoin McNeill.

No definite arrangements have yet been made, but it is probable that they will be on the following lines. On to-morrow (Monday) the remains will be brought to the Mansion House, where they will lie in state until about eight o'clock on Tuesday night. They will then be brought to St. Andrew's Church, Westland Row, where they will remain overnight. On Wednesday morning there will be Mass, after which a State funeral will take place to Glasnevin.

MR. AMERY'S TELEGRAM OF SYMPATHY.

Mr. Amery, Secretary of State for the Dominions last night telegraphed to Mr. Cosgrave expressing his sympathy with him and deeply regretting the death of Mr. O'Higgins.

THRILLS AT SEA.

Fire Outbreak On Passenger Steamer.

DASH FOR PORT

Liner Strikes Iceberg In Fog.

Liverpool, Saturday.

An exciting experience befell passengers on the steamer "Patriotic," 2,254 tons, while making her passage through the night from Belfast to Liverpool. At five o'clock in the morning an alarm, "Ship on fire," was raised. An S.O.S. was sent out and the passengers were called on deck, a stern fight proceeding between the crew and the fire, which was in No. 2 hold. The outbreak was forward of the passengers' quarters, but it was deemed advisable to acquaint all on board with the position when the outbreak was discovered.

The ship was an hour and a half from Liverpool, and the captain decided to push on to port. He meanwhile sent out wireless calls for help.

The message was picked up at Seaforth Wireless Station and immediately passed on to the Central Fire Station at Liverpool. When the "Patriotic" came alongside Liverpool landing stage with dense volumes of smoke issuing from the hold, the fire engine, with Supt. Oakes in charge, was awaiting ready to begin operations. The fire was in the furthest corner of the hold, and proved to be amongst general cargo consisting mainly of twine, hemp and cloth. The firemen were compelled to use smoke helmets in order to make their attack on the seat of the fire. After two hours' labour at the landing stage the signal, "Fire under" was given, and later the "Patriotic" was moved to Canada Dock, where the process of pumping the hold dry was entered upon. The fierceness of the fire may be judged by the fact that the saloon deck of the vessel was buckled by heat. It is impossible to estimate the damage to the cargo, but it must be considerable.

How the fire originated is a complete mystery. One of the passengers, Miss Kathleen Gillespie, of Portadown, received burns to her foot and was removed to hospital, but after treatment was able to leave.

This is the second time the Liverpool Fire Brigade has been called—once by wireless. On the previous occasion, two years ago, the Brigade with engine went out on a ferry steamer to a point off New Brighton, and attacked and vanquished a fire on a ship in mid-ocean.

LINER STRIKES ICEBERG.

Over a thousand passengers on board the C.P.R. liner Montcalm, which reached Greenock yesterday, had a thrilling experience, many women fainting, when that liner struck an iceberg in the Straits of Belle Isle, two days out from Montreal, on her voyage to the Clyde and Liverpool. Dense fogs were met in the passage down the St. Lawrence River, and at 2.30 p.m. on Sunday, July 3rd, the passengers were startled to hear a crunching noise and to find the vessel heeling over to the port side. The Montcalm had slid on to a submerged ledge of a huge berg which rose high above the funnels of the vessel.

With some way on, she slid along the ledge and eventually righted herself. The point of part of the bilge keel was scraped off and the propeller blade broken. As a precaution, the lifeboats were swung out and the ship's crews stood ready to launch them. On examination it was found that the hull of the vessel was undamaged.

The Montcalm was delayed for 44 hours in the icefield, lofty masses of ice being seen. One man who was on deck said that the berg loomed up suddenly out of the mist and was so near that he could have touched it. Others stated that when the Montcalm canted over it was like walking down a steep decline.

Prior to meeting the iceberg the Montcalm had passed several small bergs, and the Captain kept the vessel proceeding at a slow pace when, states a passenger, the large iceberg came into view, the Captain immediately steered to the right, but was unable to avoid striking the berg on the left hand side. All the passengers, who had rushed on deck, were ordered to put on their life belts. The vessel heeled over but was speedily righted.

"The quick work and action of the captain," states this eye-witness, "was greatly praised by all on board. So thick was the fog that it was impossible for the ship to proceed on its journey, and the vessel drifted about for two days. Other ships were soon alongside her, and for 48 hours they had to keep their sirens continually sounding. When the fog cleared the Montcalm was able to proceed on its journey, but she was crippled and had to sail at a reduced speed. The vessel will be repaired on the Clyde.

COLLISION WITH BARQUE.

Mishap To White Star Liner.

Owing to a slight collision in which she was involved with the Italian three-masted barque Giacomo off the Lizard in the early hours of Saturday morning, the White Star liner, Homeric, was three hours late in arriving at Southampton from New York.

A passenger on the Homeric in an interview with a Press Association representative said:—

"About 12.30 last night I was sitting in the lounge when I felt a slight shock, as though the vessel had gone aground. Almost immediately the engines were stopped and then reversed.

"I was somewhat alarmed and went to the ship's side, when I was joined by other passengers who had gone to bed earlier in the evening. They came on deck with dressing gowns over their night clothes. The Homeric was steaming round a sailing ship, and there was some shouting going on between our officers and those on the sailing vessel.

"We put a boat out, and with the assistance of our searchlight it was pulled alongside the Giacomo. They found that her bowsprit had been carried away, but she required no assistance. We then proceeded on our way to Cherbourg."

The Giacomo was on a voyage from Naples to Cherbourg.

STORM HAVOC.

Heavy Loss Of Life In Floods.

Berlin, Saturday.—Violent storms and cloudbursts caused great loss of life and damage to property in the neighbourhood of Gottleube, Saxony, this morning. The floods swept away houses, bridges, and railway lines.

About fifty persons are missing, twenty-five bodies have already been washed up, and it is feared that the loss of life will be still greater.—Reuter.

Paris, Saturday.—Additional reports from the provinces regarding the recent storm show that it caused five fatalities.

A husband and wife at Flexicourt in the Somme were killed by lightning; a woman at Montigny En Ostrevant (Nord); a man at Meuchy (Cayeux), Pas De Calais; and another at Issoudun, were killed in the same way.

At Beauvais the power station was struck and the town deprived of electricity. The same thing happened at Dunkirk, and at Poitiers the town hall was badly damaged.

In Burgundy miles of telegraph poles were blown down, interrupting communication between Paris and South Eastern France.

Trains on the main line through Burgundy arrived hours late, as they had to be held up while the poles were cleared from the line.—Reuter.

NAVAL ARMAMENTS.

Efforts For Agreement At Geneva.

THE PARITY PROBLEM.

Britain's Assurances To U.S. Government.

Geneva, Saturday.—The Japanese delegation to the Naval Disarmament Conference has issued a statement, the substance of which is, that naval limitation is their main object and that it would seem to them the adoption in principle of the minimum figure proposed by the Americans as the basis for discussion would be conducive to the speedy consummation of the task before the conference. If 450,000 tons for the United States and Great Britain is taken as the base, the Japanese would propose that the tonnage of surface auxiliary vessels to be allotted to Japan should be about 3[illegible] tons.

The more hopeful view expressed last evening as to the results of the Naval Limitation Conference is maintained this morning. The Executive Committee assembled at 10.30 a.m., Admiral Lord Jellicoe returned this morning from London and is taking part in the Committee's discussion. Reuter's correspondent understands that capital ships were also discussed at yesterday's meeting of the Executive Committee, and that it was agreed that an exchange of views on the subjects should take place at the present Conference. Sir James Parr, the Chief New Zealand delegate left last night for London, and Sir Joseph Cook, the Australian delegate, is leaving to-night for London. These personal movements, however, are not connected with the work of the conference.

SUBMARINES AND DESTROYERS.

With regard to destroyers, the British delegation have proposed that the maximum individual displacement of destroyer leaders shall be 1,750 tons, and that of destroyers 1,400 tons. They shall have five inch guns, and the age limit for their replacement shall be 20 years.

The American delegation has proposed respectively 2,000 tons for destroyer leaders, 1,500 for destroyers, and an age limit of 16 years.

The Japanese delegation has made no proposals as regards destroyer leaders, but for destroyers they suggest 1,500 tons and an age limit of 12 years.

The following limitations were finally agreed to:—Destroyer leaders 1,850 tons, destroyers 1,500 tons, five-inch guns, and an age limit of 1[illegible] years.

The American delegation preferred at present to give no definite figures as regards numbers or total tonnage of the destroyer class.

The British requirements were—221,000 tons of which not more than 25,000 tons would be composed of units exceeding 1,[illegible] tons displacement, though these figures are provisional pending a final agreement.

Regarding submarines, the Japanese have not made any proposals regarding the total tonnage of destroyers.

Concerning submarines, the recommendations deal with two types of the vessels ranging from 6[illegible] to 1,8[illegible] tons with five inch guns, and an age limit of [illegible] years.

The subject of small aircraft carriers was broached, but neither consideration was reserved. It is proposed that the age limits of warships should only apply to vessels of all classes laid down subsequently to August 17th, 1923, the date of the final ratification of the Washington Treaty.

The American delegation stated in the course of discussion that their agreement to all these recommendations was conditional upon decisions being reached upon the two following points, namely the total tonnage limitation of all categories of warships, and the methods to be adopted to provide for the transition from the status quo to the ultimate status contemplated by the Treaty.—Reuter.

CAPITAL SHIP PROPOSALS.

Geneva, July 9.—The following communique was issued at the close of this morning's sitting of the Executive Committee of the Naval Limitation Conference:—

"Discussions on the cruiser question were begun, and suggestions were made which will be given further consideration. In the course of the discussion regarding the British proposals concerning capital ships, the following statement was made by the Japanese delegation: The British proposal presents various technical problems on some of which the Japanese Government are unable to express their views without mature consideration.

"They (the Japanese Government) are of the opinion that the matter might be taken up with profit at the present conference with a view to arriving at some kind of understanding with regard to capital ships. Care should, however, be exercised in handling the question, so that it may not be allowed to stand in the way of the principal object of the present conference—the limitation of auxiliary naval armament. It would therefore be advisable that the question of capital ships should be held up until agreement has been reached on the subject of auxiliary vessels."—Reuter.

PRINCIPAL DELEGATES MEET.

Geneva, Sunday.—Mr. Hugh Gibson, head of the United States delegation to the Naval Disarmament Conference, again held no Press reception yesterday. The principal delegates to the Conference met yesterday afternoon at a tea party given at a private house, and continued their morning conversations. Owing to the fact that the large conference room at the League Secretariat is being occupied by the Conference of the International Relief Union, the second plenary session of the Naval Conference will be held in the large hall of the Hotel Des Bergues, the residence of the American delegation.—Reuter.

LIVELY CRUISER DISCUSSION.

Geneva, July 9, 12.30 p.m.—Reuter's correspondent learns that a lively discussion took place at this morning's sitting of the Executive Committee of the Naval Limitation Conference on the cruiser question. According to some delegates slight progress was made, but according to others there was no progress at all. There will be a further meeting to-day, while the plenary sitting of the Conference is fixed for 3 p.m. on Monday.—Reuter.

BRITAIN'S OBJECT.

Ambassador's Assurances At Washington.

Washington, Friday.—Sir Esme Howard, the British Ambassador, explained in a statement to-night that his call on Mr. Kellogg, the Secretary of State, on Wednesday, was in compliance with instructions from home, to give assurance of British acceptance of the principle of naval parity as outlined at Geneva. Disturbed by accounts in the Press, which pictured him as having notified the State Department that Great Britain would insist on naval superiority, the Ambassador said: "We are anxious not to be reduced below a figure considered necessary for the protection of the Empire." The difficulties which had been encountered at Geneva, he said, arose from an effort to respect and reconcile the needs of two countries "so entirely different," at the same time adhering to the parity principle.

Sir Esme Howard expressed regret that charges of bad faith had been circulated, and asserted that it was his belief that "both sides are trying in good faith to come to an agreement."—Reuter.

Page recreated

1928

The increasing profile of the Catholic Church in the fledgling state can be seen from the space the *Examiner* affords to the Lenten pastorals in February. Significant excerpts from the pronouncements of 12 different bishops are printed over four pages.
In sports, though Irish people had already won several medals in previous Olympics, Pat O'Callaghan's gold in the hammer throw in Amsterdam was the first medal won by an athlete officially representing Ireland.
He went on to also win the gold at the next Olympics, and was part of an incredible domination of the event by Irish-born athletes which saw them take six of the first eight hammer golds awarded at the Olympics.
In aviation, Commandant Fitzmaurice of the Irish Air Force joined two German crew members to complete the first ever flight across the Atlantic from east to west.
Another expression of national pride in this era was the Irish language, and efforts to revive it included its introduction as a compulsory subject at second-level schools.

NEWS BRIEFS

Feb To any lover of nature in search of an interesting pastime, trout fishing holds strong attention. There is a thrill in holding a rod, expecting every minute that a trout will rise to one's fly, or tug at one's worm, that must be experienced to be understood. (20)

Nov The ss *Lake Gorin*, one of the fleet of ten ships owned by Messers Henry Ford and Son, arrived at the Ford Wharf on the Marina yesterday from Detroit with the first consignment of machinery for the manufacture of tractors at the Marina Works. It is estimated that when the Cork factory is in full working order as many as 150 tractors will be turned out every eight hours. (9)

Ireland's first gold medal

Tuesday, July 31

One of the principal features of today's programme in the Olympic Games was the hammer throw which was won by Dr P O'Callaghan, of Kanturk, County Cork, with a magnificent effort of 168 feet 7 inches.
The popular winner was the essence of modesty when interviewed by the Press Association's special correspondent after his victory.
He is a great boyish figure of a man with a mass of golden hair and is only 22 years of age. When he emerged from the dressing tent he was given a rousing cheer by a great crowd of admirers.
Dr O'Callaghan's great achievement will undoubtedly give a considerable impetus to the revival in Irish athletics which has been apparent of recent years, and it is a matter for congratulation that a Munster man should lead the way in so notable a fashion.

World record holder Pat O'Callaghan prepares to throw the hammer at Kanturk.

Safely across the Atlantic

Saturday, April 14

In the early hours of this morning the news was circulated of the safe arrival of the *Bremen* – the German plane which left Dublin for New York on Thursday – at an island near the Canadian mainland in the Belle Isle Straits, north of Newfoundland.
During yesterday numerous reports of the sighting of the machine at various places were given out, but all lacked confirmation, and many were subsequently proved to be inaccurate.
Greenly Island, where the aviators have landed, is a Canadian fishing station, north-west of Newfoundland.
The *Bremen* was evidently driven by stress of weather far northwards of its normal course, as Greenly Island would be 400 miles from any of the points over which the plane was calculated to fly to New York.

Bishop on women's dress

Monday, May 7

On the occasion of his visitation to Clonakilty for the purpose of administering the Sacrament of Confirmation, his Lordship Most Rev Dr Roche, Bishop of Ross, referred in striking terms to the need for modesty in feminine attire.
"In modern times," continued his Lordship, "a bit of the spirit of paganism and a love of pleasure are prominent features even in the life of good Catholics. It manifests itself particularly at present in regard to female dress".
"This failing is worldwide. The Holy Father, Pope Pius XI, has again and again in recent years denounced the immodest extravagance of women's dress. Now brethren, our people have been caught in this snare of fashion, and in our towns and in the country too, many of our young girls are dressed in a manner that is to men an occasion of sin."

TEA
AND
POPULAR IN QUALITY
2/4, 2/8, 2/10, 3/-, 3/2, 3/6.
6lb. Postage Paid. 3lb. Postage 9d.
WOODFORD, BOURNE
AND CO., LTD.,
CORK.

The Cork Examiner.

NO. 23,397. TUESDAY. MORNING, DECEMBER 11, 1928. PRICE--TWOPENCE.

Registered for transmission at Newspaper Rate of Postage to Ireland and Great Britain, and at Magazine Rate to Canada and Newfoundland.

CITY SPECIAL
WOODFORD'S
REGISTERED
FOUR (****) STAR
INVALID'S
Champagne Brandy
Age and Quality Guaranteed.
WOODFORD, BOURNE
AND CO., LTD.,
CORK and LIMERICK.

BIG LINER GOES ASHORE

ON ROCKS AT ENTRANCE TO CORK HARBOUR.

EARLY MORNING MISHAP.

All Passengers Taken Off By Local Vessels.

EFFORTS TO REFLOAT.

The Scene On Board---No Panic And Splendid Discipline.

The White Star liner Celtic, 21,179 tons gross, homeward bound from New York, went ashore early yesterday morning on the Cow and Calf Rocks, about 400 yards west of Roche's Point, Cork Harbour. The liner was making the harbour when the accident occurred.

Among her two hundred odd passengers were 27 survivors of the Vestris disaster. All passengers came safely ashore on the tenders, which were quickly on the scene. A tug from Cove, as well as the lifeboat from Guileen went to the assistance of the vessel in response to wireless and telephone calls.

There was little excitement and no panic on board, the passengers being able to partake of breakfast before leaving the ship, which remains wedged between the two rocks and standing broadside to the shore. Efforts by three tugs to get her off were unsuccessful last night, but it is hoped she may be refloated to-day.

It is understood the vessel is holed and has several feet of water in some compartments. She is, however, in no immediate danger, though her position in the event of the weather conditions becoming stormy, gives cause for some anxiety.

Latest reports from Cove state that two salvage steamers are on the way—one from Falmouth and another from Liverpool—with the necessary gear for towing the Celtic off the rocks. A tug was standing by all night in case of any urgent necessity.

The earliest intimation of the mishap to the Celtic was contained in a Lloyd's report that Land's End radio station received a message from the Celtic at 5.40 yesterday morning stating that she was ashore off Roche's Point.

A Lloyd's message from Cove subsequently stated that the Celtic was ashore on the Cow and Calf rocks, about 200 to 300 yards west of Roche's Point lighthouse.

The Dutch tug, Gelezee, had been despatched to her assistance.

The Celtic is a White Star liner of 21,179 tons gross, built at Belfast in 1901. She was homeward bound from New York.

Roche's Point is on the east side of the entrance to Cork Harbour. A fine lighthouse marks the spot, and is a wellknown guide for boats proceeding out into the Atlantic. It has a fixed light, sixty feet above high water, with a visibility of thirteen miles. It also has a recurring light 56 feet above high water, which can be seen fifteen miles away in clear weather. In the ordinary way the Celtic, having reached Roche's point, would be within a very short distance of where she would cast anchor to meet the tender which goes out from Cove to meet all inward and outward liners. The tender lands or embarks mails and passengers.

Another Cove message stated—The

Previous to this the pilot, in a small boat, was lying up at the buoy inside the harbour, and a tender was also there. Presumably the sea was too heavy at the time to board the Celtic. On the liner blowing her siren the pilot went out towards the ship and boarded her. When daylight came Mr. Hill saw the Morsecock alongside, transferring the passengers, all of whom were got off. The weather was quite clear at the time. It was blowing very strong up to 4 a.m., but after that the wind moderated. There was a heavy ground sea running.

Mr. Hill communicated immediately with the Guileen life saving station. This was about half-past 5. The Guileen crew at once proceeded to Roche's Point, and stood by, but their services were not required. The tender was able to get between the rocks and alongside of the bow of the liner for the transfer of the passengers.

PROMPT ASSISTANCE FOR VESSEL.

The splendid intelligence and 'phone service of the marine branch of the Department of Industry and Commerce, by which all the lighthouses on the South coast are connected, was demonstrated on this occasion. A special word of credit is due to the Guileen life-saving crew, under Mr. R. Costin, who were on the spot prepared for action with highly commendable alacrity. Mr. John Morgan, superintendent for the Southern area of the coast life-saving service, was noti-

TOWING OFF THE LINER.

Yesterday's Futile Attempt

SALVAGE STEAMERS TO TRY TO-DAY.

POSITION LAST NIGHT.

Cove, Monday Night.—An effort at high tide this evening to tow the Celtic off the Calf rock, close to Roche's Point, proved useless, as the Gelezee, the powerful Dutch tug, which had got a hawser out of her, with the Morsecock aiding, was unable to get a stir out of her.

Another effort to get her out of her precarious position—and it is now generally regarded by competent observers as such—will not be made until to-day.

There is a great depth of water in the Celtic now, and it is sufficient to put her engines out of action completely. She is heavily laden with a general cargo, and it is absolutely essential, if salvage operations are to be successful, that the present calm weather conditions shall continue. At the same time a heavy swell prevails off Roche's Point, and this does not render the task of those engaged in taking off baggage, etc., less easy. Heavy baggage will be brought ashore early to-morrow morning, but all the mails have already been landed—over 800 sacks, most of which are for the Irish Free State. All leave here to-night for Cork and Dublin by the 9.10 p.m. train.

STEWARDS COME ASHORE.

A large number of the stewards came ashore to-night, and are being divided up amongst hotels, boarding and lodging houses for the night. All seem in cheerful mood, notwithstanding the trying ordeal they have just come through.

The manager of the White Star Line at this port, Mr. W. R. Harman, had a strenuous time since 5.30 o'clock this morning, attending to an immensity of details connected with the landing of the passengers, their baggage, and the mails. His efforts were ably seconded throughout the whole exacting duties of the day by Mr. Wm. O'Reilly and Mr. Jack Murray, of the White Star Line local office staff. In fact every member of the whole office did not spare themselves, including Miss Kane and the girl typists, in doing everything they could that would in any way tend to the comfort of the unexpected influx of passengers.

TRANSFER OF PASSENGERS.

Afloat, the marine superintendent of the White Star Line spent over sixteen consecutive hours, commencing before dawn, looking after every detail connected with the safe transfer of passengers, mails, baggage from ship to tender, special gangways for this purpose having to be improvised to safely effect this difficult work, having regard to the list of about 20 degrees which the Celtic took, and also to the heavy seas breaking on the ship's seaward side.

Lloyd's Agent at this port (Mr. A. C. Horne) left here long before dawn this morning aboard the Gelezee, which arrived at the scene of the disaster in an incredibly short time after the Celtic had struck, and did not again come ashore until many hours after another night of darkness had descended on the harbour.

Mr. John J. Brennan, of the Clyde Shipping Company, who are representatives of the owners of the tug Seafolke, is superintending arrangements connected with the arrival of that tug at this port to-night.

At 9 p.m. to-night the weather was fine and calm.

The Guileen Rescue Crew go to aid the stricken liner Celtic

Page recreated

1929

One of the major undertakings in the Free State's attempt to industrialise and modernise was the harnessing of the Shannon to produce electricity. Hugely symbolic for the Free State to underline the nation's perceived progress since independence, it was also hoped that the expensive burden of coal imports would be reduced. The scheme was completed at a cost of £10 million and was carried out by German firm Siemens.

The year also marked the centenary of Daniel O'Connell's emancipation movement winning the right for some Catholics to vote and enter parliament. The occasion stirred memories and religious fervour and sparked some of the biggest gatherings yet seen in the state.

Alarming slump in Wall Street

Friday, October 25

It is estimated that five billion dollars in market values were swept away today in the worst crash in the history of the Stock Exchange, eclipsing yesterday's crash. By 2pm 11,000,000 shares had frantically changed hands and at 3pm the tickers were nearly three hours behind. Meanwhile, all stock and commodity markets throughout the country declined in sympathy.

Pandemonium reigned today. The shouts of the brokers fighting on the floor of the exchange to sell their stocks at the best available prices could be heard in the street.

With rumours that the exchanges might be closed, and with financial disasters increasing, there was almost a panic.

In San Francisco, thousands of insufficiently margined speculators have been ruined following the stock crash. Frenzied investors bombarded brokerage houses, and pitiable scenes occurred.

In London, scenes of unprecedented excitement were witnessed tonight in Throgmorton Street. Nervousness with regard to the condition of the American market caused hundreds of brokers to remain in Shorters Court to watch events.

The Limerick Clothing Factory was one of the city's major employers. Among the company's earlier clients for uniforms were the French during the Franco-Prussian war of the 1870s and the Confederates during the American Civil War of the 1860s.

Shannon gates open

Tuesday, July 23

Yesterday, in the presence of a very representative gathering, President Cosgrave formally opened the intake gates at the head race of the Shannon Power Scheme.

Mr Cosgrave said that henceforth the Shannon would be harnessed in the service of the nation, distributing light and heat and power throughout the Free State and increasing the comfort of their homes and the productive capacities of farms and factories. It was probable that the supply of electric power throughout the Free State could be begun in early winter.

Impressive and edifying scenes

Monday, July 15

A crowd estimated at 70,000 participated in the closing ceremonies of the Catholic Emancipation Centenary Celebration in Cork yesterday.

Forty thousand men, women and children were present at this historic ceremony, while fully 30,000 others lined the streets en route.

The scene as the huge ranks wended slowly through Patrick Street under the gayest sunshine of the year in a setting of flags overhead and on every side, the harmonious volume of the hymns sung by thousands of men's and women's voices, the solemn accompaniment of the bands and, finally, the dramatic moment when the immense concourse knelt with heads bowed and bared to receive the blessing imparted by the Bishop, all will be cherished in the memory of every Catholic citizen as a glorious conclusion to a week of unprecedented homage to the Faith.

NEWS BRIEFS

July The low rate of exchange helped keep Continental buyers away from the Cahirmee horse fair, but there were a number of cross-channel buyers. Artillery horses were making £30 to £50, while high class colts fetched prices from £80 to £150. (15)

Oct Count Gerald O'Kelly, first Minister of the Irish Free State in Paris, tells the American press: "There is no country in Europe where Americans are as welcome as in Ireland. There is scarcely a family in the country which has not a relative in the United States, and today the country would be very glad to have the aid of American capital and business methods in developing the natural wealth as yet unexploited." (25)

The Cork Examiner.

NO. 23,587. TUESDAY. MORNING, JULY 23, 1929. PRICE--TWOPENCE.

Registered for transmission at Newspaper Rate of Postage in Ireland and Great Britain, and at Magazine Rate to Canada and Newfoundland.

SHANNON SCHEME

YESTERDAY'S HISTORIC CEREMONY AT PARTEEN.

SLUICE GATES OPENED.

President's Address At Memorable Function

ALL PARTIES REPRESENTED.

Power And Light To Be Available Before Year's End

Yesterday, in the presence of a very representative gathering, President Cosgrave formally opened the intake gates at the head race of the Shannon Power Scheme.

There were present members of the Senate and Dail Eireann, including Mr. De Valera and several of his party; commercial and industrial interests were also represented, and there was a big attendance from various parts of the Free State. The ceremony began with the blessing of the undertaking by the Most Rev. Dr. Fogarty, Bishop of Killaloe, and special prayers for the whole scheme.

Mr. Cosgrave said that henceforth the Shannon would be harnessed in the service of the nation, distributing light and heat and power throughout the Free State and increasing tne comfort of their homes and the productive capacity of their farms and factcries. It was probable that the supply of electric power throughout the Free State could be begun in early winter. It was known from a recent statement by the Minister for Industry and Commerce that a margin of less than 5 per cent would cover the difference between the actual and estimated cost of construction. The country would always take pride in this magnificent installation, created by arduous labour, skill in conception and tenacity in execution.

It was thus demonstrated that Saorstat Eireann could carry out rapidly, efficiently and economically a hydro-electric scheme on a scale as large as any in Europe, and thereby had been laid a firm foundation for confidence, both at home and abroad, in their capacity to realise those economic developments of wide national scope and effect to which they all looked forward. The consumption of electricity supplied from existing plants was increasing at such a rate as to leave no doubt that the anticipations of experts would be realised in full.

THE SHANNON HARNESSED.

His Lordship blessing the waters and the great canal.

GARDA SIOTCHANA SPORTS.

Page recreated

1930

In November, British motorcyclist JS Wright set a new world record of 150.736 miles an hour at the Carrigrohane Road, Cork. Col Crennan, of the J.A.P company which made the bike, later described the extremely straight road as "the best in the world", rare words of praise for Irish thoroughfares.

Several news reports throughout the year carried accounts of the suppression of religion in Russia and attacks on Irish priests by the 'reds' in China, so it probably wasn't surprising that a meeting in support of Communism in Cork should be the source of some disturbance.

Bird protection Bill

Thursday, February 12

The Minister for Justice in the Dáil last evening moved the second reading of the Wild Birds Protection Bill. The main provision of the Bill is a closed season from March 1 to August 1.

Mr Lemass (FF, Dublin), opposing the Bill, said that many people were making their living out of trapping wild birds and exporting them. Human needs should be considered before the needs of wild birds.

Mr Anthony (Labour, Cork) said that other countries were making admirable efforts to encourage the protection of wild birds, even by making artificial lakes. In this country little or nothing was done. He directed attention to the Lough in Cork, where so-called sportsmen shoot off snipe and other birds.

The second reading was carried.

A gas-cooking demonstration at Fr Matthew Hall, Cork. While gas was becoming more popular, many people would still have been using solid-fuel ranges.

Irishman's long trudge

Tuesday, December 3

Montreal – An Irishman arrived here today after a 1,500 mile trudge from Winnipeg, seeking to find a cattle boat sailing to Great Britain, in which he could find a free passage to take him home to see his fiancée lying critically ill in Ireland.

Patrick O'Shaughnessy received a cable at Winnipeg about the illness of his fiancée and without funds he immediately started on the long trek to Montreal. On his arrival here he was told that the last cattle hunt for the season had left. He has now started for Saint John, another long walk of 500 miles, under winter conditions, hoping to secure a passage there for home.

Funeral of Ireland's oldest man

Saturday, December 27

The funeral took place today in Cloughbawn Cemetery, Co Wexford, of Patrick Flood, of Killegney, who died on Monday. Flood, who was 115 years of age, claimed to be the oldest man in the British Isles. He was born in the year of the battle of Waterloo, and spent his life as an agricultural labourer in his native parish. The only occasion on which he was away from home was when he walked to Dublin, 84 miles, in the days before railways.

Flood did not attribute his longevity to any particular cause. As he often remarked, plain fare and hard work were the common lot of many people of his early days, and his survival long after their time was just his luck.

Wild scenes at Soviet meeting

Saturday, February 22

There were scenes of remarkable excitement last night at a meeting held at the North Gate Bridge, Cork, at which a man who has been advocating the political system of the Soviet Republic at other public meetings during the week was to have been the principal speaker.

A man whose name was given as Mr McLysaght, who was said to be a native of Cork, was beginning his speech when his opening sentence was interrupted by a remark from the crowd: "What about the persecution of the Christians in Russia?"

A middle-aged man who was standing near jumped on the side of a hackney car and commenced an opposition speech. "The people of Cork", he said, "should refuse to listen to or be dictated to by a Russian spy." This remark created further excitement, and in a few moments the crowd was startled by the discharge of dog bombs in several parts of the assembly.

NEWS BRIEFS

Aug Government control over motor road traffic, embodying tests for drivers, third party insurance, penalties for dangerous driving, etc was demanded by the General Council of County Councils at its annual meeting in Dublin yesterday. (6)

Nov Éamon de Valera and Peadar O'Donnell were among those who addressed a meeting in Dublin against the flagrant display of British Imperialism disguised as Armistice celebrations. At the conclusion of the meeting two Union Jacks were burned, and the crowd sang 'The Soldiers Song'. Shots were fired later in O'Connell Street when rival parties came into collision. (11)

The Cork Examiner.

For Births, Marriages and Deaths See Page Six. Column One.

NO. 24,017 TUESDAY, MORNING, DECEMBER 9, 1930. PRICE—TWOPENCE.

Registered for transmission at Newspaper Rate of Postage in Ireland and Great Britain, and at Magazine Rate to Canada and Newfoundland.

"THE INNISFALLEN WAY"

M.V. INNISFALLEN

3600 TONS 18 KNOTS

Resumes service

at Fishguard

Thursday 11th. Dec.
1930

after FIRST overhaul

Leave Cork (Penrose Quay)
MON., WED., FRID.,
at 6 p.m.

PASSENGERS ARRIVE

LONDON (Paddington)	9.45 a.m.
Birmingham	11.50 a.m.
Bristol	8.8 a.m.
Cardiff	6.35 a.m.
Plymouth	12.26 p.m.
Reading	9.0 a.m.

LATER TRAINS FROM FISHGUARD
are available for Passengers who may not require to travel by first connecting Express.

CITY OF CORK STEAM PACKET CO. LTD., Penrose Quay, CORK

1931

As can be seen from the adjacent newspage, the Government and Catholic hierarchy alike were worried about people joining organisations which might not be in keeping with the world view of the State or the Church, outlooks that were in many ways intertwined.

President Cosgrave warns parents to keep their children away from 'illegal organisations' while the bishops refer specifically to Saor Éire, the left-wing group that had grown out of the IRA. "Surely the ranks of Communistic revolution are no place for an Irish boy of Catholic instincts," implore the bishops.

In Cork, the last night of the trams in the city was turned into a social occasion. Many people predicted that the tram would now be consigned to the history books.

Incredible scenes at passing of the trams

Thursday, October 1

Buses on their first day in Cork after the retirement of the trams.

Hundreds thronged around the Father Mathew Statue last night to witness the departure of the Cork Trams, which last night made their final appearance on the streets. From 11 o'clock on, people flocked into Patrick Street to give a send-off to the trams, worthy of their 34 years' service to the citizens.

Remarkable scenes of enthusiasm were witnessed as each tram reached the Statue to complete its last journey, and then retire to the Power House, never again to be seen in active service by the people of Cork.

As the vehicles drew up at the Statue, huge crowds rushed towards them, and a scramble took place to get a good position for the last ride. The onlookers were treated to the extraordinary sight of figures clinging to the railings and sides of the top of the conveyance.

As each tram moved off, groaning under the weight of numbers and years, or who knows but that it may have been their way of sighing, the crowds, densely packed on them, cheered loudly and broke into song, this being taken up on the streets below.

One man had brought a supply of fireworks as his tribute to the work of the trams, whilst in the very last vehicle a bunch of young men beat the tin advertisements with sticks, a procedure which made a deafening noise.

As well as being a definite public convenience, the trams were in the nature of a luxury during the summer months, when hundreds of citizens availed of the top of the vehicles to carry them to the outlying districts. The Blackrock route was especially favoured in this respect, and many will miss the outings which they have hitherto enjoyed.

NEWS BRIEFS

Jan In a wide-ranging encyclical given major coverage, Pope Pius XI speaks out against contraception, abortion, eugenics and also warns against the movement towards women's 'emancipation'. The report states: "His Holiness gravely censures those who would do away with the obedience which woman owes to man."

Apr Two London-based Italians begin legal proceedings in Dublin to stop the payout of £354,544 which has been won by a third Italian man in the Irish Hospitals Sweepstakes. They claim that the winning ticket was one of a number that the trio owned as a syndicate. (2)

A priest is assaulted when he goes to the 'Cheese House' in Castleisland, Co Kerry, with a flashlight to check the goings-on at a dance being held there. After hearing the evidence against the two men involved, Justice Johnson comments: "This is the second case that I have heard in Kerry of a priest being interfered with in the discharge of his duties regarding the inspection of these dance halls. I don't propose to say very much about it, because the Commissioner has taken steps to regularise these dance halls. But I know from my own experience in the courts that the dance halls in the districts of Kerry have done more to reduce certain members of the community to a savage state than anything we have had in the country for many a long day." (25)

The Cork Examiner.

NO. 24,284. MONDAY MORNING, OCTOBER 19, 1931. PRICE—ONE PENNY.

Registered for transmission at Newspaper Rate of Postage in Ireland and Great Britain, and at Magazine Rate to Canada and Newfoundland.

THE UNMASKING OF COMMUNISM

HATRED OF GOD!

ORGANISATIONS THAT PREACH WAR ON RELIGION AND THE STATE

MENACE THAT IRELAND MUST CHECK

Bolshevist Teaching Disguised In Terms Of Nationality

IMPIOUS AND NEFARIOUS DOCTRINES

Earnest And Stirring Appeal Of The Hierarchy To The People

The following joint Pastoral of the Archbishops and Bishops of Ireland was read in all Churches yesterday:—

Dearly Beloved in Christ.

Assembled in Maynooth for our annual October Meeting, and deeply conscious of our responsibility for the Faith and Morals of our people, we cannot remain silent in face of the growing evidence of a campaign of Revolution and Communism, which, if allowed to run its course unchecked, must end in ruin of Ireland, both soul and body. You have no need to be told that there is in active operation amongst us a society, of a militarist character, whose avowed object is to overthrow the State by force of arms. In pursuit of this aim they arrogate to themselves the right to terrorise public officials and conscientious jury men, to intimidate decent citizens into silence or acquiescence, and even to take human life itself. Such methods and principles of action are in direct opposition to the Law of God, and come clearly under the definite condemnation of the Catholic Church: nor can deeds of bloodshed to which they lead be made legitimate by any motives of patriotism.

To guard against misrepresentation, it is to be clearly understood that this statement, which we feel called upon to issue, has reference only to the religious and moral aspect of affairs, and involves no judgment from us on any question of public policy, so far as it is purely political. The political issue is a matter for the country at large, and is to be decided by the votes of the people as a whole. But no policy, however good, may be prosecuted by methods and means like those we have referred to, which are contrary to Divine Law and subversive of social order.

LAWFUL CIVIL AUTHORITY.

The existing Government in Saorstat Eireann is composed of our countrymen, and has been entrusted with office by the votes of the people. If the majority of the electors are not in agreement with its policy or its work they can set it aside by their votes, and return another to take its place. But so long as the Government holds office, it is the only lawful civil authority, a proposition that would be equally true if the Government were defeated to-morrow, and if any of the opposition parties assumed responsibility. From this it follows that no individuals or combination of individuals are free to resist its decrees or its officials by armed force, violence or intimidation. If such things were lawful, if any body of people who felt that they were aggrieved, and free to set up a rival executive and a rival army, the inevitable result must be anarchy, the destruction of personal liberty and the material as well as the spiritual ruin of the country.

Side by side with the Society referred to, is a new organisation entitled "Saor Eire," which is frankly Communistic in its aims. The published programme, as reported in the Press, when reduced to simple language, is, amongst other things, to mobilise the workers and working farmers of Ireland behind a revolutionary movement to set up a Communistic State. That is: to impose upon the Catholic soil of Ireland the same materialistic regime, with its fanatical hatred of God, as now dominates Russia, and threatens to dominate Spain.

This organisation, which is but a translation into Irish life, under Bolshevistic tuition, of a similar scheme in use in Russia, proposes to attain its object by starting throughout the country districts, wherever it can, and in towns and amongst industrial workers, what they call "Working Peasant Clubs," or "Cells," disguised for the moment in terms of Nationality and zeal for Farmers and Workmen, but which are to serve as revolutionary units to infect their disciples with the virus of Communism and create social disruption by organised opposition to the Law of the Land.

WHAT COMMUNISM MEANS.

Thus are we to see, if their efforts are successful, the ruin of all that is dear to us in History, Religion and Country, brought about in the name of Patriotism and Humanity. For materialistic Communism, in its principles and action, wherever it appears, means a blasphemous denial of God and the overthrow of Christian civilisation. It means also class warfare, the abolition of private property and the destruction of family life.

In the words of Our Holy Father: "Communism teaches and pursues a two-fold aim: merciless class warfare, and complete abolition of private ownership: and this it does, not in secret and by hidden methods, but openly, frankly and by every means, even the most violent. To obtain these ends, Communists shrink from nothing and fear nothing; and when they have attained to power, it is unbelievable, indeed it seems portentous, how cruel and inhuman they show themselves to be. Evidence for this is the ghastly destruction and ruin with which they have laid waste immense tracts of Eastern Europe and Asia, while their antagonism and open hostility to Holy Church and to God Himself are, alas, only too well known and proved by their deeds. We do not think it necessary to warn upright and faithful children of the Church against the impious and nefarious character of Communism. But we cannot contemplate without sorrow the heedlessness of those who seem to make light of these imminent dangers and with stolid indifference allow the propagation far and wide of those doctrines which seek by violence and bloodshed the destruction of all Society."

SINFUL AND IRRELIGIOUS.

It is our duty to tell our people plainly that the two Organisations to which we have referred, whether separate or in alliance, are sinful and irreligious, and that no Catholic can lawfully be a member of them.

We appeal most earnestly, and with deepest anxiety, to all our people, and especially the young, who through misguided counsels or mistaken love of country, have been caught in the meshes of those evil associations, to abandon them at once, and at any price. Surely the ranks of Communistic revolution are no place for an Irish boy of Catholic instincts. You cannot be a Catholic and a Communist. One stands for Christ, the other for Anti-Christ. Neither can you, and for the same reason, be an auxiliary of Communism.

Furthermore, we appeal, and with all the earnestness we can command, to men of all political parties who love their religion and country, to forget their differences for the time being, and join their forces in an endeavour to find a solution for our social and economic problems that shall be in accordance with the traditions of Catholic Ireland.

With anxious hearts we turn to God, Who has mercifully watched over our country through the ages, to extend His protecting arm to her now; to save her from the horrors of civil strife and religious ruin; to open all eyes to the danger impending over us; and to strengthen all hearts to resist the forces of evil with unflinching faith.

We know, and it is a consolation to us, how sincerely Catholic our people are as a body; but in view of the peculiar enemies that are now

(CONTINUED ON PAGE NINE.)

HIS EMINENCE CARDINAL MacRORY.

STRIKE CRIPPLES SPAIN.

Rail And Telegraph Services Paralysed

SEETHING UNREST.

Nuncio's Efforts To Calm Catholic Feeling

Madrid, Saturday.—A thousand men are affected by the railway strike in Seville. Two hundred and fifty Army engineers have arrived there. No cases of sabotage have been reported.

The strike called by the Railwaymen's Union in Andalusia began at midnight. The Government is taking the strictest precautions to maintain order. The trains will be run by soldiers if necessary.—Reuter.

Cadiz, Saturday.—In face of the railway strike, communications between here and Seville are secured by means of a torpedo boat which travels up and down the River Guadalquiver. The strike has crippled the whole Andalusian railway system, and while the train, telegraph and station services are maintained by detachments of army engineers, the only trains still kept running are the expresses between Cadiz, Malaga, and Granada. All other services are suspended.

The authorities have adopted every possible means to ensure the running of trains, and this has only been made possible by the co-operation of Socialist railwaymen, who are on the side of law and order, with detachments of Army sappers.—Reuter.

NUNCIO NOT LEAVING.

("Chicago Tribune" Special).

Madrid, Sunday.—The Nuncio to-night called in the Press, and said he was not leaving Spain, and at the same time, without previous mention, the Government released the Pope's exhortation to Spanish Catholics.

It is understood that the call to Catholics to work within the law to defend their beliefs was sent by Rome on the Nuncio's urgent request. He is having extreme difficulty in calming Catholic elements in the North.

NEW PASSWORD OF MONARCHISTS.

Barcelona, Saturday.—Meaning glances are exchanged between Spaniards, who may be seen wearing a small badge in their button-holes coloured emerald green. They know each other for keen Monarchists, who are organising their ranks to counter the threatened interference with the property of the Church.

Green in Spanish is "verde." This word has become the password, as well as the colour of the Monarchists. The letters "v e r d e" stand for Viva el rey de Espana.—Reuter.

DIVORCE LAWS.

Fundamental and far-reaching changes in the marriage laws of Spain provided for in Article 41 of the new Constitution have been approved by the Cortes. The marriage tie will no longer be indissoluble.

The article contains the following clauses:—

(1) Marriage is based on equal rights, and can be dissolved by mutual consent or at the request of either of the parties if just cause is shown.

(2) Fathers are under an obligation to maintain and educate their children born in or out of lawful wedlock.

(3) The State will undertake the care of abandoned children.

(4) There will be no distinction between legitimate or illegitimate children.

SOCIALISING INDUSTRY.

Madrid, Saturday.—The plan for labour control in industrial undertakings has been already inscribed in the Spanish Constitution and must be carried out, declared Senor Caballero, Minister of Labour, to-day, referring to the opposition that is finding expression in a section of the Press.

Employers, he said, must show good faith in the matter. If under the new Constitution they were advancing towards Socialisation the capitalist class must train the workers for the time when Socialisation would be realised. Labour control would apply to all workers, manual and intellectual, except the engineers and managers of industrial undertakings.—Reuter.

APPEAL TO PARENTS.

Youth And Unlawful Associations

PRESIDENT'S STATEMENT.

President Cosgrave on Saturday issued the following statement in connection with the Constitution Amendment Bill, which finally passed in the Senate, on Saturday:—

"The order required to bring into operation the new article of the Constitution has now been made. The powers which the Government have been given by the Oireachtas are wide. The penalties for unlawful activities are drastic. It is our sincere hope that the goodwill and innate sanity of the people of

PRESIDENT COSGRAVE.

this country will reduce to the minimum the necessity for using those powers, or inflicting those punishments.

"I want to make a special appeal to all parents and others who have a special responsibility towards the young men and women of the country. There are, to-day, young men and women who have been induced to join unlawful associations without realising the nature of those associations, or the extent of their dastardly programme.

"The actions of those associations are condemned by every Christian-minded man, and no effort should be spared to make clear to the youth the serious crime against their country which is involved in membership of them.

"The State must protect the people from everything which involves the decay and downfall of the Irish nation. Irish parents have a real responsibility towards their children and towards the State to do all in their power to aid in the observance of the laws. Drastic laws are made only for the evildoer, and there need be no fear of punishment in the minds of those misguided young men and women if they seize this opportunity to recognise that the observance of the laws of God and of the State is the only sure means of achieving the ultimate happiness and prosperity of the people.

"The authority of the State comes from God, and every organisation that seeks to destroy the State is subversive of morality and religion."—(Signed) L. T. MacCosgair.

LEAGUE TAKES ACTION.

Kellogg Pact And Far East Crisis.

JAPAN ADAMANT.

U.S. Intervention Inflames Feeling

Geneva, Sunday.—The Council has acted promptly in the matter of reminding China and Japan of their obligations under the Kellogg Pact. Within a few hours of the decision of Council to take this step the notes had been despatched through the usual diplomatic channels. The presence of the Foreign Ministers here enabled this course to be followed without loss of time. The American observer acted in the same way on behalf of his Government. It is understood that M. Briand is communicating the text of the Note to all signatories of the Kellogg Pact not represented on the Council, leaving it to them to take similar action or not.

JAPAN'S STIFF RETORT.

Meanwhile the Japanese representative has handed to the President of the Council a strong note questioning the legality of the attitude adopted by the Council in the matter of inviting the presence of a representative of the United States. The Japanese Government points out that the Council overrode the objections of the Japanese representatives, especially his request for a juridical opinion as to whether a question of procedure was involved. It remarks that a knotty question is raised by the fact that other signatories of the Paris Pact are interested, and only the United States is singled out by the invitation of the Council.

Finally, in asking when the juridical issues will be discussed and what will be the attitude of the Council in the event of its vote of Oct. 15 not being upheld, the Japanese Government says that it "will decide upon its attitude when it has learnt the views of the President of the Council on these points."

This very stiff note of the Japanese Government is much commented upon in League circles. It is understood that M. Briand is making a conciliatory but firm reply to-day. He will emphasise that the Council is master of its own decisions. There was a private sitting of the Council this morning lasting an hour and a half. To-morrow there will be a public sitting at which both the Chinese and Japanese delegations will be present.

ANGLO-SAXON MOVE AGAINST JAPAN?

Although the likelihood of the League to resorting to Article 16 is scouted in responsible circles here, the fact that such possibility has been mentioned in recent Geneva cables has produced a most unfortunate impression among certain sections of the Japanese public. Coming on the top of American participation in the League deliberations, it has served to revive the bogey of Anglo-Saxon nation combining to seek an opportunity to deal the blow at Japan. Responsible people feel that any further talk of applying sanctions will do more harm than good, as Japan would not be frightened into submission, but reactionaries might be encouraged to anti-foreign demonstrations, thereby adding to the difficulties of the Government in seeking a peaceful settlement.—Reuter.

RUSSIA'S RIGHT TO ATTEND.

Tokio, Saturday.—The question of whether the U.S.S.R. might not take part in the deliberations of the League Council on Manchuria has, it is understood, again been raised in Government circles.

In fresh instructions sent to Mr. Yoshizawa this afternoon, the Government says that it should be emphasised that whereas the American observer will be allowed to speak only on matters in which the Kellogg Pact is involved, the situation does not constitute one which would lead to war, and, consequently, there is no need to invoke the Pact. Moreover, if it is thought that the situation requires the invocation of the Pact, why are not all signatories invited to participate instead of the United States only?

While not specifically mentioned in the instructions, it is thought the Government feels that on this basis the U.S.S.R.—which, though not a signatory, declared her intention to adhere to the Pact—was more entitled to receive an invitation as being far more closely concerned with Manchuria.

The Japanese Government says in its instructions that before declaring its final attitude to the League's decision, the Government desires to seek enlightenment on certain points. These concern the legality of the League's decision to invite the United States to participate, and the question of the League proceeding without first deciding whether it has acted legally.

While the League talks about its own existence being imperilled if it fails to act, Japan feels that her own existence is in danger if the League insists on intervention merely to settle the present dispute. Japan wants a fundamental permanent settlement, not a mere temporary patch-work truce, and considers that such a settlement is only possible by direct negotiations with China.—Reuter.

MORE BOMBINGS.

The Chinese Delegation continues to shower upon the League Secretariat telegrams received from Nanking. One, dated October 16th, reads as follows:—"The sensational report that a Japanese named Komura was brutally murdered by Chinese workmen at Tsingtao has been fully investigated by the local authorities. It has transpired that Komura was done to death on account of a love triangle case among the Japanese community, and, accordingly, the Japanese made no representations to the Chinese authorities."

Another cablegram, dated Nanking, October 16th, alleges that Japanese troops are making an aerodrome covering some 330 acres between Yangchi and Peihetawan. On October 14th four Japanese aeroplanes dropped twenty bombs near Heinglungtien. Yesterday, at 1 o'clock, Japanese aeroplanes flew towards Paitai and Heilungkiang from Taonan, the message continues, and threw two bombs, the casualties not being ascertained.

Another cablegram, dated Nanking, October 16th, states that Japanese troops were busy digging trenches and burying mines near Chohho.

SAFETY BILL IN SENATE

MEASURE PUT THROUGH THE FINAL STAGES

ANGRY SPEECHES

Mr. McGilligan's Bitter Allusions To Opposition Senators

THE PROPOSED CONFERENCE

President's Warning As To Consequences Of Membership Of Illegal Organisations

The Senate passed the Public Safety Bill on Saturday by 41 votes to 15.

On the motion that the Bill finally pass, Colonel Moore expressed strong opposition, and said the measure would mean as great a perversion of justice as anything the I.R.A. had done.

Mr. Comyn also opposed the motion and said the Minister for Defence had referred to some of the people against whom the Bill was directed as blackguards, but he hoped that the Minister did not include the I.R.A. in that category.

Mr. Dowdall said he did not regard the Bill seriously. If it were put into effect there would be such a revulsion of feeling as would drive the Government out of office.

The Minister for Education said he had never heard from Fianna Fail so much anxiety as during the past week to acknowledge that the Oireachtas was the only legitimate Government in the country. They had been deluged with statements that resistance to the authority of the Oireachtas was wrong.

There was a great deal said about coercion, but the whole stock in trade of the organisations against which the Bill was directed was coercion. They were reaping the fruits of Irregularism.

Liberty of opinion was subordinate to the safety of the State.

Mr. McGilligan said the Bill was "putting into the hands of the Executive Council loaded rifles with no safety catches, but it was putting them into the hands of those men because traitors had been going about the country with guns at half cock; and guns had gone off and lives had been lost."

Dublin, Saturday.

The Senate reassembled this morning at 11 o'clock, with Mr. T. Westropp Bennett, Ceann Cathaoirleach, in the chair.

The Chairman said that the procedure would be that the Senate would take the report stage of the Constitution (Amendment No. 17) Bill without any discussion, and leave the remainder of the time at their disposal for final consideration of the Bill.

The proposal was agreed to, and the report stage was carried, on a division, by 26 votes to 11.

On the motion that the Bill finally pass, Colonel MOORE expressed the strongest opposition, and said that the Bill would mean as great a perversion of justice as anything the I.R.A. had done. In his opinion, the death sentence, carried out under the circumstances set down in the Bill, was nothing less than murder. The Ministers who were responsible for it would be guilty of murder also. When he was in South Africa he had refused to preside at a similar courtmartial as those to be established under the Bill, and he had withdrawn his regiment so that his men would have no connection with it. These secret courts could carry out whatever decision they liked, and there would be nothing about it. The officers would be totally unfit for the job as they had been taught nothing about the law, and they were being asked to do what no other court in the world had ever done. In all other military courts there was always a legal assessor to see that things were carried out properly. If he were an officer in the Free State army he would refuse to act on any such court.

What would be the effects of these courts? A person was arrested and brought before the courts. The whole thing would be done in secret and the man would disappear. How would the bodies of those who were executed be disposed of? Would they be buried in the prison precincts or buried outside? If they were buried outside, all Dublin would march at the funerals. The Government would have to disperse those funerals, and this would give rise to further troubles all over the country. This was a most infamous Bill. In 1922 the President went over to England and signed a document whereby 49 millions of money was presented to England. He did that without anybody asking him to do it outside his own Ministry, and he kept it secret for eighteen months for fear anybody would know about it. In 1926 the Minister for Finance signed a document to pay £5,000,000 over to England. He (Colonel Moore) was not saying now whether they were right or wrong, but he strongly deprecated the secrecy with which it was done. Now these same Ministers came and told them that the rights of everyone in the country were going to be entrusted to them. He disapproved, because he had no faith in them.

MILITARY POWERS.

Mr. COMYN also opposed the Bill, and said that the occasion was one too serious for any vituperation or condemnation of the Bill. Even in a state of war, no courtmartial or military tribunal had the power which it was proposed to give to three military officers. They were not to have the assistance of legal assessors, such as were required by the laws of every civilized country, before military men did pronounce sentence of death, even in a state of war. They would not be limited by any law as to the nature of the offences for which they could inflict punishment. "You are not amending the Constitution," he said. "You are suspending the Constitution." The debate in the Senate had been most unsatisfactory. In only one point was it satisfactory, and that was an admission from the President that no death sentence could be carried out except with the consent of the Executive Council.

Mr. Comyn, continuing, said he got the definite assurance from the President and from the Minister for Finance that there would be no executions carried out under this Bill without the consent of the Executive Council. We have also got the assurance that there will be legal assistance for defendants before the tribunal, and that a copy of the charge will be given to the prisoner in sufficient time to enable him to answer that charge. Anything else would be stark, rank, mad injustice. They got a further almost admission from the President, continued Mr. Comyn, that the oath of allegiance was not imposed on the President from Great Britain, and he (Mr. Comyn) hoped that that avenue would be explored further for the benefit of the country. The Minister for Defence had referred to some of the people against whom this Bill was directed as blackguards, but he (Mr. Comyn) hoped that the Minister did not include the I.R.A. in that category, because he had been counsel of the I.R.A., and in its ranks were some of the best men that ever breathed in Ireland. He hoped that the President, who also had knowledge and experience of this matter, would not forget that fact when they came to administer the Bill. The same applied to Cumann Na mBan, and they ought to remember that depression never cured the wounds of a country. There must be healing of wounds in this country.

MILITARY COURTS.

Mr. DOWDALL said that the military courts proposed could not be used without being abused, but, frankly, he did not regard this Bill seriously. If it were put into effect there would be a revulsion of feeling in the country that would drive the present or any other Government that tried to put it into effect out of office. It was no more than an election device, to create an atmosphere suitable to the present Government. He protested against the wilful and malicious defamation of this country that had gone on in the Press in the last ten days. He referred to articles in the "Manchester Guardian" and "The Observer," and also to one in the "Sunday Times" of last Sunday, in which the "Scribe" said that the old familiar whine against coercion had been raised in the country. They ought to remember, said Mr. Dowdall, that when coercion of the Irish people was afoot, the bigots were not far distant. There had been no whine against coercion in this country—thank God, the people always stood up to it. He differentiated between this Bill and the previous Coercion Bills passed by the British regime, for at least the men who were putting this very repressive measure into force were their own countrymen, elected by the people of this country. He thought they were wrong, but still they were the responsible Government, and he regarded that as a feature in the Bill which gave it any moral justification at all. The scribes who had written of the old familiar whine had better be careful. After all, none of them wanted to rip up the past, but those who wrote about the old familiar whine against coercion might turn the "interior light" on their own past.

MINISTER'S REPLY.

Why Government Rejected The Conference.

Professor O'SULLIVAN, Minister for Education, said that if there was a state of war in this country it was a very one-sided war, with the Government and people completely defenceless against a conspiracy that was threatening the liberties of the people and the very foundations of social order. References had been made to "a few murders and a few crimes," and it had been pointed out that there were more murders in other places, and there had not been such a bother about them. It was not the number of murders or the number of crimes, but the fact that they were the product of a conspiracy aimed at the destruction of the State and at the liberties of the ordinary citizen of the State.

SUGGESTED CONFERENCE.

Nothing could be more wrong-headed than to compare murders and crimes of that kind with ordinary crimes. They were much more serious from the social point of view, and were doubly hurtful because they were aimed directly at the State for the purpose of bringing it down. To speak of these things as a few murders and a few crimes, as if they were merely incidents that might happen anywhere, was a proof of incapacity on the part of the person who used such expression. The

(CONTINUED ON PAGE EIGHT.)

1932

The Eucharistic Congress was, in terms of numbers, the biggest event ever held in the state. Devised by the Catholic Church as a major gathering of the faithful held in different locations around the world, attendances at the Phoenix Park were estimated at 200,000 for the men's Mass, 300,000 for the women's day and up to a million for the closing Mass.

While hundreds of thousands of pilgrims from Ireland and abroad converged on Dublin for the main events, towns all over Ireland also made the effort, adorning buildings with Papal flags and bunting and lighting up their streets at night with a combination of candles, gas and electricity.

As the report shows, the Congress also attracted people with less than godly intentions. The attempted con of an Australian mayor mentioned in the report refers to a case in which a man had told the mayor of Bourke, New South Wales, that he had £100,000 which he needed help with dispersing to the poor and that a deposit of £100 from the mayor would prove he was a man who could be trusted to help with the distribution.

On the political front, newly-elected Taoiseach Éamon de Valera sparked an economic war with Britain when he withheld payments of the land annuities. These payments had been agreed by both governments in the 1920s as a system where farmers would compensate British landlords for loss of the land caused by the advent of the Free State. In retaliation the British government imposed huge duties on Irish cattle and other agricultural exports.

The year also saw Ireland's greatest ever day in athletics when Pat O'Callaghan and Bob Tisdall won Olympic gold within an hour of each other at Los Angeles. O'Callaghan, winner of the hammer throw at the previous Olympics, retained his title, while Tisdall set a new world record with his time of 51.7 seconds in the 400 metre hurdles. Unfortunately, he knocked the last hurdle which, under the regulations of the time, meant that his record was not officially recognised. Ireland was also able to claim, by default, another athletics gold at the Games when Sam Ferris from Co Down won the marathon representing Great Britain.

The reports of the double-gold medal winning day were quite small by today's standards, but when they arrived back in Ireland, Tisdall and O'Callaghan were welcomed by over 200,000 people in Dublin.

Thieves at Congress

Friday, June 24

It was learned in Dublin this evening that the depredations of the gangs of pickpockets and confidence tricksters who have been attracted to the city have marred the complete harmony of the Eucharistic Congress. During last night's rejoicings in the streets the pickpockets reaped a rich harvest, as many pilgrims today ruefully realised.

It is stated that the thieves adopt particularly despicable methods: wearing the Congress Cross and robbing the victims while they are at their devotions. The more subtle methods of the confidence tricksters have also met with a good deal of success. One case of an alleged attempt to rob an Australian mayor of £500 has already come to court. Meanwhile, pilgrims have been warned to beware of plausible strangers.

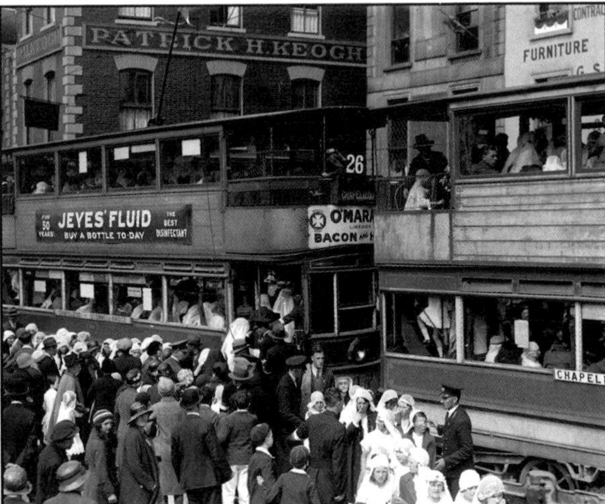

Crowds pile on trams at O'Connell Bridge, Dublin, on their way to the Eucharistic Congress.

NEWS BRIEFS

June Florence Geoghegan, a Protestant, applied in court to have her four youngest children returned to her from institutions where they had been placed after their Catholic father had died. Before he passed away, the father had asked that the children be raised as Catholics and had thus granted custody of all seven children to his sister.

In court, Justice Sullivan commented: "Surely as far as the court is concerned, we have decided they are to be brought up in the Catholic religion. We have decided that as the father is Catholic, he has the right to decide the religion in which his children should be brought up." The justices granted the application for the return of the children after demanding an undertaking from Mrs Geoghegan that the children would be raised as Catholics. (30)

CITY SPECIAL

The Cork Examiner.

NO. 24,495. THURSDAY MORNING, JUNE 23, 1932. PRICE—ONE PENNY.

Registered for transmission at Newspaper Rate of Postage in Ireland and Great Britain, and at Magazine Rate to Canada and Newfoundland.

HOLY FATHER'S PATERNAL MESSAGE TO IRISH PEOPLE

IRELAND'S GLORIOUS DAY

OPENING OF EUCHARISTIC CONGRESS BY PAPAL LEGATE.

SOVEREIGN PONTIFF'S MESSAGE.

What The Irish Race Has Done For The Faith Of Christ.

SCENES OF FERVOUR IN DUBLIN.

Archbishop's Address Of Greeting And Cardinal Lauri's Inspiring Reply.

The thirty-first Eucharistic Congress was opened yesterday at the Pro-Cathedral, Dublin, by the Papal Legate, amidst scenes of great solemnity and impressive ceremonial. The Cardinal Legate read the Holy Father's message, and subsequently pronounced the Apostolic Benediction.

In his message the Sovereign Pontiff paid glowing tribute to the services of the Irish people to the Faith, their sacrifices, sufferings and world-wide missionary labours. He exhorted them to be faithful followers of their forefathers in sending out and sustaining preachers of the Gospel in the missionary countries. They would receive abundant fruits not only for the welfare of the Catholic religion but also for the progress and glory of their illustrious country.

Cardinal Lauri said that his Holiness the Pope sent his paternal greetings to the Irish Hierarchy, clergy and people. He referred to the attachment of this great people from the time of Ireland's conversion to the Faith of Christ, and showed his desire for participation in this great International Eucharistic Congress by sending the Cardinal Legate to preside in his (the Pope's) name.

The Archbishop of Dublin delivered an inspiring address in welcoming the Papal Legate to the Archdiocese, and in reply Cardinal Lauri expressed his deep affection for the noble Irish people. He exhorted them and all the distinguished assembly to pray during the Congress that God may grant the world peace and rest from the tribulations that at present, in every land, are causes of anxiety and

AMERICA'S CALL TO WORLD

PROPOSALS FOR EASEMENT OF ARMAMENTS BURDEN.

DRASTIC ALL-ROUND REDUCTIONS.

President Hoover Sends Strong Message To Nations In Conference.

"THE TIME HAS COME—"

Cordial Approval By Principal Powers—But France Remains Hostile.

In a dramatic message from President Hoover, read yesterday at the Geneva Armaments' Conference, and published also in Washington, far-reaching proposals for the reduction of the world burden of armaments are put forward.

President Hoover emphasises that while the world economic situation grows more desperate, the cost of armaments is still further crushing the people. War forces have, he points out, grown proportionately among the nations, and an effort should be made to considerably reduce them, at the same time preserving the relative strengths.

The abolition of bombing 'planes and the total prohibition of air bombardments is put forward. Other demands are for the abolition of tanks, chemical warfare and large mobile guns, and a reduction by one-third of all land armies. Similar reductions in other war forces are also advocated.

The Italian representative announced his country's complete acceptance of the American proposals, as did the German delegate. The British spokesman welcomed them, and promised his country's careful consideration, but the French representative received the plan coldly and questioned its practicability.

International comment is strongly in support of President Hoover's gesture, and feeling in Germany is distinctly more hopeful of progress towards a situation which will give general relief to the world.

OPENING OF EUCHARISTIC CONGRESS.—Pictures show—Left—Cardinal MacRory on his way to the Pro-Cathedral. Right—Most Rev. Dr. Broderick and Dr. Mar Ivanios, Archbishop of Bethany, India, arriving for the opening ceremony. ("Examiner" photo.)

Page recreated

1933

It's easy with hindsight to believe that Adolf Hitler's accession to power in Germany should have set alarm bells ringing. It did in many quarters, including his own nation where rioting and strikes accompanied his appointment, but there was also the general impression that at least he could bring some stability to an ailing Germany.

His anti-Semitic views were well established, but less extreme versions wouldn't have been that unusual in the Europe of the time, including in Ireland. That he had compromised to form a government with his enemy Von Papen was seen as a good sign by the *Examiner*, which welcomed the coalition as an 'effective antidote' to the spread of Communism in Germany.

With the Blackshirts to the fore in Italy, and the Brownshirts now prominent in Germany, Eoin O'Duffy became leader of a group in Ireland that would adopt the colour blue as their collar of choice. While many members of the Blueshirts were not fascists, the organisation did adopt the trappings of the movement and O'Duffy himself was a great admirer of Mussolini.

Éamon de Valera was worried about the Blueshirts and he banned their march on Dublin. O'Duffy's National Guard were officially banned, but survived afterwards under a number of different names.

In the cinema, gorillas were getting a bad reputation with the release of *King Kong*.

An Irish invasion of London

Wednesday, December 6

London is being invaded today by six film stars who came from the West, but not from Hollywood. They are the islanders who played the leading parts in the new film *Man of Aran*, produced by Robert Flaherty. They have come over to complete their work at the Gaumont British Studios, Shepherds Bush.

Only one of their number has ever been further than Galway. His name is Pat Mullin, who is a great rebel, and once a Labour leader in Chicago. The other five, who have never been in a train, are Tiger, the hero; Maggie Dirane, the heroine; and Michael Dilgane, a 14-year-old boy. Tommy the Talker and Patch Ruadh (red head) are names which speak for themselves.

They are to stay in a suburban boarding house, near the studio, to be within easy reach of their work. It would be interesting to hear their stories of the big city on their return to their island home. This London visit will undoubtedly gain them great prestige among their own people, even more than the knowledge that most of them are descended from the ancient kings of Ireland.

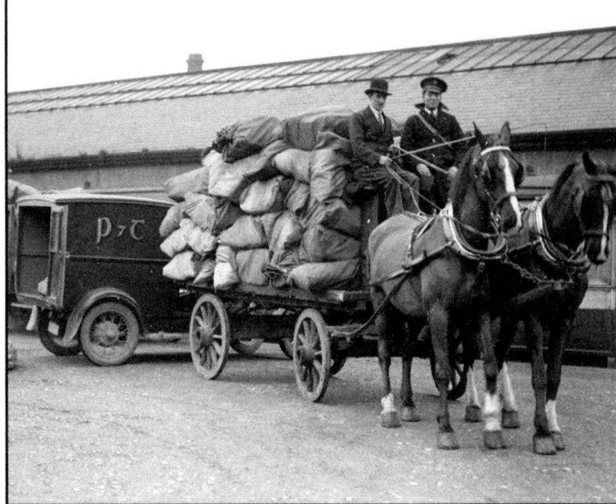

Transporting the Christmas mail in Cork.

The end of America's liquor thirst

Wednesday, December 6

Mr Philips, Acting Secretary of State, has issued a proclamation certifying that the 21st amendment to the constitution repealing Prohibition has become valid as part of the constitution.

A special police squad has been created to eradicate speakeasies, which last night had a last clandestine fling. Today 65,000,000 inhabitants of 23 states are waiting for a further celebration.

One large New York hotel will have a bar on wheels to move among the guests. Many new cocktails have been invented. In Harlem cabarets the end of prohibition will be heralded by the singing of Negro spirituals.

Special plans are being made for ladies who learned to drink during prohibition. The Ritz-Carlton has installed a ladies' bar. Even the ultra conservative Cosmopolitan Club is providing facilities for feminine thirst.

Speakeasy proprietors are unhappy. They want prohibition back because only a few of them have been able to obtain licenses.

NEWS BRIEFS

Mar Sixteen people were arrested when a mob attacked Connolly House, the headquarters of a left-wing group in Great Strand Street, Dublin. It later emerged that those who ransacked the building had been on a religious retreat and were whipped into an anti-Communist frenzy by a priest. (29)

Dec Donal O'Kelly, one of the last great Irish-speaking *seanchaís*, died in Carrignavar, Co Cork. His powers of memory were considered extraordinary and he would often spend nights by a blazing turf fire reciting stories of Fenian chiefs or Red Branch champions to an enraptured audience. (18)

CITY SPECIAL

The Cork Examiner.

NO. 24,685. TUESDAY MORNING, JANUARY 31, 1933. PRICE—ONE PENNY.

Registered for transmission at Newspaper Rate of Postage in Ireland and Great Britain, and at Magazine Rate in Canada and Newfoundland.

NAZI LEADER'S TRIUMPH.

HERR HITLER APPOINTED GERMAN CHANCELLOR.

VON HINDENBURG YIELDS.

Leader Of Storm Troops Takes Charge Of Germany.

BERLIN SUPPORTERS JUBILANT.

Communists Distribute Leaflets Calling For A General Strike.

Herr Adolf Hitler, who has for so long been perhaps the most forceful personality in German politics, has at last been appointed Chancellor.

His claims had been put aside by the President until it became clear that no other politician could hope to form a government that could rely on a majority in the Reichstag.

Hitler at once proceeded to form a Cabinet and last night this was announced and a meeting was held. Some of the newly appointed Ministers are looked upon as safeguards against possible Nazi escapades.

There is doubt as to the attitude of the Catholic Parties—the Centre and the German People's Party—but the Socialists are definitely hostile to the new Government, and a "no confidence" motion has already been tabled.

The Communists are calling for a general strike, and there were several clashes with Hitlerites last night.

The news of Hitler's triumph was received with gravity in Paris, but was welcomed by the Italian Press.

SIX-CO. M.P.S TO SIT IN DAIL?

INTERESTING DEVELOPMENT EXPECTED IN POLITICAL SITUATION.

NORTHERN NATIONALISTS' MOVE.

To Partake In Debates But Not To Vote In Divisions.

GOVERNMENT AND LABOUR.

A New Understanding—Rumour About Seat In Executive Council.

A highly interesting report is being discussed in political circles in Dublin. It is to the effect that Nationalist M.Ps. in the Six Counties may take seats in the Dail and altogether abandon the Northern Parliament. Negotiations with the leaders of the Government and the Opposition are stated to have taken place in this connection.

The matter was canvassed some time before the Free State General Election, and its revival now is regarded as indicating the possibility of some understanding being under consideration. Our Political Correspondent says in such an eventuality the Northern members would take part in the Dail discussions but would not be eligible to vote.

The relations between the Government and the Labour Party are also being speculated on, and a rumour has gone the rounds of political circles that a Ministerial post may be filled by a Labour deputy. This is not, however, receiving much credence, and the probability is that the understanding which existed in the last Dail will be resumed.

It is stated that the new Senate which the Government propose to bring into existence will comprise a small body of 35 persons whose functions will mainly be of an economic advisory character.

Leaders of the Opposition met in Dublin yesterday to consider the new situation and decide on the policy to be followed when the Dail begins its deliberations.

Senator Crosbie, B.L., opens Cork Camera Club Exhibition. ("Examiner" Photo).

Page recreated

1934

By 1934 Fine Gael and the Blueshirts were gaining plenty of support among cattle farmers for their organisation on the annuities question. De Valera's government, instead of handing on the farmers' payments to Britain, was keeping them in the Free State's own coffers. Some farmers stopped paying and the government responded with the inflammatory action of seizing cattle and reselling them to make up the debt.

The sale at Marsh's Yard in Cork was of cattle seized from farms in Bishopstown and Ballincollig, and the combined efforts of the Blueshirts and farmers to stop the proceedings met with a tragic end when police, who had been expecting trouble, opened fire on a lorry trying to break through their cordon. Michael Lynch, one of those wounded by police, died later in hospital.

The funeral brought an estimated 30,000 people to the streets of the city. General O'Duffy gave the graveside oration, while George Crosbie, the *Examiner* proprietor who was by now a Fine Gael senator, was among the other prominent mourners.

While the shootings by police and subsequent street riots were on the extreme end of the violence, the extent of the unrest at the time can be seen from the fact that on just one day in April, the *Examiner* had reports of violence in Leitrim, Enniscorthy, Dingle and Waterford.

Police baton-charge protestors trying to disrupt the sale of seized cattle in Cork.

School Blueshirt protest

Tuesday, February 27

More than 100 pupils of the Christian Brothers' Schools, Thurles, went on strike today as a protest against the wearing of blue shirts by a number of their classmates.

The strike originated in the junior section amongst the first year Intermediate pupils. A number of boys approached the principal of the school, Rev Brother Lynam, this morning and intimated that they resented certain of their fellow pupils appearing in class wearing blue shirts, and added that they would give these boys 10 minutes to remove the shirts.

Shortly afterwards 20 of the boys left school and did not return. At lunch hour when most of the pupils go to their homes, they were met by the ringleaders of the strike. A procession was formed in the Square, and upwards of 100 boys marching four deep paraded the principal streets of the town carrying a tricolour flag and singing 'The Soldier's Song' and 'We'll Crown de Valera King of Ireland'.

One of the boys said that for three weeks they had sat next to fellow pupils wearing blue shirts and they were not going to do it any longer.

Mourners give the Blueshirt salute at the funeral of Michael Lynch at Dunbollogue, Co Cork.

NEWS BRIEFS

Feb The government seeks to control the Blueshirts by introducing legislation to restrict the wearing of uniforms and the use of military titles. General O'Duffy speaks out against the laws before a crowd of 5,000 at a meeting in Kildare. "Another clause enables a member of the Garda Síochána when he sees a boy wearing a blue shirt or a girl wearing a blue blouse to remove such shirt or blouse and, if need be, by force. What do you think of that?" (26)

Apr Waterford's weekend, usually good humoured and jolly, was marked on Saturday night by disgraceful scenes, fighting and disorder. The cause of the fracas was a clash between two opposing political parties, and for close on two hours the city was in a state of seething excitement. Free fights took place in several thoroughfares and it was not until a force of 50 Civic Guards, accompanied by members of the CID, appeared on the scene that order was restored. (30)

May The Irish government says it would be "quite impossible" for the State to accede to a request from Russian exile Leon Trotsky to be granted sanctuary in Ireland. The decision not to grant the request, which had been made through the Socialist Party in the UK, was made on the grounds that the Free State is a Catholic country, with traditions entirely opposed to any form of Communism. (3)

July Heinrich Himmler, head of the SS, is put in charge of Germany's concentration camps.

The Cork Examiner.

NO. 25,163. TUESDAY MORNING, AUGUST 14, 1934. PRICE—ONE PENNY.

Registered for transmission at Newspaper Rate of Postage in Ireland and Great Britain, and at Magazine Rate in Canada and Newfoundland.

SEVERAL MEN SHOT IN CORK CITY—ONE DEAD

REVOLVERS AND BATONS.

WILD SCENES AT SALE OF SEIZED CATTLE IN CORK.

SALEYARD GATE FORCED BY LORRY.

Fire Opened By Detectives In Copley Street Repository.

ONE DEAD—SEVERAL WOUNDED.

Series Of Baton Charges By Civic Guards Extend Into South Mall.

Shooting and baton charges marked the sale of seized cattle in Cork yesterday, and for hours the area around Anglesea Street was seething with excitement.

Several men from various parts of the county were treated at the South Infirmary, eight for gunshot wounds. One, Michael Patrick Lynch, Carrignavar, died in the Infirmary last evening.

A lorry containing a number of young men crashed through the closed gates of the Copley Street repository, where the sale was to be held, and immediately it did so detectives drew revolvers and fired, a number of the occupants being wounded.

The Sheriff then adjourned the sale, but later announced that he would proceed with it. The only bidder was a man who gave the name O'Neill, and he bought the fourteen cattle for £17 15s.

Mr. E. O'Neill, T.D., protested against the proceedings, saying it was a public sale, but the public were excluded.

Meanwhile baton charges were taking place outside the repository gates, and opposite the Model Schools the crowds stood and fought the Guards. Police helmets were seen soaring in the air, some of them landing on the roof of the Farmers' Union Abattoir. The Guards were forced to fall back, but reinforcements arrived and another charge was ordered.

The crowd were beaten back across Parnell Bridge, where the Guards then took up a position. Subsequently there were baton charges along the South Mall and adjoining streets, but the retreating crowds persistently returned. Finally a charge was made by the police along the South Mall into Winthrop Street and Patrick Street.

While these scenes were being enacted wounded men were being treated at a temporary dressing station in Anglesea Street, where a protest meeting was also held. During the progress of the meeting a lorry of military arrived, and later a protest march was held through the principal streets, thousands participating.

A report reached the marchers that one of the wounded men had died and angry shouts of "where are the murderers were raised. The crowd knelt on the streets and recited the Rosary

Several arrests were made.

Scenes of indescribable excitement culminating in the shooting of several men, one fatally, marked the sale of seized cattle at Copley Street Repository in Cork, yesterday. The shooting was entirely unexpected and followed immediately a rapid move on the part of those who had come to register a protest at the action of the authorities in seizing the cattle for failure to pay annuities. Long before the hour fixed for the sale hundreds of farmers from all parts of the country assembled in the approaches to the Repository and principally in Anglesea Street. In view of the happenings at the last sale of seized cattle about a fortnight ago, the authorities took elaborate precautions to prevent any interference. A force of about three hundred [illegible] Guards in charge of half a dozen superintendents formed cordons at all [illegible] about fifty yards from the gates of the Repository which were kept closed, a [illegible] wicket gate being opened to admit [illegible] authorized to enter the sale yard. [illegible], the hour fixed for the sale, [illegible] were some fifty Civic Guards, a [illegible] detectives, three press representatives inside the yard in addition to the [illegible]. Also present were some women [illegible] of the owners of the cattle, Mr. [illegible] Desmond, T.D., Mr. E. O'Neill, T.D., [illegible] his wife, and a small group of individuals who were said to be intending [illegible]. Intimation was given to the [illegible] that some other intending buyers [illegible] coming, and he held back the sale [illegible].

THE FIRING DESCRIBED.

Rush For Shelter Inside The Yard.

[illegible] representative, who was in [illegible] yard, describes what happened as [illegible]:—We were chatting in groups in [illegible] when, suddenly, at 25 minutes [illegible] there was a wild cheer from outside [illegible]. The next moment a big lorry [illegible] upwards of a score of men) [illegible] through the gates, coming to [illegible] a few yards inside when it collided with a corner-post of the nearest [illegible].

Immediately the group of detectives [illegible] their revolvers and started firing [illegible] while the people inside rushed for [illegible] shelter afforded by stone pillars. [illegible] or three men jumped from the back [illegible] lorry and were immediately taken [illegible] by uniformed Guards. The [illegible] of the men, however, remained [illegible] the lorry and the detectives slowly [illegible], kept up their rapid fire for [illegible] minutes.

Through the burst gates a crowd of uniformed policemen could be seen and then as [illegible] as it began, the firing stopped. [illegible] of us who had been taking cover [illegible] into the open and the scene which [illegible] must read like a tale of battle.

Half a dozen young men were either staggering about the yard with blood pouring from their wounds or lying prone, pitiable objects, on the ground. Those who [illegible] unhurt immediately rushed to their assistance, and bitter taunts about shooting unarmed men were hurled at the small group of detectives standing at one corner, some with their revolvers still in their hands. When it was seen that some of the men were seriously hurt, cries were raised for priests and doctors.

Within a very short time the Rev. Fr. Cashman, C.C., of St. Finbarr's South, came rushing into the yard, and, kneeling on the ground beside a young man who was obviously badly wounded, administered the Last Rites of the Church.

The Corporation ambulance arrived soon after and made a series of trips to the South Infirmary with the injured men.

A REMARKABLE ESCAPE.

Possibly the most remarkable escape from serious injury was that experienced by Chief Supt. Fitzgerald. He rushed to the gate when the lorry was crashing through, and was all but crushed when it crashed against the post. As it was, he got out of the path of the vehicle in the nick of time, and escaped with a badly cut knee. Hastily bandaging the injured member, the Chief Superintendent immediately resumed duty

In conversation with me, the Chief Superintendent stated that shots had also been fired from outside, pointing to two broken windows in the yard as evidence of this.

Prominent in the work of succouring the wounded were Mr and Mrs O'Neill. The latter helped with hastily improvised bandages, and showed remarkable courage in the face of the firing, for she did not even wait for it to stop before helping the men. Mr. O'Neill, too, performed similar kindly actions, helped by some uniformed Guards.

Following the shooting, a great quiet prevailed, and but for the signs of conflict, it would have been difficult to realise that the whole affair had not been a nightmare of imagination.

No further attempts were made to get into the repository, and the Sheriff proceeded to where the seized cattle were penned and announced that the sale was adjourned. On receipt of this news Mr. O'Neill went outside the yard and announced to the crowd that the sale had been adjourned. In the meantime Civic Guards attempted to remove the lorry, but it was jammed too securely against the woodwork and had to be left there.

At one o'clock there was a surprising development at the Cattle Yard when the Sheriff announced that he would proceed with the sale half an hour later. At 1.35 he read the conditions of sale. The only bidder present was a man who gave his name as Mr. O'Neill, and for the first lot, a red cow, he offered £1.

The Sheriff—I could not sell it for £1. Will you increase your bid? There is a good deal of expense on these cattle.

The Bidder—No, sir.

He was then declared the purchaser, and proceeded to buy the fourteen cattle for a total of £17 15s. In each case there was only the one bid from the same man, and he was declared the purchaser at his own price. The first lot of cattle consisted of three cows, one bull and three calves, and these fetched £8 15s.; the second lot, made up of seven cows, fetched £9.

SALE TAKES PLACE.

Just as the sale concluded, Mr. Eamonn O'Neill, T.D., and Mr. T. J. O'Donovan, arrived, and the former inquired whether the sale had taken place. The Sheriff replied in the affirmative, and Mr. O'Neill said he desired publicly to protest against the entire proceedings. The Sheriff announced it was a public sale but the public were excluded. When the first sale proved abortive, a second sale was held. He had nothing to say against the Sheriff personally, but he insisted that the proceedings were not in accordance with the law. The whole of the tragedy that occurred was because the public were not admitted.

The Sheriff—I can't make any comment on your remarks at all. I can only listen to them.

Mr. O'Donovan said he also wished to protest and added that as the first sale proved abortive and information conveyed to the public that it was adjourned the second sale was illegal.

The Sheriff—The sale had to be adjourned on account of the firing.

Mr. O'Neill—I proclaimed on Mr. Kennedy's behalf that the sale was adjourned sine die or generally. Anything else from that on should become a new procedure. He then inquired for the name of the buyer.

The Sheriff—I am not supposed to furnish you with the name of the buyer.

Mr. O'Donovan—Would I be right in presuming that the name was O'Neill? When I came into this place there were six decent men—all County Councillors—with me, and I was the only one admitted.

The matter then ended and the parties left the yard.

Some of the wounded being brought to the ambulance during yesterday's scenes at the sale of seized cattle in Cork.

SCENE OUTSIDE YARD.

Lorry Crashes Through Gates.

WILD CONFUSION.

Rosary Recited In The Streets.

One man fatally shot in the stomach, six others wounded by bullets and some 30 men treated in hospital for other injuries were amongst casualties as a result of the scenes which marked the sale of seized cattle at the Copley Street Repository in Cork, yesterday, writes an "Examiner" representative who was outside the yard during the scenes.

It will be remembered that exciting scenes attended the seizure of the beasts at Ballincollig and Bishopstown last week, when the bailiffs visited the farms of Mr. John Coveney, at Bishopstown, and Mr. Corkery, at Ballincollig, and seized a total of 14 cattle.

The scenes at the last sale in Cork and foreshadowed trouble for yesterday's event and in anticipation of opposition from farmers and others, Guards were drafted into the city from all over Munster this morning. Long before 10 a.m. a cordon of Guards was on duty in front of the entrance to the Repository, and by 11.30 there were some 300 Guards on the streets in the vicinity of the saleyard. These were situated in side streets and in Copley Street, whilst within the yard detectives and Guards held positions in every nook and cranny.

FARMERS GATHER.

Lorries, special 'buses, and private cars arrived in Anglesea Street with farmers. The first of these arrived in Anglesea Street about 11 a.m., but from this up to 11.45 the arrivals were frequent, so that there were several thousand people present when the hour of sale—12 noon—was reached

The scene, however, was strangely different from that of the earlier sale at the time of auction. On that occasion farmers had been storming the gates as the auction was proceeding. Yesterday there was no excitement, no waving of sticks—not even a shout was raised up to 12.20, and it seemed that the entire proceedings would pass off without an incident worthy of note. Guards were drawn in a cordon across the entrance to Copley Street from Anglesea Street, whilst another cordon (some 80 strong) was on duty outside the Repository gates and these kept the crowd moving when groups of men attempted to congregate.

SENSATIONAL INTERRUPTION.

All was still quiet at 12.25, but a few minutes later there came a sensational interruption. The Guards in the front cordon were in conversation when shouts were heard from the direction of Anglesea St. This was followed by the roar of a lorry engine rapidly approaching, and then the crowd scattered in all directions as a lorry was seen making straight for the entrance gates.

The Guards in the cordon attempted for a moment to stop the progress of the lorry, in which were some dozen young men. They were forced to scatter to avoid being run over, however, and some Guards who attempted to grasp the sides of the lorry were beaten off by the occupants of the vehicle.

LORRY CRASHES THROUGH GATES.

Straight at the second cordon went the lorry, and here again the police scattered in all directions to avoid the oncoming vehicle, which crashed right through the gates into the yard.

Taking advantage of the disorganised state of the police, the crowd behind rushed the gates, and there followed a scene of wild confusion, as Guards with drawn batons fought men who used sticks in their efforts to get into the yard.

In the midst of all this shots rang out—several of them—and after a short interval more explosions were heard at the entrance of the repository. Spectators—amongst them many women—made a wild dash for cover, and doorways in the vicinity were congested by the rush for cover, whilst others of the onlookers made down Anglesea Street and up Infirmary Road.

The crowd at the Repository gates, however, continued the attempt to drive home an entrance behind the lorry, and it was several minutes before it broke before the charge of the Guards, scattered down and up Anglesea Street. Outside the Model Schools the crowd again stood and beat the Guards. Some of the helmets were knocked off the police, and several helmets were seen soaring into the air, some of them landing on the roof of the Farmers Union Abattoir. The Guards eventually yielded before the onslaught and fell back

(CONTINUED ON PAGE EIGHT.)

CORK'S TRAGIC EVENTS.

The Casualties In Seized Cattle Turmoil.

ONE MAN DIES FROM WOUNDS.

The following is a list of the principal cases treated in the South Infirmary:—

DIED FROM WOUNDS.

Michael Patrick Lynch, Carrignavar—abdominal injuries.

WOUNDED.

John Riordan, Macroom—injuries to lung and severe haemorrhage. Condition rather serious.

Daniel Desmond, Gurteen, Bandon—wound in neck. Condition fair.

William Crowley, Upton, Bandon—Wound in the shoulder. X-rayed. Condition fair.

James Hegarty, Clonmult—wounds in the leg. Rather serious.

Maurice Doherty, Knockroha—wounds in right thigh. Condition fair.

H. Kingston, Upton, Bandon—wound in thigh.

Timothy O'Shea, Ballyshoneen, Waterfall—shot in leg. Condition fair.

INJURED.

Several men, both old and young, and belonging to the farming class, were treated for scalp wounds and other injuries of a more or less minor nature. This casualty list includes:—

Andrew Kelleher, Butlerstown, Glanmire.
Patrick O'Sullivan, Carrigroe, Clonakilty.
John Murphy, Aherla.
William Crowley, Lispashea, Upton.
Michael Kelly, Ballinahigh.
Jeremiah Crowley, Ovens.
Denis Spillane, Ovens.
John O'Driscoll, Kilcrea.
John Hannon, Rathcormac.
Daniel Healy, Bandon.

Others included in the casualty list were two Civic Guards, but neither was detained in hospital.

EXPRESS WRECK.

Driver Of French Train Placed Under Arrest.

ANOTHER DEATH.

Avignon, Monday.—The driver of the ill-fated Geneva-Ventimiglia express which was derailed at Avignon station yesterday, with the loss of several lives, has been placed under arrest. This action has been taken following the assertion of a number of witnesses that the express was travelling at nearly forty miles an hour at the time of the accident, whereas the regulation speed at the point was twelve miles an hour. Another victim of the smash, M. Clary Giraud, aged 88, of Paris, succumbed during the night. The total death roll is now eight.—Reuter.

MOTOR FATALITY.

Man Killed When Car Swerves To Avoid Dog.

London, Monday.

A man was killed and a woman received injuries when a car in which they were passengers overturned on the Maidstone road at Ruxley, Kent, early to-day. The driver of the car, Mr. Norman Ansell, of Balham Park road, London, S.W., swerved to avoid a dog and the car struck the kerb. Mr. Joseph Cohen, of Bermondsey street, London, was killed, and the injured woman, Miss Rogers, of Perham road, West Kensington, was taken to Farningham Hospital.

MOTOR ACCIDENT.

Two Men In Cork Mercy Hospital.

Two young men were admitted to the Mercy Hospital yesterday morning suffering from severe head and facial injuries as the result of a motor car accident in the vicinity of Ballincollig.

The injured men, whose names are James Ryan, 136 Bandon Road, and Daniel Desmond, 89 Bandon Road, are still detained in a rather serious condition.

WEATHER IN CORK.

The weather in Cork yesterday was gloriously fine. A warm sun shone throughout the day and the further outlook last night was very promising.

FEAR OF TIDAL WAVE.

Coming Launching Of Liner.

DROWNING DANGER.

Chief Constable Warns Council.

Renfrew, Monday.—A tidal wave, eight feet high, is expected to sweep up the Clyde when the new Cunarder, 534, is launched by the Queen next month. To-night at Renfrew Town Council meeting a letter from the Chief Constable of Renfrewshire was read, stating that this wave would sweep over the public right of way on Clydeside, where a large crowd might be expected to gather to see the new vessel take the water. In the interests of public safety, he recommended that the right of way should be closed by the Town Council.

An animated discussion followed, one member remarking that the figures quoted by the Chief Constable were "all eyewash." Another member said that he had witnessed all the launches from Messrs. Brown's shipyard during the last 15 years, and he had never received anything worse than wet feet.

Provost Michie said that no doubt the Chief Constable was writing from technical information supplied to him, and they could not ignore the warning. A tragedy might occur, and the onus would be on Renfrew Town Council.

It was decided to inspect the right of way on Clydeside on Thursday, and thereafter to come to a decision.

STEAMER SUNK.

British Cruiser In Collision In Montreal.

Montreal, Monday.—The British cruiser Dragon, which is visiting Montreal in connection with the celebrations of the landing of Jacques Cartier in Canada 400 years ago, was in collision with the steamer Maple Branch in the harbour here to-day. The Maple Branch sank. All her crew were saved by the Dragon.

H.M.S. Dragon is a cruiser of 4,850 tons, carrying six 6-inch guns. She is on the America and West Indies station. The Maple Branch is a steamer of 1,708 tons belonging to the St. Lawrence Tankers, Ltd.

The Dragon arrived here from St. Johns after having taken the Prime Minister, Mr. Ramsay MacDonald, to Newfoundland on the completion of the first part of his holiday, which he spent in Canada. The current caught the stern of Dragon, swinging her round when she was altering her course to avoid striking another small vessel. Dragon was only slightly damaged.—Reuter.

DILLINGER HENCHMAN.

Found Asleep In Field By A Farmer.

("Chicago Tribune" Telegram.)

Paducah, Kentucky, Monday.—Alvin Karpis, "Bad man of the Middle West" and henchman of John Dillinger, who was being sought for participation in the kidnapping of Edward Bremer and William Hamm, junr., was captured in a cornfield near here last night without a shot being fired. A farmer found Karpis slumbering in the field with a newspaper for his pillow. A revolver lay beside him. The police were summoned by the farmer and they surrounded Karpis and seized his gun as he was waking from his sleep.

Although Karpis is charged with having shared in kidnapping ransoms totalling more than 300,000 dollars, he had only ten cents in his pocket at the time of his capture. Mr. Hamm, president of the Theodore Hamm Brewing Company at St. Paul, paid 100,000 dollars for his release, while Bremer's father paid 200,000 dollars for the release of his son.

POPULAR FALLACIES.

Savages Not More Healthy Than Civilized Folk.

Malvern, Monday.—At the new Health Society Summer School at Malvern to-day, the idea that it is wrong dietically to drink at meal times was contradicted by Dr. J. Neil Leitch, of the London School of Dietetics. Dr. Leitch also exploded the popular fallacy that savages are more healthy than civilised beings.

Dr. Elizabeth Sloan Chesser, in an address on "Food, Health and Character," held that diet definitely affected character. "What we eat in a sense we become," she said. "Are not overfed gluttonous old gentlemen irritable, rigid minded, intolerant of new ideas and customs? Does not the child fed on excess of fat or carbohydrates become difficult and intractable and cantankerous? Food influences for good or ill every organ and tissue of the body, including brain and nerve tissue."

NOISY DUBLIN MEETING.

County Council Scenes.

GUARDS' POSITION.

Fianna Fail Members Leave.

Dublin, Monday.

Rowdy scenes, in which personalities were frequently indulged in, marked the adjourned meeting of the Dublin County Council, held to-night.

The Chairman, Mr. P. Belton, T.D., at the outset, said that the meeting was the third attempt to hold one by the premier County Council in the country owing to the obstructionist tactics that had been adopted. It appeared to him that it was part of a plan to prevent that Council and the will of the people from functioning. He would see that any order he made as chairman that night would be obeyed and that the business would be carried through at any cost. He had taken the obvious precaution to ensure that, and had notified the Garda authorities to leave the Gardai there at that meeting. The reason why the meeting was adjourned the previous night was due to a refusal by a member to leave the chamber when the chair called upon him to do so, as it was entitled to do under statutory authority. He would ask the Secretary to bring two Guards into the chamber.

Immediately there was uproar and Mr. Carville challenged the Chairman's authority to bring in the forces of the State

The Chairman ordered the standing councillors to resume their seats, and on being refused, he asked them to leave. He was refused, and asked the Acting Secretary to bring in the Gardai.

Mr. Fogarty (heatedly)—You are one of the men who go around shouting about what you did in 1916. You never fired a shot in 1916, and you were one of the weaklings brought before a British tribunal to get your job back.

He added that if the Gardai entered the chamber his party would leave. The Chairman's party had deprived the ten Fianna Fail members, representing practically half of the county and the majority of rural areas, from being represented on the committees, and so far as he was concerned they would get no cooperation from him.

The Chairman said that any member, no matter to what side he belonged, would leave the chamber if he interrupted the business.

INSPECTOR'S INQUIRY.

The Secretary returned to the chamber and said that the Inspector wished to know if they required any man taken into custody. As matters stood at present, they had no locus standi. (A Fianna Fail member—Hear, hear.) The councillor had to be ejected from the chamber, the Secretary continued, and the Council had to provide their own means to do so. The Gardai would see that no breach of the peace would take place.

The Chairman left his seat, and immediately Mr. Mullen moved, and Mr. Brady seconded, that Councillor Fogarty take the chair.

Mr. Belton resumed the chair, and amid shouting called upon the Vice-Chairman, Mr. Good, to take the chair during his absence.

Mr. Clare moved, and Mr. Tunney seconded, that the meeting stand adjourned, but the Vice-Chairman refused to take the motion.

Mr. Belton then returned, and the business was proceeded with, but owing to the uproar it was practically impossible to follow the proceedings.

The Chairman said that the action of the Gardai in not coming in there would have to be decided in the courts (Fianna Fail cheers).

Mr. Clare (heatedly)—I will resign my seat and fight you in any area you like.

COUNSEL'S OPINION.

There were repeated cries for "Counsel's opinion" which were ordered to be obtained at the previous meeting arising out of the incidents that had occurred, and the Chairman named Councillors Fogarty and Jacob and asked them to leave the chamber. They again refused.

Finally the Chairman directed the Law Agent to read counsel's opinion, which was to the effect that the Chairman had authority to order the removal of a councillor from the chamber for refusing to obey the valid ruling of the chair or otherwise obstructing the meetings. If the removal was necessary for self-preservation or in the opinion of the Chairman of Council to preserve order, the Guards could be called to assist in the removal. If conduct was a breach of the peace the obstructionist could be given into custody. A member could be asked to withdraw or apologise for offensive observations, and if he refused the Chairman or Council could order him to withdraw from the meeting or have him removed.

Mr. Fogarty—Until such time as our party get the representation we are entitled to there will be no co-operation whatever. The will of the people is being flouted deliberately. It is preposterous that a party that got a majority in three rural areas are denied representation on the Council's committees.

The Chairman ruled the member out of order, but he continued making observations.

MEMBER LEAVES PROTESTING.

During the din, Mr. Cullen, an Independent was also ruled out of order, and on refusing to resume his seat was asked to leave the chamber. He did so, protesting against what he termed the partial conduct of the chair.

The uproar was terrific, and Mr. Good proposed, and Mr. Doogе seconded, that the meeting adjourn for ten minutes.

The Chairman would not accept the motion.

The Chairman proceeded to go through the business, heedless of the uproar, and frequent divisions were challenged by the Fianna Fail members.

At length Mr. Fogarty moved that the business be adjourned to a further meeting and that the attention of the Minister for Local Government and Public Health be drawn to the grossly irregular manner in which the Chairman was conducting the meeting.

This motion was, on a division, defeated, as was a further one to adjourn the meeting to Monday next. Ultimately the Fianna Fail members withdrew as a protest.

Mr. Jacob said that any business done would be illegal, and that they would prove it was.

The remaining business on the agenda was carried through by the Fine Gael members.

AUSTRIAN POLICEMEN EXECUTED.

Leading Actors In The Chancellery Attack.

GRUESOME WORK OF HANGMAN BY TORCHLIGHT.

Vienna, Monday.—Four Austrian policemen, who were concerned in the attack on the Chancellery, in which Dr. Dollfuss was killed, were sentenced to death this evening by the military court, and executed to-night. A police inspector was sentenced to 20 years' penal servitude and two of the other accused were sentenced to 20 and 15 years penal servitude, respectively.

The accused took the sentence motionlessly, standing to attention and without any reaction. A petition for clemency to President Miklas was filed by counsel defending them.

Giving their reasons for the varying sentences, the court said that they found that the four who had been sentenced to death must be considered leading actors in the crime, while the others had played a minor role. Immediately after the sentences were pronounced, the courtroom was cleared and the hall was closely searched for bombs and explosives by officials.

Heartbreaking scenes were observed at the main entrance of the Criminal Court, where relatives and friends of the convicted were standing and in vain tried to force their way to them.

The execution took place very slowly, as electric light is not installed in "[illegible] courtyards," and the hangman and his assistants had to do their work in the ghostly shine of torches. It was a gruesome sight, and all those present were suffering under the strain, especially the judge, Dr. Wagner, whose face was pale, his cheeks trembling, and who was hardly ever looking in the direction of the gallows.

Without any motion or reaction the four men walked up to the hangman and were executed.

VIENNA POLICEMEN ARRESTED.

Two hundred and sixty members of the Vienna police have been arrested, following the discovery of a list of members of the Nazi party during a search in a policeman's home. All the arrested men have been imprisoned in the building of the Vienna Criminal Court.—Reuter.

GERMAN ARMS DUMP FOR AUSTRIA.

Paris, Sunday.—Allegations that Germany is organising the "Nazification" of Austria are made by the Prague correspondent of the "Paris Soir," who says that he has obtained his information from excellent sources. Secret headquarters, states the correspondent, have been created at Passau, in Bavaria, with a view to supplying arms, ammunition, explosives and instructions to three Committees of Direct Action established at Vienna, Innsbruck and Linz. The principal task of these Committees, it is added, is to pick among the Austrian Nazis those most capable of carrying out confidential missions, especially preparing terrorist outrages, and penetrating into the Heimwehr to create brown cells, to ferment the disposition of the Heimwehr from within. The same method is to be applied to the railwaymen. At the same time, according to the correspondent, Dr. Goebbels, the German propaganda Minister, has issued instructions to the editors of German newspapers and Nazi propaganda agents in Austria to leave no stone unturned to foster disagreement within the Austrian Government, particularly to throw responsibility for the putsch of July 25 on Major Fey, who is to be represented as plotting to supplant Dr. Dollfuss and form an alliance with Italy.

The correspondent alleges that Herr von Papen, who has been designated as German Minister to Vienna, is fully aware of this clandestine activity, but that he is a broken man, "chained to the conqueror's chariot."—Reuter.

PRINCE STARHEMBERG IN ROME.

Rome, Monday.—Prince Starhemberg, the Austrian Vice-Chancellor, spent this morning inspecting police and Fascist militia establishments in Rome. He has not seen Signor Mussolini, who is still at his farm near Riccione.

Prince Starhemberg, it is believed, has for some time been studying Italian methods with a view to an overhaul of the Heimwehr and other Austrian organisations. In view of the close understanding and co-operation between Italy and Austria and the similarity of the two regimes, it is felt that Italy might be able to give help and advice.

Prince Starhemberg and Signor Mussolini took the opportunity of their meeting at Ostia on Saturday for a general review of the international situation as it affects Austria, but considerations of time must have prevented anything but a quick examination of the situation.—Reuter.

ARCHDUKE OTTO.

Stockholm, Monday.—Archduke Otto, the pretender to the Austrian and Hungarian thrones, spent last night in an hotel at Norrkoeping, some 80 miles South-West of Stockholm. It is understood that he will probably go on to Stockholm by car to-day.—Reuter.

INDUSTRIALIST ORDERED TO PAY £17,000.

Vienna, Monday.—The confiscation of a sum of 340,000 schillings (about £17,[illegible]) belonging to Dr. Anton Apold, chairman of the huge Alpine-Montan steel works at Leoben, Styria, has been ordered by the security director of the province, in compliance with a Government order. This development is an echo of the fighting in Styria during the July revolt, and an official report says that £6,000 of the money would be used to cover the enormous expenses on measures of security to suppress the rising in Styria.

It will be recalled that the Alpine-Montan works, the majority of whose shares are in German hands, figured largely in reports of fighting in Leoben during July. It was alleged that the Board sympathised with the Nazis and that the premises of the works were used as a hiding place for arms and fugitives. During the revolt Dr. Apold was questioned by the police, but was not arrested.—Reuter.

Page recreated

1935

In the North some of the worst rioting in decades saw over 1,500 Catholics driven from their homes by Protestant mobs. In several areas of the Free State, acts of retaliation saw Protestant targets attacked.

The ongoing situation in Germany featured regularly in the news, with a steady stream of stories regarding the violence against Jews, and Nazi warnings to Catholics, Freemasons, journalists and everyone else perceived to be a threat. Anti-Semitic laws became more extreme after Hitler's decrees at Nuremberg in September which banned relationships between Jews and Aryans and barred Jews from employment in the civil service and numerous other professions.

The Irish sporting hero of the year was Dan O'Mahony from Ballydehob, Co Cork, famous for his 'Irish twist' manoeuvre, who became undisputed wrestling champion of the world after an incident-packed bout in Boston. Some of the most sensational fighting came after the official fight ended and the referee began brawling with people who had disagreed with his decision to award the fight to O'Mahony.

Startling outrages

Monday, July 22

Amazing incidents, which are generally looked upon as a retaliation for the Belfast disorders, took place in the Free State during the weekend.

In Limerick, a mob of between two and three hundred youths appeared in the streets. The windows of a number of Protestant premises, including those of the Trinity Church, were smashed. A strong force of Civic Guards pursued the rioters, who broke windows as they ran.

The outbreak of violence assumed such serious proportions shortly after midnight on Saturday that a company of military carrying rifles with fixed bayonets were placed on duty in the streets. The latter formed a cordon across O'Connell Street, and the Guards, making a baton charge, scattered the rioters.

In Clones, County Monaghan, the Masonic Hall was completely burned down and a Gospel Hall and the Pringle Memorial were partly damaged.

The rioting and burnings, which were referred to at the Masses in Limerick and Clones, were strongly condemned by the clergy.

Locals gather at the body of a huge basking shark washed up at Carrigaloe near Cobh, Co Cork.

O'Mahony beats Don George

Thursday, August 1

Boston: Dan (Danno) O'Mahony, the Irish holder of the world's heavyweight wrestling championship, and Don George, a handsome collegian, met at Braves' Field this evening for what was termed the 'undisputed heavyweight championship of the world'.

O'Mahony was definitely superior in the first half an hour of the contest. He repeatedly clamped reverse wristlocks on George, and forced the latter to crawl through the ropes for shelter.

The bout was refereed by Jimmy Braddock, who recently won the heavyweight boxing championship of the world.

After a gruelling battle, George had twice heaved O'Mahony out of the ring, and the second time it seemed that Braddock had counted to 20 whereupon George began to leave the ring, thinking he had won. O'Mahony, however, seized George as the latter was about to make his exit and threw him outside the ropes. Again Braddock began counting and on reaching 20, raised O'Mahony's hand in victory. Several of George's seconds jumped into the ring protesting against the decision, but Braddock coolly knocked them out one after the other as they appeared.

In the presence of over 40,000 spectators, including the Governor of Massachusetts and a host of roaring Irishmen, O'Mahony gained the undisputed heavyweight title in 90 minutes flat.

NEWS BRIEFS

Jan A soldier who had been a member of the IRA and who returned home to Limerick for Christmas, told the Military Tribunal that he was chained to railings and a card was hung round his neck bearing the inscription "This is a deserter from the IRA!" Four Limerick men were charged in connection with the affair. (25)

June Japan gains control of northern China.

Aug About 12,000 pilgrims from all over the country gather at Knock to perpetuate the memory of the apparition of 1879. Among those in attendance were two of the people who saw the Virgin Mary back then, Patrick Byrne and 85-year-old Mary O'Connell. Mr Byrne tells the *Examiner* reporter of a Michael Lynch from Listowel, who was cured of a deformed foot at the shrine several years ago.

CITY SPECIAL

The Cork Examiner.

For Births, Marriages and Deaths, See Page Two

NO. 25,623. TUESDAY MORNING, FEBRUARY 19, 1935 PRICE—ONE PENNY

Registered for transmission at Newspaper Rate of Postage in Ireland and Great Britain, and at Magazine Rate in Canada and Newfoundland.

1936

The victory of the left-wing Popular Front coalition in Spain in February 1936 was, by most standards, the legitimate outcome of a democratic election. However, to many people, not least a large body of opinion in Ireland, it was a victory for godless Communism that needed to be reversed.

While editorially the *Examiner* favoured a policy of non-intervention and referred to wrongdoings on both sides, the stories that made it to the paper were primarily of atrocities committed by the leftist forces. Stories of priests being shot and nuns being forced to march naked through the streets encouraged several town councils to pass motions in support of Franco.

It is estimated that over 700 Irish people volunteered for Franco's Nationalists, and about 14 of them died in Spain. Around a third of the 200 Irish with the international brigades were killed.

News reports at the time carry more accounts of the Nationalist volunteers, not least due to the fact that many of those joining the anti-Franco forces did so in secret to spare themselves and their families censure from the pulpit.

Somerville is shot dead

Thursday, March 26

A tragic story was told yesterday by the widow of Vice-Admiral Henry Boyle Somerville, who was shot dead at the door of their residence on Tuesday night.

It was about 9.15pm, she said, when she and her husband were seated together in the dining room. They were the only occupants of the house at the time. She happened to leave the dining room to go to an ante-chamber, and while there she heard footsteps in the yard at the rear of the premises.

She returned to the dining room with a small reading lamp, and while there she again heard the footsteps. Then there was a knock and her husband went to the door. She overheard a man asking: "Are you Mr Somerville?" and her husband's reply: "I am Admiral Somerville."

"Immediately," said Mrs Somerville, "there was the sound of the firing of several shots and the accompanying sound of falling glass." Mrs Somerville called to her husband but got no reply. She heard a noise, which resembled retreating footsteps and then found Admiral Somerville lying in the porch and showing no signs of life.

A card was thrust through the door just previous to the departure of the raiders. The card had reference to the sending of Irish boys to the British Army.

In West Cork, an older conflict resulted in the killing of local resident Henry Boyle Somerville, a former vice-admiral in the British navy who had been assisting Irish people who wanted to join his old force.

Wolfhounds and pipe bands helped open the GAA's Fitzgerald Stadium in Killarney, Co Kerry.

NEWS BRIEFS

May While opening Tuam Feis, Archbishop Gilmartin describes the event as a splendid offset against the indecency of imported amusements, especially dances. He was glad to notice a rising tide of enlightened criticism against forms of music and dances known as jazz, many species of which seem like a mesmeric rhythm of sensuality. "The Irish character is naturally more spiritual than sensual," he said. (17)

Bishop Cohalan of Cork speaks out against the problems caused for farmers by the land annuities. "The small farmers in all the western parishes are greatly impoverished and are suffering a terrible injustice," he said. (25)

Nov A meeting of Limerick's County Library Committee raises the question of whether badminton is a foreign game after a request is received to use one of its rooms for the sport. "It does not come under the GAA ban," the librarian pointed out. "It sounds foreign anyway," retorted Mr Hickey, committee member. Permission to use the room was not granted on the grounds that it was needed for meetings and other functions. (20)

Clare contingent for Spain

Saturday, December 12

Affecting scenes were witnessed at Tulla prior to the immediate departure of the men, whose relatives wept as they stepped into the waiting motor cars. Holy water was sprinkled on them by Miss A Minogue, proprietress of one of the local hotels. The men themselves were in the best of spirits although fully conscious of the seriousness of their venture. Many expressed the hope that their action would not be misunderstood by political opponents and assured our correspondent that their sole object in joining the Irish Brigade was to fight for Christianity.

The Cork Examiner.

CITY SPECIAL

NO. 26,100. MONDAY MORNING, AUGUST 31, 1936. PRICE—ONE PENNY

Registered for transmission at Newspaper Rate of Postage in Ireland and Great Britain, and at Magazine Rate in Canada and Newfoundland.

IRISH BISHOP CALLS FOR CRUSADE OF PRAYER FOR SPAIN

MENACE OF COMMUNISM.

DEAN OF CASHEL ASKS FOR PUBLIC AND PRIVATE PRAYER.

THE ARCH-ENEMY OF MANKIND.

Day Of Atonement For Sacrileges In Spain Appointed By Dr. Mageean.

GENERAL O'DUFFY ON HIS PLANS.

Irish Christian Front Organised In Dublin To Give Medical Aid.

The Dean of Cashel, Right Rev. Mgr. Innocent Ryan, preaching at Cashel yesterday, appealed to the people to form themselves into a league of prayer for the deliverance of Spain, the grand old Catholic nation, from the horror of the fratricidal war at present raging in that fair land, and for the destruction of Communism, the arch enemy of mankind.

The nations stand aside, Mgr. Ryan said. They say they will be neutral, leaving the lion of Communism and the lamb of Catholic Spain to fight it out between them. There seems to be no power inclined to put a stop to the awful carnage.

He urged the faithful to prayer, public and private, "not only in charity to our Catholic neighbour, but for the safeguarding of our own shores from an invasion of this dreadful curse and enemy, Communism.

The Bishop of Down and Connor has asked for a crusade of prayer and has ordered next Sunday to be reserved throughout his diocese as a day of atonement and expiation for the sacrileges of the last few weeks in Spain.

General O'Duffy, speaking at Beal-na-Blath yesterday said he was going to Spain and was going to bring an Irish Brigade there. President de Valera, he said, was simply toeing the line with England with regard to Spain, the same way as he had toed it with regard to Abyssinia.

Speaking in Dublin, Mr. P. Belton, T.D., said the help the Irish Christian Front proposed to send to Spain was limited to medical aid for sick and wounded and to help those made destitute by the ravages of war.

Lord ffrench said that the forces in Europe to-day were lining up into two camps and peace was trembling in the balance. "If the Reds win in Spain," he declared, "then France and England will be allied with them, and that will be a bad day for this country and for its chance of independence."

THE BATTLE FOR SAN SEBASTIAN.—A detachment of insurgent cavalry on their way to take up positions on the San Sebastian front, near Andoi, where fierce fighting has been in progress for several days. (Keystone).

THE ATTACK ON IRUN

DEFENDERS SAID TO BE IMPROVING THEIR POSITIONS.

UNDER DIRECTION OF BELGIANS.

Government Claims Victory In Huesca Province.

FIGHTING WEST OF MADRID.

Neither Side Disposed To Agree To Suggested Armistice.

The fifth day of the Insurgent attack on Irun finds the attackers still held up.

The defenders, according to Reuter, are improving their positions under the direction of Belgian and other veterans of the Great War.

Yesterday morning three Insurgent planes dropped bombs on key positions around Fort San Martial

The Government forces claim to have won a "great victory" in Huesca Province and to be at the gates of its capital, the capture of which would open another route for the bringing in of supplies from France.

Fighting is taking place in the Estramadura region, a hundred miles west of Madrid, where the Insurgents are said to have concentrated the pick of their forces.

The Bishop of Tortosa is reported to be among the notabilities held captive by the Government forces on board a ship in Tarragona harbour.

Regarding the possibility of an armistice, it was declared in Spanish Government circles at Madrid last night that there could be no question of treating with the Insurgents on any terms. The proposals met with only a very lukewarm reception from the rebel leaders at Burgos.

Page recreated

1937

De Valera had already used the abdication of Edward VIII to remove references to the king from the Constitution and the entire document was overhauled in 1937. Among the major provisions of the new document were the creation of the office of Taoiseach, and the elevation of the Catholic Church and its teachings to a higher status than other religions.
De Valera's government continued a hands-off approach to the war in Spain. It supported a non-interventionist policy at the League of Nations, and resisted pressure to have Franco recognised as Spain's ruler. Meanwhile, the pro-Franco Irish Brigade returned home after spending six months in Spain.
Poverty still forced thousands of Irish people to Britain looking for work and among them were ten young potato pickers from Achill Island, tragically killed in a fire in Scotland.

Spanish town wiped out

Wednesday, April 28

The town of Guernica has now been wiped out, according to messages received today. In the last 24 hours modern warfare in its most ghastly guise has transformed the battlefield of the Basque territory into an inferno of death and destruction.
Literally hundreds of civilians were killed and the town had been reduced to a mass of blazing ruins. At 4.30pm yesterday German bombers came over in uncounted numbers accompanied by equally numerous fighters. From the first planes the crews leaned out dropping hand grenades, while the frightened population rushed to a few bomb shelters. Hundreds raced desperately for the fields where they were systematically followed and machine-gunned from the air. Next, relays of bombers dropped high explosive bombs.
The casualties cannot yet be counted, but hundreds of men, women and children must have been roasted alive, torn to pieces by explosives, and drilled with machine gun bullets. Fire fighters conducted me to the entrance of a blazing street, where they showed me a bomb shelter in which over 50 women and children had been trapped and incinerated.

Adults and children enjoying an ice cream during the summer.

NEWS BRIEFS

April Prior to his departure to Palestine, the Chief Rabbi of Ireland, Dr Isaac Hertzog, tells a reception in Dublin that Jews had never suffered persecution in Ireland, and that "unfriendly utterances in recent times" had not marred this record. Dr Herzog's Irish-born son, Chaim, would eventually become President of Israel. (8)

Aug Dr Pat O'Callaghan broke Paddy Ryan's 19-year-old world record in the hammer throw at an athletics meet in Fermoy, Co Cork. The distance of 198 feet 8⅜ inches was ratified by a "qualified engineer" who was summoned to the ground. On the same page as the *Examiner* report of the feat, a new 100-metre sprint record set at a meeting in Paris by a black American athlete is headlined 'Negro's Record'. (22)

Terrible tragedy

Friday, September 17

Ten young harvesters from the West of Ireland perished in a fire which destroyed the premises in which they were sleeping near Glasgow, early yesterday.
The party had been engaged for potato digging on a local farm, and had only arrived on Wednesday night. It included 12 men and 14 women.
They were all housed in flats in the same building at Kirkintilloch, Dumbartonshire. Two of the men, a father and son, and all the women escaped, though it is reported that one of the girls is in a critical condition.
The fire alarm was given by the youth who escaped, who lay awake suffering from a boil on the neck. Before the outbreak was noticed, the fire had got such a hold that rescue of the others was impossible.
The 10 victims are all young men from Achill Sound, Co Mayo, and include two and three members of the same families.
The girls were frantic with fear and several escaped by breaking windows with their fists. Achill Sound was plunged in sorrow when news of the tragedy was received. The Parish Priest went from cottage to cottage comforting the bereaved parents who were shocked by the terrible disaster.
A local resident said to a Press Association reporter: "The parents of the dead men and boys are all crofters, whose sons spend from June to November in Scotland seeking to add to the often scanty incomes of their parents, digging potatoes.
"One of the parents, Mrs Margaret McNeela, lost her husband some years ago in America, and another, Mrs Michael Kilhane, lost two other children, a boy and a girl, two years ago from pneumonia."

The Cork Examiner.

18 PAGES CITY SPECIAL

NO. 26,307. SATURDAY MORNING, MAY 1, 1937. PRICE—TWOPENCE.

Registered for transmission at newspaper Rate of Postage in Ireland and Great Britain, and at Magazine Rate in Canada and Newfoundland.

THE TEXT OF THE NEW CONSTITUTION OF EIRE

MAIN CHANGES PROPOSED

PRESIDENT TO SUCCEED THE GOVERNOR GENERAL

SENATE TO BE RESTORED

NO MENTION OF KING GEORGE OR GREAT BRITAIN

The text of the draft of the new Constitution which Mr. de Valera proposed to put before the people for ratification at the coming General Election was issued in Dublin yesterday.

The main changes proposed are in connection with the Legislature. With the disappearance of the Governor-General under the legislation of last December the Legislature consisted of only one House, with the Chairman having authority to sign Bills. The new Constitution provides for two Houses, Dail and Senate, and for a President as successor to the Governor-General.

The President will be apart from party politics or sectional interests and is to be invested with powers not enjoyed by the former Governor-General. In the exercise of the powers which do not come within his own discretion he will be advised by his Council of State.

There is no mention of King George or Great Britain in the new Constitution which, as Mr. de Valera has already indicated, will stand without alteration in the event of an All-Ireland Republic.

The name Irish Free State is to be altered to the name "Eire."

Article 1 says: "The Irish Nation hereby affirms its inalienable, indefeasible and sovereign right to choose its own form of government, to determine its relation with other nations, and to develop its life—political, economic and cultural, in accordance with its own genius and traditions."

Article 2 says: "The national territory consists of thewhole of Ireland, its islands and the territorial seas."

Article 12, which deals with the office of President says he shall be elected by direct vote of the people, and shall hold office for seven years.

The President shall, on the nomination of the Dail, appoint a Prime Minister, or Head of the Government, who will be called An Taoiseach.

The Senate will be composed of 60 members, of whom 11 shall be nominated by the Prime Minister, and the remainder elected as follows:—Three by the National University, three by Trinity College, and forty-three by the Dail.

It is expected, says the Press Association, that the General Election and plebiscite will take place in the last week in June.

CONFIRMATION.—Pupils of Faithlegg National School, Co. Waterford, who were Confirmed recently by his Lordship Most Rev. Dr. Kinane, Bishop of Waterford. (Phillips).

Page recreated

1938

Despite the claim by British Prime Minister Neville Chamberlain that his appeasement of Hitler had secured "peace in our time", most countries in Europe were already preparing for war. On the domestic diplomatic front, events were taking a more positive turn with an important improvement of relations with Britain. De Valera negotiated an agreement that saw the return of naval bases in Cork and Donegal, and the ending of the Economic War.

Tariffs were removed and a final payment of £10 million was paid to Britain to cover the land annuities. The return of the bases had a huge symbolic significance, but it would also ensure that Ireland could pursue a policy of neutrality in the upcoming war.

Tom Crean dies

Friday, July 29

Thomas Crean, 66, ex-petty officer in the British Navy and one of the heroes of the British Antarctic Expedition of 1910, was buried in a little cemetery in his native Annascaul, County Kerry, today.

His name recalls sad and proud memories of those who gave their lives that we might have a better knowledge of the universe in which we live. It calls forth reminiscences of those whose bodies lie in the icy tomb of the great barrier.

Commander Evans, leader of the expedition, referred to Crean some years later as follows: "When on January 17, 1912 we reached the next depot under Cloudmaker Mountain we had walked 17 miles without anything to eat except one biscuit and a mug of tea. I asked Crean and Ashley to go on without me. They replied respectfully but firmly that for the first time they would disobey my orders, and strapping me on the sledge, they dragged me 40 miles in four days.

When 35 miles from Hut Point we had a heavy snow fall which made it impossible for Crean and Ashley to move the sledge, so on February 19, Crean left us and marched for 18 hours through snow with nothing to eat but a few biscuits. He eventually reached Hut Point, and they came out and rescued us."

Crean took part in two South Pole expeditions with Scott and one with Shackleton. Despite the hardships he endured, he never lost his cheery disposition, and he was well-known and liked in the Dingle Peninsula.

Éamon de Valera and a party of ministers disembark in Cork harbour at ceremonies to mark the takeover of the remaining ports from Britain.

Priest criticises girls in commerce

Wednesday, August 17

"There are several young girls and boys going in for commerce degrees and the positions they are filling would be worth something like 24/- or 25/- a week, showing that this is a blind alley form of education. There is no market for it in this country," said Rev F McCarthy, PP, Chairman of the Cork County Vocational Education Committee when referring to the fact that there was no applicant for the position of fulltime domestic economy instructress at Castletownbere.

It was as easy for a girl to get qualified in domestic science as it was to get a commerce degree, and possibly easier, said the Chairman. There was also another aspect of the question, one to which the people of the country were not fully alive, and it was that the domestic economy ladies were very often taken into married life.

"The young men of the country," continued Father McCarthy, "in addition to having an eye for the beautiful and the aesthetic, are also influenced by what is useful in a prospective wife, and there is no better training for a wife and for a future housekeeper than a training in domestic science."

NEWS BRIEFS

Jan The Aurora Borealis, or Northern Lights, causes wonder, terror and failure of telegraph lines when it makes a rare appearance over Ireland. The phenomenon lasted for two hours over Cork in the form of streams of light in an intense crimson colour, which later changed to a silvery blue, and at times there was a tremulous motion which added to the wonder of the sight. (26)

Aug Current world wrestling champion Steve Casey from Sneem, Co Kerry, takes on former title-holder Danno Mahony at Milltown, Dublin. The fight ended in a draw. When Casey had arrived back from America to Sneem to prepare for the bout, he revealed the diet that kept him in shape: "A steak a day, fruit juices and water. I don't smoke and I don't drink. I eat lots of rye bread." (17)

The Cork Examiner.

NO. 26,680. TUESDAY MORNING, JULY 12, 1938. PRICE—ONE PENNY

Registered for transmission at newspaper Rate of Postage in Ireland and Great Britain, and at Magazine Rate in Canada and Newfoundland.

HISTORIC CEREMONY AT SPIKE

MANY THOUSANDS WATCH TRANSFER FROM BRITISH CONTROL.

GUNS BOOM IN SALUTE TO FLAG.

FIVE MINISTERS TRAVEL WITH TAOISEACH ON SPECIAL TRAIN FROM DUBLIN.

Crowds, estimated at forty thousand, gathered in vantage points all round Cork Harbour last night, saw Mr. de Valera, as head of the Irish Government, hoist the tricolour for the first time over Spike Island.

The ceremony lasted only half a minute, but it was a historic half minute which will long stand out in the memory of everybody who saw it, for it marked the passing into Irish control of the forts held by Britain for a century and a half.

The tricolour, floating in the sunshine, was saluted with the National Anthem and the firing of twenty-one guns, while at Cove a feu de joie was fired, followed by enthusiastic cheers from the thousands who thronged the town from all quarters.

Simultaneously the Irish flag broke from the three other forts in the harbour —Camden, Carlisle and Templebreedy—of which possession had been taken earlier in the day by Irish troops.

The actual handing over of Spike was a simple exchange between the military chiefs in charge of the two forces. The departing British troops were accorded a courtesy salute of guns.

Mr. de Valera was accompanied by six other Ministers:—Messrs. Aiken, Ruttledge, Ryan, Traynor, MacEntee and Boland—who came from Dublin in a special train with some hundreds of distinguished guests. The Taoiseach arrived earlier by car.

Chief Superintendent Fitzgerald chatting to Mr. Ruttledge, Minister for Justice, on the quayside. ("Examiner" Photo).

IRISH GUARDS FROM EGYPT ARRIVE IN PALESTINE

MORE DISORDER IN THE HOLY LAND.

The first battalion of the Irish Guards, the first troops ordered to Palestine from Egypt to reinforce the garrison in the Holy Land, arrived yesterday.

Despite great activity by police and military, disorders are frequent, and yesterday there were many more bombing and stabbing incidents, though casualties were fewer.

Page recreated

1939

Sunday, September 3, 1939 was a day of unprecedented high drama. World War II officially began after Britain's declaration of war against Germany, a move sparked by Hitler's invasion of Poland two days previously, while in Dublin a dramatic All-Ireland hurling final provided a temporary distraction for many Irish minds.

Weather conditions at the match between Kilkenny and Cork seemed to reflect the goings-on in Europe as a terrible storm broke out during the latter stages of what became known as the 'thunder and lightning final'. The teams themselves added to the theatre of the occasion by playing a thrilling game won by Kilkenny with a last minute point.

With the outbreak of war, the Irish government immediately declared a policy of neutrality, called up army reserves, ordered a complete night-time blackout and introduced price controls on food.

Extreme censorship measures were also introduced which particularly affected the *Examiner* because of its status as the state's only daily newspaper outside Dublin. Any doubtful matter had to be submitted to the censors by telephone at night, a procedure which caused obvious problems for publishing deadlines as staff in Cork waited for decisions.

Even mentions of the weather were censored and if the hurling final had been held a few weeks later, no references could have been made in the match report to the extreme conditions.

The Irish come home

Monday, September 4

Extraordinary scenes were witnessed at Euston and Paddington Stations on Saturday night, when thousands of Irish people, mostly young mothers with children and infants in arms, besieged a darkened departure platform to secure places on the trains for Holyhead and Fishguard.

Police in steel helmets formed long queues of anxious travellers, many of whom brought prams and cots and other of their modest belongings. Even the corridors of the trains were packed out.

There were pathetic scenes as young husbands said goodbye to their wives and children, but relief as the trains drew out in the knowledge that they would be comparatively safe in Éire.

A young Irishman to whom I spoke, and who is an air-raid warden in the Wimbledon district, said: "It's a great relief to get my wife and five-month-old baby away to her people in Cavan, because although I do not think it is any safer over there, I would be worrying about her and the baby. In Cavan she has her people to take care of her."

A cure for lonely husbands.

Leesiders out of luck in rousing final

Monday, September 4

Kilkenny 2-7, Cork 3-3

The 1939 All-Ireland Hurling Championships were played off yesterday at Croke Park under circumstances which will go down in history. It was a terrific battle between Cork and Kilkenny and practically all the second half was fought in a thunderstorm accompanied by vivid flashes of fork lightning and a deluge of rain which lashed into the faces of the Cork team and caused many spectators to seek shelter elsewhere.

It looked as if the remaining stages of the game would have to be abandoned but the players were eager on reaching a decision, and under extraordinarily abnormal conditions the match was continued to a desperate finish. The representatives of the Marble County turned up in great form and there was no mistaking their determination to win out.

Kilkenny had a pull on Cork at the interval of 2-4 to 1-1 but the Cork team launched some wonderfully good attacks throughout the second stage of the game, extending their rivals at every passage and eventually reaching level scores.

Lost time was played and in this brief period Kilkenny forced a seventy. Phelan took the free. The ball, heavy and greasy, travelled about half the distance and in a desperate clash Leahy doubled in the air and the ball sailed over the bar for the winning point.

NEWS BRIEFS

Jan Mr WB Yeats, the Irish poet, died at Mentone in the Riviera, on Saturday, aged 73. His death removes from the life of the nation one of Ireland's greatest poets and dramatists. (30)

Apr Douglas Hyde, former President of Ireland, has his name removed from the list of GAA patrons because he attended a soccer match, an action which was deemed to be in contravention of the organisation's 'ban'. (9)

The Cork Examiner.

18 PAGES

CITY SPECIAL

NO. 27,037. SATURDAY MORNING, SEPTEMBER 2, 1939 PRICE—TWOPENCE.

Registered for transmission at newspaper rate of postage in Ireland and Great Britain and at Magazine Rate to Canada and Newfoundland.

BRITAIN MOBILIZED AWAITS HITLER'S ANSWER

EIRE CALLS UP RESERVES AND SUMMONS BOTH HOUSES

GERMANY WARNED

WITHDRAW FROM POLAND ULTIMATUM

ANGLO-FRENCH ACTION

STATEMENT BY MR. CHAMBERLAIN IN COMMONS.

Britain, in a state of general mobilisation and with every city, town and village in total darkness, last night awaited Hitler's answer to the Government's "last warning" to withdraw his army from Polish territory.

The Premier's words in the House of Commons were: "If the reply to this last warning is unfavourable—and I do not suggest it is likely to be otherwise—His Majesty's Ambassador is instructed to ask for his passports. In that case we are ready."

Parliament, called specially yesterday because of the crisis, sat late and will meet again to-day at 2.45, and may also sit on Sunday.

Immediate legislation is to be introduced extending to all fit men between 18 and 41 liability to military service, and full plans have been worked out for the setting up of a War Cabinet, including Opposition leaders.

Proclamation of general mobilisation was addressed to the R.A.F., Regular Army, the Militia, Supplementary Reserves and the Territorial Army, and at the same time all A.R.P. men and women were called to duty stations.

By order of the Food Defence Department yesterday's prices of all food commodities were fixed as standstill prices until further notice. The Minister of Transport made an order taking control of all railways. A censorship on postal correspondence to places abroad was imposed by the Government.

The official correspondence between Britain and Germany was published. It told how Britain warned Hitler that conflict between the two nations might mean "a calamity without parallel in history," how Hitler spoke of "bloody and incalculable war," and finally how the Fuehrer declared his readiness to "pledge himself personally for the continued existence of the British Empire" if his colonial demands were fulfilled.

London, Friday Night.

For the third time within ten days, Parliament was recalled to hear the Prime Minister's account of the latest development in the international situation.

When the Speaker took the chair at 6 o'clock the chamber was crowded and the atmosphere was charged with a tenseness which is characteristic only of the most critical meetings of the House.

Members, many of whom had remained in London since the House met on Tuesday, following the dramatic news which had been coming from the Continent since early hours of the morning were early in their places. Both sides of the House were crowded; members flocked into the side galleries specially reserved for them and stood thickly packed beyond the bar of the House.

Both front benches were full and most of the elder statesmen, who now occupy privileged places on the back benches, were in their places.

The Distinguished Strangers' Gallery was filled with diplomats and all the other galleries were crowded.

Mr. Chamberlain was received with a loud and prolonged burst of cheering when he entered the chamber from behind the Speaker's chair at three minutes past six. He took his seat on the Treasury Bench between Sir John Simon and Sir Samuel Hoare and rose to make his speech at 6.4 p.m.

THE PREMIER'S SPEECH.

Responsibility Of The German Chancellor.

Mr. Chamberlain said:—"I do not propose to say many words to-night. The time has come when action rather than words is required (cheers).

"About 18 months ago in this House I prayed that the responsibility might not fall upon me to ask this country to accept the awful arbitrament of war. I fear that I am not able to avoid that responsibility. But at any rate I could not wish the conditions under which such a burden should fall upon me made clearer than they are to-day as to where my duty lies (cheers). No one, I think, can say that the Government could have done more to try and keep open the way for an honourable and equitable settlement of the dispute between Germany and Poland. Nor have we neglected any means of making it crystal clear to the German Government that if they insisted on using force again in the manner in which they had used it in the past we were resolved to oppose them by force.

"Now that all the relevant documents are being made public, we shall stand at the bar of history knowing that the responsibility for this terrible catastrophe lies on the shoulders of one man (cheers). The German Chancellor has not hesitated to plunge the world into misery in order to serve his own senseless ambition (cheers).

CORRESPONDENCE WITH GERMANY

"I would like to thank the House for the forbearance they have shown on two recent occasions in not demanding from me information which they recognised I could not give while these negotiations were still in progress. I have now had all the correspondence with the German Government put into the form of a White Paper. I am afraid that there are but a few copies available but I understand that they will be coming in in relays while the House is sitting. I do not think that it is necessary for me to refer in detail now to these documents, which are already past history. They make it perfectly clear that our object has been to try to bring about discussion about the German-Polish dispute between the two countries themselves on terms of equality (cheers). The settlement to be one which safeguarded the independence of Poland and which secured its due observance by international guarantee.

UNDERTAKING ASKED FOR.

But No Reply From The German Government.

"There is just one passage from our most recent communication—or a recent communication—dated August 31, which I should like to quote, because it shows how easily the final clash might have been avoided if there had been the least desire on the part of the German Government to arrive at a peaceful settlement (cheers). In this document we said this: 'His Majesty's Government fully recognise the need of speed in the initiation of discussion. They share the apprehensions of the Chancellor, arising from the proximity of two mobilised armies standing face to face. They would, accordingly, most strongly urge that both parties should undertake that during the negotiations no aggressive military movement will take place. H.M. Government feel confident that they could obtain such an undertaking from the Polish Government if the German Government would give a similar assurance.' "

"That telegram, which was repeated to Poland, brought an instantaneous reply from the Polish Government, dated August 31, in which they said the Polish Government are also prepared, on a reciprocal basis, to give a formal guarantee in the event of negotiations taking place, that Polish troops will not violate the frontiers of the German Reich, provided that a corresponding guarantee is given regarding any violation of frontiers of Poland by troops of the German Reich.

"We never had any reply from the German Government to that suggestion. It was one which, if it had been followed, might have saved the catastrophe which took place this morning.

GERMAN BROADCAST.

The Proposals Never Put To Poland.

"In the German broadcast last night—which recited the 16 points of the proposal which they had put forward—there occurred this sentence: 'In these circumstances, the Reich Government considers its proposals rejected.'

"I must examine that statement. I must tell the House what are the circumstances (cheers). To begin with, let me say that these proposals have never been communicated by Germany to Poland at all. The history of the affair is this. On

(CONTINUED ON PAGE TEN.)

THE MAP AND THE MEN.

This map shows Europe, the geographical position of the various countries, and the approximate man-powers which each country can assemble for war service.

HOW "BLACK FRIDAY" BROUGHT WAR TO EUROPE.

AIR AND LAND BATTLES AS GERMANS AND POLES CLASH.

War has come to Europe. German planes heavily bombed Warsaw yesterday as Mr. Neville Chamberlain, the British Prime Minister, was warning Germany in Parliament that responsibility of a war in which Britain would take part "rests on the shoulders of one man—the German Chancellor."

The Warsaw raid was one of five that took place during Europe's blackest Friday since the World War. German troops also appeared to be driving across the border with three definite objectives.

Herr Hitler, addressing the Reichstag declared: "I will give Poland a strong lesson," announced his grey-clad armies had crossed the Polish frontier and named Goering first and Hess second to succeed him in the event of his death.

General mobilisation was ordered in France and Premier Daladier was expected to reshuffle his Cabinet.

The Italian Cabinet announced, after a special session, that Italy "would not take any initiative of military operations," as the result of a war between Germany and Poland.

The Polish Embassy in Washington announced that Poland had called for Anglo-French aid. President Roosevelt issued a plea not to start bombing of civilians and unfortified cities.

As complete mobilisation was pput into effect in France a state of siege was declared in France and Algiers. A state of siege is a kind of martial law.

It was announced in Paris that M. Coulondre, the French Ambassador in Berlin, would last night make a demarche to the German Government similar to that which Mr. Chamberlain announced in the House of Commons was being made by Mr. Nevile Henderson, the British envoy.

Mr. Roosevelt told a Press conference in Washington that he hoped and believed the United States could keep out of a European War.

Warsaw, Friday.—German troops invaded Poland to-day, while German planes bombed Warsaw and Katowice, the highly industrialised "Manchester" of Poland; the ancient and historic towns of Cracow and Czestochowa and Tczew, and Grudziadz.

German and Polish planes fought above Warsaw City after the German bombers raided the centre of the city.

The German planes swooped over the city, apparently attempting to smash the Vistula bridges.—Associated Press.

Anti-aircraft guns opened fire on the raiders, and several German bombers appeared to fall into the river. Half an hour later Polish fighting planes attacked the German bombers. The crash of diving fighters screamed over the noise of exploding bombs. Some bombs fell two streets from the United States Embassy, and numerous explosions were heard. Low-lying misty clouds formed a temporary protection for Warsaw. There were also official Polish reports of bombing of Silesia and Polish Corridor defences. Heavy movements of German troops from East Prussia towards the Polish frontier were also reported.

Berlin, Friday.—A war bulletin issued by the German High Command to-night stated that advances by the Air Force and Army, which started from Pomerania, Silesia, and East Prussia, were well under way towards their objectives. It came just after an official announcement announced the bombing of the Polish airport at Radom, on the outskirts of Warsaw, and the bombing of troops at a Polish railway station.

The German Radio announced to-day that there would be a German naval blockade of the Baltic, and that Dr. Karl Burckhardt, League of Nations High Commissioner for Danzig, had left the Free City with his staff at 9 a.m.

REFERRED TO HITLER.

THE BRITISH WARNING TO GERMANY.

It was learned in London last night by the Press Association, that Herr Von Ribbentrop at 9.40 p.m. received Sir Nevile Henderson, the British Ambassador, who handed him the communication referred to in the Prime Minister's Speech in the House of Commons yesterday.

Herr Von Ribbentrop said he must refer the communication to Hitler.

The Swastika was immediately raised over his house to the cheers of the crowd, it was stated.—A.P.

Early in the morning, at 5.40 o'clock, while Europe still slept, Herr Hitler broadcast a proclamation that was the first announcement of war.

Making his announcement, Herr Hitler said: "From now on I have no other choice than to meet force with force."

"The German army will fight the battle for the honour and vital rights of reborn Germany with hard determination."

The following order to the Air Force by General Goering was announced: "We have suffered with clenched fists for weeks and months the provocations which have been directed against the Greater German Reich. Our cup is full. No longer can the German nation look on inactive. Every further delay would be disastrous. The Fuehrer has called. The great hour has come.

"The Air Force has now to show that it is at its post in the decisive hour. It is our pride that every one of us will justify his confidence.

"Thus we will be in the position to break down every resistance. The land forces will prepare every attack of the Air Force. Every shot of our artillery will help to fight for the freedom of our nation, of our women and our children. At our head stands our beloved leader, behind stands the united German nation."

"THE DECISIVE HOUR."

Message To The German Navy.

An order to the German Navy from Admiral Raeder was read: "The decisive hour finds us prepared. Remember our great and glorious traditions. We will fight for the greatness and freedom of the German Reich."

The German wireless has issued a warning to all ships in the Baltic stating that the "entrance to the Polish port of Gdynia is closed, and every ship entering or leaving risks the danger of being destroyed.

All civil flying over Germany has been prohibited and neutral 'planes are warned that they may be shot down if they fly over the Polish Corridor.—Reuter.

At 11.40 a.m. the German Supreme Command announced over the radio:—

"The armed forces have taken over the active protection of the German Reich.

"In the fulfilment of their task to offer resistance to Polish force, German troops have crossed all the frontiers to counter-attack.

"The air arm has also come into action. The navy has taken over the protection of the Baltic."

The following order to the German Army

(CONTINUED ON PAGE TEN.)

EMERGENCY MOVES

"BLACK OUT" ORDER FOR THE NATION

FOOD PRICES CONTROL

MR. DULANTY SPENDS BUSY DAY IN LONDON.

Eire last night called up certain classes of the Army Reserve by public and personal notice, and in many cities and towns there were scenes of activity as young men answered the call. All members of the Regular Army on leave or furlough were immediately recalled. This action followed a meeting of the Government, which also summoned the Dail and Senate to meet at 3 p.m. to-day, "to consider such measures as may be proposed by the Government for protecting the interests of the State in any emergency arising from the present international situation." Two new Bills to be before the Houses were issued last night and will be found on Page 10.

The Ministry of Defence last night ordered all private houses, factories and places of entertainment to "black out" by obscuring windows, etc., and all public lighting is to be discontinued from half an hour before sunset. Motorists, too, must take precautions about headlights.

In London yesterday it is understood that Mr. Dulanty made clear the Irish outlook on the crisis to Mr. Chamberlain, and after the statement in the House of Commons Mr. Dulanty was on the 'phone to Dublin.

It was announced in Dublin last night that by order of the Food Defence Committee, the prices of all food commodities have been fixed as standstill prices until further notice.

Following rumours that the Port of Cork was to be closed, Cove Urban Council last night made a protest.

Dublin, Friday.—The following statement was issued this afternoon by the Government Information Bureau.—

A notice is being issued summoning members of Dail and Senate to meet to-day (Saturday) at 3 p.m., to consider such measures as may be proposed by the Government for protecting the interests of the State in any emergency arising from the present international situation.

A meeting of the Executive Council was held to-day, Mr. de Valera presiding.

RESERVES CALLED UP.

The following statement was issued by the Information Bureau to-night.—

Defence Forces (Temporary Provisions) Acts, 1923 to 1939: calling out of the Reserves on permanent service.

In view of the international situation, the Government, at its meeting to-day, decided to summon the Dail and Senad for 3 p.m. to-morrow, ordered the Minister for Defence, as a precautionary measure, to call out on permanent service certain categories of the Reserve of the defence forces.

The Minister for Defence has, therefore, ordered the following classes of the Reserve to be called up by public and personal notice.—

(1) All officers of the General Reserve of Officers; (2) Officers of the Volunteer class of Coast Defence Artillery units; (3) Officers of the Volunteer class of the units of the Coast Watching Service; (4) All non-commissioned officers and men of the Reserve Classes A and B; (5) All non-commissioned officers and men of the Volunteer class of Coast Defence Artillery units; (6) All non-commissioned officers and men of the Volunteer class of units of the Coast Watching Defence; (7) All mechanical transport drivers of the Volunteers class of units of all Corps and Services.

THE REGULAR ARMY.

In addition, all officers, non-commissioned officers and men of the permanent force on leave or furlough are required to report forthwith to their units or appointments without further delay.

The Government relies with confidence upon employers, transport agencies, and the general public to do all in their power to facilitate the rapid mobilisation of the troops called up.

EIRE'S ATTITUDE.

Mr. Dulanty Sees Mr. Chamberlain.

(From Our Special Correspondent).

London, Friday.—I understand that Mr. de Valera's views were conveyed by Mr. John Dulanty, the Irish High Commissioner, when he chatted with Mr. Chamberlain, the Prime Minister, at 10 Downing Street for twenty-five minutes, before Mr. Chamberlain left for the House of Commons this evening, and that the High Commissioner pointed out that Eire will fight only in the event of her independence being threatened.

It is certain, for instance, that the British Navy will have to protect important trade routes for the shipping of food between the two countries.

Mr. Sean Leydon, Permanent Secretary of the Eire Department of Industry and Commerce, has arrived in London on what was stated to-night, in well-informed Irish quarters to be an important mission.

I understand that he is discussing the maintenance of full supplies of coal and other essential commodities for Irish life and industry in war time.

Mr. Dulanty, the Irish Commissioner, listened to Mr. Chamberlain's momentous speech, in the House of Commons to-night, from the Dominions' gallery. Afterwards he was again on the telephone to the Department of External Affairs in Dublin.

"BLACK-OUT" ORDER.

Nation-wide Instructions From Dublin.

The following was issued in Dublin to-night.—

The Government considers that it is essential that certain precautionary measures should now be taken in the matter of lighting restrictions.

All local authorities throughout the country have been requested to arrange for the restriction of public lighting in streets, highways and public places, as on and from Saturday the 2nd September, until further notice.

The Minister for Defence requests all occupiers of private houses, shops, business premises and places of entertainment to co-operate in these precautionary measures by discontinuing to use all exterior lights, and by darkening every window, skylight, glass door, or exterior opening in parts of buildings where lights are used after dark.

HOW TO DO IT.

The latter purpose can be effected by utilising opaque coverings, such as dark blinds, thick curtains, or dark material, which will cover the openings completely.

Skylights, fanlights and glass doors can readily be covered with black paint or thick dark paper. Motorists are requested to co-operate by driving with sidelights only within a radius of 15 miles of any costal urban area, and to exercise the added caution necessitated by the reduced lighting conditions. Parents and guardians are advised to keep their children off the streets and highways during hours of darkness.

CORK ORDER.

Dublin was partially blacked out last night as a precautionary measure.

Last night, the Minister for Defence notified Mr. Philip Monahan, Cork's City Manager, that from henceforth there is to be no public lighting of the streets of the city. Until further notice then, there will be no street lights lighting in Cork.

The Minister further requests that those who use electrical or other signs, as well as those whose shop windows are normally illuminated at night, should discontinue such lighting half an hour before sunset.

It is presumed that a similar notice has been sent to the Board of Health, which is the controlling authority for the lighting outside the city boundaries.

Sunset to-night is at 8.15 p.m.

WATERFORD PRECAUTIONS.

In Waterford early yesterday morning Corporation officials and Mr. Commissioner Meghen, held a conference during which communication was established with the Department in Dublin. It was felt that there was no immediate danger, but some precautions should be taken against any attacks.

Arrangements were made to shut off all sirens and hooters in the city except one, that of Denny's Bacon Factory, which would be used to give any air raid signals on a prescribed signal from Dublin. Arrangements have also been made with the E.S.B. and the local Gas Company to be prepared for an immediate black-out in the event of a sudden warning. Trials for a black-out will take place early next week. No other precautions are being taken, under the advice of the Department.

FOOD PRICES.

Dublin Provision Exchange announce that by order of the Food Defence Committee, to-day's prices of all food commodities have been fixed at standstill prices until further notice.

PARLIAMENTARY SECRETARY RESIGNS.

Mr. Sean O'Grady, T.D., has resigned his office as Parliamentary Secretary to the Minister for Defence. His resignation takes effect from the 29th August, 1939.

Mr. Sean Moylan, T.D., has been appointed Parliamentary Secretary to the Minister for Defence with effect as from the 29th August.

Mr. O'Grady continues to hold his office as Parliamentary Secretary to the Minister of Lands.

LABOUR PROBLEMS.

Dublin, Friday.—The international crisis was under consideration by the Irish

(CONTINUED ON PAGE TEN.)

1940

Unsurprisingly, by 1940 the war dominated the daily newspapers. Any ideas that the conflict would be a distant affair were also shattered in the summer when the evacuation of Allied forces from Dunkirk left much of Europe in German hands. Hitler was now within striking distance of Britain and one of the options being considered in Germany was to first invade Ireland, possibly with the help of the IRA who saw the war as a means of ending partition.

There also existed the possibility of Ireland being invaded by the Allies. De Valera assured the British that Ireland's neutrality would be benevolent in their direction, and hundreds of IRA members were interned and several executed. Army reserves were expanded and a marine service tried to watch out for any signs of invaders. Several places in Ireland were bombed by German planes and three women were killed at Campile, Co Wexford. Irish diplomats in Berlin protested to the Germans and demanded reparation for the attacks. Meanwhile, around 50,000 Irish people, motivated by ideology, a quest for adventure or a steady income, joined the British army, often by making their way over the border, while thousands more found work in the war industry in Britain.

Terrific fights in sky offensive

Monday, August 26

Screaming bombs, the glow of a huge fire started by incendiary bombs, explosions from bombs and anti-aircraft guns signalised London's first big air raid on Saturday night following three earlier raids of smaller proportions.

The Press Association, describing the raid as "one phase of the Germans' fiercest air offensive of the war," tells how the three earlier attempts were beaten off. Then, in a fourth attack, a screaming bomb started a huge fire which bathed a large part of London in an orange glow.

Fire brigades, troops and Home Guards fought the flames, while in the distance could be heard the sound of guns above the murmur of a thousand voices from people in the streets who gathered to watch the spectacle despite repeated warnings.

A whole parish in another part of the capital went to the air raid shelter and held a prayer ceremony as the bombs fell. From the numerous fires started the Press Association says it seems likely that the missiles dropped were 'Molotov Breadbaskets' – large containers of incendiary bombs.

German planes drop bombs in Wexford

Tuesday, August 27

Keeping watch: With an invasion of Ireland a distinct possibility, the Local Security Force (LSF) undergo instruction in observation duties.

Three girls, two of them sisters, were killed, and a creamery, a grain store and a restaurant were wrecked when a German bomber flew over County Wexford yesterday afternoon and dropped a number of bombs.

When the machine approached Campile, a little village about nine miles from New Ross, it was flying at about 5,000 feet and came in from the sea. It circled around the village and then dived and dropped two bombs, the first of which struck the Shelbourne Creamery, belonging to the Campile Co-operative Society.

The raider then made off, but returned shortly afterwards and dropped the third bomb which struck the railway siding, making a large opening in the ground and displacing the track.

Three of the employees of the creamery, Misses Kitty Kent, aged 23, Mary Ellen Kent, aged 28, and Kitty Hurley, aged 24, were buried beneath the debris of the restaurant, and their dead bodies were later recovered by military and Red Cross workers.

NEWS BRIEFS

June Winston Churchill, Prime Minister in Britain since May, admits that recent events in France had been a military disaster, but adds: "We shall go on to the end. We would defend Britain no matter what the cost, fighting on the beaches, in the fields, in the streets and in the hills." (4)

Aug A young Welsh lady coming over to Cork to get married told an *Examiner* reporter yesterday of her adventurous trip. Shortly before leaving her home in South Wales, a bomb fell close by, and at sea her steamer was machine-gunned from the air. Finally, driving to Cork from Rosslare, she was involved in a motor accident. When interviewed, the young lady looked little the worse for her adventures – quite the contrary in fact. (21)

Sept "Please see these four children safe to Cork." This was the inscription on a label tied around the neck of an 11-year-old girl who, accompanied by her three brothers, arrived in Dún Laoghaire. They were among 375 refugees – about 120 of whom were children – who had come from Hollyhead. (30)

The Cork Examiner.

CITY SPECIAL

No. 27,252.

WEDNESDAY MORNING, JUNE 5, 1940. PRICE—THREE HALFPENCE

Registered for transmission at newspaper Rate of Postage in Ireland and Great Britain and at Magazine Rate to Canada and Newfoundland.

THE ALLIED EVACUATION OF DUNKIRK COMPLETED

French Admiral Among The Last To Leave The Wrecked Port.

END OF FLANDERS CAMPAIGN

SEVEN DESTROYERS LOST BY FRANCE

THE FINAL STRUGGLE

TROOPS EMBARKED UNDER GERMAN MACHINE GUN FIRE.

The last of the defenders of Dunkirk have escaped to safety. This was announced yesterday by the French Admiralty, which added that before they embarked, the port was rendered useless to the Germans. Admiral Abrial, who was in command of the defending forces, was among the last to leave.

Describing the last hours of the struggle, the French communique said: "Until the last moment, first in the suburbs and then in the town itself, from house to house the rearguard put up a heroic resistance. The enemy, constantly reinforced, ceaselessly continued his assaults, and was ceaselessly counter-attacked. The last embarkations took place under the fire of German machine guns."

Seven French destroyers and a supply ship were lost out of 300 ships engaged at Dunkirk. The French War Ministry spokesman said last night that some of the Northern forces failed to escape through Dunkirk, among them General Prioux himself.

A statement issued from Hitler's headquarters last night claimed that prisoners taken in the Flanders campaign numbered 1,200,000 men, and that equipment in weapons and other war materials of from 75 to 80 divisions had been destroyed or captured.

(Press Association War Special).

Paris, Tuesday.—The French Admiralty announced to-day that the last land and naval forces defending Dunkirk were re-embarked during the night. The port had previously been rendered useless to the Germans.

The French Navy, it was added, had lost in the Dunkirk operations seven destroyers—the Jaguar, Chacal, l'Adroit, Bourrasque, Foudroyante, l'Ouragan and Sirocco, and the supply ship Niger.

The communique reads:—"During the night of June 3-4 the last of the land and naval forces, which under the command of Admiral Abrial, were defending Dunkirk, to permit the withdrawal of the Allied armies of the north, were all embarked in good order after having rendered the port unusable. By their close co-operation British and French marines have thus completed an operation unique in history—an operation which has enabled more than [illegible] men of the Allied armies to be rescued.

"Three hundred French warships and merchant vessels of various sizes, with 200 smaller boats, as well as numerous formations of the naval air arm, took part in this operation. We lost the Contre-Torpilleurs, Jaguar, and Chacal, the Torpilleurs, l'Adroit, Bourrasque, Foudroyant, l'Ouragan, and Sirocco, and the supply ship Niger. Most of the crews were saved. Other ships were damaged, but some of them have already put to sea again. The French Admiralty knows that the success of such an enterprise necessarily entails the sacrifice of a certain number of naval and air units. The crews themselves also [illegible]. They did their duty as a matter of course."

FRENCH COMMUNIQUE.

Desperate Final Struggle For Dunkirk

To-night's French official war communique states:—The embarkation of Allied troops from Dunkirk was completed to-day in conformity with the pre-arranged plan. Until the last moment, first in the suburbs, and then in the town itself from house to house, the rearguards put up a heroic resistance. The enemy, constantly reinforced, ceaselessly continued his assaults, and was ceaselessly counter-attacked. The last embarkations took place under the fire of German machine guns.

"This implacable defence and the success of these difficult and vast operations under the orders of Admiral Abrial and General Fagalde, have had a definite influence on the development of the struggle.

"Our soldiers, returning from the north, whose energy remains intact, are ready for fresh battles. During the embarkation operations our land, sea and air forces have shown an exceptional degree of co-operation to which the British land, naval, and air forces have brought untiring aid. Admiral Abrial declares that the work accomplished by the British was magnificent.

"The enemy had hoped by his enveloping movement to secure the capitulation of the British and French forces surrounded by him. From this trap they escaped by their own redoubtable energy. Fighting occurred this morning on the lower Somme, in which we took some prisoners."

BRITISH ADMIRALTY.

Tribute To Seamen "From Every Walk Of Life."

London, Tuesday.—The following signal has been sent out by the Admiralty to-day:—

"The Board of Admiralty congratulates all concerned in the successful evacuation of the B.E.F. and the soldiers of the Allied armies from the Dunkirk area. Their Lordships appreciate the splendid endurance with which all ships and personnel faced the continuous attack of enemy aircraft, and the physical strain imposed by long hours of arduous work in narrow waters over many days. The magnificent spirit of co-operation between the Navy, Army, Royal Air Force and Merchant Navy alone brought the operation to a successful conclusion. The ready willingness with which seamen from every walk of life came forward to assist their brother seamen of the Royal Navy will not readily be forgotten.

"Their Lordships also realise that success was only rendered possible by the great effort made by all shore establishments, and in particular by the Dover Command, who were responsible for the organisation and direction of this difficult operation."

WAR OFFICE ANNOUNCEMENT.

The War Office announced to-night: "The evacuation of the Allied forces from the Dunkirk area has now been successfully completed, the last troops being withdrawn during the night of 3rd-4th June.

"The outstanding success of this operation, which must rank as one of the most difficult operations of war ever undertaken, has been due to the magnificent fighting qualities of the Allied troops, to their calmness and discipline in the worst of conditions, to their devotion to duty of the Allied navies, and to the gallantry and exertions of the Royal Air Force.

"As the result, although our losses have been considerable, they are small in comparison to those which a few days ago seemed inevitable.

"South of the Somme our troops are now operating in conjunction with the French. To-day has been a quiet day on the British front."

NAVY THANKS R.A.F.

"Devotion Of Our Comrades In The Air."

A message expressing the gratitude to the R.A.F. of those engaged on the Dunkirk evacuation has been sent by the Vice-Admiral, Dover, to the Commanders-in-Chief of the Fighter, Bomber and Coastal Commands of the R.A.F.

The message says: "I and the forces under my command, who have been engaged on the evacuation of the Allied armies, owe a deep debt of gratitude to the R.A.F. for the support and protection which they have given to us. We are fully conscious of the severe strain these operations have imposed on all taking part, and we are filled with admiration for the courage and devotion of our comrades in the air."

Air Chief Marshal Sir Cyril Newall, Chief of the Air Staff, said in reply: "I express to you my warmest congratulations on the magnificent success which you have achieved."

KING'S MESSAGE TO FRANCE.

The King to-day addressed to the President of the French Republic the following telegram:—

"Our armies of the North, fighting side by side, have with the help of the fearless and unflinching efforts of the Allied navies and air forces come through an ordeal that has proved their courage, discipline and fighting power. The gallantry of this comradeship in arms has shown the enemy the measure of Allied bravery and resolution which will meet him in the battles that are to come.

"May I express to you, Monsieur le President, the profound gratitude and admiration with which I and all my peoples have followed the great part played in these historic events by the French armed forces. We sympathise in the losses that France has sustained, but recognise in them the measure of French heroism and devotion.—George, R.I."

APPEAL TO BELGIANS.

"Fight For Liberation Of Your Country."

A moving appeal to Belgian soldiers to fight on for the liberation of their country was issued to-day by General Denis, the Belgian Minister of National Defence.

"All that made up your happiness in life has passed into the hands of the invader in spite of the heroic resistance of the army against an enemy twenty times superior in numbers," states the appeal. "You have had the luck to escape from the inferno of the German occupation, from the threats and moral torture which that brings in its wake.

"United to the cause of the Allies by the same ideal of justice and liberty, Walloons and Flemings, fraternally re-assembling under the folds of the national flag, must henceforth cherish only one object, one thought—to drive the odious invader from the national soil.

"Soldiers of Belgium, let us swear all

(CONTINUED ON PAGE SIX.)

"RAIDERS PASSED!"

Wreckage in a French village near the front caused by heavy calibre bombs dropped by German planes. (A.P.).

REPRISALS RAIDS.

ALLIED AIRMEN REPAY FOR 906 PARIS RAID CASUALTIES.

MUNICH, FRANKFORT AND THE RUHR BOMBED.

Paris, Tuesday.—Military objectives in Munich, Frankfort-On-Main, and the Ruhr were bombed by Allied warplanes as a reprisal for yesterday's raid on Paris, the official Havas Agency announced to-night. It has now been established that 25 of the German bombers taking part in yesterday's raid were brought down. It was officially announced to-night that the casualties in yesterday's raid on Paris numbered 906—254 killed and 652 wounded. Of the dead 195 were civilians and 59 members of the military forces. 545 civilians and 107 military were wounded.

Categorically denying the claim of the German High Command regarding the number of French planes destroyed in the raid, the Paris radio in its German broadcast to-night said: "The truth is that four French planes were shot down and ten damaged on the ground. Seventeen German planes were brought down, and in addition several were destroyed by British fighters who intercepted them on the way home."

Earlier to-night it was officially stated that it had now been established that 25 German bombers had been brought down. To-day's German High Command communique claimed that 104 French planes were shot down during the raid, and 300 to 400 planes were destroyed in hangars, or on the ground. According to French sources many more than 25 German planes were seen to be in difficulties. Parisians did not turn a hair when they heard the official result of the great air attack. Dress shops in Paris were as crowded as ever to-day with women ordering new frocks, and all other spheres of life are back to normal. The police have cordoned off the bombed areas and spectators are not welcomed. A 1,000 kilogramme bomb, it is now learnt, destroyed one building of a factory. The place was still burning this morning. Several unexploded bombs were dismantled by experts in the same building.

THE REPRISAL QUESTION.

French And German Views.

Paris, Tuesday.—Authorised sources in Paris this afternoon said that in view of the fact that the Paris raid was held to have been directed at military objectives, aerodromes and factories, and that the resulting civilian casualties were not deliberate, the French could, therefore, "justifiably attack factories around Berlin, but not civilians themselves."

Berlin, Tuesday.—Nazi authorised sources, replying to a question whether yesterday's Paris air raid was a retaliation for the repeated Allied air raids on Western German localities, stated to-day: "It was not a retaliatory operation, but merely one directed solely at military objectives."

The official German News Agency continues to publish details of alleged Allied air raids on non-military objectives in Germany. The German *Press*, while maintaining that yesterday's raid on Paris was only on French Air Force establishments, scornfully rejects the Allies' assurance that only military objectives have been attacked in Germany.

GERMAN ATTACKS.

Raiders Start Fires In Le Havre.

Fires were started by incendiary bombs in Le Havre when German bombers continued their recent attacks on the port last night and to-day. While the people of Paris were still mourning their dead and injured in yesterday's raid, and the tragic task of searching the debris of destroyed and battered buildings continued, the sound of anti-aircraft gunfire and the drone of aeroplane engines overhead were again heard in the capital early this morning, but no alarm was given. Some bombs dropped yesterday had a delayed-action fuse and were still exploding this morning, said a French military spokesman. Factories, aerodromes and railway lines in the Paris region had been bombed.—Associated Press.

OVER RHONE VALLEY.

Berne, Tuesday.—German bombers were reported to-night to have attacked French Rhone Valley bases again. The exact objectives could not be learned. It was presumed that the bombers shot down by the Swiss strayed from these squadrons and had crossed the Swiss frontier despite anti-aircraft fire. A number of Swiss fighters promptly attacked them.—Associated Press.

THE ALLIES' REPLY.

Industrial Targets Bombed In Reprisals Raid.

Oil depots and storage tanks in Western Germany were attacked by a strong force of R.A.F. heavy bombers on Monday for the third night in succession, states the Air Ministry News Service. Direct hits with high explosives and incendiary bombs were registered on many of the targets, and trails of fire, followed by violent explosions, made evident the success of the night's operations, which also included attacks on industrial targets and communication centres. These attacks, states the Press Association, were part of the operations carried out by the Allies in reprisal for the raid on Paris. The area covered by the raiders extended from Emmerich, in the North, to Frankfurt in the South. At Emmerich several groups of oil tanks were set on fire. For miles around the glow of the fires enabled later raiders to locate their targets with ease. In another attack a series of explosions was followed by a pall of smoke so dense that a large part of the target area was entirely covered. At Monheim several attacks were made on a munitions works. Hundreds of incendiary bombs were released and fires burst with a bright green flame all over the target. High explosive bombs caused "large green explosions." At many points in the Ruhr fuel plants, oil tanks and munition works were successfully bombed.

Strong opposition was encountered from guns of light and heavy calibre, all working in close co-operation with searchlights. At Krefeld one large concentration of searchlights ceased to operate after a number of bombs had been dropped near them, while elsewhere other searchlights were machine-gunned and put out of action.

GHENT RAIDED.

At least three big oil tanks were set on fire when aircraft of the Coastal Command raided Ghent last night. The flames floodlit the countryside for the British aircraft flying at 10,000 feet, says an Air Ministry bulletin. Other Coastal Command aircraft again raided other military objectives in Holland. Pilots and crews said on their return that the display of searchlights, pom-pom fire and high explosives put the Crystal Palace fireworks to shame.

DEFENCE FORCES

The Services Of Ex-Officers In Ireland

The Government Information Bureau has issued the following:

The Department of Defence is at the moment receiving large numbers of enquiries from ex-officers in relation to the present expansion of the Defence Forces.

The General Headquarters staff are anxious that all such applicants should understand that the essential first step to joining the forces in any capacity is to complete National Service Enrolment Form No. 1, which can be obtained at any Gardai station. It has been arranged that all forms completed by ex-officers or other citizens deemed suitable for commissioned rank will be expeditiously segregated and classified and further action, if necessary, will follow with the minimum of delay.

The submission of personal letters to the Department or to individual officers, T.D.s, Senators, etc., is not required and only results in adding to the difficulties of already overworked staffs.

All applications made on the standard National Service Enrolment Form No. 1 will receive full and careful consideration, and ex-officers and others concerned will facilitate the army authorities if they follow these simple instructions.

BAN ON "DERRY JOURNAL" LIFTED.

Belfast, Tuesday.—The Northern Ireland Minister of Home Affairs (Sir Dawson Bates) to-night withdrew the ban on the circulation within Northern Ireland of the "Derry Journal," a tri-weekly Nationalist newspaper, published in Derry. The order imposing the ban was issued on Saturday last.

ITALY STILL SILENT.

Reynaud Says "Door Still Open."

FRENCH OFFER.

Rome Cabinet Meets—No Announcement.

Rome, Tuesday.—The Italian Cabinet assembled to-day for what was expected to be a fateful meeting, but no announcement of any fresh war decision was made afterwards. An American comment was that obviously the Allies were doing better and keeping Mussolini out. It was stated that the Cabinet approved ordinary administrative measures. These included tightening up war organisation. Many people here believe that the Cabinet could not have failed to discuss graver questions than those mentioned in the announcement which followed its meeting. The net result appears to be that Italy's position with regard to the war is unchanged. One rumour current here to-night is that members of the Services must be at their posts by June 16. Rumours that the Fascist Grand Council and the Supreme Defence Council are to meet are not confirmed.

The Fascist Press for days past has been giving prominence to shoals of telegrams from organisations and private persons clamouring in general terms "for the privilege of fighting for the country's independence." Some of these emanate from the finest bodies of Italian troops, such as the Alpine regiments. The emphasis given to these telegrams is apparently aimed at whipping up enthusiasm among the general public. Another feature of the Press is a mass of telegrams from Berlin expressing gratitude for the "efficient help that Italian non-belligerence has brought to Germany." Readers are asking: "If that is so, why not let us continue as non-belligerents."—War Special.

RADIO COMMENT.

Rome radio in its English broadcast to-night said:—"The results of this meeting are by no means to be taken as an indication that Italy has changed her intentions. She is still prepared to take up arms and fight for her rights at any time she thinks fit."—Press Association War Special.

Mr. Paul Reynaud, French Premier, told the Senate Foreign Affairs Commission that if Italy entered the war she did so deliberately to wage war, adding that the door to discussion of outstanding questions was still open and had never been closed.

A significant article in the Soviet paper, "Trud," describes Italy's "anti-Allied hullaballoo" as a smoke-screen to cover her Balkan aspirations. Yugoslavia well understands "the Italian menace," it was added. "However peaceful Italian assurances are Yugoslavia can only pretend to believe them."

LONDON VIEW.

London, Tuesday.—As was to be expected, no decisive statement emerged after the meeting of the Italian Cabinet to-day, the reports sent out from Rome regarding the meeting referring almost entirely to internal affairs, writes the Press Association diplomatic correspondent. This is not to say, however, that more important matters were not under discussion. At any time Signor Mussolini may announce at short notice his final decisions. He may at any moment decide to plunge Italy into war, or he may continue his present attitude of non-belligerency and thus help his Axis partner by immobilising a large French army on the Italian-French frontier, and by giving such supplies to Germany as he is able.

COMMONS STATEMENT.

Britain May Raise Parachutists.

Mr. Eden, British War Minister, replying to a question in the House of Commons, yesterday, as to whether he intended to organise a corps of parachutists and gliders, said that recent operations were being carefully studied in order to decide if any changes in the organisation of the army were required. It would not be in the national interest to make any further announcement at this stage.

Replying to further questions, Mr. Eden pointed out that he had referred to recent operations. It was these recent operations, which were a new development of a method practiced before, which was now being studied. Mr. Eden stated in reply to questions that during recent operations the enemy had deliberately bombed hospital carriers in circumstances which admitted of no mistake. He was not at present prepared to remove the red cross or other distinctive markings from hospital accommodation in England. He further stated that the desirability of transporting internees and prisoners of war to places remote from the British Isles was under consideration.

"WE SHALL GO ON TO THE END"

STATEMENT BY BRITISH PREMIER

THE BATTLE OF THE PORTS

"COLOSSAL MILITARY DISASTER" SAYS MR. CHURCHILL.

Mr. Winston Churchill told the House of Commons yesterday the story of the battle of the ports. He disclosed that British losses exceeded 30,000 killed, wounded or missing, but confessed that he feared only a week ago that "the whole root and core and brain of the British Army" was doomed to perish or be led into ignominious captivity. The Navy, however, using nearly a thousand ships, had carried 335,000 men—British and French—out of the jaws of death back to their native land—and to the tasks immediately before them.

"But our thankfulness at the escape of our Army must not blind us to the fact that what had happened was a colossal military disaster," he added.

There were now more troops in Britain than they had ever had, but they would not be content with a defensive war. He announced, too, that the defences of Britain would be discussed in secret session, and concluded:—"We shall go on to the end. We would defend Britain no matter what the cost, fighting on the beaches, in the fields, in the streets and the hills. We would never surrender, and, even if this island were subjugated and starving, the Empire would carry on the struggle until in God's good time the new world, with all its power and might, sets forth to the liberation and rescue of the old."

In a statement on the war situation made in the House of Commons yesterday afternoon, the Prime Minister, Mr. Winston Churchill, said that from the moment that the French defences at Sedan and on the Meuse were broken, at the end of May, only a rapid retreat to Amiens and the south could have saved the British and French armies who had entered Belgium at the appeal of the Belgian King.

But this strategical plan was not immediately realised. The French High Command hoped they would be able to close the gap, and the armies of the north were under their orders. Moreover, a retirement of this kind would have involved almost certainly the destruction of the fine Belgian army of over twenty divisions, and the abandonment of the whole of Belgium.

Therefore, when the force and scope of the German penetration was realised, and when the new French Generalissimo General Weygand, assumed command in place of General Gamelin, an effort was made by the French and British armies in Belgium to keep on holding the right hand of the Belgians, and to give their own right hand to the newly created French army, which was to have advanced across the Somme in great strength to clasp it.

GERMAN SURPRISE.

The German units, however, swept like a sharp scythe, aiming at our armies of the North. They consisted of eight or nine armoured divisions, each of about 400 armoured vehicles of different kinds. This force cut off all communications between us and the main French army. It severed our communications for food and munitions. It ran first to Amiens and afterwards to Abbeville and turned its way up the coast from Boulogne and Calais—almost to Dunkirk.

Behind this armoured and mechanised onslaught came German divisions and lorries, and behind again came plodding the dull, brute mass of the German army—always so ready to be the lead to the trampling down of any other land which has the liberty and comfort that they have never known in their own.

This armoured scythe-stroke almost reached Dunkirk—almost, but not quite. Boulogne and Calais were the scene of desperate fighting. The Guards defended Boulogne for a while and were then withdrawn by orders from this country. The Rifle Brigade, the 60th Rifles, and the Queen Victoria's Rifles, with a battalion of British tanks and a thousand Frenchmen (in all about 4,000 strong) defended at Calais to the last.

The British commander was given an hour to surrender. He spurned the offer and four days of intense fighting passed before a silence reigned over Calais.

Only thirty unwounded survivors were brought off by the navy, and we do not know the fate of their comrades. Their sacrifice was not, however, in vain. At least two armoured divisions which otherwise would have been turned against the British Expeditionary Force had to be sent for to overcome them. They have added another page to the glory of the light division, and the time gained enabled the Gravelines water line to be held by the French troops, and thus it was that the port of Dunkirk was kept open.

"FORLORN HOPE."

When it was found impossible for the armies of the North to re-open their communications through Amiens with the main French armies, only one test remained. It seemed, indeed, forlorn. The Belgian, British, and French armies were almost surrounded; their sole line of retreat was through a single port, and through its neighbouring beaches. They were pressed on every side by heavy attacks, and far outnumbered in the air.

When a week ago to-day I asked the House to fix this afternoon as the occasion for a statement, I feared it would be my hard lot to announce the greatest military disaster in our long history. I thought, and some good judges agreed with me, that perhaps 20,000 or 30,000 men might be re-embarked, but it certainly seemed that the whole of the French first army, and the whole of the B.E.F. north of the Amiens-Abbeville gap would be broken up in the open field, or else have to capitulate for lack of food and ammunition. These were the hard and heavy tidings for which I called upon the House and the nation to prepare themselves a week ago. The whole root and core of the brave British army on which we were to build, and are to build, the great British armies of the later years of the war seemed about to perish upon the field or be led into ignominious and starving captivity. That was the prospect a week ago. But another blow, which might well have proved fatal, was yet to fall upon us.

BELGIAN DEFECTION.

Mr. Churchill recalled that it was the Allies who rescued Belgium from extinction in the last war. Had they not sought refuge in what has proved to be a fatal neutrality the French and British armies might well at the very outset have saved not only Belgium but, perhaps, even Poland. Yet at the last moment, when Belgium was already invaded King Leopold called upon us to come to his aid, and even at the last moment we came. His brave and efficient army, nearly half a million strong, was on our eastern flank and was upon our only line of retreat to the sea.

Suddenly, without prior consultation with the least possible notice, without the advice of his Ministers, upon his own personal act, he sent a plenipotentiary to the German Command surrendering his army and exposing our whole flank without the means of retreat. (Cries of "Shame").

"I asked the House a week ago to suspend judgment, because the facts were not clear. But I do not feel that any reason now exists why we should not form our own opinion upon this pitiful episode (cheers and shouts of 'Treachery').

"The surrender of the Belgian army compelled the British, at the shortest notice, to cover a flank to the sea, more than 30 miles in length; otherwise they would have been cut off, and all would have shared the fate to which King Leopold had condemned the finest army his country had ever formed.

"In doing this he closed his flank. Contact was lost inevitably between the British, and two out of the three corps forming the First French Army, who were still further from the coast than we were, and it seemed impossible that any large number of Allied troops could reach the coast. The enemy attacked on all sides in great strength.

BATTLE ON BEACHES.

"Their main power, the power of their far more numerous air force, was thrown into the battle or concentrated on the beaches of Dunkirk. The enemy began to fire with cannon on the beaches. They sowed magnetic mines in the Channels and seas, and sent repeated waves of hostile aircraft, sometimes more than 100 strong, to the coast to bomb the troops as they were arriving. U-boats, one of which was sunk, and motor launches, took their toll of the vast traffic.

"For four or five days an intense struggle raged. Great masses of German

(CONTINUED ON PAGE SIX.)

WESTERN SEABOARD!

"Air And Submarine Attack Via Eire."

London, Tuesday.—Sir Henry Morris-Jones (L., Denbigh) asked the Prime Minister in the House of Commons to-day whether he was satisfied that, in our measures of defence in this country adequate safeguards had been taken to protect us from an attack on and through our western seaboard by air and submarine via the Dominion of Eire, and whether, in particular, adequate armed [illegible] and personnel was provided for the Isle of Man, Anglesey, Bardsey, Lundy, [illegible] and Walney Islands.

Mr. Attlee referred Sir Henry on the first part of his question to a reply made last month to a similar query. As regards the second part, he said that he did not think it would be desirable to enter into particulars.

1941

The war escalated on all fronts in 1941, but December saw two events that marked the turning of the tide in favour of the Allies. The Japanese attack on Pearl Harbor brought the USA into the conflict and, more significantly for the fight in Europe, the Soviet Union began to make some gains against the invading Germans. Hitler had overstretched himself with an invasion of the Soviet Union that had come within 40 miles of Moscow, and was now paying the price as a fierce winter helped Stalin's forces gain the upper hand.
In April, bombing raids on Belfast killed around 700 people and prompted the Irish Government to send ambulances and fire-brigades across the border, while hundreds of refugees flowed in the opposite direction. All the more dangerous animals at Belfast Zoo were shot in case they escaped. A few weeks later, searchlights and anti-aircraft guns went into action in Dublin as German planes dropped bombs that led to 34 deaths.

The 'big push' is on

Monday, March 24

Cork's 'big push' has begun. On city streets, along suburban avenues, on country roads, morning and evening, the bicycle – the push bike, whose doom was said to have been sealed by the advent of the motor car – is coming back to its own with an unprecedented rush.

The variety of circumstances which have helped to make complete the 'come back' of the lowly bicycle were pithily summarised by one of the new cyclists who said last week: "Petrol stocks have gone down, bus fares are going up, spring is here, so it's wheel and saddle for me."

The aftermath of a train crash near Farranfore, Co Kerry, in which two railway guards lost their lives when the bridge they were crossing collapsed during raging floods.

Japan declares war on US and Britain

Monday, December 8

Japan has declared war on Great Britain and America. This dramatic boiling-over of the Pacific cauldron of tension which sets the whole world in flames was heralded by a lightning thrust by Japanese warships and bombers on US naval and military bases in the Hawaiian and Philippine Islands. Heavy casualties were inflicted, one bomb on an airfield killing 350.
Almost simultaneously, Shanghai International Settlement was occupied by the Japanese who sank a British gunboat. Big sea battles are developing. The American Air Force has taken to the air and their army is mobilising. Congress has been recalled, and last night it was announced from London that the British Parliament will meet today.
News of the attacks on American bases was given to the world by Mr Roosevelt from the White House. Pearl Harbor, Cahu, and Honolulu in the Hawaiian Islands are being subjected to repeated air attacks with heavy damage and loss of life. Naval and military centres in the Philippines are being similarly attacked, Manila, a big US naval base, being the chief target. An American transport has been sunk and the battleship *Oklahoma* is ablaze in Pearl Harbor.

NEWS BRIEFS

Jan Zurich – The family announced today that James Joyce will be buried tomorrow with a non-denominational religious service in the Cemetery Chapel. (15)

Apr Belfast buried its dead, or rather continued doing so today. Van after van of their burden of death were to be seen wending their way to different cemetaries. Nine big military lorries, each containing from eight to ten coffins, and more, were necessary to convey the unidentified dead. (22)

May Disturbances have broken out in Baghdad, where Arab irregulars fill the streets, 'shooting up' passers-by, and making the night hideous with their cries. Looting is widespread. Foreigners only venture out under a strong police escort. (31)

The Cork Examiner

NO. 27,[illegible] MONDAY MORNING, JUNE 2, 1941. PRICE—THREE HALFPENCE

Registered for transmission at newspaper Rate of Postage in Ireland and Great Britain and at Magazine Rate in Canada and Newfoundland.

PROTEST TO BERLIN AS DUBLIN'S DEATH ROLL MOUNTS

Eire Asks For "Definite Assurances" Of Future Bomb Immunity.

MORE BODIES IN THE DEBRIS

TWENTY-NINE PEOPLE STILL MISSING

SUNDAY ALARM

ANOTHER BOMB DROPPED IN CO. WICKLOW.

The Dublin bombing death roll has mounted to 30 and 29 other people are still unaccounted for, the "Cork Examiner" learned late last night. About 80 were injured and their was considerable damage to property.

While the rescue work was still proceeding, yesterday, the Government having established that the bombs dropped were of German origin, directed a protest "in the strongest terms" to Berlin, demanding compensation and reparation.

The Charge d'Affairs in the German capital is being further directed to ask for definite assurances that the strictest instructions will be given to prevent the flight of German aircraft over Irish territory and territorial waters.

A bomb was dropped at 1.7 a.m., yesterday, near Arklow, but no lives were lost. Planes also passed over Dun Laoghaire during the night.

Our Dublin representative wrote [illegible] the death-roll among [illegible] were victims of the bombing at North Strand road on Saturday has reached thirty; one [illegible] to-day in [illegible] some bodies [illegible] throughout [illegible] the demolition [illegible] the ruins [illegible] The bodies still [illegible] twenty houses [illegible] result of the bomb [illegible] bodies have been [illegible]

[illegible] have been identified [illegible] Mrs. Browne (75), 21 North Strand [illegible] (Grace Browne (son), [illegible] Mary Browne (35), wife of Harry Browne; Maureen Browne (7) do.; [illegible] Browne [illegible] do.; Edward [illegible] Angela Browne (2), [illegible] Fitzpatrick, 28 North [illegible] Ellen Fitzpatrick, his [illegible] Madge Fitzpatrick, do.; [illegible] Mrs. McNally, [illegible] road; J. Murray, [illegible] Strand road; Mrs. Ellen [illegible] North Strand road; [illegible] 162 North Strand [illegible] Elizabeth Daly, 162 North [illegible]

[illegible] 11 North Strand [illegible] Richmond Hospital.

[illegible] all the other [illegible] satisfactory [illegible]

[illegible]—Six bodies [illegible] Morgue—one body [illegible] about 11 in the Mater [illegible] bodies (a man and a [illegible] to be Mr. and Mrs. [illegible]

[illegible] Thomas Carroll, [illegible] and the bodies of a [illegible] woman were removed from [illegible]

Capt. McDonagh, the A.R.P. Area Warden, informed a "Cork Examiner" representative late last night, when searching ended for the night, that twenty-nine people, believed to have resided in the demolished houses, are still unaccounted for.

[illegible] that there are still a [illegible] uncovered bodies. The [illegible] searching will be resumed [illegible]

GOVERNMENT STATEMENT.

[illegible] statement was issued [illegible] Information Bureau [illegible] regrets to announce [illegible] of the bombs dropped [illegible] during the early hours of [illegible] at least 27 persons [illegible] and about 80 received [illegible] considerable damage to [illegible] caused. A further bomb [illegible] near Arklow on this [illegible] No lives were lost, [illegible] was some damage to [illegible]

Investigations having shown that the bombs dropped were of German origin, the Charge d'Affaires in Berlin is being directed to protest in the strongest terms to the German Government against the violation of Irish territory and to claim compensation and reparation for the loss of life, the injuries suffered and the damage to property.

[illegible] being further directed to ask [illegible] assurances that the strictest [illegible] will be given to prevent the [illegible] German aircraft over Irish [illegible] and territorial waters."

RADIO APPEAL.

The following message was broadcast [illegible] Radio Eireann to-night:—"Four [illegible] who resided in house 133 [illegible] North Strand Road, Dublin, are [illegible] missing. It is possible that [illegible] of them may be staying with friends in Dublin or somewhere in the country. Will these persons please communicate at once with [illegible] J. McDonagh, Area Warden, telephone number, Dublin 76923, or any [illegible] station."

In a second message the Government, on behalf of the whole nation, expresses its sympathy with all who have been bereaved or have suffered injury or loss in the bombing.

The Government also wishes to express its appreciation of the splendid services rendered by the Gardai, A.R.P. organisation, L.S.F., the first-aid medical services, and in particular the Red Cross and St. John Ambulance Brigade and the staffs of the city hospitals who gave such devoted care to the injured.

THE ARKLOW BOMB.

The bomb dropped near Arklow fell in a field at Lamberton, about a quarter of a mile from Arklow, causing a crater measuring 15 feet by 12 feet. The field was under wheat and there was no injury to human life or livestock.

Twenty houses in the neighbourhood had their windows shattered by the force of the explosion, which occurred at 1.7 a.m.

Planes which searchlights failed to locate passed over Dun Laoghaire early yesterday morning also.

AIR RAID SHELTERS IN USE.

During the bombing on Saturday morning Dublin air raid shelters were used by the public for the first time.

When the first bombs dropped wardens in various districts opened the shelters, and in the North Strand area where death and destruction struck so suddenly, people sought protection in the shelters.

No air raid sirens were sounded, however. This is in accordance with the practice of a neutral country where citizens naturally do not expect bombing from the planes of belligerents.

An appeal for funds, clothing, and any other forms of help has been issued by the Irish Red Cross Society and the St. John Ambulance Brigade, who have dealt with hundreds of cases since Friday, and are definitely short of funds. A statement from Mr. Justice Conor Maguire and Sir John Lumsden, the respective chairmen of the organisations, says they "cannot carry on their work with empty hands."

BOMBING DESCRIBED.

The impression gained by a Corkman who was in Dublin during the bombing was that the first explosion heard was terrifying in its effect.

He said that about 1 o'clock he heard the aeroplanes coming over the city, and then the searchlights began to criss-cross in the sky in an endeavour to locate them.

"I jumped out of bed and dressed," he said, "and then I heard the ground defences going into action. The planes seemed to pass out from the city, but after a short while they returned. Then I saw some flares and tracer shots and once again the ground defences got busy, and there were several explosions.

"This continued for about fifteen minutes, and then there was a tremendous explosion, followed by vivid flashes, which illuminated the entire city. By this time everybody was out on the streets, standing at doors or looking out windows."

He added that he could not get beyond Amiens Street owing to crowds, but from there the flames could be clearly seen on the top of North Strand. He remarked that from what he saw in the early hours of the morning a tremendous amount of damage must have been done.

The military, A.R.P., L.S.F., and other casualty workers were very quickly in action, and in particular he was struck by the efficiency of the A.R.P. personnel, which included young and old men, women and girls, who remained on duty on the streets throughout the night.

On Saturday morning German planes were over Northern Ireland, but no bombs were dropped.

Cove, Sunday.—Prayers for the repose of their souls were requested at all the Masses in St. Colman's Cathedral, to-day, for the victims of the Dublin bombing yesterday.

LIMERICK SYMPATHY.

At a meeting of the Limerick County Council a resolution of sympathy was passed to the bereaved families.

COUNTY CORK DEPUTY'S ACCOUNT.

A County Cork deputy, who was in Dublin during the raid, said that he had not retired to bed when he first heard the aeroplanes. "I could hear the 'planes distinctly," he said, "and at the same time I saw the searchlights. I could hear our own anti-aircraft guns I went to bed, also I was not long there when I heard one terrific explosion. This was about 2 o'clock in the morning, and it rocked the whole city, and I think it must be the explosion that damaged the houses beyond Annesley Bridge." He added that after that he remained about for some time but he heard no further explosions.

"IRAQ TROUBLES OVER."

Britain Grants An Armistice.

The news of the armistice was revealed when the following communique was issued from British G.H.Q. yesterday:—"Following our acceptance of an armistice, which was asked for by the committee set up to administer Baghdad after the flight of Rashid Ali and his gang, the situation in the city remains quiet."

A Press Association message says that the terms of the armistice published in Cairo include the return of the Iraqui Army to a peace-time basis, the release of all British prisoners and the internment of all German and Italian prisoners, who are stated to number several hundred. Iraqui prisoners are to be handed over to the Regent.

The Regent of Iraq was given an enthusiastic welcome when he returned to Baghdad yesterday, says a London report. He was greeted by the British Ambassador and the British Commander-in-Chief of the Forces in Iraq, a few minutes after his arrival.

The Commander-in-Chief paid a glowing tribute to the work of the R.A.F., who had given an excellent example of the co-operation between an army in the field and air forces. It was possible that the attack made on the Iraq machine-gun nests by the R.A.F. on Friday night was the cause of the final break in their morale, for an hour or two afterwards they asked the British Ambassador to find out what would be the terms of an armistice.

The armistice was signed yesterday evening.

The six-year-old boy King, Feisul II, is reported to be safe in Baghdad.

It is also learned that the Governor of the Mosul area, where the oilfields are situated, is an opponent of Rashid Ali's movement so it is considered that the Iraq trouble is virtually at an end.

IRAQ OIL FIELDS "INTACT."

Vichy, Sunday.—A Baghdad despatch received here says that the Mosul oilfields are intact. Police have had no trouble for the past 48 hours in Baghdad, where the situation is quiet.—Press Association.

BRITAIN WILL RESPECT IRAQI INDEPENDENCE.

Sunday.—Britain will abstain from any infringement of Iraqi independence and will afford the Regent every help in re-establishing the legal government of the country, says the Press Association. These are the chief provisions of the armistice signed in Iraq yesterday afternoon, it is learned in London to-day. Drawn up in accordance with the British Government's declared policy, it is further designed to assist the Iraqi nation to resume its normal and prosperous existence.

BRITAIN SHOULD TAKE SYRIA, SAYS TURKS.

Ankara, Sunday.—Turkish unanimity that Britain's next move should be to take over Syria has become stronger since Mr. Eden's remarks about Arab independence. The man in the street does not want to see German troops on yet another frontier, but on the contrary, would welcome Britain, an ally and friend, as a neighbour, even if only for the duration of hostilities. Cyprus, most Turks say, will be the next German objective, and then Syria, where, according to some reports, the Germans have more materials, and their plans are more advanced than is generally supposed.

The position of Egypt, the Turks feel, is safe.

They point out that the Germans have not yet reached the Western Desert defences of Mersa Matruh or reduced the British-held fortified Libyan town of Tobruk, while the Navy is constantly menacing the German lines of communication.—Press Association.

A Teheran (Iran) message says Rashid Ali crossed the frontier on Friday at the Iranian frontier town of Kasr I Shirin. He was accompanied by Sherif Sharaf, by Amir Zaki, his chief of staff, and a group of officers.

The German news agency says that the British garrison at Habbaniyah is reported to have had considerable reinforcements of large troop and material transport from Transjordan.

Before leaving Baghdad Rashid Ali appointed his Minister for Economics, Yunis Al Sebawi, the Military Governor of the city. The new Governor has formed a Commission of Internal Security, which has ordered the dissolution of all military formations whose members are instructed to surrender their arms to the police and "resume civilian clothes."

A proclamation issued by the Commission appeals to the population to remain calm and disciplined.

GERMAN PLANS FOR SYRIA.

Ankara reports that the Germans are making preparations to land forces in Syria. Certain barracks have been evacuated by French troops, and many boats are being assembled north of Tripoli, and are being overhauled under German supervision. It appears that Germany's leading Near Eastern expert, Von Hentig, who is reported to have returned to Syria, travelling under a false passport and is now operating along the strip of Syrian territory traversed by the Turkey-Iraq railway line, where he is attempting to organise bands of volunteers.

IRISH RED CROSS

Flag Day Collection In Cork City

The annual flag day of the Cork City and County Branch of the Irish Red Cross took place on Saturday. The collectors were early on the streets and the public response to the appeal was very satisfactory.

LORD HUGH BERESFORD MISSING.

Telegrams received by his mother, the Duchess of St. Albans, and by his sister-in-law, the Marchioness of Waterford, announce that Lord Hugh Beresford, Lieut.-Commander, British destroyer Kelly, sunk in recent naval action in the Mediterranean, is missing and believed drowned.

DUBLIN BOMBING.

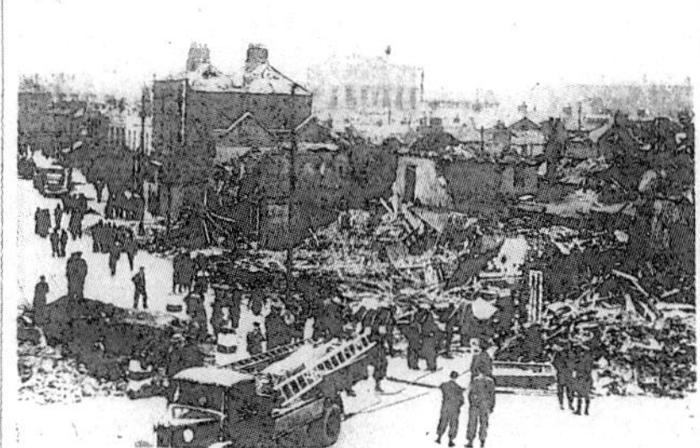

View of the wrecked houses in North Strand Road, Dublin, after Saturday morning's bombing. (Merriman).

POPE PIUS XII SPEAKS.

THE STATE AND "THE EXERCISE OF OTHER RIGHTS"

PONTIFF ON FREEDOM OF THE INDIVIDUAL.

Pope Pius XII broadcast from Vatican radio yesterday an address to commemorate the 50th anniversary of the Encyclical Rerum Novarum issued in 1891 by Pope Leo XIII says Reuter.

It was followed by Benediction "Urbi et Orbi" and the granting of a plenary indulgence.

Translations into European languages were broadcast later.

The Pope began his broadcast by sending Whitsuntide greetings to the followers of the Church throughout the world. He described his message as being one of love and comfort in the present difficult times. Wireless transmission which for many to-day amounted almost to a weapon of war, was for the Vatican an instrument of Providence in the nonstop task of pacification, said His Holiness. Thus it would appear that the miracle of Pentecost was renewed. Just as the many different peoples assembled in Jerusalem were able to hear the voice of St. Peter and the other apostles, so the Vatican across the ether called to the Catholic community.

"Within the general framework of labour and the reasonable development of all physical and spiritual energies of individuals and their free organisations," the Pope said, "a vast field of multiform activities is opened in which the public authority collaborates firstly by means of local cooperative or professional organisations, and then by reason of the State itself, whose superior and moderating social authority provides for a general economic equilibrium. It is, on the other hand, within the competence of the Church in that aspect of the social order into which moral considerations enter, to decide whether such social order is in accord with the unchangeable order of the Creator manifested by means of natural laws and the revelation. This is the twofold manifestation to which Leo XIII. appealed and with reason in his Encyclical. The Encyclical Rerum Novarum went deep into the hearts of the working classes. This call evoked a powerful response, and it is the clear duty of justice to recognise the progress which has been achieved in the lot of the workers through the pains taken by civil authorities in many lands. Hence it can be well understood that the Rerum Novarum became the magna charta of a Christian social endeavour."

Meanwhile, the Pope went on, half a century passed, leaving deep furrows and grievous disturbances both in nations and society, until the years finally poured their dark and turbulent waters into the sea of war "whose unforeseen currents may affect our economy and society."

The Pope then dealt with the problems likely to arise after the war, beginning with social evolution. Goods were created by God for all men and "the natural right to the use of material goods provides man with a secure basis of the highest import on which to rise with reasonable liberty to the fulfilment of his moral duties.

"To safeguard the rights of the human person and to facilitate the fulfilment of his duties," the Pope went on, "should be the essential office of every public authority.

"It follows that the care for such a common good does not imply a power so extensive over the members of the community that in virtue of it the public authority can interfere with the evolution of that individual activity which we have just described, to decide on the beginning or ending of human life, determine at will the manner of its physical, spiritual, religious and moral movement in opposition to the personal duties or rights of man, and to this end abolish or deprive of efficacy his natural right to material goods.

"The economic riches of a people did not properly consist in the abundance of goods but in that fact that such an abundance represented the material basis sufficient for the personal development of its members. If the scope of national economy is correctly considered it will become a guide for the efforts of statesmen and people and will enlighten them spontaneously to follow a path which does not call for continual exaction in goods and blood, but which will give fruits of peace and general well-being.

"The right to work was conceded to the individual in the first place by nature and not by society. From which it resulted that the right to organise labour belongs, above all, to those immediately interested, the employers and workers. Every legitimate and beneficial interference of the State in the field of labour should be such as to safeguard and respect personal character.

"This would happen if the State did not abolish or render impossible the exercise of other rights and duties equally personal: the worship of God, the right to marry, the right of husband and wife or father and mother to lead their married domestic life, the right to a reasonable freedom in the choice of a condition of life and of the fulfilment of a true vocation."

The Pope urged the more favourable distribution of men on the earth's surface, and a spirit of confidence between the countries of emigration and immigration.

The Pope urged the need for the co-operation of all. Failures common to all human activity should not make mankind forget the inspiring message of the Rerum Novarum which "to-morrow when the ruin of this world hurricane is cleared may be the outset of a reconception of a new social order worthy of God and man will keep living the noble flame of a brotherly social spirit.

"Nourish it, keep it burning even more brightly, carry it wherever a cry of pain reaches you," the Pope concluded.

THE POPE'S NAME DAY.

Vichy, Sunday.—Pope Pius XII. to-day received the College of Cardinals, who brought His Holiness their good wishes on the occasion of his name day, says a Vatican City despatch. The Cardinals were received separately in the Pope's library. The Festival of Saint Eugene falls to-morrow. The Pope's name is Eugenio Pacelli.—Reuter.

WATERFRONT FIRE.

U.S. Barges For Britain In Danger.

New York, Sunday.—A big fire broke out to-night on the Hudson River waterfront. So far there is no evidence of sabotage.—Reuter.

According to the Associated Press, G-men (United States Federal Government police) are investigating the fire. Nation-wide measures were taken during the week-end to guard vital defence factories and docks from a threatened outbreak of sabotage. Coastguard officials said that first reports indicated that barges loaded with war materials for Britain had not been damaged. Two American liners berthed were towed up the Hudson River to escape the flames, and firemen turned hoses as a precautionary measure on five Italian steamers seized several weeks ago by the U.S. Government.

The fire damaged a section of a warehouse filled with war orders of grain and rubber. How much of this material was destroyed has not yet been determined.

SPANISH PRISONERS.

Vichy, Sunday.—The Spanish Cabinet has decided to grant provisional liberty to 1,755 prisoners, according to a Madrid telegram.

Senor Benolio Manuel Santos has been appointed General Commissioner of Public Order, while Senor Francisco Greno is made Director-General of Social Welfare.—Reuter.

DUBLIN HOUSES COLLAPSE.

Three Dead In The Ruins.

SUNDAY ALARM.

Many Injured In Hospital.

Dublin, Sunday.—Three people were killed and a number of others injured when three houses collapsed this morning in Old Bride street at the rear of Jacob's biscuit factory.

The dead are Mrs. Bridget Lynskey (45), Old Bride street; her five months old baby, Noel, and Samuel O'Brien, a 72 years old pensioner of Messrs Arthur Guinness, Son and Co., who lived alone in the top back room of No. 46.

Shortly after 10 o'clock this morning the occupants of Nos. 45, 46 and 47 were startled when the walls of their houses began to bulge and the ceilings collapsed on top of them. Nos. 45 and 46, both of which are two-storeyed tenement houses, fell completely and sixteen residents were buried in the debris. Several succeeded in crawling out and four were rescued by the Fire Brigade.

Demolition squads, which had been working almost non-stop since Saturday morning at the scene of the bomb explosions were called from the North Strand and assigned the task of extricating Mrs. Lynskey and her son and Mr. O'Brien.

Doctors from the Adelaide Hospital pumped oxygen into the debris in the hope of keeping the Lynskeys alive, but when they were reached at 1.30 p.m. they were found to be dead. Samuel O'Brien was not discovered until half an hour later. He was alive when released, but died shortly after admission to the Meath Hospital.

No. 47 Old Bride street is occupied by a Mr. Harvey, his wife and six children and his mother-in-law. Only part of his house collapsed and all the occupants escaped uninjured. The house has since been razed as dangerous.

George Leigh, 16 Parnell road, a member of the Fire Brigade, was one of the first into the ruins, and although suffering badly from gas poisoning himself, he succeeded in dragging Mrs Georgina O'Brien, who was similarly affected, to safety. He was subsequently treated in the Adelaide Hospital. Mrs Georgina O'Brien and Miss Margaret Lawler were detained in the Adelaide Hospital and Miss Mary Lawler was detained in the Meath Hospital. The other injured, who, however, were allowed out after treatment, were Joseph Atkinson, Elizabeth O'Brien, Mary Doyle, Patrick Hodgins, James Doyle, Mary Doyle, Thomas Lynskey (husband of the dead woman), Esther Lynskey, Fray Lynskey and Patrick O'Brien.

Most of the injured lived in No. 46. Ambulances sent by the Red Cross Society were early on the scene and brought those who had been rendered homeless to the Hall at Merrill road, where they will be cared for until accommodation has been found for them.

A sad feature of the affair is that Mrs Lynskey had yesterday been given the key to a new Corporation house at Kimmage and she and her family were to have moved there on Tuesday next.

THIS LITTLE SCOUT'S GOOD DEED WAS FATAL

London, Sunday.—Two men and a boy Scout gave their lives in a brave but vain attempt to rescue a girl of seven who had fallen into a gas filled cavity in a North-Eastern town on Saturday.

Told that little Irene Page had slipped through the opening, which was only two feet wide, Mr. Edward Corbett sent for help, and the first to answer his call was Ernest Smith, a nine-year-old scout. "Put a rope round me and I'll go down," said Smith. He was lowered but collapsed. Then John Tulip, the girl's uncle, descended, but he, too, became unconscious. George Wanless, a fireman, was the next to make the attempt. He had a gas mask, but, although he was able, with the help of a man named Percy Wardle, to rescue Smith, he himself collapsed just afterwards. Eventually the girl and her uncle were brought to the surface. All efforts to revive the four insensible people failed.

BRITISH TROOPS REMOVED

THE WITHDRAWAL FROM CRETE

END OF STRUGGLE

"THE FIERCEST FIGHTING OF THE WAR."

The withdrawal of British troops from Crete was announced in London, yesterday. Some 15,000 have been taken to Egypt. The announcement adds: "It must be admitted that our losses have been severe." It is not indicated how many troops Britain had in Crete.

It is assumed, says the Press Association, "that General Freyberg came out with the troops that have been withdrawn." The Germans had previously claimed that he had been killed.

Yesterday's German communique claimed that 10,000 British and Greek troops had been taken prisoner and that "mopping up" was continuing, while the German radio, heard in New York, said that the British troops were attempting to reach Egypt in small fishing boats.

London, Sunday.—After twelve days of the fiercest fighting of the war, British troops have been withdrawn from Crete. A communique issued in London to-day states that "some 15,000 British troops have been removed to Egypt, but our losses have been severe."

The communique says:

"After twelve days of what has undoubtedly been the fiercest fighting in this war, it was decided to withdraw our forces from Crete.

"Although the losses we inflicted on the enemy's troops and aircraft have been enormous, it became clear that our naval and military forces could not be expected to operate indefinitely in and near Crete without more air support than could be provided from our bases in Africa.

"Some 15,000 of our troops have been withdrawn to Egypt, but it must be admitted that our losses have been severe."

GERMAN AIR SUPERIORITY.

Against overwhelming odds of air superiority the British forces put up a terrific struggle. The German troops, landing from troop carriers, gliders and by parachute, were mown down by the defence; but still they came, their planes maintaining a minute by minute time table, and each new arrival being preceded by the most ruthless and devastating bombing of the war.

It was the first large scale air borne invasion attempt in history and put into practice all the tricks by which the Germans have threatened to invade Britain. But the deciding factor was Britain's lack of fighter aircraft within reach of the battle area.

Against the devastation of the German air armada, British fighters had to be withdrawn from the weakly defended aerodromes, and from that point onwards Germany flung in large numbers of bombers of every kind, particularly dive bombers to blast a way for her paratroops. Aerodromes and beaches were littered with the blazing wreckage of Junkers troop carriers and the dead bodies of Germans, many of whom were shot before they landed. Still Germany maintained her non stop offensive. British fighters operating from bases in Egypt took heavy toll of the troop carrying planes and bombers, but the disparity in distances between the British and German bases from Crete proved too great a handicap.

Attempts by the Germans to transport troops and material by sea and convoys were smashed or turned back and many ships sunk.

VICTORY IN IRAQ.

It is not yet known how many troops Britain had in Crete, or whether the evacuation is completed or is still being continued. One factor that has been proved beyond doubt is that the magnificent resistance of the British and Greek troops in Crete has not only struck heavy blows at the German forces, material and equipment but it has also given Britain a victory in Iraq. Finding the opposition much more stubborn than was expected, the Germans were unable to fulfil the promise to supply large numbers of aircraft and other forms of aid to Raschid Ali in Iraq.

Meanwhile, General Wavell has had an invaluable breathing space in which to strengthen his positions on other fronts.

GENERAL FREYBERG.

It is assumed that General B. C. Freyberg, famous New Zealand V.C., who was Commander-in-Chief of the Allied forces on the island, came out with the troops who have been withdrawn, as the latest statement about him said that he was alive and well. The Germans had previously claimed that he had been killed.

The number of troops withdrawn, 15,000—is believed to relate only to British troops and does not include Greek forces. It is not yet known what proportion of Dominion troops are among the men saved.

NEARER BRITISH BASES

The German occupation of Crete will give them anchorages and airfields much nearer the bases which Britain is still firmly holding at the eastern end of the Mediterranean, but if they wish to exploit them they will find themselves up against stiff opposition, writes a Press Association military correspondent.

From a naval point of view it is unlikely that the use of certain harbours will give the Germans any appreciable advantages as the distance from Crete to Libya (about 200 miles), is too great for E boats to operate with success against any ships of Britain's which might be in the vicinity.

They might seek to carry troops from Greece via Crete to North Africa, but transports would still require about 12 hours sailing time between Crete and Libya, which is longer at any rate than the hours of darkness when they might slip through unperceived.

The possibility of German dive bombers operating from Crete is a factor which must be considered in any naval operations, however. If Cyprus is the next stage of the German push, they will find new problems of air combat for, operating from Crete they will have approximately the same distance to fly as the British did from Egypt to Crete.

Just as Britain needed long distance fighters in Crete, so will they need them over Cyprus unless operating from Syria. But the British should be able to protect Cyprus much more easily with fighter planes as they have adjacent bases in Palestine.

"MOPPING UP" IN CRETE.

Berlin, Sunday.—To-day's official German communique states:—

"In Crete the mopping up of the remnants of British and Greek troops in the southern part of the island is progressing. Near Harapetra yesterday German troops joined up with the Italian troops advancing from the east. Up to now, roughly, 10,000 British and Greeks have been taken prisoners.

"South of Crete German bomber formations attacked light British naval units, heavily damaged a destroyer with bombs, and shot down four Hurricane fighters without suffering losses.

"In the same sea area the German Air Force sank a merchant ship of 3,000 tons and a coastal schooner laden with munitions, and heavily damaged a small troop transport ship."

"ANOTHER DUNKIRK."

(The Associated Press).

New York, Sunday.—The German radio, heard here, claimed that British and Greek troops were attempting to reach Egypt from Crete in small fishing boats in "another Dunkirk."

"The first group of fugitive soldiers has already arrived in Egypt," the radio added.

ITALIAN REPORT.

Rome, Sunday.—To-day's official Italian communique states:—"Operations for completing the occupation of Crete are being continued with success. Italian detachments which yesterday made contact with the German forces, are closely pursuing the retreating British troops towards the southern part of the island."

BRITISH COMMUNIQUE.

Cairo, Sunday.—The following communique was issued by the R.A.F. to-day:—

"Eastern Mediterranean.—During patrols by a large force of our fighters in the Eastern Mediterranean contact was made with a big formation of enemy aircraft. Two Heinkel IIIs were shot down into the sea, one by a Free French pilot and a considerable number of other enemy aircraft were badly damaged. The enemy immediately took evasive action and retired with all possible speed to their bases and it is highly probably that many of them did not get back.

"During the night of May 29/30, our heavy bombers attacked the aerodrome at Scarpanto causing a number of fires. The aerodrome and the beach at Maleme (Crete) were also raided. On the same night the aerodrome at Kattavia (Rhodes) was bombed, but detailed results were not observed."

CRETE METHODS.

(Mr. Edward Kennedy, Associated Press War Correspondent.)

Cairo, Sunday.—The air supremacy which swept the Germans through Yugoslavia and Greece, and into Crete, cannot continue beyond that island, a high spokesman of the R.A.F. declared here to-day. "There is no chance for further German operations like those in Crete," he said. "If the Germans carry the Luftwaffe to the mainland of Africa or Asia Minor, the situation will be largely reversed, and even should they attempt an air invasion of Cyprus, they will not have the same vantage positions for bases as in the attack on Crete," he said.

"The essence of air operations, as in

(CONTINUED ON PAGE SIX.)

1942

For the Nazis, the 'final solution' to exterminate the Jews went into full effect in 1942 and, as well as the use of mobile gas chambers in Poland, the deportation began of German Jews to Auschwitz concentration camp. Censorship regulations meant that the *Examiner* could print no accounts of such events. De Valera did speak out against the treatment of the Jews but Ireland had only accepted a handful of Jewish refugees after the Nazis came to power.

The first American troops to land in Europe arrived in Northern Ireland in January, though again censorship regulations prevented the publishing of any details of where they were stationed or of de Valera's objections to their presence. The difficulty of getting supplies across the Atlantic was underlined when 33 Irish sailors were killed when the *Irish Pine* was torpedoed off New York.

Most private cars were put off the road in May and clothes and soap were added to the ration list. In international music, Bing Crosby sang 'White Christmas', while Vera Lynn released her wartime classic, 'We'll Meet Again'.

No more coal for domestic use

Tuesday, March 31

Owing to the fall in coal imports, none will be available henceforward for domestic purposes, and only barely sufficient for the minimum requirements of industry. Our political correspondent says that in a few cases proprietors of industrial concerns have tried to force the hands of the Department of Supplies by threatening to close down unless they get an increased quantity of coal, and that the Government is considering what punitive action should be taken against anyone who puts the threat into effect.

Owners of commercial vehicles are warned that if they carry passengers to race meetings or other sports fixtures they will get no further supplies of petrol or tyres. Imports of white flour have now virtually ceased.

The blessing of the nets at the village of Blackrock, Cork. This annual ritual was common in fishing communities around the country.

Books that have been banned

Thursday, November 19

Sir John Keane moved in the Senate yesterday: "That the Censorship of Publications Board has ceased to retain public confidence." *The Tailor and Ansty*, one of the most recent books banned by the Board, had aroused a great deal of interest, and protests had been voiced by people who had never raised their voices before. The book, undoubtedly was somewhat Rabelaisian. It described country folk talking at their own fireside and they were somewhat coarse in their expressions.

Sir John Keane proceeded to read passages from *The Tailor and Ansty*. He said *Ansty* was not in its general tendency indecent, and was not intended to corrupt or deprave, or excite sexual passion, or unnatural vice. He then referred to a book entitled *Land of Spices* by Kate O'Brien, which had been censored. In the 13 years during which the Act had been in operation, some 1,600 books had been censored. Generally speaking the Board of Censors are too academic and detached from the stream of life and the outlook of youth. I suggest that their outlook, generally speaking, like that of many of us here, is merely on account of their age – Victorian – and I think it is important to realise that the standard of judgement on moral questions has changed.

Senator Goulding said that not alone was *The Tailor and Ansty* silly and indecent, but tiresome. Senator P Ó Maille said that the trouble with third-rate scribblers was that they had a slap at religion and public decency to sell their books.

NEWS BRIEFS

Mar The Alliance and Dublin Consumers' Gas Company announced last night that the supply of gas in Dublin will be restricted as from 8.30am today. Thereafter the hours during which supply of gas will be available will be 7am to 8.30am; 11.50am to 3.30pm; 5.30pm to 10.30pm. (3)

May Crimes of theft were increasing, it was stated in the Dáil yesterday. General MacEoin suggested that there should be some form of bicycle registration to overcome bicycle stealing, which was becoming a racket.

Dec The SS *Irish Pine*, considerably overdue at her Transatlantic port of call, is presumed lost. (5)

The Cork Examiner

CITY SPECIAL

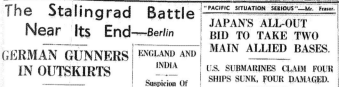

NO. 27,984. FRIDAY MORNING, SEPTEMBER 18, 1942. PRICE—TWOPENCE

Registered for transmission at Newspaper Rate of Postage in Ireland and Great Britain and at Magazine Rate in Canada and Newfoundland.

The Stalingrad Battle Near Its End—*Berlin*

GERMAN GUNNERS IN OUTSKIRTS

REDS SUCCESSFUL IN STREET FIGHTING.

German Tommy-gunners are in the north-western suburbs of Stalingrad, only ten miles from the wide squares adorning the centre of the city. The decision now rests on the ability of the Soviet troops to bring the Germans to exhaustion before they themselves are worn down by the forces thrown against them without an hour's respite on land or in the air.

At the suburbs edging this vast city, sprawled for 32 miles along the river bank and over the little hills and gullies lining the steppe country, in the "egg-cup" between the Don and the Volga, fighting of incredible fury goes on night and day.

Berlin's most definite statement is that "mopping-up continues in the town districts," but an earlier announcement spoke of delay in "mopping-up" and said that the official report of Stalingrad's fall could only be expected after this was completed.

(By Harold King, Reuter's Special Correspondent.)

Moscow, Thursday.—The Germans, with their preponderance of men and armour, are to-day relentlessly pressing forward into Stalingrad, where their tommy-gunners are already installed in houses in the north-west outskirts. German tanks, straight from revitalising bands in the rear and with fresh crews, are rumbling forward on zig-zag courses. The battle for Stalin's city increases in fury, and rain is now falling on the scene of the greatest slaughter of the Eastern front. Fighting is going on in the streets of Stalingrad, which sprawls for 32 miles along the banks of the Volga. At the same time the battle rages among the hills and valleys beyond the town, where fighting has now lasted for nearly four weeks.

There is no doubt that the most critical moment in the defence of Stalingrad has been reached.

Beyond the north-western outskirts Soviet units yesterday launched counter-attacks to retake some tactically important hills. Simultaneously the German Command was pressing in from the south-west, but their attacks were staved off. The defenders of Stalingrad are now faced with some extremely urgent tasks:—

(1) They must hold on at all costs for the longest possible time to the defensive positions outside the city;

(2) They must fight wherever they ...

... a powerful counter-attack, drove the Germans back at the point of the bayonet and restored the position. Subsequent German attacks have all been repulsed.

The threat to Stalingrad from the north-west is still considerable with the Germans entrenched at the very edge of the city, but Stalingrad is not cut off. Reinforcements for the defence are still arriving.

SOVIET COMMUNIQUE.

To-night's Soviet communique states: "During September 17 our troops fought fierce engagements with the enemy on the north-western outskirts of Stalingrad and the area of Mozdok ..."

By the end of the day all enemy groups were repulsed and the Germans were forced to retreat.

GERMAN REPORT.

"The Russians attempted in vain to break the choking loop of the German attack, and all Soviet counter-attacks were repelled."

"A MATTER OF TIME."

The Germans have now reached positions where they have at least severely interrupted railway transport from North to South Russia through Stalingrad. That is a severe blow to the Red Army.

RUSSIAN RESISTANCE.

SOVIET REPORT.

A Soviet front line dispatch says that the German effort to achieve a major break-through into Stalingrad from the north-west has failed.

ENGLAND AND INDIA

Suspicion Of Promises

(The Associated Press.)

GIRLS GO TO PRISON.

GENERAL WAVELL.

"OFFER WITHDRAWN."

IN MADAGASCAR.

French Resistance To Continue.

RESISTANCE TO CONTINUE

MYSTERY OF RAFT ON LONG ISLAND SHORE.

"LISTEN TO BERLIN."

CANADIAN PLEA FOR SPEEDY SECOND FRONT.

"MINOR" ENGAGEMENTS IN CHINA.

BRITISH WERE WAITING

FRENCH SOCIALISTS ESCAPE TO BRITAIN.

IRISH LADY'S WILL

"PACIFIC SITUATION SERIOUS"—Mr. Fraser.

JAPAN'S ALL-OUT BID TO TAKE TWO MAIN ALLIED BASES.

U.S. SUBMARINES CLAIM FOUR SHIPS SUNK, FOUR DAMAGED.

COINCIDING with the statement yesterday of Mr. Peter Frazer, New Zealand Premier, on his return from the U.S. that "it is obvious that the present situation in the Pacific is serious," comes a report from Sydney that Japanese forces massed in the South-West Pacific are making an all-out bid to smash their way into the Allies two main bases.

In New Guinea they are now only 32 miles from Port Moresby, while further attacks are expected shortly on the vital Solomon's airfield island of Guadalcanal.

According to a Washington Navy communique last night, U.S. submarines have sunk four Japanese ships, two of them large freighters, and damaged four other vessels, including a large transport. These actions, it was stated, are not related to operations in the Solomons.

Yesterday's Allied communique mentioned "serious fighting in progress" in the Owen Stanley mountains, with the Japanese exerting heavy pressure.

At Buna Allied aircraft bombed barges and the beach, with results that could not be observed. At Rabaul, the communique adds, "Our medium ..."

The U.S. bases in the Solomons—which the Japanese are endeavouring to retake.

U.S. NAVAL CLAIMS.

AUSTRALIAN LOSSES.

MR. FRAZER'S VIEWS.

"BROKEN HARMONY OF MANKIND."

The Pope On Miseries Of The War.

U.S. ENVOY WILL RETURN TO VATICAN.

CANADA PROTESTS TO FRANCE.

LAND LULL CONTINUES IN EGYPT.

ALLIED AND AXIS BOMBING RAIDS ON SUPPLY BASES.

LAND LULL CONTINUES.

RAIDS ON MALTA.

F.F. DEPUTIES MEET.

Early General Election?

(From Our Political Correspondent.)

INDIA "MENACE TO JAPS."

U.S. WAR PRODUCTION

Full Flow Early Next Year, Says Mr. Nelson.

SHAH'S FIRST FLIGHT.

AIR RAID WARNING IN U.S.

NEW BRAZILIAN CONSUL FOR EIRE.

TAOISEACH AND CORK TRADES COUNCIL.

Workers And High Prices.

GENERAL GIRAUD WITH WEYGAND.

JAPAN AND THE AXIS.

SUPPORT FOR U.S. NON-INFLATION DRIVE.

39 PLANES MISSING AFTER BIG R.A.F. RAID ON RUHR.

"VERY STRONG FORCE" USED

BERLIN'S CLAIMS FOR NEW A.A. METHODS.

"A VERY strong force" of British bombers took part in Wednesday night's attacks on the Ruhr, when it was stated six fires were left burning. This was the ninth big raid this month on German targets. Light bombers also attacked the Weisbaden area. It was stated in London that 39 machines were missing—the heaviest losses suffered by the R.A.F. in the present series of attacks, the most sustained yet undertaken.

Two Axis ships were attacked off the Norwegian coast yesterday by the R.A.F. and hits with torpedoes were claimed.

The German Radio claimed last night that entirely new anti-aircraft methods accounted for the British loss of 'planes which, it asserted, represented 25 per cent. of the total number engaged.

Of two German 'planes which raided Britain yesterday, one was claimed to have been shot down after a chase of 80 miles across the Channel towards France.

An Air Ministry communique last night stated:—"A very strong force of bombers attacked objectives in the Ruhr. Many fires, some of them very large, were left burning. At dusk light bombers attacked industrial objectives in the Wiesbaden area. From these operations, thirty-nine bombers are missing."

... many, the British Air Force yesterday lost four aircraft.

"During the night British bomber formations attacked the Rhenish-Westphalian area. There were casualties among the population. Fires, material damage and destruction to buildings were caused in residential areas of several places. Thirty-seven of the attacking bombers were shot down.

DAY RAIDERS CHASED.

A British Air Ministry and Ministry of Home Security communique last night stated:—"Two enemy fighters dropped bombs at a place on the South Coast this afternoon, causing some damage and a small number of casualties. One of these aircraft was destroyed by our fighters."

NIGHT RAIDS ON BRITAIN.

SHIPS ATTACKED OFF NORWAY.

"NEW GERMAN A.A. METHODS."

WAR ON SHIPPING

Many German Vessels Sunk Off Norway

BIG ARMS DUMP FOUND NEAR BELFAST.

Six Young Men Charged.

JEHOVAH'S WITNESSES.

More Meetings Banned By British Home Secretary

TRAIN CRASH CASUALTIES

BINDER TWINE FOR TRUSSING STRAW PROHIBITED.

1943

While life in Ireland was extremely easy in comparison to many parts of Europe, the nation did have it's share of tragedies. In February, the *Examiner* reported heart-breaking scenes from Cavan where 35 children and an elderly cook died in a fire at an institution run by the Poor Clare Order.

Daily life in Ireland became that much more austere as clothing joined the list of restricted items and the government issued instructions on everything from how many pockets were allowed in jackets to styles of women's underwear. The news was better for bread as December brought relief from the unpopular brown loaves that had been filling the rations until then. Perks of the job for an *Examiner* reporter meant getting a sneak preview of the newsworthy new loaf. Overall, supplies from America to Europe improved during the year as convoys improved their defences against German submarines. This was achieved through the increase in escort ships freed up by successes in the African campaign and improvements in technology such as Asdic for locating the subs and better depth charges for destroying them.

NEWS BRIEFS

Jan Soviet forces achieve victory at the formerly besieged cities of Stalingrad and Leningrad.

Apr A Dublin fire brigade officer tells the inquiry into the Cavan fire that, in a three-month period, there had been 170 fire outbreaks in the capital. Half of them were domestic fires, and the officer blamed the increased use of turf which he said was more dangerous than the unavailable coal. (28)

Sept Italy surrenders to the Allies. Mussolini had been deposed a month earlier after Sicily was invaded by Allied forces. An invasion of the mainland looks likely to follow. (8)

Irish seaside disaster

May 12

Seventeen men were killed and five injured when a mine, which drifted ashore at the little seaside resort of Ballymanus, on the West Donegal coast, exploded on Monday night.

The disaster, which occurred at 10 o'clock, has plunged the countryside into mourning. Several of the dead are boys, and include three brothers of one family. Two other families lost two sons each.

Accounts vary as to the immediate cause of the explosion. One report states that, not realising the danger, some of the men threw stones at the mine. Another version is that the mine, although ashore, was rising and falling with each incoming wave, and that the explosion was caused by contact with some rocky outcrop in the sand.

Word was sent to Civic Guards at Anagry, but before any steps could be taken for the protection of the people the mine exploded with a terrific detonation. It caused a veritable shambles among the group of men who had approached close by in order to examine it. Many of them were blown into the sea, and in some cases the mutilation was so appalling that identification of the remains was difficult.

Keeping in shape: The army's Construction Corps gymnastics team strut their stuff at Collins Barracks, Cork.

Improved quality of new bread

Saturday, December 11

The 'new' bread and flour, composed of 85% extraction of wheat, with a barley admixture, will be on sale and in general use as from Monday next. Naturally the burning question of the hour is what the new loaf is going to be like. Yesterday an *Examiner* reporter was able to see some of the trial loaves baked with the new flour at a well-known Cork bakery. There is a very considerable improvement in the colour of the bread compared with that to which we have become accustomed, but the new loaf cannot properly be described as white. 'Off white' would be a better description of the colour. The disappointment of those who anticipated a return to the snowy pre-war loaf will, in all probability, be offset by the big improvement in flavour, texture and keeping qualities of the new product. Externally the new loaf is similar to the white loaf; it has a tempting crust of biscuit colour at the sides and bottom.

"A baker does not judge bread by eating it," said the master baker. "He smells it. If the smell makes him think, 'I would like a slice of that', it's good. Get your nose deep into this." The reporter found that a day-old half-loaf smelled very appetisingly in fact, with just a suspicion of an odour of barley.

The Cork Examiner

CITY SPECIAL

NO. 28,119. THURSDAY MORNING, FEBRUARY 25, 1943. PRICE – TWOPENCE

Registered for transmission at Newspaper Rate of Postage in Ireland and Great Britain and at Magazine Rate in Canada and Newfoundland.

Thirty-Five Children Die In Blazing Orphanage

AGED WOMAN ALSO VICTIM

APPALLING TRAGEDY IN CAVAN.

TRAPPED in an inferno of flame and smoke, thirty-five children and a woman, aged 87, lost their lives in a fire which practically destroyed the Poor Clares Girls' Orphanage at Cavan early yesterday. Out of the 85 children living in the institution 50 were saved, though some are injured and detained in hospital. Frantic with terror, the children crowded the windows, crying to the people below to save them. Rescuers attempting to reach the children through smoke-filled corridors were choked by the fumes and forced back.

The fire swept the dormitories with terrifying rapidity. Some of the children jumped from windows and were injured. Others, in a wildly frightened condition, ran out into the fields adjoining the town. The Poor Clares' Convent, which adjoins the orphanage, was saved by firemen, who cut away part of the roof to prevent the spread of the flames.

The fire broke out in St. Joseph's Orphanage buildings in Pearse Street, Cavan, about two o'clock yesterday morning. There were 85 children in the institution, a Press Association report says, and of these, 35, of ages ranging from four to eighteen years, are missing.

Others escaped by jumping from the windows, some at a height of forty feet. Thirteen were taken to the County Hospital. The building is a four-storey one.

HUGE BLAZE.

In a matter of minutes after its first discovery, the fire assumed huge proportions, and children in their night clothes rushed screaming from the building.

Civic Guards, the Fire Brigade, and townspeople, all worked desperately to quell the flames and break through to the children inside the burning building. The Dundalk Fire Brigade reinforced the local fire-fighters, and at 5 a.m. the fire was brought under control. Doctors and nurses and first aid workers were standing by.

Among the missing is Maggie Smith, an 87-years-old servant, who had been employed at the Orphanage for over 50 years.

Yesterday was observed as a day of mourning in the town, and all business premises were closed.

The children who escaped into the street were accommodated in the neighbouring houses. Some of them were in a wildly frightened condition and ran out into the fields adjoining the town. One farmer found four little girls crying piteously outside his house.

CONVENT SAVED.

The Convent of the Poor Clares adjoining the orphanage was saved by firemen who cut away part of the roof to prevent the spread of the flames from the orphanage. The nuns together with the orphanage staff who had reached safety helped to pacify and care for the rescued children.

When the flames were under control rescue workers, including soldiers, searched the smouldering debris for the bodies of children.

One of the Dundalk firemen, Patrick Maguire, was taken to hospital with a back injury caused when a beam fell on him.

HEROIC WOMAN.

A message from Cavan last night indicated that the death roll had been finally established at 36. Of these, 35 were children, and the remaining one was the 87 years' old retired domestic servant, Margaret Smith. Despite her great age, this heroic woman, according to many of the rescue workers, did everything she could to get the children out of the blazing building, regardless of her own safety. Five of the children are detained in hospital seriously injured as a result of jumping from the windows.

His Lordship, Most Rev. Dr. Lyons, Bishop of Kilmore, was amongst the numerous callers during the day at the convent to express the sympathy universally felt as a consequence of the dreadful tragedy.

FURTHER DETAILS.

Further details show that the outbreak developed in the lower portion of the four-storeyed building and quickly involved the entire orphanage. The Convent was saved. Military, Civic Guards, Civil Defence Services, and many civilians joined in the frantic efforts at rescue and in fighting the flames. Dundalk Fire Brigade arrived at 5 a.m.

Meanwhile the Priests of Cavan Cathedral and the De La Salle Brothers hurried to the scene and helped in the rescue work. Members of the Irish Red Cross Society co-operated with the nuns in doing everything for the children, and the County Manager placed at their disposal the newly constructed County Sanatorium as a temporary residence for the survivors. Lady members of the Red Cross helped to prepare the building for their reception.

During yesterday all business premises in Cavan remained closed and the atmosphere was one of general mourning.

HEARD CHILDREN CRYING.

Miss Riley, who lives next door to the convent, and was the first to raise the alarm, told the Press Association:—"I saw fire through the smoke and banged on the door of the convent, which adjoins the orphanage, until some nuns opened it. They did not know the place was on fire. A lot of people were shouting outside. A Civic Guard and some neighbours forced their way up the stairs towards the dormitories. The smoke got thicker, and when we got into the corridors we could neither see nor breathe. We could hear the children crying and calling out that they were burning. We were choking and had to get back. In the meantime neighbours had got a ladder up to the windows and men were climbing up to bring the children out. I think about 25 children were brought down the ladders. They were crowding about the windows and crying: 'Oh take us out.' People cared for them at their homes until the ambulances arrived." Miss Riley first noticed the outbreak at about two a.m.

The nuns, with the orphanage staff, except Miss Smith, reached safety and helped to pacify the rescued children.

THE INQUEST.

An inquest was opened and adjourned last night, by Dr. S. Stuart, on the victims of the tragedy.

Dr. J. Clarke said the condition of the victims was such that it rendered them beyond recognition.

Mr. P. N. Smith, solicitor, on behalf of the Mother Abbess and Convent Community, said he could not find words to express how deeply they all felt about the tragedy, which had caused the loss of so many young lives and shattered the happiness of relatives and friends of the victims. His clients would give every assistance in the inquiry. He also expressed the deep gratitude of the nuns to all who had helped in the work of rescue.

Supt. J. Bradley paid tribute to the wonderful rescue work performed by the military and the ladies of the Red Cross Society.

Adjourning the inquest, the Coroner expressed sympathy with the relatives, the Sisters in charge of the orphanage, and with Most Rev. Dr. Lyons, Bishop of Kilmore, patron and guardian of the institution. "It is," said the Coroner, "a grand feature of the Irish character that at a time of tragedy like this, so many people rally to the help of those involved."

The Taoiseach and the Minister for Education have sent messages of sympathy to the Bishop of Kilmore.

The last big fire in Ireland was at a cinema in Drumcollogher, Co. Limerick, in September, 1926, when 49 people lost their lives.

CHURCHILL ON GANDHI

Pleas For Release Turned Down

Mr. Churchill, the British Prime Minister, in a reply conveyed to Sir Tej Bahadur Sapro, the Indian Liberal Leader, through the Viceroy, states, says Reuter: "There can be no justification for discriminating between Mr. Gandhi and other Congress leaders. The responsibility, therefore, rests entirely with Mr. Gandhi himself." The text of his reply is:

"The Government of India decided last August that Mr. Gandhi and other leaders of the Congress Party must be detained for reasons which have been fully explained and are well understood. The reasons for that decision have not ceased to exist and H.M. Government endorse the determination of the Government of India not to be deflected from their duty towards the peoples of India and United Nations by Mr. Gandhi's attempt to secure his unconditional release by fasting. The first duty of the Government of India and of H.M Government is to defend the soil of India from the invasion by which it is still menaced, and to enable India to play her part in the general cause of the United Nations. There can be no justification for discriminating between Mr. Gandhi and other Congress leaders. The responsibility, therefore, rests entirely with Mr. Gandhi himself."

The British Premier's cable was in reply to a resolution from the Committee of the Indian Leaders' Conference, which urged "the immediate release of Mahatma Gandhi, whose condition is fast approaching a crisis."

The resolution sought to "explain to the British public that the Mahatma is fasting only to be able to review the situation as a free man and advise people accordingly, and not on the issue of independence. We are convinced that his letter of September 23rd, recently published, amounts to unequivocal disapproval on behalf of himself and Congress of all acts of violence."

"We are convinced that wise and liberal statesmanship will solve the Indo-British problem more speedily and effectively than stern repression."

The resolution was signed by representatives of many organisations in India.

EXPECTED TO LIVE.

Cabling from Poona, last night, the Associated Press said:—Gandhi, whose 73-year-old life was despaired of four days ago unless he broke his fast, is now expected to live through the remaining six days of the scheduled twenty-one days. While Gandhi grows a little weaker each day, he was more cheerful on his fifteenth foodless day and is suffering less acute distress. "Every day he pushes back the devil we are much happier," say his friends, who feel that their constant prayers are being answered by a miracle.

Authoritative medical sources, while recognising the possibility of a further crisis, nevertheless declare that "if he has been able to manage it for fifteen days, there is no reason why he should not manage six days more." Visitors say that Gandhi's voice seemed stronger. He himself is so sure that he is going to live that he is already planning what he is going to do when his fast is ended.

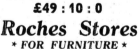

Page recreated

1944

As early as January, 1944, the *Examiner* was reporting on German beliefs that the Allies were preparing to invade France. An increase in bombing raids on coastal defences and a build-up of landing boats in southern England were obvious signs that something was being planned. However, the Allies were anxious that no intelligence about the planned D-Day landings should come from Ireland, where both Japan and Germany had consulates and where American troops in the North were training for the invasion. Phone connections to Britain and Irish shipping movement were therefore halted.

Earlier in the year, the impending Allied attack on Rome had been a source of much concern for the Catholic hierarchy and de Valera had made representations to the Allies not to bombard the city.

By now, newsprint shortages meant that the *Examiner* only had four pages. Mainline trains were reduced to two days per week, while those that did run were turf-powered and could take 10 hours to travel between Dublin and Cork.

How the battle began

Wednesday, June 7

Guns are belching flame from more than 600 Allied warships, thousands of bombers are roaring overhead, fighters are weaving in and out of the colludes as the invasion of Western Europe begins. Rolling clouds of dense black and grey smoke cover the beaches south-east of Le Havre, as the full fury of the Allied invasion force is unleashed on the German defences.

It is the most incredible sight I have ever seen. We are standing some 8,000 yards off the beaches of Bernière-sur-Mer, and from the bridge of this little destroyer I can see vast numbers of naval craft of all types. The air is filled with the continuous thunder of broadsides and the crash of bombs. Great spurts of flame come up from the beaches in long, snake-like ripples, as shells find their mark.

It is now exactly 7.25am, and through my glasses I can see the first wave of assault troops touch down on the water's edge and fan up the beach. Conditions are not ideal. A fairly high sea is running, and the sky is overset.

The army helps with the cutting of turf at Nadd, Co Cork.

NEWS BRIEFS

Jan The crew of a German ship torpedoed off the coast of Ireland are brought to Cobh, Co Cork and, in keeping with usual government policy, are interned. (3)

June Anti-aircraft guns were in action continuously over Britain during the weekend, meeting German 'robot' raids, whilst fighters were on patrol in the sky waiting to attack the pilotless planes which dropped at various points along the south coast of England on Saturday night. (19)

Aug The Germans in Paris have surrendered to the Allied forces. French armour and American troops are at Notre Dame in the heart of Paris. General De Gaulle has entered Paris and last night he made a speech to the populace, which was broadcast by Paris Radio. (26)

Vatican radio broadcast

Friday, September 22

Messages from Irish residents in Italy to relatives and friends at home were broadcast yesterday afternoon by the Vatican radio. The reception was generally good:

To Mrs Thos Cook, Bottomstown, Co Limerick, from Fr Thos Cook, Irish College, Rome: "I am getting on well here now. I received your letter dated June 9th. Please keep on writing and be sure to give all the news, with God's help we shall meet again soon, at least for a short period. Give my heartiest greetings to all at home and at Knockaney, also to Fr Meaney and all the neighbours. Good bye and all the best – Tommy." There was a postscript saying: "I was sorry to hear that Canon Humphreys died. I have already said Mass for him."

Fr Peter to Mrs W Flannery, Nenagh: "Hope all is well with you. Perhaps may see you before Xmas. Departure extremely difficult. Kindest regards to yourself, Bill and children."

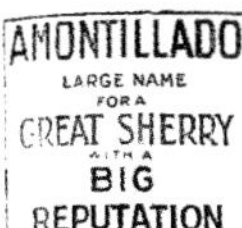

The Cork Examiner

NO. 28,518. WEDNESDAY MORNING, JUNE 7, 1944. PRICE—TWOPENCE

Registered for Transmission at Newspaper Rate of Postage in Ireland and Great Britain, and at Magazine Rate in Canada and Newfoundland.

CITY SPECIAL

ALLIED AIR AND LAND TROOPS STRIKE INLAND AFTER A DAWN INVASION OF FRENCH COAST

AT DAWN YESTERDAY THE ALLIED INVASION OF THE CONTINENT BEGAN WITH LANDINGS OF MANY ALLIED DIVISIONS BOTH BY SEA AND FROM THE AIR. THE LANDINGS FOLLOWED A TERRIFIC AIR BOMBARDMENT DURING THE NIGHT, IN WHICH 10,000 TONS OF BOMBS WERE DROPPED BETWEEN MIDNIGHT AND 8 A.M. YESTERDAY.

The position early this morning was still confused, with reports pouring in from all quarters, many of them contradictory. However, the position appeared to be that the main Allied landings from the sea were concentrated around the mouth of the River Orne at first, and later spread along an area roughly between Arromanches and Trouville (see map).

The official German News Agency stated last night that the Allies had secured a coastal bridgehead between Villiers-Sur-Mer and Trouville, about 20 kilometres (16½ miles) in length and a few kilometres in depth. "Although they brought up reinforcements from the waters around Le Havre," the Agency added, "the Allies could not prevent the Germans from sealing off the bridgehead on all sides and even from narrowing it down locally."

Other reports said that landings had been made at Dieppe and Boulogne, while to the West the main landing of glider and parachute troops took place between Valonge and Carpentan on the Cherbourg peninsula,—a move which might be interpreted as being aimed at cutting off the Axis troops on the peninsula from the main body of the defending forces.

The road from Carpentan to Valognes (route Nationale 13) is the main highway from Paris to Cherbourg. It leads straight to the great port of Cherbourg 12 miles from Valognes.

The deepest Allied penetration seems to have been to Caen (see map), where fighting was taking place in the streets, according to Axis reports. Later it was reported that heavy Allied landings west of Le Havre were made with the intention of screening the bringing up of more Allied forces to the bridgehead north of Caen.

Reports received from Allied agencies up to early this morning indicated that Axis air support was not very extensive, but the Allies were using the greatest air screen ever seen in action.

Mr. Churchill in the House of Commons said that casualties were so far much lighter than expected, and the Axis obstructions built under the sea along the coast had proved less dangerous to the Allies than had been foreseen. Some 4,000 ships and thousands of small craft participated in the landing.

A few minutes after midnight a communique from Allied Supreme Headquarters announced: "Reports of operations so far show that our forces succeeded in their initial landings." These landings, according to German accounts, are taking place at a series of points extending over a 100 miles line from Cherbourg to Le Havre.

TROOPS LANDED BY PARACHUTE AND GLIDER HEAVILY ENGAGED
REPORTED LANDINGS
MAIN LANDINGS FROM SEA REPORTED BETWEEN THESE POINTS
LARGE AIR BORNE LANDINGS HERE
ALLIED LANDING REPORTED BY GERMANS
TANK BATTLES IN PROGRESS
HEAVY STREET FIGHTING
GERMANS REPORT 16 MLS OF COAST OCCUPIED
GUERNSEY
CHANNEL
SARK
ISLANDS
JERSEY
Cherbourg
Valognes
Carentan
Isigny
Arromanches
Bayeux
St Lo
Granville
Avranches
Vire
Conde
Caen
Orne
Villers
Trouville
Lisieux
Le Havre
Harfleur
Bolbec
Fecamp
St Valery
Dieppe
Le Treport
Abbeville
Amiens
Boulogne
Rouen
Seine
Beauvais

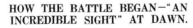

The above map gives an impression of the situation in France last night, according to the confused reports available

SOVIET ATTACK EXPECTED

Lower Dniester Army.

THE GERMANS FALLING BACK IN ITALY.

BRITISH PREMIER'S TRIBUTE TO ALLIED ARMIES.

"However, General Alexander's prime object has never been the liberation of Rome great as are the moral, political and psychological advantages of that episode.

"This is a memorable and glorious event, which rewards the intense fighting of the last five months in Italy," Mr. Churchill said.

INVASION WAS DELAYED.

"D-day" Planned For Monday.

FLASHES FROM THE FRONT

A German war correspondent on the West last night said: "The enemy is aiming straight at the heart of France—Paris."

The German air force flew only 50 sorties up to about noon, but airmen were warned that a violent reaction was expected from the Luftwaffe soon, says the Press Association.

An Allied naval officer said, last night: "It has not been very great worry and thing we are still going on. It is the weather."

PRESERVATION OF ROME.

Expressions At Cork Corporation.

DAIL MEETING

Religious Services In Dublin

OLANN NA TAL'HAN.

P.O. WORKERS

The Cost Of Living Bonus

SENATE ELECTION.

PORTUGUESE DECISION

"HEAVY FIGHTING WILL BEGIN," SAYS MR. CHURCHILL.

ALLIED LOSSES LESS THAN EXPECTED.

MR. CHURCHILL, speaking in solemn tones, announced in the House of Commons yesterday, that landings had begun.

After other speeches had been made, Mr. Churchill rose from the front bench as Mr. Lloyd George, who was sitting on the front Opposition bench, rose to leave the Chamber. Mr. Churchill crossed the floor of the House and he and Mr. Lloyd George shook hands vigorously.

"The obstacles which were constructed in the sea have not proved as difficult as was apprehended. The Anglo-American Allies are sustained by about 11,000 first line aircraft, which can be drawn upon as may be needed for the purpose of the battle.

"We have captured various bridges which are important and which have not been blown up by the enemy, and fighting is even proceeding in the town of Caen, inland.

"The landings along the whole front have been effective, and our troops have penetrated in some cases several miles inland. Lodgements exist on a broad front.

10,000 TONS OF BOMBS IN EIGHT HOURS.

HOW THE BATTLE BEGAN—"AN INCREDIBLE SIGHT" AT DAWN.

DESMOND TIGHE, Reuter's special correspondent, aboard a British destroyer off Berniers-Sur-Mer, at dawn yesterday described the opening stage of the invasion thus:—Guns are belching flame from more than 600 Allied warships; thousands of bombers are roaring overhead; fighters are weaving in and out of the clouds as the invasion of Western Europe begins. Rolling clouds of dense black and grey smoke cover the beaches south-east of Le Havre, as the full fury of the Allied invasion force is unleashed on the German defences. It is the most incredible sight I have ever seen. We are standing some 8,000 yards off the beaches of Berniers-Sur-Mer, and from the bridge of this little destroyer I can see vast numbers of naval craft of all types. The air is filled with the continuous thunder of broadsides and the crash of bombs. Great spurts of flame come up from the beaches in long, snake-like ripples, as shells, ranging from 16ins. to 4ins., find their mark. In the last ten minutes alone, more than 2,000 tons of high-explosive shells have gone down on the beach-head.

It is now exactly 7.25 a.m., and through my glasses I can see the first wave of assault troops touch down on the water's edge and fan up the beach.

It is giving away no secret now to say that weather conditions for the landings were not perfect, but despite high running seas and a strong north-westerly wind, a bold decision was taken to go ahead with the operation.

It was just after four o'clock when we reached a position some 18 miles off the coast of France. The night bombing was in full swing, and from that distance we could see enormous blood red explosions and hear the rumble of the bursting bombs.

The bombardment continues and by now big fires are burning ashore. Clouds of black smoke rise hundreds of feet into the air.

07.25—The first wave of landing craft have reached the shore. I see them touch down. Red tracers from close range. German weapons are searing across the beach. Men leap out of the craft and move forward. Tanks follow them. By now everything is an inferno.

Over 10,000 tons of bombs were dropped on the invasion coast between midnight and 8 a.m.

Page recreated

1945

At last came the headlines announcing the end of the war, but 1945 also brought new horrors with reports on the use of the Atom Bomb attacks on Japan and conditions at the Nazi concentration camps. At least the lifting of war-time censorship restrictions in May meant that *Examiner* readers could get better accounts of such events. Earlier tales of the concentration camps had been suppressed by Irish censors and the lifting of restrictions also allowed stories expressing the mixed feelings around the world about the use of the A-bombs. One *Examiner* story was headlined with the quote 'Anglo-Saxon War Criminals', an opinion that couldn't have been published before May. An item that didn't make the paper was an advertisement in January for men's skating trousers, which fell foul of the censors' fixation with not giving away weather information.

As Britain celebrated the end of the war in Europe, Churchill's victory broadcast took a few swipes at Éire's policy of neutrality. "We left the de Valera Government to frolic with the German, and later the Japanese, representatives to their hearts' content," he said, and made reference to Britain's self-restraint in not resorting to violence to change Éire's position. De Valera's riposte a few days later became part of the legend of Ireland's great statesman putting Churchill in his place.

In Dublin, end of war celebrations by students at Trinity College sparked incidents when people were offended at the raising of the Union Jack and an attempted burning of the Irish Tricolour.

Tremendous havoc in Hiroshima

Thursday, August 9

Tokyo yesterday gave a picture of tremendous havoc in Hiroshima. All living things, human and animal, were "literally seared to death" when the atom bomb burst in Hiroshima, said Tokyo radio. "Those outdoors were burned to death and those indoors killed by the indescribable pressure and heat. The major part of Hiroshima is destroyed. The city became a disastrous ruin. The destructive force of the new weapon is indescribable as is the terrible devastation it has caused. The dead were burned beyond recognition. The authorities are still unable to obtain a definite check-up on the casualties."

Reconnaissance photographs show that fires were still burning in Hiroshima, it was stated at General Spaatz's headquarters on Guam, yesterday. Heat comparable to that of some stellar body was generated when the bomb burst in the heart of the city. The photographs disclosed that four square miles of the city – 60 per cent of the whole built-up area – had been wiped out with such awful thoroughness it was as if some giant bulldozer had swept across it.

A taste of peace: The first post-war consignment of oranges arrives.

Famous Irish tenor dies

Monday, September 17

We regret to announce the death of Count John McCormack which took place at his home in Dublin, at 11.15 last night after a short illness. He was aged 61 years.

The late Count McCormack, like many Irishmen who won fame in the New World, came of humble origin. He was born in Athlone in 1884 and it was typical of the man that even during the height of his success he should always speak of Athlone as "up in my home town".

Wherever this famous tenor went on tour his programmes included a group of Irish folk songs, which he sang with a tenderness and sweetness surpassing even his treatment of Gounod's 'Ave Maria' – which was acclaimed by one famous critic as "a standard for all time".

On the occasion of his retirement, he stated that the greatest occasion of his life was when he sang the 'Panis Angelicus' at the Eucharistic Congress in Dublin in 1932.

NEWS BRIEFS

May Former Dolphin rugby club scrum-half Archie Ryan tells of the gratitude of Polish prisoners at receiving provisions from the Irish Red Cross in the German prisoner of war camp where he was held. They came to the Irish prisoners thanking them on behalf of their nation. "They were very moved and showed great emotion," he said. (23)

Sept The *Examiner* publishes accounts of mass killings, starvation and cannibalism in Belsen Concentration Camp. (21)

The Cork Examiner

NO. 28,804. WEDNESDAY MORNING, MAY 9, 1945. PRICE—TWOPENCE

Registered for Transmission at Newspaper Rate of Postage in Ireland and Great Britain, and at Magazine Rate in Canada and Newfoundland

Midnight Cessation of Hostilities In Europe

King George's Plea For Just And Lasting Peace

MR. Winston Churchill and President Truman broadcast statements from London and Washington, respectively yesterday, announcing that hostilities in Europe would end officially at midnight last night. No statement was issued from Marshal Stalin yesterday, but after midnight, last night, a Reuter message stated that Moscow Radio had issued an announcement and that to-day (Wednesday) would be regarded as Victory Day.

In his broadcast, Mr. Churchill stated that the cease fire had been ordered on Monday. He added that the Germans were still, in places, resisting the Russian troops, and warned that if they continued to do so after midnight, they would deprive themselves of the protection of the laws of war and would be attacked from all quarters by Allied troops.

After saying that the German war was at an end, Mr. Churchill in a reference to Japan, said that after a brief period of rejoicing they must devote all their strength and resources to the completion of their task, both at home and abroad.

In his announcement from the White House, President Truman said: "We must work to finish the war. Our victory is but half won. The West is free but the East is still in bondage to the Japanese. Our blows," he said, "will continue until the Japanese lay down their arms in unconditional surrender."

The President then read a Proclamation in which he appointed Sunday next as a day of prayer.

According to the Associated Press, White House sources later made it clear that for the U.S. no formal victory day had been proclaimed.

King George in his broadcast last night also pledged Britain's resources in the war against Japan, and after paying tribute to all who died, fought and served in the European conflict, he said: "We shall have failed and the blood of our dearest will have flowed in vain if the victory which they died to win does not lead to a lasting peace founded on justice and established in good-will."

Late last night, the German High Command ordered all German armed forces in all theatres of war to cease hostilities, not to sink ships, nor destroy ammunition, equipment, etc., with effect from midnight, last night.

"PEACE FOUNDED ON JUSTICE" —King George.

King George said:—

"To-day we give thanks to God for a great deliverance. Germany, who drove all Europe into war, has been finally overcome. In the Far East, we have yet to deal with the Japanese, a determined and cruel foe. To this we shall turn with the utmost resolve and with all our resources. But at this hour, when the dreadful shadow of war has passed far from our hearths and homes in these islands, we may at last make one pause for thanksgiving and then we must turn our thoughts to tasks all over the world which peace in Europe brings with it. First, let us remember those who will not come back. With those memories in our minds, let us think what it was that has upheld us through nearly six years of suffering and peril. The knowledge that everything was at stake—our freedom, our independence, our very existence as a people; but the knowledge also that in defending ourselves we were defending the liberties of the whole world. We knew that if we failed or faltered the last remaining barrier against a world-wide tyranny would have fallen in ruins. But we did not falter and we did not fail. We kept faith with ourselves and with one another; we kept faith and unity with our great Allies. That faith, that unity, have carried us to victory, through dangers which at times seemed overwhelming.

"So let us now resolve to bring to the tasks which lie ahead the same high confidence in our mission. Much hard work awaits us both in the restoration of our own country after the ravages of war and in helping to restore peace and sanity to a shattered world.

"There is great comfort in the thought that years of darkness and danger in which the children of our country have grown up are, please God, over forever.

"We shall have failed, and the blood of our dearest will have flowed in vain if the victory which they died to win does not lead to a lasting peace founded on justice and established in good will.

To that, then let us turn our thoughts on this day of just triumph and proud sorrow and then take up our work again, resolved as a people to do nothing unworthy of those who died for us and to make the world such a world as they would have desired for their children and for ours. This is the task to which now honour binds us.

"In the hour of danger we humbly committed our cause into the hand of God and He has been our strength and shield. Let us thank Him for His mercies and in this hour of victory commit ourselves and our task to the guidance of the same strong hand."

"JAPAN REMAINS UNSUBDUED" —Mr. Churchill.

Mr. Churchill said:—

"Yesterday morning at 2.41 a.m., at General Eisenhower's Headquarters, General Jodl (representative of the German High Command and of Grand Admiral Doenitz (designated head of the German State) signed an act of unconditional surrender of all German land, sea, and air forces in Europe to the Allied Expeditionary Forces, and, simultaneously, to the Soviet High Command.

"General Beddell Smith (Chief of Staff of the Allied Expeditionary Force), and General Francois Seve, signed the document on behalf of the Supreme Commander of the Allied Expeditionary Forces, and Gen. Suslapatov signed on behalf of the Russian High Command.

"To-day this agreement will be ratified and confirmed at Berlin, where Air Chief Marshal Tedder (Deputy Supreme Commander of the Allied Expeditionary Force) and General Tassigny will sign on behalf of General Eisenhower. Marshal Zhukov will sign on behalf of the Soviet High Command. The German representatives will be Field Marshal Keitel (Chief of the High Command), and Commanders-in-Chief of the German Army, Navy, and Air Forces.

"Hostilities will end officially at one minute after midnight, to-night, Tuesday, 8th May, but in the interests of saving lives the 'cease-fire' began yesterday, to be sounded all along the front, and our dear Channel Islands are also to be freed to-day.

"The Germans are still, in places, resisting the Russian troops, but should they continue to do so after midnight, they will, of course, deprive themselves of the protection of the laws of war, and will be attacked from all quarters by the Allied troops.

"It is not surprising that on such long front as in the existing disorder, the commands of the German High Command should not in every case be obeyed immediately. This does not, in our opinion, with the best military advice at our disposal, constitute any reason for withholding from the nation the facts communicated to us by General Eisenhower of the unconditional surrender already signed at Rheims, nor should it prevent us from celebrating to-day and to-morrow (Wednesday) as Victory-in-Europe days.

"To-day, perhaps, we shall think mostly of ourselves. To-morrow we shall pay a particular tribute to our Russian comrades, whose prowess in the field has been one of the grand contributions to the general victory.

"The German war is, therefore, at an end.

"After years of intense preparation, Germany hurled herself on Poland at the beginning of September, 1939, and in pursuance of our guarantee to Poland, and in agreement with the French Republic, Great Britain, the British Empire and Commonwealth of Nations declared war upon this foul aggression. After gallant France had been struck down, we, from this island, and from our United Empire, maintained the struggle single-handed for a whole year until we were joined by the military might of Soviet Russia, and later by the overwhelming power and resources of the United States of America. Finally, almost the whole world was combined against the evil doers who are now prostrate before us. Our gratitude to our splendid Allies goes forth from all our hearts in this island and throughout the British Empire.

"We may allow ourselves a brief period of rejoicing, but let us not forget for a moment the toil and efforts that lie ahead. Japan with all her treachery and greed remains unsubdued. The injury she has inflicted on Great Britain, the United States, and other countries and her detestable cruelties call for justice and retribution. We must now devote all our strength and resources to the completion of our task both at home and abroad. Advance Britannia. Long live the cause of freedom. God save the King."

Mr. Churchill's message was followed immediately by the ceremonial sounding of the end of the war in Europe by the buglers of the Scots Guards.

SIGNED IN BERLIN.

The German unconditional surrender to the Soviet forces was signed in Berlin on May 8 by Field Marshal Keitel, Generals Friedeburg and Stumpf on behalf of Germany, and by Marshal Zhukov and Air Chief Marshal Tedder on behalf of the Allies.

UNION JACK DESTROYED.

A Union Jack, flying from the home of Mrs. Mackimmon, caretaker of the Scriptural School, Downshire Road, Newry, Co. Down, who lost a son in the war, was pulled down and destroyed during Monday night.

"VICTORY IS BUT HALF WON" —President Truman.

President Truman, in his American broadcast statement, announcing the end of the war in Europe, said:—

"This is a solemn but glorious hour. My only wish is that Franklin D. Roosevelt had lived to witness this day.

"General Eisenhower informs me that the forces of Germany have surrendered to the United Nations. The flags of freedom fly all over Europe. The Western world has been freed of the evil forces which for five years and longer have imprisoned the bodies and broken the lives of millions upon millions of free-born men.

"The power of our peoples to defend themselves against all enemies will be proved in the Pacific war, as it has been proved in Europe. Our blows will continue until the Japanese lay down their arms in unconditional surrender."

Stressing the task still ahead, President Truman said:—"If I could give you a single watchword for the coming months that word is work, work, work. We must work to finish the war. Our victory is but half won. The West is free, but the East is still in bondage to the treacherous tyranny of the Japanese."

"The job ahead is no less important, no less urgent, no less difficult than the task which now is happily done. I call upon every American to stick to his post until the last battle is won. Until that day let no man abandon his post or slacken his efforts."

The President then read a proclamation, in which he said: "The Allied armies, through sacrifice and devotion, and with God's help, have won from Germany final and unconditional surrender. For the triumph of the spirit and of arms which we have won and for its promise to the peoples everywhere who join us in our love of freedom, it is fitting that we as a nation should give thanks to Almighty God, Who has strengthened us and given us the victory.

"Now therefore I, Harry S. Truman, President of the U.S.A., do hereby appoint Sunday, May 13th, 1945, to be a day of prayer. I call upon the people of the United States, whatever their faith, to unite in offering joyful thanks to God for the victory we have won, and to pray that He will support us to the end of our present struggle, and guide us into the way of peace."

In announcing the victory in Europe, said an Associated Press Washington message, President Truman carefully avoided any use of the popular term "V-Day," and White House sources later made it clear that for the United States no formal "V-Day" had been proclaimed. Instead, the President set aside next Sunday as a day of prayer.

RUSSIA'S VICTORY DAY.

MOSCOW radio announced last night the signing of unconditional surrender by Germany. Reuter adds: "This is the first announcement from Moscow of Germany's unconditional surrender."

Moscow radio said:—"The unconditional surrender of all German armed forces on land, sea and air has been signed. The German High Command will immediately issue orders to all forces on sea, land and air under the German High Command to cease military operations after 11.01 p.m. Moscow time."

Moscow radio broadcast a special Order of the Day announcing that to-day (Wednesday) will be Victory Day in Russia.

THANKSGIVING FOR PEACE.

Instruction By Archbishop Of Dublin.

The Archbishop of Dublin, Most Rev. J. C. McQuaid, D.D., in a statement yesterday, said: "In thanksgiving to God for the cessation of the war in Europe, the prayers Pro Gratiarum Actione (Tamquam Pro Re Gravi) shall be substituted for the prayers Pro Pace in all Masses where the Rubrics permit, in the Diocese of Dublin, until the end of May. After that date until further notice, the prayers Pro Quacumque Necessitate (Tamquam Pro Re Gravi) shall be said in all Masses where the Rubrics permit, that the truth and charity of Our Divine Lord Jesus Christ may be the basis of the enduring peace for which we pray. The May devotions shall continue to be offered for the intention that God in His mercy may, by the intercession of Our Blessed Lady, grant peace to all the world.

"GERMAN REICH ENDED" —Admiral Doenitz.

Broadcasting to the German people on the Flensburg radio yesterday, Admiral Doenitz said:—

"German men and women,—When I addressed you on the evening of May 1 to announce the death of the Fuehrer and my appointment as his successor, I told you that my first task would be to spare the lives of German men and women. In conformity therewith, I ordered the High Command of the German Wehrmacht on the night of May 6 to arrange for the unconditional surrender of all German fighting troops in all theatres of war.

"From 23.00 D.B.S.T. on May 8, the guns will be silent. German soldiers, veterans of countless battles, are now treading a bitter path to captivity and thereby making the last sacrifice for the life of our women and children and for the future of our nation. We bow in respect to their gallantry—which they have proved a thousand times. We remember the fallen and the prisoners.

"I have promised our brave men, women, and children to provide them with endurable living conditions so far as it is in my power to do so in the coming difficulties. I do not know yet what I shall be able to do to help you in these hard times.

We have to face the facts. The foundations on which the German Reich was built are a thing of the past. The unity of State and Party no longer exists. The Party has disappeared from the scene of its former activity.

"With the occupation of Germany, power has passed into the hands of the occupation forces. It depends on them whether I and the Reich Government formed by me will be able to continue in office or not. If I can be of assistance to the Fatherland by continuing in office, I shall do so until the German people have a chance to express their will by appointing a head of State, or until the occupation Powers make it impossible for me to continue in office. My love for Germany and my sense of duty keep me at my difficult post without regard to personal considerations. I shall not remain an hour longer than is compatible with the dignity which I owe to the Reich.

"There is a difficult road ahead for every one of us. We must tread it with the dignity, gallantry, and discipline which the memory of our dead demands. We must be inspired by the will to do our best in work and achievement without which there can be no basis for a future life. We want to march along this road in unity and justice, without which we cannot survive the hardships of the times to come.

"We may tread the road in the hope that the time will come when our children will live a free and secure life in a Europe at peace. I do not want to lag behind you on this thorny path. If my duty calls me to remain in office, I shall try to help you all I can. If, however, duty requires me to depart, this will be taken in service to the people and Reich."

NEW ORDERS TO ALL GERMAN FORCES.

New orders to the German armed forces, broadcast from Flensburg radio by the German High Command last night, said that with effect from 00.01, May 9, "all parts of the armed forces in all theatres of war must cease all hostilities. No destruction of ammunition, equipment, etc., must be carried out. No ships must be sunk. Acts to the contrary are an offence against the terms accepted by the High Command. The order applies to everybody who had no knowledge of it before. From 00.01, May 9 onwards, all wireless messages must be in open language—no code to be used."

SERVICES IN DUBLIN CHURCHES.

Special Thanksgiving Services for the return of peace to Europe were conducted last evening in Church of Ireland, Presbyterian and Methodist Churches in Dublin. In all Church of Ireland Churches in the Diocese of Dublin, Glendalough and Kildare, there will be special thanksgiving for the return of peace at the ordinary services on Sunday next.

MOURNING FOR HITLER.

Addressing a Unionist meeting in Belfast, Major J. M. Sinclair, Northern Ireland Minister of Finance, said, yesterday, that he had heard of girls going to work in a linen factory wearing mourning bands for Hitler. They were not pro-German but anti-British. "If the whole country had been neutral during the war, Ireland might have come under Nazi domination in 1940. It would not only have been Belfast, but Dublin, Cork, and Limerick."

GOVERNMENT BUREAU STATEMENT.

GERMAN LEGATION CLOSED IN DUBLIN

[illegible] following official statement was issued by the Government Information Bureau yesterday afternoon:

"Dr. Hempel, the German Minister, called on the Minister for External Affairs this morning and informed him that in view of the events which had occurred he regarded his mission as terminated.

"Dr. Hempel stated that he was vacating the Legation premises and that he wished the Irish Government to take charge of them and all the German Government property contained therein until the assumption of the Government of the Reich by the new authority."

[illegible] Hempel was appointed [illegible] and Minister [illegible] Eire on July 23, [illegible] to the late Herr von [illegible] was born in Saxony, [illegible] early education. [illegible] Law he obtained [illegible].

[illegible] as an officer in the first [illegible]. After being wounded he [illegible] headquarters. He entered [illegible] the Foreign Office [illegible] where he held different [illegible]. From 1930 to 1935 he [illegible] of the German Legation [illegible]. Frau Hempel is a daughter of a General of the former German Army.

It was learned, last evening, that the Legation premises have actually been vacated.

In addition to Dr. Hempel the following four officials were also in the Legation: Herr Henning Thomsen, Counsellor, appointed 1/11/'38; Dr. Carl Heinz Petersen, appointed 3/9/'38; Herr Johannes Bruchhaus, appointed 10/5/'38, and Herr Wilhelm Muller, Consular Secretary, appointed 1/10/'38. All the officials are married and their wives live in this country.

COMMONS QUESTION.

Mr. Walkden (Labour) asked the British Dominions Under-secretary, in the House of Commons, yesterday, whether he is aware that the Prime Minister of Eire, accompanied by the Secretary of External Affairs called on the German Minister in Dublin to express his condolences on the death of Herr Hitler, and whether any protest had been conveyed to the Government of Eire?

Mr. Evans, in a written reply, stated:—No. Mr. de Valera can safely be left to realise for himself the universal feeling of indignation which his action has aroused in this country and throughout the United Nations.

CAPITULATION IN NORWAY PROCLAIMED.

[illegible] Prince Olav, as Commander[illegible] of the Norwegian armed forces, [illegible] proclaimed the capitulation [illegible] Germans in Norway. He added [illegible] had placed all the Norwegian [illegible] at the disposal of the Allied [illegible] Command, says the P.A.

[illegible] Haakon, in a broadcast to Nor[illegible] night, sent his and the [illegible] "warm greetings to all [illegible] men and women on this [illegible]. Our difficulties are still not [illegible]," he said, "but when we [illegible] work again, it will be in [illegible] land, where together we shall [illegible] Norway's future for ourselves [illegible] our children. Let us hold [illegible] that unity which has brought [illegible] victory. And let us at this [illegible] remember those who offered [illegible] lives in the fight for Norway. [illegible] unite in the pledge—all for [illegible]."

LONDON'S DAY OF REVELRY.

"With all its memories of big [illegible] stretching back a thousand [illegible] London could never before have [illegible] a day and night like this," said Arthur Booth, P.A. staff reporter, last [illegible].

There were three focal points—Buckingham Palace where King George and Queen Elizabeth again and again made a balcony appearance; Whitehall, with its Cenotaph and an impromptu speech from the Prime Minister from the verandah of a Government building, and, finally, Piccadilly Circus, packed with an almost immovable mass of cheering, singing men and women.

"In all our long history we have never seen a greater day than this," Mr. Churchill told the vast assembly in Whitehall.

It was in many ways a celebration very different from that of the first Armistice Day. There was much singing and shouting, but less of the hysteria and none of the blind, unthinking over-optimism of November, 1918. It was remembered, too, that one powerful enemy was still unvanquished.

Taxis and private cars came to a standstill early. Crowds along Regent Street and Piccadilly held up traffic for hours, and many cars had to be abandoned by their owners for a time.

"The manager of a Knightsbridge [illegible] firm said: 'Half of our cars have been pushed over or turned upside down. The remaining drivers refuse to go out.'

Mr. Churchill made another speech from the balcony on the Ministry of Health building in Whitehall just after 10.30 p.m.

With the approach of 'Cease fire' at one minute after midnight, great crowds renewed the singing and [illegible], roaring, dancing, in West End centres and in other parts of London, where famous buildings were floodlit and turned the city into fairyland. It was London with the lid off."

"THEN GO TO POLAND"

Minister's Reply To Journalist

Professor Pragier, Minister of Information to the Polish Government in London, said to Press correspondents as he heard cheering yesterday from the crowds in Piccadilly beneath his [illegible] floor office:—

"I am happy, but I would be much happier if we thought the future of the world was as safely in our hands as the victory is."

He stigmatised as without truth Russian statements that arrested Polish Leaders had been engaged in "diversionary acts" against the Soviet armed forces. When one journalist at the conference said: "We are trying to elucidate a mystery and want the facts," Professor Pragier retorted:

"Then go to Poland. You can go to France and Belgium and Holland. Go to Poland as well."

The Polish Government in London, on Sunday sent to Mr. Stettinius, as Chairman of the San Francisco Conference, an urgent appeal to the United Nations' Governments to induce the Soviet Government to set free the arrested men and to guarantee personal safety to them and to their families, says the Polish Ministry of Information, in a statement issued yesterday.

U.S. ARMY CASUALTIES.

Washington, Tuesday.—The American War Department announces that, according to latest available figures, the U.S. Army has suffered a total of 695,247 casualties, of which 135,284 are killed, 421,365 wounded, 67,092 missing, and [illegible] are prisoners of war.—Reuter.

POPE WILL BROADCAST.

Vatican City, Tuesday.—The Pope will make a brief address over Vatican Radio at 12 o'clock to-morrow (Rome time), the Vatican announces.—A.P.

WINDOWS IN U.S. AND BRITISH OFFICES BROKEN.

Dublin Incident.

Dublin, Tuesday.—The following official statement was issued by the Government Information Bureau this afternoon:—"Windows in the British Representative's Office and the American Consulate-General were broken last night by stones thrown by a member or members of a disorderly crowd, which paraded the streets after the disturbances at Trinity College.

"The Secretary of the Department of External Affairs called this afternoon on the British representative, Sir John Maffey, and the American Consul-General, Mr. McEnelly, to express the regrets of the Minister for External Affairs at the occurrence, which he greatly deplored."

MORE SCENES.

There were some scenes in Dublin again last night, in the vicinity of Trinity College, when large crowds gathered in College Green and other districts around the college. There were cheers and catcalls from various elements as youths made attempts to snatch emblems from the coat lapels of some passers by. A large force of Guards was present and on several occasions drew batons, but on such occasions the crowds scattered swiftly and although the atmosphere was lively for several hours, the incidents were never outside the trivial category.

THE WEATHER.

Britain Issues First Forecast Since The War.

For the first time since the war began it is possible to tell the world what weather Britain is having while it is having it.

Rain fell practically everywhere on V.E. Day, stated the British Air Ministry. Winds off the sea kept day temperatures down to around 50 degrees along the East coasts of England and Scotland, but inland and in western districts the day was warm, 70 degs. being exceeded at most places in South-east and South England, South Midlands and East Anglia. London was the warmest place, with 78 degs.

VIOLENT THUNDERSTORM IN CORK.

A severe thunderstorm raged over Cork City and County last night. Shortly after 7 o'clock the sky became overcast and for the best part of an hour vivid flashes of lightning illuminated the sky, while peal after peal of thunder was heard. During the storm the electric lighting system all over the city failed for about ten minutes, but no cases of serious damage to cables were reported. Telephonic communications in and around Cork were not interrupted.

Story Of The Surrender

Marshall Yarrow, Reuter's special correspondent at Rheims, France, in a message dated Sunday and received last night, said:—Around a plain wooden table, painted in battle-ship grey, in a drab, commonplace schoolroom in the heart of France, the greatest surrender in history took exactly five minutes to sign. Seated at the table were three American, three British, three Russian, one French and three German officers.

The surrender took place in the 30ft. square war room at General Eisenhower's H.Q. in the red brick Coeducational Industrial College of Rheims. The documents had been prepared on plain, legal forms. There were four copies, all in plain manila folders, without ribbons, seals or trimmings. At about two o'clock in the morning staff cars began to pull up at the H.Q. and an air of excitement spread throughout the building. Clerks and drivers off duty, and many junior officers, gathered in the halls and stairways.

When all were seated, Genl. K. W. D. Strong (S.H.A.E.F.) placed the documents for signature in front of General Smith, who said: "These are the terms of unconditional surrender," and asked formally whether the Germans were prepared to sign. Genl. Jodl nodded slightly. Special brown-coloured fountain pens with gold nibs, which Genl. Eisenhower had kept specially for this occasion since the landing in North Africa, were handed to the delegates. Genl. Jodl scrawled his name on all four copies. Copies were then passed to Genl. Sevez, who was followed by Genl. Suslopatov, and finally Genl. Bedell Smith signed.

The signing of the historic documents began at exactly 2.40 a.m. and all was over by 2.45. The official time on the document is 2.41 a.m.

As he laid aside the fountain pen with which he had signed his country's total defeat, Genl. Jodl snapped to attention and spoke in English: "I want to say a word." Then he continued in German (his speech has already been published).

There was no reply to his remarks, and Genl. Jodl, after another stiff bow, looked towards the British escort and with his two colleagues left the room.

Genl. Eisenhower did not see the German delegates until the ceremony was completed. Fourteen minutes after the signing, the Germans were escorted into the Supreme Commander's office. Air Chief Marshal Sir Arthur Tedder, Deputy Supreme Commander, was with him.

Genl. Eisenhower asked the Germans sternly if they fully understood the terms of surrender and were prepared to carry them out. They answered in the affirmative, bowed, and left the room.

THE TERMS.

Robert Eunson, Associated Press war correspondent at S.H.A.E.F., Paris, said yesterday: The text of the German unconditional surrender document, entitled "Act of Military Surrender" is as follows:—

"(1) We, the undersigned, acting by authority of the German High Command, hereby surrender unconditionally to the Supreme Commander, Allied Expeditionary Force, and simultaneously to the Soviet High Command, all forces on land, sea, and in the air who are at this date under German control.

"(2) The German High Command will at once issue orders to all German military, naval, and air authorities and to all forces under German control to cease active operations at 23.01 hours Central European Time, on the 8th of May, and to remain in the positions occupied at that time. No ship, vessel or aircraft is to be scuttled, or any damage done to their hull, machinery or equipment.

"(3) The German High Command will at once issue to the appropriate Commanders, and ensure the carrying out of any further orders issued by the Supreme Commander, Allied Expeditionary Force, and by the Soviet High Command.

"(4) This act of military surrender is without prejudice to, and will be superseded by any general instrument of surrender imposed by, or on behalf of the United Nations and applicable to Germany and the German armed forces as a whole."

"THE EAST IS STILL IN BONDAGE."

U.S. PRESIDENT'S CALL TO BATTLE AGAINST JAPAN

THE United States President, in his broadcast yesterday announcing the end of the war in Europe, said: "The West is free, but the East is still in bondage to the treacherous tyranny of the Japanese. Our blows will not cease until the Japanese military and naval forces lay down their arms in unconditional surrender."

General MacArthur, Commander of all army forces in the Pacific theatre, in a broadcast message yesterday said, according to Reuter: "I rejoice that this Command will now be reinforced by those vast and powerful resources which were previously employed on the battlefields of Europe. Through this additional strength the Japanese Empire will be more speedily vanquished, with greater economy of American and Allied life than would otherwise be possible."

Tokyo radio reported yesterday, the A.P. says, that 65 to 70 Mustangs, "led by a few Superfortresses," attacked an airfield and munitions plants in the Tokyo area yesterday. Another report said that Superfortresses earlier raided airfields and installations on the home islands of Kyushu and Shikoku.

Tokyo radio told the Japanese people yesterday that Germany had surrendered to the Allies. The radio referred on Monday to the surrender, but only in broadcasts beamed abroad in an English language transmission, according to the A.P. Yesterday's broadcast said that "along with the surrender of the entire German forces, the German forces garrisoned in Norway also surrendered." The broadcast was based on a Domei report from Stockholm.

Vice-Admiral Teijiro Toyoda, Japanese Minister of Munitions, told the Japanese people yesterday that it was "now or never" so far as increases in war production were concerned.

In a speech quoted by the Japanese News Agency, the Minister said: "Make as many aircraft as possible, and rush them to the battlefront of Okinawa without delay."

The Japanese News Agency yesterday, says Reuter, quoted Japanese newspaper articles accusing Germany of "betrayal" of the Axis and reiterating Japan's determination to continue the fight against the Allies.

The "Tokyo Asahi" said, "Foreign Minister Togo's statement yesterday made clear that the Japanese Government is prepared to denounce the three-power alliance upon further [illegible] of the German [illegible]. The tripartite alliance is deemed to have a natural death as a result of the collapse of the German and Italian nations. "Japan should free herself of the Axis ideology, which is now a thing of the past, both at home and abroad."

Japanese [illegible] between [illegible] and [illegible] troops at [illegible] of Rangoon [illegible] eastward [illegible] Reuter from [illegible].

Farther north in Central Burma, there has been a [illegible] along the road [illegible] Toungoo, 14 miles east of M[illegible] the Japanese are trying to [illegible] a way into the [illegible] rearguard. [illegible] Army made [illegible] Irrawaddy [illegible] advance from Prome [illegible] Prome-Rangoon [illegible] north-west of Rangoon.

The Australian Army [illegible] fighting in the [illegible] gainville, where Australians [illegible] inflicted the heaviest [illegible] Japanese since the [illegible] Easter offensive. In New [illegible] gainville [illegible] landed [illegible] on Nashin Bay. The Japanese [illegible] suffered heavily [illegible] Guinea coast. Eight [illegible] R.A.A.F. [illegible] have been landed on Tarakan, off Borneo.

TRANSATLANTIC FLIGHT.

New York, Tuesday.—The first Transatlantic airplane, whose departure could be made public under the security regulations since 1941, to-day left Laguardia Field, New York, for Foynes. It was an American export liner carrying 21 passengers, including the Duchess of Leinster and M. Alain du Parc, the Belgian Minister to the United States.—Associated Press.

SURRENDER OF GERMAN NAVAL FORCES.

A special communique, issued from Supreme Allied Headquarters yesterday afternoon, said:—

"All German land, sea, and air forces in Europe were unconditionally surrendered to the Allied Expeditionary Forces and, simultaneously, to the Soviet High Command at 01.41 Central European time, May 7th.

"The surrender terms, which will become effective at 23.01 hours Central European Time, 8th May, were signed by an officer of the German Command.

"Allied Expeditionary Forces have been ordered to cease offensive operations, but will maintain their present position."

A supplement to the German communique yesterday said:—

"The British have in several places prohibited the use of the German (Nazi) salute by the Wehrmacht. Military discipline makes it advisable to have a unified form of salute, and therefore, the army salute is being made compulsory for all parts of the Wehrmacht."

A British Admiralty announcement says that the following orders have been issued for the surrender of the German Fleet:—

"All German and German-controlled warships, auxiliaries, merchant ships, and other craft at sea are being ordered to report their position in plain language to the nearest Allied wireless telegraph station, and are being given orders to proceed to such Allied ports as directed. They will remain in these ports until further directions are received.

"All warships, auxiliaries, merchant ships, and other craft in harbour are being ordered to remain in harbour; U-boats are being ordered to surface, to fly a black flag or pennant, and to report their position in plain language to the nearest Allied wireless telegraphy station. They will then proceed on the surface to such port as they may be directed.

"All warships and merchant ships, whether in port or at sea, are being instructed to train all weapons fore and aft. Breech blocks will be removed from guns, and torpedo tubes will be unloaded. In harbour all ammunition, explosives, torpedo warheads, and all portable weapons will be landed.

"Mine-sweeping vessels and salvage vessels, though similarly disarmed, will be instructed to complete with fuel (if necessary) and to prepare themselves immediately for mine-sweeping or salvage service as directed. Instructions will be given for boom defences at ports and harbours to be kept open.

"All personnel will be ordered to remain either on board their ships or in their establishments until other directions are received."

RIOTING IN NOVA SCOTIA.

Halifax, N.S., Tuesday.—Rioting broke out here anew, to-day, as 500 persons, mostly sailors, smashed every window on the west side of Granville Street. Thousands of dollars damage was caused. Three liquor stores have been looted and wrecked since the celebrations started yesterday.—Reuter.

OLD HEAD OF KINSALE AND EROSION.

Danger From Taking Of Beach Material.

A PART of the County Cork seashore near Kinsale, which some years ago was stated to be in danger of being inundated by the sea, cutting off the Old Head of Kinsale from the mainland, was mentioned in Kinsale District Court yesterday in cases brought by the Cork County Council against a number of defendants.

Timothy Manning, Kilcolman, Kinsale, Co. Cork, was fined £1, with £1 costs, for removing beach material on March 9, 1945, from the White Strand, Co. Cork, in respect of which a prohibitory order had been made.

Christopher O'Donovan, Ballymackeen, Co. Cork, was fined £1, with £1 costs, for a similar offence on the same day. The evidence against both defendants was that they had removed sand from the strand in question.

Michael Mulcahy, Asst. Co. Surveyor, said that if this particular beach were lowered the sea would encroach, as it had been doing for the last few years. In the years 1938 and 1939 the Co. Council had had to construct two large groynes on this stretch of seashore. From the records it appeared that the coast road running by the shore had had to be shifted twice, the last time in 1917, and the sea had continued to move in since then. The effect of removing material from the strand would be to cause the sea to encroach still further.

DRESDEN CAPTURED BY SOVIETS

Marshal Stalin, in an Order of the Day to General Eremenko, to-night, said, according to Reuter: "Troops of the Fourth Ukrainian Command, after stiff fighting to-day, occupied the large town and railway junction of Olomouc." Olomouc, 35 miles south-west of Moravska Ostrava, is an important road and rail communications centre on the main road to Brno. It is 128 miles south-west of Prague.

In an Order of the Day to Marshal Koniev he said: "Troops of the First Ukrainian Command, after a battle lasting two days, broke [illegible] and took [illegible] important communications [illegible] strong [illegible] in Saxony."

An Order of the Day to Marshal Malinovski, last night stated:—"Troops of the Second Ukrainian Command to-day captured in Czechoslovakia the town of Jaromerice and the town of Znaime, and in Austria the towns of Hollabruenn and Stockerau, important communication centres and strong bastions in the German defences."

Znoimo, or Znaim, is 30 miles south-west of Brno, and six miles [illegible] the Austrian frontier. Jaromerice is 32 miles west-south-west of Brno.

A supplement to the German communique yesterday said: [illegible] our troops have withdrawn [illegible]. While the Russians continued to keep quiet on the southern sector of the eastern front, American formations are advancing eastwards from the Linz area. In Moravia, the fierce defensive battles are continuing south-east of Brno and in Moravia generally. The towns of Olomouc and Sternberg were lost. American formations reached Beraun.

"On the Frische Nehrung the situation is unchanged in spite of continuous strong enemy attacks. In Courland the Soviets confined themselves on Monday also to local thrusts."

An agreement for German capitulation in Prague and the surrounding area starting at 8 p.m., last night, has been signed, said Prague radio.

The agreement, said the radio, was signed by representatives of the Czechoslovak National Army and the German General commanding the forces in Prague. According to this agreement all Wehrmacht units, S.S. troops, German police and all German State organs in Prague and surroundings had to start leaving by 8 p.m.

The Germans in the Dodecanese Island have surrendered, it is officially announced, says Reuter from Cairo. General Wagener, Commander of the German garrison in the Dodecanese surrendered his forces to a British Brigadier on Tuesday at 10.10 a.m. All hostilities were due to cease at 1 p.m. yesterday. The surrender, signed on Simi, one of the islands, was unconditional. An immediate return of Allied prisoners of war has been arranged.

The only German outpost in the Mediterranean still unaccounted for is Crete, where it is believed that at least one division is still holding out, says the Associated Press from Cairo. The Germans had approximately 10,000 troops in the Dodecanese Islands.

CORK WILL.

Mrs. Ellen Moloney of Elsinore, Currie Ave., Dun Laoghaire, Co. Dublin, who died on August 6th last, widow of D. J. Moloney of Sydenham, Wellington Road, Cork, left personal estate in England and Eire valued at £3,054. She left £100 to her devoted friend Nelly Barry, £100 each to her sister Ann and her grand-daughter Dorothy Black, some smaller legacies and the residue to her daughter Mary Black of Elton[illegible], [illegible] Park, Sandycove, Co. Dublin, to whom probate has been granted.

1946

The immediate period after the war brought little improvement in the living conditions for most Irish people. It is estimated that only one in four homes had running water, many imported items were still hard to get and a terrible summer ensured a poor harvest and further shortages of home-produced goods. Fuel shortages were exacerbated by the worst winter that century. Prices rose, wages didn't, bread rationing was re-introduced and the butter ration was halved. Discontent led to a long strike by national school teachers in Dublin and around 30,000 people emigrated, mainly to Britain.

In Europe, war crime trials had been restricted to the losing side and 10 prominent Nazis were hanged in October. Hermann Goering cheated the gallows by swallowing cyanide. An Irish angle on post-war justice was the execution of Nazi propagandist, William Joyce. However, the *Examiner* report of his trial and death makes no mention of the fact that Joyce's father was Irish and that he had lived for a time in Mayo. There had been government suppression of this fact during the war and there was probably a continued desire not to be associated with him.

NEWS BRIEFS

Jan William Joyce, the infamous Lord Haw Haw, who had broadcast German propaganda during the war, is hanged in Wandsworth Prison, London, after being found guilty of treason. (4)

Mar Winston Churchill signals the start of the Cold War by warning of how "a shadow has fallen upon the scenes so lately lighted by an Allied victory." He also states that an Iron Curtain has descended across Europe. Stalin condemns the speech as a call for war. (6)

Voluntary harvest aid ends

Tuesday, October 8

Helping with the harvest.

The work of the Cork City Harvesting Committee has been terminated. This was announced at a meeting of the committee, held at the City Hall last night. The following statement was read: "Operations were unexpectedly prolonged because of the persistently broken weather. From the 25th September to the 4th October there was not a day without rain, and at times torrential rain that made a sodden mess of corn in stooks and corn uncut. Much of such crops have suffered serious devastation, even though with some improvement in the weather, they have now been mainly dried out. In all it is thought that 16,000 men were sent out from this city for harvesting work."

Bishops denounce modern craze for pleasure

Monday, March 4

In their Lenten Pastorals this year, the members of the Irish Hierarchy warn the people against evils which tend to undermine the Catholic life of Ireland. Particular stress is laid upon the growth of the drink habit and the craze for pleasure amongst the younger generations, the grave issues at stake being brought forcibly to the notice of parents and guardians.

On the subject of immoderate drinking, Most Rev Dr Cohalan, Bishop of Waterford and Lismore, writes: "This undesirable phenomenon is alleged to be noticeable on the occasion of socials, dances, reunions, etc, and also in bars and lounges where intoxicating drinks are available. Such behaviour is a definite and conscious lowering of family and national standards and often begins out of mere bravado and cowardice."

His Grace, Most Rev Dr McQuaid, Archbishop of Dublin, writes that no Catholic may enter Trinity College, Dublin, without the previous permission of the Ordinary of the Diocese. The Pastoral continues: "The National University of Ireland with its three constituent colleges, is by its charter a neutral educational establishment. For that reason it must be regarded by Catholics as failing to give acknowledgement of the one true Faith. In view, however, of the measure taken by the Ecclesiastical Authorities to protect faith and morals, University College, Dublin, in our diocese may be considered sufficiently safe for Catholic students."

The Cork Examiner.

SUICIDE WHILE SENTINEL WATCHED PRISONER

Goering's Death Mystery Still Puzzles The World

THE great mystery of how Herman Goering was enabled to die by self-administered poison two and a quarter hours before he was to die on the scaffold at Nuremberg yesterday morning was still unsolved and agitating the world late last night.

Goering, with a sentry watching him constantly, with the aid of a bright light shining through a peep hole in the door of his cell, was able to transfer a phial of cyanide to his mouth, grind the glass between his teeth, and swallow the poison. He was dead within a few minutes.

Last night the earlier propounded theory, that Goering's wife had passed him the phial when kissing him farewell on the occasion of her last visit, was exploded. Major Teich, a security officer in Nuremberg, said: "She never kissed him. It would be impossible, as there was a thick plate glass window dividing them, and Goering was manacled."

"The barber, dentist and doctor—all Germans—who came into contact with Goering in his cell, as far as we are concerned, are not under suspicion," Major Teich added. "They are only three of a possible twelve persons who had daily contact with Goering. A report that an American guard traded the phial with Goering, in return for one of his rings, is impossible. All his jewels were taken from him."

Asked where he thought Goering got the phial of poison, Major Teich replied: "I think he had it ever since he was taken into custody."

Major Teich accepted as a possibility that Goering might have had the phial passed to him in a pancake during meals.

Major Teich ruled out the possibility that Dr. Stahmer, Goering's counsel, could have passed him the phial during the trial. "When counsel passed documents or notes to their clients they had to do so through a U.S. court official," he said.

The phial was 2½ inches long and ½ inch in diameter; the glass ampoule was in a brass container, with a plug at each end. He did not think it possible it could have been thrown into the cell through the window.

There was a daily "shakedown" of Goering's cell which, from the time that sentence was pronounced, had contained the minimum of equipment and clothing. "I could not say whether a thorough search was made yesterday, but the cell was searched," he said.

[illegible] Binder, Security Officer, [illegible] yesterday that Goering had [illegible] to take any exercise for the [illegible] days of his life.

[illegible] now surmised that if Goering [illegible] phial of cyanide already in [illegible] possession, he would not want to [illegible] to physical contact with his [illegible] if he could avoid it. An accidental jostle while he was being [illegible] for exercise would have [illegible] sufficient to break the fragile [illegible] the phial.

Goering made what appeared to be [illegible] "joke" about suicide eight days [illegible] the incident, it was disclosed yesterday. An official of the Palace [illegible] Justice at Nuremberg said that [illegible] given something to sign, [illegible] took the paper-clips off the document, and said, "You had better take these back—the guards might [illegible] I'll hang myself with them."

[illegible] facts now pieced together are [illegible] to show that Goering decided [illegible] suicide as soon as he heard the [illegible] of the International Tribunal. [illegible] is also thought that he may have [illegible] suicide by cyanide with [illegible] who was found to have a [illegible] phial strapped to his groin [illegible] captured by the British in Hamburg.

Asked about Goering's refusal to take his daily exercise, Major Teich said "He made this request on the grounds that he was handcuffed."

On the question of precisely how Goering managed to take the poison, he said: "As he was apparently asleep, it was not the sentry's duty to go into the cell.

"This sentry has not been arrested. In fact no one has so far been arrested."

Nor did he think that Goering could have concealed the phial in his long Bavarian pipe. "He smoked his pipe regularly, and could not have done this if the phial had been concealed in it. I do not think the other condemned men knew that Goering had committed suicide when they went to the scaffold. Goering may have learned the time of execution from his wife, or he may have worked it out on the basis that it would be 15 days after the sentence."

Prison Chaplain D. F. Gerecke, of St. Louis, who talked to the former Reichsmarshal every day for four months, believes he carried the phial of potassium cyanide with which he ended his life from the time he was captured.

The Chaplain was backed in his [illegible] by a member of the prison [illegible] detail, who said that top-[illegible] officers had been trained in [illegible] deadly poisons.

[illegible] Berghold, counsel for Bormann, [illegible] he felt that Goering had had the [illegible] for months, because of his [illegible] assurance that although he [illegible] receive a death sentence he [illegible] never hang.

On the other hand, medical authorities say that if the poison were stale, [illegible] could not have acted as quickly as [illegible] did.

[illegible] of the correspondents present [illegible] Nuremberg Prison for the execution [illegible] told how the news of Goering's [illegible] was first broken. He wrote:—

[illegible] the Nuremberg clocks were [illegible] midnight, Colonel Andrus, the [illegible] governor, came hurrying into [illegible] rooms through the deserted [illegible]. His face was white, and [illegible] panting.

[illegible] any notes, he started [illegible]: "I have news for you. I [illegible] sorry, I cannot release it yet, but [illegible] is the Control Council's orders."

Then, with a slight pause, he burst out: "Goering is dead—by suicide, at 10.45 p.m. The sentinel never saw him put his hand in his mouth.

"He was lying in bed with his hands above the clothes. The sentinel saw him twitching, and heard him make a strange noise. He called the corporal of the guard and rushed into the cell. The corporal called Dr. [illegible] (German ex-P.O.W. doctor working in the prison) and the chaplain, who were on the floor at the time, and an assistant doctor rushed in at the same time. They heard Goering making a strange noise in his throat which the prison doctor believed was a death-rattle.

"The examination of the remains revealed a small envelope torn open at the top marked in pencil simply 'H Goering.' It contained three pencilled notes and had a small brass cartridge case. One of the notes seemed to be a message to the prison commandant from Goering."

"The documents," Colonel Andrus said, "are being translated under the supervision of the Four-Power Commission. Examination of Goering's body revealed bits of glass in his mouth, and an odour which doctors said indicated the presence of cyanide of potassium. The container was standard equipment for Nazis."

Colonel Andrus then revealed that one such vial had already been taken away from Goering shortly after his arrest. He did not say whether any check had been made "to see whether the first vial was still in safe keeping. A similar poison cartridge was taken from the convict Goering on his arrival at Mondorf, where it was found concealed in a tin of 'Nescafe' in his possession," he said.

"How he obtained this second one, and concealed it after the daily detailed searches to which his cell and his person have been subjected, has not yet been determined."

Colonel Andrus disclosed that after Goering's suicide the other condemned men had been manacled.

Half an hour before Goering had copied Himmler and crushed the phial in his mouth, I watched him lying in his bed, apparently peacefully sleeping, the correspondent continues.

We were being taken on a tour of the prison. We passed along the wooden runway through which the prisoners passed for their daily ordeal in Court, until we entered the actual "death wing" by a barred gate. The wing was one hundred yards long with three tiers of cells and wire-netted gangways. Lights high in the ceiling threw criss-crossed shadows on the cells doors.

At eleven of the doors guards were leaning forward with a lamp shining into the cell and looking through a foot square grated opening at the condemned men. None of the men knew then that he would be dead within six hours, except perhaps Goering, jealously hiding his suicide phial.

Goering was in cell five. Although it was only 9 p.m. he was already in bed. He seemed to be asleep. His hands, covered in the blue silk pyjama coat rested quietly on the khaki army blanket which was soon to be his shroud. His military jackboots were placed tidily in a corner of the small whitewashed cell.

Reuter's special correspondent says that Colonel Burton C. Andrus, Chief Nuremberg gaoler, told him that the phial of poison with which Goering took his life was identical with the one he had found on Goering when he was arrested at Mondorf. "On that occasion he had it in a tin of coffee," Col. Andrus said.

The butt of Goering's grim joke was Colonel Andrus, whose proud boast since the suicide last year of Robert Ley, Nazi Labour leader, had been that self destruction was impossible in "his" prison, says Reuter.

American security officers at once began investigating the suicide and questioned all persons who came into contact with Goering.

Goering's suicide bears out earlier observation that the former Reichsmarshal has had an intense dread of hanging ever since the public hanging of Mussolini. In his cell Goering told Doctor Douglas M. Kelly, Chief Psychiatrist, attending the Nuremberg trials: "I wish I had surrendered to the Russians. They would either have killed me outright or treated me like a hero. I never dreamed you Americans would treat a marshal like a common criminal. You are starting a precedent with these war trials. I thought you would want to go easy in case you are the ones to be tried next time."

Doctor Kelly then said to Goering: "Apparently Hitler did not share your belief in the easy way out." Goering replied: "Hitler. He had his own ideas about dying. You remember the Mussolini incident. We got complete pictures of Mussolini dead in the gutter with his mistress, and hanging in the air upside down. We all looked them over. They were awful. Hitler went into a frenzy. He seized the picture and went up and down shouting: 'This will never happen to me.'"

A German who spent four years in a concentration camp declared:—"The Allied Press has made martyrs of these men. From the scaffold they have thrown forth the seeds of another war."

A Czech broadcaster announced to Czechoslovakia:—"If the Allied Control Council had devoted as much energy to seeing that Goering was not allowed to commit suicide as they did to guarding the eight correspondents from witnessing the executions, Goering might not have cheated justice."

PROBLEM OF THE ACQUITTED

Mr. Bevin On The Situation

Mr. Ernest Bevin, the British Foreign Secretary, stated in the House of Commons yesterday, that the Government had no responsibility for the disposal of Schacht, Papen, and Fritsche, who were acquitted at Nuremberg.

Mr. Skeffington-Lodge (Lab., Bedford) asked whether the Foreign Secretary would take steps to ensure that these three men were given safe conduct to, and sanctuary in, a place where their victimisation by their own fellow countrymen or others would be impossible. Would not the Minister use his very vital influence to secure that these men are not chased up for new charges until passions have died down, this being both vindictive, and, in my judgment, indecent."

Mr. Bevin—I think we must leave it to the American authorities.

Mr. McKinlay (Lab., Dumbarton)—Will the Foreign Secretary place nothing in the way of the persons mentioned joining their fellow-countrymen in hell.

When Mr. Stokes (Lab., Ipswich) asked whether it was not the responsibility of the Four Powers to protect people whom they had already tried and acquitted, Mr. Bevin said: "I don't think any accusation has been made that the American Government, responsible for the zone in which they are residing, is doing anything else."

WORLD PRESS OPINIONS

The following are some world Press reactions to the hangings:—

The "New York Post" dramatised the Nazi hangings by depicting on its front page 10 figures dangling from a swastika. White letters on a red background said: "Paid, 16 11 '46." The "New York World-Telegram" dismissed the hangings with the shortest leading article within American memory. In two lines it said: "Nuremberg hangings. We're glad they used good strong rope."

Dutch newspapers did not comment on Goering's suicide but the Socialist, "Het Parool" said of Seyss-Inquart, former Commissioner for occupied Holland: "The Proverb" says: Of the death nothing but good' but the Dutch people will be quite unable to apply these words to Seyss-Inquart."

The Paris Communist paper "Ce Soir" said: "World public opinion will demand to know who allowed Goering to escape a hanging which he deserved one hundred times.

In South Africa the Nationalist "Die Volksblad" said: "To-day we do not witness the end of the tragedy of Nuremberg. It is only the beginning. Hate stirs up hate. Vengeance creates new vengeance. The generation after us will pass judgment on October 16th, 1946."

VATICAN JOURNAL'S VIEW

"Osservatore Romano," the official Vatican journal, said yesterday that Goering, like Rosenberg, died an atheist. The pair, it said, denied God to the end, one by refusing a minister of religion, thereby confessing the atheistic principle of which he was master; the other, his pagan disciple, by refusing life in whatever it still offered him of expiation and salvation, thereby confessing in practice the same atheistic principle.

The "Johannesburg Star" said the Nazi chiefs had paid with their lives for the enormities committed in the past. Whether the world is to be a better and sweeter place hereafter, is no longer in their keeping. It is the affair of all of us who remain."

In Spain, the privately owned "Madrid": "Russia emerged from Nuremberg as one o fthe accused but nobody is going to hang Stalin, Molotov and Company."

The Left-Wing Belgian paper "Cite Nouvelle said: "Without a doubt a victory for Goering, who thus rejoins Hitler, Goebbels and Himmler in the Nazi's Valhalla . . . The repercussions of this event on German psychology must not be underrated. Goering's suicide constitutes an appeal, a non-submission to defeat. It will haunt Germany's dreams."—Reuter.

NEXT TRIALS SOON

Trials of Nazi industrialists, politicians, S.S. chiefs and others—now that the major criminals have been executed—will begin "some time next month," Mr. Peterson, U.S. Assistant Secretary of War, predicted in Nuremberg yesterday.

He discussed detailed plans for these new trials yesterday with Brigadier-General Taylor, who was appointed last spring as Justice Jackson's deputy in charge of subsequent proceedings.

Reflecting an "intense interest" on the part of War Department officials in these next trials, Mr. Peterson said that

Washington officials were "specially anxious that subsequent trials be prosecuted with the same aggressiveness that characterised the first trials."

PROTEST IN BRITAIN

German Prisoners Wore Black Ties.

German prisoners on a Dunmow (Essex) farm went on a "sit-down strike" yesterday. They had heard the news of the Nuremberg hangings, and turned up for work in the potato fields wearing black ties, made from old bits of rag.

Mr. Paratridge, the farmer, said: "These Germans work hard as a rule, but to-day I can get nothing out of them. They seem dejected and apathetic."

LONDON HOTEL WORKERS RESUME

Workers at hotels and restaurants involved in the 8-day London strike went back to work yesterday.

The Strikers Committee in a statement, yesterday, say that the return to work was carried out smoothly with the exception of one establishment where there was no food. One striker was told to go home as his place had been filled, but on the intervention of Mr. Arthur Lewis, M.P., the man was reinstated.

CAPTAIN ILL.

Ship To Put Into Cork Harbour.

Arrangements were made in Cove last night for the despatch of a launch to meet a vessel, believed to be the s.s. Veaggus, which was expected to put into the harbour early to-day, to land her captain, who is seriously ill.

BELFAST STRIKE ENDED.

The strike of 60 crane drivers which has been holding up unloading of coal in Belfast, is over. The men will return to work to-day pending negotiations. Their return is apparently not a whit too soon, for coal importers, it was stated yesterday, had only a week's supply in stock.

KALTENBRUNNER said: "I regret that my people were not led by soldiers only, and that crimes were committed in which I had no share."

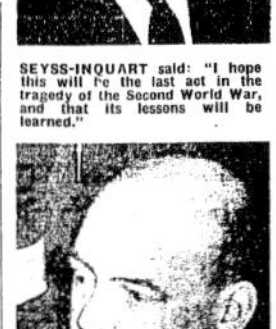

SEYSS-INQUART said: "I hope this will be the last act in the tragedy of the Second World War, and that its lessons will be learned."

FRITZ SAUCKEL said: "God protect Germany, and may God make her great again."

STREICHER told the priest standing beside him on the scaffold: "I am with God, father."

—AND ROSENBERG, the philosopher, was the only one who had nothing to say.

MOLOTOV "GRATEFUL TO BRITAIN"

Why He Declined Offer Of Cruiser

Mr. Molotov, who is travelling to the United States on board the Queen Elizabeth, told a Press conference yesterday that he hoped the work begun at the Paris Conference would be completed in New York.

Mr. Molotov thanked the British Government for the offer of a cruiser to bring him from France, but added: "I could not avail myself of the very kind offer. The position is that we were busy until late at night, and I could not accept. We expected to finish work before the evening, but, unfortunately, were too late.

I hope there won't be any misunderstanding. I am very grateful to the British Government for its kind offer."

Mr. Molotov spoke in the crowded corridor outside the door to his cabin. He said he was going to New York because the Soviet delegation hoped to complete the work begun at Paris.

Asked—"Do you go to America with good hopes?" Mr. Molotov replied: "As always."

The Soviet Embassy in London issued a statement last night on reports about the cancelled trip of the Soviet delegation from France on the British cruiser Dido, which was on similar lines to the statement made by Mr. Molotov.

STEPINAC RELEASE PETITION

Cardinal Griffin's Action

CARDINAL GRIFFIN, Archbishop of Westminster, yesterday suggested the drawing up in every Catholic parish throughout Britain of a petition asking Mr. Bevin, the Foreign Secretary, to make the strongest possible representations to the Yugoslav Government to secure the immediate release of Archbishop Stepinac of Zagreb.

The following notice was sent to the clergy of the Westminster Diocese yesterday, and similar notices were being sent out in other dioceses:—"We wish prayers to be said publicly in all the churches of the diocese next Sunday, October 20, for the release of the Archbishop of Zagreb, who has been most unjustly condemned. We suggest, if no action has already been taken, that a petition be drawn up in every parish and signed by Catholics and non-Catholics alike asking the Foreign Secretary to intercede for the Archbishop's release. When the petition has been completed it should be forwarded to your local member of Parliament asking him to place it before the Foreign Secretary. The petition should be on the following lines: 'We, the undersigned, fervently request the Secretary of State for Foreign Affairs to make the strongest representations possible to the Yugoslav Government to secure the immediate release of Archbishop Stepinac of Zagreb.'"

BRITISH PROBLEM.

Plight Of 125,000 Homeless Children.

Three British Cabinet Ministers—Mr. Chuter Ede, the Home Secretary; Miss Ellen Wilkinson, Minister of Education, and Mr. Bevan, Minister of Health—yesterday took action following the disclosures by Miss Myra Curtis's Committee on the plight of some of the 125,000 children in institutions and official homes, stated the P.A. Lobby correspondent.

The Ministers have set up an Inter-Departmental Committee which is at once going into the Curtis Report and drawing up a number of recommendations as to how things could be put right to be submitted to the Cabinet for final decision.

So far, the Cabinet have never considered the problem of children who are without normal home life. The Inter-Departmental Committee will have full access to the identities of those responsible for the bad cases described in the report, and will be able to take remedial measures.

SIR P. BATES

Cunard Chairman's Unexpected Death

Sir Percy Bates, chairman, Cunard White Star Line, died yesterday at his home, Hinderton Hall, Neston, Cheshire, says the P.A. He was 67.

Sir Percy Bates had a heart attack in his Liverpool office on Tuesday and was taken to his home.

He was to have sailed on the Queen Elizabeth on her first peace time voyage from Southampton to New York yesterday.

PROPAGANDA WAR IN THE NEAR EAST

London-Moscow Exchanges On Persian Issue

AFTER Mr. Bevin, in the British House of Commons yesterday, had denied that the British Consul-General at Ahwaz, in Persia, had been implicated in a recent tribal rising in his district, the Foreign Secretary commented adversely on Russian Press and radio publicity regarding the incident.

Last night, in an unusually strong comment, Frank A. King, Press Association Diplomatic Correspondent, described Soviet Press and radio reports of the Persian situation as a campaign of calumny and "a red blaze of propaganda."

"It is," he wrote, "becoming increasingly clear that this Russian propaganda campaign against Britain is merely a curtain to cover extensive interference by the Soviet Government in Persian internal affairs. This was revealed by the assistance Russia gave to the Azerbaijan revolt, her control and subversion of the Tudeh Party, and her financial aid to and control of a section of the Persian Press."

Mr. Bevin's House of Commons' statement referred to recent events in Persia affecting relations between the British and Persian Governments in connection with the recent arrests by the Persian authorities of tribal leaders in South Persia, and the disturbances which had occurred in that area.

The Persian Government, said Mr. Bevin, having certain information, concluded that the British Consul-General at Ahwaz, Mr. Trott, had been implicated in a plan for a tribal rising. After full investigation of the matter, the British Government had assured the Persian Government that there was no justification for the charges against Mr. Trott. The Persian Government have accepted the British Government's assurance with goodwill, and the case may, therefore, be regarded as closed.

The British Diplomatic and Consular officers in Persia had categorical instructions not to interfere in the internal affairs of that country. The Government had satisfied itself that no British official there had contravened, or was contravening, these instructions, and that no British official had given subversive elements reason to suppose that they could hope for British support.

The British Government had noted how the Soviet Press and Soviet broadcasts to Persia had given considerable prominence to these baseless allegations made against British officials, and it had taken steps to ensure the true facts of the situation were brought to the knowledge of the Persian people.

Frank A. King, P.A. Diplomatic correspondent, wrote from London last night: The statement in the House to-day on recent events in Persia reveals only a fraction of the wide and sustained campaign of calumny waged by the Soviet Press and wireless against Britain, all designed to show that the British Government is interfering in the internal affairs of Persia.

The astonishing part of the campaign is that while this Red blaze of propaganda is focussed on alleged British Imperialism, the Soviet Government, both now and for a long time past, has shown a strong dislike to any publicity being given to its own activities in Persia.

So long ago as last January, when the Security Council met in London, it was obvious that the Russian Government were embarrassed by the publicity then given to their Persian activities to such an extent that they offered certain concessions in their attempts to get it discontinued.

The whole campaign is designed to distract attention from Soviet activities in North Persia, and to throw a blanket of oblivion over their activities there in the past.

The Russian line throughout has been to attempt to manufacture a threat to Persia by "British Imperialism," while at the same time proclaiming Russia as the champion of Persian independence.

The correspondent describes as "completely baseless" other Russian stories that Britain has been landing arms by air in Baluchistan, and has been sending wheat from south-east Persia to India, and landing arms from warships at Bushire. The fact that the request for the recall of Mr. Allan Trott, British Consul in Ahwaz, has been withdrawn, shows that the Persian Government are satisfied.

Latest reports from Teheran, I am informed, make it clear the present Russian activities in Persia are "particularly unsuitable for public scrutiny." These activities are now extending to the economic field, and include the selling of sugar in the black market at exorbitant prices, and of reported Russian demands for excessive use of Northern Persian aerodromes. There are signs also of heavy pressure on the Persian Government in connection with Persia's elections. Only a day or two ago, Belinkov, on Moscow radio, was referring to the "chief instigators and organisers of the anti-Government conspiracy in Persia, Trott and Gault." In wild language he was referring to "unbridled reactionaries again spreading their campaign of lies and rumours."—P.A.

GOERING photographed in the cell in which he swallowed the fatal phial

ONLY THE PHILOSOPHER SAID "NEIN."

Grim Morning Scene As Ten Walked To The Scaffold

GOERING'S suicide led to a last-minute change of procedure in the executions of the other ten condemned men. They were to have been allowed to walk freely to the gallows, but instead they were marched manacled to guards.

The men walked in turn to the scaffold—Ribbentrop coming first at 1.09 a.m. and the others following at short intervals into the dirty bomb blasted prison gymnasium, its walls illuminated by ten blazing lights in the ceiling.

Two scaffolds were used, a curtain being hung over the swinging body of the preceding prisoner, as each new accused entered the gymnasium for execution. The ten bodies were in turn placed behind another curtain at the rere of the scaffolds, and were later photographed for official purposes.

The accused, said the correspondents attending the grim scene, died calmly and with dignity. Each was given an opportunity of saying last words from the scaffold. Ribbentrop availed of this to say: "My last wish is that the German unity should remain and that an understanding between the East and West should come about and peace for the world." Streicher, just before the hood was placed over his head, turned to Fr. Sixtus O'Connor, the Franciscan chaplain, and said: "I am with God, Father." Sauckel's last words were: "May God protect my family." Seyss-Inquart, bespectacled and club-footed, said: "I hope this execution will be the last act in the tragedy of the second world war."

It was 1.11 a.m. when Ribbentrop, first to be hanged in Goering's place, walked through the gymnasium door, his face white but set.

It was 2.45 when Seyss-Inquart, shouting: "I believe in Germany," fell to his death. Twelve minutes later two American soldiers entered the death chamber with its three ugly purple-blanketed scaffolds of rough wood carrying a stretcher. A body covered with a khaki American Army blanket was on it. Two bare feet, white and stiff, stuck out beneath it. The soldiers put their burden on the floor, and the thirty-three persons present at the executions—the Four Power Commission from Berlin, doctors, American Army officers and men and with eight Allied reporters chosen by lot. The blanket was whipped off. Goering's body lay there wearing disarrayed black silk pyjamas trousers and a pale blue silk pyjamas coat. Doctors examined him. Then an American colonel said: "O.K., take him away," and the body was taken behind the black cloth screen where his dead comrades were already being placed in rough light brown pine coffins.

The ten who had followed him into death died bravely. Not one of them broke down, not one of them whimpered or made any appeal. Each was given a chance to say a last word.

Only Alfred Rosenberg, the Nazi Party philosopher and most prolific writer of them all, could find no word except a murmured "Nein" to leave to history.

On the way to the gallows they walked with their hands manacled behind them down past "Death Row," out through the wing door, and then through an improvised wooden door into the open air. American security guards with shining steel helmets and chinstraps like Roman sentries lined the short route across the prison yard.

The condemned men passed slowly under the trees, and the cold wind shook autumn leaves on their heads as they walked, breathing the fresh air, and with clouds scudding across the moon above their heads.

In front of them were three scaffolds fourteen feet high, purplish black, of thick, unplaned wood and roughly painted. The crossbeam, with its curled hook and dangling rope with thirteen turns at the noose end, was supported by two square wooden columns.

The platform was eight feet square, and leading to the place on the trap from the floor were thirteen steps, wide enough for three men to mount at once.

Two of the scaffolds had ropes; the third was a reserve, only for use should one of the others break down. Each had a three-foot iron lever to spring the trap. The floor of the gallows hall was dirty. Some of the climbing rungs were broken. The grimy walls were spotted by the round patches left by the basketball. In one corner was a rusty, useless stove, and near it a chipped enamel sink.

At 1.06 a.m. an American colonel—by order of the Council, no names of those present have been released—asked: "Is there anybody who isn't ready?" There was no answer. He gave a sign and said "O.K."

The two hangmen—an American sergeant and lance-corporal—stood at ease on the platform.

Three minutes later there were two knocks on the door. It opened a crack and a voice said: "Stand by!" There was some mumbling outside. Then the door opened wide and Ribbentrop with a guard on each arm and his hands manacled behind him walked into the execution chamber and looked straight at the gallows. His face was dead white, his hair ruffled, and his eyes half closed, but he held his chin. There was a delay as his manacles were removed.

His hands were tied behind him with two black shoe-laces. Ribbentrop, still held by the guards, was then marched up the thirteen steps to the platform.

The colonel said—"State your name." The interpreter repeated it in German. Ribbentrop asked, puzzled—"Why should I state my name?" The demand was repeated. Ribbentrop—"Joachim Von Ribbentrop."

Then he cried—"God protect Germany. Thank God that he is merciful."

The colonel asked—"Have you any last words?"

Ribbentrop did not understand. Anxiously he repeated—"May I say something?" Then he cried firmly—"My last wish is that the German unity should remain and that an understanding between the East and West should come about and peace for the world."

From the time Hitler's former Foreign Minister had come into the execution chamber until he fell to his death two minutes and a half had elapsed. The two executioners went to the second gallows on the right. We all waited.

Three minutes passed, then the same procedure—the standby warning, the double knock, and Wilhelm Keitel, wearing his field marshal's uniform stripped of all insignia, his jackboots polished, and his grey hair carefully brushed, stopped at the door and clicked to attention. He walked steadily up the steps.

The American colonel asked—"Have you anything to say?"

Keitel lifted his chin and shouted—"I call on the Almighty: May he have

(CONTINUED ON PAGE SEVEN.)

U.S. STOPS CREDIT TO CZECHOSLOVAKIA

The U.S. State Department has blocked a £12,500,000 credit to Czechoslovakia from the Export-Import Bank of Washington and stopped the sale of surplus American property to Czechoslovakia, it was officially announced in Washington, yesterday, according to Reuter.

A State Department spokesman said the credit was blocked indefinitely, because Czechoslovakia misunderstood the objects of the United States in granting such credits, and had not yet agreed about compensating U.S. nationals for their rights and properties in Czechoslovakia.

DISABLED FRENCH VESSEL

Towed To Dunmore By Irish Ship.

The s.s. Irish Larch (3,192 tons) on a voyage from Montreal to Dublin, arrived in Dunmore East, Co. Waterford, about 2 p.m. yesterday, with the disabled French fishing vessel, Le Cabellon, in tow.

A pilot cutter met them at the entrance to the harbour and towed the fishing vessel into the bay, where she remained overnight. There is a crew of ten aboard.

It is understood that the Le Cabellon developed engine trouble while fishing somewhere in the waters between France and Ireland. Repairs will be carried out to-day.

TITO SAYS TRIESTE "UNSOLVED"

BELGRADE Radio last night broadcast answers by Tito, Yugoslav "Premier," to a series of questions put to him by a correspondent of the "New York Times."

Asked if Yugoslavia would accept the Paris Conference decision about Trieste, Tito replied: "This question cannot be considered as having been solved.

"As it stands, we cannot accept it. This means, of course, that we do not exclude further discussions about the problem."

Asked to comment on Yugoslav-United States relations, Tito said: "There is on our part the greatest desire to have good relations with all countries, far and near. But there have been a series of incidents and problems, which show that this desire is not shared by the United States.

"On our part, we have done everything to improve relations, but the recent attitude of the United States on the Trieste issue and on the questions of reparations, as well as on the question of our Danubian ships, shows a contrary standpoint on the part of the United States."

Other answers were:—

Ægean Macedonia: "Our Government has brought up this question, but the persecution of the Slavs by the Greek authorities goes on, and if it continues we shall, of course, take certain steps. That is obvious."

He added that for the present "There is no mention of a Balkan Federation."—Reuter.

CAIRO REPORT.

Plot To Blow Up Premier's Plane.

Unconfirmed reports in Cairo last night, from usually reliable sources, said that a threat to blow up the plane on which Sidky Pasha, Egyptian Premier, was due to leave for Britain yesterday, caused a change in plans. The decision to leave by flying boat, instead of by a land plane, from Almaza, was made because the Premier's advisers thought it would be safer to change the route and place of departure, the sources added.

According to unconfirmed reports from usually reliable sources, Abdul Fattah Uhia Pasha, former Foreign Minister, and independent member of the Egyptian Treaty delegation, has received a letter threatening him with death if he supports Sidky Pasha in the delegation.—Reuter.

DEATH OF SIR G. BANTOCK.

The death was announced, yesterday, of Sir Granville Bantock, the composer, at the age of 78, following an operation. He was Emeritus Professor of Music at Birmingham University, and Vice-Chairman of the Corporation of Trinity College of Music, London.

1947

The deaths of Henry Ford and Jim Larkin in 1947 marked the passing of two sons of emigrant Irish stock who both had an influence on the country's development, albeit from different sides of the negotiating table. Ford, the ultimate industrialist with a knack for invention, amassed the world's biggest fortune by making cars accessible to the 'common man', even if the £340 price on an Anglia was still beyond the reach of most Irish people. Larkin, the campaigner for social justice, founded the union that fought for the rights of workers all over the country, including at Ford's factory in Cork.
The bad winter continued with turf shortages being reported in towns and non-producing areas. Even when surplus turf was available in some regions, inclement weather and lack of transport infrastructure sometimes prevented it from being distributed. Ireland did achieve a world transport first when Shannon became the world's first duty-free airport. Internationally, 1947 saw the end of the British Raj with independence for India and Pakistan.

NEWS BRIEFS

Feb The Cork Board of Fishery Conservation offers a bounty of 10 shillings a head for any seals killed in the River Lee. These pests are causing great damage to fish and nets. (10)

July De Valera hits out at the Soviet Union for blocking Ireland's membership of the United Nations on the grounds that Ireland had sympathised with the Axis powers during the war. (31)

Aug British rule in India ended last night in a great midnight symphony of roaring guns, temple bells, and fireworks reverberating through the teeming cities and villages of the new-born dominions of India and Pakistan. (15)

Sept Cavan beat Kerry in the All-Ireland football final played in the Polo Grounds, New York, before a crowd of 40,000. Scenes of jubilation described as "more thrilling than anything seen in Croke Park" greeted the final whistle. (15)

Nov The UN General Assembly votes to partition British-ruled Palestine and create a state for Jews, a state for Palestinians and an international administration for Jerusalem. (30)

No fuel of any kind

Monday, February 10

"At the present moment off the coast of West Cork, the islanders are burning their hay and straw to cook their food," declared Mr TF O'Driscoll, TD, at Saturday's meeting of the Cork County Committee of Agriculture. "They have no fuel of any description," he added, "and as well as burning their hay and straw, which means they will have no feeding for their cattle, the people on Cape Clear, nine miles off the coast, are also burning their bits of furniture and their doors."
Earlier at the meeting, references had been made to the continued shortage of kerosene supplies in West Cork and a reply had been received from the Department of Industry indicating that temporary shortages had been caused by transport difficulties experienced by the distributing companies. Mr Roycroft said west of Skibbereen kerosene formed the only means of lighting the houses of the people. Although they had paid their share, the people of West Cork had never seen the Shannon scheme or any other scheme.
Mr O'Driscoll: "The only light they have west, around Crookhaven, is the flashes from the Fastnet Lighthouse."

A Traveller woman prepares a meal at a site near Killorglin, Co Kerry, during the Puck Fair.

World's first free airport opened in Shannon

Monday, February 10

At 3pm yesterday Shannon Airport became the world's first customs-free airport when, following a special luncheon held to mark the occasion, An Tánaiste, Mr Seán Lemass, Minister for Industry and Commerce signed an Order declaring the Shannon Airport customs-free to the world.
In his address, Mr Lemass said that the inauguration of the first free airport might even be worth the passing notice of the ordinary man in the street, whose sense of national pride would be touched by the knowledge that at least in this one instance we had not waited to follow the example of others but had taken the lead ourselves.
Having referred to the advantages which they hoped would result from the setting up of the free airport, Mr Lemass said that with the passing into law of the Customs-Free Airport Act, transit passengers would in the future receive as a right what they had hitherto been given as a privilege. "Furthermore," said the Minister, "we may be giving a lead to other airports where, perhaps, the transit passenger is regarded with a less kindly eye than at Shannon."

The Cork Examiner

CITY SPECIAL

NO. 30,498. WEDNESDAY MORNING, APRIL 9, 1947. PRICE—THREE HALFPENCE.

Registered for Transmission at Newspaper Rate of Postage in Ireland and Great Britain and at Magazine Rate in Canada and Newfoundland.

NEW PARTY FOR de GAULLE

France Between Two Minds

MAJORITY AGAINST DE GAULLE

Many ordinary people are undoubtedly still in two minds about General de Gaulle's appeal. They believe in his patriotism and integrity, but are afraid lest the force of events carry him outside the limits of Parliamentary democracy.

GIRL SERIOUSLY INJURED.

Unusual Accident In Waterford.

MR. WALLACE AT SHANNON AIRPORT.

SHARP CRITICISM AT CORK I.N.T.O. CONGRESS OF GOVERNMENT'S ATTITUDE TO EDUCATION

Age Of "Despotism Without Enlightenment"

"THE Government's attitude to educational expenditure and thus to education itself, is shown clearly by two events of the past year: the refusal to use the principle of third-party arbitration to settle the teachers' salary dispute, and the declaration made officially during the strike, that money spent on education is not in the nature of capital expenditure," declared Mr. D. J. Kelleher, B.A., Dublin City, in the course of his presidential address to the seventy-ninth annual I.N.T.O. Congress which opened at the City Hall, Cork, yesterday.

"One period of European history," he continued, "is known as the 'Age of the Enlightened Despot,' but now we have despotism without enlightenment and it is obvious that there can be no real educational progress in this country until the Government's present attitude to educational expenditure is challenged, discredited and abandoned."

In a reference to the recent teachers' strike, Mr. Kelleher said that the part played by the authorities prior to and during the strike deserved the strongest condemnation. While they strongly urged conciliation, or arbitration for outside bodies and set up elaborate State machinery for the settlement of disputes, they themselves would have none of it, he said.

A Civic welcome was extended to the delegates by the Lord Mayor of Cork (Mr. M. Sheehan).

Joining in the welcome, the Bishop of Cork, Most Rev. Dr. Cohalan, expressed his appreciation of the services rendered by the teachers of the diocese and, in a reference to the rule concerning married women teachers, His Lordship said that the loss of the married woman teacher—the mother teacher—would be very much felt.

That was a grand and glorious thing that the teachers should be convinced that they had the apostolate.

Rev. Fr. J. Forde, Diocesan Inspector, said that he did not think that in any country in the world there was such a high moral standard among teachers as amongst the teachers of Ireland.

If such a Council was set up he hoped that their Protestant fellow citizens would act similarly, as their wishes were the same in this matter.

(CONTINUED ON PAGE SEVEN)

EXTRA BREAD FOR TRACTOR CREWS

Needs Of Tillage Workers

CITY ARCHITECT.

Co. Dublin Man Secures Cork Post.

At last night's meeting of the Cork Corporation, the Law and Finance recommendations contained the following item: "Directed that Mr. Eamonn O'Byrne ... Ballybrack, Co. Dublin, be appointed City Architect and Town Planning Assistant, Cork Corporation, as from 1st March, 1947, at remuneration at the rate of £700 per annum rising by annual increments ... per annum, in accordance with recommendation of Local Appointments Commissioners."

The recommendation was adopted.

KING LEOPOLD 'REPORT' READY

The report of the special committee appointed last July by King Leopold of the Belgians to investigate "the truth of the King's attitude since 1936" has been completed and is to be submitted to the Presidents of Belgium's Chamber of Deputies and Senate, it was announced yesterday in Brussels. It will be made public later, the announcement from the exiled King's secretariat said.

WORLD TRADE CONFERENCE.

U.S. Delegation At Shannon Airport.

ROME CONGRESS.

The Church Discusses Existentialism.

30 LOST IN SUNK STEAMER.

SON OF CO. CORK MAN WHO "PUT THE WORLD ON WHEELS"

World's Richest Man Dies By Candlelight

WHILE Henry Ford, the world's richest man, lay dying by candle and lamplight at his flooded estate at Dearborn, Michigan, on Monday night, one of his employees ran half-a-mile to his engineering laboratory to summon a doctor. All telephones to the estate had been disrupted by the flooding of the River Rouge, which had cut off power and light. Before a doctor could reach him, Henry Ford had died of cerebral haemorrhage. He was 83.

In his last hours his room was warmed only by a wood fire and lighted by a paraffin lamp and candles, it was disclosed last night. While America mourned the industrial genius who "put the world on wheels," there was speculation on the disposition of his personal fortune, estimated at £50,000,000 to £125,000,000.

The Ford industrial assets, estimated at the end of 1946 at £182,500,000, will go to his 80-year-old widow, Clara Bryant, his daughter-in-law, Mrs. Edsel Eleanor Ford, and her four children, Henry Ford the second, Benson, William and Josephine.

Mr. Ford and his wife are understood to have held 58 per cent of Ford voting stock.

MR. HENRY FORD

(CONTINUED ON PAGE SEVEN)

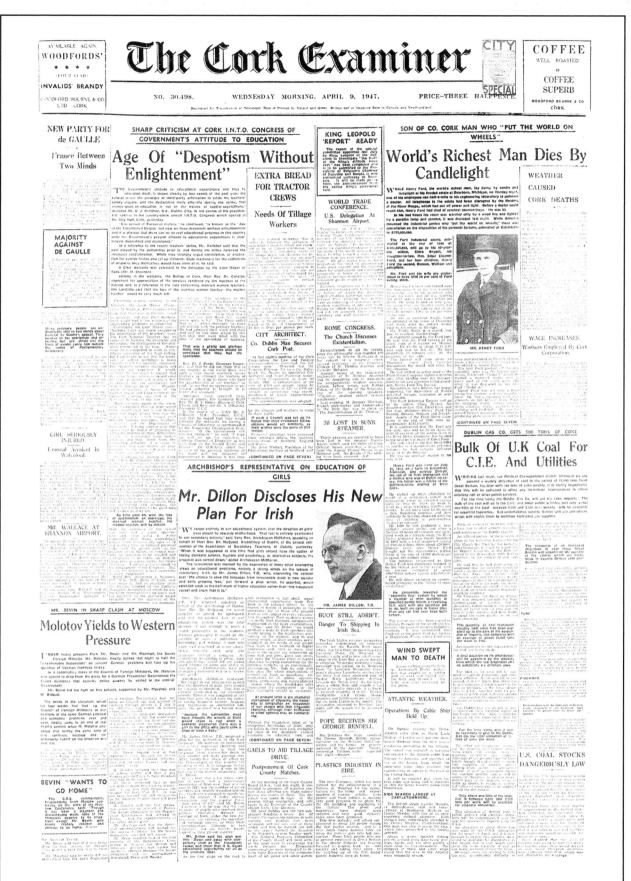

WEATHER CAUSED CORK DEATHS

WAGE INCREASES.

Workers Employed By Cork Corporation.

DUBLIN GAS CO. GETS 500 TONS OF COKE

Bulk Of U.K Coal For C.I.E. And Utilities

WRITING last night, our Political Correspondent stated: Although we are assured a weekly allocation of coal to the extent of 11,000 tons from Great Britain, together with 500 tons of coke weekly, it is highly improbable that this will be sufficient to effect any immediate improvement in either existing rail or other public services.

For the time being the Dublin Gas Co. will get the coke imports. The bulk of the coal will go to the C.I.E. and other public utilities, and only about one-fifth of the total—between 2,000 and 2,500 tons weekly—will be available for essential industries. Gas undertakings outside Dublin will get allocations which will enable them to maintain restricted gas supplies.

The prospects of an increased allocation of coal from Great Britain will depend on the success of the efforts which are being made to expand British coal production.

This quantity of coal represents roughly half what had been supplied up to the date of the suspension of imports, and compares with an average of about 15,000 tons per week in 1946.

Arrangements for the importation of the coal are being made.

A final decision on its distribution will be governed by the districts from which the coal originates and its suitability for different uses.

For the time being also it will be necessary to give to the Dublin Gas Co. the total allocation of 500 tons of coke per week.

Only about one-fifth of the total, that is between 2,000 and 2,500 tons per week will be available for essential industries.

U.S. COAL STOCKS DANGEROUSLY LOW

ARCHBISHOP'S REPRESENTATIVE ON EDUCATION OF GIRLS

Mr. Dillon Discloses His New Plan For Irish

"WE forget entirely in our educational system, that the direction of girls' lives should be towards motherhood. That fact is entirely overlooked in our secondary schools," said Very Rev. Archdeacon McMahon, speaking on behalf of Most Rev. Dr. McQuaid, Archbishop of Dublin, at the annual convention of the Association of Secondary Teachers, in Dublin, yesterday. "When it was suggested at one time that girls should have the option of taking domestic science, hygiene and psychology, as alternative subjects, the proposal was turned down," added Archdeacon McMahon.

The convention was marked by the expression of many other interesting views on educational problems, notably a strong attack on the system of compulsory Irish, by Mr. James Dillon, T.D., who, expressing the opinion that "the chance to save the language from irrevocable death is now slender and daily growing less," put forward a plan which, he asserted, would establish Irish as the hall-mark of higher education rather than "the fraudulent racket and sham that it is."

MR. JAMES DILLON, T.D.

"because the authorities must have thought the wheels of State would cease to run when a bachelor discovered there was a girl in the office who could cook a chop or bath a baby."

Mr. Dillon said his plan was this: Down and away with compulsory Irish as the fraudulent racket and sham that it is. Equal educational opportunity for all as the ultimate ideal.

At present Irish is the shameful instrument of imposing the necessity of emigration on thousands of our people who lack linguistic capacity, although their brilliance in other spheres may be outstanding.

(CONTINUED ON PAGE SEVEN)

BUOY STILL ADRIFT.

Danger To Shipping In Irish Sea.

WIND SWEPT MAN TO DEATH

ATLANTIC WEATHER.

Operations By Cable Ship Held Up.

SICK SEAMEN LANDED AT CASTLETOWNBERE.

POPE RECEIVES SIR GEORGE RENDELL.

PLASTICS INDUSTRY IN EIRE.

GAELS TO AID TILLAGE DRIVE.

Postponement Of Cork County Matches.

At the meeting of the Cork County Board G.A.A., held last night, it was decided to postpone all matches (except those affecting city clubs solely) during the month of April. The decision was taken in view of the present tillage emergency, and will apply to all Divisions of the County except Cork City Division.

MR. BEVIN IN SHARP CLASH AT MOSCOW

Molotov Yields to Western Pressure

UNDER heavy pressure from Mr. Bevin and Mr. Marshall, the Soviet Foreign Minister, Mr. Molotov, finally agreed last night to halt the "interminable discussions" on current German problems and take up the question of German frontiers to-day.

In a conciliatory move in the Council of Foreign Ministers, Mr. Molotov also agreed to drop from the plans for a German Provisional Government the Soviet insistence that security police powers be vested in the central Government.

Mr. Bevin led the fight on this subject, supported by Mr. Marshall and M. Bidault.

The break in the stalemate which for four weeks had tied up the Council of Foreign Ministers on discussions of the same German political and economic problems over and over, finally came to an end at last night's session when M. Molotov proposed that to-day the same kind of talk continue, because one co-ordinating report on the situation was still out.

—Associated Press and Reuter.

BEVIN "WANTS TO GO HOME"

The C.B.S. commentator, broadcasting from Moscow yesterday on the work of the Moscow Conference, said: "Though it has been a stagnant and discouraging week, none of the Ministers appears to be impatient except Mr. Bevin, who seems frankly restless and anxious to go home.—Reuter

1948

The creation of Israel in 1948 can be viewed from two very different perspectives.

For most Jews it was an occasion for great rejoicing. At last, after the horrors of the Holocaust and centuries of anti-Semitism in many countries, they would have a homeland. It also fulfilled the promise contained in the Old Testament that the land was theirs. For Palestinians, the creation of Israel is known as 'al Nakba' - the catastrophe - the start of decades of ethnic cleansing and powerlessness. For them, the new immigrants from Poland, Germany, etc had no rights to land that had been in Palestinian hands for centuries.

The fighting between the two sides increased as soon as the British mandate ended and an attack by Arab armies looked like it would wipe out the fledgling state. Despite their numerical inferiority, the Jewish forces emerged victorious and were able to seize a much larger amount of land than that awarded by the UN for the new state. Hundreds of thousands of Palestinians were forced from their homes into refugee camps, while Jews who had lived in Arab states fled to Israel.

In Ireland, de Valera's 16-year reign as Taoiseach came to an end when his surprise general election call backfired and the other parties combined to form a new government.

In sport, the Irish rugby team won their first Triple Crown in nearly half a century, a feat made all the more special as the team also went unbeaten against France to record the nation's only ever grand slam. As well as Chris Daly from Youghal, among the other heroes of the campaign was Clontarf's Barney Mullan who finished top scorer over the four matches.

Welsh bogey laid at Ravenhill

Monday, March 15

Forty-nine years is a long time to wait between one Triple Crown win and another, but for the 20,000 persons who saw Ireland achieve the highest honour in rugby, last Saturday, it was nearly worth all the years of defeat and near misses when the final whistle announced at Ravenhill with Ireland leading Wales by two tries (6 points) to one try (3 points), and with a string of successes since the international season opened on January 1st behind this latest victory, the crowd went wild with enthusiasm. The field was a sopping mass of humanity and for a moment players were lost. Then the men in green were hoisted, shoulder high and chaired to the pavilion, some, among them JC Daly, who played a very notable part in Ireland's win, losing their jersey to the souvenir-seeking crowd.

The Ireland team are mobbed by fans after their first Triple Crown win of the century, achieved with a victory over Wales.

India has lost a great leader

Saturday, January 31

Mr de Valera interrupted his election tour at Boyle, Co Roscommon, last night to pay a tribute to the memory of Mahatma Gandhi. He said: "I have got news which has made me sad at heart. I have learned of the death of Mahatma Gandhi, the Indian leader. In the latter phases our struggle for freedom and that of India coincided and our two peoples felt they were brothers in a common cause.

The Indian people are grieving tonight and we grieve with them. Gandhi was not merely a great Indian leader, he was a great leader of mankind, teaching the world in the words of our poet 'the might of moral beauty'. We pray to God to grant eternal rest to his noble soul. I ask you to stand in sympathy with the people of India and in tribute to one of the truly great men of our age." The audience then stood for a minute in silence with heads uncovered.

NEWS BRIEFS

Feb A new government is formed from an ideologically-diverse coalition of Fine Gael, the two Labour parties and Clann na Poblachta. John A Costello was appointed Taoiseach, Seán MacBride as Minister for External Affairs and Noel Browne as Minster for Health. (19)

Apr Irishwoman Mary O'Shaughnessy, a former inmate at Ravensbrueck concentration camp, gives evidence in the trial of five women guards. Miss O'Shaughnessy described how she survived numerous line-ups in which the SS guards would choose batches of about 50 women for the gas chambers. She had been a children's governess in Paris when the war started and had been sent to the camp for helping downed British airmen. (15)

The Cork Examiner

NO. 30,842. MONDAY MORNING, MAY 17, 1948. PRICE—THREE HALFPENCE.

Registered for Transmission at Newspaper Rate of Postage in Ireland and Great Britain and at Magazine Rate in Canada and Newfoundland.

FIVE ARAB ARMIES DRIVE INTO PALESTINE—PORT OF TEL AVIV DESTROYED

Egyptian Forces Less Than Forty Miles from Jewish Capital

EGYPTIAN forces, unofficial reports said last night were fighting the Jewish Army less than 40 miles from Tel Aviv, the Jewish capital. According to these reports says Reuter from Cairo, the Egyptians were in action with the Jewish forces for the first time and were advancing under artillery and mortar fire along the coast road. The Jews were resisting and the Egyptians pushing on from Gaza, occupied on Saturday, were up against opposition from fortified settlements.

Earlier Tel Aviv's harbour was said to have been destroyed by dive bombing Spitfires of the Egyptian Royal Airforce. The Jewish capital was bombed four times yesterday and has had eight air attacks since Friday night.

... children. The women and children were sent to the Red Cross at Jerusalem and the others interned in P.O.W. camps.

"On Saturday the Lydda airfield was captured by the Liberation Army," it said. "Kalundiya colony and the adjoining airfield between Jerusalem and Ramallah were captured also."

Map of Palestine with arrows indicating the direction of trusts by the Arab armies.

Nokrashy Pasha, Egyptian Premier, announced in Cairo that the vanguard of the Egyptian forces had entered the historic all-Arab city, one-third of the way from the Egyptian border to Tel Aviv.

These appear to be the electric power installations of Naharayim, only one of its kind in Palestine, some ten miles south of Lake Tiberias, on the Jordan.

JEWISH CLAIMS.

Jewish authorities in Tel Aviv claimed last night the capture of a number of Bren guns from the Egyptian forces invading from the south and to have killed at least 30 of the invaders.

Fierce fighting was reported in a Tel Aviv despatch last night to be going on for the French Trappist Monastery commanding the approaches to Latrun. Arab forces are strongly entrenched in the monastery's massive stone buildings.

BRITISH SOLDIERS WOUNDED.

MUFTI FLIES TO CAIRO

Haj Amin El Husseini, Mufti of Jerusalem and Chairman of the Arab Higher Committee, and other Committee members left Damascus yesterday by air for Cairo with the intention of entering Palestine.

New York radio, in a Palestine dispatch, reported that the Mufti had moved his headquarters into Palestine behind the invading Arab forces.—Reuter.

PRINCESS AND DUKE IN PARIS

Royal Couple's Visit To Races

Police advised her not to go to look at the horses in the paddock as had at first been planned, and this deprived the great crowd of a chance to see her at close view.

ATTACKED IN BELFAST SHOP

ISRAEL'S APPEAL TO U.N.

Intervention By Egypt

The new Jewish State of Israel appealed to the United Nations Security Council last night to step Egypt's intervention in Palestine. The appeal was made by Mr. Moshe Shertok, Foreign Minister of the new State.

SOVIET PRESSURE ON FINLAND

Terms Of Recent Pact

ISRAEL ASKS FOR WORLD RECOGNITION

Israel is applying to the 58 members of the United Nations, as well as to some other Governments, for explicit recognition, Mr. Moshe Shertok, Foreign Minister of the new State, disclosed in Tel Aviv last night. He told reporters such a request had already been sent to Britain.

£12,000 GRANT "INADEQUATE"

Roscommon Requests To Government

YOUGHAL PREMISES ENTERED

CORK AND DUBLIN IN DARKNESS

E.S.B. Failure

FR. FLANAGAN

Body To Be Flown To The United States

FORD WAGE RATES MAY BE CUT

While 75,000 Chrysler workers, members of the C.I.O. United Auto Workers, are striking for higher pay, the Ford Motor Company, yesterday, asked the Union to consider a wage reduction for Ford workers, reports the Associated Press from Detroit.

The Company notified the Union that it would fight the demand for a two shillings and sixpence hourly increase, and said one of the Company's five specific proposals in the contract negotiations would be to eliminate wage differentials between Fords and major competitors.

GOVERNMENT PLANS FAIR DEAL FOR MINORITIES

Ovation To General Mac Eoin

SPEAKING at a demonstration of welcome and congratulations to General Sean MacEoin, Minister of Justice, at Ballinalee, Co. Longford, yesterday, Mr. James Dillon, Minister for Agriculture, said that no citizen of the State would be victimised because he had voted for Fianna Fail.

Should such happen, "our name," said Mr. Dillon, "will forever be disgraced in this country, whether the minority be a Fianna Fail minority or a Unionist minority."

Gen. MacEoin said that the inter-Party Government gives fair representation to everyone. "This is an example to our fellow countrymen in the North that if they come in here, we will give them a fair share of Government and responsibility."

Speaking at a demonstration of welcome and congratulations to General Sean MacEoin, Minister of Justice, at Ballinalee, yesterday, Mr. James Dillon, Minister for Agriculture ...

... M.C.C.; M. J. Timlin, N.T., U.D.C.; P. J. Herety, Robert Belton. Mr. L. H. Reynolds presided and an address of welcome and congratulations on behalf of the people to General MacEoin ...

"NO REAL DISPUTE."

KEEPERS SAVED FROM BURNING LIGHTHOUSE

Lifeboat Goes To Rescue

DR. T. F. O'HIGGINS

Minister For Defence In Cork

MISSING NEWSMAN

Body Washed Ashore At Salonika

CATHOLIC PRINCIPLES AND TRADES UNIONS

Dr. O'Rahilly's Address To C.Y.M.S. Delegates

THE Catholic Church to-day was the only organised corporate defender of the fundamental principles on which trades unionism rested and they did not admit that there was any such thing as neutrality in religion, declared Dr. A. O'Rahilly, President, U.C.C., addressing the Annual Convention of the National Council of the Catholic Young Men's Society of Ireland at Cork yesterday. Dr. O'Rahilly added that in the general activities of trades unionism to-day they had to be guided either by Catholic social principles or else slip into Communism, which was being thrust forward by the small well organised minorities in these countries. Referring to their association with British trades unions, Dr. O'Rahilly said, it certainly added to their difficulties in Ireland and therefore an increased measure of cultural protection was required. The Convention which was the seventeenth annual event of the Society, opened at the C.C.Y.M.S. Hall, Castle Street, on Saturday night and concluded yesterday evening.

The annual report of the Central Executive Committee stated that while Communism in Ireland was practically negligible, it had some adherents, and if Ireland was to safeguard her sacred heritage, her people must elevate the Christian moral code.

Dr. O'Rahilly, whose address was on "Catholic Principles and Trades Unions," said the Catholic Church to-day was the only organised corporate defender of the fundamental principles on which Trades Unionism rested, and they did not admit that there was any such thing as neutrality in religion. In the general activities of Trades Unionism to-day they had to be guided either by Catholic social principles or else slip into Communism, which was being thrust forward by the small, well organised minorities in these countries. Catholics to-day had the choice that the early Christians had, the choice between Christ and Caesar ...

The big issue to-day was could they prove to people who called themselves Socialists that they could even go up towards Christ and carry out all that was good in their programme or else go down and develop into Communists. Socialism was only the half-way house.

Referring to the social problem of the mass emigration of Irish domestic servants, Dr. O'Rahilly asked would any sane country allow its trained workers to emigrate, who were an asset to the nation.

OPERATION OF NEW CONSTITUTION

Importance Of Cork Convention

Welcoming the delegates at the opening session on Saturday, Rev. D. J. Donovan, Spiritual Director, Cork Branch, apologised for the unavoidable absence of the Lord Mayor, Councillor M. Sheehan, T.D., who, he said, wished the Convention every success in its deliberations.

Mr. J. W. Moore (Dublin), Vice-President who presided owing to the absence through illness of the President (Mr. C. M. Drum, Dublin) said that the latter had prepared the following telegram which he hoped the convention would agree to send to His Holiness, the Pope: "The National Council of the Catholic Young Men's Society of Ireland, meeting at Whitsuntide in Cork City, tenders to the Holy Father the loyalty of its members and humbly begs the Apostolic Blessing."

The telegram was unanimously endorsed.

Continuing, Mr. Moore said that the convention was of particular interest in that it marked the 21st anniversary of its foundation and they were all agreed that the Society could look back with a certain amount of pride at the progress which had been made ...

YEAR'S PROGRAMME.

(CONTINUED ON PAGE SEVEN)

Mr. J. W. Moore, Vice-President, speaking at the Annual Convention of the National Council of the Catholic Young Men's Society of Ireland in Cork on Saturday. ("Examiner" Photo).

KNOCK PILGRIMAGE

Bishop's Appeal For Prayers For The Pope

CIVIL SERVICE SALARIES

IRISH CYCLE TRADE'S SHOW

BIG INFLUX OF VISITORS

The Whit Week-end In The South

Saturday's brilliant sunshine from a cloudless sky, which gave promise of a summerlike Whit Week-end, was not fully realised yesterday, and thousands of holiday-makers who trekked to seaside and country by train, bus, car, bicycle and afoot, must have had some misgivings yesterday ...

INFLUX OF VISITORS.

1949

After already being known as the Free State and Éire, the 26 counties underwent another name change in April, 1948, when it became the Republic of Ireland. Masses and military parades marked the occasion which was part of the final severing of formal colonial links with Britain that also saw Ireland leave the Commonwealth.

Pride in the new republic was further enhanced in September when the nation's soccer team became the first ever foreign side to inflict a home defeat on England. The Irish team which won 2-0 in Liverpool included the previous season's player of the year in England, Jackie Carey of Manchester United.

Ireland was still an occasional stopping point for desperate refugees attempting to leave post-war Europe and one of the ships to visit Cork this year was the *Victory*. The over-crowded ship, mainly carrying Poles and people from the Baltic countries, was on its way across the Atlantic to Canada.

Welcome for war refugees

Monday, October 3

Crowds gather in Cork to view the refugee ship, the **Victory.**

The refugee ship *Victory*, with 385 displaced persons on board including nearly 100 children, arrived in Cork Harbour from Gothenburg on Friday and was an object of considerable interest at her berth at the south jetties during the weekend. While in Cork, they intend taking on a supply of fuel oil as well as provisions.

Yesterday afternoon all the Catholics amongst the refugees - most of this group were Poles - assembled on the quay to meet Rev Mgr J Scannell, Dean of Cork. The Dean, speaking in German, expressed pleasure that the refugees had been able to reach Cork in safety, and said on behalf of the Catholics of Cork he was very glad to welcome their Polish fellow-Catholics to this country.

The general position on board is that there is only sufficient food for one full day. The refugees sleep four and five in space usually allowed for a single berth on a ship, each little family trying also in that sleeping space to store their few clothes and food utensils.

Ireland's fantastic international win

Thursday, September 22

One of the most astonishing upsets of form in an international match took place at Goodison Park, Everton, yesterday, where England met their first defeat on their own soil against a side other than from one of the home countries.

The crowd seemed bewildered all through the second half as the Irish goal underwent a series of such remarkable escapes that eventually the situation became laughable. Fully half the play after the interval occurred in the Irish penalty area, yet the England forwards could not force the ball home. Godwin, in goal, was always in the right spot. The attendance was 51,000. Ireland must be given credit for a great display against superior individual footballers.

Martin put Ireland ahead from a penalty after 34 minutes awarded for a tackle from behind on Desmond. England piled on the pressure on the resumption, but Ireland packed their goal and denied their rivals a clear shot.

Five minutes from the end came the crushing blow. The ball came out to O'Connor who angled in and gave Farrell a perfect pass and as Williams advanced Farrell cleverly lobbed the ball over his head into the net.

NEWS BRIEFS

Feb The Dáil is told of a major slump in the Gaeltacht tweed industry. Despite strenuous efforts, no new markets had been found for the 120,000 yards of surplus homespun products. In addition, the kelp-making industry which had been revived during the war as a source of potash, was again almost wiped out. (25)

May Outrage at the imprisonment of Catholic Church leaders in Hungary and other areas of Eastern Europe brings an estimated 140,000 people onto O'Connell Street in protest.

Oct Mao Tse-tung, victorious in China's civil war, declares the world's most populous nation will be a Communist Republic. (1)

The Cork Examiner

NO. 31,101. MONDAY MORNING, APRIL 18, 1949. PRICE—THREE HALFPENCE.

Registered for Transmission as Newspaper. Rate of Postage in Ireland and Great Britain and at Magazine Rate in Canada and Newfoundland.

CITY SPECIAL

NEW ERA OF NATION'S HISTORY OPENS

Guns Salute, Trumpets Herald The Republic Of Ireland

WHEN at one minute past midnight last night the inauguration of the Republic of Ireland was heralded by salutes of guns, a new era was opened in the nation's history.

The ceremonial ushering in of the era of the Republic was for Cork as for the rest of the country an event of historical importance. Long before midnight crowds converged on the City Hall and there, as they counted out the closing minutes of the old regime, they presented to the close observer a cross section of the most eventful period of modern Irish history.

In that gathering were greybeards who had watched at the death bed of the constitutional movement, and who, in their own way had effectively advanced the cause of Irish freedom. There were the middle aged, who, in the enthusiasm of their youth had snatched the torch from older hands, and whose readiness to sacrifice all for the cause gave substance to the dream of insurrection. Deprived, as the great majority were through no fault of their own, of the honour of fighting in 1916, they seized the later opportunity with both hands and helped to write a glorious page of Irish history in 1920-1921. The generation which has grown up since then was also fully represented, there to witness the transition from partial to full independence.

"WELCOMED BY ALL THE NATIONS"

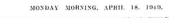

IRISH PROTEST MEETING IN LONDON

IRELAND'S DEAD HONOURED

Many Commemoration Ceremonies

LIMERICK FIRE

BAN ON EASTER PARADE DEFIED AT NEWRY

Police Cordons Pushed Back

The order of the Six Counties' Minister of Home Affairs, Mr. E. Warnock, banning the parade of Easter Week was defied at Newry yesterday.

Extra police had been drafted into the town to enforce the ban but yesterday morning almost 10,000 people, led by their public representatives, paraded to St. Mary's Cemetery, following Mass in the Cathedral for the repose of the souls of those who gave their lives for Ireland.

Twice the police threw cordons across the street in an attempt to stop the procession and twice they were pushed aside.

Finally they gave up the attempt to stop the procession, which moved off through the main streets of the town decorated with the Tricolour, to the cemetery.

At the cemetery an oration was delivered by Mr. Fionan Breathnach (C. na P.) who said they were that day "attending the political funeral of Sir B. Brooke."

KILLORGLIN.

Killorglin, Co. Kerry, the scene of the first 1916 casualties. A special Mass for the Ballykissane Pier casualties, a parade of Old I.R.A. men and the general public, and the placing of wreaths on the monument to the first casualties of the rebellion who died on Good Friday night, 1916. A band parade and the reading of the 1916 Proclamation.

CHARGED BY POLICE

At Carrickmore, Co. Tyrone, 400 people assembled to hold a similar ceremony, but they were charged by the police and several were injured on the head by blows of batons. Afterwards, however, the ceremony was held in a field some distance from the village.

BLESSINGS TO IRELAND BY RADIO

"IMPORTANT MILESTONE"

Mr. MacBride's Comment In U.S.

BELFAST WOMAN ATTACKED

IRISH LIFEBOAT RESCUES DUTCH YACHT

DEFIED STORMONT BAN

KING GEORGE'S GOOD WISHES.

Message To The President Of Ireland.

King George sent this message, dated April 18th, to President O'Kelly:—

"I send you my sincere good wishes on this day, being well aware of the neighbourly links which hold the people of the Republic of Ireland in close association with my subjects of the United Kingdom

"I hold in most grateful memory services and sacrifices of the men and women of your country who rendered gallant assistance to our cause in the recent war and who made a notable contribution to our victories.

"I pray that every blessing may be with you to-day and in the future.

Signed, GEORGE R."

CHEERING CROWDS WELCOME THE REPUBLIC

Midnight Scenes In The Capital

TO the accompaniment of a fanfare of trumpets, a rolling of drums, a booming of guns and the singing and flag waving of thousands of joyous people, the Republic of Ireland came into being in the capital at midnight.

In such terms did the seat of our national Government declare to the world that the waiting of many years was at last ended and that this proud and valiant little country had won its right to recognition by Powers, great and small, as a sovereign independent nation.

Throughout the world this historic event will be chronicled to-day, and wherever there are freedom-loving peoples it will be hailed with almost as much delight as here at home. True, none can be blind to the sole remaining problem yet to be solved before the final aspirations of those age-old struggles are realised. But we have come by far the greater part of the way, and hope is virile and alive in the efforts at present being pursued so strenuously by our leading statesmen to clear away this last vestige of injustice.

... their beams. Satisfied that it had done its duty well and nobly in the ushering in of this new era in the country's history, the great throng melted away into the night. To help them homewards, special bus services ran to all parts up to 1 a.m.

TO-DAY'S CELEBRATIONS

This morning those same people will be early astir. They will want to participate also in the Church and State honours to the newly declared Republic.

SALUTE SEARCHLIGHT DISPLAY AT COVE

NEW MINISTER TO IRELAND

Appointment By The Indian Government

SIX DROWNED IN HOLIDAY TRAGEDIES.

The guard of honour from the Fourth Infantry Brigade drawn up outside the City Hall for this morning's ceremonies.—("Examiner")

"VALUABLE AID TO CHURCH IN REVEALING TRUTH TO FAIR MINDS"

Pope Pius Televised For First Time

POPE Pius XII. was televised yesterday for the first time, when a film sent from the Vatican was transmitted by the French Television Service, says a Reuter message from Paris. After stressing the valuable aid which television could give to the Church, the Pope closed by giving his Benediction to viewers.

MOTOR-CYCLIST INJURED IN COLLISION

IRISH MEAT FOR DENMARK.

SHIP ATTACKED BY PIRATES.

MANY MESSAGES OF GOODWILL

Greetings From All Parts Of The World

FROM such personages of eminence as His Holiness the Pope, President Truman, King George VI., Mr. Attlee and the heads of the Governments of many countries have come messages of congratulation directed either to the President or the Taoiseach on the coming into operation of the Republic of Ireland Act.

His Holiness imparts to the President and the people of Ireland the Apostolic blessing.

THE POPE'S MESSAGE

BRITAIN

UNITED STATES

CANADA

ITALY

SOUTH AFRICA

AUSTRALIA

BURMA

SWEDEN

NEW ZEALAND

INDIA

NORWAY

OTHER MESSAGES

TEST PILOT KILLED.

FOOD SHIP BATTERS WAY TO LABRADOR.

CHRISTUS REX SOCIETY

SOVIET OFFICIALS RESTIVE.

Page recreated

1950

Barely five years after the end of World War II, major hostilities broke out in the Korean peninsula when the communist north invaded the south of the country in June. The United Nations condemned the attack and the United States and Britain soon entered the fray. By November, China was involved on the opposite side and thousands of lives were being lost every week. Officially, Ireland stayed neutral but, as was the case with other overseas conflicts, Irish people were involved in other nations' armies and also through the Catholic missionaries who had a significant presence in Korea.

Many other Irish people on the move during the year went to Rome, the then venue for a major Catholic pilgrimage. Tens of thousands made the journey across the continent by plane, train, car, motorbike and even bicycle.

In November, 94-year-old Irish genius George Bernard Shaw died at his home in England.

World tributes to Shaw

Friday, November 3

The world paid tribute to George Bernard Shaw, who died yesterday. Leaders, organisations, press and radio of many political hues mourned his loss and praised his genius.

President Truman declared: "The world of letters has lost a prominent figure. As critic, essayist and dramatist, he left the indelible print of his genius on a prodigious literary output during more than two generations."

George Bernard Shaw.

New York's Broadway, scene of many of his triumphs as a playwright, switched off its brilliant lights for several minutes when the news came through. Theatre audiences in Australia stood for two minutes in silence.

Moscow radio announced his death briefly, but Marxist intellectuals behind the Iron Curtain joined in the world chorus of praise.

George Bernard Shaw was born in Dublin in July 1856 and was married to a West Cork Lady, Mrs Charlotte Frances Payne-Townshend, who died in 1943. One of his best known later plays, *St Joan*, was written in Glengarrif and Parknasilla in areas where he holidayed. Some years ago, when Mrs Shaw was alive he was often to be seen in Cork bookshops and was ready to talk 'shop' with anyone who would take him on.

Local people in Enniskeane, Co Cork, carry a 25ft cross for erection on nearby Corran Hill.

NEWS BRIEFS

Mar The number of new houses completed this year will be about 10,000, said Mr Keyes, Minister for Local Government. He was speaking at Waterford where he opened new houses at Bernard Place. Waterford workers banded together to build the houses which cost approximately £640 each. (21)

June At present, only the 'big swanks' with money to burn could buy tomatoes, said Capt Giles (FG) when he spoke during a debate in the Dáil yesterday. (23)

Oct Chinese Communist army units have been ordered to advance into Tibet "to free three million Tibetans from imperialist oppression and to consolidate the national defences of China's western corner," according to a New China (Communist) News Agency dispatch from Peking yesterday. (28)

Adventures of Irish pilgrims in Rome

Monday, October 16

It is estimated that more than 1% of the population of the Republic of Ireland will have visited Rome for the Great Pilgrimage by the end of the Holy Year. Many of the pilgrims have had adventures, some comic, some tragic and quite a big percentage have been the victims of thieves.

The Irish Legation staff at Rome has been kept busy attending to unfortunate pilgrims, the latest being an 82-year-old Irishman, who arrived by plane from Shannon, apparently suffering from loss of memory.

A Legation spokesman estimated yesterday that one in 15 of Irish pilgrims are robbed – some of all but the clothes they wear. Many have lost their precious bicycles as they slept in fields on the way to Rome.

The most unfortunate class of pilgrims so far appears to have been the motor cyclists. A large proportion have underestimated the distance and almost all underestimated the wear on brakes and engines of the long pull up and sharp run down the Alps. They have arrived in Rome in numbers with motor cycles written off or needing repairs which they cannot afford.

The Cork Examiner

NO. 13,989. SATURDAY MORNING, JULY 1, 1950. PRICE—THREE HALFPENCE

Registered for Transmission at Newspaper Rate of Postage in Ireland and Great Britain, and at Magazine Rate in Canada and Newfoundland.

G.I.s ADVANCE HURLED BACK

U.S. Cruiser Sunk —Reds Claim

An American counterthrust 10 miles into Communist-held territory was hurled back late last night when North Korean infantry sprang a trap on the American patrol, A.P. reports.

The Americans driving north to regain some territory lost in the deep withdrawal on Thursday, were forced to go back.

[illegible]

The North Korean army also claimed yesterday it had sent the 24th Battalion of the American 24th infantry division reeling back with heavy losses in a battle for an important railway town south of Seoul.

[illegible]

The sudden reverse came after the Americans had prodded northward easily.

They had two minor exchanges of gunfire at villages along the way but had advanced 10 miles against meagre opposition. Then the Communists sprang the trap.—A.P.

Backed by rocket-carrying invader bombers, the Americans were earlier said to have met the Red tanks and troops head-on just north of Chonan and counter-attacked northward.

Earlier General McArthur reported that the Red forces in the drive south had reached the American front line north of Chonan to Magung, 25 miles east of Yongtaek, to Chungju, 40 miles east of Pyontaek and thence east to the coast.

The Red first, third and fourth divisions were spearheading the advance.

Meanwhile, British warships with the U.S. 7th Fleet bombarded bridges and oil tanks behind the Red lines north of Samchok on Korean's north-east coast.

A Washington announcement said that the British ships encountered fire from the beaches and retaliated.

[illegible]

Two B26 light bombers were lost and two crewmen in returning planes were wounded.

[illegible]

U.S. RATIFIES TREATY WITH IRELAND

Unanimous Action In Senate

The U.S. Senate has ratified the Treaty of Friendship, Commerce and Navigation between the United States and Ireland signed in Dublin last January, it was announced yesterday in Washington.

The Treaty, ratified without debate and by voice vote, binds the two countries in formal ties of friendship for the first time in history.

President Truman sent the Treaty to the Senate with a message saying: "I consider this Treaty to be an important manifestation of the friendly relations between the United States and Ireland. The Treaty is now effective."

Irish Ambassador Mr. John Hearne said in a statement: "It is a special pleasure to note not one dissentient voice was raised in the Senate and the treaty was passed unanimously.

It is true the friendship which exists between our two countries was not hitherto recorded in any legal pact and formal registration of the feeling of amity which has been in being between our two countries for so many generations is naturally a source of gratification to the Irish people."—Reuter and A.P.

Americans To Be Called Up For Korea, Mr. Truman's Decision After Talks With Service Chiefs

AMERICANS are to be called up for the war in Korea. The U.S. Government yesterday ordered conscription to bring military forces to the strength needed, said a Washington announcement by the Defence Department. All three armed services were authorised to exceed the overall budget ceiling for military personnel, and the Department said that overall ceilings on branches of the services, which had restricted their expansion had been lifted. Military enlistments will also be used to step up the size of the various services.

The conscription order followed a White House meeting between President Truman and his Congressional and military leaders.

After this there was a White House conference attended by members of the National Security Resources Board, of which Mr. Stuart Symington is chairman. This Board is responsible for national mobilisation of industry.

The U.S. announcement ordering conscription said:—

"This action constitutes a first step to build up to full operating strength the units of the Army, Navy and Air Force to be used in the Korean operation, to provide further maintenance and support therefor, and to replace units to be moved to Korea.

"The use of selective service has been authorised. Voluntary enlistments also will be accepted."

The announcement did not contain any estimated figure for the new military expansion.

The latest total strength figure given for the armed forces was about 1,370,000. Of that, the army had 593,000, the navy and marines 427,000 and the air force 350,000.

An armed forces spokesman said that while the reserves are not being called, they will be accepted for active duty if they volunteer.

A Navy spokesman said: "There is no intention on the part of the Navy to recall reserves to active duty, but reserves who volunteer will be welcomed with open arms."

After seeing the President, Senator Tydings, the Democratic Chairman of the Senate Armed Services Committee said that new legislation would not be necessary. Under existing legislation, the President would be empowered to disregard the budgetary ceiling in the administration of conscription legislation.

He said that future action "depends on where the situation goes."

Senator Tydings said he felt "a little better about it", now he had heard the President's report.

The Conscription Act, which last week was renewed for one year, calls for the registration of men between 18 and 26. Only those from 19 to 25 can be drafted.

Major-Gen. F. L. Parks, Chief of Army Public Information, told reporters that if the armed forces were brought to full strength "without use of selective service, we will be very happy."

Gen. Parks added that, as far as he knew, "the decision has not been made to call the National Guard."

A decision had not been made to order up Army reserves, but that those volunteering would be welcomed.

Exactly how many men Mr. Truman has decided to add to the armed forces was kept secret, but 635,882 draftees or volunteers would be needed to bring the services up to authorised strength, says the A.P.

After the "emergency" meeting at the White House, Senator Bridges told reporters that Mr. Truman asked them to keep secret the number to be called up.

"That might enable the enemy to gauge what we are planning," Senator Bridges said.

U.N.O. COMMANDER TO BE APPOINTED

The U.N.O. Security Council last night asked the U.S. to appoint a Commander-in-Chief over all Allied forces fighting in aid of the Republic of South Korea.

Voting was seven in favour with three abstentions, and as in all other Security Council meetings since the Korean crisis began, Russia boycotted the session.

[illegible] United Nations flag—a wreathed globe on a light blue ground—alongside national flags.

NO MILITARY AID FROM FRANCE.

France yesterday informed the United Nations that in view of her own struggle against Communism in Indo-China, she would be unable to send any military assistance to Korea.

In a letter to Mr. Trygve Lie, Secretary-General, the French delegate, M. Chauvel, said that, nevertheless, the French Government was considering what measures it could undertake to comply with the United Nations appeal for help.—Reuter and A.P.

U.S. HAS ONLY 11 DIVISIONS.

The latest total strength given for the armed forces was about 1,370,000. Of that the army had 593,000, the navy and marines 427,000, and the air force 350,000.

The army's combat strength has been whittled down from the war-time peak to only 11 divisions—and four of these are in the Far East.

The army, in building up its combat forces in terms of divisions, must have for each far more than the nominal 16,500 or 18,000 men. All of the supporting services which keep the division operating require as many as four men to each one in the division.

The authorised strength for all branches of the armed services is 2,005,882, compared with the 1,370,000 now in uniform.—Reuter.

EXTENSION OF LIMERICK CITY

More Members For City Council

Moving the second reading of the Limerick City Management Bill 1950, **the Minister for Local Government, Mr. M. J. Keyes,** said in the Dail yesterday, that in March last the Oireachtas confirmed a provisional order to extend the area of Limerick City by the addition of approximately 3,000 acres. The existing population of 42,987 was increased by approximately 4,799.

The corresponding population and members of the other county boroughs were Cork City, population 75,361 and the City Council has 21 members; Dublin City population 506,635 and there are 45 members of the City Council; Waterford City, population 28,332 and there are 15 members of the City Council.

By reason of the extension of Limerick City, the City Council had requested that the existing City Council of 15 members should be increased to 17 members, and the request was unanimous.

[illegible] must necessarily be considered on its merits, regard being had to the views of the local authority. As regards the Local Government electorate in Limerick City, the old city on the present register contained 24,954 Local Government electors, and in the added area there were 3,591 Local Government electors, so that the increase of two members sought by the City Council was exactly proportionate to the increased electorate. He considered that the request of the City Council was quite reasonable and justified, and he commended the proposal to the House.

The Bill passed all stages.

"GREATEST ACHIEVEMENT IN HISTORY OF INTERNATIONAL CO-OPERATION."

West European States Agree On Trade Payments Scheme

EIGHTEEN West European States agreed in Paris yesterday on a trade payments scheme which Sir Stafford Cripps hailed as "the greatest achievement in the history of international co-operation."

Finance Ministers of the Organisation for European Economic Co-operation announced complete agreement on the European Payments Union after meeting yesterday morning. America will provide a working fund of dollars linked with the Marshall Plan.

The Union is designed to secure the effects of a multilateral system of payments in Western Europe and dependent territories.

All bilateral surpluses and deficits between particular member countries will be offset against one another in a sort of clearing house, so that each country will finish up with a net credit or debit position against all the other countries together.

These net positions will be settled by a combination of credits and gold payments.

Each country is given a quota within which its surplus or deficit will be settled by credit or gold payments roughly reflecting the country's importance in intra-European trade.

Britain's quota, reflecting the trade of the whole sterling area, will be 27 per cent. of the total—roughly one thousand million dollars.

Experts will now draw up the text of the agreement which will be signed within a few weeks. It will be retrospective from July.

M. Marjolin, O.E.E.C. Secretary-General, said the decision reached in monetary matters yesterday was the most important since the Bretton Woods agreements setting up the World Bank and International Monetary Fund.

The common unit in which all accounts of the payments union will be kept will be equal to one-thirtyfifth of an ounce of fine gold.

The working capital to be made available to the European Payments Union by America through the Economic Co-operation Administration will amount to 350 to 400 million dollars (about £125 to £142 million sterling).

WILL HELP TRADE.

The agreement announced in Paris yesterday by the European Payments Union may lead eventually to some revision of travel provision for British visitors to the Continent, writes a financial correspondent.

The scheme is primarily devised to facilitate trade among member countries. It places no obstacle on such day to day use of sterling as may be thought appropriate in Europe, and it does not affect the existing use of sterling as an international trading currency.

There are four main objectives of the scheme:—To facilitate a return to multilateral trade in Western Europe by making surpluses earned by one country in any other expendable in all the other member countries;

to remove restrictions on trade that were unavoidable in the absence of a multilateral payments system;

to secure these objectives without hindering the efforts of the members to become independent of dollar aid, and without impeding the development of high and stable levels of trade and employment; to provide multilateral payments facilities without impeding the steady growth of the still inadequate gold and dollar reserves of the member countries.—Reuter and P.A.

STRENGTH OF THE ARMY

Sharp Reply To F.F. Deputy

On the motion for the adjournment of the Dail last evening, **Major V. de Valera** (F.F.) raised a question which he had asked the Minister for Defence on Thursday. Dr. O'Higgins, in reply, had given the total strength of the defence forces exclusive of chaplains, cadets, nursing staff and reserves on June 28th last as 7,934. Major de Valera said that in February last the Minister had made a statement to the effect that he had a stronger defence force than he had previously, and that the defence forces were being built up. The statement made in the Taoiseach at Tullamore on June 9th, that there were over 12,000 men in the forces was incorrect.

Was the Government trying to create the impression that the forces were growing when, in fact, they were not?

The first line strength was below that of 1949 and the F.C.A. strength was also falling. From January to March the Minister had got 1,000 recruits, but the strength had remained static since that month. He accepted the Minister's explanation that the Taoiseach was speaking of the established strength, but the fact was that misleading information had been published.

Dr. O'Higgins (Minister for Defence), replying said that everybody knew that the strength of an army based on short-term attestation and volunteering was liable to variation from week to week and from month to month. No one was entitled to toss a two-headed penny. The Deputy said that it was criminal for the Taoiseach to quote the establishment figure, but it was no harm for the leader of the Opposition to make the same mistake and repeat it. The Deputy had stated that in 1948 they aimed at an army of 12,500, but the Book of Estimates showed that they only arranged for that number, less a reduction of 25 per cent. The Book of Estimates was made out in exactly the same way this year, and the only difference was that he was asking for 8,000 soldiers, and had the honesty to tell the people that.

"I have never stopped recruiting," said Dr. O'Higgins. "The Deputy is only a small boy in the big campaign to discredit this army in the eyes of people at home and abroad. He gets quite hot under the collar in case anybody might think that the Army is slightly larger than it was. He must tell people at home and abroad that we are unprepared and defenceless, that we are not prepared for our job, and that that is in the national interest.

"I am standing for the same army as my predecessor, and more honestly than my predecessor, because I am prepared to say what I am looking for and not to shelter behind a paper establishment."

The Minister denied that the strength of the F.C.A. was reduced. It was, he said, "watered down" to its effective strength so that they would know where they were.

The House adjourned until 2 p.m. on Tuesday next.

SENTENCED MAN BEFORE TRALEE COURT

Sydney Webber, 66-year-old Englishman serving a sentence of three years penal servitude for having stolen by false pretences sums amounting to about £2,000, was present at Tralee District Court yesterday when Supt. Glavey made an application under the Police Property Act in respect of £13 found on accused when arrested in Dublin in March last.

Webber, in reply to District Justice Johnson, said he was an undischarged bankrupt in England.

The Justice made an order directing the Supt. to hold the money until he got a valid order to part with it and to hold the money on trust for the estate of Sydney Webber.

£93 Millions For More Atomic Bombs

PRESIDENT'S REQUEST TO CONGRESS.

PRESIDENT Truman asked Congress yesterday for 260,000,000 dollars (about £93,000,000) to speed development of atomic bombs and push experiments on the hydrogen bomb.

He said the money would be used to enable the Atomic Energy Commission "to build additional and more efficient plants" to carry out his directive of January 31 ordering work on the hydrogen bomb.

Mr. Truman said the fundamental objective was to use atomic energy for peace but added: "Until this objective is achieved, however, we must strengthen our own defences by providing the necessary atomic energy capacity."

In a statement, he pointed out that his January directive called on the A.E.C. "to continue its work on all forms of atomic weapons, including the hydrogen or fusion bomb."

[illegible]

The new plants to be built with the money, he added, would be "of advanced design" and their operation would "provide new knowledge that will feed the progress of the atomic energy programme."

"Expansion in the scope of our atomic energy programme gives added emphasis to the fact that atomic energy has great potentialities both for destruction and for the benefit of mankind."

The U.S. Atomic Energy Commission has completed dispersal and expansion of plant capacity for the manufacture of components for atomic weapons, Senator O'Mahoney disclosed yesterday. He was making public information in a report of the Commission made to the Senate Appropriations Sub-Committee behind closed doors on March 21.

The report said that American atomic weapons production was in "better shape" than ever before.

"New processes are expected to come into operation during 1951 and will enable us to re-use uranium that has been irradiated in the piles," the statement presented by Mr. Sumner T. Pike, the Commission Chairman, said. "This means we can now look forward to production of a good deal more fissionable material per pound of virgin raw material."

In a statement, Mr. Pike said that for some years the Belgian Congo would continue to be the chief source of raw uranium. More and more could be expected from other foreign sources which might include South Africa, where uranium development was under way.

The Chairman of the United States [illegible] Board, Mr. Hubert E. Howard, said yesterday that [illegible] 256 plants built by the Government [illegible].

[illegible]

Mr. Howard gave the information in a report in "Commerce Magazine," a publication of the Chicago Association of Commerce and Industry.

Ottawa, Friday.—Defence Department officials said yesterday that details of a course being given in home defence against atomic and bacterial attack were strictly secret.

Civilians who took it would apparently have to be screened for security purposes.

American business firms were yesterday promised easier access to non-secret atomic energy technical reports.—Reuter and A.P.

NO REQUEST YET FOR MORE TROOPS IN GERMANY

—*Mr. McCloy*

'If We Show Weakness Aggression Likely.'

U.S. High Commissioner John McCloy, said last night in Frankfurt—"I do not believe the Korean situation will have any consequences for the West German Republic."

He said: "Our own (Allied) actions will determine to a large extent whether there will be any aggression in Europe.

"If we show weakness, aggression is likely.

"But I think that war can be avoided, chiefly by showing strength in the West and convincing the world that we are ready to fight if necessary."

He had no reports of any unusual troop movements in Russian-occupied Eastern Germany or any other indications of early military action.

There were some reports of troop movements in the Balkans, but he could not evaluate their significance.

Asked whether he was satisfied with the strength of Allied forces in Western Germany, Mr. McCloy said: "You had better ask the Generals about that."

"As far as I know, there has been no request for more troops in West Germany.

"But I don't think the West has enough troops yet in all of Western Europe. I think we should continue to increase these as rapidly as possible."

Appealing to the German people to "maintain their balance" in these turbulent times, he said "The poise of the German people is important."—A.P.

"IN INTERESTS OF FOREIGN POWER"

Threat Of London Haulage Strike

With the aim, "Not a lorry on the road on Monday morning," delegates of some 25,000 trade unionists in general haulage in the London area called, last night, for paralysing action in support of the Smithfield Meat Market workers who have been on strike a fortnight.

Transport Union leader Mr. Arthur Deakin countered later with a declaration that "these people are completely irresponsible," and advising members to disregard the decision.

"They are acting very clearly with the support of active members of the Communist Party, who are out to create the utmost confusion at this time in the interests of a foreign Power," he said.

He stated there was no reason for a continuance of the strike, and immediately work was resumed, negotiations would go on.

The meeting aimed at a hold-up of all forms of road transport except passenger services in the Greater London area and called for emergency week-end meetings of all branches and depots.

U.S. STOCKPILES METALS.

The United States foreign trade gap narrowed during May with an increase in imports of 75,000,000 dollars (£25,142,000 sterling), and in exports of 15,000,000 dollars (£5,678,400 sterling).

The Commerce Department said that the sharp rise in imports was due chiefly to increased receipts of metals which the United States was stockpiling against a war emergency.

The U.S. Air Force said yesterday that military transport flights to Europe have been cut to meet demands for the Far East.—Reuter

IRISH GENERAL IN KOREA

Gen. MacArthur's headquarters last night released the names of the following three general officers assigned to the headquarters:—

Major-Gen. William F. Dean, Commander U.S. Forces in Korea;

Brigadier John H. Church, deputy Commander U.S.A.F.I.K.

Brigadier Crump Garvin, Base Commander in Korea.

General Dean comes from Belmullet, Co. Mayo. He fought as a junior officer with the U.S. forces in World War One and was Lieut.-Col in World War Two. His sister, Mrs. T. Flanagan, lives in Enniskillen.

U.S. PILGRIMS IN DUBLIN

Nearly 1,000 American pilgrims en route to Rome landed at Dublin yesterday from the specially chartered liner Liguria. They are due to leave for Liverpool this evening and from thence will continue their journey to Rome overland, except for the English Channel crossing.

The Liguria, formerly the yacht of Kaiser Wilhelm, has an Italian crew and is the largest pilgrim ship to call at Dublin since the Eucharistic Congress.

The pilgrims, who left New York eleven days ago, are members of the Apostleship of Prayer and are led by Rev. J. C. Faulkner.

"THERE SHOULD BE ONLY ONE ARMY..."

Reference In Dail To "New Volunteer Force"

REFERENCE to a volunteer force which is being organised by a T.D., was made in the Dail yesterday during the debate on the estimate for the Department of Justice.

Mr. G. Boland (Fianna Fail) said that under the Constitution there should be only one army, and whether the body that Deputy Cowan was trying to form was called a volunteer force or otherwise, it should not be allowed. They all know that Deputy Cowan was more or less play-acting but some of the people induced to take part might not be play-acting. So far the force had displayed no arms, but surely the Government were not going to wait until they began shooting. They all know that there was another organisation which was naturally taking full advantage of all that.

Mr. P. J. Little (Fianna Fail) said there could be only one authority in control of military activities.

Capt. P. Cowan (Ind.) said that the significant thing about the new volunteer force was that it had increased substantially in strength since it had been subjected to certain criticism by Deputy Boland in the country, and his leader in the House.

General MacEoin (Minister for Justice), moving an estimate of £45,720 for his Department, said that the aggregate Vote for the Department was £3,528,220, a decrease of £191,340 on last year's estimate. [illegible]

[illegible]

months there had been only one promotion from sergeant to inspector, and that the last examination for sergeants was in 1942.

"CONFIDENTIAL REPORT."

Mr. Boland said that Deputy Lehane had produced in the House what, he said, was a confidential police report, given to a judge before people were tried.

The Minister had a bounden duty to investigate that whole matter and find out whether the judge did in fact let that document out of his hands or whether the document was stolen.

"My information," said Mr. Boland, "is that it was stolen, either from the judge's pocket or from his office, and by a solicitor at that, and sent by post to Deputy Lehane. The person who stole that could only be described as a thief, but what could be said about the receiver?"

"ONLY ONE ARMY."

Mr. Boland said that under the Constitution there should be only one army, and whether the body that Deputy Cowan was trying to form was called a volunteer force or otherwise, it should not be allowed. Competent legal men had told him (Mr. Boland) that it was definitely contrary to the Constitution and to Section 6 of the Offences Against the State Act. They all knew that Deputy Cowan was more or less play-acting. [illegible]

[illegible]

Captain Cowan—And you cooperated with gun during the emergency.

Mr. Boland—I had a vote in 1935 when I was a member of the Sinn Fein Party [illegible]

[illegible]

Captain Cowan—The Government cannot break the law.

Mr. Boland—This House can make the law, and if there is any doubt about the law it is the bounden duty of the Government not to allow the position to drift.

Captain Cowan—Deputy Boland is the defender of Basil Brooke in this House.

Mr. Boland—Deputy Boland did his damnedest to prevent this happening [illegible] Deputy Cowan and people like him. Deputy Cowan's colleagues gave the [illegible] Basil Brooke, and that [illegible] of a Government recognised by the [illegible]

(CONTINUED ON PAGE EIGHT)

MR. NORTON ON THE NEW HOUSING BILL

Speaking at a meeting of the Naas Divisional Council of the Labour Party, An Tanaiste, Mr. Wm. Norton, T.D., said that the Housing Bill before the Dail was the most radical effort yet made in this sphere to assist people to build houses for themselves by means of a five per cent. deposit. Honest and credit-worthy citizens with limited resources, with Government aid and the assistance of local authorities, could undertake the building and purchase of their own homes on terms that would not impose an onerous burden upon them. [illegible]

[illegible] but would also provide outstanding dividends in rural areas in the drainage of lands and improving amenities generally.

While the repeal of the County Management Act would not take place before the next local elections, stated Mr. Norton, the Government's declared policy was to restore the powers taken from local representatives and thus restore, in a most democratic way, the will and initiative of the representatives of the people to work for local communities. The experiment in local dictatorship by the late Government had been a ghastly failure and now there was no question of any person with intelligence attempting to justify its continuance.

Civilians making their way along the road from battle scared Suwon. —(I.N.P.)

Page recreated

1951

Through the 1940s and early 1950s, TB was on the increase in Ireland and claiming up to 4,000 deaths per year, mostly of people in their twenties. An extremely poor health service was proving ineffective against the disease, and Minister for Health Noel Browne - who had watched several members of his family die from TB - decided to do something about it. He had used money from the Hospitals Sweeps draws to build sanatoria and was also planning a new health bill to provide free medical care to all mothers and to children up to the age of 16. These plans would prove to be his undoing. Doctors were against the bill as they feared their income would be reduced with state interference in the health arena, but the really significant objections came from the Catholic Church. The hierarchy felt that the state had no right to interfere in the family, and also feared the bill would lead to contraception or even abortion being introduced.

Browne had also fallen out with other members of the cabinet and had little support when the bishops raised their objections to the bill. His resignation led to the downfall of the government and a general election which brought de Valera back to power.

Cong, Co Mayo, delayed the arrival of the rural electrification scheme which was spreading across the country so that the village could provide the setting for *The Quiet Man*, starring John Wayne and Maureen O'Hara.

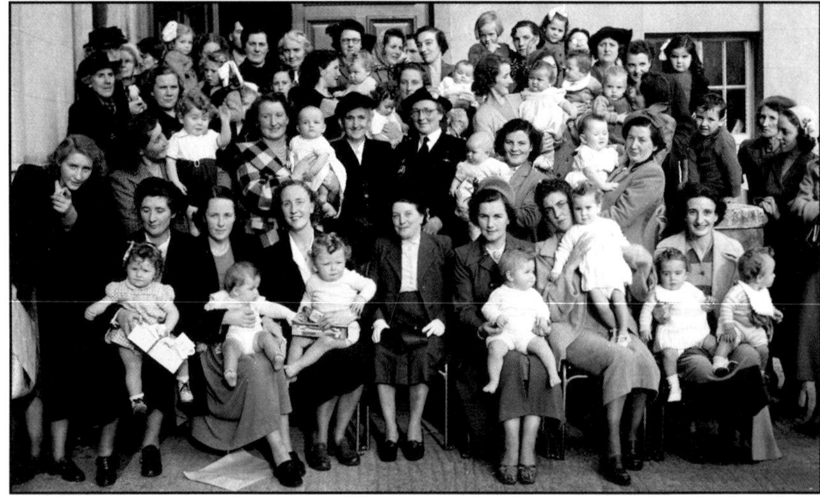

The winners of a baby show at the City Hall, Cork.

Pope saw Fatima vision

Monday, October 15

Moved by disclosures that the Pope last year saw four visions, nearly 2,000 Italians thronged the Vatican Palace last night to see His Holiness Pius XII carried shoulder-high on his golden throne from an audience with Catholic lay workers.

Cardinal Federico Tedeschini told nearly a million pilgrims at Fatima, near Lisbon, Portugal, that the Pope had the visions immediately before and after proclaiming the Dogma of the Assumption of the Blessed Virgin Mary.

According to the Cardinal, the Pope saw the sun "break through the clouds and dance about the heavens" on four occasions as he walked through the Vatican gardens. This was a peculiarity of the visions at Fatima in 1917, when three shepherd children saw the Blessed Virgin on May 13 of that year, and on the same day of the month for the next five months.

After describing the 'Dancing of the Sun' at Fatima, Cardinal Tedeschini said: "Another person has seen this miracle - the Pope. Who can gaze at the disc of the sun surrounded by its halo? But he was able to do so. Under the hand of Mary, he was able to watch the life of the sun - the sun agitated, all convulsed, transformed into a pattern of life, into a spectacle of celestial movement, into a transmitter of mute but eloquent messages to the Vicar of Christ."

NEWS BRIEFS

Jan Plans get underway for a major census that would reveal some very interesting trends in Irish life over the past few decades. Despite a small increase in population in the Republic to 2,961,000, about 120,000 people - more than half of them female - had emigrated between 1946 and 1951. Migration rates were highest in the 15 to 19 age group. Statistics also revealed that women outnumbered men in urban areas, but the reverse was true in the countryside. The extent to which Ireland was still a rural country can be seen from the statistic that more than half the population did not live in towns or villages. However, there had been a 23% decline in the amount of people involved in agriculture since 1926.

June Éamon de Valera was elected Taoiseach in a minority government last night after receiving the votes of several independent TDs, including Noel Browne. (14)

Dec Troops on the Korean front were last night observing a virtual cease-fire. They failed to shoot at Communists who came within sight. At least one Eighth Army Corps issued an order to the troops to confine action to the defensive and soldiers on the front were briefed accordingly.
The feeling spread among Allied soldiers that Tuesday's cease-fire line agreement means the cessation of practically all fighting. (29)

The Cork Examiner.

THE CORK EXAMINER, THURSDAY, APRIL 12, 1951.

BETTER PRICES FOR CATTLE AND SHEEP

And Remunerative Market For Pigs

CATTLE, SHEEP, PIGS

SENATE AND LAND WORKERS' HALF-DAY.

BRITAIN'S MEAT PURCHASES IN IRELAND

—M.P.'s Question

RADIO RECITAL AWARD AT FEIS MAITH

CLIMAX TO CONTROVERSY OVER MOTHER AND CHILD SCHEME

Dr. Browne Resigns Post As Minister For Health

DR. NOEL BROWNE yesterday resigned his portfolio as Minister for Health. He handed the letter personally to the Taoiseach at Leinster House at 4.30 p.m. The Taoiseach subsequently drove to Arus an Uachtarain where he informed the President of Dr. Browne's resignation. Later the Taoiseach informed the Dail and said that he himself would take over the Ministry temporarily.

Dr. Browne's resignation followed days of intense activity behind the scenes in an effort to persuade the Minister to alter the terms of his proposed Mother and Child Scheme. On Friday last, the Government having fully considered reasoned criticism of the scheme by the ecclesiastical authorities, sent a direction to Dr. Browne to prepare without delay a new scheme which would be in the fullest accord with Catholic teaching and principles.

I understand that Dr. Browne, wrote our Political Correspondent, from Dublin last night, was not prepared to concede that his proposals were in any way in opposition to the moral law and that accordingly he was not prepared to make any amendment.

LETTER TO DR. BROWNE.

MR. COSTELLO'S STATEMENT

DEPUTIES MOTION.

MR. McBRIDE'S LETTERS.

(CONTINUED ON PAGE NINE)

RAILWAY GATE SMASHED AGAIN

PRESIDENT SAW MR. COSTELLO AND NUNCIO

WATERFORD PROJECT

CORRESPONDENCE BETWEEN BISHOPS, TAOISEACH AND MINISTER

Mother And Child Scheme "Opposed To Catholic Social Teaching"

LAST night Dr. Browne released for publication the correspondence which passed between the Bishops and the Taoiseach and himself. In the course of the correspondence it was stated that the Hierarchy regarded the Mother and Child Scheme proposed by the Minister for Health "as opposed to Catholic social teaching."

"The elimination of private medical practitioners by a State-paid service has not been shown to be necessary or even advantageous to the patient, the public in general or the medical profession.

HIERARCHY'S LETTER.

DR. BROWNE JOINS INDEPENDENTS

Dr. Browne has resigned his membership of the Clann na Poblachta, but will retain his seat in the Dail as an Independent.

(CONTINUED ON PAGE SIX)

FIRE OUTBREAK IN CORK

DUBLIN THEATRE GROUP TO VISIT CORK

REPLIES IN THE DAIL

CIVIL DEFENCE

PRICE OF BACON

AGRICULTURAL OUTPUT.

(CONTINUED ON PAGE NINE)

INFECTIOUS DISEASES

I.M.A. And Department Of Health

SCHOOL-LEAVING AGE

Minister's Reply To Dail Question

Social Welfare Bill Gets Second Reading By Four Votes

AN AGREED SCHEME WOULD BENEFIT THE COUNTRY—Mr. de Valera

THE Social Welfare Bill passed its second reading in the Dail last night, by seventy-one votes to sixty-seven. Motions that the Bill be refused a second reading were defeated by 71 votes to 66. The Fianna Fail Party voting for en bloc, the only Independent deputies voting were Messrs. P. D. Lehane, P. Cogan and P. J. O'Reilly.

There were cheers from the Government benches and shouts of "do you want an election now" and F.F. shouts of "yes," you have thrown Dr. Browne to the Fine Gael wolves."

A division was challenged on the motion that the Bill be given a second reading and this was carried by 71 votes to 67. Dr. Noel Browne voted with the Government in both divisions.

During the debate, Mr. E. de Valera said there should be some effort to try and get discussion in order to have the whole question considered between them. A proposition had already been put to him, he said, by Mr. Norton. It would be a great thing for the country to have an agreed scheme.

Mr. Norton said there could be a broad discussion on the Committee stage and they could have free play for their different views on that stage.

(CONTINUED ON PAGE NINE)

NO CHANGE IN U.S. POLICY ON KOREA

But Secret Talks Start At U.N.O.

SIR GILBERT LAITHWAITE IN LONDON

MacArthur's Dismissal May Start Anti Truman Moves

Republicans Support General

U.S. House of Representatives Republicans decided at a party meeting last night to defer for the time being any formal action to initiate impeachment proceedings against President Truman over the dismissal of General MacArthur.

The Republican group voted unanimously to support a proposal for a full Congressional investigation of foreign and military policy. They also approved inviting MacArthur to address a joint session of Congress.

The Senate Republican Policy Committee agreed at a secret meeting to get General MacArthur "back here as soon as possible" to discuss the Korean war and Far East policies. The Senate group also agreed to call a general conference of all Republican Senators on Monday to discuss the MacArthur dismissal and related policies.

President Truman announced his dismissal of the United Nations Supreme Commander in a dramatic early morning Press conference yesterday.

Swiftly a storm of controversy broke throughout the U.S. and rumbled all over the world. Amid the storm, General MacArthur indicated he would not accept his dismissal without public protest.

(CONTINUED ON PAGE NINE)

MR. TRUMAN'S BROADCAST.

18 NEW CHINESE DIVISIONS

Slow U.S. Advance In North Korea

'BUS CONDUCTOR'S DEATH

Manslaughter Charge At Waterford

NEW ACT WELCOMED

1952

Africa really was the 'dark continent' for Irish newspaper readers in 1952 when several missionaries fell victim to the colonial struggles there. In South Africa, an Irish nun was killed when a strike meeting called by the African National Congress (ANC) in East London was banned and a riot ensued. Irish people were also caught up in Kenya's Mau Mau rebellion, a nationalist attempt to drive out Europeans.

Still in the pre-television age, newspapers were now experiencing more competition in the media arena with increasing sales of radios. The government regarded radios as a useful source of revenue and detector vans travelled the countryside looking for unlicensed sets.

The death of Britain's King George VI was marked in Ireland with special church ceremonies and the flying of flags at half mast, including on the GPO in Dublin.

Let there be light

Thursday, December 4

The 21st area to receive the benefit of rural electrification in the Cork No 2 District was 'switched in' last night when in Carrignavar village, Rev C O'Brien threw over a switch which lighted a public street lamp. Simultaneously lights appeared in most of the houses in the village and the surrounding countryside.

After he had made the official switch on, Fr O'Brien said rural electrification was an amenity which lessened the disparity between city and country. The people of the area thoroughly deserved such amenities because they were hard working: they were suppliers of milk to the city and had to rise early with the dawn. They would no longer have to work in the dark. They would also have heat and the other benefits that electricity brought.

Mr J Ware, District Engineer, first spoke of the co-operation which was needed before a district could be electrified. He then recalled that five years had passed since the first area of Co Cork - Inniscarra - had received rural electrification. At that time the ESB was told that farmers were too conservative to take to electricity and that the charges were too high.

Fr O'Brien switches on the power as the Rural Electrification Scheme comes to Carrignavar, Co Cork.

Minister at opening of radio exhibition

Wednesday, October 29

The Cork Radio Exhibition, the first ever to be held in the city, was officially opened in the City Hall yesterday. The Lord Mayor, Ald P McGrath, said wireless was a particular joy to the aged and the sick, for it provided for them the only form of entertainment they could enjoy.

The Minister for Posts and Telegraphs, Mr Erskine Childers, said Radio Éireann always liked to see everything possible done to stimulate the radio industry. At the moment there were nearly 4,000 licence holders in the country, and that number included 35,000 listeners who, last year, were unknown to the Department of Posts and Telegraphs, and whom they regretfully had to compel to pay their licence fees.

Rat nibbled her nose

Saturday, February 16

Awakened from her sleep at 2am one morning to find a rat nibbling at her nose was the unnerving experience of Mrs Mary O'Loughlin of Ennis, Co Clare, who subsequently received medical treatment for four rat bites and shock.

Mrs O'Loughlin, when first awakened, did not know what was wrong, and then came the horrible realisation that a rat was gnawing at her nose with its sharp teeth. She screamed and woke her husband. The rat vanished immediately.

Since this occurrence a trap has been baited in the house, and last night a rat, stated to be as big as a well-nourished kitten, was caught in the trap.

The unusual occurrence caused a fluster amongst other housewives in the town where old disregarded rat traps and poison preparations are being hurriedly pressed into service.

NEWS BRIEFS

Jan Twenty-three people died when an Aer Lingus Dakota bound for Dublin from Northolt nosedived into a bog on the slopes of Moel Slabod in Snowdonia last night. There were no survivors. (11)

Sept An attempt to murder an Irish priest, who had denounced the secret African society, Mau Mau, in Kenya was revealed yesterday. Another priest, Fr J O'Donoghue, of Tipperary, had a spear hurled at him during a night raid by members of the society. (13)

Dec An outbreak of polio has occurred at Ballyvourney, Co Cork. Three cases have been confirmed and one has since proved fatal. (4)

The Cork Examiner.

MINOR MIRACLE REPEATED

A 2½ year old MORRIS MINOR covers 1,000 miles in 24½ hours

An average speed of 41.1m.p.h. Petrol consumption 45.6 m.p.g.*

Leaving the Phoenix Park, Dublin, on June 23rd, Mr. Eric Fry, a Director of G. A. Brittain Limited, with his co-driver, Mr. T. Davidson, and a Press observer, covered 1,000 miles around Ireland in 24 hrs. 25 mins.

A truly remarkable performance, made all the more remarkable because the Morris Minor used by Mr. Fry is the same car in which he covered the same distance in 1950.

This car has now done over 50,000 miles with the original engine, and is standard in every detail. Before the trip the car was in every-day use, throughout the country, by one of G. A. Brittain's representatives.

This map shows the route taken in the test — roads of every type were covered

A picture taken at the start of the endurance test (left to right): Mr. T. Davidson; a Press Observer; Mr. E. A. L. Fry. A very full load was carried—in addition to spare wheels, petrol, tools and food, the driver and passengers weighed almost 40 stones.

Proof of the Morris Minor's *endurance, dependability and all-round economy*

This performance by a standard Morris Minor, without any special tuning or alterations, identical, in fact, with thousands on the roads of Ireland to-day, proves beyond doubt that it can equal the performance of bigger cars at a surprisingly low running cost.

The car used by Mr. Fry has not had an 'easy' life—since it was built it has been used for the following jobs: (1) As a demonstration car. (2) For Mr. Fry's first 1,000 miles round Ireland. (3) As a hire car. (4) As a traveller's car. That it is still in perfect condition, after such hard usage, and a further 1,000 mile trip is proof indeed that the Morris 'Minor' is built to last.

** On actual running time the average speed was 42.6 m.p.h.*

MORRIS MINOR

2 Door £439-10. 4 Door £470

G. A. BRITTAIN LIMITED DUBLIN

Young

1953

A few days before Queen Elizabeth II was crowned Queen of England, a Nepalese porter and a New Zealand beekeeper became the first people to reach the summit of Mount Everest. The lack of pictures and first-hand accounts from Nepal limited initial coverage of the feat by Tenzing Norgay and Edmund Hillary, while the news from London on the day of the coronation was very much from the angle of the Catholic Church's involvement in the event.

The use of Cóbh as a port of call for transatlantic liners continued to provide access for locals to world figures in politics, sports and entertainment and also gave the *Examiner* a wealth of stories. This year, the American comedy duo of Stan Laurel and Oliver Hardy came ashore while on their way to a tour of Europe, hoping in vain that "no fuss" would be made about their visit.

Oliver Hardy and Stan Laurel with Cork Lord Mayor Patrick McGrath. Laurel and Hardy are mobbed by hundreds of children at Cóbh who ruffle their ties and beg for autographs. Twenty-three stone Hardy comments: "There scarcely ever was a film scene like it. They are grand children, and Stan and I are grateful to them." Later, the portly comedian would be the only member of the party not to kiss the Blarney Stone, expressing the fear that: "Nobody would hold me up. I am too big".

NEWS BRIEFS

July The war in Korea ends. An estimated two million people were killed in the conflict. (27)

Aug Dr Alfred O'Rahilly, President of UCC, warns that Ireland would "go Communist" much more quickly if the country gave up its religion. The prominent Catholic academic also says that the State has no right to interfere in the family. (17)

Nov A man from Galway serving in Berlin with the British Army defects to East Germany. A statement from the East German government quotes Martin Nee from Inveran as saying he wanted to do all he could to prevent a third world war: "That is why I have come here." (13)

Turbulent seas prevent evacuation of Blaskets

Wednesday, November 18

Some of the last islanders to be evacuated from the Blaskets arrive at Dunquin.

In a remote corner of County Kerry, where the huge Atlantic breakers pound relentlessly on the rugged coastline around Slea Head and Dunquin, and where seldom a word of English is spoken by the hardy, weather-beaten inhabitants, a drama of no little moment to its participants was enacted yesterday.

It was the beginning of the final stage of the total evacuation of the historic Blasket Islands, stronghold of an ancient and distinctive Gaelic civilisation, home of peerless storytellers and sages like Peig Sayers and Tomás Ó Croimhthin, and a place of pilgrimage for generations of Irish scholars and students. Yesterday was the day fixed for the final exodus, but the weather decreed otherwise, and only six out of 21 were able to leave the island owing to the huge swell in the rolling seas.

For years past, it had been regretfully realised that the Blaskets' days of glory were no more. Not for the younger generation were the rigours of life on the dreary, windswept and often stormbound 'Oileán Mór' which had been borne and overcome by their forbears. Emigration, death and dwindling population all took their toll, and for a long time past, the Government have been arranging to transplant the remaining 30 or so residents to the mainland at Dunquin.

When our representative visited Dunquin school yesterday, nothing but Irish was to be heard from the 20 or so young children playing in the school yard. One of the gayest of them was young Gearóid Ó Cathair, the school's newest pupil, who up to a week or so ago was the only child living on the Blaskets.

He played and laughed and shouted with the others, entirely unaware of the fact that in a language he does not understand he had won headlines in the newspapers as "the loneliest boy in the world".

The Cork Examiner.

THE CORK EXAMINER, TUESDAY, JUNE 2, 1953.

NEWS CHEERED BY LONDON CROWDS

British Team Reached Summit Of Mount Everest

NEWS of the successful attempt of the British expedition in reaching the summit of Mount Everest was given by announcers who broke into United States radio and television programmes last evening.

The radio station of "The New York Daily News" broadcast reported that the men who conquered Everest were E. P. Hillary and the Sherpa guide, Tensing.

Reports that Everest had been conquered drew cheers from the squatting crowds in London. Some people were told by police and others got it from passers-by.

Hillary (34) is a New Zealand beekeeper, who joined the expedition in India. He has wide climbing experience in the New Zealand Alps where heavy snowfalls and peculiar icefalls make conditions not unlike those in the Himalayas.

Tensing (39), leader of the Sherpa guides (members of a tough caste of mountain dwellers on the southern slopes of the Himalayas) is the stalwart veteran of more Everest attempts than any man on earth.

He made an epic ascent last year with the tireless Swiss climber, Raymond Lambert, reaching the previous record height of 28,215 feet.

... oxygen equipment, without which no expedition ever tried to climb the last few thousand feet battling against wild gales in rarefied air and lashing snow.

Colonel Hunt's party took an improved type of equipment of two kinds—a closed circuit system by which the climber receives 100 per cent oxygen from the cylinder, and an open circuit, in which a certain proportion of fresh air is absorbed as well as pure oxygen.

RESULTS OF EARLIER EXPEDITIONS.

THREE FLAGS.

"PUT NEW ZEALAND ON THE MAP"

ELEVENTH ASSAULT.

Coronation Crowds Wait In Rain

Some of the thousands of people who waited throughout the night for to-day's Coronation Procession. This picture shows a corner of Trafalgar Square with the Coliseum in the background. Heavy rain fell in London during the night. (Wired Picture)

Pope's Envoy, Catholic Peers And Diplomats At Te Deum

MR. BOLAND AT PONTIFICAL MASS BY CARDINAL GRIFFIN

IN brilliant pageantry, Cardinal Griffin, Archbishop of Westminster, with the Papal Ambassador to the Coronation, Archbishop Cento, Nuncio to Belgium, presiding, last night sang the Pontifical High Mass at Westminster Cathedral, London, in the presence of a mighty crowd of dignitaries and overseas visitors, hundreds of simple men and women, scores of children and row after row of nuns and priests.

It was the climax to the three days of prayer ordered by the Hierarchy of England and Wales for the Coronation.

Two minutes before Archbishop Cento arrived at the north door, the Duke of Norfolk, the Earl Marshal, in morning dress, who himself is a Catholic and last night represented Queen Elizabeth, walked to his place of honour beneath the Sanctuary steps.

SOUTHERN PRIESTS PRESENT.

CROWDS GREET CARDINAL.

CARDINAL D'ALTON'S MESSAGE.

Hopes That Border May Go During This Reign.

His Eminence Cardinal d'Alton, Archbishop of Armagh and Primate of All Ireland, issued the following statement last night:—

"I am sure that Irishmen of all shades of opinion, with their innate sense of chivalry, will join in good wishes to the young Queen who was called to the throne in circumstances of great personal sorrow.

"It is my earnest prayer that her reign may be the opening of a new era of prosperity for her people. All of us who love the old historic Ireland sincerely hope that during it we may see our own country restored to its natural unity."—P.A.

MOVES TO SAVE ATOM SPIES

Judge Refuses Reprieve

DAIL MEETS TO-DAY

OBLATE FATHER JOINS CISTERCIANS

Thousands Wait In Rain For Coronation

VATICAN PAPER PAYS TRIBUTE

AS darkness fell last night, a damp but cheerful multitude settled down for the night along the Coronation route in London's West End. They wanted to have good places for viewing to-day's Coronation procession.

Mr. F. H. Boland, the Irish Ambassador in London, yesterday attended Queen Elizabeth's reception and lunch in Buckingham Palace for Commonwealth Prime Ministers, Governors and other diplomats. Lord Brookeborough, Premier of Northern Ireland, was also present. After the reception, Queen Elizabeth and the Duke of Edinburgh moved informally amongst the guests.

The Vatican newspaper, "Osservatore Romano," yesterday hailed the Coronation with glowing words of praise for Queen Elizabeth, saying: "The Catholic world is not extraneous to the homage of so large a part of the world." Five Cardinals were amongst those who attended the special Coronation eve Mass in Rome's Church of the Holy Apostles.

CARDINALS AT SPECIAL MASS

VATICAN PAPER'S TRIBUTE.

AER LINGUS CORONATION TRAFFIC.

MR. DULLES SUMS-UP HIS RECENT TOUR

"Allow Self-Government To Develop"

SECRETARY OF STATE Dulles said in Washington last night that the United States Government should pay more attention to the Near East and South Asia, where people suspected that the United States was trying to preserve the old colonial interests of Britain and France.

Mr. Dulles was speaking to the nation by radio and television on his recent twenty-thousand-mile trip through twelve countries in the Near East and South Asia. Most of the people there, he said, were "deeply concerned" about political independence. He believed that the Western Powers could gain rather than lose from "an orderly development of self-government."

Reporting on the Anglo-Egyptian dispute, he said he was convinced there was "nothing irreconcilable" between Egyptian sovereignty and the international concern over the future of the Suez base, which had an importance to Western security.

Turning to the question of colonialism, Mr. Dulles said most of the people of the Near East and South Asia were "deeply concerned" about political independence for themselves and others.

IRISH COUPLE HURT IN FRENCH CRASH

WHALE CHASER AT COBH

INQUEST ON CHILD KILLED BY VAN

MR. BERGEN MEETS THE TAOISEACH

Plans To Make Million Bog Acres Productive

Tanaiste Stresses Value Of Present Experiment

THE economic and social consequences to this country of success in the Sugar Company's experiment on Gowla Bog were so great that exaggeration was hardly possible, said Mr. Lemass, Minister for Industry and Commerce, at the opening yesterday of the Sugar Company's grass-drying plant at Gowla Bog, Co. Galway.

If they succeeded in doing what they were convinced could be done—the bringing of a wider area of hitherto derelict bogland into cultivation,—it opened up a new future for wide areas in all our Western counties. It held out the prospect, in time, of the addition of about a million acres of productive land located in just those counties where the pressure of population on available resources was the greatest.

THREE MILLION ACRES

It was roughly estimated that there were three million acres of bog in Ireland, of which only a small percentage was suitable for large-scale mechanised fuel production by the methods heretofore perfected by Bord na Mona.

ECONOMIC METHODS SOUGHT

MORE TOURISTS FOR IRELAND.

The Irish Tourist Office in Lower Regent Street has been inundated during the past few days with personal inquiries from tourists in London for the Coronation—mostly Australians and Americans anxious to go to Ireland immediately after to-day's event, reports our London editor.

IRISH EXHIBITS SOLD OUT

Business Boom At Toronto Fair

THREE PLAYERS KILLED

Lightning Strikes Cricket Pavilion

CAR CRASH VICTIMS

Improved Condition Of Injured

RISK WAR WITH RUSSIA

U.S. Senator On Korean Crisis

WOMAN GOLFER STRUCK.

EDEN'S FORTHCOMING OPERATION

LINERS FOR COBH

VISCOUNT SETS UP AIR RECORD

IRISH DELEGATES FOR GENEVA

New South Korean Proposals To U.S.

—REPORT

MUTUAL DEFENCE PACT SOUGHT

SOUTH KOREAN Government officials said last night that President Rhee and his Cabinet had reached agreement on an "important and final" decision on the Korean war. President Rhee was reported in Washington yesterday to have proposed that President Eisenhower should sign an agreement promising a mutual defence pact with South Korea if the Seoul Government would drop its opposition to the United Nations truce terms.

The proposed agreement would also promise American military and financial help to South Korea. The White House and State Department refused comment.

The South Korean Government would shortly make an "important statement on the cease fire in Korea."

Salute Guns Won't Hit Chinese.

These orders went out last night to British Commonwealth division artillery firing a 101 gun Coronation salute this morning in Korea.

"Be careful not to hit the Chinese."

Though the guns will be pointed towards the enemy, division officers explained yesterday that the barrage has been carefully plotted so that the shells fall on "dead ground."

One officer said: "We didn't think it would be quite sporting to hit them with the Queen's salute." A.P.

1954

The Marian Year drew thousands of devotees to religious ceremonies dedicated to the Blessed Virgin, but none of those events could match the All-Ireland hurling final in terms of crowd. Almost 85,000 people, a record back then, witnessed Christy Ring win his eighth and final championship medal. It was the days before organised ticketing, so huge queues formed outside the ground from 8am.

Cork's win was their third in a row and was to mark the end of a period of Munster dominance of the competition which had also seen a Tipperary three-in-row and victories by Limerick and Waterford, and the McCarthy Cup had left the province only once since 1940.

While all seemed well in sport and religion, literature was still taking a hammering in Ireland from the censor. This year had the unenviable record of having the most books banned by the censor - over a thousand titles were prevented from reaching the eyes of the Irish public.

Christy Ring wins another All-Ireland

Monday, September 6

Cork's nineteenth All-Ireland hurling title, Christy Ring's eighth All-Ireland medal and a crowd of 84,856 who paid £10,661 were three new records established at Croke Park yesterday when Cork, in a vigorous exciting finish, defeated Wexford by 1-9 to 1-6 in the final of this season's campaign.

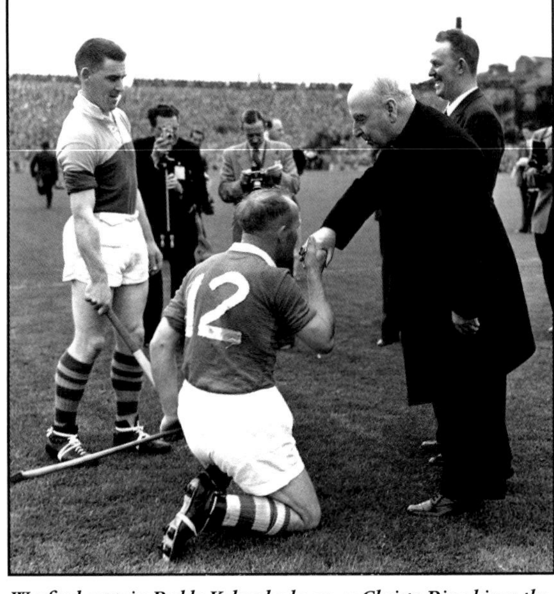

Wexford captain Paddy Kehoe looks on as Christy Ring kisses the ring of Dr Kinane, Archbishop of Cashel, before the All-Ireland hurling final.

The final will be recorded as one of the most colourful and finest for many years and it fully satisfied the appetites whetted as the teams fought their way to the final. Wexford led 1-3 to 0-5 at the interval and after the resumption they still continued to force the pace. The Cork defence gradually blunted the Model County's thrust and with the Cork forwards beginning to get the better of the Wexford half-backs, the Leesiders got the upper hand in a welter of intense excitement and inch by inch fought their way to victory.

All during the night numbers of young people, and some not so young, continued to arrive in Dublin, both by bicycle and by motor car. CIÉ ran no fewer than 35 special trains, not to mention countless numbers of special buses.

As early as 8am there was a queue outside Croke Park. Every effort was made to pack the ground so as not to disappoint people, but despite all these efforts the entire number of entrances had to be closed at 2.37pm.

It was, despite everything, a good humoured and sporting crowd and it is pleasant to report that, on the whole, the arrangements worked smoothly, and though many hundreds and even thousands failed to gain admission, there was no disturbance of any kind.

At three o'clock sharp the Wexford team came bouncing on to the pitch to the accompaniment of a mighty cheer. Their splendid physique won the admiration of every spectator. They were quickly followed by the Cork hurling team, led by their incomparable captain Christy Ring. Though slightly smaller in build, the members of the Cork team looked a wiry, lithesome and well-trained lot.

While the teams reached the centre of the pitch the two captains, Christy Ring and Paddy Kehoe, were introduced to His Grace, Most Rev Dr Kinane, Archbishop of Cashel and Emly. Following the singing of 'Faith Of Our Fathers' and 'The Soldiers Song', His Grace threw in the ball and from that moment until the final whistle the crowed got what must be a surfeit of thrills.

NEWS BRIEFS

Apr Michael Manning becomes the last person to be executed in the state. The 25-year-old Limerick man was hanged by executioner 'Pierpoint' at Mountjoy two months after being found guilty of murdering Catherine Cooper, a 65-year-old nurse. The previous execution had been in 1948. (20)

Sept Twenty-eight people are killed when a KLM plane crashes in the Shannon estuary. Most of the victims were suffocated by fumes from a cracked petrol tank. Criticisms were raised that it took nearly three hours to start a rescue attempt. Nobody knew about the crash until the plane's navigator made his way to shore and walked the two miles back to the airport where he raised the alarm. Twenty-nine people survived. (5)

Dec Road deaths for the year reach 267. Of these, 103 were pedestrians while 81 were cyclists. Most fatal accidents occurred between 7pm and 8pm.

The Cork Examiner.

THE CORK EXAMINER, MONDAY, SEPTEMBER 6, 1954. 5

TWENTY-EIGHT DIE IN SHANNON AIR CRASH

Plane Plunges Into River After Leaving Airport

TWENTY-EIGHT people are dead as a result of an airliner crash in the Shannon estuary before dawn yesterday. Twenty-five were drowned in an unconscious condition in the ill-fated plane; two other men were drowned after jumping or falling from the aircraft and a woman died later last night in Ennis Hospital.

Most of the victims were rendered unconscious by fumes from a cracked perol tank, and then drowned by the rapidly-rising tide. Including the woman who died in hospital, twenty-nine people—seven of the crew of ten, and 22 of the 46 passengers—got out of the aircraft alive because a large hole torn in the roof let in the life-saving air.

They swam to the mudflats, or reached them by rubber dinghies. Rescuers later could hardly tell whether they were men or women until they spoke, so covered were they by black slime.

The plane, the K.L.M. Super Constellation aircraft "Triton" left Shannon just before 3.30 a.m. Triton in Greek mythology is the God of the Sea, and yesterday a few minutes after it had left the airport the sea claimed its own for the aircraft met a watery grave in the middle of the river Shannon.

This was the second crash of a K.L.M. aircraft within a fortnight and the fourth actual crash within the vicinity of Shannon Airport since it opened in October, 1945. Yesterday morning's crash with its heavy loss of life was described as the most mysterious crash since the post-war records of civil aviation.

STUMBLED ASHORE.

The great mystery is that until the navigator of the plane John Tieman, stumbled ashore, wet, weary and exhausted and made his way over the two-mile journey to the airport, the officials, though puzzled by the stop of communications, did not know that a plane had crashed within a mile and a quarter flying distance from the airport.

Following a day of conferences and Press statements, it was not clear up to late last night the reason for the delay from the time of the crash to the time the rescue crews went into action.

The plane had just made the take off, came down, skimmed the water and came to rest on a submerged sandbank.

Neither passengers nor crew were aware that the vessel had come to a stop until they were overcome or partially overcome by petrol fumes and the water of the river poured into them.

The crash occurred at 3.38 a.m. and it was two and a half hours later before the navigator staggered in to tell the airport staff that the plane had dived into the river.

Passengers made their escape by dinghy and some more were taken off by a launch.

Two men who spent four hours in rain and darkness clung to the tail of the aircraft for over four hours and then as a launch came alongside one of them slipped, lost his grip and plunged to his death into the angry waters.

All day long the watchers waited until the tide receded in the late afternoon to go to the aid of the men and women trapped in the doomed plane. Hope was at its lowest ebb then as was the tide.

TWO MISSING.

When the rescuers got alongside twenty-one bodies, many of them clung to their seats, were taken off and brought to the airport and Limerick City. Last night four more bodies were recovered. Two bodies were still missing and it is expected that they are those of men who had jumped from the plane when the crash occurred and were drowned.

Of the four people who joined the aircraft at Shannon all are alive. They included Mrs Elizabeth Carolan, who had been holidaying with relatives in Co. Sligo. Her daughter, Betty, had come to the aircraft to see her off on her journey to New York and when Mrs. Carolan was numbered among the survivors her daughter was the first to rush into her arms and spent the day by her side.

Aer Lingus placed a plane at the disposal of General Isaac Alers, President of K.L.M., who had been visiting Dublin and he flew into Shannon in the forenoon. Later he talked to reporters and gave a dramatic account of the death-dealing dive of the plane.

Irish Departmental officials under Mr. R. W. O'Sullivan are conducting an enquiry into the cause of the accident and Dutch officials are also conducting an enquiry.

WOMAN DIES

Most of the survivors suffered from petrol scorches and many of them also suffered from shock.

One of those seriously injured, Mrs. Caroline Platz, an American, was removed to Ennis Hospital with a fractured spine. She died at the hospital later last night.

The Ennis Red Cross ambulance brought her to the Clare Co. Home. She was pulseless when brought

(CONTINUED ON PAGE SEVEN)

"SHOULD HAVE BEEN ON ALERT."

A spokesman for K.L.M. said last night that some emergency should have been sent out when the 'plane failed to report after passing Kilkee. "It only takes 25 minutes to reach the radio marker at Kilkee, and when no communication was received from the aircraft after that time Shannon should have been on the alert."

Photographer's Plane In Difficulty.

AN Auster aircraft, carrying an amateur photographer who wished to take pictures of the airliner crash, made a forced landing in a field half-a-mile from the Super-Constellation.

The two men on board escaped injury.

Mr. Sam Pratt, the photographer, an American from Shannon Airport, was accompanied by Mr. Joseph Creigh. The Auster took off from the Shannon Aero Club half-a-mile from the crashed 'plane.

When half-a-mile from the Constellation the engine cut out and they landed in a field, damaging the under-carriage of the Auster.

"Groggy" From Fumes, Drowned

The dramatic story of the "Triton's" last two-minute flight was told at a Press conference at Shannon last night by General Isaac Aler, President of K.L.M. Airlines. There were tears in his eyes as he spoke.

General Aler confirmed that the air liner carried 46 passengers and a crew of 10. Twenty-two passengers and seven members of the crew were rescued. There were 24 passengers and three cabin crew members—two stewards and a stewardess—missing.

"I am sorry to say that now they must be considered as casualties," said General Aler. Hope of further survivors had been given up.

"I understand that those who died were rendered unconscious by petrol fumes and were not able to get out, with the result that they were drowned," said General Aler.

"I am told by the crew and everyone I interviewed that the fumes made them groggy and almost unconscious. I think that a number of the passengers fainted because of the smell of the fumes. Nobody died by the impact with the water."

The crew were not sure of the altitude, said General Aler, and there was no noticeable bumpiness. The plane took off at 3.38 a.m. local time.

"Two minutes later the plane hit the water two miles from the end of the runway. There was no such thing as trying to make an emergency landing. Everything was completely unexpected. The aircraft skimmed the water. It was lucky that it did come down on water and not on land at that speed.

"It was then a rising tide," went on General Aler. "It was so unexpected that the co-pilot had his landing gear up and was reaching to do his normal checking. It was only when the Flight Engineer came into the cockpit that they realised that they were on water.

PETROL TANK BURST.

"There was a heavy smell of petrol in the cabin. This was brought about

(CONTINUED ON PAGE SEVEN)

PREVIOUS CRASHES AT SHANNON

In December, 1946, thirteen people were killed when a Trans-World Airlines Constellation crashed near the airport. In April, 1948, 30 people were killed—including five women, and a 13-months old baby, when a Pan-American Airways Constellation crashed there.

In October, 1949, a Viking aircraft became firmly embedded in the river mud when it ran off the taxi strip on landing. No one was hurt.

Recovery Of 21 Bodies From Ill-fated Plane

HEAVY rain, and a southerly gale were the adverse weather conditions which prevailed when the tug Flevo I, captained by Skipper Schlikker, left Limerick docks yesterday afternoon to go to the scene of the crash of K.L.M.'s blue, white and red Constellation Triton.

On board the tug was an "Examiner" reporter who had the experience of being present at the recovery of twenty-one bodies from this ill-fated airliner.

The scene of the crash was about nine miles down river from Limerick in a broad but lonely stretch of the Shannon. The plane struck a sandbank about 1½ miles from Fergus Island, and approximately one mile from Shannon Airport. She was lying in Middleground, between the North and South Channels, the former of which is now being dredged by Blankevoort Whittaker Ellis Ltd., owners of the tug Flevo.

On arrival at the scene of the crash at 3 p.m. the tug dropped anchor to see what assistance it could render to Limerick's Harbour Master C. J. Hanrahan, who had been on the scene for several hours with his launch, St. Munchins. With the Harbour Master was Mr. James Wallace, Thomond Road, Limerick, who gallantly volunteered to go inside the Constellation and see if he could help. On his first attempt Mr. Wallace penetrated about two-thirds of the way down the fuselage but failed to find anything except papers, flight documents diplomatic papers, brief cases and many personal belongings.

Half an hour later, Mr. Wallace, accompanied by Mr. Pat Hickey, a Harbour Board worker from Limerick, set off from the launch St. Munchins, in a big rowing boat. They entered the body of the plane, and succeeded on this occasion in penetrating into the after portion, from which, with the help of many others, including Mr. Prior (Limerick), Frank Tolton (Cobh), a deck-hand on the tug Flevo, and W. Wallace (Limerick), all the twenty-one bodies were eventually recovered. One body was taken aboard the tug, but on the arrival at 4.30 p.m. of a rescue launch from the Airport with K.L.M. officials aboard, this, with all the others, was transferred to the latter vessel.

Of the twenty-one bodies recovered all were passengers with the exception of two who were crew members. The body of one other passenger who had succeeded in getting out of the plane, and was swept away by the strong current of the river, has not yet been recovered.

UNSELFISH COURAGE

One feature of the whole tragic episode stands out, namely the unselfish courage of the men who despite gasoline fumes went into the doomed plane and helped to recover the bodies. High praise must also go to Mr. D. G. G. Maynard, who is at present in charge of the Dutch dredging operations in the Shannon, and who ordered the tug Flevo, with himself aboard, to go to the scene of the crash, and see what help they could give. All the crew of this vessel, which included three Dutchmen, worked like slaves with others to recover the bodies, and when later the rescue launch appeared they continued to give all possible assistance.

Mr. James Wallace, Thomond Road, Limerick, handing over some of the valuable documents which he recovered from the ill-fated plane.

The wrecked airliner as it appeared at high tide in the Shannon yesterday.

Survivors' Stories

"Yesterday morning," writes an "Examiner" reporter, "I visited the hospital, where I saw Airport Doctor Bill Flynn attending to a man and his wife who were the occupants of beds in the corner. These were the only occupants as the rest had been taken to the Airport hostel, where, after being treated, in most cases for minor injuries, they told investigators of their experiences as the plane crashed on the sand bank."

The pair were Mr. George W. Swallow of Waterbury, Des Moines, U.S.A., and his wife. Mr. Swallow, a sales engineer, said that he was about to settle down for a quiet sleep when he felt gasoline fumes. Then somebody pushed him through an open window and he was hauled on to a rubber dinghy.

His wife said: "Please tell my relatives that I am safe. They will be worrying." She kept repeating this.

In the hospital was a collection of mud-spattered clothing taken from the plane, while Dr Flynn, who had rushed to the scene on being informed of the crash and did a hero's work in tending to the injured, was also covered with mud. In the corridor outside was a collection of water-soaked mail, including diplomatic letters which had been taken from the doomed plane.

Dr Charles Farrington of St. Petersburg, Florida, who was returning from the International Surgeons Conference in Berne, Switzerland, with his wife and two children, all of whom were saved, said:

"I pushed my family out on the first dinghy. I stayed back on the aircraft myself as there was not room for me. I got on to the next dinghy and was glad to rejoin my family."

Dr Farrington was shivering beneath the Red Cross blanket which he held around him, and there were tears in his eyes as he spoke of being rejoined with his family.

Another American surgeon who had been at the same Conference, Dr Ernest H. Bettman, White Plains Hospital, New York, sat on the side of his bed in the emergency hospital and told an almost similar story. He could not get on the first dinghy and waited, clinging to the window of the plane, until the second dinghy was launched.

Capt. Viruly said that the reason that he did not get in touch with the Airport immediately at the crash was that the radio communications were out of action by the crash. He circled the scene in a dinghy four times before he was satisfied that nobody else could be taken off the sinking airliner.

HOLLAND MOURNS.

Holland was in mourning last night for the 27 people killed. One newspaper in The Hague issued a special broadsheet reporting the crash in heavy black type. It was distributed free in streets, trams and restaurants.

The crash came as a stunning blow to the Dutch less than a fortnight after another K.L.M. airliner, the Willem Bontekoe, plunged into the North Sea, killing all 21 aboard.

The two Dutch Broadcasting Corporations yesterday decided to cancel their programmes of light music and give serious music instead, following the news of the crash.

MOUNT TABOR ROAD OPENED

A road leading to the summit of Mount Tabor, traditional site of the Transfiguration of Christ, was dedicated yesterday by Msgr. Alberto Gori, O.F.M., Latin Patriarch of the Holy Land.

He cut a ribbon to open the road and a long motor convoy climbed the steep and winding new mountain highway to the Catholic Monastery and Basilica at the top.

The new road, only half-an-hour's drive from Nazareth, will make it easier for Christian pilgrims to visit the heights of Mount Tabor.—A.P.

Two Priests Intervene Between Police And Newry Crowd

APPEAL TO PEOPLE TO DESIST

THE intervention of two priests, who placed themselves between a police cordon and an angry crowd estimated at 10,000, prevented serious developments in Newry, County Down, yesterday.

The police had drawn a demarcation line between the Nationalist and Unionist areas of the town when a meeting was held by the Nationalists as a protest against police action in recent rioting in Pomeroy, Co. Tyrone, at the homecoming of Mr. Liam Kelly, the Six Counties abstentionist M.P., who was released from jail last month. For three hours, and long after the meeting ended an angry crowd of some hundreds faced the cordon.

The meeting, attended by 12 bands, was held in the town square, one side of which opens on the Unionist area of the town. Shortly after it started a group of people on the Unionist side began to interrupt the speakers, and were immediately rushed on by near sections of the crowd.

Police reinforcements were called and the cordon of 25 men stretched across the roadway. The two priests, the Rev. E. Campbell Administrator of Newry and the Rev. J. P. Burke, his curate, placed themselves between the cordon and the crowd and appealed to the people to desist. In fact a number of sporadic rushes were made and the cordon breached and at one time a constable threw his baton.

About 100 yards away in a side street six tenders of police stood at the ready, and a very large crowd of people had gathered nearby in the Unionist quarter. The organisers of the demonstration left the platform, and crossing to the troubled area, appealed to the crowd to retire.

U.S. Fleet Increases Patrols Near Quemoy

Reds Kept Up Bombardment Of Island Base

THE U.S. Seventh Fleet yesterday strengthened its patrols near Quemoy Island as the Chinese Reds continued for the third day their bombardment of the Nationalists only three miles from the mainland.

Usually reliable Nationalist sources reporting this said the Seventh Fleet did not at present include Quemoy and other Nationalist islands off the shore under its protection, unless it had specific orders from Washington to do so.

President Eisenhower has conferred with defence officials in Washington and later it was said that orders to the fleet to protect Formosa have not been changed.

In Washington, Mr. Fred Seaton, Assistant Secretary to the Defence Department, told a Press Conference that America was "alert to our responsibilities" towards Quemoy, but he knew of no specific orders to the Seventh Fleet to defend the island.

Nationalist military sources said yesterday the intensity of the Communist shelling had decreased considerably after "daredevil" attacks on their shore batteries by Nationalist bombers earlier.

They said Nationalist planes attacked the batteries with bombs and rockets again yesterday, in a determined effort to knock them out.

Three Nationalist fighters were reported to have been shot down in low-level attacks.

Nationalist intelligence officers were reported to be checking rumours that Communist troops were massing along the coast opposite Formosa, the Nationalist headquarters, and in Communist-held islands near Tachen Island, about 200 miles south of Shanghai.

The Nationalist acting Chief of Staff, General Peng Meng Chi, spent most of yesterday in the "War Room" at the Defence Ministry studying latest reports from Quemoy and issuing new orders to his service chiefs.

U.S. OFFICERS KILLED.

The bodies of two American officers killed by Communist shells at Quemoy on Friday have been flown to Taipeh and identified as those of Lieutenant-Colonel Frank Lynn (39), of Chicago, and Lieutenant-Colonel Alfred Medendrop (47), of Grand Rapids, Michigan.

Peking Radio said yesterday that a number of seats in the first Communist Chinese National People's Congress had been reserved for "future Deputies" from Formosa, which had "not yet be[illegible]n liberated."

EISENHOWER DISCUSSED QUEMOY.

President Eisenhower conferred by telephone with U.S. Defence Department officials in Washington yesterday on the Communist shelling of the Chinese Nationalist held island of Quemoy off the Chinese mainland.

The Presidential Press Secretary, Mr. James C. Hagerty, told reporters of the conversations.

Replying to questions, he said that the President's orders to the U.S. Seventh Fleet to protect Formosa (the Nationalist base) from Communist attack "have not been changed."

Mr. Hegarty declined, however, to say whether those orders are broad enough to call for U.S. protection of Quemoy, which is between the mainland and Formosa.

It is pointed out in Washington last night that American support, to be fully effective, would probably involve counter-battery fire, which would entail shelling the Communist mainland.

A week ago when Communist "frogmen" killed three Nationalist defenders in a commando-type raid on Quemoy, American naval officials were quick to say that Quemoy did not fall under the shield of the Seventh Fleet.

In Washington the Navy Department clamped down on movements of U.S. warships in the Pacific theatre. Naval authorities are giving serious consideration to the possibility that the Communists may launch a seaborne assault on Quemoy after a softening up bombardment — Reuter and A.P.

BREAK DIPLOMATIC RELATIONS—Senator.

Senator William Knowland, the U.S. Senate majority leader, has called on the United States to break off diplomatic relations with Russia after the shooting down of an American bomber off Vladivostok.

He called the shooting a new example of Russian arrogance and aggressiveness.

Senator Knowland telegraphed President Eisenhower, on holiday at Denver, Colorado: "I strongly urge that the Soviet Ambassador and his staff be sent home."

"Our own Ambassador should be recalled from Moscow as notice to the Russian people that so long as the present Communist dictatorship rules them, their country can no longer be treated as a member of the family of peace loving nations of the world or entitled to the respect of the free nations."

NORTHERN LORRY DRIVER CHARGED WITH MURDER

Samuel Johnston, a forty-seven years old foreman lorry driver, Albert St., Lurgan, was at a special court yesterday in Lurgan Police Barracks, charged with the murder of Jack Abraham, of Lurgan, and was remanded in custody to September 13th.

Only formal evidence of arrest was given by Head Constable Langan, who said he arrested and charged Johnston that morning with murder and he made no reply.

Abraham was aged fifty-three and a small farmer and jobbing gardener, unmarried and living with his mother and sister. He was admitted to Lurgan Hospital on Saturday night about eight o'clock, and was transferred to the Royal Victoria Hospital, Belfast, after midnight, where he died yesterday morning from suspected fracture of the skull.

SEARCH FOR EASY LIFE

Pope Warns Against Materialism

The Pope yesterday warned against the dangers of materialism which was "little by little" invading society, its institutions and activities.

Broadcasting in French from his summer place in Castelgandolfo to a rally of Catholics in Brussels, culmination of a Marian congress,

the Pope declared that materialism "reveals itself in many people by the search for a comfortable life, with full insurance for the future but closed to supernatural realities and to any call to devotion, and incapable of feeling the sometimes crying need of other social classes or other peoples.

"It is so easy to forget that temporal well-being is not the principal aim of human life and that there exist other riches, infinitely more precious and more lasting—those of divine charity, which make man forget himself in order to attach himself to God and to God's work."—(Reuter).

26 MARINES HURT IN FIGHT

A hundred Royal Marine Commandos fought a five-hour pitched battle with Maltese police and civilians in the streets of Valetta yesterday. At least 26 marines were injured as well as two policemen and two civilians. Police said that 60 of the Commandos, singing "Rule Britannia," had marched through the streets breaking shop windows. The fight started when they attacked a police sergeant and four constables with broken bottles. Later yesterday, police were patrolling Valetta following complaints that English-speaking civilians were being molested.

Mrs. Muriel Anderson Hallinan, of Glandalane House, Fermoy, Co. Cork, who died on March 8th last, wife of Joseph A. Hallinan, left estate in England and the Republic valued at £21,707 (duty paid, £3,240). Probate has been granted to John J. Horgan, solicitor, of 30, South Mall, Cork.

IRELAND CONSUMES MOST MILK

—U.S. REPORI

Families used more milk and dairy products last year in the 15 primary diary producing countries, though production exceeded consumption, the U.S. Department of Agriculture said yesterday.

Ireland has taken over from New Zealand, the pre-war leader, as the leading per capita consumer of milk and dairy products, consuming 1,382 pounds of milk per person per year.

Consumption of milk in the 15 primary countries was 704 pounds per person; a 10-pound increase over 1952. But production was 808 pounds per person, a 35-pound increase over last year.

The competition which margarine gave to butter, reducing the use of milk, was "responsible for a large part of the loss in milk consumption."

New Zealand led the 15 countries in the consumption of butter with a 44 pounds per person per year.

Sweden was the leader in fluid milk consumption at 513 lbs. per person and Norway was the first ranking cheese consuming nation at 17.9 pounds per person.—(Reuter).

KILLED TRYING TO BEAT OWN RECORD

Jet Pilot Crashes At 649 m.p.h.

Major John Armstrong was killed at Dayton (Ohio) yesterday when his F86 Sabrejet fighter crashed only a few minutes after an Air Force announcement that he had set up a new speed record for the 500 kilometre (310 miles) closed course.

He was trying to beat his record of an average of 649.302 miles an hour (set up on Friday) when his plane hurtled to earth.

A big crowd at the National Aircraft Show saw the crash.—Reuter.

TWO INJURED IN CORK ACCIDENT

Two men, William Hook, 18 Avon Crescent, Bristol, and Michael Dinneen, 62 High St., Cork, are at present detained in the North Infirmary, Cork, suffering from injuries received in an accident on the Blarney Road, last night.

On inquiry at the hospital it was ascertained that Mr. Hook was suffering from severe head injuries and Mr. Dinneen from leg injuries.

Soviet Jets Shoot Down U.S. Plane

AMERICANS FIRED FIRST SAYS RUSSIAN NOTE

THE United States announced yesterday that an American jet naval patrol plane was shot down on Saturday in the Sea of Japan, east of Vladivostok "apparently by M.I.G.-15 type aircraft."

In Moscow, the Soviet Government handed over a note to the United States Ambassador, Mr. Charles Bohlen, admitting that Soviet fighters fired on the aircraft over the Sea of Japan.

The plane was last seen heading "in the direction of the sea," the Russians said.

The note claimed the American plane fired first. The Russians demanded the punishment of those responsible for the alleged "violation" of Soviet air space.

The U.S. Defence Department said that nine survivors were rescued at sea, but Ensign Roger Henry Reid, of Alameda, California, was reported missing.

Seven rescue planes were despatched to the scene by U.S. Far East Forces.

The plane, a U.S. Navy Neptune, on routine patrol, was attacked about 100 miles east of Vladivostok and 44 miles from the Siberian mainland, the Defence Department said.

The Russian protest note said that a twin-engined military aircraft of the Neptune type, bearing U.S. Air Force identification marks, had opened fire on two Russian fighters which approached it.

"The Soviet planes were forced to open fire in return, after which the American plane flew off in the direction of the sea," the note said.

PREVIOUS INCIDENTS.

There have been several instances of somewhat similar incidents in the past two years.

On January 12th, 1953, an American Superfortress was shot down and eleven of the crew captured, the Communist New China News Agency reported.

The incident was said to have taken place ten miles north-west of Antung.

The United States denied that the plane had flown over Manchuria. This incident was followed by a Communist Chinese claim that an American jet fighter was shot down by the Chinese Air Force on January 23rd, 1953, in Liaotung Province, Manchuria.

The pilot, who baled out, was captured.

In February, 1953, the New China News Agency said five of 48 American fighters which "invaded Manchuria" had been shot down.

In the next month—March, 1953, an American plane on a routine weather reconnaissance flight from Alaska, was intercepted by two MIGs 25 miles east of Kamchatka, and one of the MIGs fired at it.

On July 26th this year, the State Department in Washington reported that two United States carrier planes of the rescue type had shot down two Chinese Communist planes at sea outside the 12-mile limit, which attacked them while they were searching for survivors of the British Skymaster shot down off the [illegible]munist controlled island of Hainan.

Three Americans, including two children, aged four and two, lost their lives in the Skymaster, and three, including a child of six, were injured.—Reuter.

RAIN-SOAKED PILGRIMS AT KNOCK

Thousands of rain-soaked pilgrims gathered at Our Lady's Shrine, Knock, Co. Mayo, yesterday. The traditional Stations and Rosaries were conducted by the local and visiting priests and the devotions ended with Benediction given by Father Murphy. Pilgrims were present from Kilkasa, Co. Clare, Ballingarry, Moyvane, Kerry and other distant places.

Free Yugoslavia "Soon"—Ex-King Peter.—A message of hope for the "liberation of our country in the near future" was given by ex-King Peter of Yugoslavia to more than 2,000 Serbians who travelled to Leicester yesterday from all over Britain and also from France to take part in his 31st birthday celebrations. The ex-King, who flew from Paris on Saturday night, attended a special church service yesterday morning and a programme of national folk-singing at the De Montfort Hall, where he said: "We have waited a long time for the liberation, but we shall not have to wait much longer."

LINER HULK BREAKS AWAY FROM MOORINGS

—While Sheltering In Dublin Bay

Forced to put into Scotman's Bay, Dun Laoghaire, for shelter on Saturday, the salvaged hulk of the 20,000 ton liner Empress of Canada, which sank in Gladstone Dock, Liverpool last year, broke away from her moorings yesterday and nearly ended up on the rocks off Howth, on the opposite side of the Bay. The ship was being towed from Liverpool to Genoa for scrap.

When the hulk broke away from her moorings, she was pursued by the accompanying tugs.

There was never any danger to shipping in the harbour, but heavy seas drove the hulk off course and for a time it was in danger of piling up on the rocks off the Bailey Lighthouse, Howth. The tugs, however, pulled her clear and she left the Bay last night.

1955

By the mid-1950s there were enough cars on Irish roads to merit a road safety week. On the political front, the big news was the entry of Ireland into the United Nations. Previous attempts to join the organisation had been blocked by the Soviet Union, ostensibly because of Ireland's non-participation in the fight against the Axis powers in World War II, but also because of Cold War politics where the Republic leaned towards the Western powers. Ireland's membership, along with that of 15 other countries, was approved by the Security Council in December.

Pigeon enthusiasts get ready for a race in Cork.

Opera House destroyed

Tuesday, December 12

The final curtain has fallen. The Cork Opera House is no more. Over 100 years of stage history has come to an end. Never had the last moments of any drama played on this stage such an audience as last night's farewell one. In heavy rain a vast crowd stood silently as flames enveloped a proud landmark. They watched it from the short first burst of fire on its roof until the building crumbled before their eyes.

Bishop attacks emigration

Friday, March 18

There was no country today doing so little for its sons and daughters as Ireland was doing. One out of every three of them was left to find a livelihood in foreign parts and celebrated St Patrick's Day in exile from St Patrick's land, declared Most Rev Dr Lucey, Bishop of Cork, when he addressed the annual St Patrick's Day luncheon given by the Lord Mayor yesterday.

Later in his address, his Lordship, having referred to partition as an evil thing, said that those who talk ever of partition and never of emigration, and those who put the ending of partition before the ending of emigration had their scale of values altogether wrong.

NEWS BRIEFS

Mar Four of the first eight horses in the Grand National at Aintree are Irish. Among them was the winner Quare Times, trained by Vincent O'Brien and ridden by Pat Taafe, which was the third Irish horse in a row to win the race. Taafe's brother Toss rode the third place finisher, Carey's Cottage. Bonfires blaze on the Rock of Cashel, a few miles from O'Brien's stables, to welcome them back. (29)

Oct Twenty-two thousand people attend a soccer match between Yugoslavia and the Republic of Ireland at Dalymount Park, despite an appeal by Archbishop McQuaid of Dublin to boycott the game as a mark of protest against the treatment of the Catholic Church in the communist country. A far superior Yugoslavia side beat Ireland 4-1. (19)

Dec A report to Cork Corporation mentions the increased incidence of infant mortality in November which has seen 18 babies die in the city. The city's medical officer reports that 13 of the deaths had occurred in hospitals, and five at home. Prematurity and congenital defects accounted for most of the deaths. The unusually high figures raised the infant mortality rate way beyond the figure for 1954 of 23 per 1000 births (The 2004 average was around 5.5 per 1000 births). (14)

Justice condemns cock-fighting

Friday, September 23

"If there is one other case of cock-fighting in Westmeath, not only will there be fines but imprisonment as well. All those present at cock-fighting are as guilty as those in charge, and in future they will get similar treatment as those promoting the event, together with imprisonment."

So said District Justice Beatty of Ballynacargy Court yesterday, when he imposed fines amounting to £25 each on the five men charged with participating in cock-fighting at Painestown on 24th May. Sergeant Byrne told the court he saw two cocks being prepared for battle. There were steel spurs tied on each cock's legs by means of adhesive tape. These spurs were very sharp and measured from two to three inches. The cocks were then taken to an adjacent paddock, placed in a ring and the fight commenced.

The Cork Examiner

NO. 34,292 WEDNESDAY MORNING, OCTOBER 5, 1955 PRICE—TWOPENCE

CITY SPECIAL

Two very ~~small~~ *Big* reasons for driving safely

SOMETIMES A MAN at the wheel forgets. His hands grip the circle of plastic; but his mind is miles away.

Then—a boy tries to beat the first bell, and doesn't remember how he was taught to cross the street. A little girl pushes her way out of the bus and races towards her afternoon milk and cookies. A gang of happy small fry let off steam on the way home; only a motorist with his mind on the job can save them.

Why do design engineers strive endlessly to build more safety into cars? Why must "Safety First" mean more than a slogan? Why does any driver have more than a wheel in his hands?

Look at children for a moment, and you know why.

A cherished ball will roll onto the street, closely pursued by its pint sized owner. Some of the most exciting races in history are run on the way to and from school, often past the safety of the sidewalk. And hop-scotch boxes are nearly always drawn but a laugh away from a stream of traffic.

When children are on the streets, a driver *must* go slowly, extra slowly.

The Irish Road is your road. Every highway, every byway, every main thoroughfare and every back street. And all the children on it are your children. The fate of so many is in your hands—when your hands are on the wheel of a car.

ROAD SAFETY WEEK
OCT. 2nd—OCT. 8th

See your Ford Dealer for a FREE Safety-check Inspection.

HENRY FORD & SON LIMITED · CORK

ESTABLISHED 1917

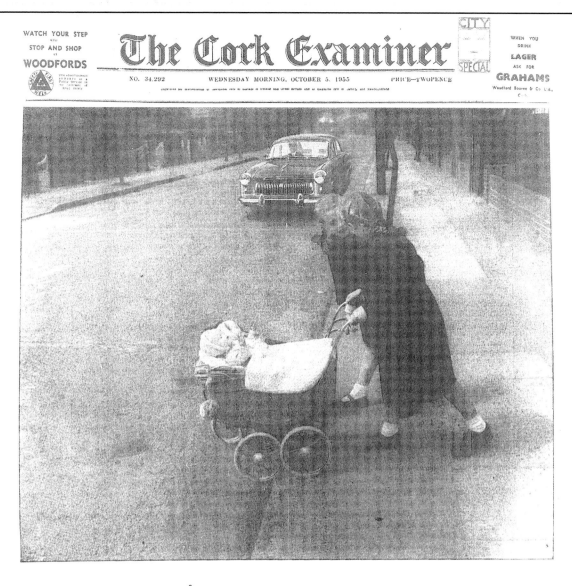

PASSENGER CARS · COMMERCIAL VEHICLES · TRACTORS
AGRICULTURAL IMPLEMENTS · INDUSTRIAL ENGINES

1956

The Soviet Union's crushing of the popular uprising in Hungary caused outrage across the world. While the Soviet actions dominated the headlines in Europe, they were also in people's thoughts in Melbourne where the Olympics were being held. Several athletes from Hungary defected and their animosity towards the Soviet Union was evident when both nations reached the water polo final – fighting between the two teams left the pool tinged red with blood.

These events didn't take from what was a joyous Games for Ireland. A team of just 12 athletes returned with five medals. The haul was such an immense achievement that nobody could have predicted that Ireland wouldn't win another Olympic medal until 1980.

In Northern Ireland, the IRA began a new campaign with a wave of attacks in 11 different areas one night in December, targeting a BBC relay station, bridges and the security forces. Of the five people arrested during the first attacks, two were from Armagh and three were from Cork.

The hidden issue of abortion made a rare appearance in the news when a Dublin woman died after a 'back-street' operation performed by Nurse Mary Cadden. Cadden was charged with murder, found guilty and sentenced to death. The execution was never carried out and she died later in psychiatric care.

Ronnie Delany's magnificent victory

Monday, December 3

21-year-old Ronnie Delany, the youngest man to run a mile in less than four minutes, put up the greatest performance of his career at Melbourne on Saturday in scoring a magnificent victory in the 1,500 metres, smashing the existing record in the process and gaining for Ireland her first Olympic gold medal for 24 years.

Our other finalist on Saturday, boxer Fred Teidt, fought magnificently in the welter-weight decider against Rumanian Necolae Linca, but failed to gain the verdict. The decision was loudly booed and seemed to surprise most ringside observers.

However, our team of 12 has much to be proud of in their achievements at Melbourne and will return home with five medals – Delany's gold, Teidt's silver and three bronze won by boxers Fred Gilroy, John Caldwell and Tony Byrne.

Delany said he felt he had the race won when he took the lead in the final stretch: "And when I saw that tape in front of me I knew I had it. I never felt so good in all my life."

Dublin went wild with delight on hearing the news. Busmen, milkmen and newsboys shouted the news to suburban residents and windows flew open to hear, cheer and then pass on the glad tidings.

Ronnie's mother could hardly speak with excitement. "Thank God it's all over," she said. "He's a wonderful boy."

Garda Coleman Carey, the first of the new motorcycle unit operating for the first time in Cork city.

Abortion nurse sentenced

Friday, November 3

At the Central Criminal Court yesterday, Mary Anne Cadden was found guilty of the murder of Mrs Helen O'Reilly. She was sentenced to death.

As Miss Cadden was helped to her feet and asked if she had anything to say as to why sentence should not be passed on her, she replied: "This is not my country and I am reporting this to the president of my country. This is the third time I was convicted in this country falsely. But for my council I would say something you would not like to hear."

Mr Justice McLoughlin then donned the black cap and sentenced Miss Cadden to death, and fixed the date for execution for November 21.

When he uttered the words: "And you shall then be taken to the common place of execution in the prison in which you shall then and there be hanged by the neck," Miss Cadden exclaimed: "You won't get the chance."

When he came to the final words: "And may the Lord have mercy on your soul", Miss Cadden said: "I am not a Catholic. Take that."

NEWS BRIEFS

May Thousands of people gather outside the Savoy Cinema on Patrick's St, Cork, for the opening of Ireland's first international film festival. Stars at the occasion include Peter Finch, Noel Purcell and Maureen Swanson. Finch comments: "Cannes was, Venice is, and Cork will be the fairest city of the three." (21)

Oct The world's first nuclear power station opened at Calder Hall, Cumberland in Britain, at a site that would later house the Windscale/Sellafield reprocessing plant. (17)

Egypt's nationalisation of the Suez Canal and blockading of the Gulf of Aqaba provided the spark for an attack by the combined forces of Britain, France and Israel. While militarily successful for Britain, the fall-out from the war led to the resignation of Prime Minister Anthony Eden.

The Cork Examiner.

THE CORK EXAMINER, FRIDAY, NOVEMBER 9, 1956

IRELAND CALLS FOR SPEEDY U.N. ACTION ON HUNGARY

Mr. Boland Urges Use Of Moral Authority

Observers To Be Appointed

UNITED Nations observers are being appointed to investigate the situation in Hungary, Mr. Hammarskjoeld, the U.N. Secretary General, said yesterday.

He told the Hungarian Delegate to the special session of the General Assembly now debating the Hungarian situation, that he intended to proceed with the selection of the observers on the assumption that the Hungarian Government would admit them.

Mr. F. H. Boland, the Irish representative told the Assembly that the United Nations must not "sit back" now that it had passed the resolution calling for the withdrawal of Soviet troops from Hungary, but should use its moral authority which had proved such a potent factor in Egypt.

Mr. Hammarskjoeld's aide memoire to Hungary was in line with a resolution approved by the Assembly last Sunday that the Secretary-General should "observe directly through representatives named by him" the Hungarian situation.

The Assembly at the same time called on the Soviet and Hungarian Governments to permit observers to enter and travel freely in Hungarian territory.

The Secretary-General asked the Hungarian delegate, Mr. Janos Szabo, for an early reply as to whether his Government would admit the observers.

The resolution also asked the Secretary-General to investigate the situation caused by foreign intervention in Hungary, and Mr. Hammarskjoeld said: "I have taken steps for such an investigation on the basis of available and confirmed material."

The Secretariat was also actively considering the Assembly's request that Mr. Hammarskjoeld should suggest methods to bring an end to the foreign intervention. But he said it was not possible to reach a final result before the end of the investigation he had mentioned and without the co-operation of the Hungarian Government. He made another appeal to Hungary for such co-operation.

Later the Assembly was urged to pass another resolution calling on Russia to withdraw her forces from Hungary without delay and to propose the holding of free elections under United Nations auspices as soon as law and order was restored. The resolution, introduced by Italy, was also sponsored by Cuba, Ireland, Pakistan and Peru.

IRELAND'S CALL

Referring to the resolution calling for the withdrawal of Soviet troops from Hungary already approved by the Assembly, the Irish delegate, Mr. F. H. Boland, said the United Nations must not just "sit back" now that it had passed the resolution, but should continue to use its moral authority, which had "proved such a potent factor" in Egypt.

"We are profoundly confident that the gallant Hungarian nation, which has won the respect of the world, will arise again," Mr. Boland said.

"I know that for us in Ireland, and for many other of the smaller nations, any mention in the future of national independence or anti-colonialism or the right of self-determination by any Soviet spokesman will always evoke in our minds a single name—the name of Hungary," he said.

Mr. Boland called what has happened in Hungary "one of the blackest chapters in human progress."

He declared: "As we in Ireland know, the spirit of nationhood never dies. It is handed on from generation to generation."

ATTACK ON RUSSIA

Senor Nunez-Portuondo, the Cuban delegate, said that his Government would not recognise the Janos Kadar

(CONTINUED ON PAGE NINE)

PATRIOTS STILL FIGHTING

Flare-up In Central Hungary

The new Soviet backed Communist Government of Hungary yesterday admitted, for the first time since it took power last Sunday, that armed rebels were still fighting, reports Reuter from Vienna. The Government, using Budapest Radio as its main link with the population, said starvation was threatening. It appealed to workers in the food industry to go back to work immediately.

Reports from Belgrade, unconfirmed in Vienna, said that insurgents were still resisting Soviet forces in the Gyoer area in the northwest and near Pecs in the south, and that Soviet tanks were in action against them.

Budapest Radio announced measures to disband or severely curb the revolutionary committees formed as the uprising swept the country.

VIOLENT FIGHTING

Violent fighting has flared up in Central Hungary near the post-war steel centre of Sztalinvaros (Stalin Town), according to reports which reached Belgrade last night.

Little further news was available last night of the fate of the two main insurgent groups, near Gayer and Pecs. Since Wednesday the Russians have been attacking the Gyoer area with some 300 tanks.

The Pecs insurgent radio was not heard yesterday.

In various parts of the south and south-east Hungary, the Russians were reported to be harassed by groups of partisans, after the cessation of organised resistance.

FIRES IN BUDAPEST

Inside Budapest, reports said there was little food, little water, little medicine, no gas and three quarters of the city without electricity. Fires were still burning.

The Russians and survivors of the Hungarian secret police were said to have arrested in the course of yesterday over 2,000 Hungarians in Budapest on the grounds of aiding and abetting the "Fascist counter-revolution", according to the Belgrade reports.

Communications throughout the country were reported to be paralysed. The Government appealed to railway workers to repair railway lines and get trains back into running order.

HOUSE TO HOUSE SEARCHES

Reports reaching Belgrade said Soviet forces by yesterday had advanced seven miles in an offensive by about 300 tanks which started at dawn on Wednesday against one of the main insurgent concentrations in the Gyoer area. They were reported to be conducting house-to-house searches and executing any inhabitants found with arms in their possession.

Austrian frontier guards reported from Nickelsdorf last night that a group of 45 Hungarian rebels who held out for three days in the customs house at Hegyeshalom crossed into Austria, bringing their weapons with them. They were immediately disarmed and interned.—(Reuter and A.P.)

PROPOSALS FOR RELIEF OF DISTRESS

Red Cross Broadcast To-night

Mrs. Tom Barry, Chairman of the Irish Red Cross Society, will speak from Radio Eireann to-night at 6.25 on the subject of the Red Cross proposals for the relief of distress in Hungary.

SUNDAY'S APPEAL

The Irish Red Cross Society and the St. John's Ambulance Brigade of Ireland launch a national appeal for the relief of those suffering from aggression, on Sunday next, November 11th.

The Archbishop of Dublin, Most Rev. Dr. McQuaid, has authorised a special collection in churches of the diocese on Sunday next towards alleviation of distress in Hungary.

MASS AT U.C.C.

The following statement was issued by University College, Cork:—

Requiem Mass was celebrated yesterday morning in St. Finbarr's Collegiate Chapel for the repose of the souls of those who lost their lives innocently in Hungary while the people of that nation were defending their human rights against unjust aggression. Prayers were offered beseeching Almighty God to bless the Hungarian nation and to restore to it peace and liberty, above all the liberty to worship God freely. Prayers were also offered that human rights may be respected everywhere and that God may avert from mankind the horror of another world war. The Mass was celebrated by Very Rev. J. Canon Bastible, Dean of Residence, U.C.C. There were present at the Mass the President, the officers and members of the teaching staff, together with an overflow congregation of students.

A Church of Ireland religious service was held at the same time and was conducted by Rev. C. W. C. Quin, B.D.

A special meeting of the Academic Council was held yesterday, at which the following resolution was passed unanimously:—

"We, the members of the Academic Council of University College, Cork, extend our heartfelt sympathy to the people of Hungary in their struggle for human freedom against Russian aggression. We call on the Government to concert measures with other small nations — non-European as well as European—for keeping constantly before the United Nations and world opinion the cause of Hungary, which is the cause of all men who believe in human freedom."

It was also decided at this meeting that a collection would be made among members of the staff for transmission to the Irish Red Cross Society.

CANON HAYES' STATEMENT

The following statement has been issued by Very Rev. J. Canon Hayes, Chairman of the National Executive, Muintir na Tire:—

"All guilds of Muintir na Tire will have followed with deep feeling the tragic and glorious struggle of the gallant people of Hungary. As a practical expression of our sympathy, we urge all our guilds to co-operate wholeheartedly with the Irish Red Cross national appeal to help the Hungarian victims of aggression. Where a collection is organised by the local branch of the Red Cross, the Muintir na Tire Parish Councils should offer co-operation. Where no local branch of the Red Cross Society exists, the Parish Council should volunteer to organise a collection. They should secure the necessary authorisation from Church and Garda authorities, being careful to avoid a clash with other organised collections. Lists of subscribers should be kept, and the proceeds of the collections should be sent to the County Committee of the Irish Red Cross Society, or, if this is not convenient, to Muintir na Tire National Headquarters, Tipperary, for transmission to the Irish Red Cross."

NORTHERN AID

Contributions to the Hungarian Relief Fund soared in Belfast yesterday. The Presbyterian Church appeal has reached £5,000. Lady Brookeborough's appeal for the refugee children has brought an immediate response.

The Guild of Catholic Teachers at a meeting voted £100 to aid Hungarians.

Two Escape From The "Scrubs."—Two prisoners escaped from Wormwood Scrubs Prison last night after breaking into a workshop and stealing a ladder, which they used to scale the prison wall.

DELAY MAY BE FATAL

Vatican On Duty Of U.N.

Vatican Radio said yesterday that the United Nations had "an undeniable duty" to take action in Hungary. "The peoples still look to U.N.O. as the only instrument empowered to impose a fair solution of international differences. Among these they place the problem of Hungary in the first rank.

"But the free peoples are impatient. Because the cry of justice which comes from their Hungarian brothers is heard even more faintly, suffocated by the inexorable descent of the Iron Curtain.

"They fear that that cry may be extinguished before it can be heard in time. They fear that delay may be fatal . . .

"They turn not to one person, or to a particular nation. But to an international authority—the United Nations Organisation.

"We hope that it will give practical effect to the voice of public opinion which has rarely called with such strength, soundness and unanimity. It is an undeniable duty."—Reuter.

OFFERS OF HOMES FOR REFUGEES

Offers to accommodate Hungarian refugees have been flooding into the office of the British Council for Aid to Refugees in Grosvenor Crescent, S.W. London, a spokesman said. "It looks as if we shall have quite enough offers to accommodate the 3,500 refugees who are coming to this country."

U.S. TO TAKE 5,000

President Eisenhower yesterday ordered admittance to the United States of up to 5,000 refugees from Hungary.

The Canadian immigration office in Vienna has been instructed to give priority to applications from refugees from Hungary. Assisted passage loans would be available on the same terms as to other immigrants from Europe.

Action on the problem of the 15,000 Hungarian refugees was reported by Reuter from several centres yesterday.

Australia is to provide sanctuary for 1,020. Switzerland 1,000. Holland will receive 1,000 next week and Italy will take 2,000 on a temporary basis.

Britain, Belgium, Italy, Holland, Sweden and Switzerland are sending representatives to Vienna to discuss aid for the refugees.

The international committee of the Red Cross has appealed to Russia by cable for a truce to succour the wounded in Budapest.—(Reuter).

Protest In Dublin

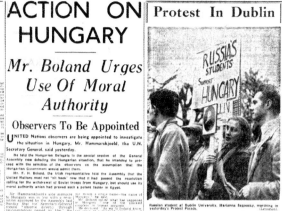

Russian student at Dublin University, Marianna Sagousky, marching in yesterday's Protest Parade. (Lensmen).

Students Attack Bookshop During Dublin Parade

Anti-Soviet Demonstrations In Many Countries

A BOOKSHOP in Pearse Street, Dublin, which sells Communist literature was attacked yesterday by a group when some 4,000 students who marched through the streets of the city in a protest demonstration against the Soviet attack on Hungary. The windows were smashed and a man was injured.

The students, stated to be from University College, Dublin, Trinity College, the Royal College of Surgeons and the National College of Art, had paraded up and down O'Connell Street carrying placards and banners with slogans such as "Save Crucified Hungary", "Down With Communism", "Aggression, We Know What It Means".

Extra police were on duty to control the parade, which included Ukranian, White Russian, Dutch, American, English, Danish, Swedish, Spanish, Nigerian, Canadian and Indian students.

Large crowds watched as the parade passed from Stephen's Green through O'Connell Street, circling the Parnell Monument and returning through O'Connell Street. Traffic was disrupted.

FUNDS COLLECTED

The parade was orderly and members of it detached themselves to collect funds for the Red Cross appeal for Hungary as they passed through the streets.

At Pearse street, outside a shop, which is known as "New Books," the parade stopped and the students began to boo loudly. A young man, while attempting to reach the shop, was stopped by a Garda.

Other students threw stones and sticks at the windows of the shop and three large windows were broken.

Another attempt was made to rush the seven policemen outside the shop, but this also failed, and cries of "Burn it down" were heard. The students began to mill around the front of the shop and completely blocked traffic on the street.

When two of the policemen were hit by missiles batons were drawn and the police made an effort to clear the street. The owner of the tobacconist and sweet shop next door to the bookshop was injured by a stone thrown by one of the crowd, which glanced off a gutter and fell on his head when he attempted to put metal shutters against the window of the shop.

PETITION TO U.S.

The Gardai after about ten minutes succeeded in dispersing the students, who moved down the street and re-formed the parade. They then marched to the American Embassy where a petition was left for forwarding to the President of the United States. From there they marched to the Department of External Affairs, where a petition was presented to the Minister for forwarding to the United Nations Organisation.

Following this the students observed a one-minute silence and then dispersed quietly.

On inquiry at the Garda station, Pearse street, it was learnt that two young men had been detained. It was also learnt that a man had been taken to Sir

(CONTINUED ON PAGE NINE)

MR. COSGRAVE ARRIVES IN U.S.

Irish Sympathy With Hungarians

Mr. Liam T. Cosgrave, Minister for External Affairs, who arrived in New York by air yesterday, said: "The Irish people sympathise deeply with the Hungarian people in their trials and great struggle for liberty."

Mr. Cosgrave, who is leading this country's delegation to the United Nations' General Assembly, said that Ireland, through the Irish Red Cross, was ready to give aid to Hungary and to accept Hungarian refugees. Ireland supports the resolutions passed by the General Assembly in the emergency session on the Middle East and Hungarian crises, Mr. Cosgrave said.

Mr. Cosgrave recalled Ireland's own struggle for independence and said: "We in Ireland can appreciate the desire of the Hungarian people for political and religious freedom."

Ireland has not yet decided on the question of sending voluntary troops to the Middle East.

Mr. Cosgrave, on his first visit to the United States, will be Ireland's first representative to address the General Assembly. His father, Mr. William T. Cosgrave, then Ireland's President, was the first Irishman to address the League of Nations in September, 1923. Mrs. Cosgrave arrived with her husband.

The regular session of the Assembly opens next Monday.

Fire Destroys Cork Offices, Studio

Residents Evacuated From Adjoining Building

FIRE completely destroyed the premises of the New Ireland Assurance Co., Ltd. and the studio and dark room of Mr. Liam Kennedy, photographer, at 48 McCurtain Street, Cork last night.

But for the very commendable actions of one man, who declined to give his name to the Press, much more damage would have been caused.

RAISED ALARM

This man raised the alarm when he saw smoke coming from the building as he left the Metropole Hotel directly opposite. He roused and helped to evacuate people living next door to the blazing building, assisted in salvaging valuable equipment from the Headquarters of the Cork Blood Bank, which was for a period in danger of being burned, and removed motor cars parked at the scene of the fire.

Four rooms on the upper storey of the building, three belonging to the Assurance Co. and one which contained the whole of Mr. Kennedy's equipment were destroyed; while water caused extensive damage to the C and S Stores and Messrs. Mulcahy's, Newsagents and sweet shop on the ground floor.

WELL ABLAZE

The alacrity with which the Fire Brigade arrived on the scene could not prevent the destruction of the building which was well ablaze seconds after the fire was first discovered.

The man who raised the alarm told our reporter that after he had seen the smoke he ran back into the hotel and phoned the Fire Brigade.

"I estimate I was back on the street again within 20 seconds" he said, "that time the upstairs of the premises across the street was burning rapidly and flames were shooting through the roof into the sky."

He then told how he raced to arouse people living next to the burning building and helped to evacuate them and how with the assistance of members of the Cork Blood Bank he brought containers of blood plasma, microscopes and other valuable equipment to safety.

ALL EQUIPMENT LOST

Mr. Liam Kennedy, whose first information of the fire came from a phone call, said that he had lost all his equipment and cameras.

"I intended coming back to the studio later in the evening to do some work," he said, "and I left my cameras there. All I saved was a tripod which I had in the car."

The fire was first reported at 9.35 p.m. and within twenty minutes had claimed the whole upper storey. There was no evidence last night of where or how it originated.

Picture below shows the premises involved in the outbreak.

TRUCK, WITH HORSES, HITS BRIDGE WALL

Mitchelstown-Cahir Road Accident

At Kilbeheny Bridge yesterday, on the Mitchelstown-Cahir road, a truck proceeding with horses to the Clonmel Race Meeting, struck the left wall of the bridge on the village side.

The collision demolished portion of the wall and the front of the truck went downwards towards the river bank, its rear wheels ending high up towards road level. Fortunately, the vehicle remained in an upright position, and the occupants and animals sustained no injury. Later the horses were removed to another vehicle.

This bridge has been the scene of many accidents.

RAIN IN THE DAIL

Mr. O. Malley (F.F.) intervened during a debate in the Dail last evening to point out that rain was falling from the ceiling of the chamber on to the bench in front of him and asked the Leas Ceann Comhairle to tell the Board of Works to have the roof repaired.

Mr. Dillon (Minister for Agriculture)—I am sure the Government will be pleased to supply the Deputy with an umbrella.

IRISHMEN'S APPOINTMENTS

Mr. R. O'Connor, principal officer Aviation Division, Department of Industry and Commerce, has been made chairman of the Airport Charges Office at the I.C.A.O. meeting in Montreal.

Mr. J. Algar, permanent Irish representative at I.C.A.O., has been elected chairman of the Transport Committee.

U.N. Police Force To Move In Soon

Israel Agrees To Withdraw Forces From Egypt

THE world's first international police force will probably move into Egypt in strength within ten days, usually reliable sources said at the United Nations Headquarters in New York last night.

They said giant American transport planes operating under United Nations control were expected to begin a airlifting the first troops into Egypt in five days time. Canada, India, the Scandinavian countries and Pakistan would supply the first teams, amounting to about 4,000 men.

Meanwhile, in Cairo Major-General Burns, of Canada, Palestine Truce Supervision Chief of Staff, saw top Egyptian officials and formally took up command of the new force with an initial token unit of observer officers.

Sources in New York said a Canadian group would probably spearhead the force. Canadian Air Force transports were expected to take in the first men, while the aircraft carrier Magnificent would be used to take in the bulk of them.

ISRAEL TO WITHDRAW

It was planned to keep the carrier off Port Said as a supply and hospital ship, though the Canadians were quick to add "for sick, not wounded men. We expect no fighting."

It was announced last night in Jerusalem and New York that Israel was ready to withdraw her armed forces from Egypt and to co-operate with the proposed U.N. Police Force.

The U.N. delegation informed Mr. Hammarskjoeld of the decision, while President Eisenhower was also informed.

Israel's decision to withdraw her forces was seen in New York yesterday as the removal of a major obstacle to quick, effective action by the International Police Force.

Mr. Ben-Gurion, the Israeli Premier, made the announcement of Israel's readiness to withdraw in a surprise broadcast after midnight last night. He said Israel was ready to withdraw her forces from the Sinai Peninsula after the entry of an international force into the Suez Canal.

Mr. Ben-Gurion's speech followed two Cabinet meetings yesterday to decide Israel's next moves. The Jewish state has been under pressure from East and West alike to give up the Sinai Peninsula which Israeli troops captured last week.

INFLUENCE OF MODERATES

The Prime Minister told Parliament on Wednesday that Israel would not give up the territory she now holds—an area nearly three times the size of Israel. But moderate political elements are understood to have persuaded him to modify his earlier stand.

President Eisenhower last night sent a telegram of appreciation to Mr. Ben-Gurion on his decision.

In Port Said, battered by the first battles of the Anglo-French attack, the ceasefire was temporarily broken on Wednesday when an Egyptian patrol fired on a British tank, which returned the fire, an Allied communique said yesterday.

Apart from this General Sir Charles Keightley, Allied Commander-in-Chief, said: "There has been no fighting since the ceasefire became operative." Egyptian Press reports, however, continued to report fighting and air raids at Port Said.

Britain informed Switzerland yesterday that she was consulting other interested governments about the Swiss proposal for a five-power "summit" conference to safeguard world peace.

The Israeli Government last night issued the texts of what purported to be captured Egyptian military documents ordering "the annihilation of Israel".

The documents were said to be directives of the third Egyptian Infantry Division to field units.

SOVIET WEAPONS

The Anglo-French military action in the Suez Canal Zone and the joint policy of the two Governments were seen in diplomatic quarters in Paris last night as nearing a state of collapse.

There was widespread belief that the French and British troops would

CONTINUED ON PAGE NINE

SOVIET PLANES LAND IN SYRIA

The French Foreign Minister, M. Pineau, yesterday affirmed to the Foreign Affairs Commission of the National Assembly that Soviet war planes had landed in Syria a few days ago. This statement from so official a source has reinforced the belief in Paris that the British and French Governments had been forced under threats to abandon their projects in the Suez Canal zone.

ANOTHER MINISTER RESIGNS

Some Back-benchers Critical Of Eden

Sir Edward Boyle, 33-year-old Conservative M.P., has resigned his position as Economic Secretary to the British Treasury because of disagreement with the government policy in the Middle East. He was the youngest member of the government.

In the course of his letter to Sir Anthony Eden he stated: "I fully realise the very great difficulty of the problem which the government have had to face in the Middle East. But I do not honestly feel that I can defend, as a Minister, the recent policy of the government, and I feel bound to associate myself with that body of opinion which deeply deplores what has been done."

Sir Edward Boyle is the second member of the Government to resign because of disapproval of Britain intervention in Egypt.

Last Saturday night Mr. Anthony Nutting's resignation from the post of Minister of State for Foreign Affairs was announced for the same reason.

The announcement from 10 Downing Street of Sir Edward Boyle's resignation came at the end of a day in which the Government had had several critical jolts from dissatisfied Conservative back benchers.

OTHERS CRITICAL

Colonel Cyril Banks, M.P. for Pudsey, had announced that he will from now on sit as an independent in the House of Commons because of his disapproval; Sir Frank Medlicott, M.P. for Norfolk Central, had said that he must withdraw his support unless the Government complied with the United Nations demands; the Hon. J. J. Astor, M.P. for Sutton, Plymouth, had made a critical speech in the House in which he said the Government's action had been neither necessary nor right.

There are other Conservatives, including Mr. Nigel Nicolson, M.P. for Bournemouth East and Christchurch, who are known to be critical.

Estimates of the number of these ranged from a dozen to 17 last night. That is not a large enough number to imperil the Government if they abstain from voting. But it is a body of defection which is, no doubt, causing Sir Anthony Eden some anxiety.

SICK MEMBER OF TANKER TO BE LANDED

The Norwegian tanker Erling Hogenes (9,215 tons gross) is due in Cork Harbour at approximately 8 o'clock this morning to land a member of the crew, who was taken ill.

The Clyde Shipping Coy. (Cork), the vessel's agents, have made arrangements for a doctor and nurse to journey out by launch to Whitegate Roadstead where the vessel will anchor.

TRAWLER MAN INJURED

A crew member of the Spanish trawler, Mar Mayor, who was landed at Bantry yesterday, is being treated for a thigh injury, suffered at sea. He was removed to the Bon Secour Hospital, Cork, where it was learned that his condition was not serious, but that he would be detained.

Equality For Wives In Law

Provisions Of Married Women's Bill Explained

THE Minister for Justice, Mr. Everett, moving the second reading of the Married Women's Statute Bill, 1956, in the Dail yesterday, said it was a co-edification of all the law concerning married women, except the law relating to income tax and intestacy, though in one small respect the law of intestacy was being changed.

The object of the Bill, he said, was to put married women in the same legal position as single men and women.

Mr. McGilligan, Attorney General, who later explained the technical provisions of the Bill, said it was proposed to change the law completely in regard to woman's rights. Husbands and wives, he added would, if and when the Bill was enacted, be on an equal footing before the law for every purpose practically except the devolution of property in intestacy.

The House would welcome the statement that the law of inheritance was to be brought up to date so that they could look forward to another comprehensive reform measure in the not too distant future.

The debate was adjourned until next Wednesday week.

Mr. Everett said the Bill meant to get rid once and for all of the disabilities under which married women at present suffered, not alone in regard to their property, but also in regard to their ordinary rights in contract and tort.

At common law, a married woman's existence was treated as being merged in that of her husband.

A married woman could not own any property, and all her property became either absolutely or temporarily the property of her husband, and it did not matter whether the property was hers at the time of the marriage or was acquired thereafter.

Personal property became the husband's absolutely, and, even if the wife earned money by her own labours, the husband could take it as his own.

The theory of the law was that in consideration of the husband's undertaking to support and maintain his wife, he became entitled to her property.

A married woman could not make a contract at law, and, if she committed a tort or private wrong during the marriage, her husband could be made liable for it, and he could also be made liable for her ante-nuptial contracts, debts and torts.

She could not make a will of the real estate so as to deprive her husband of his estate, by the curtesy or her heir-at-law, of his inheritance, and if she made a will of personal estate, it could only be enforced with her husband's consent.

To give some relief to married women from the rigors of the common law, the Court of Chancery, through the institution of the Trust, devised the doctrine of separate use. When the legal interest in land was transferred to trustees to be dealt with for the benefit of a married woman the Court of Chancery compelled the trustees to carry out the Trust, and in that way evolved what was still known as a married woman's separate property.

A clause was provided to protect the property of a married woman from her husband, and also to protect it from her creditors.

Subsequent changes made were concerned with the property of a married woman and not with her status as a person.

SUEING AND BEING SUED

The Minister said that the idea of separate property was being abolished and a married woman would be in the same position as a single woman in so far as acquiring and disposing of property and sueing and being sued was concerned. She would in addition be subject to the bankruptcy laws in all respects as if she were unmarried. A married woman might sue her husband in tort and he might likewise sue her. The matter had been given the most careful consideration and the

(CONTINUED ON PAGE NINE)

"STOPPED WAR" SAYS MINISTER

Egypt Action Defended

The House of Commons last night expressed its confidence in the Government's Middle East policy by a majority of 58. By 320 votes to 262 M.P.s rejected the Opposition "censure" amendment regretting that the Government did not propose to call forthwith a Commonwealth Prime Ministers' Conference for support of the authority of the United Nations.

In a vigorous final defence of the Government's action in Egypt, Mr. Peter Thorneycroft, President of the Board of Trade, said that something else had been achieved than a cease fire in seven days.

"There is one explanation of the Russian dismay at these events," he said. "Her plans included—and I think are now shown to have included—the take-over of the Middle East, using Nasser as her instrument.

"Our intervention showed that Egypt had been armed to the teeth by Russia. The truth is apparent. We intervened to stop a war and we perhaps stopped it in the nick of time before the Egyptian Air Force, organised by Russia, ran amok in the Middle East."

Mr. Thorneycroft then declared: "If we stopped war prematurely we make no apology either to Russia or to the opposition."

Mr. Anthony Head, Minister of Defence, stated that information so far suggests that British casualties for all three services in Egypt have not exceeded 85, of whom not more than 30 were killed.

A British army doctor said in Cairo yesterday that Egyptian dead might number up to 1,000.

Amongst the list of injured issued yesterday by the British War Office was Guardsman J. Murphy of Dundalk.

AER LINGUS HALF-YEAR SURPLUS UP

New Routes Planned

Mr. J. F. Dempsey, General Manager, Aer Lingus, told a large gathering of the company's staff in Dublin last night that the airline had made a surplus of £344,000 in the first half of the current financial year. This showed a substantial increase of £31,000 or almost 10 per cent on the surplus for the same period of last year.

Reviewing the six months operations, Mr Dempsey said that the company had carried 314,856 passengers. This exceeded the number carried in the first half of last year by 41,436. The cargo figure for the period 3,062 tons showed a decrease of 5 p.c. (156 tons) on the figure for the corresponding period of the previous year. Import levies introduced last March cut down the volume of imports especially in the type of goods handled by Aer Lingus.

The volume of mail carried (837 tons) during the period was down by 42 tons.

Explaining how the surplus of £344,000 had been earned, Mr. Dempsey stated that revenue from all sources amounted to £1,882,400, an increase of 12 p.c. or £206,500. Costs were up under almost every heading and in comparison with the same period in 1955-56 expenditure had risen by £177,500 or 13 p.c.

Due to improved scheduling, combined with an increase in the number of revenue hours flown a load factor of 71 p.c. was achieved, the highest for many years.

PROSPECTS BRIGHT

Examining the outlook for the current financial year as a whole Mr. Dempsey said that the prospect of finishing up with as good a result as last year seemed bright. In the financial year 1955-56 Aer Lingus made a nett surplus of £41,438.

Referring to the recent air agreement, Mr. Dempsey said that this would mark an important change in the pattern of operations. Preparations are well advanced for the opening of new routes to the continent. He added that it was hoped to establish some if not all of these new routes next year.

1957

For a week in November, the fate of a little Russian dog named Laika dominated the headlines. The terrier was the first living creature sent to space when he blasted off on board the *Sputnik 2*. Irish interest in this leg of the space race had been increased a few weeks earlier when the first *Sputnik* satellite was widely sighted over the country. However, it soon became apparent that the four-legged hero was unlikely to survive the trip and the Soviets' technological strides in the space race were almost forgotten as speculation about Laika's health became the main news angle.

At home, the IRA campaign which had started in the latter part of 1956 continued with an attack on Brookeborough RUC station in Co Fermanagh. In the ensuing gun battle, IRA members Seán South of Limerick and Fergal O'Hanlon from Monaghan, along with 23-year-old police officer John Scully, were killed. No mention of the IRA appears in the *Examiner's* reports of the three deaths or in accounts of other incidents during the campaign. This was due to censorship regulations which prevented the paper from mentioning the IRA by name. Instead journalists had to constantly use the phrase 'an illegal organisation'.

While the raid the men took part in was not a 'success', the Seán South legend soon began to grow as huge crowds turned out through the country to see his body being brought back to Limerick, where thousands more attended the funeral.

In Britain, a fire at the Windscale plutonium 'factory' caused a release of radiation and subsequent banning of the production of milk within an area of 200 square miles. The lack of understanding at the time of the hazards of radiation was evident when the accident at the plant, 60 miles across the sea from Dundalk, is reported as a UK news story with no mention of any implications for Ireland.

Thousands attend Seán South's Funeral

Saturday, January 5

Thousands of citizens lined the streets of Limerick from the city boundary to St Michael's Church when the remains of Seán South, the Limerick man killed in the attack on Brookeborough Barracks, were brought to the city last night.

It was one of the largest funerals seen in the city since the death of Ald Ml O'Callaghan and Mr George Clancy in 1921.

St Michael's Church was filled to capacity during recitation of the Rosary after the remains had been laid in the mortuary. Hundreds remained outside and made the responses which were conveyed over a loudspeaker system.

The hearse had come on the long journey from St Macartan's Cathedral, Monaghan, where the remains had laid with those of Fergal O'Hanlon, the other victim of the raid.

When the funeral of the Limerick man passed through Dundalk yesterday morning, 1,500 workers from the local GNR works and other factories left their employment to march in procession after the hearse. Many shops were shut at the request of men who called on the owners.

Bareheaded crowds lined the streets of Dublin as the hearse bearing the remains passed through the streets today. Some 7,000 people met the funeral in Roscrea last night and a guard of honour of men marched beside the hearse to the outskirts of the town.

A Christmas treat for these children was a visit to Santa and a spin on the Showboat.

NEWS BRIEFS

Mar The Treaty of Rome establishes the European Common Market with six members: Belgium, Holland, Luxembourg, France, Italy and West Germany. (25)

May Ireland just miss out on a World Cup play-off after drawing 1-1 with England at Dalymount Park before a crowd of 47,000. Ireland needed to win the game to go through and were up 1-0 until England equalised in injury time. Fans of Denmark, the other team in the group, had battered Ireland with fruit in protest at their rough play during an earlier match in Copenhagen. (19)

July Internment is introduced in the Republic in response to the IRA campaign. (8)

The Cork Examiner.

MOSCOW MAKES NO MENTION OF LAIKA

Space Dog May Already Be Dead Or In Orbit

U.S. Trying To Decode Satellite Signals

LAIKA, the space dog, may be dead—or her container may be the "faint object" reported by a U.S. scientist yesterday to be moving ahead of the second Soviet satellite.

Last night's Soviet communique on Sputnik Two (as quoted by Tass) made no mention of Laika although a reference to her condition had been included in all previous announcements.

A study of Soviet official statements about Laika suggests that the dog is nearing the end, if she is not already dead.

Two days ago the dog was described as "satisfactory." On Wednesday night the Tass communique said telemetric measurements of the dog's reactions were continuing—but nothing was said about his condition being satisfactory.

This communique was repeated by Moscow Radio earlier last night. A study of Soviet official statements about Laika suggests that the dog is nearing the end of its duration...

...whereabouts are now guarded like state secrets.

Dr. John Rinehart, assistant director of the Smithsonian Astrophysical Observatory at Cambridge, Massachusetts, yesterday reported seeing a faint object 50 to 75 miles ahead of Sputnik 2. He declined to speculate what the object might be.

Dr. Hagen, director of the U.S. earth satellite programme, said yesterday that American scientists...

MYSTERY OBJECT SEEN

MIGHT ADVISE SCIENTISTS

MAN CAN BE BROUGHT BACK FROM SPACE

MOVE TO INCREASE EXPORTS

New Credit Insurance Agreement

In August, 1957, a new agreement was concluded between the Minister for Industry and Commerce and a group of four Irish insurance companies under which these companies are in a position to extend the area of application of the political risks of credit insurance cover for Irish exports. Ordinary commercial risk cover is already being made available by the companies.

The new agreement extends to most countries to which exports from Ireland are likely to be consigned the political risk credit insurance cover, available since December, 1955, for exports to dollar areas. The agreement between the Minister and the insurance companies provides that the Minister will reinsure the total liability involved.

Policies will be issued only to persons or firms carrying on business in the State, and only in respect of goods made or produced in the State. The policies cover 90 per cent of the insured loss.

The object of the scheme is to enable Irish exporters of goods to the countries specified to get insurance cover which is not available commercially against the following risks: (a) The prevention or restriction of transfer of payments from the buyer's country; (b) the operation of a law preventing the buyer from securing delivery of the goods; (c) the occurrence of war, civil war, rebellion, revolution or similar disturbance in the buyer's country; (d) the imposition of export controls or the cancellation of an export licence.

It is hoped that the extension of the scheme will encourage more firms to enter export markets and induce existing exporters to seek...

POULTRY HATCHERIES' REGULATIONS

Deeds Not Words Wanted From Russia

"Current Actions Seem Designed To Cause Maximum Trouble"

THE British Foreign Secretary, Mr. Selwyn Lloyd, yesterday challenged Russia to show by deeds rather than words, that they desired a co-existence that would really be peaceful.

He told M.P.s in a foreign affairs debate in the House of Commons yesterday that all Russia's current actions seemed designed to cause the maximum trouble for Britain and her friends.

"If the Soviet Union wants to end the cold war," said Mr. Selwyn Lloyd, "they should (1) stop seeking to undermine us throughout the world; (2) stop the campaign to increase tension in the Middle East; (3) stop making propaganda out of their decisions on disarmament, and (4) stop using the United Nations purely as a platform for an attack on the West."

Russia should show that they are prepared to work for a settlement...

...has made concessions to the Western point of view," he said.

"It is easy for the Russians," added M. Spaak, "with their directed economy to produce ballistic missiles and sputniks by depressing the standard of living of their people. We cannot do this. We cannot choose between the sputnik and the washing machine. The security of the United States will not be endangered if they entrust their allies with secrets which their possible enemies already possess."

BAFFLING PROBLEMS

"FUNDAMENTAL" CHANGE

CORKMAN DIES FROM INJURIES

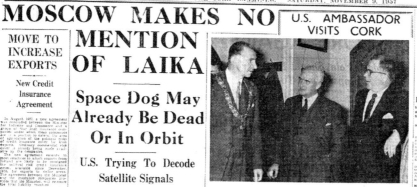

DUBLIN COLLISION

U.S. AMBASSADOR VISITS CORK

Mr. Scott McLeod, U.S. Ambassador (right), who lectured at U.C.C. last night, is seen here chatting to Dr. H. St. J. Atkins, President of U.C.C., and the Lord Mayor of Cork, Mr. R. V. Jago. —("Examiner")

Ireland Not 'Ganging Up' With Communist Bloc

Bishop Of Cork And Recent U.N.O. Discussion

"THERE is an impression abroad that Ireland is going Communist or at any rate is 'ganging up' with the Communist bloc. It is a wrong impression, and if it is the impression created by our representatives at the recent U.N.O. Assembly then very definitely the people of Ireland were misrepresented at U.N.O. The Irish at home, no matter what an individual or two may say or do abroad, have no wish to 'gang up' with the invaders of Hungary, or the persecutors of our missionaries in China. Quite the contrary."

This statement was made by Most Rev. Dr. Lucey, Bishop of Cork and Apostolic Administrator of Ross, at a reception given by the Lord Mayor of Cork (Mr. R. V. Jago) to mark the first official visit to Cork of the United States Ambassador to Ireland, Mr. Scott McLeod, yesterday.

STARRY EYED "LIBERALS."

CITY HALL RECEPTION

U.S. Envoy's First Official Visit To Cork

Lecture On Sport At U.C.C.

PROMINENT ATHLETE

NEW JERSEY PARTY TO TOUR HERE

U.S. Missile Chief

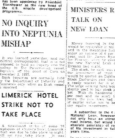

DR. JAMES R. KILLIAN, who has been appointed by President Eisenhower as the new head of the U.S. missile development programme.

12 Die In U.S. Tornadoes

Fallen Lines Impede Rescue Work

NO INQUIRY INTO NEPTUNIA MISHAP

NEW DUBLIN COLLEGE OPENED BLESSED

TANAISTE FOR TRADE TALKS IN LONDON

MINISTERS RADIO TALK ON NEW LOAN

LIMERICK HOTEL STRIKE NOT TO TAKE PLACE

CO. LIMERICK P.P.'s APPOINTMENT

Another A-Bomb Exploded

Britain's Tests Continue

REPLY TO JAPAN

LIMERICK CLOCK BREAKS SILENCE

Improvements At Shannon

Work On New Runway To Begin Soon

IT was announced some months ago that the Government had decided to equip Shannon Airport to receive the large new aircraft which will begin to operate on the transatlantic air routes in the near future. This decision was in accordance with the policy of maintaining Shannon as a first class international airport.

Work will shortly commence on the new runway at Shannon capable of being used by the most modern aircraft now planned.

The Minister for Industry and Commerce has been giving special consideration to other measures beyond the provision of landing facilities so as to ensure that the potentialities of the Airport are fully developed and utilised. Great possibilities exist in the comparatively undeveloped field of air freight traffic.

Shannon is considered to be favourably located as a centre for freight traffic. The possibility of industrial development within the Customs Free Airport...

...bility of further increases in terminal traffic. The advantages of the Airport as a transit stop are already well known and in recent years travel agents are reporting that an increasing number of transatlantic travellers are requesting to be routed through Shannon.

The improvement of terminal traffic may be expected as a consequence of the growth of Ireland's tourist industry.

APPOINTED BY MINISTER

NEW OPPORTUNITIES

FISHING VESSEL IN TROUBLE

EARLY WINTER SUNSHINE

The imposing tower of St. Mary's Protestant Cathedral, Limerick, makes a striking picture in the early winter sunshine. —(Echo Photo Service)

Atom Power Choice Facing Mankind

—Eisenhower

PRESIDENT EISENHOWER said yesterday that the destructive capacities of the atom contain terrible possibilities if left in the hands of "wicked men." Dedicating a new headquarters building for the U.S. Atomic Energy Commission, he said that if mankind had one wish, "it would be that the curse of the atomic explosion may pass" and only the peaceful uses of nuclear energy be remembered for the future.

"Man's judgment and intelligence must measure up promptly to his inventive genius," the President said. The terrible destructive power of atomic energy "should awaken man's conscience and appeal to his common-sense."

A-BOMB SHELTER

U.S. ARMY TO LAUNCH SATELLITE

MEETING COUNTRY'S TEA REQUIREMENTS

Formation Of New Body Proposed

French Trawler Arrested Off Kerry Coast

MORE SWINE FEVER IN SIX COUNTIES

1958

As was common among newspapers of the time, the front page of the *Examiner* was taken up with advertisements and news only appeared on the inside pages. Only a major event would change this tradition and the accession of a new Pope in October was one of those events deemed worthy of a full front page. Even the death of Pope Pius XII a few weeks before had been announced on inside pages.

The retrospective coverage of Pius's 23-year reign was, as to be expected, overwhelmingly positive. No mention was made of criticisms of his reluctance to make a stand against fascism in the lead-up to and during World War II but several references were made to his strong anti-Communist feelings. It took 12 ballots to elect the new Pope, John XXIII, the son of an Italian peasant and widely seen as a progressive pontiff.

In April, Aer Lingus began flying to the United States. As the *Naomh Pádraig* was given a rousing send-off by thousands of onlookers, the Taoiseach Éamon de Valera recalled Cardinal Newman's vision of Ireland as being at the crossroads of the world.

This image was given further weight in September when the first commercial jet making the trip from the USA to Europe made a stopover at Shannon. For those who could afford it, the travel time between America and Ireland was suddenly six and a half hours, as opposed to the many weeks or even months it had taken by ship since travel between the continents had begun.

In the education sector, the marriage bar for female national teachers was lifted. The year was also the wettest on record so far, with 53.7 inches of rain.

Pope's minder mourns

Thursday, October 9

Among the world's 400,000,000 Catholics mourning Pope Pius XII, the most tragic figure is that of a German nun, Sister Pasqualina, the Pope's housekeeper for over 40 years, and the first woman ever to live in the private Papal apartments on the third floor of the Vatican Palace.

With the help of three Swiss nuns who lived there with her, the diminutive Sister Pasqualina ran the Papal apartments with fierce precision. She was one of the sternest disciplinarians the Vatican has ever known.

It is said that whenever Pope Pius XII was working late in his study Sister Pasqualina would knock on his door punctually at 1am. With a pronounced German accent, she would announce: "Santita, e l'una." (Your holiness, it's one o'clock.)

People who saw them together reported that she seemed to know his needs before he himself became aware of them.

At the great mass audiences which the Pope gave, Sister Pasqualina lurked watchfully in the background. Every now and then she would dart forward, with a small bottle in one hand and a swab of cotton wool in the other. The Pope would seem entirely unaware as she seized his right hand and quickly rubbed disinfectant over his Papal ring and the back of his hand, kissed by hundreds of people in the course of an audience.

Sister Pasqualina made sure that the Pope had just the food he needed and that he did not lack the only company he allowed himself when eating - his canaries. She would free the canaries from their cage in the early morning and shepherd them to bed at night.

An exhibition of how a Hula-hoop works at Dunnes Stores, Cork.

NEWS BRIEFS

Feb Dubliner Bill Whelan is among the eight Manchester United players killed when their plane crashes at Munich airport. Eleven other people die in the accident. (6)

Apr Ireland's first fish farm is opened by Minister for Lands, Erskine Childers, at Roscrea, Co Tipperary. Trout, carp and tench will be bred to help restock inland waterways. (28)

Jun An Irish international team has its first involvement in the World Cup finals when Northern Ireland qualify for the tournament in Sweden. The North, featuring Danny Blanchflower and Billy Bingham, win one, lose one, and draw one. There had been a certain amount of controversy in the province when it emerged that the team would have to play on a Sunday.

Aug All 99 people aboard a KLM Super Constellation are killed an hour after take off from Shannon Airport when their plane crashes into the Atlantic about 90 miles from the coast of Ireland. (14)

Sept A large crowd gathered at Shannon to witness the landing of the first commercial jet to cross the Atlantic. The noise was far less than expected and PanAmerican Airway officials at the airport did not have to use the rubber ear plugs with which they had been supplied. (9)

The Cork Examiner

NO. 44,306 WEDNESDAY MORNING, OCTOBER 29, 1958 PRICE THREEPENCE

Registered for transmission at newspaper rate of postage in Ireland and Great Britain and at magazine rate in Canada and Newfoundland.

His Holiness Pope John XXIII

1959

A campaign against tuberculosis in cattle had begun in the mid-50s as part of the attempt to increase Irish agricultural output. Despite huge amounts of money invested in the problem in the decades since, the debilitating disease has never been wiped out, though it has been brought down to an almost acceptable level.
On the motoring front, Ford released its new Anglia. Retailing at £535, the car was assembled in Cork, though the four-speed gearbox was manufactured in Ford's Dagenham plant. The eight horsepower Anglia incurred a tax of £13 and boasted 49 miles to the gallon at 40mph. It remained one of the most popular models in Ireland for many years.
Two major films produced extremely different perspectives on the nation in 1959 with the release of *Mise Éire*, a very serious 'epic' history, and *Darby O'Gill and the Little People*, a light-hearted Disney movie with leprechauns, shillelaghs and the fantasy Irish-American view of Ireland.
Two world leaders came to prominence in 1959 – Fidel Castro in Cuba and Tibet's Dalai Lama who went into exile in India – while Ireland's own political phenomenon, Éamon de Valera, resigned the post of Taoiseach and was subsequently elected as the country's president.
In sport John Giles scored on his international soccer debut for Ireland and a Kerry team captained by Mick O'Connell beat Galway in the All-Ireland football final.

Disney film premieres

Thursday, June 25

A galaxy of stars and the producer himself, Walt Disney, graced the world premiere of *Darby O'Gill and the Little People* at the Theatre Royal, Dublin, last night. A plane full of stars arrived from Britain shortly before the show opened and flew back again at 2am after a banquet which was served by waiters dressed as leprechauns.
The stars included Albert Sharpe, Jimmy O'Dea and Sean Connery. The film is a fantasy which deals with the delusions of an old man with an unmarried daughter and his dealings with the little people.
Walt Disney said last night: "I am a brave man to come over here tonight with this film I have done about Ireland and the peoples, legends and suspicions." The film was regarded as highly entertaining.

Japanese delegates Ms Kawakita and her mother at the Cork Film Festival.

100,000 at pioneer rally in Dublin

Monday, June 16

In a hosting that was reminiscent of Dublin's great International Eucharistic Congress of June, 1932, close on 100,000 members of the Pioneer Total Abstinence Association of the Sacred Heart made Croke Park their rallying centre yesterday. They were celebrating the Association's Diamond Jubilee through the recital of the Rosary, listening to addresses by Most Rev Dr Conway and as a final act participating in Solemn Benediction of the Blessed Sacrament.
One could not describe better the impressiveness and motive of it all than through the Reverend's words – "Through you," he told the Pioneers, "Ireland today gives an example to the world."
In the course of his jubilee address he referred to the world concern at the grave social problem of alcoholism, the growth of drinking among women and girls, and the problem of the drunken motor car driver.

NEWS BRIEFS

April The Dalai Lama is greeted by thousands of Tibetan refugees when he arrives in India after sneaking out of Lhasa and making his way across the Himalayas to escape the Chinese. (19)

June Aer Lingus advertise economy class return flights from Dublin to New York for £155. 5s. 'Emigrant fares' (one-way) are £60. 8s.

July The first female recruits are accepted to the Irish police force when 12 future Bean Gardaí are sworn in at a ceremony in Dublin. "I wanted an opportunity for an outdoor career. I could not work in a shop or office," says Miss Mary Philomena O'Donnell of Kilmallock, Co Limerick. (10)

Oct *Mise Éire*, the first ever feature-length film in Irish, gets its world premiere at the Cork Film Festival. Produced by Gael Linn, the film is a documentary on the history of Ireland between 1893 and 1918. During the festival, American film director Ralph Florio comments: "Ireland is the one place in the world where a man can relax on a hill and forget all his troubles." (30)

Nov Gales of up to 90 miles per hour lash Ireland, resulting in widespread loss of electricity and phone communications. Three women are killed when a wall is blown over at Bachelor's Quay, Cork. (19)

The Cork Examiner

NO. 44,081 SATURDAY MORNING, FEBRUARY 21, 1959 PRICE THREEPENCE

Registered for transmission at newspaper rate of postage in Ireland and Great Britain and at magazine rate in Canada and Newfoundland.

Births, Marriages, Deaths, In Memoriam, Etc., On Page Two

CITY SPECIAL

WHY WE MUST GET RID OF BOVINE T.B.

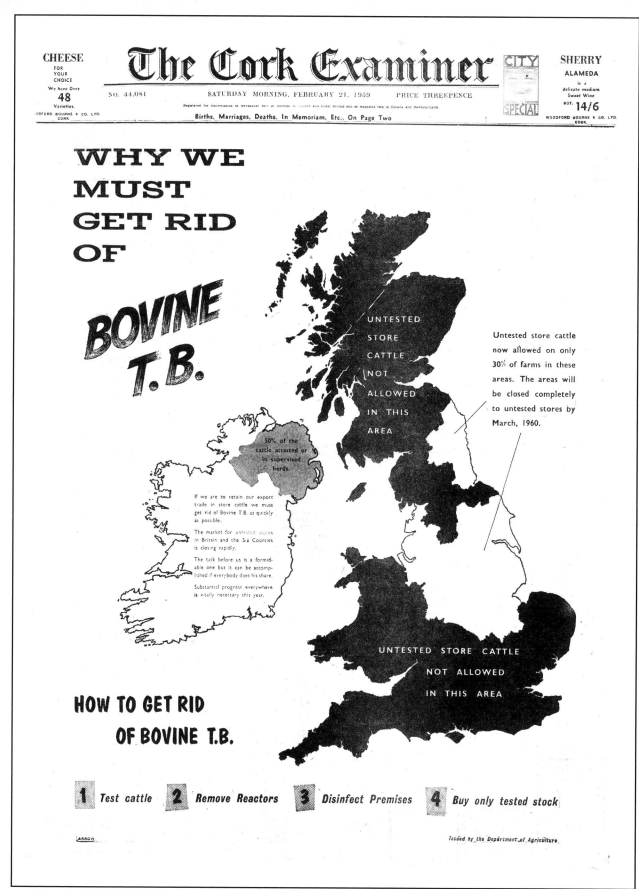

UNTESTED STORE CATTLE NOT ALLOWED IN THIS AREA

Untested store cattle now allowed on only 30% of farms in these areas. The areas will be closed completely to untested stores by March, 1960.

50% of the cattle attested or in supervised herds.

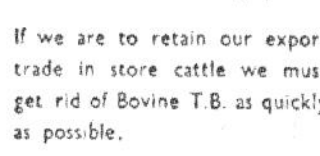

If we are to retain our export trade in store cattle we must get rid of Bovine T.B. as quickly as possible.

The market for untested stores in Britain and the Six Counties is closing rapidly.

The task before us is a formidable one but it can be accomplished if everybody does his share.

Substantial progress everywhere is vitally necessary this year.

UNTESTED STORE CATTLE NOT ALLOWED IN THIS AREA

HOW TO GET RID OF BOVINE T.B.

1 *Test cattle*

2 *Remove Reactors*

3 *Disinfect Premises*

4 *Buy only tested stock*

ARROW

Issued by the Department of Agriculture

1960

Ireland's efforts to help the United Nations operations in the breakaway Katanga region of Congo (later Zaire) had tragic consequences when ten Irish soldiers were killed in an ambush at Niemba. The soldiers were part of UN efforts to crush a rebellion in the mineral-rich province of the recently independent nation.

The tragic news of the ambush took away from what should have been a happy day for Ireland's fortunes overseas with the announcement of John F Kennedy's narrow victory in the US presidential elections. Kennedy had strong Irish ties and was the first Catholic to hold the office.

In South Africa, demonstrations against the 'Pass Laws' which required non-whites to carry identity cards were met with a response from the police that left 56 people dead at what came to be known as the Sharpeville Massacre. The agency report published by the paper is interesting in that there is no tone of outrage that such an account would likely contain today, and the only opinions quoted in the piece are those of the police and government.

Over 60 killed in African riots

Tuesday, March 22

More than 60 persons were killed and nearly 200 wounded in South Africa yesterday as police, armed with rifles and sten guns, fired on thousands of Africans who staged violent demonstrations in the Johannesberg and Capetown areas against the Government's pass laws.

Brendan Behan on his return to Ireland from a few months in New York .

Reports from both areas last night said that blood ran in the streets and women screamed and wailed as the police fired on the crowds in a drastic bid to restore order. The toll in the riots was the highest in recent years in the Union, where there have been several racial disturbances since 1958.

Mangled bodies of men, women and children lay sprawled on the roadway in the square of Sharpeville. One policeman said it was "like Delville Wood (a world war one battle) all over again".

The police seemed to be rather shocked themselves at the scene. A newspaper photographer said he "took pictures of more bloodshed than I have ever before seen in South Africa." The clash came after thousands in the square, facing police Saracens, began to hurl stones. Police replied with rifle and sten gun fire. Roads outside the police station were literally covered in blood.

Anti-Communist stand reaffirmed by Synod

Thursday, January 28

The Synod of the Roman Clergy yesterday remembered the "suffering Church of Silence" (Catholics in Communist-ruled countries) when it ended its three days work behind closed doors. One of the many articles read yesterday was that Communists and others who propagate and defend anti-Christian principles may not be married in the Catholic churches of Rome.

Another article read yesterday warned Roman Catholics that they will be considered "public sinners" if they marry in a civil rite, even though they may intend to be married later in a religious ceremony.

NEWS BRIEFS

Jan A decrease in crime in Dublin is reported for the last quarter of 1959. The total number of indictable crimes, exclusive of bicycle stealings, was 1,782, as compared with 2,105 for the last quarter of 1958. Housebreakings (447) and larcenies (1,557) accounted for most of these. (18)

May Radio Éireann's schedule is mainly comprised of shows featuring Irish history and music, while Radio Luxembourg has *The Pat Boone Show* and *This Week's Top Discs*. (5)

Court threat for Kavanagh

Monday, January 18

New York Public Library officials said they were considering legal action against an Irish writer who made daily trips to the library, memorising the letters of the late John Quinn, and then published them in his own volume of *The John Quinn Letters*.

The writer is Dr Peter Kavanagh, a brother of poet Patrick Kavanagh. Dr Kavanagh told reporters he spent 13 days in the library reading a thick volume of manuscripts of Quinn, early patron of writers and artists. Then, with his head full of words from letters Quinn exchanged with world-famous artists and writers, he returned nightly to his New York tenement room – where he also makes his own shoes – to jot down everything. Finally, on a home-made hand-press he produced a 32-page volume.

Legal action is being considered by the library because Quinn, who died in 1924, had bequeathed his letters to the library on condition that they were not published before January, 1988.

The Cork Examiner.

THE CORK EXAMINER THURSDAY, NOVEMBER 10, 1960

Army Names Victims Of Congo Ambush

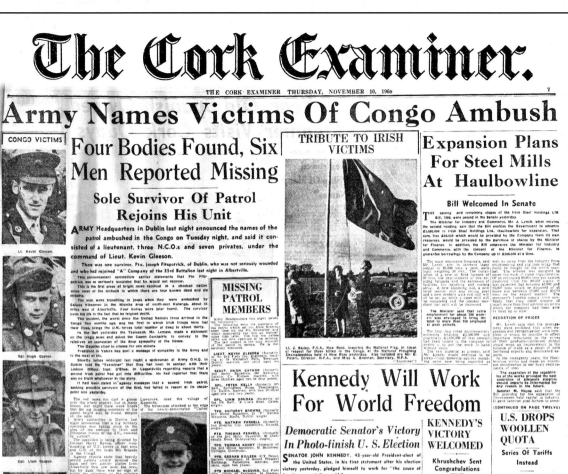

CONGO VICTIMS

Lt. Kevin Gleeson.

Sgt. Hugh Gaynor.

Cpl. Liam Dougan.

Trooper Thomas Kenny.

Tpr. Thomas Fennell.

Cpl. Peter Kelly.

Pte. Michael McGuinn.

Four Bodies Found, Six Men Reported Missing

Sole Survivor Of Patrol Rejoins His Unit

ARMY Headquarters in Dublin last night announced the names of the patrol ambushed in the Congo on Tuesday night, and said it consisted of a lieutenant, three N.C.O.s and seven privates, under the command of Lieut. Kevin Gleeson.

There was one survivor, Pte. Joseph Fitzpatrick, of Dublin, who was not seriously wounded and who had rejoined "A" Company of the 33rd Battalion last night in Albertville.

This announcement contradicts earlier statements that Pte. Fitzpatrick was so seriously wounded that he would not recover.

This is the first piece of bright news received in a shocked nation since news of the ambush in which there are four known dead and six missing.

The men were travelling in jeeps when they were ambushed by Baluba tribesmen in the Niemba area of north-east Katanga, about 25 miles west of Albertville. Four bodies were later found. The survivor owes his life to the fact that he feigned death.

The incident, the worst since the United Nations force arrived in the Congo four months ago, and the first in which Irish troops have lost their lives, brings the U.N. forces total number of dead to about thirty.

In the Dail yesterday the Taoiseach, Mr. Lemass, made a statement on the tragic news and asked the Ceann Comhairle to convey to the relatives an expression of the deep sympathy of the House.

The Deputies stood in silence for one minute.

President de Valera has sent a message of sympathy to the Army and to the next of kin.

Shortly before midnight last night a spokesman at Army G.H.Q. in Dublin told the "Examiner" that they had been in contact with their Liaison Officer, Capt. O'Shea, in Leopoldville regarding reports that a second Irish patrol had got into difficulties. He had reported that there was no truth whatsoever in the story.

It had been stated in agency messages that a second Irish patrol, seeking possible survivors of the first, had failed to report at its checkpoint late yesterday.

The sad news has cast a gloom over the whole country, but in many homes last night there were hopes that the six missing members of the patrol might still be found, despite all the odds.

Army authorities in Dublin last night announced that a big military operation was taking place in the area of the ambush by Irish and Ethiopian troops of the U.N., assisted by aircraft.

The operation is being directed by Colonel Harry Byrne, officer commanding all U.N. forces in that area and C.O. of the Irish 9th Brigade in the Congo.

Agency reports state that heavily armed patrols slowly scoured the bush and two spotter planes from Albertville flew low over the area, but by dusk there was no sign of either the attackers or the missing men.

SURVIVOR'S REPORT

In a telephone interview an Irish sergeant at Albertville said that the survivor, Private Fitzpatrick, had saved his own life by playing dead after the ambush. He went on: "As far as I know, the ambush took place when the boys came across a roadblock on that bridge. They all got out of their jeeps to remove it when they were suddenly surrounded by about 100 Balubas.

"Our chap who escaped said the others who were taken were still alive. We can only pray for them," the sergeant said.

He added that he had had some experience of Baluba rebels and had found that when they took prisoners they always tortured them to death. "It would have been better if all the boys had been killed. These Balubas are just savages. They will torture them for sure."

A military source in Elisabethville said the Irish troops had apparently "put up a good fight" against drug-crazed marauders.

They had gone out on patrol to clear a roadblock erected by the Balubas at a bridge over the River Luweyeye, near the village of Kamanda.

The tribesmen attacked at the edge of the newly-demarcated "United Nations Defence Zone." The actual place of the ambush is on a stretch of road slightly east of the geographical limit of the zone, but linking two points within it.

Pte. Joseph Fitzpatrick. (Survivor).

COULD ARREST THEM

Under the new agreement delimiting the zones, any movement of

(CONTINUED ON PAGE TWELVE)

MISSING PATROL MEMBERS

Army Headquarters last night issued the following:—

The following were the members of the patrol which set out from Niemba some time on the 8th November and which apparently ran into an ambush some time later. The first ten names listed are now reported to be missing. The last named is the only member of the patrol to escape. He is not seriously wounded.

LIEUT. KEVIN GLEESON (formerly of the 2nd Field Coy. Engineers, residing at 55 Wainsfort Park, Terenure, Dublin, married, one child aged six years).

SERGT. HUGH GAYNOR (formerly 2nd Motor Squadron, 340 Newtown, Leixlip, Co. Kildare, married, with three children aged two to four years).

CPL. PETER KELLY (formerly 5th Batt., Springfield House, Templeogue, Co. Dublin, married, with two children aged one and two years).

CPL. LIAM DOUGAN (formerly of the 5th Batt., 14 Cuala Road, Cabra, single).

TPR. ANTHONY BROWNE (formerly 2nd Motor Squadron, 25 "F" Fatima Mansions, Rialto, Dublin, single).

PTE. MATHEW FARRELL (formerly 2nd Hospital Coy., Jamestown, Swords, single).

PTE. THOMAS FENNELL (formerly of the 2nd Motor Squadron, 46 Clanranald Road, Donnycarney, single).

TPR. THOMAS KENNY (formerly of the 2nd Motor Squadron, 61 Ballinteer Cottages, Dundrum).

PTE. GERARD KILLEEN (C.T. Depot, Eastern Command, 93 Mount Pleasant Buildings, Rathmines, married, one child, aged two years).

PTE MICHAEL McGUINN, 2nd Field Coy., Corps of Engineers, 54 Staplestown Road, Carlow, married.

Survivor:

PTE. JOSEPH FITZPATRICK (2nd Infantry Batt., 55 Claremount Street, Dublin, single).

The Army statement does not mention that four bodies have been found.

CELEBRATIONS CANCELLED

Open air dancing and other celebrations which it was intended to hold at New Ross Quay last night to celebrate the election of Senator Kennedy in the U.S. Presidential election were cancelled in the historic Co. Wexford town when news of the deaths of the Irish soldiers in the Congo was learned.

At the ploughing competitions the National Flag was lowered to half mast.

TRIBUTE TO IRISH VICTIMS

Lt. J. Bailey, F.C.A., New Ross, lowering the National Flag, in token of respect for those killed in the Congo, at the National Ploughing Championships held at New Ross yesterday. Also included are Mr. G. Peters, Director, N.P.A., and Miss A. Brennan, Secretary, N.P.A. ("Examiner")

Gave Their Lives In Most Noble Cause

Taoiseach's Dail Statement On Congo Tragedy

IN the Dail yesterday Mr. J. M. Dillon (F.G.) asked the Taoiseach if he would make a statement in relation to the sad news emanating from the Congo.

The Taoiseach, in reply, said the members of the House had, no doubt, already heard the tragic news which had reached this country from the Congo.

Despite the efforts of the Minister for Defence to ascertain the full facts, the information available was not yet complete. It appeared, however, that a patrol of eleven members of "A" Company, 33rd Batt. of the Irish contingent to the United Nations force operating from Niemba was attacked on Tuesday.

It had been reported that some bodies were seen at the scene of the attack. One member of the patrol escaped with injuries and was believed to be in hospital. Strong forces had now been despatched to recover the bodies and to locate the missing members of the patrol. Aircraft were being used in the search, which was also being assisted by the Ethiopian batt. located in the area.

He said the relatives of the missing members of the patrol were being informed and every effort was being made to get further particulars with the least possible delay.

"I know," said the Taoiseach, "that every member of Dail Eireann is profoundly grieved by this event. The men who have died have bravely given their lives in a most noble cause—the maintenance of peace.

"I would ask you, Cheann Comhairle, to convey to their relatives an expression of the deep sympathy of Dail Eireann."

MR. BOLAND'S MESSAGE

The deputies stood in silence for one minute.

The President of the U.N. General Assembly, Ireland's Mr. F. H. Boland, yesterday cabled the Chief of Staff his "profound condolences on the tragic loss of the members of the defence forces."

Mr. Boland said their memory would "be honoured everywhere as men who gave their lives in a noble and unselfish cause."

Mr Frank Aiken, Minister for External Affairs, conferred with the Secretary-General, Mr. Dag Hammarskjoeld, on the ambush incident.

STATEMENT AT ARD-FHEIS

At the Fianna Fail Ard Fheis in Dublin, yesterday, Mr. Lemass intervened to make the following statement:

"I regret to have to inform the Ard-Fheis that a report has been received by the Minister for Defence that a patrol of Irish soldiers serving with the United Nations forces in the Katanga province of the Congo has been ambushed, and some of them killed.

"Information is not yet precise as to the extent of the casualties.

"This is very distressing news indeed and I am sure the Ard Fheis will wish to record our sorrow that Irish lives have been lost and to have our deep sympathy conveyed to the relatives of those who died.

"I ask you as an expression of sympathy that you stand in silence." All the delegates stood in silence.

U.N. PEACE MISSION FOR CONGO

General Assembly Halts Debate

The General Assembly last night abruptly halted its Congo debate so that an Afro-Asian conciliation commission might visit the troubled land and report back.

The Assembly endorsed a Ghanaian resolution for suspension of discussion, over-riding objections by the United States which wanted only an over-night adjournment so that delegates might consider the situation.

Britain supported the simple adjournment and voted with the United States and France among the 30 nations which opposed the Ghanaian motion. Some 48—including Russia—were in favour of it, while 18 abstained, and there were two absentees.

The purpose of the 15-nation conciliation group's trip to the Congo is to try to reconcile opposing political factions and facilitate the resumption of parliamentary government.

The commission may leave for Leopoldville next week.

BILL TO PERMIT TROOPS TO BE SENT ABROAD

The first stage of the Defence (Amendment) (No. 2) Bill, 1960, was moved in the Dail yesterday by the Minister for Defence, **Mr. Boland.**

The next stage was provisionally fixed for next Wednesday.

The Bill authorises subject to the approval of Dail Eireann the despatch of contingents of the permanent defence force for police duty outside the state with international forces established by United Nations.

Mr. W. Norton (Lab.) asked the Minister if the Bill extended the period of service in the Congo.

The **Minister** said that it did not but it enabled them to send troops abroad in certain circumstances.

The committee and remaining stages of the International Development Association Bill were passed.

The Pensions (Increase) Bill, 1960, was also passed.

Kennedy Will Work For World Freedom

Democratic Senator's Victory In Photo-finish U. S. Election

SENATOR JOHN KENNEDY, 43-year-old President-elect of the United States, in his first statement after his election victory yesterday, pledged himself to work for "the cause of freedom around the world."

At the drill hall in his home town of Hyannis Port, Cape Cod, he said the next four years would be "difficult and challenging years for us all" and that a supreme national effort will be needed in the years ahead to move the country safely through the 1960s.

Senator Kennedy won victory for the Democrats after one of the longest and tensest neck and neck struggles this century for the Presidency of the United States. He will be the first Catholic to occupy the White House.

Although he looked assured of victory when he retired to bed at Hyannis Point early yesterday morning it was not until 12.35 p.m. (5.35 p.m. Irish time) that his victory became assured.

The President-elect in his statement also said:

"I can assure you that every degree of mind and spirit I possess will be devoted to the long range interests of the United States and to the cause of freedom around the world.

"Now my wife and I prepare for a new administration and for a new baby," he added.

His attractive wife, Jacqueline, who expects her second child within three weeks, stood by his side.

Mr. Kennedy's prepared statement was addressed to all citizens of the United States. In it he said: "It is a satisfying moment for me and I want to express my appreciation to all of them and to Mr. Nixon personally."

YOUNGEST PRESIDENT

The boyish-looking Senator from Boston thus became the youngest man ever elected to the highest office in the western world and the first Catholic.

The Mid-Western farm State of Minnesota clinched it for him by voting Democrat and giving him the 11 electoral votes needed to make his total 272, three more than he needed for a majority in the electoral college.

A few minutes later his rival, Republican Vice-President Nixon, sent him a telegram of congratulations—his formal concession of defeat. There were also congratulations from President Eisenhower and many other American leaders.

Six States were still outstanding—with Kennedy leading in California, Illinois and Alaska, and Nixon in New Mexico, Washington and Montana.

The Senator's campaign leaders claimed California, but counting was still going on to decide the fate of the 32 electoral votes in this key State.

A PHOTO-FINISH

It was a real photo-finish. In the early stages the 47-year-old Vice-President swept into the lead, but with two million votes counted, Kennedy took over. From then on he kept the lead but in some cases only by a narrow margin.

Shortly after 3 o'clock yesterday morning (8 a.m. Irish time) Vice-President Nixon, smiling bravely as the tide went against him, issued a statement from his hotel in Los Angeles: "If this present trend continues, Mr. Kennedy will be the next President of the United States."

"I want Senator Kennedy to know, and all of you to know, that if this present trend does continue and he becomes the next President, all of us here will wholeheartedly support him."

But his wife, Pat, was in tears as

(CONTINUED ON PAGE TWELVE)

POPULAR VOTE

Popular vote returns early this morning showed:—

Kennedy 33,600,259 (50.2 per cent)
Nixon 32,679,260 (49.8 per cent)

Kennedy was leading in 25 States with 332 electoral votes, Nixon in 24 States with 185.

…nator Kennedy making his statement at Hyannis Port after his election yesterday. With him is his wife

KENNEDY'S VICTORY WELCOMED

Khrushchev Sent Congratulations

Senator Kennedy's win was generally welcomed throughout the world yesterday—in the West, among the "uncommitted" countries and by the Communist bloc, with the exception of Peking. Amongst the messages of congratulation was one from Mr. Khrushchev, the Soviet Prime Minister.

The Soviet News Agency Tass said last night Mr. Khrushchev said he hoped Soviet-American relations would follow the line along which they were developing in President Roosevelt's time, "which would meet the basic interests not only of the peoples of the Soviet Union and the United States, but of the whole of mankind, which is longing for deliverance from the threat of a new war."

Mr. Nehru, the Indian Prime Minister, said he would be "very happy" to co-operate with Kennedy.

VATICAN: "HIGH PRINCIPLES"

Vatican City: The Director of the newspaper "Osservatore Romano" said Kennedy's win "strenghtens appreciation for the high democratic principles of freedom which guide American public life."

Paris: Reaction was dominated by the Algerian question, and it is assumed that France can count on Kennedy's support in implementing de Gaulle's Algerian self-determination policy.—(Reuter)

ELECTRICITY SUPPLY BILL IN DAIL

The Dail yesterday passed the Committee Stage of the Electricity Supply (Amendment) Bill, 1959, and the Report Stage was fixed for Wednesday next.

Expansion Plans For Steel Mills At Haulbowline

Bill Welcomed In Senate

THE second and remaining stages of the Irish Steel Holdings Ltd. Bill, 1960, were passed in the Senate yesterday.

The Minister for Industry and Commerce, Mr. J. Lynch, when moving the second reading, said that the Bill enables the Government to advance £3,500,000 to Irish Steel Holdings Ltd., Haulbowline for expansion. That sum, less £89,000 which would be provided by the Company from its own resources, would be provided by the purchase of shares by the Minister for Finance. In addition, the Bill empowers the Minister for Industry and Commerce, with the consent of the Minister for Finance, to guarantee borrowings by the Company up to £500,000 at a time.

The main expansion proposals, said Mr. Lynch, are: to increase ingot output to 80,000 tons a year, each ingot weighing 30 cwt., The installation of a new oil fired furnace of 60 tons, the improvement of two existing furnaces and the extension of facilities for handling and casting scrap. A new blooming mill, a new large section mill and rolling gear and a new modern wire rod mill will all be set up while a sheet mill will be completed and the present merchant bar mill will be improved.

The Minister said that extra employment for about 200 workers was envisaged to bring the total to more than 700 employed at peak periods.

The Dail had voted supplementary estimates totalling £1,500,000 and practically £1,000,000 of that amount had been issued to the company to enable it to put the work in hand without delay.

The raw material at present, said Mr. Lynch, would continue to be scrap—from domestic sources including some now being exported as well as scrap from the industry from shipbreaking and pig iron scrap that could be bought on the world market. The scheme was designed to cover the bulk of home requirements. Of an estimated 65,000 tons per annum produced from the 80,000 ingots, it was expected that between 45,000 and 50,000 tons would be disposed of at home and between 15,000 and 20,000 tons on the export market. The company's London agents were confident that they could dispose of much more than that amount on terms which the company had been able to meet up to now.

REDUCTION OF PRICES

Mr. Lynch said that the management were confident that when expansion and reorganisation were complete, it would be possible to effect important reductions in the prices of their products—increased output would mean an improvement in the balance of trade as a result of both increased exports and diminished exports.

In the emergency years, the Haulbowline works had made an important contribution to our basic requirements of steel.

The expansion of the capabilities of the works provided the best assurance of adequate supplies should imports be interrupted for any reason in the future.

Senator M. Hayes said that the Bill provided for the expansion of Government held capital in industry. It gave sanction post factum to some-

(CONTINUED ON PAGE TWELVE)

U.S. DROPS WOOLLEN QUOTA

Series Of Tariffs Instead

The United States is to abandon its controversial quota system for woollen fabrics imports on January 1, and introduce instead a series of standard tariff rates.

Announcing this, the State Department said in Washington that the quota system, which has been in effect since 1956, had disrupted normal marketing practices in the woollen goods trade.

The new U.S. tariffs will be slightly higher than the rates under the quota system.

ACCEPTABLE

American officials said the new rates, although higher, were believed to be generally acceptable to the chief nations supplying woollen and woven fabrics to the United States.

Britain led the suppliers last year. Smaller supplies came from France, The Netherlands, Belgium and Luxembourg, **Ireland,** Switzerland and Uruguay.

BRITAIN FIRES FIRST OVERLAND MISSILE

The first overland launching of a live missile in Britain took place at Larkhill on Salisbury Plain (Wilts) when "Honest John", a 27ft. American artillery weapon was successfully fired yesterday.

The warhead, designed to carry a 13cwt. atomic bomb, was yesterday packed with concrete. It was fired completely according to plan and fused to explode and destroy itself—which it did—5,000 feet up over the Plain.

Bill Criticised In Dail

Fluoridation Of Water Supplies

WHEN the debate was resumed in the Dail last evening in the Committee Stage of the Health (Fluoridation of Water Supplies) Bill, Opposition deputies criticised the measure.

A division was challenged on one of a number of amendments designed to give local authorities the right to choose whether they would or would not add fluorine to public water supplies and was defeated by 74 votes to 45.

The debate was adjourned.

Mr. Mi. O'Higgins (F.G.) spoke to a number of amendments designed to give local authorities the right to choose whether they would or would not add a fluorine to public water supplies. He said the Minister had made the point that he was introducing the measure because the Fluorine Consultative Council had recommended that legislation should be introduced. The amendment suggested that it should not be made mandatory on public authorities to add fluorine.

Mr. MacEntee, Minister for Health, said that in his view, Deputy O'Higgins had misinterpreted the purport of the Council's report. As the law stood, local authorities could not instal fluoridation plant or incur the expense of operating it. That was the whole significance of that part of the Council's report.

There was a specific recommendation that piped public water supplies should be fluoridated.

Mr. F. Loughman (F.F.) said he believed the Minister was taking a wise course in view of the competent experts who tried to save the people of this country from the immense expense and damage suffered because of dental caries.

Mr. T. F. O'Higgins (F.G.) argued that the Council which he, when Minister for Health had set up to consider this vexed question, had recommended only that local authorities who desired to do so would be given enabling powers to introduce fluorine to their public water supplies and that there was no intention of making it obligatory on local authorities to do so.

"I urge the Minister to take care where he is going," Mr. O'Higgins said. "It is but ordinary elementary justice that the strong feelings which certain people hold on this matter should not be disregarded."

Mr. MacEntee said that if the council of experts wanted to make the legislation merely permissive for local authorities they would have made that quite clear in their recommendations.

The observations of individuals which were not based on scientific fact, should not be allowed to deprive children of the protection from a disease which was rampant among them and which was by unanimous opinion of the medical profession, a source of general ill-health.

These overies. [illegible] mass of high [illegible] in favour

DUBLIN, N.E. [illegible] (F.G.) said th[illegible] to prev[illegible]

[illegible] E TWELV[illegible]

1961

By 1961, the Cold War was in full swing and the 'space race' was just one manifestation of the efforts of the two superpowers to show their superiority. With Yuri Gagarian's flight into orbit, the Soviets had won this particular battle and it would take eight years and the first moonwalk for the United States to gain the upper hand in the propaganda stakes. The *Examiner* reported the Soviets' achievements quite objectively, but perhaps an indication of the paper's sympathies can be seen from some of the headlines of the time. The name of Soviet leader Khrushchev seems to have been deemed too long and is often shortened to 'K' in headlines. 'Kennedy' continued to be spelt as normal. The US president was beginning to show his tougher side with his anti-Communist pronouncements after the Bay of Pigs invasion failed to oust Castro in Cuba.

In July, the *Examiner* underwent a major shift in how it was presented when news replaced advertisements on the front page.

83 die near Shannon

Monday, September 11

In darkness and fog, 83 people died in the tidal waters of the Shannon Estuary in the early hours of yesterday morning, when a chartered air liner crashed within seconds of take-off from Shannon. One 25-year-old female student survived the crash itself, but later died from her injuries. The US air liner was on a flight from Dusseldorf in Germany to Chicago, via Gander and New York.

Rescuers sift through the debris of the President Airlines plane on the mudflats at Shannon.

The 77 passengers in the President Air Lines DC 6 silver-coloured air liner were mainly German and Austrian farmers and their wives on a visit arranged between German and American agricultural machinery firms. The aircraft carried a crew of six, including two hostesses.

The cause of the disaster, one of the biggest in aviation history, is believed to be engine failure. Battling against darkness and tidal conditions, teams of rescue workers had last night recovered 63 bodies.

Reports said that people at Shannon Airport remarked on an unfamiliar raucous sound made by the engines of the plane shortly after it had become airborne. Within a few moments of leaving the Airport, two loud bangs were heard followed by sirens.

Launches were quickly on the scene of the crash on the mudbank. One launch took on board a young woman. Judged to be about 25, it is not known how she was thrown clear. Mr Ralph Parkes, who was in charge of the rescue launch service, said that he saw the girl flapping about in the water a short distance from the crash. "I pulled her into the launch. She was badly injured. I whispered an Act of Contrition into her ear. I think she understood, as her lips were moving," said Mr Parkes. She died about four hours after the crash as she was about to be transferred to hospital.

NEWS BRIEFS

Aug As construction begins on the Berlin Wall, East Germans make last-gasp efforts to get to Western side of the city. (20)

Sept German driver Wolfgang Von Trips – 'Count Crash' – is killed, along with 12 spectators, when his car ploughs into the crowd at the Italian Grand Prix at Monza. (11)

Dec It is reported that Dr Conor Cruise O'Brien has been "released" from his position as UN representative in Katanga, Congo. The Irish diplomat had received much criticism from Western powers for his attempts to suppress the province's secession, but his work there had won praise from African and Asian states. (2)

It is reported that only 156 salmon have passed through the counter at the Inniscarra dam this year, meaning the Lee is almost wiped out as a fishery.

In 1960, 803 salmon had been counted, and the 1959 figure was 2,994. (11)

Full backing for effort to avert nuclear war

Friday, December 1

The United Nations' main Political Committee yesterday adopted by acclamation an Irish resolution calling on the nuclear powers to work out an agreement to stop the spread of atomic or hydrogen bombs. This action assured adoption of the resolution by the General Assembly.

It represented a personal triumph for Ireland's Minister of External Affairs, Mr Aiken. For the first time he had the backing of both the United States and the Soviet Union in his initiative, which he first began pressing at the UN in 1958.

Mr Aiken told the Committee that if non-nuclear countries became one by one possessors of nuclear weapons, he was convinced "nuclear war is inevitable."

The Cork Examiner.

"Road To Planets Is Open" After First Manned Space Flight

Russia Wild With Joy At Historic Conquest

Honours Showered On Soviet Air Force Major

RUSSIA yesterday celebrated the successful landing of the first man in history to journey into space. "The road to the planets is open," declared a leading Russian scientist.

The Soviet Union went wild with joy over the epoch-making voyage of the cosmonaut, 27-year-old Major Yuri Alexyevitch Gagarin, dubbed by Moscow Radio "the Columbus of interplanetary space." He is a married man with two small daughters.

Early yesterday his spaceship Vostok (East) roared into orbit at 18,000 m.p.h., made rather more than one complete circuit of the earth and landed at a prearranged spot in Western Russia 108 minutes later—decisively winning the long space-race with America.

Yesterday Gagarin was undergoing rigorous medical examination to ascertain all the effects of his amazing journey in regions never before accessible to man. He will probably be in Moscow to-morrow to receive the plaudits of Moscow and the world.

Honours are already showering upon him. Scientists and poets paid tribute to him, painters and sculptors promised to portray his achievement, a street and new-born child were named after him, massed choirs sang "The First Flight", the Komsomol Youth Movement inscribed Gargarin's name in a book of honour, and he was awarded the title of "Master Of Radio Sport Of The U.S.S.R."

But Russian statements emphasised the collective nature of the space triumph and claimed it as a victory of the Socialist system. The Communist Party made it the text of a peace appeal.

Moscow Radio last night broadcast a recording of the voice of Major Gagarin "coming from the cosmic spaceship during the flight." It lasted about 30 seconds. Gagarin could be heard speaking against a noisy background.

This was translated as "Major Gagarin said that the flight was going on successfully and normally, visibility was good, and that he himself was feeling good as well."

Tass, reporting the effect of the spaceman news on Muscovites, said: "The usual rhythm of the city's life is disturbed. Strangers smile at each other in the streets and congratulate one another on the great accomplishment. Everyone is very much excited and agitated, which is uncommon for the usually composed Muscovites."

Despite the snow and cold, windows were left open with radio sets on the sills to give the latest news to passers-by. Cars were stopped with their radios switched on, and bus drivers used their microphones to keep passengers informed of the space flight progress.

STAMP ALREADY.

The Soviet Ministry of Communications already has issued a stamp devoted to Soviet man's flight into space, Tass said.

The stamp depicts part of the globe and the Soviet space ship flying into interplanetary space. At the top of the stamp is the inscription "Soviet Man in Space" and the date "April 12, 1961."

The Russians surprised experienced students of Soviet affairs by the way they played up the "human interest" of the event.

From the very outset Tass and the radio threw overboard the long-winded style normally used for Sputnik announcements with all the "in accordance with the research programme" introduction, and gave the outstanding facts, including Gagarin's name, within the first 30 or so words.

The announcement was terse and to the point, and soon after Tass and the radio began to issue items of interest, such as Gagarin's biography.

Between the launching and re-

(CONTINUED ON PAGE TWELVE)

First Spaceman

This picture of 27-year-old Soviet cosmonaut Major Yuri Alexyevich Gagarin was received by radio from Moscow last night.

'Key Figure' In Extermination Of The Jews

Court Listens To Demand For Eichmann's Trial

ADOLF EICHMANN, as head of the Gestapo's Department of Jewish Affairs, was the key figure in the Nazi extermination of the Jews and as such "succeeded in part in committing the crime of genocide".

This was the heart of the prosecution statement on the second day of Eichmann's trial in Jerusalem, for the alleged war-time murder of millions of European Jews.

Mr. Gideon Hausner, Israeli Attorney-General, quoted from the Bible and marshalled legal precedents from Britain, the United States ,and half a dozen European countries to support his rebuttal of Tuesday's defence submission that an Israeli court was incompetent to try Eichmann.

Eichmann, slumped on his chair in the bullet-proof glass dock, remained impassive, with his head slightly tilted to the left, as Mr. Hausner cited the trial of the Commandant of Auschswitz extermination camp, Rudolf Hoess, to support his case.

Eichmann has said in memoirs published in an American magazine that he was a close friend of Hoess, hanged by the Poles for war crimes.

The prosecutor cited another Nazi supporter hanged after the war—William Joyce, "Lord Haw-Haw," the Briton who broadcast from Germany during the war.

And he went back to the Old Testament Book of Esther for the first example of genocide—the persecution of Persia's Jews by a Minister named Haman.

DRY TECHNICALITIES

Yesterday, as on Tuesday, the courtroom atmosphere was one of dry technicalities, with occasional moments of emotion as when Mr. Hausner declared: "For the man who carried it (the extermination of the Jews) out, there is no pardon, forgiveness, or atonement. There can only be hope and trust that the children will be different from their parents and that the son shall not be punished for his father's sins."

The Attorney-General discounted the defence claim that Eichmann was "free of guilt" and was being prosecuted for things he was drawn into by the Nazi state.

"Our argument is that Eichmann was not just an ordinary cog in the wheel," he said. "We shall attempt to prove that he initiated, planned, organised, and implemented the extermination of the Jews in Europe."

When Mr. Hausner described him as the "man who succeeded in part in committing the crime of genocide," Eichmann showed slight signs of agitation.

He rubbed his hand over his forehead, shook his head slightly, and vigorously blew his nose.

Eichmann (55), former S.S. Lieut.-Colonel, faces 15 charges, of which the first 12 carry the death penalty.

The prosecution devoted all yesterday to rebutting the defence submission that the 1950 law for the punishment of Nazis and Nazi collaborators under which Eichmann is being tried was unacceptable because it provided punishment for actions committed before the founding of the State of Israel in 1948, outside the borders of Israel, and

(CONTINUED ON PAGE TWELVE)

COMMONS REJECT MOTION ON HANGING

The age for hanging in Britain is to remain at 18, for last night the House of Commons rejected, by a majority of 85, a move to have the minimum raised to 21.

Although 144 M.P.s voted for the change, there were 229 against.

The bid to amend the present law was made on the Report Stage of the Criminal Justice Bill, when Labour M.P.s failed to get a new clause, incorporated in the measure, which would have had the effect of raising the age.

The Home Secretary opposed the proposal for two reasons (1) that it was too soon to draw conclusions about the result of the Homicide Act; and (2) the increase of violence by persons of 17 to 21.

BRITISH BUYERS VISIT SHANNON FACTORIES

A specially chartered aircraft with 30 British buyers and salesmen from industrial concerns flew into Shannon Airport yesterday to look over the industrial estate.

A number of them were buyers from the British War Department, and the British and American armed forces. They toured the factories and saw a variety of goods produced before returning to London.

NEW PRESIDENT OF FORD MOTORS

Mr. John Dykstra was named yesterday to succeed Mr. Henry Ford as President of the Ford Motor Company. Mr. Dykstra has been Vice-President in charge of manufacturing at Fords, Detroit.

Mr. Ford, grandson of the founder, took over as President on a temporary basis after Mr. Robert McNamara resigned to take up another position. Mr. Ford is to continue as Chairman and Chief Executive Officer.

Mr. Dykstra, who will be 63 next Sunday, was born in Holland.—(Rtr.).

Great Conquest Which Honours Man

—VATICAN RADIO

THE Vatican City newspaper "Osservatore Romano" said the flight was a memorable moment in history, which did not disturb Catholic beliefs, but rather comforted them.

Signor Manzini, the newspaper's director, said scientific progress reflected "the superior image of man as a spiritual creature endowed with liberty and reason, capable of a growing mastery of the exterior world, according to the Divine Commandment."

Signor Manzini continued: "Scientific truth has no frontiers and technical conquest is a universal good. To-day's great stage, in any case, does not surprise nor does it perturb our religious vision, but it gladdens and comforts it."

HONOURS MAN

The Vatican Radio said: "It is a great conquest which honours man, documents his intelligence, and rewards his labour.

"Science has to-day achieved what belonged to science-fiction yesterday. All growing mastery of nature's energies puts man before new and higher responsibilities."

The Vatican Radio continued: "Man does not create, he discovers and finds energies and laws. The secrets God expressed in the Universe when He created the world are all within man's reach. God invites him to discover them in order to know him and serve him better.

"Technology, making man live in a universe which is his handiwork, exposes him to the peril of feeling himself almost its creator."

OTHER COMMENTS

In Ottawa yesterday, the British Premier, Mr. Macmillan, who was leaving for home, described the orbiting as "a very notable achievement." He added that he was sending a message of congratulations to Mr. Khrushchev.

President Kennedy said in Washington, the flight was "an outstanding technical accomplishment." He issued a statement saying: "We congratulate the Soviet scientists and engineers who made this feat possible."

"SO NEAR AND YET . . ."

As he spoke the Redstone rocket which is to take the first American into space was standing on its launching pad at Cape Canaveral, Florida, a technician there commented: "So close and yet so far.

"We've kept our fingers crossed all along that we would get our rocket off before the Russians. But you have got to give the Russian scientists credit," he added.

The next phase in the U.S. "project mercury" space programme is planned for later this month—perhaps April 28—when an American astronaut is due to make a "sub-orbital" flight along the missile range from Cape Canaveral.

All-night U.S. radio services broadcast the news of the Russian feat in special "flashes."

Two American astronauts yesterday admitted they were "disappointed" that they had been beaten in the race to be the first spaceman.

The Americans—Lieut.-Comdr. Alan Shepard (35), navy test pilot, and Virgil Grissom (33) air force captain—two of the three men "short listed" for the first U.S. flight were sleeping as Major Gagarin whirled round the earth.

COUNTY CORKMAN DIES IN TRACTOR ACCIDENT

Mr. Patrick Kelleher, aged 40, of Lahanna, Macroom, has died in a Cork hospital from injuries received in a tractor accident. He was found lying in a field by a neighbour; and it is believed that the tractor rolled on him.

Space Major Is A Family Man

Major Uri Gagarin is a kindly-faced family man, the son of a carpenter, and born on a collective farm. He celebrated his 27th birthday last month.

His wife, Valentina, a medical graduate, is one year younger. Their daughters are Elena, aged 2, and Galina, one month.

WAITED IN FLAT

There were tears of joy in the eyes of Major Gagarin's wife when she was told of her husband's epic flight, "Izvestia" said last night.

The newspaper, whose reporters were in the Gagarin flat while the father of the family was orbiting the earth, said his two small daughters were sleeping. Major Gagarin had said goodbye to them a few days ago.—(Reuter).

NO REPORT OF PERSONAL REACTION

Summarising the space-man flight, "The Guardian's" Science Correspondent says that, since two laconic sentences broadcast by the space traveller during his flight, there has been no first-hand report of his personal reaction to the flight.

Major Gagarin's survival implies that the sequence in which he experienced the forces due to deceleration (and to acceleration during the launching of the capsule) are within the limits of human tolerance. Information of what exactly those forces were will be of great value in the planning of future journeys into space. These forces are the main hazard of this work.

Their exact magnitude depends on the design of the rocket, but must always be something like eight times the force associated with a man's weight.

Further development of rocket power, of guidance and control equipment, and of radio communications will be needed before still more ambitious journeys, as for example to the neighbourhood of the moon, will be possible.

NO WEEK-END SPORT

Landing on the moon will be still more difficult and will require further radical improvements of rocket engines. It is possible—but only just—that all this might be accomplished within a decade. A more realistic target would seem to lie at least twice as far ahead. And for the rest of this century if not indefinitely ,it is likely that space travel will never become a week-end sport.

RUSSIA MAY FREE U-2 PILOT

Mr. Oliver Powers, father of Gary Powers, American U-2 pilot imprisoned in Russia, said yesterday that there probably would be a report concerning the release of his son. He said he had no further comment.

There have been London reports, denied by the pilot's wife, that Powers would decide to stay in Russia if he were freed.

The White House spokesman, Mr. Salinger, said he had absolutely no information about the report of a statement or about reports that Powers would be released. "We know nothing about that," the President's press secretary told Reuter.

Rural Water Supplies

Mr. P. J. Meghen (right), Co. Manager, Limerick, and Vice-President, Muintir na Tire, speaking at the opening session of the conference on rural water supplies in the Mansion House, Dublin, yesterday. Mr. Neal Blaney, T.D., Minister for Local Government, who opened the conference and the "Turn of the Tap" Exhibition, is centre, and Mr. J. Barry, Consultant Engineer, is on left. (Report on page 13.)

COSMONAUT AT HOME

Soviet cosmonaut Major Gagarin is seen with his wife Valentina and daughter Lena in this picture received by radio from Moscow last night.

Balance Of Payments Position Improved

Economic Statistics Give Bright Picture Of Nation's Economy

THERE was an improvement in the balance of payments position last year compared with 1959, according to the economic statistics published by the Central Statistics Office.

The estimated deficit on current account last year was £800,000, compared with £8,700,000 in 1959. As there was a deficit of £1,000,000 in 1958 and a surplus of £3,200,000 in 1957, external payments were thus roughly in balance over the four-year period 1957-1960.

The import excess (adjusted for balance of payments purposes) on merchandise trade rose from £53.2 million in 1957 to £68.2 million in 1958 and to £82.2 million in 1959, but declined to £74.2 million in 1960. At the same time net invisible receipts increased steadily from £62.4 million in 1957 to £73.5 million in 1959; for 1960 the estimate is £73.4 million.

There was a net increase of £2.4 million in receipts from tourism, travel, etc. in 1960. Expenditure by visitors to the State rose from £37.8 million in 1959 to £42.4 million in 1960. At the same time there was an increase in the expenditure of Irish residents outside the State from £13.0 million in 1959 to £15.2 million in 1960.

Net income from investments, profits, etc., increased by £2.4 million. This was the result of a rise of £3.0 million in the inflow of investment income, profits, etc., offset by an increase of £0.6 million in the outflow in respect of these items.

Receipts from emigrants' remittances and pensions from abroad were £0.7 million and £0.3 million higher, respectively, and there was also an increase of £0.7 million in other known current items. The balance unaccounted for fell from £8.8 million to £2.2 million.

RECORD LEVELS.

The increased activity in the economy in 1960 led to increases in the values of both imports and exports, so that both attained record levels.

Imports, aggregating £226.4 million in 1960, showed an increase of £13.7 million over the 1959 level, while exports, at £152.3 million, were £21.7 million higher than in the previous year.

The import excess for the calendar year 1960 rose somewhat to £74.0 million.

PRICE CHANGES.

Though the price changes of both exports and imports over the past two years have not been large, the trend in domestic export prices has, in general, been slightly downwards in 1960, while import prices, after remaining fairly stable for the first half of the year, showed a slight tendency to rise in the last six months of 1960.

As a result of the movements of import and export prices, the terms of trade, which were more favourable to the country in 1959 than in 1958, deteriorated somewhat in 1960, particularly towards the end of the year.

The increase in the cost of imports

(CONTINUED ON PAGE TWELVE)

NO RISE IN BUS FARES PLANNED

C.I.E. To Meet Wage Awards Out Of Revenue

The Minister for Transport and Power, Mr. Childers, told Mr. L. Cosgrave (F.G.) in the Dail yesterday that the cost of implementing the award of the court of inquiry into the recent bus dispute, like other wage or salary costs, fell to be met by C.I.E. out of revenue. In so far as revenue was not sufficient to meet all revenue charges of the Board, they fell to be met from the annual grant-in-aid provided under the Transport Act 1958 for each of the five years 1959/60—1963/64.

He was informed by C.I.E. that while final figures for the year ended March 31, 1961 were not yet available, further appreciable reductions in the Board's revenue losses for the year were assured.

In the confident expectation that the improvement in the revenue earning position of the undertaking would continue during the coming year, the Board had decided to meet the cost of implementing the recommendation of the court's award without resorting to an increase in bus fares.

Belgian Composer Dies — Francis de Bourguignon, Belgian composer who accompanied Dame Nellie Melba on her world tours, died in Brussels yesterday, aged 71.

New Electoral Bill Criticised

Government Accused Of Gerrymandering

THE Government was accused of gerrymandering and of attempting to "fix" the electorate to protect themselves, by Deputy J. M. Dillon (Fine Gael) and other Opposition speakers in the Dail yesterday, during the debate on the second reading of the Electoral (Amendment) Bill 1961.

The debate had not concluded when progress was reported.

Mr. Blaney, Minister for Local Government, moved the second reading of the Bill, the purpose of which is to replace the Electoral (Amendment) Act, 1959, parts of which providing for the revision of Dail constituencies were held by the High Court to be repugnant to the Constitution.

Mr. Blaney said it had been decided in fixing the total membership of the Dail to apply the lower ratio of population per member permitted by article 16 of the Constitution and accordingly the total membership of the House as proposed in the Bill had been fixed at 144, the same total for which the Act of 1959 provided. If this proposal was approved the next Dail would have three fewer members than the present House.

The Bill, he said, proposed to increase the existing representation of Dublin City and County by four members and to add a further member to the constituency of Kildare which was being extended to incorporate some electoral divisions in Meath and Westmeath. To compensate for these gains and to provide for the reduction in the total membership of the House, it was necessary to propose reducing by one member in each case the present representation of constituencies in Cavan, Donegal, Galway, Kerry, Longford, Westmeath, Sligo-Leitrim, Wexford and Waterford.

The number of constituencies provided for was 38 as against 40 under the Act of 1947.

This resulted in an increase from nine to 12 in the number of four-member constituencies and a reduction from 22 to 17 in three-member constituencies. The number of five-member constituencies would remain unchanged at nine.

The Bill, Mr. Blaney said, contained provisions of a transitory nature to enable existing polling schemes to be adopted where necessary to relate to the new constituencies. The provisions would apply only until such time as revised schemes could be prepared conforming to the new constituencies. While the decision of the High Court was that only sub section (1) of section 3, section 4 and the schedule to the Electoral (Amendment) Act 1959 were repugnant to the Constitution it was considered that the appropriate course was to repeal the Act entirely and to re-enact the provision of that measure

(CONTINUED ON PAGE TWELVE)

U.N. SEIZES ARMS PLANE

White Woman Signed For Katanga Cargo

United Nations authorities at Leopoldville have seized a charter aircraft which flew more than seven tons of arms and ammunition to the Katanga forces of President Tshombe.

A United Nations spokesman said the crew, believed to be German, have been questioned in Leopolddville but are not in custody.

The arms were loaded into the aircraft at Brussels and were signed for at Kolweizi by a white woman of unknown nationality.

The U.N. official said the aircraft—a Douglas DC-4 belonging to a German firm—was on charter to the Belgian airline, Sabena. It arrived at Kolweizi, about 200 miles west of Elizabethville, on Monday, after beginning its flight at Hamburg. It later flew to Leopoldville, where U.N. officials, who had heard reports of illicit gun-running, took the crew to headquarters for interrogation, and seized their aircraft. The crew are not being detained.

(In Brussels, a spokesman for Sabena said last night the company "categorically" denied having chartered any foreign plane to carry arms to Katanga).

The British Ambassador in Leopoldville is being instructed to make arrangements for warning those British subjects known to be already serving in the Congo, but not under U.N. command, that unless they leave the Congo at once, their passports will be invalidated.—(Reuter and P.A.).

Miss Catherine Mary Ball Carew, of Peraki, Nelson Place, Youghal, who died on October 25, 1959, left estate in England and the Republic valued at £8,637 (duty paid £347). (£3,024 being gross personal estate in the Republic). Probate has been granted to John B. Jermyn, solicitor, of 67 South Mall, Cork.

Miss Annie Gleeson, of Boheragecla Lodge, Bruff, Co. Limerick, who died on September 2, 1959, left estate in England and the Republic valued at £810 (duty paid £196). Probate has been granted to her nephew, James F. Gleeson, of the same address.

Dublin Gas Talks Break Down

The talks between the Dublin Gas Company and the trade unions have broken down. The strike which took place last week-end was deferred until Sunday next to allow the two sides to work out an agreed shift work schedule in line with recommendations of the Labour Court.

The talks began on Tuesday and were resumed yesterday at the Labour Court, but they broke down shortly after 6 o'clock.

A union spokesman said last night that so far no arrangements have been made for further discussions. The position is now that unless the talks are resumed and agreement is reached the shift workers will resume their strike next Sunday night.

While no official statement was issued it is understood that the talks broke down on a question of a 42-hour week which the men are claiming.

FARMER DIES ON ROADSIDE

Fifty-seven-year-old farmer, Denis Condon, Duincha, Banteer, collapsed and died on the roadside at Kilnacurrane, Banteer, yesterday.

He was returning from the Millstreet Mart and was found in a dying condition.

SWING TO CONSERVATIVES CONTINUES

With 14 of the 62 British County Council election results declared, the Conservative Central Office claimed yesterday a net gain of 40 seats, with a net Labour Loss of 39 seats.

The Conservatives said the state of the parties was—Conservatives and supported candidates, 391 seats (53 gains, 13 losses). Independents—205 seats (12 gains, 15 losses). Labour—329 seats (10 gains, 49 losses). Liberal—8 seats (2 gains, no losses).

1962

For people in Ireland, the Cuban missile crisis was much more than some foreign diplomatic incident. There was a genuine fear that it would spark a nuclear war and many people prayed daily for a peaceful resolution to the crisis. As the front page from the first day of the blockade shows, views among the public as to which side was 'right' were mixed as demonstrators marched on the US embassy, and an *Examiner* reporter put a Cuban woman in Shannon right about 'our' feelings on Communism.

At a political level, Taoiseach Seán Lemass was adamant that Ireland was not neutral in the situation and lined up with the United States and the other Western nations. This stance was reinforced with our application to join the European Economic Community. Fortunately for everyone, Khrushchev backed down in his attempts to place nuclear missiles on Cuba and the situation was defused.

While Telefís Éireann moved into its first year of broadcasts, televisions were still a luxury item and it was quite normal for people in an area to gather in the house of a neighbour who was lucky enough to have one.

Literary censorship was still going strong in Ireland, with Joseph Heller's worldwide bestseller *Catch 22* joining the list of banned books.

Television come to Ireland

Monday, January 1

Everything went according to plan with the new Irish Television Service's first programme from the precise stroke of 7pm when the St Brigid's Cross motif vanished and viewers in Dublin and other parts of the country saw the national colours being hoisted by an Army lieutenant.

A family watches President de Valera on the television during Telefís Éireann's inaugural broadcast.

Reception in the South, however, varied from "perfect" in Limerick, to "practically none" in Cork city. The specially-arranged music of the National Anthem was interspersed with scenes of O'Connell Street, Dublin, and various aspects of Irish endeavour, including agricultural and industrial.

Then, as the music faded away, viewers saw the President, Mr de Valera, seated in Áras an Uachtaráin. He spoke first in Irish, and then in English, welcoming the new service, in which he said he had great hopes. Then the Taoiseach, Mr Lemass, and the Minister for Posts and Telegraphs, Mr Hillard, made short speeches in which they wished the service well.

The inaugural programme fittingly concluded with an address by his Eminence Cardinal D'Alton, Archbishop of Armagh, Primate of All Ireland.

Bishop of Cork on 'nests' of foreigners

Monday, April 30

"Nobody would object to a non-national here and there among us. It is a different matter when they tend to come in numbers to a particular area – when there are nests of them." This reference to the widespread purchase of land, specially coastal land, in West Cork, by non-Irish persons was made by His Lordship Most Rev Dr Lucey, Bishop of Cork and Ross, yesterday, when he preached at Skibbereen before confirming 120 children.

The Bishop said: "At Confirmation here two years ago I deplored the catastrophic decline in population over the country as a whole and more especially in West Cork. That decline is still going on. According to the recent census figures, the number of people in the urban district of Skibbereen fell from 2,202 in 1956 to 2,013 in 1961, or by 8.5%, while the fall in the rural district was from 12,031 to 11,153, or a fall of 7.7%."

"At the time I said – 'It is a fair and fertile land, this Emerald Isle of ours. With the population pressure what it is in other countries, it is inconceivable that so favoured a country can remain for long half-inhabited. Either we populate Ireland with the Irish or some other nation will colonise us. But this is a fear for the future.' In this last I was wrong. The colonisation was, in fact, just about to begin. We have a welcome for foreigners when they come among us as tourists; we have a welcome for them when they come to work here or to start work here. But we have no welcome for them when they come to take over our Irish land. And if the state will do nothing, or, perhaps, can do nothing about it, we might do something ourselves. People could let them see that they are not wanted. Farmers should be patriotic enough not to sell to the foreigner."

NEWS BRIEFS

Feb The IRA campaign in Northern Ireland, which had been in effect since 1956, is called off.

Aug Marilyn Monroe is found dead in Los Angeles, with a large number of medicine bottles on her bedside table. She had recently compared her fame to caviar: "good to have, but not when you have to have it every meal and every day." (5)

Dec British scientists Francis Crick and Maurice Watkins receive the Nobel Prize for Science for their discovery of the structure of DNA. (10)

The Cork Examiner

NO. 45,852 — WEDNESDAY MORNING, OCTOBER 24, 1962 — PRICE THREEPENCE

Massive American Armada Awaits Soviet Ships Sailing To Cuba

BLOCKADE STARTS 2 P.M. TO-DAY

Russia Warns U.S; Stops Forces' Leave

PRESIDENT KENNEDY last night ordered a blockade by United States land, sea and air forces to prevent missiles, bombers and other offensive weapons from reaching Cuba from the Soviet Union. The President, in a special proclamation, ordered U.S. forces to begin action from 2 p.m. G.M.T. to-day "to interdict . . . the delivery of offensive weapons and associated material to Cuba."

America last night awaited a showdown with Russia as the massive U.S. armada was deployed to halt "large numbers" of Soviet ships steaming for Cuba. America has said Soviet ships will be fired on should they run the blockade.

The Soviet Union gave America a "serious warning" on her Cuban policy, stopped all leave for the forces and halted releases from strategic rocket, submarine and anti-aircraft forces. Both the Soviet and Warsaw Pact higher commands ordered increased combat readiness in their forces.

Cuba has already been placed on a "war footing" even before President Kennedy's blockade announcement on Monday night.

A fleet of more than 40 aircraft carriers, cruisers and destroyers sailed overnight from San Juan, Puerto Rico, to join naval forces which left southern Atlantic seaboard bases on Monday.

In Berlin, the British garrison was placed under curfew as a "precautionary measure." About 4,000 U.S. soldiers began a four day "on guard" exercise in the Grunewald Forest.

CASTRO TO SPEAK

Cuba waited tensely for a promised television broadcast by Prime Minister, Dr. Fidel Castro, who is also Commander-in-Chief, at 8 p.m. last night (2 a.m. to-day Irish summer time).

In West Havana military zone civilians were not allowed to enter or leave—even if they lived there.

The Cuban Government notified Pan-American World Airways and K.L.M. Royal Dutch Airlines that Havana Airport was closed to civilian traffic and the companies suspended their flights.

All the armed forces were ordered to battle stations—"an order issued only in cases of most critical danger."

The United States' Latin American allies yesterday threw their full support behind President Kennedy and formally agreed to take joint action "including the use of armed force" to bar Soviet shipments of offensive weapons to Cuba.

The member states of the Organisation of American States (O.A.S.) approved a U.S. resolution to this effect at an emergency session of the O.A.S. Council.

Observers believed this opened the way for the issuing of a presidential proclamation last night putting the blockade into effect.

The O.A.S. members approved the resolution by a vote of 19 in favour, with one abstention—Uruguay, who was expected to add its vote in favour later.

Adoption of the resolution represented a major diplomatic victory for the U.S. in its goal of obtaining inter-American backing for the naval blockade.

RUSSIA CALLS FOR NEGOTIATIONS

Mr. Zorin last night presented a Soviet draft resolution asking the U.N. Council to insist that the U.S. revoke its decision to inspect ships bound for Cuba. It also called for negotiations between Russia, the U.S. and Cuba to remove the threat of war.

BRITAIN ACCUSES RUSSIA

Britain, in a Foreign Office statement yesterday accused Russia of "deception and deliber-

(CONTINUED ON PAGE 10)

GARDAI BREAK UP DUBLIN PROTEST

A demonstration organised by the National Progressive Democrat Party and the Irish Campaign for Nuclear Disarmament, outside the American Embassy in Dublin last night, was broken up by a force of about 20 gardai with two police dogs.

The demonstration was said to be against President Kennedy's decision to blockade Cuba and the marchers had intended to deliver a letter of protest at the Embassy.

As the demonstrators, about 50 in number, approached the Embassy, gardai cordoned off the roadway and some scuffling broke out between police and marchers. The demonstrators were gradually moved back and three of them were taken to College garda station.

Prominent among the demonstrators was Dr. Noel Browne, T.D.

IN LONDON

Struggles broke out outside the U.S. Embassy in Grosvenor Square, London, last night when demonstrators tried to rush the Embassy's steps. The demonstrators, over 2,000 strong, broke through an arm-in-arm police cordon 100 yards from the Embassy steps and ran towards the building. There, dozens of police who had raced with the demonstrators succeeded in forming a line at the top of the steps and repelling the demonstrators. The demonstration was organised by the Committee of 100.

A crowd of several hundred marched from Grosvenor Square to the Russian Embassy, half a mile away. There several small deputations were allowed in. They presented batches of letters, written mainly by individuals, to a senior Russian official.

The Committee of 100 plan a constant picket day and night, of the Russian, American and Cuban Embassies until Sunday when a demonstration march to the three embassies will be held.

An aerial picture issued by the United States Embassy in London last night showing "surface to air missile assembly facility in Cuba."

No Contact Yet With Soviet Ships

The United States armada of blockade ships is now on station ready to halt "large numbers" of Soviet vessels headed for Cuba, a U.S. Defence Department spokesman said yesterday.

The spokesman said there had been no contact so far between U.S. navy ships and foreign vessels proceeding to Cuba, whether Soviet bloc, allied or neutral.

SOVIET SHIPS ON WAY

The spokesman declined to say how many Soviet ships were steaming towards Cuban ports, but said emphatically that there were "large numbers." The spokesman said that to his knowledge the Russian ships were not proceeding in convoy.

The Defence Department spokesman said it was impossible for him to say at this time when the first "confrontation" between a U.S. warship and a Russian freighter would take place.

Washington sources said the first Soviet ship to be intercepted might be the Poltavia, apparently designed to carry missiles. The Poltavia was said to be bound for Cuba, and the navy was keeping a special watch for her. Reconnaissance planes had taken photographs of the vessel.

Two Soviet freighters entered Havana Harbour yesterday morning coming from the West, apparently on the way from other Cuban ports. One British freighter is also docked there.

CONTENTS

Stop "Ominous Adventure" U.S. Warns K.

IN a tense emergency session of the United Nations Security Council in New York yesterday, the United States called on Russia to halt its "ominous adventure" in Cuba, and warned Mr. Khrushchev against thinking America lacked the will or nerve to use its weapons.

The Council heard Mr. Adlai Stevenson, chief U.S. delegate, declare that no threat to "the vision of peace" since the end of World War II had been so profound as the Soviet military build-up in the Caribbean Island.

He told a hushed standing-room-only audience that Cuba had made herself an "accomplice in the Communist enterprise of world domination."

If the Western hemisphere nations accepted this new phase of aggression, "we would be delinquent in our obligations to world peace," Mr. Stephenson said.

Failure to stand firm now would "guarantee a heightening of the world civil war to new levels of intensity and danger."

The threat lay in the submission of the Castro regime to the will of an aggressive power.

"The crucial fact is that Cuba has given the Soviet Union a bridgehead and staging area in this hemisphere—that it has invited an extra-continental, anti-democratic and expansionist power into the bosom of the American family—that it has made itself an accomplice in the Communist enterprise of world domination," Mr. Stephenson declared.

VAST PLAN OF AGGRESSION

"The time has come for this Council to decide whether to make a serious attempt to bring peace to the world—or to let the United Nations stand idly by while the vast plan of piecemeal aggression unfolds, conducted in the hope that no single issue will seem consequently enough to mobilise the resistance of the free peoples.

"For my own government, this question is not in doubt. We remain committed to the principles of the United Nations Charter, and we intend to defend them."

Mr. Zorin, Soviet Deputy Foreign Minister and chief U.N. delegate, presided over the 11-nation Council, which met at the separate requests

(CONTINUED ON PAGE 10)

Taoiseach Clarifies Stand On Two Major Issues

From "Examiner" Staff Reporter In Bonn

AT a crowded Press conference in Bonn yesterday, the Taoiseach, Mr. Lemass, made very clear Ireland's situation in regard to two major issues — our part in the European Community and the country's position in the East-West conflict.

Referring to Ireland's application to join the E.E.C., Mr. Lemass said that our reason for desiring to join was primarily political, but backing up that political decision was the recognition that there would be no economic future of any kind for Ireland in the circumstances in which the other countries of Western Europe would be combined in the Common Market.

He said: "We hope to be able to participate in this effort which is being made to build up the unity of Western Europe, and to ensure by common action future progress in the economic and every other sense.

"I was very glad to learn this morning that governments of the Community have now decided to accept our application in principle, even though the actual conduct of the negotiations may be delayed for some time.

"We ourselves will not press for immediate negotiations, because we recognise that negotiations with Great Britain must have priority, and because of our trade relations with Britain we would wish to know the outcome before completing our own negotiations".

The Taoiseach made clear Ireland's position in the East—West conflict: "We are not neutral, and we wish to remove any misunderstanding about Ireland's position in the world. It is true that for reasons which would take rather long to elaborate that we are not in N.A.T.O., but that does not mean that we should be regarded as neutral — on the contrary, we have emphasised over and over again that we are on the side of the Western democracies".

Mr. Lemass told an American questioner that responsibility of reducing withdrawal from points of conflict was put forward by the Irish representative of the U.N. "Unfortunately, in my opinion, the idea made little progress. We do not wish to push

(CONTINUED ON PAGE 10)

Ireland Favours Inspection

Ireland will certainly support in the United Nations Organisation any proposal for the abolition of weapons of aggression in Cuba and for some system of inspection to ensure that the wishes of the U.N. would be observed. An Taoiseach, Mr. Sean Lemass, told this to a crowded Press conference in Bonn yesterday, writes an "Examiner" staff reporter. The Taoiseach added: "There is at least some similarity in regard to Cuba vis-a-vis the U.S. as in our own country vis-a-vis Britain. It has been our policy for many years to give specific undertakings to the British Government that we will never allow our territories to be used as a base to mount an attack on Great Britain. It seems to me to be reasonable for the U.S. Government to seek some similar assurance from Cuba."

The Taoiseach added that the situation which was now developing in Cuba was "very serious and the consequences are unpredictable."

SHIPYARD OUTLOOK "SERIOUS"

The present position and future outlook for the shipyards in Britain are serious, says the British Shipbuilding Conference in a statement on the third quarter.

An intake of 563,000 tons gross of new orders in the last 12 months compares with completions of 1,111,000 tons gross, a figure which in itself falls considerably short of the average annual rate of completions in recent years.

"This points to conditions becoming progressively worse for the industry unless there is a marked upswing in ordering by British shipowners, of which there is no indication at the present time. Future prospects are overshadowed by excess capacity throughout the world in shipping and in shipbuilding."

K. AT OPERA

A smiling Mr. Khrushchev last night led the applause at the Bolshoi Theatre, Moscow after a performance of Boris Mussorgsky's opera "Boris Godounov".

The American singer George Hines took the leading role.

Mr. Khrushchev, accompanied by Mr. Gheorghi Dej, the Rumanian President, went backstage after Hines had taken four curtain calls and personally congratulated the tall American singer.

"Six" Chief's Note To Lemass

SIGNOR EMILIO COLOMBO, Chairman of the E.E.C. Council of Ministers, yesterday sent a note to the Taoiseach, Mr. Lemass, in Bonn, officially confirming the earlier reported agreement on the opening of negotiations on Ireland's application for full membership of the Common Market.

The Council unanimously agreed on the text of the following letter at a late-night session on Monday:

TEXT OF LETTER

"Mr. Prime Minister,

"I have the honour to inform you that the E.E.C. Council of Ministers made a decision at its meeting of October 22/23, 1962, on the demand of the Irish Government to open negotiations with a view to adhering to the Treaty of Rome, according to the provision of Article 237 of this Treaty.

"I am happy to inform you that the Council of Ministers has agreed unanimously to this request for the opening of negotiations.

"The date on which the negotiations will open will be fixed through diplomatic channels by common agreement between the Irish Government and the governments of the member states of the European Economic Community".

Article 237 of the Treaty provides for full membership.

Signor Colombo told reporters last night that the decision to open negotiations on Ireland's application did not necessarily mean that Ireland was bound to become a full member. The door would be left open during the negotiations for alternative arrangements, such as association, if these should prove to be more suitable, Signor Colombo said.

Official sources in Bonn last night said that it was expected the negotiations would not begin until 1963.

"TOTAL WAR" DANGER

The Japanese National News Agency Kyodo yesterday in Tokyo quoted the Director-General of the Soviet News Agency Tass, Mr. Dmitri Goryunov, as saying that if the United States sank a Soviet ship there would surely be total war".

In a report from Hiroshima, Kyodo also quoted Mr. Goryunov, who is visiting Japan as head of a seven-member delegation of Soviet journalists, as saying that if the U.S. attacked Cuba the Soviet Union would help Cuba.

Cubans At Shannon Hit At U.S.

The first Cuban airliner to fly on the only open route linking Moscow with Cuba passed through Shannon Airport shortly before midnight last night.

It was a Cuban National Airlines Britannia with 72 passengers and fifteen crew members aboard. Two of the crew did not wear uniform and are believed to be political security men who frequently pass through Shannon.

The passengers included East German and Czechoslovakian military technicians, young Cubans returning after technical training in Moscow and Prague as well as a party of returning Cuban tourists who have been in the Communist countries.

Two of the East Germans who stood apart from the others said that they were going to Cuba because the money was good and they did not think there would be a war.

One Cuban woman wearing a green beret of the Cuban Militia, travelling with her husband and three young children said: "We don't mind going back in the face of war clouds. We are going back to defend our freedom which we so dearly won". Her husband is a doctor.

Speaking perfect English she said on behalf of another group of passengers: "What right have the Americans to blockade any country and search their ships?"

Reminded by an "Examiner" reporter that they might have missiles on board, she replied: "How many missile bases have America throughout Europe?" She then added: "What a pity after your fight for freedom that Ireland has not given us any sympathy."

She was told that we did not agree with their Communist manifestations.

New Move To Re-organise Industry Here

THE setting up of a new branch of the Department of Industry and Commerce which will devote itself exclusively to activity in connection with the re-organisation of industry was announced by the Minister for Industry and Commerce, Mr. Jack Lynch, last night.

The Minister was speaking at the annual dinner of the Dublin Chamber of Commerce in the Gresham Hotel.

"This branch is now in existence and has begun its work," he said. "It will co-operate with industry in every way, particularly with the adaptation councils; it will give all possible encouragement and assistance, and will guide and steer the action which will be necessary to re-organise the various industries in the light of the recommendations made by the Committee on Industrial Organisation. It is my intention that this branch should be a vigorous and active unit, which will be a live force in all sectors of industry.

CO-OPERATION NEEDED

"If this branch is to achieve its aims, it must have the full co-operation of every sector of industry and of every firm. It will not be sufficient for industry to accept passively the existence of the branch and to look to it for an easy solution of the various problems. Re-organisation is primarily a matter for the industries themselves.

"The function of the branch will be to co-operate and to energise. Industry's approach must be active and whole-hearted if we are to achieve what we all desire to achieve," he said.

"I feel confident that industry will make the efforts that are necessary,

Mr. J. Lynch
Minister for Industry and Commerce

and I believe that the assistance which the new branch of the department will provide will be a positive benefit for industry at this crucial stage."

GOOD EXAMPLE

Mr. Lynch said that the linen and cotton industry was now setting up an adaptation council, and he con-

(CONTINUED ON PAGE 10)

BISHOP CONFIRMS INJURED GIRL

Two sisters were rushed to Dungarvan Hospital yesterday in a serious condition following an accident at Curradoon Hill, Ballinamult, Co. Waterford. They are Josephine McGrath (11) and her eight-year-old sister, Mary.

The accident occurred when their bicycle crashed at the end of the hill and they were thrown on to the road. The bicycle was driven by Josephine, with Mary on the carrier.

GOING TO SCHOOL

They are daughters of Mr. and Mrs. Peter McGrath and they were going to school at the time of the accident. They were found at the scene by a passing motorist and taken to the hospital.

Following an inquiry from the hospital, His Lordship the Bishop of Waterford, Most Rev. Dr. D. Coholan, travelled to Dungarvan and confirmed Josephine, who was later taken to the Richmond Hospital in Dublin in a critical condition. She was described as being in a semi-conscious condition and under observation at the hospital early this morning.

The condition of her sister, Mary, was stated to be "fairly comfortable" at Dungarvan Hospital early this morning.

CORK WOMAN DIES

Mrs. Alice Murphy, 23 Abbey Street, Cork, who sustained serious injuries in a street accident on Thursday last, died in the South Infirmary Hospital yesterday.

Mrs. Murphy was struck by a driverless car at the junction of Evergreen Street and Barrack Street.

WEST BACKS KENNEDY

President Kennedy's announcement of a partial blockade of Cuba touched off world-wide reaction ranging from unqualified support to fierce condemnation, Reuter correspondents round the globe reported. Most of America's allies in Europe and Asia at once voiced their support for President Kennedy's decision.

In Ottawa, Mr. Diefenbaker, the Prime Minister, said Canada had no doubt at all that the U.S. allegations were correct. His earlier suggestion that a neutralist fact-finding mission should visit Cuba was intended only to allay doubts in other countries, he told reporters.

NATO headquarters in Paris said only that "appropriate measures" were being taken in connection with the crisis.

Paris—French newspapers as a whole expressed sympathy and approval of President Kennedy's action.

The French Government did not publish an official statement on its attitude towards the American decision. Diplomatic sources said General de Gaulle had told Mr. Acheson the United States could count upon the general support of France in any subsequent developments.

Oslo—The Norwegian Government expressed its support for the U.S. move in bringing the matter before the Security Council.

Stockholm—The Swedish Government was meeting to consider the situation.

Copenhagen—The Danish Prime Minister, Mr. Krag, said he could see no reason at present for Danish military precautions.

TITO URGES SOLUTION

President Tito said: "A way out from this kind of situation can be found only by seeking a solution by peaceful means and not by relying on force.

"We believe that the United Nations offers the most favourable and only way of finding the corresponding solution in the spirit of the charter of this organisation."—(Reuter.)

CHINESE ADVANCE INTO INDIA

Advancing Chinese troops are threatening Tawang, India's main administrative centre in the area between Bhutan and Tibet, the Defence Ministry stated last night in New Delhi.

Its communique said Chinese forces had attacked positions in Bum La Pass, 12 miles east of the Thag La Ridge, and advanced about eight miles down the Nam Yang valley.

Observers said it appeared the Chinese were trying to use a pincer movement to outflank Tawang—a Buddhist monastery and trading centre 50 miles south of the border, where the Dalai Lama found refuge after fleeing Tibet.

CHINESE AIM

They added it appeared the minimum Chinese aim was now to occupy the Tawang area and control the Nam Yang river valley running south-west through Bhutan to the Brahmaputra plains. A Defence Ministry spokesman last night said further Chinese reinforcements had been seen at Longju, and Monday's attack on Kibitoo—at the eastern end of the frontier near Burma — was continuing.

NEHRU ANSWERS MR. K.

Mr. Nehru yesterday answered a letter from Mr. Khrushchev which suggested talks to settle the border crisis. The Soviet Prime Minister's letter was given to Mr. Nehru by the Soviet Ambassador on Saturday. Mr. Nehru's reply was not disclosed.

THE WEATHER

From 6 a.m. to midnight

General Inference—South-westerly airflow covers Ireland as troughs of low pressure approach from the west.

Munster and South Leinster—Mainly fair but rather cloudy; moderate, locally fresh, south-westerly winds, mild.

Ulster, Connacht, North Leinster—Mainly cloudy; outbreaks of rain or drizzle reaching the north-west about midday and spreading slowly south-eastwards during the afternoon and evening; moderate or fresh south-westerly winds; mild.

Further Outlook — Outbreaks of rain or drizzle in most places to-morrow.

THE TIDES

Cobh—3.31 a.m., 4 p.m.
Rise—Cork 11ft 6ins, Cobh 10ft 3ins

To obtain the time of high water at the other southern ports, add or subtract the appropriate period as shown in the table below to or from the time of high water at Cobh

Port	Minutes	Port	Minutes
Ballycotton	−5	Dunmore	+13
Baltimore	−29	Fenit	−37
Bantry	−55	Foynes	+31
Cahirciveen	−36	Glandore	−28
Castlet'nb'nd	−26	Kenmare	−32
Clonakilty	−23	Kinsale	−12
Cork	+29	Limerick	+50
Courtmac'	−5	Schull	−45
Crookh'v'n	−25	Valentia	−56
Dingle	−18	Waterford	+37
Dungarvan	+8	Youghal	+6

Lighting-up time (Cork)—6.32 p.m.

1963

John F Kennedy dominated the news of 1963. His visit in June brought thousands of people on to the streets in Dublin, Cork and Wexford and his smiles and gracious manner further increased his popularity. Kennedy shook hands, made time for informal chats with 'ordinary' people and drank tea by the fireside. Journalists struggled with vocabulary to find enough good things to say about the US president. 'Home' was the hero, one of our own who had done so well for himself. So, when he was assassinated just five months after his momentous visit, many Irish people were genuinely saddened. It wasn't just the normal celebrity fascination involved in such an event; it was as if a family in the parish had suffered the tragic loss. As one of his relations in Wexford put it at the time: "Isn't it terrible. If we had not seen him it would not be half as bad as it is. He was such a fine young man."

Great welcome for JFK

Friday, June 28

A journey which began over a century ago ended yesterday in a great welcoming home when President John Fitzgerald Kennedy stood on the sod from which his great-grandfather emigrated to the United States 115 years ago. With the end of the joyous pilgrimage, which took Mr Kennedy 6,000 miles from the gilt and glitter of his presidential court in Washington to the humble homestead in Dunganstown, the wheel had turned the full circle – the legend had become a reality.

In Wexford, in New Ross, in Dunganstown, there were fantastic scenes as the happy, smiling President repeatedly shattered the nerves of his security men by calling the people to come to him; losing himself in the crowds which swarmed around him to shake his hand as he stood chatting to young and old, rich and poor.

In Dunganstown, for the first time in a long century, the two branches of the far-flung family were once again reunited when the President kissed the cheek of his cousin, Mrs Mary Ryan, who still farms the old family smallholding, and shook the hands of 23 of his blood relations who still remain on their native heath.

John F Kennedy takes some tea with his cousin Mrs Mary Ryan and assorted onlookers at the family homestead in Dunganstown, Co Wexford.

As the President said as he partook of a cup of tea poured for him by Mrs Ryan in her farmyard: "Let us drink to the health of the Kennedys who stayed and the Kennedys who went away."

NEWS BRIEFS

Jan One of the worst blizzards in living memory exacerbates an icy spell which has gripped the country for a month. Snowdrifts of up to five feet are common in many places, water shortages in Limerick force people to use melted snow and the army is called in to bring food supplies to families in the Nire Valley, Co Waterford, who have been cut off for five weeks. (28)

May Noel Cantwell captains Manchester United to a 3-1 victory in the FA Cup final against Leicester City. Other Irish players in the winning team are John Giles, Tony Dunne and Maurice Setters. (25)

Oct A one-day strike ensues at the Dunlops factory in Cork when 90 men are suspended for taking time off without permission to watch a televised soccer match between England and the Rest of the World. (31)

Dec Session 2 of the Second Vatican Council permits Mass to be said in languages other than Latin and stresses the need for greater lay participation in the ritual.

Near hysteria erupts as The Beatles sing in Dublin

Friday, November 8

Cars were damaged and a number of people were injured, as teenage crowds pressed on the Adelphi Cinema, Middle Abbey Street, Dublin, last night, where the Liverpool vocal group, The Beatles, were making its first appearance in the country.

Amid shouts of "We want the Beatles", about 50 gardaí started to push the crowd back towards O'Connell Street, but an unruly section of the crowd resisted and tried to overturn parked cars. Some gardaí drew their batons, but their efforts to clear a way for traffic and pedestrians met with little success.

A number of girls fainted in the crush and were given medical assistance by members of the St John Ambulance Brigade. Most business firms shuttered their windows hours before the show started.

At the press reception one of the four confided: "I hope you have brought your earplugs. We always bring ours." And when the show got under way it was obvious that many in the audience had wished they had. When The Beatles were on stage the screaming reached a deafening pitch, and at times only snatches of the songs could be heard.

The Cork Examiner

CITY SPECIAL

NO. 45,189 — SATURDAY MORNING, NOVEMBER 23, 1963 — PRICE THREEPENCE

PRESIDENT KENNEDY ASSASSINATED

Wife By His Side As He Is Shot By Sniper's Bullets

A SNIPER'S bullet fired in Dallas, Texas yesterday ended the life of 46 years old John Fitzgerald Kennedy, 36th President of the United States, and plunged the whole world into mourning. The assassin shot and killed the President as he drove in an open car beside his wife Jacqueline.

The gunman presumably used a rifle with a telescopic sight. One was found nearby.

Shots rang out as the President's motorcade passed through the city's main business section. President Kennedy collapsed face down in the car.

Mrs. Kennedy threw herself over her stricken husband, crying "oh, no." She cradled his bloody head in her arms as the driver sped to hospital.

The car drove to Parkland Hospital, where the President died 25 minutes after the shooting. Governor John Connally of Texas, also in the car, was hit by shots and is critically ill.

Vice-President Lyndon B. Johnson is now President.

First Catholic President of the United States, Mr Kennedy had been in office for two years and ten months.

Police later arrested 24-year-old Lee Harvey Oswald, a Texan who defected to Russia in 1959 but returned to the U.S. last year. He is still being questioned in connection with the assassination.

Oswald was hauled screaming from a cinema after a policeman had been shot soon after the Kennedy assassination. He was said to have worked in the building from which the assassination shots were fired.

Police quoted Oswald, a wiry, blonde man, as saying: "Well, it's all over now."

The President, concerned about his unpopularity in the South over his bid to ensure civil rights for negroes, was halfway through a three-day tour of Texas to rally support for the Democratic Party and a second term for the President.

He and Mrs. Kennedy were driving from the airport to the trade mart in this centre of Conservative politics where Mr Kennedy was to have made a speech.

Reports of the actual shooting are still confused. One reporter said he heard three shots as the President's car approached a road underpass.

A senator who was in the third car behind the President said: "It seemed to me that at least two shots came from our right rear. I [illegible] about the third."

Immediately, an enormous police dragnet was ordered to catch the assassin, who may well have changed the course of history.

Police found a British .303 rifle with telescopic sights near a window in a building used by the [illegible]. Three empty cartridges [illegible] on the floor.

Later a Dallas policeman was shot dead some distance from where the President was assassinated. N.B.C. radio said a car the assassin was believed to have used for a get-away had been seized in Fort Worth, Texas, and that the suspect, Oswald, had been detained.

Oswald has a Russian wife and a child.

N.B.C. News said he had been identified as president of the pro-Castro "Fair Play for Cuba Committee."

WORLD SHOCK

The death of the President whose "New Frontier" programme and tough but realistic line with the Russians had boosted American prestige everywhere, caused grief and shock all over the world.

Other members of the Kennedy family flew to Dallas within an hour of the shooting.

An hour after he died the President's body was removed from the hospital in a tightly-curtained cream ambulance. Mrs. Kennedy was with him. She appeared dazed and in a state of shock.

Her clothes had been covered in blood as she entered the hospital with her dying husband, but she never became hysterical.

Doctors said the President was hit in the neck and head and did not regain consciousness.

He died at 1 p.m. (7 p.m. G.M.T.), the fourth American President to have been assassinated.

After the fatal shots were fired, the stricken President's Secret Service driver raced away from the scene at top speed—heading for the nearest hospital and trying to get the presidential party out of range of further gunfire.

Mr Kennedy, Governor Connally

TURN TO BACK PAGE, COL. 8

THE WEATHER

General inference—A trough of low pressure is almost stationary over Ireland.

Leinster, Munster and South Connaught—Mostly cloudy with outbreaks of rain or drizzle at times, generally light. Fresh south or southwest winds. Rather mild.

Ulster and North Connaught—Some bright intervals but generally rather cloudy with periods of rain at times. Moderate variable winds. Near average temperatures.

Further Outlook—Mainly dry at first to-morrow. Rain spreading eastwards during the evening.

THE TIDES

Cobh 5.38 a.m.; 18.3 p.m.
Sun—Cork [illegible] Sun; Cobh [illegible]

To obtain the time of high water at the other southern ports, add or subtract the appropriate period as shown in the table below to or from the time of high water at Cobh.

[illegible]	—5	Dunmore	+13
[illegible]	—39	Fenit	—37
Bantry	—35	Foynes	+31
[illegible]	—36	Glandore	—38
[illegible]	—25	Kenmare	—33
[illegible]	—27	Kinsale	—12
[illegible]	—23	Limerick	+35
Cork	+20	Schull	—46
[illegible]	—8	Valentia	—38
[illegible]	—15	Waterford	+57
Dingle	—58	Youghal	+6
[illegible]	+8		

Lighting-up Time (Cork)—4.45 p.m.

CONTENTS

Crime Brings Horror And Grief Over World

THE world reacted with horror and grief at President Kennedy's assassination yesterday. The general mood was summed up by Italy's President, Antonio Segni, who said: "The execrable attack which has cut down President Kennedy's young life is a crime against all mankind."

He added: "His figure will remain in history as a strenuous defender of liberty, peace and justice."

Negotiations for a new Italian government were suspended as a sign of mourning.

Cardinal Spellman of New York [illegible] shaking with emotion said in Rome that he was "shocked and grief-stricken." President Kennedy's death was "a great loss to the country and to the world."

In **Paris**, President de Gaulle —who has himself survived several assassination attempts— said "President Kennedy died like a soldier, under fire, for his duty and in the service of his country. I salute this great example and this great memory."

In **Ottawa**, Canadian Prime Minister Mr Lester Pearson, told a shocked House of Commons, "the world can ill afford at this time to lose a man of his courage. It is a tragedy not only for his family but for all of us." The House adjourned until Monday as a mark of respect.

MOSCOW REACTION

Moscow: The Soviet radio broke into its programme to make the following announcement: "Comrades, radio listeners, we have interrupted our broadcast because of a sorrowful report which has just been received from New York."

It then gave the news of the shooting of President Kennedy.

It did not resume its normal programme later but began broadcasting solemn organ music.

Mr. Gromyko, Soviet Foreign Minister, telephoned U.S. Ambassador Foy Kohler at midnight "to express his shock and great sympathy towards the American people," an American Embassy spokesman said.

The spokesman said he thought Mr. Khrushchev's condolences would be published this morning.

United Nations: Diplomats from 111 nations stood in silence as the U.N. General Assembly adjourned in token of the world's grief.

Bonn: Former Chancellor Adenauer sent a telegram to Mrs. Kennedy saying her husband "will go down in the history of mankind"

TURN TO BACK PAGE, COL. 5

Mrs. Jacqueline Kennedy standing at his side, Vice-President Lyndon Johnson (55) raises his hand as he takes the oath as President of the United States on board the Presidential aircraft at Dallas Airfield, Texas, last night.

The casket containing the body of President Kennedy is shown here being moved to a navy ambulance from the Presidential plane at Andrews Air Force Base, Washington, last night. Mrs. Kennedy is behind on an elevator.
(A.P. wire photo)

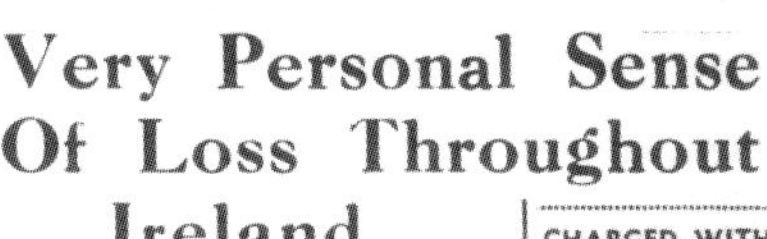

Very Personal Sense Of Loss Throughout Ireland

A DEEP sense of very personal loss followed the terrible shock of President Kennedy's death here in Ireland, where the first American President to visit our shores was regarded with love and affection as a "true Irishman" as much as First Citizen of the United States.

Throughout the country, but especially in those places which he visited during his triumphal journey in June, people stood silent, stricken by the awful news, and then rushed for a special edition of an evening paper or to watch or listen to Telefis and Radio Eireann.

In **Cork**, the people gave him the freedom of their city and their hearts with a demonstrative warmth which was perhaps unparalleled in his return to the home of his people. They welcomed him with the honour due the leader of a free world, but with a fierce pride of race. They welcomed him for himself, because he was young and capable and because the aura of his personality reached out to bind them to him with a sense of vital living affection.

"ONLY A BOY"

"I remember the anxious face of an old lady, straining for a glimpse of John Kennedy when Cork took him to its heart," writes a "Cork Examiner" reporter, one of a team who covered his visit. "She said: 'Ah sure he's only a boy.'"

That now is how Cork grieves. This loss for them was a private thing, the death of a young man who in an incredibly short space of a few hours made them his friend.

The tumult and wild enthusiasm of that moment when John Kennedy moved triumphantly through the acclamation of the thousands who lined the streets of the city was sadly contrasted last evening in the quiet brought by the news of his death.

Groups of people stood silently watching in city shops the television tribute to the late President or gathered in groups to read a special edition of the "Evening Echo" which brought the first fragmentary but so irrefutable tidings of his death.

Long queues formed in this office to purchase the edition and read of his assassination.

A young girl said to the writer: "I find it hard to believe."

The Lord Mayor of Cork, **Mr. Sean McCarthy**, T.D., said last night: "The death of President Kennedy who was so recently amongst us and made a freeman of our city, has shocked us deeply. We extend to his widow, his family and to the American nation our most heartfelt sympathy and prayers."

Ald. Sean Casey, T.D., who was Lord Mayor when Mr. Kennedy

TURN TO BACK PAGE, COL. 7

BODY ARRIVES IN CAPITAL

"I will do my best. That is all I can do." President Lyndon Johnson pledged last night as he arrived in Washington with the body of his murdered predecessor.

Thousands of people stood silently behind the barriers at Andrews Air Base as the bronze coffin bearing the President's body was lowered gently from the big silver-and-blue air force plane which brought it from Dallas, Texas.

Grim-faced, Mr. Johnson, Vice-President to Mr. Kennedy, went to the microphone to address the nation.

"We have suffered a loss that cannot be weighed," he said. "I ask for your help and God's."

A guard of honour carried the bronze coffin from the air force jet plane as a mourning nation watched solemnly on television screens.

Mrs. Kennedy and the President's brother, Attorney-General Robert Kennedy, accompanied the coffin as it was transferred in a naval ambulance to the naval hospital at nearby Bethesda, Maryland, where it was to remain overnight.

It was announced that all U.S. Navy ships and shore stations throughout the world would fire salutes at half-hourly intervals from 8 a.m. to sunset to-day in honour of the dead President.

CHARGED WITH PATROLMAN'S MURDER

Oswald was charged with the murder of patrolman J. D. Tippett after witnesses had identified him.

Police said it had not been established that he was Mr. Kennedy's killer. But at the time of the assassination he was in the schoolboy depository from where the shots were fired, police said. Oswald fired a shot from a gun when police seized him. He was disarmed. A policeman was hit in the struggle.

POPE TO OFFER MASS

HIS HOLINESS POPE PAUL prayed last night "that the sacrifice of John Kennedy may advance the cause which he promoted and defended for the freedom of peoples and the peace of the world."

The Pope said he would offer his Mass to-day "for the peace of President Kennedy's soul, for the comfort of those who mourn his death, and that love and not hatred shall reign among humanity."

DEEPLY BEREAVED

"We are deeply bereaved by the tragic and sad news of the assassination of the President of the United States, John Fitzgerald Kennedy and the grave wounding of Governor Connally, and we are profoundly saddened for such a shameful crime which, through the person of its chief, has struck a great and civil nation, and for the sorrow which it inflicts upon Mrs. Kennedy, their children and their family.

"We deplore this event with all our heart. We express the hope that the death of this great statesman shall not harm the American people, but reinforce their moral and civic sense, and strengthen their feelings of nobility and concord and we pray to God that the sacrifice of John Kennedy may advance the cause which he promoted and defended for the freedom of peoples and the peace of the world.

GREAT WISDOM

"He was the first Catholic President of the United States. We remember having had the honour of a visit by him and having recognised in him a great wisdom and high regard for the well being of mankind."

TRAGIC WIDOW AT 34

Jacqueline Kennedy, tragically widowed yesterday at the age of 34, met her husband while working as a Washington newspaper's "inquiring camera girl."

The daughter of a New York banker, Mr John Vernon Bouvier, she was educated privately in Connecticut, at Vassar, and also spent a year at the Sorbonne

CHILDREN NOT TOLD

President Kennedy's two children, Caroline (five) and John (nearly three) have so far not been told of their father's death, a White House spokesman said last night.

He said the children were at the White House in the care of their nurse.

before graduating from George Washington University in 1951.

She speaks excellent French, and is fluent in Italian and Spanish.

Slim and elegant, with soft brown hair and eyes, she has been a leader in the world of fashion. In 1961, when she accompanied her husband to France, Parisians went wild over her.

For all her easy poise, she sometimes appeared a little uncomfortable in the limelight.

A skilled horsewoman, her tastes are for music, reading, painting and other intellectual pursuits.

She married Mr. Kennedy in Newport, Rhode Island on September 12, 1953. She has two children, Caroline (born in 1957) and John Fitzgerald Junior (born in 1960). A son, Patrick, born prematurely earlier this year, died shortly afterwards.

FIRST IN LINE FOR THE PRESIDENCY

Mr John McCormack, 71 years old speaker of the House of Representatives, is now first in line for the presidency.

A Secret Service guard was posted at his office an hour after President Kennedy's death.

Like the late President, the white-haired speaker is Catholic and comes from Massachusetts.

He would succeed to the White House if, for any reason, President Johnson did not serve out the remaining 13 months of Mr. Kennedy's term.

Story of President's Career on page 14.

Whole Irish Nation Mourns —Mr. de Valera

SPEAKING in a recorded message to the nation, broadcast by Telefis Eireann last night, President de Valera spoke of the Irish people's sorrow.

"You will all have heard of the tragic death of President Kennedy," he said. I am here simply to give public expression to our common sorrow. We sympathise with all the people of the United States, but in particular with his grief-stricken wife and the other members of his family.

"During his recent visit here we came to regard the President as one of ourselves, though always aware that he was the head of the greatest nation in the world to-day.

"We were proud of him being of our race, and we were convinced that through his fearless leadership the United States would continue increasing its stature amongst the nations of the world and its power of maintaining world peace.

Our consolation is that he died in a noble cause, and we pray that God will give to the United States another such leader."

MESSAGE TO MRS. KENNEDY

President de Valera has sent the following telegram to Mrs. John F. Kennedy.

"The whole Irish people mourn in sympathy with you. Their hearts go out to you and we pray that the soul of your husband who had become so dear to us here may now be with God in Heaven and that the Holy Spirit may give you consolation in this hour of terrible sorrow for you."

The President sent the following telegram to President Lyndon B. Johnson.

"The whole Irish nation grieves at the death of President Kennedy. During his visit here we

TURN TO BACK PAGE, COL. 8

A Secret Service man holds the rifle with which it is believed the President was shot.

1964

In Ireland, 1964 saw the passing of two of the nation's literary giants. While Sean O'Casey is considered a more important literary figure than Brendan Behan, the latter's death was afforded more coverage by the *Examiner.* As can be seen from the bank holiday report, Ireland also had enough cars by then to make complaints about heavy traffic.

Overseas, the Gulf of Tonkin incident had forces from North Vietnam and the United States clash in what would provide the prompt for Lyndon Johnson to send more troops to the area at the start of what would be the precursor to an ill-fated war.

At the time, events in Cyprus were still more of a worry as Irish troops formed part of a UN force to keep peace between the Turkish and Greek communities.

In sport, the Tipperary team that won the All-Ireland championship that year are recognised as one of the greatest hurling teams ever. Their success came in the midst of a golden era for the county which saw them reach five All-Ireland finals between 1960 and 1965, and win four of them. The 1964 victory was also important in that it gave Tipperary one more championship than rivals Cork, and meant a seventh medal for John Doyle who would go on to equal Christy Ring's record the following year.

NEWS BRIEFS

Mar Scientists in the United States warn that rising temperatures has led to the melting of the polar ice caps and a rise in sea levels which may cause a problem "by the turn of the century". (13)

June Nelson Mandela, leader of the African National Congress, is jailed for life for sabotage and plotting to overthrow the South African government. (14)

Oct Khrushchev is deposed as leader of the Soviet Union and replaced by Leonid Brezhnev. (15)

Brendan Behan dies in coma

Saturday, March 21

Brendan Behan's struggle for life ended at 8.00 last night. His wife was at his bedside in the Meath Hospital, Dublin, but the playwright – 41 only last night – never knew: he was still in the coma which overtook him on St Patrick's Day. In and out of hospitals in recent years, Behan was admitted for the last time earlier this month with jaundice and diabetes.

Playwright, minstrel, songster and raconteur, Behan became a national figure following the stage success of *The Quare Fellow* in 1956. The fame brought to him by his plays was accompanied by a degree of notoriety resulting from his drinking escapades. He himself once described his recreations as drinking, talking and swimming.

In August, 1960, he said he had "beaten the bottle" but this image of a "reformed character" was never permanently etched – later that year he interrupted *The Hostage* in New York after drinking champagne.

The Irish-Americans banned him from the St Patrick's Day parade in New York in 1961 but he turned up – coatless, hatless and gripping a shillelagh.

He was the complete extrovert himself, and was ever ready to burst into song. He had a commanding knowledge of French, which he wrote with great skill, and he was also a fine Irish speaker.

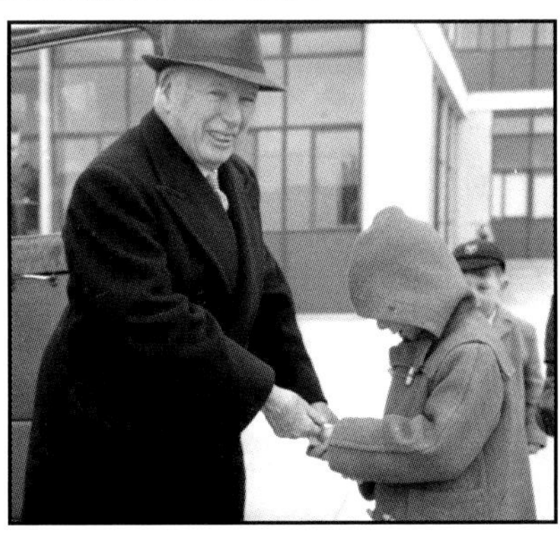

Charlie Chaplin signs an autograph in Cork Airport before heading for a family holiday in Kerry.

Tipp indeed the Premier County

Monday, September 7 **Tipperary 5-13, Kilkenny 2-8**

Consistently good, occasionally brilliant, incomparably dedicated, Tipperary at Croke Park yesterday crushed Kilkenny in a victory which achieved a record 20 All-Ireland senior hurling titles for a now undeniably Premier County. It was, despite the inference of the score, for three-quarters of an hour an exciting and inhumanly hard game in which fitness and courage had as much a part as hurling. If, with 15 minutes remaining, Tipperary held a 3-12 to 1-7 lead, it was only because they had been pushed to as near the peak of their powers as they would have hoped.

There was this quality of success about Tipperary yesterday which seemed proof against set back, an aura of invincibility even when Kilkenny were most dangerous. Always the Munster champions possessed reserves of hurling and determination and almost inevitably, it seemed, they wore down their opponents. Although with nine minutes remaining Kilkenny had bridged a distressing gap to the size of seven points, even their optimists in the crowd of 71,282 could not have been too hopeful of victory. Instead came the last lash of two goals scored by Doney Nealon in the 54th and 55th minutes followed by Jimmy Doyle's point and a humbling moment for the champions.

Tipperary: J O'Donoghue, J Doyle, M Maher (Lonergan), K Carey, M Burns, A Wall, M Murphy, T English, M Roche, J Doyle, L Kiely (Devaney), M Keating, D Nealon, J McKenna, S McLoughlin.

The Cork Examiner

NO. 45,404 — TUESDAY MORNING, AUGUST 4, 1964 — PRICE THREEPENCE

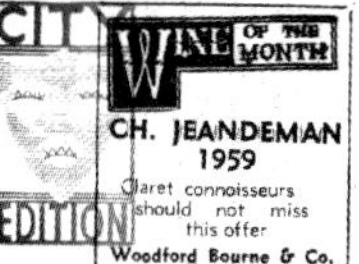

Washington Plans Diplomatic Protest Over Destroyer Incident Off North Vietnam

U.S. FORCES STRENGTHENED

"Destroy Any New Attackers," Says Johnson

PRESIDENT JOHNSON announced yesterday that he had increased naval and air power off the coast of North Vietnam and had ordered U.S. forces there to destroy any new attackers.

The President called reporters to his office to disclose the moves following Sunday's unsuccessful attack by three torpedo boats on the U.S. destroyer Maddox about 30 miles off North Vietnam.

It was announced in Washington later that the U.S. intended to make a diplomatic protest over the "unprovoked attack" on the destroyer.

President Johnson issued four specific instructions to the Navy. They were:—

1.—Continue patrols in the Gulf of Tonkin, where Sunday's attack took place.

2.—Double the force there by sending an additional destroyer to patrol with the Maddox.

3.—Provide a combat air patrol over the destroyers.

4.—Issue orders to the commanders of the destroyers and the

President Johnson

aircraft to retaliate in force in the event of an attack in international waters and to retaliate with the objective not only of driving off the hostile force but of destroying it.

The President said his instructions were conveyed on Sunday to the appropriate authorities, and he added: "They will be carried out."

The President declined to answer questions and dismissed reporters by saying that was all he had to tell them.

There was an air of calm at the White House, and officials said the attack was not regarded as a major crisis which called for anything but retaliatory action in the event of future threats to U.S. ships and planes in the area. The U.S. Seventh Fleet has been patrolling the area for some time, and the President's new instructions made it clear that the force would stay there with new strength.

The Navy announced later that the destroyer Turner Joy had been assigned to join the Maddox in patrolling the Tonkin Gulf and that planes from the carrier Ticonderoga would fly protective cover for the two ships.

U.S. PROTEST

The U.S. State Department announced later that the United States planned to make a diplomatic protest over the "unprovoked attack" on the American destroyer.

The Department's spokesman

TURN TO BACK PAGE, COL. 4

PEACE PLEDGE BY MR. K

Mr. Khrushchev yesterday pledged himself to spare no effort to get rid of international tension. The conclusion of the Moscow partial nuclear test ban treaty, he said, had fostered the easing of international tension, but countries must not rest content with what had been achieved. New steps to reduce tension should be possible, Mr. Khruschev said, because of the international confidence built up since the treaty was signed a year ago.

Agreements in "various international spheres" should be possible, he said, but did not elaborate.

Mr. Khrushchev was answering questions from "Pravda" and "Izvestia" and his comments were broadcast in the Moscow Radio home service.

Mr. Khrushchev called for the "peaceful normalisation" of the German problem. Without this, it would be difficult to make a start on general and complete disarmament, he said.

He also urged conclusion of an international agreement to outlaw the use of force in settling territorial and border disputes.

The Soviet Union would not lag behind in working to rid the world of international tension and to help consolidate peace, he said.

NIGERIA RAISES IMPORT DUTIES

The Nigerian Government has revised certain customs and excise tariffs with effect from yesterday to "remove a number of anomalies" an Nigerian Information Ministry statement said.

Duties are increased on some imported products, such as beer, bicycles, radio and television sets, carpets, jewellery, fuel oils and paints to encourage and protect local manufacturing industries.

BEATLES FILM A SELL-OUT

The Beatles' film, "A Hard Day's Night," is already a sellout in 43 cities in the U.S., distributor James Velde announced in New York yesterday.—(A.P.)

TURKEY PROTESTS TO GREECE

Turkey has protested to Greece over an alleged concentration of Greek forces near the Turkish border, a Greek Foreign Ministry spokesman said in Athens yesterday.

He said the protest was considered "unacceptable" by the Greek government and Turkey was informed that all movements of the Greek armed forces had been "duly notified" to the North Atlantic Treaty Organisation headquarters in Paris.

The spokesman said the Turkish protest was handed over to the Greek charge d'affaires in Ankara.

It is believed in Athens to concern the deployment near the Greco-Turkish border along the River Evros (Maritsa) of Greek armoured units.

Greek military sources in northern Greece claimed last week that the Turks had concentrated on their own side of the frontier about three infantry regiments.

SHOOTING IN CYPRUS

Sporadic firing has been going on throughout Kyrenia mountain range, a United Nations spokesman reported in Nicosia yesterd[ay].

Shooting, he said, was taking [illegible] sides of the Kyrenia Pass, through which passes the key road, held by Turkish Cypriots, between Nicosia and Kyrenia.

CONTENTS

Alice Followers Outlawed After New Rampage

DR. KENNETH KAUNDA, Northern Rhodesian Prime Minister, yesterday outlawed the fanatical Lumpa Church sect, following a fresh rampage by its followers, resulting in at least 150 deaths.

Alice Lenshina

Declaring the sect unlawful throughout the country, he said in a broadcast he hoped to be able to revoke the ban in about a month provided he was satisfied law and order had been restored.

Followers of the sect, led by "Prophetess" Alice Lenshina, killed at least 150 people in Northern Rhodesia's Eastern Province early yesterday and troops have been flown to the area.

Dr. Kaunda told a mass rally in Lusoka yesterday: "They burned people alive."

Yesterday's order provides for up to seven years' imprisonment for anyone assisting in the management of a Lumpa Church branch or acting as a member or indicating his membership in public or attending a Lumpa Church meeting.

Mr. Kaunda said Government policy was still not to suppress the Lumpa religion.

"My Government has no quarrel with the Lumpa religion as a religion," he said. "But the events in the Chinsali district last week and the happenings in Lundazi in the past 24 hours have satisfied me

TURN TO BACK PAGE, COL. 6

FIRES AS QUEEN WATCHES POLO

Two small fires started underneath the stands adjoining Queen Elizabeth's platform at Windsor Park yesterday, while the Duke of Edinburgh was playing polo. Queen Elizabeth's car, which was parked nearby, was quickly driven away.

Earlier, the Duke damaged his open car when it scraped a gatepost as he entered the enclosure.

The royal party, which included Prince Charles and Princess Anne, watched a display of Canadian cutting-in horses, and met the rider, afterwards. The Queen presented the prizes.

DROWNS WHEN CANOE CAPSIZES

A visitor, Mr. David Mole, of Nuneaton, Warwicks, was drowned last night when a canoe in which he was an occupant capsized at Llanaber, Barmouth, Merionethshire.

CONGO REBELS IN NEW ADVANCES

Insurgent forces were reported advancing in the Stanleyville and Bukavu regions of the Congo last night as the National Army completed a mopping up operation against other groups in the north-west of the country.

Reports reaching usually reliable sources in Leopoldville said the situation in Stanleyville, the Congo's third largest city, was tense as rebels attacked the town of Wanie Rukula, about 30 miles to the south-east.

United Nations headquarters in Leopoldville told eight of its staff in the Stanleyville area to evacuate at their discretion into Stanleyville itself.

EUROPEANS KILLED

Unconfirmed reports said four Europeans had been killed in the rebel-held town of Kalima, a mining centre in Maniema province due west of Central Kivu.

But diplomatic observers are finding it difficult to assess the importance of the insurgent advances as there is no clear picture of the numbers involved.

Both the Bukavu and the Stanleyville areas gave Premier Moise Tshombe a rousing welcome when he visited them a week ago.

SOS FROM MANONO

The rebel-threatened town of Manono, 350 miles north of Elisabethville, has sent an SOS to Air Congo asking for immediate evacuation of women and children, officials of the national airline said yesterday.

Reports received in Elisabethville said the rebels were now within 40 miles of the important Katanga mining town.

SOUTH AFRICAN POLICE RAID UNION OFFICES

Security police raided the offices of the multi-racial South African Congress of Trade Unions in Johannesburg, yesterday, a Congress spokesman stated.

They took away 10,000 leaflets which, the spokesman said, were printed for purposes of organising workers.

In Pretoria security police, for the second time in a week, raided the home of the Chairman of the Pretoria branch of the Liberal Party, Mr. Walter Hain. After a 30-minute search of the house and grounds the police left, taking nothing.—Reuter.

ANNA SEEKS HER BLACKBIRD

Fiery Oscar-winning actress Anna Magnani last night searched a Rome square near her penthouse apartment for her talking blackbird "Tutu" which escaped on Sunday.

She had received many telephone calls in response to an appeal she made through the newspapers but none of them was genuine. "I can't bear to think that he may be dead," she said.

August Monday holidaymakers on the beach at Fountainstown, Co. Cork.

Weather Gave Holidaymakers A Great Break

YESTERDAY'S glorious sunshine, following on that of Sunday, gave week-end holidaymakers one of their greatest breaks for many years and, despite heavy traffic and a few fatalities, the overall accident figures are expected to be lower than those of previous August week-ends.

Yesterday morning dull, hazy skies slightly delayed the trip to the beaches for many, but from early afternoon traffic on all roads was extremely heavy. Last night there were again reports of busy roads all over the country as the throngs of holidaymakers made their trek back home. The worst traffic in the south was on the Cork-Youghal road, with thousands heading for this popular resort where last night there was the additional attraction of two of the country's most popular and greatest showbands.

Kinsale Regatta, which has always been a very popular attraction during August week-end, attracted thousands of tourists and natives, and late yesterday afternoon cars were bumper to bumper as the crowds poured in.

The Cork-Crosshaven road was also extremely taxed, with many of the late travellers choosing the nearest strand to avail of the brilliant weather. There were 40 busloads to the resort yesterday bringing some 2,000 people, and it is estimated that double that number travelled in private cars and on motor cycles.

C.I.E. had put on extra services to the various resorts and a spokesman for the company said last night that their expectations had been fully realised. During the two days some 8,000 people availed of the regular road and rail services.

On the Ennis-Limerick road 940 cars were said to be leaving the

TURN TO BACK PAGE, COL. 1

SNOW IN POLAND

More than two inches of snow fell on Sunday night in the Tatra Mountains in Southern Poland, the Polish Press agency reported last night.

Police Attacked By Youths

"Mod" and "Rocker" trouble broke out on the main sands at Margate (Kent) last night.

Rival gangs chased each other backwards and forwards across the beach. At one time about 20 youths were engaged in a hard fight.

Police officers standing by ran along the beach with drawn truncheons to break up the fight and arrested at least one youth.

As he was being taken away by two officers, they were set upon by about six other "Mods" but the officers defied them and put their prisoner into a police van.

For 90 minutes scores of police using dogs kept the gangs on the move on opposite sides of the sea front. A police spokesman said "the position is still explosive."

CORK YOUTH'S FATAL COLLAPSE

Shortly after midnight last night a Cork youth, Denis Quinn, of 12 Geraldine Place, collapsed at Lapps' Quay, Cork, while walking home from a dance with his brother James, and was dead on admission to the South Infirmary, to where he was removed by fire brigade ambulance.

Quinn, who was aged 17, was a member of the Cork minor basketball team and played soccer with Blackrock.

MARRIAGE WILL LINK NOBEL PRIZE FAMILIES

Two Nobel prize-winning families are to be linked by marriage.

They are also the only families in which the prize has gone to fathers and sons.

In 1915, Sir William Bragg and his son, Sir Lawrence Bragg, won the prize for Physics. In 1937, Sir George Thomson won it—also for Physics—31 years after his father, Sir Joseph Thomson, had got the same award.

Now, Sir George Thomson has announced in Auckland, New Zealand, that his younger son is to marry the younger daughter of "my very good friend, Sir Lawrence Bragg."

"But don't ask me if their children will be physicists," Sir George said.

DAM THREAT TO 2,000 PEOPLE

The entire population of Harvey—a hamlet of 2,000 people 100 miles south of Perth, Western Australia — was evacuated today when floodwaters threatened to burst a dam and engulf them.

Irish Beauty Queen In U.S. Contest

GIRLS from Britain and Ireland led another invasion of international beauty queens into the U.S. just as the first group was preparing to leave.

The first Miss International competitors to arrive yesterday were Miss Ireland, Miss Wales and Miss Scotland.

Miss Wales, 18-year-old Pamela Mary Martin, a secretary, of 345 Carhilly Road, Cardiff, arrived with Miss Scotland, Miss Dorothy Smallman, a 21-year-old model, from 26 Manor Road, Lanark.

Miss Martin expressed a desire to see Harlem while she was in New York, declaring: "I saw some pictures of it in a magazine and I want to see where all those brawls are going on." Observers predicted that pageant officials would discourage her.

Miss Ireland, 19-year-old singer Joan Power, of 21 Hawthorn Road, Bray, Co. Wicklow, flew in for a two-day stay in New York before going on to California.

She told reporters at Kennedy International Airport that she was not optimistic about her chances of winning the title. Irish representatives, she said with a smile, were selected not so much for their figures and looks as because "we speak fluent Gaelic and know all about Irish politics".

Entombed Miners Can Hear Drill

THE noise of the rescue drill boring down to save nine miners entombed for a week in a limestone mine at Champagnole, France, reached the trapped men yesterday afternoon.

A rescue official said that Andre Martinet, foreman of the entombed shift, had told the rescue party he and his workmates could hear the drill quite distinctly.

If all goes well, the drill will reach them to-night, the officials said.

Engineers working on the Forez One drill said they had reached a depth of 61 metres (200 feet) at 5 p.m. (I.S.T.) yesterday and had about another 21 metres (70 feet) to go before reaching the roof of the gallery.

SLOW AND DIFFICULT

They cautioned that the last few feet would be slow and difficult for technical reasons.

The abrasive sludge used in the drilling process will have to be pumped out of the 23-inch escape

TURN TO BACK PAGE, COL. 2

"A Matter For The U.N."

Mr Harold Wilson, returning yesterday from a conference of European opposition leaders in Sweden, said he was cheered by support he received for the suggestion of international control of second-hand arms.

Arriving at London Airport, he said: "This problem was raised with Khrushchev this June and my colleagues in Sweden whole-heartedly endorsed it. There are unscrupulous people who buy up second-hand arms, such as fighters, bombers, tanks, and sell them to all sorts of people.

"Something must be done to regulate this and I think there must be proper control with guarantees. This must be a matter for the United Nations."

NEW RIGHTS LAWS 'WILL CHANGE U.S.'

Mr. Carl Rowan, director of the United States Information Agency, who is himself a negro, claimed yesterday that the new civil rights laws "would change America" and bring "new opportunities" to the negro minority.

He hit out at the press which he said had given the impression that Rochester and Harlem had a "monopoly on racial prejudice and violence."

"We are trying, as no society ever tried before, to build into our system enough safeguards to ensure that one man's prejudice cannot deprive another man of that to which he is entitled . . ."

The final contingent of state police were yesterday ordered to leave Rochester, following the withdrawal on Sunday of about 1,500 national guardsmen (territorials) brought in at the height of racial rioting there two weeks ago. Local police are now solely responsible for law and order in the town, which has remained quiet for the past week.—Reuter.

BODIES BROUGHT DOWN FROM EIGER AFTER YEAR

Swiss Alpine guides braved snowstorms on the Eiger this week-end to bring down the bodies of three Britons, who died climbing the mountain's north-west wall a year ago.

Long searches failed when the climbers, Victor Tilley, Peter Mitchell and Tony Ansett vanished in July, 1963, but a week ago a team of German Alpinists found the bodies in a hollow 9,000 feet up.

Police said yesterday the bodies were buried immediately the guides brought them to Grindelwald.

Woman Killed In Gap Of Dunloe Pony-Trap Crash

A TRAGIC accident occurred at the Gap of Dunloe, Killarney, yesterday when a pony trap was involved in a collision with another trap and five people were thrown on to the road, one woman being killed and three other people injured.

Shortly after midnight last night six people were injured in a collision between a car and a van near Ballincollig, Co. Cork.

Dead is Mrs. Louise Baker, Richmond, Ballyvolane Road, Cork, and injured are Mr. Maurice Lyons, 33 Victor Street, Ravenhill Road, Belfast; his wife, Mrs. Mary Lyons, and the driver of the trap, 17 years old Pat Healy of Derrycarna, Black Valley. All the injured are in St. Catherine's Hospital in Tralee and last night they were stated to be satisfactory.

These injured and the dead woman were in one trap and had come through the Gap. They were only a mile from Gearhamee, where they were to embark on a boat trip through the lakes.

It appeared that a dog snapped at the pony, causing it to shy and bolt. It crashed into a stationary trap further down the hill.

Some minutes after the accident, two sisters of the dead woamn, Miss A. McNamara of Cork, and Mrs. Cassidy of Dublin, came on the scene in another trap. The three ladies had been staying at the Lake Hotel in Killarney since last Saturday.

Mr. and Mrs. Lyons and a daughter were members of a C.I.E. bus tour and had booked into the Great Southern Hotel on Sunday, being due to remain until tomorrow. Miss Maura Lyons, their daughter, was uninjured.

Dr. William O'Sullivan gave medical aid at the scene of the accident and Rev. Fr. O'Callaghan, C.C., gave spiritual assistance.

SIX INJURED

Six people were rushed to hospital in Cork shortly after midnight last night following a collision between a van and a car on a stretch of road near Ballincollig. The vehicles, which were going in opposite directions, were both badly damaged, but no one was seriously hurt.

Injured are the driver of the van, Mr. Denis O'Regan, Aglish, Coachford, and the occupants of the car, Mr. and Mrs. Lucey, Mr. and Mrs. O'Brien and Miss Mary O'Connell, all of Clasels, near Ballincollig.

Within minutes of the crash, the

TURN TO BACK PAGE, COL. 3

Dead Woman In Wood

Police are investigating the death of a young coloured woman whose body was found in a wood near Bishopbriggs (Lanarks) yesterday. The woman is thought to be in her twenties.

A post-mortem examination was being carried out last night in Glasgow by Glasgow police surgeon Dr. James Imrie.

In a statement early yesterday, Chief Superintendent Muncie of Bishopbriggs said that the post-mortem examination had revealed that the woman died from natural causes.

He would not be disclosing the girl's identity until her parents, who lived abroad, had been informed of her death. The girl had been a nurse in a Glasgow hospital.

1965

The biggest news item in Ireland was the return of Roger Casement's body from Britain. Casement had been arrested on Good Friday, 1916, as he attempted to import arms from Germany to support the Easter Rising. He was subsequently tried for treason and hanged. Still a powerful figure in memories of an event which had happened in Dublin less than 50 years previously, huge crowds turned out as his coffin was borne through the city on a tricolour-draped gun carriage. More-modern heroes, The Rolling Stones, created news when gigs on a mini-Irish tour caused great excitement among 'frenzied teenagers'. Just like the Beatles' concert in Dublin two years previously, Gardaí had to be called in Cork when the audience began to get out of hand.

In domestic music Brendan Boyer and the Royal Showband had a huge hit with 'The Hucklebuck', while in sports Ireland's great steeplechaser Arkle ran to his second of three victories in a row in the Gold Cup at Cheltenham.

NEWS BRIEFS

Jan Tributes to Jimmy O'Dea continued to pour in last night, as his many friends mourned Ireland's most famous and best-loved comedian, who died yesterday morning in Dublin, aged 66. (8)

Mar More than 25,000 people yesterday wrote a new page in the turbulent racial history of America's Deep South, when they marched with Negro leader Dr Martin Luther King to Alabama's capital in a massive 'freedom' demonstration. (26)

May Dublin priest Desmond McCarthy calls for peace as skirmishes between rival groups of dockers lead to one man's death and several injuries. (22)

June First official American offensive in Vietnam sees troops in action against the Viet Cong near Saigon. (29)

Rolling Stones create frenzy at Savoy

Saturday, January 9

Police were called to Cork's Savoy Cinema last night when frenzied teenagers dashed from their seats and tried to climb on to the stage during a concert by the British beat group, The Rolling Stones.

The Stones' 20-minute, eight-song, top of the bill spot was drowned by the screaming teenagers. The group, long-haired and untidy, and the bane of mums and dads in Britain because of this, took the theatre by storm from the moment they stepped on to the stage at 10.35pm. But after four numbers, girls dashed from their seats and swarmed to the organ pit screaming and waving. Two of them jumped over the rail and entered the stage door.

Another, a young man, climbed on the cinema organ but moved when Savoy manager Jimmy Campbell ordered him back. But when he again moved to the organ, uniformed Gardaí were called and marched him out of the cinema.

The Rolling Stones, the biggest pop attraction ever to appear in Cork and second only to The Beatles in the beat business, sang through it all even though they were almost impossible to hear. At times they were pelted with programmes and jelly beans.

The Stones' appeal and undoubted impact last night was due as much to their reputation as anything, for only in the tremendous finale 'It's All Over' were they really impressive. That of course is a man's viewpoint.

The Rolling Stones at the Savoy, Cork.

Mighty Arkle humbles Mill House

Friday, 12 March

Ireland's wonder horse Arkle swept to new heights and, cheered by a delighted crowd, once again humbled England's pride, Mill House, to win his second Gold Cup at Cheltenham yesterday. Before the last three fences had been crossed Arkle began his remorseless annihilation of Mill House, steadily building up a lead that amounted to 20 lengths by the time he cruised majestically past the post.

"What is inside my horse? It must be jet engines," laughed the proudest of owners, Anne, Duchess of Westminster. "Talk about those jet engines at London airport – wasn't that simply wonderful."

Yesterday Arkle not only confirmed his supremacy but became the record prize winner under NH rules as far as England and Ireland are concerned. This was his 19th victory and the total of £36,818 places him well above former record holder, retired National winner Team Spirit.

The Cork Examiner

NO. 45,580 MONDAY MORNING, MARCH 1, 1965 PRICE THREEPENCE

Dramatic Moment As Cortege Halts At G.P.O. To Honour Other Fallen 1916 Leaders

THOUSANDS PAY TRIBUTE

The scene outside the G.P.O., headquarters of the 1916 Rising, as the patriot's remains are borne on a gun-carriage to the Pro-Cathedral.

Roger Casement's Remains Borne Through Dublin

TO the measured tread of slow-marching feet, the beat of muffled drums, and the solemn strains of the "Dead March in Saul," the remains of Sir Roger David Casement were yesterday borne with full ceremony from Arbour Hill Military Church, past silent thousands lining the Dublin streets, to the Pro-Cathedral in the heart of the capital.

There were many poignant scenes during this tribute nearly 50 years delayed. Little children to whom the patriot is yet but a name were lifted head-high to see the Tricolour-draped gun carriage; many of the soldiers wore the blue berets denoting Congo service, in fitting tribute to a man who had done so much for the oppressed people of that country, and as the cortege passed the G.P.O., it halted for a moment in dramatic, silent tribute to the patriot's other fallen comrades of 1916.

The ritual took place in bright sunshine which hinted at spring, and seemed to epitomise a season of new beginnings and new hopes.

The normally quiet Sunday afternoon atmosphere was absent, as for an hour before the ceremony, 600 gardai drafted into the city shepherded the orderly crowds to their positions along the route.

Breakdown vehicles were used to tow away parked cars blocking the route, and rope barriers were set up.

Flags swayed at half-mast in the gentle breeze. A solemn hush descended on the city.

Around the Church of the Sacred Heart at Arbour Hill, the silent, bare-headed crowd heard the murmured responses to the brief prayers recited by Rev. Patrick Duffy, Head Chaplain to the Forces.

Then the coffin, borne on the shoulders of ten tall N.C.O.s, was carried with measured tread from its bier, through the church, and out to the waiting gun carriage.

MOURNING BANDS

Ten colonels, under Colonel Brian Moran, Army H.Q., the plain green of their right sleeves broken by black arm bands, the hilts of their swords ribboned with black crepe, were the pall bearers. As they flanked the jeep-drawn gun carriage, the 600 soldiers in the procession moved off at a slow pace to the music of the "Dead March in Saul."

The main escort consisted of a 450-strong infantry battalion made up of three companies, drawn from the Southern and Western Commands and the Curragh Training Camp.

The Colour Party was in charge of Second Lieut. Michael Lucey, 2nd Infantry Battalion, with a colour escort of 27 in charge of Lieut. Seamus Duffy, 5th Battalion.

The band of the Curragh Training Camp, with muffled drums, played ceremonial music. Then came five jeeps laden with wreaths from the President, Taoiseach, Government Ministers, the Army, the Gardai, and many organisations.

Lilies and Tricolour ribbons predominated, and the green, white and orange motif was repeated in various patterns and floral arrangements.

After the jeeps came the battalion escort with their rifles reversed, and it was noted that

TURN TO BACK PAGE, COL. 6

Lenten Pastorals

The Lenten pastorals of the bishops of Ireland will be found on pages 4 and 5.

His Eminence Cardinal Conway, Archbishop of Armagh and Primate of All Ireland, will issue his pastoral letter at a later date.

Dispute Stops R.E., T.E. News Bulletins

IN a statement last night Radio Eireann stated that owing to the withdrawal of services without notice by members of the N.U.J. employed in the news division of Radio Eireann it was not possible to broadcast the regular news bulletins from Radio Eireann and Telefis Eireann last night.

Asked what would be the position of to-day's broadcast on the Casement funeral a spokesman said: "I cannot comment on what might happen."

The dispute is believed to have arisen over the employment of a lecturer at U.C.D., to give a commentary on the removal of Roger Casement's remains to the Pro-Cathedral yesterday.

The National Union of Journalists (Dublin Radio Branch)

TURN TO BACK PAGE, COL. 2

AUSTRIA'S PRESIDENT DIES

President Adolf Schaerf, chief architect of Austria's post-war independence, died in Vienna last night, aged 74. A liver failure had followed a three-week bout of influenza.

Dr. Schaerf, former Socialist Party leader, became President in May, 1957. He was regarded as chief architect of the State Treaty that ended the Allied occupation and restored Austrian independence after World War II.

Son of a Viennese glass blower, he was born on April 20, 1890, in the Moravian town of Nikolsburg, and was educated in Vienna. There he joined the Socialist Democratic Party at the age of 16 and organised a Socialist student group before graduating as Doctor of Laws and Philosophy in 1914.

EAGLE AT LARGE IN LONDON

"Goldie," the seven-year-old male golden eagle which flew out of its cage at the London Zoo, Regent's Park, on Saturday, was still at large last night despite new efforts to recapture it.

The bird, which has a six-foot wing-span, spent the afternoon 80 feet up in a tree in Regents Park, near Chester Gate, after passing Saturday night in trees in the park.

A spokesman for the Zoological Society said there was no question of danger to the public.

The spokesman added: "It is hoped that the bird will return to the zoo when it gets hungry, but this may be several days.

"There is also the possibility of it being attracted back to its mate in the zoo since it is, in fact, slowly moving towards the zoo."

Pope's Request To Cardinal

The Pope has asked that public discussion on contraception should end, according to Cardinal Heenan, Archbishop of Westminster.

The Cardinal was asked about birth control on his arrival at London Airport yesterday after his elevation at the Vatican last week.

He said: "The Pope has requested that there should be an end to public discussion on contraception.

"We were also informed that it was not for us to make further public statement on the subject."

Young Man Loses Fingers After Cottage Explosion

A young Dublinman had two fingers amputated at the Mater Hospital, after an explosion in a cottage in Glenmacnass, eight miles from Glendalough, Co. Wicklow, late on Saturday night.

The man was Mr. Gerard Heasley (21), Clonliffe Gardens, off Clonliffe Road, Dublin, who, with two other unidentified companions, had gone to Glendalough on a week-end hiking expedition.

Gardai are investigating the accident, which is believed to have happened when the men were experimenting with weed-killer and sugar.

After the accident, the men drove in their car to the Dublin Fire Brigade substation at Dolphin's Barn, where the injured man asked to be taken to hospital and specially requested to be taken to the Mater Hospital.

Mr. Heasley's badly-injured hand and arm were swathed in makeshift bandages and he was bleeding profusely. Members of the brigade gave him a temporary dressing and took him to hospital where yesterday he was stated to be "comfortable."

Cardinal Takes Possession Of Titular Church

HIS EMINENCE CARDINAL CONWAY yesterday took possession of his titular church, St. Patrick's at Villa Ludovisi, near the Via Veneto, in Rome at an hour-long ceremony attended by hundreds of Irish seminarians and the members of Rome's Irish colony.

Irish Augustinians maintain St. Patrick's, which was built in 1911 on land that once formed the huge estate of the Ludovisi noble family.

By ancient tradition each new Cardinal, no matter where he lives, has powers in a church in Rome itself where his own portrait and coat of arms hang along with those of the Pontiff.

Hundreds of Irish seminarians and members of Rome's Irish colony crowded the church to see Cardinal Conway, in the bright scarlet robes he began wearing only last Thursday, take possession in an hour-long religious ceremony.

The Irish Embassy to the Holy See held a big reception last night in tribute to the Cardinal and his guests, including many of his relatives who flew to Rome for the week-long spiritual and social festivities honouring him.

DEEP EMOTION

In a brief speech at St. Patrick's, Cardinal Conway said:

"This is for me a moment of deep emotion, the moment when I take canonical possession of a Titulus Presbyteralis in the heart of Rome, in the See of Peter and of the successor of Peter, in this city which is the symbol and centre of Catholic unity throughout the world.

"From this moment, I can say: In hac alma urbe, in Ecclesia Romana quae est omnium ecclesiarum

TURN TO BACK PAGE, COL. 1

FLU EPIDEMIC

The Board of Medicine in Helsinki has appealed for extra nurses to deal with cases admitted to hospital due to an influenza epidemic. One hospital has admitted 70 patients who caught pneumonia while suffering from flu.

DUTCH CABINET CRISIS OVER TV

Queen Juliana will meet political leaders today in an attempt to settle the Cabinet crisis caused by a dispute over commercial radio and television.

The Coalition Government stated on Friday it had decided to resign because ministers had failed to agree on a new radio and television system worked out by the Minister of Education, Mr. Theo Bot.

The crisis was generally believed to have been caused by the popularity of commercial radio and television beamed from "pirate" stations in the North Sea.

One of these, "TV North Sea" was recently closed by the authorities.

The other, the radio ship Veronica, is still operating and is estimated to have the biggest audience in Holland.

The Government has been under pressure to introduce commercial broadcasting in Holland. Of the five broadcasting corporations already in existence, four have religious and political affiliations.

500,000 AT FAMILY ROSARY CEREMONY

More than 500,000 Catholics attended a ceremony yesterday closing the family Rosary crusade which began in Barcelona in August and whose director is the Irish priest, Rev. Fr. Patrick Peyton.

Monsignor Gregorio Modrego Casaus, Archbishop of Barcelona, presided and local authorities and church officials attended.

During the meeting Fr. Peyton appealed to the people to pray for family unity, peace and happiness.

The Papal Nuncio to Spain, Monsignor Antonio Riberi, read a message from Pope Paul closing the crusade.

Pope Has Plan To Boost Irish Role In World

THE Pope had expressed ideas as to how Ireland's influence for good in international affairs might be more more effective, said the Taoiseach, Mr. Lemass, describing his audience with Pope Paul, on his return from the Vatican to Dublin yesterday.

He said that at the moment, however, it would be understood that he could not disclose what these ideas were.

Mr. Lemass said that the ceremony in connection with the public consistory was very impressive, but for people in Ireland the outstanding feature of it was the reference made by the Holy Father in his address, to the missionary work of the Irish people.

"OUTSTANDING EVENT"

"For me the outstanding event of the whole visit was the private audience I had on Saturday with the Pope," he said.

"In the course of our discussions we covered a wide range of affairs, and I was very gratified that he expressed appreciation of the manner in which Irish influence has been used throughout the world, particularly in the United Nations.

"The Holy Father had ideas which he hoped we would consider as to how our influence for good might be made more effective.

"He asked me to convey a message to the Irish people expressing his paternal interest in their welfare, and his assurance that he would pray for our prosperity and progress."

Referring to his luncheon with the Italian Prime Minister, Signor Moro, the Taoiseach said that from his point of view it was very informative in disclosing the attitude of the Italian government on a number of matters of international concern, and covering particularly the movement of events in Europe with reference to the Common Market.

Mr. Lemass, who was accompanied by Mr. H. McCann, Secretary to the Department of External Affairs, and Comdt. J. O'Brien, was met at the airport by the Tanaiste, Mr. MacEntee, the Minister for Agriculture, Mr. Haughey, Most Rev. Dr. Sensi, the Papal Nuncio; the Italian Ambassador, Baron Guarciardi, and the Deputy General Manager of Aer Lingus, Capt. J. C. Kelly-Rogers.

"Satisfactory."—The condition of the Duke of Windsor, who underwent an operation for detachment of the retina of the left eye on Friday was stated yesterday to be "satisfactory." Yesterday's bulletin from the London clinic stated: "He had a comfortable night and his condition continues satisfactory."

Five Young Men In Hospital After Collision

FIVE young men are in St. Finbarr's Hospital, Cork, with serious injuries sustained when two cars in which they were travelling were involved in an almost head-on collision near Little Island Cross on the Cork-Youghal Road on Saturday night. Early this morning two were still in a "critical" condition and a third was "serious."

The accident, the second in this area within two weeks, occurred on the city side of Little Island Cross at approximately 10.30 p.m.

The cars were travelling in opposite directions. One finished up on its roof and the other on its side. Both were very heavily damaged and both were practically new.

One of the cars, driven by Mr. Jerry Higgins, of 13 St. Lappin's Terrace, Little Island, Co. Cork, was travelling in the Midleton direction, while the other vehicle was going in the city direction. The occupants of the second car were Mr. Michael O'Sullivan, Churchfield Avenue, Gurranabraher, Mr. David Lynch, 41 St. Teresa's Road, Gurranabraher, Mr. John Murphy, 373 Lower Blarney Street, and Mr. Edward Jones, 281 Cathedral Road, Gurranabraher.

Mr. Higgins and Mr. O'Sullivan were said to be in a "critical condition" at the hospital this morning, while Mr. Lynch was stated to be in a "serious condition." Both Mr. Murphy and Mr. Jones were described as "comfortable." Another occupant was not taken to hospital as he was only slightly dazed.

The accident took place on a straight stretch of newly constructed roadway. Both cars, which ended up almost 75 yards apart, were, according to one onlooker, "complete write offs."

Rescue operations led by Garda P. Dolan of Glanmire, began almost immediately. With the help of local residents and

TURN TO BACK PAGE, COL. 3

CONTENTS

Honour For Lady Harbour Master

IRELAND'S only woman Harbour Master yesterday received at the Parochial House, Rath, Co. Cork, what she described as "the most wonderful birthday present imaginable." She was offered and has accepted an invitation to Baltimore, Maryland, U.S.A., for this year's St. Patrick's Day celebrations.

Mrs. Margaret Davis, Harbour Master and Secretary of Baltimore and Skibbereen Harbour Board, was 36 yesterday. The bearer of the invitation from the citizens of Baltimore was Prof. Michael Grimes, who lectures at Ales University, Iowa.

GUEST OF A.O.H.

Mrs. Davis will be the official guest of the Ancient Order of Hibernians in Baltimore, which has a population of two million people, about 40 per cent of whom are Irish or of Irish descent.

The A.O.H., with the co-operation of Carling Brewery, Baltimore, and Pan American Airways, are financing the trip, which will begin on March 11 and end on March 19.

When asked about her reaction to the invitation yesterday, Mrs. Davis said: "It is the most wonderful birthday present imaginable. I hope to be a worthy representative of Baltimore and Ireland in this great American city."

Mrs. Davis, whose maiden name was Miss Margaret Connery, of Kilmallock, Co. Limerick, met her husband, Mr. Eugene Davis, of Baltimore, in London. They have two children.

She will fly out from Shannon on the afternoon of March 11, carrying with her messages of greetings from the Chairman and members of the Baltimore and Skibbereen Harbour Boards to the Governor, Mayor, Cardinal and harbour authorities of the American city. She will also carry 100 sprays of shamrock and give some Waterford Glass to the religious and civic dignitaries of Baltimore.

She will stay overnight in New York, and on arrival at Baltimore Airport on the following afternoon, will be accorded a civic reception. After being entertained at lunch at Carling's Brewery, Mrs. Davis will be the guest of the Baltimore Harbour Authority, who will take her on a tour of the port. On Saturday morning, March 13, she will be received at the City Hall by Mayor McKeldon, who will present her with the key to the city. Later in the day she will visit the Governor of the State, who will make her an honorary citizen of Maryland.

SEAT OF HONOUR

She will also be received by His Eminence Cardinal Shehan, Archbishop of Baltimore. She will occupy the seat of honour on the reviewing stand at the St. Patrick's Day Parade in which 100,000 people will take part. She will also appear on radio and TV, and hopes to boost the tourist attractions of West Cork.

Her visit was suggested in Irish circles in Baltimore, Maryland, last November, and Prof. Grimes was contacted. He got in touch with the Parish Priest of Rath and the Islands, Very Rev. Patrick O'Donovan, who referred the matter to the Harbour Commissioners. The arrangements were finalised yesterday by Prof. Grimes in the Parochial House in the presence of Fr. O'Donovan, Mr. T. D. Burke, M.C.C., chairman of the Harbour Commissioners, and Mrs. Davis.

(Picture on Page 14)

1966

While 1966 was the year that London was branded a 'swinging' city, Ireland's own cultural change can be seen in the debate about a mention of a wife's nightdress on *The Late Late Show*. On one side you had the still-powerful Catholic Church, on the other a young broadcaster by the name of Gay Byrne who'd go on to bring several other taboo topics into the public arena.

Wales was close enough that the Aberfan disaster which killed 144 people, mostly children, caused deep sadness in Ireland and prompted prayers and collections. The deadly slide by a coal-tip covered an infants' school and several houses. The deputy headmaster of the buried school was found with the bodies of five children in his arms.

Two more of Ireland's literary giants passed away during the year, with the death of Brian O'Nolan taking his alter-egos Flann O'Brien and Myles na gCopaleen to the grave, and Frank O'Connor's demise depriving Ireland of one of its great short story writers.

Bishop 'disgusted' with *Late Late Show*

Monday, February 14

During *The Late Late Show* from Telefís Éireann on Saturday night, the Bishop of Clonfert, Most Rev Dr Thomas Ryan, sent the following telegram to the show's compere, Gay Byrne: "Disgusted with disgraceful performance." At the same time, the Bishop's secretary, Very Rev MH O'Callaghan, telephoned the studios registering a protest on behalf of the priests of the diocese against the show, which he described as "immoral".

In St Brendan's Cathedral, Loughrea, yesterday, where he celebrated Mass, His Lordship said: "Many of you, I am sure, will have seen the programme; the fewer of the younger people who saw it the better. I know you will all agree with me when I describe it as most objectionable."

His Lordship added: "Surely we are entitled to a show, if you want to look at it, that is more in keeping with the traditions of Catholic Ireland."

Gay Byrne, commenting on the part of the show to which the Bishop raised objections, said yesterday: "We just played a little game with a husband and wife in the form of asking one questions while the other was out of earshot and then asking the partner the same questions on return."

Gay Byrne was in trouble after the discussion of a woman's nightie on **The Late Late Show.**

Mrs Eileen Fox, who, with her husband, Mr Patrick Fox, had been asked questions concerning the night wear she wore on her honeymoon, said: "There was absolutely nothing objectionable about it. I thought it was all in good fun. When I was asked what kind of nightie I wore I replied 'none' just to be sporting, and then added 'white'. It is just too ridiculous for words for anyone to find it in any way objectionable."

Author Frank O'Connor dies of heart attack

Friday, March 11

Cork-born author Frank O'Connor, died of a heart attack yesterday at his Dublin home. He was 63.

O'Connor, whose real name was Michael O'Donovan, was also a playwright, broadcaster and a witty and entertaining talker.

He was born in 1903 in a little house in Harringtons Square, not far from what is now Collins Barracks, where his father was a drummer in the Munster Fusiliers. In his autobiography, *An Only Child*, O'Connor describes vividly his childhood in that area.

At the height of his literary career, when he had already published several collections of short stories, including *Guests of the Nation* and the biography of Michael Collins, *The Big Fellow*, he went to the US and became a regular contributor to the *New Yorker*.

Séamus Murphy, RHA, who went to school with O'Connor said: "He was the quintessence of Cork. He loved and hated it, and his work reflected the stratified life of a small city like this."

Writer Frank O'Connor.

NEWS BRIEFS

Mar Twenty people are injured in a crush at Dublin airport as fans mob Dickie Rock on his return from the Eurovision. (8)

Oct While Mr Neil Blaney was replying to the debate on the vote in the Dáil for his Department of Local Government yesterday, his parliamentary secretary, Mr Paudge Brennan, handed him a note and Mr Corish (Lab) challenged him to read it. After a moment's hesitation, Mr Blaney, who had placed the note downwards on his desk, took it up and read it: "Baby boy born 9pm" and "it is mine," he said. Mr F Coogan (FG), amid laughter: "Put his name down for a house." Mr Blaney: "I already have."

The Cork Examiner

NO. 45,859 WEDNESDAY MORNING, MARCH 9, 1966 PRICE FOURPENCE

A Reckless Act, Says Mr. Lenihan; Providential No One Was Killed

PILLAR BLAST IS CONDEMNED

Six Men Still Held

A RAGGED stump, starkly unfamiliar in its ring of granite debris, was all that remained last night of Dublin's most famous landmark, as thousands of dumbfounded citizens strained at the garda rope barriers to see the effects of a shattering blast which finally unseated Lord Nelson after a century and a half.

Throughout a day of tragic chaos, development followed quickly on development, culminating in the news that six men had been detained for questioning in connection with the affair.

The Minister for Justice, Mr. Brian Lenihan, has condemned the explosion as a "reckless act".

In a statement last night, the Minister pointed out that the explosion was timed for 1.30 a.m., when it was well known that many persons, including late-night workers in restaurants and dance halls, would be in the O'Connell Street area.

"There can be no doubt" he said, "that the outrage was planned and committed without any regard for the lives of the citizens and it was providential that nobody was killed or injured. As it was, there was wanton damage to property in the immediate vicinity and the disruption of traffic has already inconvenienced thousands of Dubliners."

TO BE DEMOLISHED

The Dublin Assistant City Manager, Mr. Ruairi O Brolchain, declared that the remaining 84 feet of the pillar would be demolished.

- Major developments yesterday were an announcement by the Garda Traffic Department that it may be a week before normal traffic in O'Connell Street is resumed.
- Six men were detained in a series of Special Branch raids and further arrests are expected.
- The Irish Republican Publicity Bureau stated that it had no connection with the demolition of the pillar.
- A guard has been mounted on Wellington monument in Phoenix Park, and the British war memorial at Islandbridge.
- The guard on the British Embassy and the homes of members of the Diplomatic Corps has been reinforced.

Yesterday Special Branch detectives under the direction of Det.-

TURN TO BACK PAGE, COL. 4

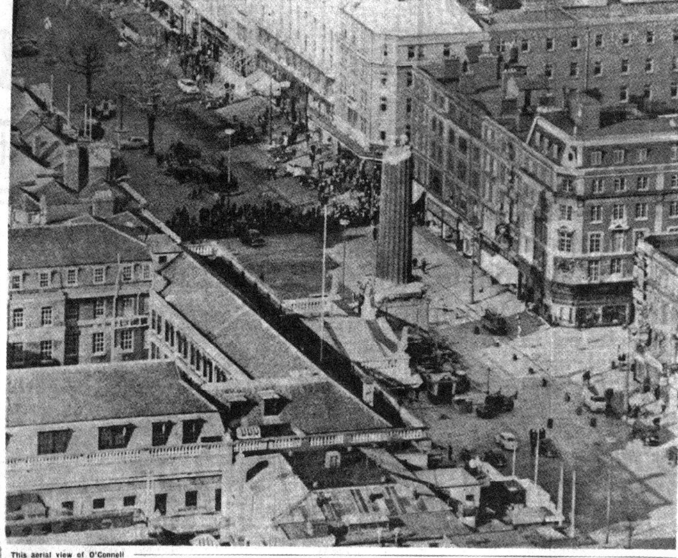

This aerial view of O'Connell Street, taken yesterday by an "Examiner" staff photographer, shows the shattered monument

Higher Taxes All Round

INCREASED taxes right across the board are expected in the budget today, writes our political correspondent. This viewpoint was reflected in all the comments one heard in Leinster House last night, as speculation continued as to how the Minister for Finance, Mr. Jack Lynch, will provide for the national housekeeping for another 12 months.

There was even the question as to whether with the budget a month earlier than usual, the Minister might have an autumn budget under consideration as well should the economic demands not be contained as the year progresses.

This is Mr. Lynch's first budget. Though he introduced last year's budget, it was generally conceded that in the main it was the handiwork of his predecessor, Dr. Ryan.

The big question is whether the Minister will be content to take enough to meet the gap. To close it would require about £9 to £10 million in extra taxation. Over estimation would probably bring in the balance to take the income up by £12½ million, the actual size of the gap.

The feeling in Leinster House last night was that the Minister would opt for a larger slice in taxation so as to provide for a sizeable surplus.

But how will he get it? If I knew the answer to that question I would not be writing this commentary. It appears, however, that the Minister will have no option but to increase taxes all across the board.

It will be about 4 p.m. to-day in Leinster House when the Minister rises to tell us how he proposes to rake in the extra millions.

TURN TO BACK PAGE, COL. 2

70,000 MILES FLYING WITHOUT A HITCH

British Aircraft Corporation's B.A.C. One-Eleven demonstration aircraft landed at Gatwick Airport yesterday after a 70,000 tour which has taken it to ten countries in a little more than six weeks.

Mr. S. B. Oliver, captain of the aircraft throughout the tour, said: "The One-Eleven went like a bird. All the 125 route flights and demonstration flights went off without a hitch."

JOHNSON'S 'NO' TO DE GAULLE

President Johnson has told General de Gaulle that the United States will not agree to putting its forces in France under French command, diplomatic sources reported in Washington yesterday.

The French Leader, who sent a message to President Johnson on Monday, ultimately wants American military bases in France to be French controlled as part of his plan to withdraw France from the N.A.T.O. Military Command in Europe.

Mr. Johnson replied on Monday night to the letter, but officials said it was not a simple "no" as reported by the "Washington Post."

Before President Johnson gave a final answer there would be consultations with other members of the alliance, diplomatic sources said.

CHARGED WITH MURDER OF CAFE OWNER

A 55-years-old Galway man was remanded in custody for a week when he appeared in the Dublin District Court yesterday charged with the murder of a Dublin cafe owner.

He is Martin Meagher, of no fixed address, and the District Justice said that he would arrange legal aid for him.

He was charged with the murder of John Finn, who was injured in a shooting incident at the Banba Cafe, in Talbot Street, on Wednesday last, and who died in hospital on Sunday.

To Boycott Dutch Royal Wedding

More than half of Amsterdam's councillors—24 out of 45—will boycott the civil wedding ceremony in Amsterdam tomorrow of Crown Princess Beatrix and Claus von Amsberg, officials said yesterday.

This move is the latest development in the bitter controversy touched off by the wedding of the 28-year-old princess and the 39-year-old former West German diplomat.

All six Communist councillors have turned down invitations. The rest are Socialist, Liberal and Pacifist Socialist members of the city council.

Pamphlets appeared on some walls yesterday sarcastically calling for unity round the Dutch throne, "even though it will be joined by a former member of the Wehrmacht."

SIX AGREE ON MEAT PRICES

Agriculture Ministers of the Six European Common Market countries reached agreement on milk and meat prices for the marketing year 1966-67.

The last obstacle to the agreement was cleared when the West German delegation agreed to a progressive reduction of part of her national milk subsidies in the coming year.

Member states will be able to fix their national prices in the coming year within the upper and lower limits decided by the Ministers in Brussels yesterday.

The price ratio between beef and milk proposed by the Commission—that beef should be seven times higher than milk—has also been respected.

The Commission is trying to stimulate meat production in the Community in view of an expected deficit of about 630,000 tons in 1966.

No General Rise For Those Over £1,200

THE Government cannot afford any more than an average increase of approximately 3% in wages this year and do not contemplate any general increase for persons earning more than £1,200 annually, says a statement issued by the Government Information Bureau.

The Government, says the statement, have now reviewed the situation which might develop in relation to wage and salary claims following the inability of employer and worker interests to negotiate a national agreement which could have ensured, within what the economy could bear, an orderly progression in money incomes.

The statement goes on to say:—"The economic considerations which make moderation essential for the future well-being of the community were fully discussed in a recent Dail debate on an incomes policy and on the prospect for 1966. The best advice available to the Government shows that the economy can afford no more than an average increase of approximately 3 per cent in money incomes in 1966, without starting inflationary tendencies, endangering employment and the expansion of production.

"By and large, wage and salary rates and other working conditions in this country are fixed by negotiation. It is important, there-

TURN TO BACK PAGE, COL. 1

BELGIAN CRISIS WORSENS

Belgium's Socialists yesterday refused to accept Premier-designate Paul Vanden Boeyants as head of a new two-party coalition, deepening still further the country's 26-day-old political crisis.

Socialist Party President Leo Collard, announcing the refusal in a letter to M. Vanden Boeyants, criticised the Social Christian Premier-designate for submitting his coalition plans last week to the Socialists as well as the Liberal "party for liberty and progress."

M. Collard said M. Vanden Boeyants should have made up his mind earlier whether he wanted the Socialists or Liberals as coalition partners. The Socialists were opposed to a three-party coalition.

But the Socialists main criticism of M. Vanden Boeyants is his intention to form a Social Christian Cabinet if his coalition offer is refused, M. Collard said.

Financial Merger Move By Three Irish Distilleries

IT was announced in Dublin yesterday that agreement has been reached in principle between the directors of Cork Distilleries Co. Ltd., John Jameson & Son Ltd., and John Power & Son Ltd., to form a strong association between these companies. It has been agreed to recommend a financial merger, which is now being formulated, so as to create a group comprising the three companies.

Detailed particulars will be sent to shareholders within the next few weeks and it is expected that the company will be formed by early April. It is intended that the form of financial merger will be such that the shareholders of Cork Distilleries Co. Ltd., and John Jameson and Son Ltd., and the stockholders of John Power and Son Ltd., will have the ordinary shares in the new group.

Applications will be made for quotations for the new shares on the Dublin and Cork Stock Exchanges.

As the stock of John Power and Son Ltd. is already quoted on the Dublin and Cork Stock Exchanges, the directors of the merging companies consider that they should now state that, under the proposals for the new group, the stockholders of John Power and Son Ltd. would receive by way of dividend the same total distribution in respect of the current year as they received in respect of the year ended June 30, 1965.

Mr. F. J. O'Reilly, chairman, John Power and Sons, told an "Examiner" reporter in Dublin, yesterday, that the merger meant that the companies involved were getting ready for free trade, and for entry into the Common Market. They would also be enabled to increase exports in line with Government policy.

Shareholders, he said, were bound to benefit. The merger

TURN TO BACK PAGE—COL. 6

AMERICAN JAILED ON SECRETS CHARGE FREED

John George Gessner, a former nuclear weapons engineer in the U.S. Army, was released from prison in Kansas yesterday where he was serving a life sentence for passing nuclear secrets to the Russians.

Late last year, Gessner won a new trial, on the grounds that a confession presented as evidence at his original trial was involuntary and should not have been allowed.

Yesterday the Government announced that it was dropping charges against him since the prosecution did not have sufficient evidence to try him again without the confession.

Gessner (29) was convicted by a federal court on June 9th, 1964.

Couple Sue Hospital. — A couple filed a one million dollars (about £357,000) suit in Chicago yesterday against a local hospital from which their new-born baby was kidnapped nearly two years ago. The baby has not yet been found.

Astronauts' Space Walk Rehearsal

Gemini astronauts Neil Armstrong and David Scott performed weightless tumbling acts in a high-flying jet transport yesterday as they entered the final week of training for one of man's most exciting space flights.

Two important tests arranged for to-day and to-morrow are the last major hurdles which must be cleared before the astronauts rocket into orbit next Tuesday for a three-day trip.

For the first six hours Armstrong and Scott are to chase an Agena space vehicle in an attempt to achieve man's first link-up with an orbiting satellite.

On the second day, Scott is to take a record space walk of nearly 2¼ hours, during which he is to evaluate how well man can manoeuvre and work outside a space ship. He is to float about on the end of a 100-ft. lifeline, guiding himself about with a gas-propelled jet gun.

BIG COPPER FIND SUSPECTED

A major copper find is believed to have been made on a group of islands off the northern New Zealand coast. Some estimates say the deposits of high grade ore may be 30 million tons.

The islands are Coppermine Island and the other is in the "Hen and Chicken" group off Whagarei.

Irish Farmers Not Favoured, Commons Told

In the British House of Commons yesterday Mr. Patrick Wolrige-Gordon (C.) asked the Minister of Agriculture, Fisheries and Food, if, with a view to equalising the opportunities of farmers in the Republic of Ireland and the United Kingdom for producing beef for the British market, he would take steps to ensure that the United Kingdom trading arrangements do not favour Irish farmers.

Mr. James Hoy, Joint Parliamentary Secretary, in a written reply says: "The trading arrangements recently agreed with the Republic of Ireland do not give any advantage to Irish farmers over those in the United Kingdom as regards the supply of beef to the U.K. market."

DUKE STARTS U.S. TOUR TO-DAY

The Duke of Edinburgh, who is in Miami, begins to-day a 10,000 miles coast-to-coast tour of America, which will help children throughout the world.

Besides giving British exports to the United States a boost, the 11-day visit aims to raise a million dollars (£357,000) for international children's charities.

LORD ASTOR'S BODY BEING FLOWN HOME

Viscount Astor (58), one of Britain's richest men and a member of a famous political family, has died of a heart attack in hospital at Nassau, Bahamas. His body is to be flown to London.

Lord Astor, the third Viscount, arrived there three days ago for a holiday with his wife, the former model, Bronwen Pugh. He was taking coffee on Monday with some old friends when he complained of pains. A doctor was called and he was rushed to Princess Margaret Hospital, where he died shortly after.

Diplomats' Test 'Dip' In Mediterranean

THE American Ambassador in Madrid and Spain's Information Minister went for a diplomatic dip in the chilly Mediterranean in Palomares, Spain, yesterday, to show there was no radioactive danger in the waters.

As they swam, hundreds of U.S. Air Force and Navy men continued their search for a missing hydrogen bomb lost after an atomic bomber crashed seven weeks ago.

It was the second swim for Ambassador Angier Biddle Duke, who had earlier braved the cold waters with three other diplomats, a general and six children.

Mr. Duke and Information Minister, Manuel Fraga Iribane, had come to Palomares specially from the capital to calm fears of lingering danger from the lost bomb.

Mr. Duke was accompanied on his first unseasonal swim by his two children, three embassy staff members, General Stanley Donovan, commander of the 16th U.S. Air Force in Spain, and his son, two children of Senor Fraga Iribane and the son of an American correspondent.

The Ambassador said afterwards: "Our presence here is proof in action that there is no danger of radioactivity in this area."

The B-52 bomber which crashed on January 17 after being in collision with a jet tanker carried several unarmed nuclear weapons. One of them has not yet been recovered and is believed to have fallen into the Mediterranean. Two bombs were found blown open, blasting nuclear material over a small area.

Mr. Duke said contaminated soil was being sent to the United States and clean-up operations would continue until Spanish and U.S. scientists were convinced that "we are leaving Spain as we found it."

CONTENTS

1967

While the war between Israel and its Arab neighbours in 1967 lasted just six days, its consequences would be felt for many years after and the world is still trying to deal with the outcome. In a humiliating defeat for Egypt, Jordan and Syria, Israel was able to capture vast tracts of Arab land, including East Jerusalem and the Old City, the Gaza Strip, the West Bank and the Golan Heights. The occupation of these areas still fuels the conflict in the Middle East today.

Sex was continuing to cause problems for the Catholic Church and when members of the flock in Tralee were about to turn out in droves to see a risqué cabaret by Jayne Mansfield, it was time to intervene. The resulting statements from the hierarchy in Kerry led to the cancellation of the American actress's show.

The world's ongoing fascination with the Kennedy family led to scenes of modern paparazzi proportions when Jacqueline Kennedy and her two children spent a month holidaying in Ireland. Some photographers even put on bathing suits so they could get close-up shots of the family swimming at a Waterford beach.

Bishop puts stop to Jayne Mansfield Show

Monday, April 24

Jayne Mansfield, the American actress, did not appear in a cabaret at the Mount Brandon Hotel, Tralee, last night. Statements were made by the Bishop of Kerry and the Dean of Kerry at Masses yesterday. The Bishop's (Dr Moynihan) statement said: "Our attention has been drawn to an entertainment tonight in Tralee. The Bishop requests you not to attend."

Monsignor John Lane, Dean of Kerry, told his parishioners that while he was their servant he should guard the interests of Christ. He had an unpleasant task and unpleasant duty from which he would run if he could because he was a moral coward but it was his duty as a priest to condemn in the strongest possible terms the entertainment that was being billed to take place that evening in the town.

He said he wanted to bring home to the people the teachings of their Faith. Within the last few years the Vatican Council had published documents on entertainment which would tell people how to assess such things.

At a press conference which commenced two and a half hours late, Miss Mansfield appeared carrying a chihuahua in each palm and said: "There seems to be a problem."

Jayne Mansfield addresses the media after her controversial cabaret was cancelled in Kerry.

Jayne said she had one very beautiful moment while travelling to Tralee. While a flat tyre was being changed on the car she entered the parish church at Castleisland and lit a candle for her son who was mauled by a lion. "I felt a great peace, happiness and satisfaction for this," she said.

Earlier a huge crowd turned up at Shannon Airport for the arrival of Miss Mansfield who was dressed in an emerald green trouser suit, high-heeled cowboy boots studded with jewels and a large matching green bow in her flowing flaxen hair.

NEWS BRIEFS

May Biafra announces its intention to break away from Nigeria, providing the spark for a protracted war in the region that would kill over a million people through violence and starvation. (30)

June A 20-year-old Mallow man who two weeks earlier was reputed to have won the world beauty personality championship for beauticians at Zagreb, Yugoslavia, admits that he had never been there. On arrival home he had been met at Mallow railway station by several hundred townspeople and a pipe band. He was also given a civic reception by members of Mallow urban district council.

He said he had been met in London by a Mr Sweetman of the International Syndicate des Beauties. "He told me there was no competition. At this stage I intended going to the police but he warned me not to. He told me not to go to the police, as there was someone watching me. He told me he would fix everything and the public would never know." (3)

Sept British group Pink Floyd play at the Arcadia in Cork. Advertisements for the gig promise 'psychedelic lighting'. (16)

Nov Patrick Kavanagh dies, aged 63, of pneumonia in Dublin. (30)

Jacqueline Kennedy arrives at Shannon Airport accompanied by her children John and Caroline.

The Cork Examiner

NO. 46,477. THURSDAY MORNING, JUNE 8, 1967. PRICE: FOURPENCE

Dayan's Troops Hold Jerusalem, Re-Open Blockaded Gulf Of Aqaba

ISRAEL CLAIMS TOTAL ROUT OF EGYPT

ISRAEL last night announced major victories over the Arab nations, claiming to have completely routed Egypt, re-opened the blockaded Gulf of Aqaba, captured the entire old walled city of Jerusalem and taken control of a wide sector of Arab territory, ranging from the west bank of the River Jordan to the Suez Canal In addition, Israeli Chief of Staff, Major-Gen. Rabin, announced that Jericho had fallen to his troops.

In a declaration in Tel Aviv, Major-General Rabin said: "The Egyptians are defeated. All their efforts are aimed at withdrawing behind the Suez Canal, and we are taking care of that. The whole area is in our hands. The main effort of the Egyptians is to save themselves."

The three-day whirlwind conquest by Israel exceeded the speed of its 100-hour victory in 1956. Cairo was a city of fear last night as Nasser's troops withdrew before the fierce Israeli onslaught, but the Israeli Defence Minister, General Dayan, said his country had achieved its primary aim by re-opening the Gulf, and probably would not press on to the Suez Canal.

The major feature of yesterday's battle was the capture by Israeli forces of the Egyptian stronghold of Sharm El Sheik, at the entrance to the Gulf of Aqaba.

It was Egypt's closure of the Gulf on May 17, after securing the withdrawal of the U.N. peace-keeping force, that led to the current conflict.

The fort was one of Israel's main objectives, and its capture yesterday meant that the country could re-open its vital trade route to the Red Sea.

JERUSALEM TAKEN

Another major Israeli achievement yesterday was the capture of the old walled city of Jerusalem, held by Jordanian troops for over 19 years.

A few hours after tanks and infantry took the old walled city, containing such holy shrines as the Church of the Holy Sepulchre and the site of Calvary, Gen. Dayan stood in the shadow of the arch at "Wailing Wall" and declared: "At this hour, we extend our hand in peace, but we have returned here never to part with Jerusalem."

As he spoke, soldiers knelt and prayed, and some wept openly at the Wall.

One said: "For many years I have seen it from the roofs on our side, and now for the first time I am here."

Some of the black-garbed Orthodox Jews, who have been cool toward the secular Jewish state, gathered about the victorious Israeli tanks to cheer the soldiers. Others, their side curls flying, danced in the streets.

In Tel Aviv, Israel's Premier, Mr. Levi Eshkol, gave orders for preserving the sanctity of holy places in the old quarter of Jerusalem. He conferred with the leaders of all religious communities to inform them of the capture of Arab Jerusalem.

On the battlefront, Israeli forces

TURN TO BACK PAGE, COL. 1

HUSSEIN SAID TO HAVE LEFT FOR LONDON

Rumours swept Rome last night that King Hussein had left Jordan by plane and would land at Rome's Ciampino military airport.

Crowds of reporters who rushed to the airport were blocked at the entrance by unusually heavy guards of police and carabinieri, who cordoned off the entire airport.

The head of the foreign division of Rome police headquarters, Signor Marino la Mela, was among the officials at Ciampino. The Jordanian Ambassador to Rome, Mr. Abdel Hamid Siraj, said: "I know nothing about this and I don't believe it".

The rumours alleged Hussein was on his way to London for talks.

The Israeli flag being hoisted at El-Arish Airfield in Sinai. —(A.P. Radiophoto)

Taoiseach To Visit Holland Soon

IN reply to Mr. S. Dunne (Lab.), the Taoiseach said in the Dail yesterday that he hoped to visit Holland soon in connection with his tour of E.E.C. capitals. He hoped to be able to give more information next week. Now that the situation in the Middle East had reached a crisis it was not easy to make arrangements at this time.

Mr. L. Cosgrave (F.G.) asked the Taoiseach if he had received any communication or indication from E.E.C. Commission, suggesting some form of transitional arrangements between this country and the E.E.C. other than actual membership.

Mr. Lynch replied that the answer was "No".

Mr. Cosgrave asked if the Taoiseach could yet say when formal negotiations were expected to start on our application for membership?

Mr. Lynch—I'm afraid I cannot.

Mr. B. Corish (Lab.) asked if the Taoiseach had taken any initiative to find out if the suggestion contained in Mr. Cosgrave's question as to a form of association could be applied to Ireland?

Mr. Lynch said he had not. This suggestion had apparently emanated in France and had not found approval in the minds of the British government.

Mr. Corish asked if in the event of our application for membership being rejected, the government would negotiate for association.

Mr. Lynch said there was no such thing as association. Any association was a temporary arrangement leading to full membership.

The Taoiseach told Mr. Cosgrave that our negotiations would

TURN TO BACK PAGE, COL. 1

BRITONS LEAVE E. NIGERIA

Britain yesterday launched a full-scale evacuation of British women and children from the secessionist eastern region of Nigeria as key army leaders met in Lagos for crisis talks under the Nigerian federal leader, Major-General Yakubu Gowon.

Borrowed Ghanian airplanes were pressed into service to join a chartered DC-6 airliner which has airlifted more than 1,000 foreigners from the breakaway territory since Sunday.

Two DC-3 aircraft brought in from Ghana flew to Port Harcourt on the coast of Eastern Nigeria yesterday, and the British High Commission in Lagos said it hoped to fly in an extra DC-6 and a Viscount to raise the daily air-lift capacity up to 1,400 people.

Most of those who have flown out of the Eastern Region so far are Americans. There are more than 4,000 British and Commonwealth expatriates in the region, which is threatened with military action by the Gowon Government following its breakaway announcement last week.

LUXURY HOTEL BLAZE

Fire yesterday badly damaged the upper storeys of the luxury Palace Hotel in St. Moritz, Switzerland—famous haunt of show business celebrities, but no one was reported injured.

Kiesinger Plea On U.K. Market Entry

West German Chancellor Kurt George Kiesinger yesterday called on the five Common Market countries which favoured Britain's entry to the Common Market to try dispel the doubts of the sixth—without mentioning France by name.

He recalled there had been differences of opinion during the Rome summit meeting of Common Market heads of government about the influence Britain would have on the community's present form and its future development.

He said the Common Market countries should examine this issue and added: "The five countries which favour entry should try in open and thorough discussion to dispel the doubts of the other partner".

British Protest To China

BRITAIN last night delivered [illegible] strong protest [illegible] time for not [illegible] the British diplomatic [illegible] in Peking from a [illegible] yesterday.

[illegible] Chinese Acting Charge [illegible] Mr. Shen Ping, who [illegible] to see Mr. W. T. [illegible] Parliamentary Under [illegible] for Foreign Affairs, at [illegible] Office in London, re[illegible] the protest.

Chinese and foreign demonstrators smashed their way into the mission in Peking and tussled with British diplomats during massive demonstrations over the Middle East war.

A crowd of about 100 tore down [illegible] Union Jack and ripped it to [illegible] before smashing the locked [illegible] of the mission and entering [illegible] ground floor. They swept a [illegible] of Queen Elizabeth from the wall, smashed the glass and [illegible] to pieces.

The crowd included British, American and Arab Communists [illegible] in a special friendship [illegible] in Peking. The mission's [illegible] first secretaries, Mr. Anthony [illegible] and Mr. Raymond Wh[illegible] were punched.

The third secretary, Mr. [illegible] Appleyard, and the wife [illegible] Mr. Bishen, who left the compound before the crowd broke in [illegible] punched and battered by [illegible] crowds outside for several minutes. None of the mission staff was injured.

KICKED DOOR

The crowd which went into the [illegible] hurled potted shrubs [illegible] windows and kicked the [illegible] before entering.

A portrait of Mao Tse-Tung was [illegible] against the wall inside [illegible] when the demonstrators departed leaving behind [illegible] broken glass, mud and [illegible] wood.

It was pointed out to Mr. Shen [illegible] last night that Britain reserved the right to demand compensation. It was emphasised that members of the Chinese mission [illegible] London were afforded full protection and the British Government expected the same treatment [illegible] British diplomats in Peking.

MORE CLASHES IN ADEN

Sporadic firing between British troops and Arab gunmen was renewed in Aden yesterday afternoon in a fresh outbreak of violence inspired by the Arab-Israeli conflict.

Police said four Arabs were wounded in the shooting in the Sheikh Othman suburb. There were no British casualties.

The firing started shortly after British security authorities lifted a two-day-old dusk to dawn curfew in the Sheikh Othman and Mansoura areas.

On Tuesday night a British soldier was killed and another wounded in outbreaks of violence. Six Arabs were also wounded in at least 30 grenade, mortar, bazooka and other attacks on British troops.

The security authorities yesterday imposed a night curfew on Arab residential areas about 25 miles west of Aden where a British petroleum refinery is situated.

RUSSIAN SATELLITE FOR TV SHOW

Russia will show live pictures of the earth's surface, using one of two satellites launched in February and April this year, in the first round-the-world television programme "Our World," on Sunday, June 25, the B.B.C. announced last night.

"Our World," to be seen live on B.B.C. 1 between 8 p.m. and 10 p.m. on June 25, will be seen in 31 countries linking five continents, said the statement. Some [illegible] people will watch the £250,000 project using [illegible] television cameras and [illegible] million miles of telephone lines.

Egyptians Surrender At Gaza

Gaza had the appearance yesterday of a city after a battle, with bodies of dead soldiers still lying around and smouldering wrecks of tanks and vehicles standing where they were hit in pitched battles.

The Egyptian commander of the Gaza Strip yesterday took part in a formal ceremony, surrendering to the Israelis. The Commander, General Abdul M. Husni, signed a surrender document.

"UNCONDITIONALLY"

Written in Hebrew it said: "I, General A. M. Husni, Governor-General and Officer Commanding the Egyptian forces in the Gaza Strip, surrender unconditionally to the defence forces of Israel."

General Husni issued orders for all Egyptian troops in his command to discontinue any resistance to Israeli forces. Gaza remained under curfew last night and Israeli troops carried out house-to-house searches for arms.

Israel Would Agree To U.N. Truce Call If . . .

THE U.N. Security Council yesterday demanded that Israeli and Arab troops stop their war by observing a truce from 9 p.m. (Irish time) and, up to late last night, the only response had come from Israel. The U.N. call was proposed by Russia and approved unanimously.

Late last night Israel announced its consent to a ceasefire but only on condition that the Arab nations also agreed.

An official announcement after midnight said that the Israeli Government "decided to authorise the Foreign Minister Abba Eban to notify the United Nations Security Council of the consent of the Israel Government to a ceasefire if the other countries concerned should also announce their agreement to a ceasefire."

SECOND CALL

This was the United Nations' second ceasefire call to the Arabs and Israel in less than 24 hours. The first request was met by rejection from Egypt, Iraq and Saudi Arabia.

Jordanian Prime Minister, Saad Jumas, said he had accepted, but the Jordanians complained the Israelis were ignoring it, and King Hussein called on his troops to "fight to the last breath."

This time however the U.N. call was a "demand" in stronger terms, and this time there was a precise time for it to go into effect.

Earlier, in Tel Aviv, when asked if Israel would accept the ceasefire proposals being pressed at the United Nations, Gen. Dayan, the Defence Minister, had said: "Other sides have to stop fighting in order for us to stop."

The announcement was made by the Israeli Security Ministerial Committee after hearing a report from General Dayan and Army Chief-of-Staff Major General Yitzhak Rabin. The committee acted with the authority of the Government to make the decision.

It was reported earlier yesterday that a Paris official had been informed by the Egyptian Foreign Office that Egypt would accept a ceasefire only on condition that both sides returned to the old armistice demarcation line.

This would mean that Israeli forces would have to go back over all the ground they have occupied since fighting began, including relinquishing control of

TURN TO BACK PAGE, COL. 1

EGYPT FIGHTS ON

Soon after the deadline of the U.N. Security Council's new call for a Middle East ceasefire, a senior spokesman in Cairo declared: "Egypt will fight on".

His terse comment came in response to a request put to the Ministry of Information for Egypt's reaction to the U.N. bid to end the war.

Cairo Radio continued to blare martial music and commentaries urging the Arabs to throw themselves unsparingly into the struggle.

Chichester's Satisfactory Progress

Sir Francis Chichester, admitted to the Royal Naval Hospital at Plymouth on Tuesday night after a haemorrhage from a duodenal ulcer, was said by the hospital last night to have maintained satisfactory progress throughout the day.

"At the moment he is responding well to medical treatment," said a hospital statement.

The 65-year-old round-the-world yachtsman was visited by Lady Chichester during the day. He will remain under medical care for at least a month.

Queen Elizabeth immediately agreed to the postponement of the ceremony of knighthood, which was to have taken place at Greenwich next Tuesday.

Royal Naval doctors have ordered complete rest and visitors will be limited to members of Sir Francis' family.

30 Years For U.S. Secrets Soldier

Herbert Broeckenhaupt (24), a German-born Air Force staff sergeant, was sentenced in Alexandra, Virginia, yesterday to 30 years in prison on charges of conspiring to provide U.S. defence secrets to the Russians. The maximum sentence could have been death.

Boeckenhaupt was sentenced to 20 years on a charge of conspiring to transmit defence secrets and 10 years for conspiring to obtain national defence information illegally. The sentences were consecutive.

Notice of appeal was given when Broeckenhaupt was found guilty last month.

DAY OF THE MINI-SKIRT "DOOMED"

The day of the mini-skirt is doomed according to a survey carried out among women aged between 16 and 24, to be published in Britain at the end of June.

The report, called "The Bird Market", was conducted on behalf of Griggs Lander Associates Limited by a leading psychologist specialising in the teenage group, supported by an independent research organisation.

Its aim was to establish the whole perspective of teenage attitudes to clothing and cosmetics.

One conclusion is that although teenage girls are not yet ready to revert to the ultra-feminine look represented by maxi skirts, skirts will, nevertheless, get longer. They are reacting against extremes in mini-skirts.

Assurance To Irish Speaking Senators

ON the order of business in the Senate yesterday, **Senator D. O Conallain**, speaking in Irish, asked the Cathaoirleach whether he could guarantee that Senators speaking in Irish on the business proposed for discussion would have their speeches recorded in the official report. If the Chair could not give this guarantee it would raise a serious issue involving the infringement of the constitutional rights of the individual members who elected to speak in Irish.

It was his experience at the last meeting of An Seanad on May 10 that when he had spoken in Irish on a motion affecting the secondary teachers' superannuation scheme he was informed that not a word he had said was on record as there was no means at hand, human or mechanical, of doing so. He was subsequently requested by the editorial department to submit his speech in writing for inclusion in the official report.

This was not the first time that he had experienced this treatment of the Irish language in Seanad Eireann and he resented this method of pressurising people into using English when Irish was the language of their choice.

He did not know how far the failure to record speeches in Irish in An Seanad affected the publicity given in the press but it was significant that, on the occasion in question, Senators who had spoken in English on the same subject were reported in the newspapers the following morning whereas he got no mention whatever.

He recognised fully that the press had no obligation in this regard, but on the more serious issue of official recording, he would ask the Chair to state unequivocally whether Senators speaking in Irish would continue to be victimised or whether he could give a guarantee to the contrary.

The **Cathaoirleach** said he was grateful to the Senator for raising the matter and he assured him that it would not happen again.

Senator J. B. O'Quigley said he would like the same assurance to be given in relation to speeches in English.

GARDA STATION DEATH INQUEST ON THURSDAY

The inquest on Mr. Liam O'Mahony, the 40 years old retired seaman, of O'Connell Avenue, Turner's Cross, Cork, who died in the Bridewell Garda Station last week, will be held in the Courthouse next Thursday.

It is expected that the proceedings will be lengthy in view of the order from the Garda Commissioner that all the evidence be made available to the coroner.

For more than a week gardai and detectives have conducted a full-scale investigation into the death and have taken several statements.

CONTENTS

1968

After Saturday, October 5, 1968, Ireland would never be the same again. If the years of sectarian bitterness between the Catholic and Protestant communities in the North, combined with the fractious relationship between Ireland and Britain that resulted in the Troubles, could be said to have started on a single day, this was it. The Northern Irish Civil Rights Association, which had been campaigning against discrimination towards Catholics in housing and employment, defied a ban on one of its marches in Derry. The police response to the holding of the march left about 50 people requiring hospital treatment. Riots followed and the spiral into violence had begun.

Of course, Ireland was just one of a number of areas to experience major upheaval during 1968. The United States had civil rights demonstrations, the assassinations of Martin Luther King and Bobby Kennedy and major anti-war protests; Britain also had anti-war riots; Czechoslovakia had its 'Prague Spring' crushed by Soviet tanks; and the French government almost collapsed after a student-led uprising in Paris.

61 killed in horrific Aer Lingus crash

Monday, March 25

Aer Lingus said last night that little hope could be entertained of finding any survivors from the worst tragedy in the history of its operations when a Cork-London Viscount aircraft with 61 people – including two babes in arms – plunged into the sea off Strumble Head, near Fishguard, Wales just before noon yesterday.

On the aircraft were a crew of four and 57 passengers – 36 of whom were from Cork city and county. Despite an intensive air and sea search which was continuing through the night, no trace of the ill-fated plane had been found late last night.

Aeronautical experts were baffled by the crash, and especially by a garbled message, given in "matter-of-fact" tones, which contained the phrase: "Am spinning through 1,000 feet." An expert at Cork Airport yesterday said that he could not conceive how a Viscount could spin unless there had been a structural failure in the craft.

An early civil rights march in Northern Ireland.

US on brink of racial explosion

Saturday, April 6

America last night trembled on the brink of a nationwide explosion of violence as the country reeled under the shock of the assassination of negro leader Dr Martin Luther King. All appeals for calm appeared to have been fruitless, and militant negroes, led by Stokely Carmichael, were warning that a major outburst was imminent. President Johnson, putting off his Vietnam peace-seeking plans to deal with race violence at home, ordered army troops into the heart of Washington last night in the face of renewed negro rioting.

In Memphis, the body of Dr King was put on public view yesterday just 30 minutes before it was to be taken to the airport for the journey back to Atlanta, Georgia. Negroes, who somehow seemed to know about the unannounced viewing, filed past mournfully for a last look at the man who had made non-violence, and the song 'We Shall Not Be Moved', the two major factors in the American civil rights movement.

NEWS BRIEFS

Apr The 17-storey County Hall in Cork, Ireland's tallest building, opens after a three-year construction period. The 'skyscraper' was built floor-by-floor, without the use of scaffolding, and cost £500,000. (17)

June Robert Kennedy is fatally wounded by Sirhan Sirhan, a Palestinian student who had objected to the American senator's support of Israel. (6)

June A general election in France results in a landslide victory for Charles de Gaulle, effectively ending unrest that had seen thousands of students fight pitched battles with police in Paris and a general strike by workers. (30)

The Cork Examiner

NO. 46,840 MONDAY, MORNING, OCTOBER 7, 1968 PRICE: FIVEPENCE

CITY SPECIAL

Petrol Bombs Thrown As Police And Demonstrators Clash

MORE VIOLENCE FLARES IN DERRY

MORE violence flared in Derry last night as angry Nationalists, still inflamed by Saturday's incidents, renewed their demonstration. Police fought running battles with demonstrators, who smashed almost every window in one street, as they retreated from the walled area of the city centre.

The demonstrators made repeated sallies up the steep street running parallel to one of the city's walls, engaging the police in stone-throwing battles. Police sheltered on the walls and behind one of the archways in the walls. Violence then spread to other parts of the city and ambulances were running a shuttle service to take scores of demonstrators and many police to hospital. Four petrol bombs were thrown at a police car and an armoured water wagon was called in to help disperse the crowd.

Earlier yesterday afternoon a crowd of about 200 youths were dispersed by the police after they began throwing stones and smashing shop windows in the city centre. Last night's clashes followed allegations of extreme police brutality when Northern Ireland Civil Rights Association marchers clashed with police in the Waterside area of the city on Saturday, as they attempted to hold a protest march which had been banned by the Minister of Home Affairs, Mr. Craig.

It began when the 2,000-strong parade ran into a barrier of police and vans. Batons and fists flew in a brief clash and Mr. Gerry Fitt, Westminster M.P. for West Belfast, was one of the first to be struck down.

Violence flared again after a number of speakers had addressed the marchers appealing for them to go home. Then as a section of the crowd surged forward the police launched a baton charge striking out at men, women and children.

Placards were hurled at the police in a brief counter-attack by the marchers who found themselves hemmed in by another police barrier about 100 yards down the narrow street.

SMALL BOY KICKED

Grim-faced policemen made repeated charges against the trapped demonstrators. Then armoured water wagons moved in firing at everyone in sight including onlookers and women returning home from shopping in the city centre.

Two babies in prams and their mothers were soaked and when the crowd of onlookers booed the police they launched a baton charge. One small boy was kicked in the stomach by a policeman and had to be rescued by a passer-by. A youth who was grabbed by three policemen was dragged across the street, thrown into a police van and then struck several times with batons.

Shortly afterwards a section of the marchers reached the city centre and began marching around the War Memorial. Police once again used batons to disperse them and as they retreated outside the city walls they hurled stones at the police and smashed shop windows. The crowd then retreated to the foot of a street below the city walls where they threw up a barricade and set it alight. Police did not attempt to follow them despite repeated taunts.

Later in the evening as the crowd behind the barricade was swelled by large numbers of youths it advanced repeatedly up

TURN TO BACK PAGE, COL. 5

RIOTS CAUSED 96 CASUALTIES

Early this morning, Altnagelvin Hospital, Derry, reported that the total number of riot casualties over the week-end was 96, including six policemen and a fireman.

The figures were, for Saturday afternoon, 30; Saturday night and Sunday morning, 46; Sunday night, 10.

Among those detained in hospital were three children.

A total of 17 men and two women were arrested and charged during the week-end.

British M.P.s Cannot Raise N.I. Matters

Although many M.P.s who object to the present electoral laws in Northern Ireland have complained about a system which permits Northern Ireland M.P.s to comment on internal affairs of the U.K., there is no way in which Northern Ireland questions can be raised on the floor of the House of Commons.

Constitutionally the Northern Ireland Government is entirely responsible for internal law and order. Britain's only responsibility is for external security through the armed forces.

Unlike Scotland and Wales, there is no allotted day for Northern Ireland matters to be discussed at Question Time.

M.P.s who wish to raise constitutional issues concerning Northern Ireland can only do so by making an appointment to see the Home Secretary of the day.

The power of the Northern Irish Parliament to make its own laws for maintaining peace, order and good government derives from the original 1920 Act, which resulted in the partition of Ireland between the North and the South.

U.K. legislation is applicable to Northern Ireland only if specific provision is made for this in the Bill and the Northern Ireland Parliament passes enabling legislation.

Demonstrators scatter as the police begin a baton charge in Duke Street, Derry.

Hardliners Are Returning In Prague

CZECH conservatives who are critics of party leader Dubcek but who still retain some popular appeal are the men Moscow is likely now to want in key jobs in Prague, informed sources said yesterday.

The sources said Moscow's leaders hope these men will be found within the present party Central Committee, although they had excluded those branded as arch-conservatives or collaborators after the August 20 invasion.

With the outcome of the tough negotiations in Moscow last week between Czechoslovak and Kremlin leaders, Dubcek is now faced with Soviet demands for further purges of progressives from the party ranks.

Moscow's new conditions for normalisation — the price of a withdrawal of the Warsaw Pact forces from Czechoslovakia—also include the reinforcement of party and state organs with men firmly adhering to Marxism-Leninism.

This is taken to mean the return of conservatives and hardliners to ranking positions in party and public life.

Communist sources believe the men the Soviet Union may be eyeing are conservatives and officials in the Central Committee who have not become thoroughly unpopular with the people.

Two of the men mentioned in this category are the former Deputy Defence Minister, General Otakar Rytir, and the ousted rector of the Communist Party college, Vilim Novy.

Both attacked Dubcek personally at the Central Committee meeting at the end of August, blaming the First Secretary for the events which led to the Warsaw Pact invasion.

MITTERAND WON'T LEAD NEW PARTY

M. Francois Mitterand, head of the French Federation of the Left, announced yesterday that he would not lead the single Democratic Socialist Party due to be formed next year.

M. Mitterand told the annual congress of the Convention of Republic Institutions — the group he led into the federation three years ago—that one of the essential factors of the new party would be the "renewal of men".

The new party is a projected fusion of the three main factions at present loosely allied within the Federation—the Socialists, the Radicals, and M. Mitterand's Convention of "Political Clubs".

But the Federation, rent by discord after the invasion of Czechoslovakia and a crushing electoral defeat last June, now look much more like splitting up than merging as planned.

As M. Mitterand apparently remains leader of the Federation until it is replaced by the new party, it is uncertain if his withdrawal will become effective.

The new party, M. Mitterand stressed, must be led by new men. "I shall not be a candidate for any post in this new party to which I shall belong," he said.

It had been reported that M. Mitterand was considering stepping down as a gesture of disillusionment with the state of France's anti-Gaullist opposition.

Taoiseach Deplores Incidents

THE Taoiseach, Mr. Lynch, has deplored Saturday's incidents in Derry, while the leader of the Labour Party, Mr. Corish, has sent a telegram to the British Prime Minister, Mr. Wilson, asking for a special inquiry.

Speaking at Kilkenny Mr Lynch expressed the hope that the root cause of such demonstrations would soon be eliminated so that people of different religious beliefs and political convictions would be treated as equals in every respect and would be permitted to live with each other in peace and harmony, free to exercise and enjoy their lawful democratic rights.

The following is the text of Mr. Corish's telegram to Mr. Wilson:

"Outraged at police brutality in Derry Civil Rights march. Request you set up special committee of inquiry immediately into injustice and discrimination in Northern Ireland. As Socialist am prepared to participate with you in discussion on this issue."

Mr. Corish has also sent the following telegram to the Taoiseach:

"Request you ask Capt. O'Neill to meet you for immediate talks to lodge strongest protests against police brutality in Derry. Further request that all future meetings with Northern Ireland Ministers should concentrate on matters of civil and political rights and ignore public relations trivialities."

CORK SUPPORT

Mr. C. O'Donovan, chairman Cork Borough Constituency Council, has sent the following telegram to Mr. Gerry Fitt, Republican Labour M.P., Belfast: "Congratulations on stand for civil liberties and democratic principles. Support and sympathy."

The Labour Party is also calling for the convening of the Council of Labour, representative of the Twenty-six Co. Labour Party, the Republic Labour Party in the Six Counties and also the Six County Labour Party.

Members of the Dublin Labour Group, composed of members of the Labour Party in the Dublin region last night sent the following telegram to Mr Gerry Fitt: "Derry's own 1913. Admiration and solidarity. Dublin Labour Group."

NIXON FORGES AHEAD

Mr. Richard Nixon has strengthened his commanding lead in the presidential election race, the "New York Times" reported yesterday.

The newspaper said in a survey it had conducted in all 50 states showed the Republican candidate leading by varying margins in 34 states with 380 electoral votes. To win an election, a candidate must receive 270 of the 538 electoral votes.

The third party candidate, Mr. George Wallace, was reported leading in seven states with 66 electoral votes and the Democratic nominee, Mr. Hubert Humphrey was ahead in four states and the District of Columbia (which includes Washington) with 28 electoral votes.

In five states with 64 electoral votes the three candidates were running too close for any definite trend to be discernible, the survey said.

The report, based on interviews with political leaders, said the figures represented a net gain of 34 electoral votes for Nixon over a similar survey conducted three weeks earlier.

The Humphrey total dropped 14, the Wallace total 11 and the indefinite total nine.

A "Washington Post" survey yesterday said a Republican presidential victory would be a "near certainty" if the election were held now.—Reuter.

Violence As 'Torch' Arrives In Mexico

Paratroopers beat back an estimated crowd of 100,000 with their rifle butts when the Olympic torch borne thousands of miles across land and sea from Mount Olympus, Greece, was carried ashore in Vera Cruz, Mexico, yesterday by a relay of Mexican swimmers.

They went into action when the festive, cheering crowd lining the waterfront tried to break through a cordon of navy guards who had clasped hands to hold back the throng. For a time it looked as if the crowd would get out of hand and surge on to the reception platform. But they fell back before the paratroops, who clubbed several people to the ground.

The waterproof torch was brought ashore from the Mexican frigate Durango, anchored about 800 yards offshore, by a relay of 17 Mexican swimmers. The swimmers were protected from sharks prowling the waters outside this tropical port in the Gulf of Mexico by navy frogmen armed with spear guns.

The authorities had to drop plans to use a huge aluminium net to keep out the sharks because tests showed it was too cumbersome. The frogmen were called out when a shark repellant ordered from Mexico City failed to arrive on time.

MOSCOW 'CONCERN' OVER YEMEN

The Soviet Union is concerned at alleged constant outside attempts to interfere with internal affairs of the Yemen and South Yemen Republic, a communique said in Moscow yesterday.

The communique, issued jointly by the Yemen Republic and the Soviet Union, and published by the official news agency Tass, followed talks by the Yemeni Prime Minister, Hassan Al-Amri, and President Podgorny and Prime Minister Kosygin. The Arab leader's delegation visited Moscow from October 1 to 5.

The communique said the two countries had discussed the problems of Soviet aid to the Arab Republic in strengthening its defences against "imperialist and other reactionary forces."

Both Yemeni and Soviet leaders said they regarded the United Nations' Security Council resolution of November 22, 1967—which calls for Israeli withdrawal from occupied Arab territories—as a basis for settlement of the Middle East problem.—Reuter.

NIGERIAN KILLINGS 'INEXCUSABLE'

A four-man international team of observers in Nigeria has said the killing of four relief workers in the civil war zone last Monday was "unprovoked and inexcusable".

The killings "could have been avoided, had an as-yet unidentified officer taken action to quell the excited soldiers", the team said in a report published on Saturday.

Two British missionaries, Mr. and Mrs. Albert Savory, Dr. Dragan Hercog, a Yugoslav, and Mr. Robert Carlsson, a Swede, were shot dead by a Federal Nigerian soldier outside a hospital at Okigwi.

Three Swedish Red Cross men were wounded in the incident which the Red Cross in Geneva described on Saturday as "murder".

The Commonwealth Office in London said yesterday that if current inquiries in Nigeria confirmed that the deaths of two British missionaries were not accidental, assurances should be given that "prompt steps will be taken to bring to justice those responsible for their deaths".

Exchange Of Fire Across The Jordan

Israeli troops and Arab guerrillas exchanged bursts of automatic fire across the Jordan River near the Israeli village of Ashdot Yaacov yesterday after a mine exploded under a half-track vehicle, an Israeli army spokesman said.

The guerillas opened fire from the east bank when the half-track ran over the mine on a dirt track on the Israeli-held west bank, the spokesman said.

There were no Israeli casualties and the vehicle was only slightly damaged. A second mine was later found nearby and exploded by troops.

Meanwhile an Arab communique issued in Beirut claimed Arab guerillas killed or wounded about 18 Israeli soldiers in a clash in the Jordan valley on Saturday. —(Reuter).

£16,000 Worth Of Gold Found — French police found about £16,000 worth of gold ingots in two suitcases at the bottom of the hold of a West German freighter in Marseilles on Saturday night, they disclosed yesterday.

EX-KING IN LONDON FOR OPERATION

Elaborate security arrangements came into force at Heathrow Airport, London last night for the arrival of ex-King Ion Saud of Saudi Arabia.

The 72-year-old ex-King arrived aboard a chartered jet with 40 relations and wives. He is in London on a private visit to have an operation on his knee.

As the plane taxied on to its aircraft stand, it was ringed by hired guards and police.

310 DIE IN FLOODS

The death roll from Darjeeling district's four days of pounding rain and landslides was officially stated to be 310 last night.

The spokesman said nothing was still known of the fate of 400 families living along the river banks because two bridges, the Teesta and the Balasun, had been washed away.

The governor of West Bengal, Dr. Dharma Vira, said all tourists in Darjeeling, India's best-known hill-station, were safe.

Despite the disrupted communications, there was no shortage of food, he said.

From Katmandu it was reported that rains and landslides in Eastern Nepal had taken 20 lives. Landslides also damaged a hydro-electric power project completed in Nepal three years ago with Soviet help, stopping its generators.—Reuter.

TWO EX-WIVES CLAIM £12½M.

Two of the 11 ex-wives of late playboy - heir Tommy Manville have started a legal battle over his estimated 30 million dollar (£12,500,000 sterling) will. Manville died last year aged 73, leaving a fortune from asbestos.

The legal battle will be between his eleventh and last wife Christina and Mrs. Manville number nine, Anita. According to a will dated 1962, Manville left the bulk of his fortune to Christina. But Anita has now produced a ten-page document claiming she is entitled to a half share under a will made in 1961 and never revoked.

Anita told reporters on Saturday night she had instructed her lawyers to file a suit to have the 1962 will declared void. She claimed Manville "was not mentally competent" when he wrote it.

Astronauts Will Circle Earth For 11 Days

The United States will launch three astronauts into space in the Apollo-7 craft next Friday to circle the earth for 11 days as a prelude to a future moon landing.

Walter Schirra, Donn Eisele and Walter Cunningham will cover 4,500,000 miles as they go round the world 162 times.

The Apollo-7 mission, costing 145 million dollars (about £60,000,000) will decide the exact target of Apollo-8, which is to be the first manned flight launched by the giant Saturn Five moon rocket.

The Apollo-8 mission could send three astronauts flying round the moon during the Christmas holidays, but much will depend on the outcome of Apollo-7.

SAFETY MEASURES

The astronauts are paying particular attention to safety. On January 27, 1967, astronauts Virgil Grissom, Edward White and Roger Chaffee died in an Apollo spacecraft with a similar rocket on the same pad as will launch Apollo-7.

The new spacecraft is devoid of inflammable material and has a quick-release escape hatch.—(Reuter).

Russians To Visit Cambodia— President Podgorny and Prime Minister Kosygin of the Soviet Union have accepted an invitation to visit Cambodia at a date still to be fixed, it was announced in Phnom Penh yesterday.

CARBERY WIN SENIOR FOOTBALL CHAMPIONSHIP

Carbery, drawn from the junior teams of Cork's South-West division, won the Cork S.F. Championship final replay at the Athletic Grounds yesterday when they beat Clonakilty 1-9 to 1-6 in an all-West Cork decider.

The attendance of 11,352 was almost identical to that which saw the sides draw a week earlier. Carbery won their only other title in 1937.

The Lord Mayor of Cork (Ald. John Bermingham) was present at the game.

BLUE CARS IN MORE ACCIDENTS

Blue cars are involved in more accidents than cars of any other colour, according to a world survey by a tyre company. The survey by Goodyear Tyre and Rubber showed that blue cars, the most popular colour, were involved in 25 per cent of more than 2,000 accidents investigated. Green cars were second in the accident list, with 20 per cent, white cars, which are almost as popular as blue, were involved in 12 per cent. Safest colour was bright orange.—(Reuter).

INSTITUTE'S NEW PRESIDENT

Sir Derek Pritchard, chairman of Allied Breweries Ltd., and chairman of the British National Export Council, is to be the next president of the Institute of Directors. He succeeds Sir Paul Chambers, former I.C.I. chairman, and now chairman of the Royal Insurance Company, the Institute announces.

Sir Derek, who is 58, will take over the presidency after the Institute's annual conference on November 7, when Sir Paul completes his five-year term of office.

"MISSING" CLIMBERS MEET RESCUE PARTY

A man and a woman—who did not know that search parties were looking for them—met their would-be rescuers as they came down the mountain yesterday. What had happened was that they had found themselves engulfed by fog and mist on Saturday night and decided to wait until daylight before descending.

On Saturday, three climbers were found injured by expert rescue team and taken to the Caernarvon and Anglesey Hospital, Bangor, with injuries received in falls.

Richard Sagar (19), a Washam (Oxford) college student, from Mead Way, Coulsdon, Surrey, fell 150 feet in Llanberis Pass and injured his head and pelvis. His condition yesterday was described as "fairly comfortable." Two other climbers—Leslie John Goodman (20), student, of Gordon Road, Reddish, Stockport, and Neville Sanderson (26), of Hall Close, Macclesfield — were also found injured by the Ogwen Cottage mountain school rescue team.

Goodman's condition was reported yesterday to be "only fair," but Sanderson was "fairly comfortable."

Benny's Bar Won't Be The Same Again

NOW that Henry McAllister has left for Dublin, Benny's Bar will never be the same.

"Kiss the Blarney Stone for me, Henry", one of the bar's regular patrons told the white-haired 69-year-old Irishman at a tumultous tearful going-away party in Los Angeles on Friday night.

The regulars at Benny's bought Mr. McAllister's plane ticket to Dublin. They decided to do it when he told them he wanted to go home to die. He went to Los Angeles from Dublin in 1959.

Mr. McAllister, suffering from arteriosclerosis, had a leg amputated in 1963. Now doctors say the other leg must come off.

In March, Henry used the money saved from his social security cheques to send his wife, Lily, back to Ireland. He promised to join her by next March to celebrate their 50th wedding anniversary.

After Lily left, Mr. McAllister said he spent his evenings "drinking a few Irish whiskeys, playing a few games of pool" and telling stories to the patrons at Benny's neighbourhood bar.

Then the fund-raising campaign began. The regulars pitched pennies and dollars into a jug on the bar. Last week they raffled a clock radio. Finally the collection totalled 355 dollars (about £150) — the cost of a plane ticket to Dublin.

Henry left Los Angeles on Saturday.

At his party, he read a poem he had written. It ended with the lines: "Dublin — now the only place my old heart wishes to be is where the River Liffey flows right down to the sea."

"Society Man" Offered Editor Queen Photos

THE editor of the West German magazine "Stern" said yesterday that the man who offered him photographs of Queen Elizabeth in bed soon after the birth of Prince Edward was "a man with a very good position in English society."

"I can only laugh when people say that the pictures were stolen," said Herr Henri Nannen. "But I cannot say who the man is or how he came to possess them."

He told Reuter in a radio-telephone conversation from his yacht in the Baltic that the man had delivered the photos to him personally in his Hamburg office, before offering them to the French magazine "Paris Match."

Today's edition of "Stern" will carry a front page colour picture — hitherto unpublished — showing the Queen and Prince Andrew, and six or seven black and white photographs, some of which have already appeared in "Paris Match."

Herr Nannen said the man, whom he had not known personally, rang the Hamburg offices directly and asked if they wanted the world rights of the 25 pictures.

"He came to Hamburg to deliver the photos personally to make sure they did not fall into the wrong hands," he said.

Herr Nannen said he told the man "Stern" only wanted the German rights and took seven or eight prints of the pictures, while the man retained the negatives.

He had then sent the man on to "Paris Match," Herr Nannen added.

Asked if he had hesitated before publishing in view of the rumpus which the "Paris Match" pictures had already caused in London, Herr Nannen said: "I did not hesitate for a minute—I would have hesitated if it had not been a man of absolute integrity and the pictures had not been decent."

"The photos are most decent, they are the most human photos we have ever seen of Queen Elizabeth. Before, she was an institution rather than a human being," he said. "It would be absurd if the Queen were offended."

He said the magazine would only publish a short text with the pictures today, but next week's edition would carry a description of life at Buckingham Palace written by a "Stern" magazine journalist.

When asked how much "Stern" had paid for the German rights of the photos, Herr Nannen replied: "I cannot say. But it was not a question of money."

ITALIAN MINISTRY MEN ARE SPY SUSPECTS

Police have detained four men, including two employees of the Italian Foreign Ministry, suspected of spying for the Soviet Union, Foreign Ministry sources said in Rome yesterday.

Counter-espionage agents alleged they had caught one in the act of handing over secret documents to another Italian he met on a street.

The two others detained were identified only as "private citizens."

The Rome newspaper "Il Tempo" said a Soviet diplomat was also involved but the Foreign Ministry declined to comment on this pending further investigations.

Two Soviet officials have been expelled from Italy in the last two years for espionage.

CONTENTS

1969

While most of the world had their eyes fixed on the moon in 1969 for Neil Armstrong's landing, that event was almost eclipsed in Ireland by the Troubles north of the border. The tone for the year was set as early as the first week of January when a civil rights march from Belfast to Dublin was attacked along the way by unionists and the police.

In August, as battles between nationalists, loyalists and the police spiralled out of control in Derry, the decision was taken to send 300 British soldiers to the city. When the soldiers arrived at the nationalist Bogside area, they were actually cheered by locals who were relieved to see the withdrawal of the RUC and B-Specials.

For several months, trouble had also been flaring in Belfast with Catholics and Protestants alike being forced from their homes amidst vicious street battles as the situation edged towards all-out civil war. In the Republic, Taoiseach Jack Lynch warned that his government would no longer "stand by" and called for a UN peace-keeping force to be sent to the North. In the meantime, the Irish army set up field hospitals at the border.

At least parts of Kerry did look spectacular for the filming of *Ryan's Daughter* and the movie, starring Robert Mitchum and Sarah Miles, went on to win two Oscars and was a great tourist advertisement for the area. In music this year, Joe Dolan made it to number three in the UK charts with 'Make Me An Island'.

Hail of petrol bombs in Derry riots

Wednesday, August 13

Derry erupted into a running battle between stone-throwing mobs and baton-charging police last night after a day of mounting tension. And later, senior police officers in the battle-torn city said the rioting was the worst since the troubles began in Northern Ireland a year ago.

Police, steel helmeted and carrying shields, had faced a vicious hail of stones and petrol bombs in the clashes between Catholics and Protestants. Police carried running battles for the predominantly Catholic Bogside area last night after the rioting flared in the afternoon near the end of the annual Orangemen 'Apprentice Boys' parade.

One youth told a Press Association staff reporter that on top of the block of flats on Bogside, there were men with about 900 petrol bombs. "There are more bombs than people in Bogside tonight."

Bernadette Devlin.

The mobs were forced back into Bogside by successive police charges, followed closely by Protestants who took the opportunity to smash windows and throw bricks at the retreating Catholics.

Then the Bogsiders counter-attacked and forced the sandwiched police back towards the city. At a huge barricade at one of the roads into Bogside yesterday, Miss Bernadette Devlin, Independent Unity MP for Mid-Ulster, had called on the people of the district to get behind the barricade and be prepared for any trouble.

Staff of CMP Dairies in Cork welcome the National Dairy Council's Milk Maids to their premises. The Maids used to travel the country promoting the use of dairy products.

NEWS BRIEFS

Jan A massive sales force gets to work gathering advertisements for Ireland's first *Golden Pages*, which is due to be published in April 1970. (7)

Apr The 176th edition of popular RTÉ series *The Riordans* is broadcast. (27)

Aug A three-bedroomed semi-detached house in Douglas, Cork, is advertised for £3,600. A new Vauxhall Ventora car, with 3.3 litre six-cylinder engine, is £1,510.

Dec Samuel Beckett is awarded the Nobel Prize for Literature. (10)

The Cork Examiner

NO. 47,088 MONDAY MORNING, JULY 21, 1969 PRICE: SIXPENCE

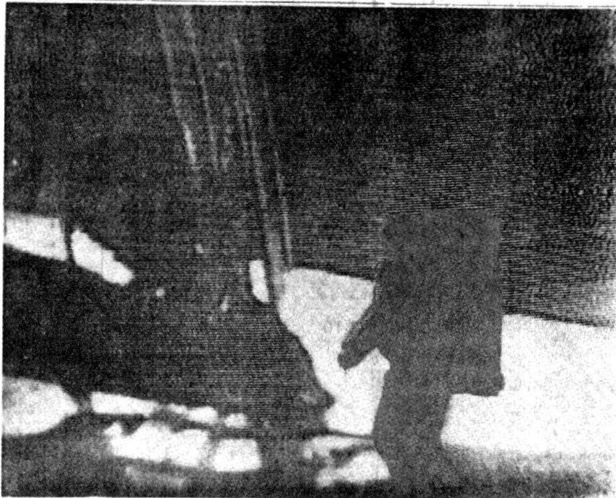

Neil Armstrong seen at the base of the lunar module after he had stepped on to the "powdery grey" surface of the moon this morning.

Three who made history: Astronauts Neil Armstrong (left), mission commander; Michael Collins, command module pilot (centre), and Edwin Aldrin, lunar module pilot, seen against a background of the lunar surface.

APOLLO MEN WALK ON MOON'S SURFACE

His 1,000/1 Bet Was A Winner

DAVID THRELFALL (26), Preston personnel officer, who five years ago placed a £10 bet at 1,000 to one, last night received a cheque for £10,010 on the London Weekend TV programme "Man on the Moon" from Air Commodore W. J. Brooks, of the William Hill Organisation.

Bachelor David, of Broadgate, Preston, bet on a human being setting foot on the moon or any other planet, star or heavenly body of comparable distance from the earth before January 1, 1971.

FIRST BET

It was his first bet apart from the football pools and the sum is tax-free, the bet being made before the betting tax came in.

He said: "I think I've had my share now. I don't think I will bet any money on people getting to Mars."

David, who has a steady girl-friend—"but it's not serious"—is spending some of his money on a three-week holiday in Nassau starting August 1st.

He is the biggest single winner on the moon landing.

A William Hill spokesman said: "We stand to lose more than £41,000 if both the Americans and Russians land before 1971."

Eleven Rescued From Island

A PARTY of 11 people and a four-month-old child were rescued from the Blasket Island yesterday by the Valentia Island lifeboat. They had been on the island since Tuesday last and had been without food since Wednesday.

The party were taken to the Blaskets on Tuesday by Kerry Boats Ltd. and arranged to be taken off on Wednesday. The boat did not return, however, and they had to spend five more days on the island before being taken off. They had originally gone on the island as part of a research to count the wild bird life and had taken food for only one day with them. They tried to attract attention from the mainland, but it was not until yesterday that they eventually managed to attract the attention of a passing

TURN TO BACK PAGE, COL. 2

CONTENTS

APOLLO mission Commander Neil Armstrong made history early today when he took the first trembling steps on to the surface of the moon, watched on television by millions of viewers throughout the world.

The realisation of a dream as old as mankind came after the lunar module had made a perfect landing, while the command capsule, piloted by astronaut Michael Collins, orbited overhead. Space agency officials were jubilant at the success, so far, of the mission, but the Apollo trio took it camly and recorded the historic event in laconic, matter-of-fact tones.

Armstrong stepped on to the moon at 3.56 a.m. after some delay in opening the module's hatch because of de-pressurisation. His first words as he put one foot on the lunar surface were: "One small step for man."

He reported the surface was fine like powdered charcoal, and his feet were "going in an eighth of an inch." He had "no difficulty" in moving around. Television pictures relayed back to earth were of very good quality, and Armstrong could be seen plainly as he moved around near the spacecraft.

At 4.14 a.m. Armstrong was followed down the ladder by "Buzz" Aldrin, who gingerly negotiated the rungs and jumped the last feet or so on to the moon's surface. So history was made, and another crucial stage in the epic journey was accomplished.

The flight plan calls for the ascent stage of the lunar module to lift off the moon surface at 6.55 p.m. (I.S.T.) today. The astronauts' chief physician, Dr. Charles Berry, said the spacemen might use up their spare time as a rest period after climbing back into the moonship.

GENTLE TOUCHDOWN

The astronauts put the spider-like Eagle gently on to the moon after controlling it by hand to avoid obstacles on the lunar surface.

It was part of the plan that the landing pilot should control the craft to choose the best spot to land. Armstrong said that going straight down on the target "would have taken us right into a football field sized crater with a large number of big boulders and rocks for about 100 feet around it."

"So we flew manually over the rock field to find a reasonably good area."

Mr. Thomas A. Paine, Director of the National Aeronautics and Space Administration (N.A.S.A.), told a press conference later that the fact that Eagle had to steer round obstacles meant that perhaps N.A.S.A. had been lucky with its unmanned space probes.

Immediately on landing, Armstrong and Aldrin began describing the lunar scene around them.

"BRIGHT, BEAUTIFUL"

With the cool efficiency and lack of emotion which has marked the whole historic journey of Apollo 11, Neil Armstrong and Edwin Aldrin told mission control and the world: "It looks like a collection of every variety of shape, angularity, granularity—a collection of about every kind of rock."

Then Armstrong, commander of man's first mission to the moon's surface looked through the other hatch at earth and declared: "It's big and bright and beautiful."

When the congratulations came from Houston, as Eagle settled firmly on its four legs after a virtually perfect horizontal landing, the two pioneers in Eagle at once replied: "Don't forget that one in the module." That was Michael Collins, piloting Columbia, the main Apollo space ship, 60 miles above the moon's surface. And Collins's comment was also laconic—"I heard the whole thing. Good show."

The immensity of the whole achievement was perhaps conveyed best by the sight of the crescent of the moon, hanging in the July sky as it has hung through man's previous history, seemingly unattainable.

ANCIENT LEGEND

Mission control earlier noted one headline alerting astronauts to watch for a lovely girl on the moon with a big rabbit.

"An ancient legend says a beautiful Chinese girl named Chang has been living there for 4,000 years," mission control read. "It seems she was banished to the moon because she stole the pill of

TURN TO BACK PAGE, COL. 4

FLASH APOLLO
APOLLO LANDED ON MOON
— 2117

How the historic news of the landing was flashed to newspapers throughout the world last night. Mission control gave the touchdown time unofficially as 102 hours 45 minutes and 42 seconds into the Moon mission (9.17 p.m. I.S.T.; July 20).

HOW THEY REACHED THE MOON

Here is how Reuter's News Agency, in a direct link with Mission Control at Houston, reported the historic moon landing last night:

Houston, Texas, Sunday. Astronauts Neil Armstrong and Edwin Aldrin began their hazardous eleven and a half minute final descent to the surface of the moon.

At 46,000 feet above the moon Mission Control told the moonship Eagle "everything is looking good to us." Aldrin replied: "Looks real good."

"YOU ARE GO"

Mission Control: "Eagle, you are go to continue power descent. You are go to continue power descent" (with seven minutes to go).

Eagle: Roger.

(Two and a half minutes to go)

Control: 3,000 feet (1,000 metres) Eagle you're looking great ... you are go for landing.

As the Eagle descended the following dialogue came over the radio:

Ground Control: Eagle you're looking great coming up nine minutes ... you are go for landing.

Eagle: Roger, understand. Go for landing.

"LOOKING GREAT"

Control: Eagle looking great. You're go.

Eagle: 75 feet, looking good. 30 seconds lights on. Down 2½, forward, forward 40 feet down two and one half, picking up some dust ... just move to the right a little. Engine stop.

Houston: The Eagle has landed.

Control: We copy you on the ground. We got a bunch of guys about to turn blue. We're breathing again.

Eagle: Roger, we'll be busy for a minute. Thank you. Very smooth touchdown.

Control: Eagle you are stay for T one (touchdown plus one hour).

Eagle: Roger, we understand, stay for T one.

Control: Roger, read you Columbia. Eagle has landed. It is at Tranquility base. Eagle has landed at Tranquility.

"Glory To God In Highest" Says Pope

AS the world last night greeted news of the lunar landing, His Holiness Pope Paul, in an emotional and unprecedented speech declared: "Glory to God in the highest, and peace on earth to men of good will."

In a dramatic, unscheduled speech from his summer retreat in the Alban Hills, the 71-year-old Pontiff, who followed the telecasts of the Apollo flight on colour television, said:

"We, humble representatives of that Christ, who, coming among us from the abyss of divinity, has made to resound in the heavens this blessed voice, today we make an echo, repeating it in a celebration on the part of the whole terrestrial globe, with no more unsurpassable bounds of human existence, but openness to the expanse of endless space and a new destiny.

"Glory to God."

"And honour to you artifices of this great spacial enterprise," the Pope continued. "Honour to those responsible, to those who have studied for it, created it, organised it, operated it."

"HONOUR TO ALL"

"Honour to all those who have made this bold flight possible. Honour to all of you who have been in some way involved. Honour to you who, seated behind your awesome instruments are controlling (the mission), to you, who notified the world of the feat and the hour, which feat spreads to the heavens — the wise dominion and courage of man. Honour, salutes, and blessings."

"STUPENDOUS"

After watching the Apollo touchdown, Sir Bernard Lovell, Director at Jodrell Bank, said: "The moment of touchdown was one of the moments of the greatest drama in the history of man. The success in this part of the enterprise opens the most enormous opportunities for the future exploration of the universe.

"Those of us who have watched the development of the space programme will wish to convey our heartfelt congratulations to the Americans on this demonstration of their tremendous superiority."

CROWD CHEERED

A crowd of about 5,000 in Trafalgar Square clapped and cheered as they heard the news of the touch down, via a huge

TURN TO BACK PAGE, COL. 6

Surface Is "Grey And Rocky"

Neil Armstrong last night gave a graphic, first-hand account of what the moon looks like at close quarters:—

"The colour of the local surface is very comparable to that we observed from orbit at a 10 degrees sun angle. It's pretty much without colour. It's grey and very white, chalk grey ... and it's considerably darker, more like an ashen grey, as you look out 90 degrees to the sun".

He said some rocks, apparently broken open by the descent engine firing, showed a darker grey inside. He said it could be basalt, a rock which in its earthly form has been transformed by volcanic activity.

There did not appear to be too much general colour at the moment but the rocks looked as if they were going to have more interesting colours later.

BIG BOULDERS

Armstrong reported: "Boulders and very little else," and those who had believed that the landing area had been picked because it was billiard table smooth were shaken to hear him and Aldrin refer to craters "five to 70 feet", ridges 20 feet high, a hill dead ahead, and great angular chunks of rock.

ALDRIN: "PAUSE AND THINK"

Aldrin yesterday interrupted his work inside the moon landing craft on the surface of the moon to ask people throughout the world to pause and "consider the events of the past few hours — each in his own way."

Aldrin: "This is the lunar module pilot: I'd just like to ask that everyone around the world who might be listening pause and consider the events of the past few hours.

"I'd like to ask everyone to contemplate these events, each in his own way."

LUNA-15 MYSTERY DEEPENS

The Soviet Luna-15 satellite last night swung into a new orbit bringing it only 10 miles from the lunar surface, the closest any Russian space probe has ever been to the moon.

The announcement in Moscow, only a few hours before the American astronauts were to land, deepened the week-long mystery of Russian intentions as the two rival stations went around in different orbits.

But the Soviet Union maintained its strict silence on the purpose of its probe as it moved closer to the Apollo-11 module's landing site.

A bland announcement issued by the official Tass news agency said Luna-15 was continuing "scientific exploration in near-lunar space" but gave no indication whether it would attempt to land on the Moon or not.

In the usual absence of explanation from the Russians, all the informed speculation on Luna-15 was coming from the British observatory at Jodrell Bank.

AFTER ORBIT, A 1,000 DOLLAR ORB

A 1,000 dollar, 24 carat gold orb, two and a quarter inches in diameter and weighing five ounces, is to be presented to each of the astronauts and to Mrs. Rose Kennedy, mother of John, Robert and Edward Kennedy, to commemorate the moon landing.

It has a diamond to mark the exact landing spot in the Sea of Tranquility, and is made by Mr. Louis Osman, who designed and made the Prince of Wales's investiture crown. It is being presented to Mrs. Kennedy to mark President Kennedy's decision to put a man on the moon by 1970.

MEDALS FROM BRITAIN

The British Interplanetary Society is awarding gold medals to each of the Apollo 11 team. The medals are three inches in diameter with a symbol of the earth, a space rocket and a human figure on one side, and an inscription on the other.

Other B.I.S. medals have gone to Yuri Gagarin, in 1961, and Valentina Tereshkova in 1964.

Aldrin Took Communion Bread To Moon

ASTRONAUT ALDRIN went to the moon yesterday with a piece of Communion bread he will use there to symbolise fellowship with his home church on earth.

The safety of Apollo 11 crewmen and the success of the mission were included in prayers of all space centre churches. "Pray for Neil, Mike and Buzz," said the Rev. M. Dean Woodruff, Minister of the Webster Presbyterian Church where Aldrin is an Elder.

Mrs. Aldrin and their three children listened to the sermon from a pew near the front. When Rev. Woodruff brought out the bread for Communion, a portion of the loaf had been broken away.

The Minister explained that Aldrin took it with him on the moon trip and at some time during the afternoon, after the moon landing was made, Aldrin would symbolically join the other parishioners in Communion during one of his rest periods. "This was Aldrin's idea," Rev. Woodruff said.

Members of St. Paul's Catholic Church, where Mrs. Michael Collins and both her children attended Mass, offered a special prayer for "a safe landing and ascent from the moon."

At the beginning of the mid-morning Mass, it was announced that all Masses yesterday were offered for the safety of the astronauts and the success of Apollo 11. Mrs. Collins, in a white suit with a black head veil, sat near the front and was one of the first to take Communion.

Mrs. Neil Armstrong remained in her home yesterday morning, listening closely to reports from mission control centre. The only activity outside the house occurred when Mary (6) went out to get the Sunday newspaper.

A Space Agency spokesman who had been in the home said Mrs. Armstrong, Mark and Eric (12) "had their morning devotional together, alone" in a bedroom while guests in the house waited in other rooms.

After the service, Mrs. Aldrin was surrounded by a pushing group of newsmen, photographers and spectators. Finally, apparently almost in tears, she broke through those surrounding her and ran to her car.

1970

That Fianna Fáil ministers could become involved in a plan to smuggle guns to nationalists in the North might seem ludicrous today but, taken in the context of events on the island around 1970, such a move would at least fit with the mindset of a huge number of people south of the border. Rather than the revulsion at IRA violence which would come later, there was a strong feeling of sympathy and solidarity with the nationalist population.

The 'Arms Crisis' began when Taoiseach Jack Lynch fired Charles Haughey and Neill Blaney from the cabinet after he received reports alleging their involvement in gun running. However, when the matter was investigated further, both men were found to be innocent.

Richard Nixon, another politician about to be tainted with scandal, met with a mixed response when he came to Ireland. He visited Limerick, Dublin and wife Patricia's Irish relatives at Ballinrobe, Co Mayo. 'Nixon Charm Captures Irish Hearts' was the *Examiner* headline, but coverage was also given to the protests against the ongoing war in Vietnam. A small home-made bomb exploded in Drumcondra along the route the American president was to take to Dublin airport.

Government sending plane for Dana

Monday, March 23

The government are sending a plane to Amsterdam today to fly Dana, Ireland's Eurovison Song contest heroine, to Dublin for a special reception. From there she will be flown later to Ballykelly Airport outside Derry, her home town.

Top executives of RTÉ and public representatives are expected to go to Dublin Airport to greet the 18-year-old singer whose success with 'All Kinds of Everything' before an audience of an estimated 450 million on Saturday night is likely to bring her a small fortune before she has even gained her General Certificate of Education (the equivalent of our Leaving Certificate).

In one respect Dana's gain will be RTÉ's loss because with the honour of winning comes that of holding next year's Song Contest, and Mr Thomas P Hardiman, RTÉ's director general, says that if the contest is to be continued, RTÉ would certainly mount it and do a first class job on it, and in colour too. The cost would be about £20,000.

Dana, Ireland's Eurovision winner.

No flat for man with coloured family

Tuesday, January 13

There has been a great controversy in the newspapers, television, radio and indeed word of mouth, about apartheid in South Africa, culminating in a mile-long protest march before the Ireland v Springboks Rugby game in Dublin on Saturday last.

But how many care that apartheid is being practised on our own doorstep and by our own people?

The Cooper family from Leeds – Ted (29), his pretty wife Violet and their two babies, Simon, who is just 12 months old, and Christopher, who is three – are a living reproach to all who boast concern or have a conscience about apartheid.

Because his wife and children are coloured, Ted, who came to Cork to work for a well-known building firm and who is earning good wages, cannot get a flat for his wife and family.

"We rented this caravan as a temporary measure and straight away I began phoning flat owners who had advertised vacancies and who had given their telephone numbers," said Ted. "On many occasions I went along and discussed terms, but when they heard that my wife was coloured they suddenly remembered that the flat had been let to somebody else. I have seen the same flats re-advertised as vacant a few days later."

NEWS BRIEFS

Jan As Nigerian forces mop up the last of Biafran resistance in a war that has ravaged the area since 1967, 80 Irish priests and nuns refuse to leave the people they had been helping. Three of the children of new Biafran leader Philip Effiong are in school in Dublin. (13)

May A Maoist bookshop in Cork is attacked by a crowd of about 1,000 local people who feared that their children were being affected by it. (23)

May Bishop Lucey of Cork warns of the importance of early baptism for babies: "To keep the child longer than a week without baptism, unless in very special circumstances, is to risk the child's eternal salvation at least a little." (24)

The Cork Examiner

NO. 47,333 THURSDAY MORNING, MAY 7, 1970 PRICE SIXPENCE

Shock report to Dail on sacking of Blaney and Haughey

MINISTERS IN GUN-RUNNING PLOT, SAYS TAOISEACH

AS the Dail sat into the early hours of this morning, an extraordinary story of attempted gun-running by two Ministers, Mr. Haughey and Mr. Blaney, dismissed from the Government yesterday, was unfolded, first by the Taoiseach, Mr. Lynch, with Mr. Liam Cosgrave, the Fine Gael leader, filling in the details.

Mr. Lynch told a crowded House, which sat until 2.30 a.m., how over a fortnight ago the security forces had brought him information about an alleged attempt to import arms from the Continent involving prima facie Deputy Blaney and Deputy Haughey.

Mr. Lynch, reading from notes, described to a silent House how he took steps to prevent the unauthorised importation of arms and then interviewed both Ministers who denied that they had "instigated in any way the attempted importation of arms".

Mr. Boland and Mr. Blaney listened on the back benches as the Taoiseach said that Deputy Blaney and Deputy Haughey had asked for time to consider their positions. He had given them that time and when he asked them for their resignations "because he was convinced that not even the slightest suspicion should attach to any member of the Government", both Ministers had told him they would give their resignations that morning (Wednesday) but not having received them, he then requested the President under the Constitution to terminate their appointments.

The Taoiseach assured the House that this was the only attempted importation of arms of which he had evidence and which the two Ministers named, were associated, that these arms had not been landed in this country and that the steps he had taken ensured that they would not be landed.

Mr. Liam Cosgrave described the situation as being without parallel in the history of the State.

He then went on to describe how he had, some time ago, received information that the arms importation involved a number of members of the Government. The value of the arms was £80,000, and they were for use by an illegal organisation.

This had involved making arrangements with the Department of Finance for getting the arms through customs at Dublin Airport without a check.

It involved an Army officer and when this came to the notice of a senior Garda officer, an official in the Department of Finance stated that the Minister had authorised the passage of the arms through customs.

Mr. Cosgrave said that eventually, after a lot of dithering, the authority from the Department of Finance for this purpose was dropped.

He said that he had received a document on official Garda notepaper which had supported the information already at his disposal. It included some additional names and stated that there was a plot to bring arms from the Continent worth £80,000 and mentioned a Captain Kelly, the former Ministers for Finance and Agriculture and two associates.

The very security of the State was threatened, the lives of the northern minority had been put in jeopardy and the country was drifting into anarchy. What action was proposed to take against these people, he had mentioned, and whose names he had brought to the notice of the Taoiseach.

CRIMINAL PROCEEDINGS

Mr. Brendan Corish, the Labour leader, asked bluntly if criminal proceedings were to be taken, and would these three Ministers be asked to answer the accusations by the Taoiseach?

Mr. Corish said that the Taoiseach had stated that no arms had been brought in, but there were rumours that arms had been brought in and he suggested that the Taoiseach should have further conversations with his dismissed colleagues to learn the actual facts.

The only thing for the Government to do was to decide to go to the country within the next 24 hours.

Mr. T. F. O'Higgins (F.G.) said that only when it became clear that the facts were known to the Opposition was a bomb put under the Taoiseach.

CHARGES DENIED

When Mr. O'Higgins said that when they had learned from an evening newspaper that the Chief of Staff had attended at a meeting of the Government that day to make a protest against what was happening to the armed forces, Mr. Lynch retorted that was not true.

When Mr. O'Higgins further alleged that in recent times Gardai had been asked to lay off prosecutions, Mr. Lynch again said that this was not true.

Dr. Conor Cruise O'Brien (Labour) who agreed that the matter would not have been exposed but for the efforts of Deputy Cosgrave, declared that Fianna Fail should not continue to hold on to office with "these tainted votes" of people on whom grave charges rested.

Technically the House was discussing a motion to approve the nomination of Mr. Desmond O'Malley as a Minister of the Government. Mr. Lynch had confirmed that he was assigning him to the Department of Justice, but this was one of the few references to Mr. O'Malley.

VACANT MINISTRIES

The Dail will resume at 10.30 a.m. tomorrow, and the Taoiseach will then name the Deputies he will propose for Ministries to fill the vacancies caused by the recent crisis. Four Ministries and one Parliamentary Secretaryship are vacant.

Deputies have been so preoccupied with the startling disclosures yesterday that the question of successors to the deposed Ministers has not got much consideration. It is thought, however, that Mr. Lynch will bring in Mr. George Colley as his Finance Minister, which would be a promotion and that he will make consequential shuffles of other Ministers and may consider Mr. G. Collins, Parliamentary Secretary to the Minister for Industry and Commerce and Mr. Gerry Cronin, Parliamentary Secretary to the Minister for Agriculture as Junior Ministers, while Mr. Michael O'Kennedy and Mr. David Andrews are still mentioned for Parliamentary Secretaryships.

● Dail report on Back Page.

Mr. Blaney and Mr. Boland outside Dail Eireann yesterday.

Lynch is master in his own house

By Anthony Ring

THE TAOISEACH, Mr. Lynch, emerged last night victoriously in full command of the leadership of a united Fianna Fail parliamentary party after a day of incredible happenings when it appeared certain that the party would be irreparably split.

The transformation from a party on the verge of ruin took just less than one hour in the Fianna Fail party's fifth-floor room in the new wing of Leinster House. The deputies came crowding out of the lifts smiling and joking, obviously relieved that once again the party's discipline had triumphed in the face of adversity.

THE MASTER

It seemed almost impossible to believe it, but the deputies claimed it was so, and their party's official statement said it. Time alone will prove whether the wounds inflicted over the past two days can heal without scars. Certain it is now that following the resignations or sackings of four long-standing and influential Ministers Mr. Lynch is now master without question in his own house.

A statement issued after the meeting which was chaired by Cork deputy Mr. A. A. Healy said that the special meeting unanimously endorsed a motion by the Taoiseach that the party approve such nominations as he may make to replace the members of the Government whose appointments had been terminated.

Each of the three former Ministers, Mr. Blaney, Mr. Haughey and Mr. Boland and the former parliamentary secretary to the Minister for Local Government Mr. Paudge Brennan expressed unreservedly his loyalty to the Fianna Fail Party and the Taoiseach, the statement added.

The meeting expressed its confidence in the Taoiseach and the policies of the Government and although there was no vote, neither was there dissent. Deputies Haughey, Blaney and Boland were present and I understand conceded publicly the Taoiseach's right to decide who he would have in his Government. Mr. O Morain was absent. He is still in hospital.

I was informed also that one

TURN TO BACK PAGE, COL. 6

Day's events precipitated by Cosgrave visit?

Speaking outside the Dail chamber at Leinster House last night, Mr. Cosgrave said the Taoiseach's timing of his dismissal of the two Ministers and the resignation of the third suggested that his (Mr. Cosgrave's) visit to Mr. Lynch with the information at his disposal precipitated the day's dramatic events.

The Taoiseach, he pointed out, had had his discussions with

Mr. Cosgrave

the Ministers, had requested their resignations, but had taken no action.

According to his information, about five or six tons of arms had been involved, and a figure of £80,000 had been put on them.

DISSOLUTION

He held there was an absolute duty on the Taoiseach to dissolve the Government, since it was relying on the support of men whom he had considered unfit to serve as members of the Government.

It was most important to the cause of national unity that the people of the North should know that the South had a responsible Government and a policy that was enforced.

Another call for the dissolution of Parliament came from Mr. Corish, who said the Government had lost the confidence of the people in relation to their policies.

Attorney General free to act

—CHILDERS

THE Tanaiste, Mr. Childers, said last night that the Attorney General is absolutely free, on the basis of any facts he can get, to take whatever action he wishes against any person in the State who imports arms illegally. In this case the arms were not imported, that was prevented.

In an interview, Mr. Childers said that it was unthinkable that a government formed by Fine Gael or Labour, together or separately could face all the challenges that this year would present, a year in which the situation in Northern Ireland was expected to become extremely difficult. It was one of the examples of a great party that it could purge itself.

UNREASONING FEAR

"I myself believe that these two men were blinded by some unreasoning fear that they in some way had to come to the rescue of certain elements in the North, whereas they should have in fact realised that there is no responsible body in the North to whom arms could be given and whose policy could be definitely known in advance, whose attitude could be known in advance.

"The only thing we know about the North is that the only way of preventing violence there is that a great body of moderate opinion both nationalist opinion and Unionist, would be able to hold its sway over the extreme elements, that is the only way that a blood bath can be avoided.

NOT IN FORCE

"I think a lot of people, not sufficiently long in politics, seem to have forgotten that this has been the policy of the Fianna Fail party right from its inception, that Partition could not be

TURN TO BACK PAGE, COL. 7

CONTENTS

"MACHINE PARTS" WERE ARMS FOR IRELAND

Recently a pilot who was sent to collect a cargo in Vienna found that the "machine parts" of the cargo consisted of about ten tons of small arms.

He refused to take it to Ireland, returned to London and reported the matter, which was taken up through diplomatic channels.

The first information about the alleged plot to smuggle arms reached Scotland Yard's Special Branch towards the end of last year.

It was discovered that agents of the I.R.A. were visiting Irish communities in London, Liverpool and other cities, writes the P.A. Chief Crime Reporter.

The exiles were asked to give to arms funds.

Later I.R.A. agents contacted arms dealers in England and meetings took place in West End hotels, where the buyers were lavish with their entertainment and indicated they had big money to spend.

Some deals were made but before arrangements could be ended sentences were passed on I.R.A. men for offences in the Midlands. These were not connected with the deals but frightened the would-be suppliers.

Reports noted in Whitehall

The sensational reports coming out of the Republic of Ireland were being carefully noted in Whitehall, writes a Press Association political correspondent.

But there was no immediate reaction from the British Government over the astounding stories because, predictably, government sources stressed that the whole matter concerned a country which had complete sovereignty over its own affairs and naturally would not welcome intervention.

Minister since day he entered Dail

Mr. Kevin Boland who has resigned is the 47 year old son of Mr. Gerald Boland, former Minister for Justice and nephew of Harry Boland one of the leading republican figures in the Anglo Irish struggle.

Mr. Boland has been a Minister since the first day he entered the Dail in 1957. He was named Minister for Defence by Mr. De Valera. Under Mr. Lemass he became Minister for Social Welfare in 1961, and under Mr. Lynch, Minister for Local Government in 1966.

Mr. Blaney a 45 year old teacher and a deputy for Donegal since 1948 when he succeeded his father was appointed Minister for Posts and Telegraphs by Mr. De Valera in 1957 and later Minister for Local Government, a portfolio he retained when Mr. Lemass became Taoiseach in 1961. He became Minister for Agriculture under Mr. Lynch.

Mr. Charles J. Haughey, son of an army officer and son-in-law of Mr. Lemass was first elected in 1957, became Parliamentary Secretary in 1960, Minister for Justice in 1961, Minister for Agriculture in October 1964 and Minister for Finance in 1967. He is a chartered accountant.

Later yesterday it was learned that Mr. Paudge Brennan, Parliamentary Secretary to the Minister for Local Government, who is a close associate of Mr. Boland, had handed in his resignation.

TRACTOR CLERKS WALK OUT

Tractor assembly at Massey Ferguson's Coventry factory was halted yesterday, by an unofficial strike by 14 clerical workers.

About 350 day shift workers were sent home and 200 on the night shift told not to come in.

The strikers took action after complaining about working conditions in their office, said a company spokesman. They are due to meet today.

CORK SUPPORT FOR TAOISEACH

The following telegram was sent to Mr. Lynch last night.

Cork City N.W. and S.E. Comhairle Dail Ceanntair Fianna Fail wish to express our congratulations and assure you of our wholehearted support in the measures you have taken.

WHY I QUIT

—BOLAND

Mr. Kevin Boland said early morning that he thought the Taoiseach had made an error in sacking Deputies Blaney and Haughey.

Mr. Boland said he had resigned because he did not agree with the manner in which the Six County situation had been handled by the Taoiseach and he did not agree with the methods by which the government was being conducted.

He said he fully agreed with the policy on the Six Counties as announced by the Taoiseach at the Fianna Fail Ard Feis but he saw a difference between the manner in which this matter had been handled and the policy announcement. He said he didn't think there was any reason for the Taoiseach to believe Mr. O Morain, Mr Blaney or Mr. Haughey did not subscribe to Government policy on the Six Counties as announced at the Ard Feis and therefore there was no reason for requesting resignations.

Mr. Blaney said yesterday afternoon: "I have not handed in my resignation, and I don't plan to. Only time will tell if I hand it in at any stage."

UNAWARE OF IMPENDING CHANGES

A FEW hours before the sackings Agriculture Minister, Mr. Blaney attended a private dinner party with agricultural journalists covering the Royal Dublin Spring Show. I sat opposite him at the dinner table, writes PA agricultural correspondent Leonard Moxon.

Mr. Blaney was obviously unaware of the impending changes. He was completely relaxed.

He chatted and joked, and discussed Ireland's farming problems and plans for the future. He was particularly concerned by the decline in Ireland's sheep population, which has followed a similar pattern to that in Britain.

It was an early dinner by Irish standards, starting about 7 p.m. after a reception. Mr. Blaney left immediately after the meal to keep a previously-made appointment. There was no hint of urgency in his departure.

Yesterday Mr. Blaney was to have paid an official visit to the show.

1971

The introduction of internment in 1971 was another milestone in the slide into prolonged violence in Northern Ireland. Most of the 'suspects' taken away in those infamous raids were not even involved in IRA activity, and the actions of the security forces further fuelled resentment amongst the Nationalist community, and sympathy in the Republic as refugees streamed over the border.

In the South, the struggle for 'women's lib' was also gaining momentum as Nell McCafferty and other members of the Irish Women's Liberation Movement targeted the ban on any form of artificial contraception in the Republic.

Women's Libbers flout contraceptive law

Monday, May 24

About 40 members of the Irish Women's Liberation Movement, some of whom had never seen a contraceptive, walked past customs officials at Connolly Station, Dublin, on Saturday night last with a horde of pills and other contraceptive devices.

Earlier in the day, the women had travelled to Belfast and purchased contraceptives in an attempt to focus attention on legislation banning contraceptive devices in the Republic.

On return to Dublin, customs officials when told by the women that they possessed contraceptive devices, asked for them. The women handed them over but demanded receipts.

Others refused to hand them over, however, and when one official said he was "not interested" when told by a "Liberationist" that the contraceptives were in her handbag, the women cheered and shouted: "he's not interested."

They all then marched towards the exit gates throwing their devices aloft to show the 200-strong crowd who had come to lend support. Some of the women waved some of the devices at the Gardaí but no action was taken.

Paul McCartney with his wife Linda, daughters Heather and Mary, and the family dog at Cork Airport where they had just missed their plane.

Where they live – at 25 in a hut

Wednesday, August 11

Confusion, bewilderment and a look of hopelessness showed on the faces of the latest group of refugees from the North, who arrived at Kilworth Camp, Co Cork, last night. The majority of the 134 men, women and children had left Belfast on Monday, and were still suffering the shock of events of what they termed "Bloody Monday".

One 24-year-old woman with a seven-month-old baby in her arms told how residents in the Ardoyne area were awakened by the sound of soldiers shouting: "Internment is in and we've got you now."

People tried to build barricades while the women gathered bottles and stones and anything they could use as weapons, she said. But the soldiers retaliated with rubber bullets and threatened that once they had interned the men, they would rape the women.

One of the most heartbreaking sights at the camp was the arrival of the 97 children in the group, many of them too young to grasp the situation. One 11-year-old girl said, with tears in her eyes, that she wanted to go back to her home in the Falls Road area to be with her five brothers and sisters who had remained behind to defend their homes.

NEWS BRIEFS

Jan Sixty-six people are crushed to death at a match in Glasgow between local rivals Celtic and Rangers when crowd barriers on the terraces collapse. (2)

Feb Ireland goes decimal with the change from £.s.d to £.p, bringing an end to the 'old money' system. (15)

Feb Robert Curtis from Newcastle becomes the first British soldier to be killed in the Troubles when he's shot by the IRA in Belfast. (6)

Mar Road deaths for the first three months of the year in Ireland reach 123.

Apr The GAA congress at Queen's University, Belfast yesterday deleted Rule 27, which for 66 years banned its members from playing, promoting or attending soccer, rugby, hockey and cricket. (12)

A British naval launch is blown up in Baltimore, West Cork. The Cork command of the Official IRA claim responsibility. (21)

Aug Twelve Cork dockers sweep up mounds of poisoned grain on the city's quays in an attempt to stop the "slaughter" of pigeons by grain handling firms. (9)

The Cork Examiner

NO. 47,726 TUESDAY MORNING, AUGUST 10, 1971 PRICE: 3½p.

Day-long violence erupts after dawn internment raids

WOMEN, CHILDREN DIE IN BLOODBATH

British troops pinned down by sniper fire in the Ardoyne area of Belfast last evening.

SUDDEN DEATH stalked the narrow, bloodstained streets of Belfast last night. Twelve—including two women — have been killed in an orgy of shooting, rioting, burning and looting which has shocked and shaken even the trouble-torn province.

The day-long frenzy of blood-letting followed dawn swoops in which more than 300 were detained under new wide-ranging powers of internment.

Besides the two women, one British soldier has died, one Ulster Defence Regiment private, two boys — one age 15 — a security guard, and five civilians. Eighteen troops have been hurt—about 11 with gunshot wounds.

Violence returned to the streets of Belfast last night when a group of more than 70 attacked an Army post in the Lower Falls.

In another incident, a number of houses occupied by Protestants on the edge of the predominantly Catholic Ardoyne area were burned down after the families had been ordered to leave.

A thick black cloud of smoke hung over the area as the houses burned. Most of them were in just two streets, Farrington Gardens and Velsheda Park, in the middle of the Catholic area.

As firemen fought the blaze, gunshots could be heard in the background.

The firemen made two attempts to get at the fires but they were thrown back each time by hostile crowds.

A spokesman commented: "We did our best to get in but it was just impossible."

It was reported that Roman Catholic families had left Mayo Street, off the Springfield Road after they had been threatened by Protestants.

HOUSES SET ON FIRE

There were also reports that vans marked I.R.A. had driven around Protestant streets delivering a "get out ultimatum."

It was in the Ardoyne area that the first woman was killed. An army spokesman said: "She was found by a military patrol and taken to hospital. But she was found to be dead from a gunshot wound on arrival.

"We believe she may belong to one of the Protestant families who have left their homes in the area.

"We have heard that some have set fire to their houses they left and others have had it done for them."

The dead woman, a 60 years old widow, has been named as Mrs. Worthington.

A soldier in the part-time Ulster Defence regiment was shot dead last night at Clady on the Co. Tyrone-Republic border. The soldier, who was not named, was in a patrol that was fired on from a passing car.

He was the first member of the Ulster Defence Regiment to be killed during the present unrest.

In a Belfast gun battle at New Barnsley Estate, two men died from gunshot wounds and a woman was also believed killed.

Police reported that the woman's body—which lay in the road outside the army post—was spirited away.

A priest was wounded by a bullet as he made his way to administer the last rites to a dying man, according to unconfirmed reports from army and police reports.

It was believed that Fr. Hugh Mullan, of the Corpus Christi Church at Ballymurphy, Belfast, was shot as he was walking across fields to see the bleeding man.

It was thought the priest was not seriously wounded, but this was also unconfirmed.

"WAR OF ATTRITION"

Last night, Maj.-Gen. Robert Ford, Commander, Land Forces, said: "Since early this morning, the security forces have been engaged in a constant war of attrition against terrorists armed with automatic weapons, petrol and gelignite bombs."

He appealed to everyone living in the troubled areas to remain indoors and not to become involved.

A spokesman for the Belfast Royal Victoria Hospital denied casualties were being prevented from entering the hospital.

"We have had some threats and the army has been investigating but there has been no indication that casualties have been prevented from getting here.

"There has been a steady flow of casualties, both civilian and military," he said.

BUS HIJACKED

A bus was hijacked and set alight by a group of youths in Armagh last night near the end of a protest meeting attended by about 500 people.

It happened at Irish Street corner, in the predominantly

CONTINUED ON BACK PAGE, COLUMN SIX

Eleven soldiers injured in Derry

AFTER 15 hours continuous fighting in Derry, 11 soldiers were injured, five by gunfire.

One soldier was lying in Althalgelvin Hospital dangerously ill after being shot by a mystery gunman.

The fighting started before dawn when troops made a surprise swoop on possible troublemakers.

Cars screamed through the city yesterday morning with headlights blazing to warn people of the searches.

The crowds concentrated their

Paisley Church burned

A church at Banbridge, Co. Down, belonging to the Free Presbyterian Church of Ulster—the Rev. Ian Paisley's denomination — was "burned to the ground," an army spokesman said early today.

attacks there on Rosemount police station, which has been swept by machinegun fire several times.

About 80 people were taken from their homes for questioning and possible detention under internment. ...

Since then crowds kept up a continuous barrage of stones, bottles, bullets and nail-bombs.

Late last night an army spokesman reported that the city was relatively quiet, although rioters had hijacked and burned a number of motor vehicles behind barricades erected across entrances to the Bogside.

Apprentice Boys' Order accept ban

The Apprentice Boys Order have "accepted" the ban on their parade on Thursday "in view of the situation now facing our country."

A statement by the order's general committee pledged "fullest co-operation and support in the efforts to restore peace and safety to our people."

UNION JACK BURNED

The Union Jack, soaked with petrol, was burned by members of Sinn Fein (Gardiner Place) near the British Embassy last night. They were prevented from reaching the steps of the Embassy by a cordon of about 50 Gardai stretching about two deep across Merrion Square.

Earlier more than 300 members of Sinn Fein and the Socialist Labour Alliance marched from the G.P.O., where they had held a protest against the introduction of internment.

Lynch calls for a new form of government

THE TAOISEACH, Mr. Lynch, has called for a conference of all interested parties in the North in order to obtain a new form of administration for the area.

Mr. Lynch in the course of a hard hitting statement issued through the Government Information Bureau calling for the conference said that there was no other way to avoid further deaths and injury.

The introduction of internment was strenuously deplored by the Taoiseach. He announced that Irish Army authorities will make accommodation at several of their camps available to dependants of detainees.

DEPLORABLE

"The introduction of internment without trial in the North this morning is deplorable evidence of the political poverty of the policies which have been pursued there for some time and which I condemned publicly last week" said Mr. Lynch's statement.

"Even if it succeeds in damping down the current wave of violence it does nothing to forward the necessary long term solutions.

"The sympathies of the Government and of the vast majority of the Irish people North and South go to the Nationalist minority in the North who are again victimised by an attempt to maintain a regime which has long since shown itself incapable of just Government and contemptuous of the norms of the British democracy to which they pretend allegiance.

HARDSHIP

"Hardship will be suffered by many families as a consequence of internment and I have instructed the Army Authorities to make accommodation available at Army camps to any dependants of internees who seek such accommodation.

"In the present situation in the North it is imperative that further parades be now banned there and that the law be administered impartially and that a conference of all the interested parties take place in order to obtain a new form of administration for Northern Ireland. There is no other way to avoid further deaths and injury".

U.K. Envoy tells Taoiseach of internment

News of internment in the North was officially conveyed to the Irish Government by the British Ambassador in Dublin.

The Ambassador, Mr. John H. Peck, called on the Taoiseach yesterday morning and informed him of the decision to intern.

The Irish Ambassador in London, Dr. Donal O'Sullivan was called to the Foreign Office yesterday and formally told of the internment measures.

NORTH TOPS CABINET AGENDA

By Tony Cadogan

THE critical situation in the North will figure urgently on the agenda when the usual weekly Cabinet meeting is held in Government Buildings in Dublin this morning.

The severe backlash to internment and the possible disintegration of the Northern situation into anarchy and chaos will be uppermost in the mind of the Taoiseach and his Ministers when they come to discuss what has become the gravest threat to Stormont since its establishment fifty years ago.

Today's Cabinet meeting could be a crucial one in many respects. For if the situation further deteriorates, Mr. Lynch may seek the approval of his Government for urgent discussions with his British counterpart, Mr. Edward Heath on the situation.

The two leaders are scheduled to hold two days of talks in London on October 20-21 but observers in Dublin feel, urgent and immediate talks are necessary because of the strong reaction to internment and the threat of a massive sectarian confrontation unless some action is taken.

BACK FROM HOLIDAYS

Contingency plans in the event of complete disorder and anarchy in the North are also likely to be discussed, as is the Army's state of preparedness in manning refugee camps and other factors. Already a number of Army officers have been called back from holidays to help in the administration of the camps.

Opposition party reaction to internment came swiftly in Dublin yesterday. Fine Gael called for impartial international observers to be sent into the North immediately to see that justice was administered.

Labour leader Brendan Corish

TURN TO BACK PAGE, COL. 2

500 REFUGEES AT ARMY CAMPS

Nearly 500 refugees from the North had reached Irish Army camps last night, a Government official in Dublin disclosed.

There were 160 at a camp at Kilworth, Co. Cork; 46 registered at Gormanstown, near Dublin, and another 273 at Finner Camp near the border in Donegal.

SHOTS ACROSS BORDER

Shots were fired at police and troops as they inspected a "bomb" at a bridge near Belcoo, Co. Fermanagh, yesterday.

The shots came from the Republic side of the border and for 15 minutes the security forces were pinned down under a river bank.

The army said later that the shots came from south of the border. No soldier was injured, and the firing was not returned.

The incident was at about 4.15 p.m. at Lattone Bridge, near Kiltyclogher. The shots, according to army authorities last night, included .22 and high velocity calibre.

The "bomb" which was being investigated turned out to be a hoax.

CARDINAL DEEPLY DISTURBED

His Eminence Cardinal Conway, in a statement last night, said that he fully understood the deep emotion, frustration and forboding which grips the Catholic population in the North.

He said: "I have been deeply disturbed by reports of some events during the course of the day."

Girl, 4, among those arrested

A four-year-old girl was held in yesterday's internment swoop in the North, her mother claimed last night.

Mrs. Mary Davey said troops had taken her daughter Marie and 39-year-old husband John from their beds at their home in Gulladuff, Maghera, Co. Derry.

When her daughter was returned home by police six hours later, "she was in a hysterical state and I had to give her a sedative to calm her down," added Mrs. Davey.

When night nurse Mrs. Davey returned from work early yesterday she found her home empty. Police did not know where her husband or daughter were, she said.

Mrs. Davey claimed her daughter had told her she had been separated from her father and taken to an army camp. The only food she had had was an apple given to her by one of the soldiers.

CONTENTS

Wrecked cars used as barricades in the Leeson Street area of Belfast

Heath at sea but keeps in touch

The British Premier Mr. Ted Heath at sea in his yacht Morning Cloud, has been kept in touch with the situation by radio telephone writes a Press Association reporter.

He was well aware of what was intended by Stormont before he left Plymouth at the weekend to take part in the Fastnet race, which will keep him afloat until either late today or early tomorrow.

Mr. Heath, captain of the British Admiral's Cup team, and Morning Cloud, were hidden in sea mists and low cloud as they headed across the Irish Sea towards the Fastnet Rock.

SILENCE

There was no news about the position of the British Prime Minister's yacht for, while many of the contenders were spotted during the day, Morning Cloud was never once mentioned.

The last time she was reported was east of The Lizard in the middle of the afternoon on Sunday. Since then—nothing.

There were reports yesterday from Royal Navy and R.A.F. aircraft and H.M.S. Undaunted, the frigate whose duties are to shepherd the fleet of Fastnet race contenders, but all remained silent on Mr. Heath's whereabouts.

1972

All around the world, 1972 is primarily remembered as being the year of the Munich Olympics and the botched rescue attempt of Israeli athletes from their Palestinian captors. The *Examiner*, like other media outlets, had been given misleading information immediately after the attempted rescue and, on Wednesday September 6, had led with the front page story: 'Hostages Freed After Gunbattle'. It was later that the terrible truth became known.
In Ireland, the year is remembered for Bloody Sunday. The immediate aftermath of the killings saw passions in the Republic reach their all-time peak in relation to events in the North. A national day of mourning was declared, schools closed, workers downed tools and anger on the streets climaxed with the burning of the British Embassy in Dublin.
The official Widgery Tribunal set up by the British government to investigate the shootings largely supported the soldiers' version of events - that they had been acting in self defence - but this account was widely dismissed in the Republic as a whitewash.

Protests, flags burned

Tuesday, February 1

Thousands of workers left their jobs in Cork yesterday, and numerous protest marches were held in the city. Twice during the day British flags were taken by the protestors: one was burned at a meeting in Patrick Street and the other was taken from the bow of a ship in Cork port.
Work in Cork docks ceased early in the morning as dockers took part in a one-day stoppage to show their concern for the 'Sunday massacre'. In the region of 1,000 workers at the Ford plant on the Marina paraded to the City Hall where they handed in a petition calling for the withdrawal of British troops from the Six Counties. Six hundred workers from the Pfizer plant at Ringaskiddy marched to the City Hall.
Maintenance and re-fuelling workers at Shannon Airport have decided not to service British aircraft. More than 2,000 people attended a protest meeting in Limerick city last night.

A Union Jack is burnt in Cork in the aftermath of Bloody Sunday.

Ali wins in Dublin

Thursday, July 20

The Muhammad Ali – Al 'Blue' Lewis heavyweight contest at Croke Park last evening, before an estimated attendance of 18,000, was stopped by the referee in the 11th round when Lewis was reduced to near insensibility. Early on, some of the crowd slow handclapped Ali when he idled, but eventually there was as much appreciation for his skill as for Lewis's gameness.
Whether the 18,000 people who attended the show will finance the promoters and meet the boxers' bills is another question. Ali is reputed to get £80,000.
Afterwards, Ali, surprised to learn that the Taoiseach, Mr Jack Lynch, was at the ringside said: "If I had known he was there I would have finished the contest in the third round."

Muhammad Ali at Dublin Airport.

NEWS BRIEFS

July 'Bloody Friday' in Belfast sees 11 people killed in a series of IRA bomb attacks in the city. (21)

Sept An advertisement for a secretary in the appointments section of the *Examiner* offers an annual wage of £1,000. (4)

Air of gloom and sadness surrounds Olympic Village

Thursday, September 7

Munich was a shocked city yesterday following the horrible Olympic shooting horror, a city of gloom and sadness. Germans were reluctant to talk about it; they felt it was a severe blow to their prestige in the world.
Then, too, there was the confusion surrounding the airfield gunbattle in which nine Israeli athletes so tragically died. Many questions hung over it. Could it not have been avoided? Why did nine peace-loving sportsmen have their lives terminated in such brutal fashion? Nine men who had first spent 18 hours as prisoners of a force of guerrillas in the Olympic Village where all men were living as brothers.
A major row was in progress over the handling of the affair by the Munich police, and the finger of suspicion was being pointed directly at them by the world press.
The shock of the tragedy was lightened by the news in the early afternoon that the games were to continue. But when the contests did get under way at 4pm, there was a subdued atmosphere about the place that is likely to linger now until the closing ceremonies on Monday.

The Cork Examiner

NO. 47,873 MONDAY MORNING, JANUARY 31, 1972 PRICE 3½p

MASSACRE IN DERRY

Paratroopers jumped over a barbed wire barrier as they chased the crowd into the Bogside.

13 civilians shot dead by troops

AN EYE-WITNESS REPORT FROM WALTER ELLIS

AT LEAST 13 men were killed and 17 others wounded by gunfire in Derry yesterday when soldiers of the Parachute Regiment appeared to open fire indiscriminately on a crowd of about 3,000 demonstrators gathered at Free Derry corner in the Bogside.

They were there to listen to speeches from Lord Fenner Brockway, the British Labour peer and others, after their attempt to march to Guildhall Square had been blocked by soldiers using a water cannon, rubber bullets and C.S. gas.

Late last night, four of the 17 injured in Altnagelvin Hospital were said to be serious and undergoing emergency operations. Two were a woman and a girl who was believed to have been run over by an army vehicle. Another of the wounded was a soldier, whose injuries were described as "only minor".

Lord Brockway was just about to speak when the first bullets ripped into the crowd, sending everyone diving for cover and causing widespread hysteria.

The commander of land forces in Northern Ireland, General Ford, said that his men had come under attack from snipers firing from behind the rubble of a deserted house, but this, even if true, could never justify the response of the paratroopers under his command.

They stood at the far end of Rossville Street, firing their automatic weapons at a civilian crowd, and it is likely that the death toll resulting from their actions will rise during the night at Altnagelvin Hospital, where a number of emergency operations were being performed.

When the shooting stopped, people could be seen dragging blood-strewn figures into the comparative safety of nearby houses.

FROM WALLS

Up on the walls of the city, overlooking the Bogside, other soldiers were seen crouched with their rifles pointed at the mass of people below, and occasionally they fired. The army say that they were only acting against snipers, but if this is so they will have to prove that a 15-year-old boy, a man of 60 and at least two women were in action against them in Derry yesterday.

A fleet of cars, as well as ambulances of the Order of Malta, were needed to transfer the dead and injured to Altnagelvin Hospital. One nurse working in the Order was herself fired upon when going about her work of helping the injured.

Earlier, the planned march had set off from the Creggan Estate to proceed to Guildhall Square. Leading the 8,000 or so demonstrators was Mr. Kevin McCorry, senior C.R.A. organiser, standing on top of a lorry. Lord Brockway, Miss Bernadette Devlin, Mr. Eamonn McCann and Mr. Ivan Cooper were all following close behind.

When the march had gone about four miles, in an attempt to find an unblocked exit, it came upon two Saracen armoured cars and a detachment of riot troops at the junction of William Street and Rossville Street.

March organisers tried to turn the crowd away from the soldiers in the direction of Rossville Street. About 200 youths ignored the order, however, and began jeering and throwing stones at the troops.

Immediately, rubber bullets began smashing into the demonstrators, and a water cannon was called up to spray them with purple dye. Snatch squads rushed into the front ranks and began dragging as many away as they could.

Later, they announced that 60 arrests had in fact

TURN TO BACK PAGE, COL. 2

Cabinet talks after Lynch phones Heath

THE Taoiseach, Mr. Lynch, made a dramatic phone call to Chequers last night and discussed the Derry killings with the Premier, Mr. Heath. Apparently, however, the outcome was by no means satisfactory from Mr. Lynch's point of view.

A statement from the Government Information Bureau said: "The Taoiseach has been in touch with Mr. Heath, but in the light of Mr. Heath's response, the Taoiseach will discuss the position with his Cabinet colleagues tomorrow".

A G.I.B. spokesman would not enlarge on the statement but it appears obvious that had Mr. Heath's response been sympathetic, the need would not so quickly have arisen for a Cabinet discussion.

Meanwhile, Mr. Heath has received a preliminary report from Mr. Maudling and the Defence Secretary, Lord Carrington. He will get fuller reports this morning and will study these before deciding what action the Government will take, whether there will be a statement in the Commons and whether the facts of the situation merit holding an inquiry.

SAVAGELY INHUMAN

Earlier in a strongly worded statement, the Taoiseach described the actions of the British soldiers in Derry as "savagely inhuman".

Mr. Lynch said he had been in contact with Mr. John Hume, the Derry member of the Social Democratic and Labour Party, to find out the facts of the shootings.

The statement added: "I am appalled and stunned that British soldiers should shoot indiscriminately into a crowd of civilians who were peacefully demonstrating, resulting in the death of 13 young men.

"Even if they were in technical breach of a recently imposed ban on demonstrations, this action by British troops was unbelievably and savagely inhuman".

APPALLING

The Fine Gael leader, Mr. Liam Cosgrave, described the Derry shootings as an appalling tragedy and said it must surely jerk the British Government into immediate action to find a political solution which would get the British Army out of this country for ever.

"If this happened, Irishmen, irrespective of politics or religion, will be compelled in the common interest of all to find a solution that will enable all Irishmen to live together.

"Tonight our deepest sympathies go to the families of those so wantonly killed in Derry today. May God comfort them in their sorrow".

The leader of the Labour Party, Mr. Brendan Corish announced last night that he was sending the Party's spokesman on Northern Affairs, Dr. Conor Cruise O'Brien, to London today to press the British Labour

TURN TO BACK PAGE COL. 7

I.R.A. PLEDGES TO AVENGE ALL DEATHS

The Provisional Wing of the I.R.A. in Derry pledged itself last night to avenge the deaths of everyone killed yesterday.

The officer commanding said: "At no time did any of our units open fire on the British army prior to the army opening fire.

"In order to avoid any possibility of danger to civilians, the Derry Provisional Command of the I.R.A. ordered all weapons out of the total route march area this morning.

"The British army murdered innocent civilians in Derry today—we leave the world to judge who are the real terrorists."

600 marchers defy ban in Dungannon

On Saturday, 600 marchers defied the Stormont ban on parades by marching from Dungannon to Coalisland.

They marched through fields but dodged back to the roads for lengthy periods. Troops fired CS gas and rubber bullets at them as they twice swept past army barriers.

Meanwhile, a Protestant rally in Derry planned to coincide with yesterday's march was called off on Saturday after organisers were given Stormont government assurances that the march would be stopped. The rally was to have taken place in the Guildhall.

Security chiefs warned that organisers of marches will be brought to court. A joint army-police statement over the weekend said that because some parades were allowed to proceed for a distance, it could not be regarded as a victory for the demonstrators.

One high-ranking army officer said: "We will choose the time and place to stop a march."

Army shooting was indiscriminate—priest

FR. EDWARD DALEY, a Bogside parish priest, said: "The British Army should hang its head in shame after today's disgusting violence. They shot indiscriminately and everywhere around them without any provocation."

Fr. Daley, who has been a priest in Bogside for the past 10 years, said the demonstration was "reasonably peaceful". It appeared as though the paratroopers were under orders to move in and shoot away at anyone.

"A 16-year-old boy was shot dead beside me, and others were badly injured by the firing. I crawled to him and gave him the last rites for there was no hope of saving his life", he said.

Fr. Daley said: "The quicker the British army get out of Northern Ireland after today's violence, the better for everyone concerned. It is the only way to achieve peace.

"There has been a terrible amount of blood, and no public relations job by the British army will cover this up. I intend to protest to the highest people in the strongest way possible".

Labour Peer Lord Fenner Brockway, who was about to address the meeting when the shooting began, said "Bernadette Devlin, who was with me on the lorry where we were standing, told everybody to lie down and I was pulled down.

"The firing went on for some time and when it stopped Bernadette told the crowd of about 2,000 to disperse.

"I did not take part in the march but it seemed a perfectly peaceful procession to me. In fact, I've never seen a more peaceful march."

CRAWLED AWAY

Another eye-witness, civil rights leader Finbarr O'Kane said "Lord Brockway was on the platform waiting, when a bullet hit a wall opposite Derry Corner.

"People didn't realise what it was at first. But more shooting started and everybody hit the ground. The shooting seemed to stop after a bit and everybody got up on all fours and started to crawl away. But it started again.

"I've never seen anything like it. Everybody was trying to crawl away, hitting walls and stumbling. I was fleeing like hell".

Mr. William O'Connell — a member of the SDLP—said: "I saw a detachment of three armed personnel carriers come up Rossville Street.

"Paratroopers jumped out and started to fire at the people — including people lying on the ground. It was completely indiscriminate.

"After a while they shouted: 'Move and you're dead' and everybody who had been running away when they saw the paratroopers arrive stopped running. Troops told the people to come towards them — and they arrested them".

Mr. Tony Smythe, leader of Britain's National Council for Civil Liberties, made a bid to reach Derry for the anti-internment rally—but he was held up at Army checkpoints and arrived late.

"WE'LL USE THEM"

He was to have headed a team of observers at the rally. "People have already started taking statements from eye witnesses — and we'll use them", he said.

Mr. Ivan Cooper, a SDLP M.P., who was among those to come under fire in the Bogside claimed: "I was shot at even though I had raised a white flag as I tried to help a wounded man".

His shirt and suit still dirt-

TURN TO BACK PAGE, COL. 6

A Derryman on a stretcher, having received the Last Rites from priest, on left.

Six injured in blast after border fill-in

SIX people were injured and taken to Monaghan County Hospital following an explosion at about 5 p.m. yesterday evening at the British customs post at Clontivern, a mile from Clones on the Enniskillen road, writes an "Examiner" correspondent. A crowd of about 300 had been engaged in filling in a road crater.

They set fire to a caravan serving as a temporary customs post. A domestic gas container in the caravan exploded, scattering the crowd in all directions. One man was blown off the road across a hedge into a field.

The injured men are suffering from burns and shock. Four are detained in hospital but two were discharged after treatment.

AFTER the explosion, a British Army helicopter hovered overhead and dropped canisters of marker dye on the crowd standing near the border. Amongst those who were splashed with the dye was a garda inspector and members of the gardai on duty on the Co. Monaghan side of the frontier.

The crowd also attempted to burn two private cars belonging to British customs officers but the Sinn Fein member of Clones Urban Council, Mr. Frank McCaughey, intervened and prevented the destruction of the cars.

Earlier, about 600 civilians had a brief confrontation with the British Army while filling in a border road crater in Co. Fermanagh a mile from Rosslea on the Clones road.

Four trees were felled to block the approach roads to the crater and when two British Army ferret cars arrived a section of the crowd armed with heavy sticks attacked them and

TURN TO BACK PAGE, COL. 4

CARDINAL 'DEEPLY SHOCKED'

In a statement issued in Armagh, last night, referring to the Derry deaths, Cardinal Conway said: "I am deeply shocked at the news of the awful slaughter in Derry this afternoon. I have received a first hand account from a priest who was present at the scene and what I have heard is really shocking.

"An impartial and independent public enquiry is immediately called for and I have telephoned the British Prime Minister to this effect.

"Meanwhile, I call on the whole Catholic community to preserve calm and dignity in the face of this terrible news. If an impartial and independent public enquiry is held, the world will be able to judge what has happened".

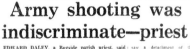

1973

Ireland slipped quietly into the European Economic Community at the start of 1973. The nation had voted by a margin of about five to one the previous year to join the Community, tempted by promises of cheaper prices, more jobs and a major boost for agriculture.

The other stories on the first front page of 1973 were to set the tone for the rest of the year: the continuing Troubles in Northern Ireland, including the arrest of "young republican" Martin McGuinness; and US actions in Vietnam.

Big hunt for 'Copter escapees

Thursday, November 1

In one of the most intensive manhunts ever carried out in the Republic, thousands of Gardaí and troops last night combined in a joint exercise to track down three Republican prisoners who were taken to freedom when a hijacked helicopter snatched them from inside Mountjoy Prison, Dublin, yesterday afternoon.

The helicopter, owned by Irish Helicopters Ltd, was hired by an American who gave his name as Mr Leonard. He wanted it, he said, to film ancient monuments in the Midlands. In Co Laois the helicopter touched down at Mr Leonard's request and immediately armed men surrounded the machine. Mr Leonard got out and one of the men got in and ordered the pilot at gunpoint to fly to Dublin. Over Mountjoy prison eyewitnesses saw it descend over the exercise yard.

The armed man jumped out and ordered prison officers to hand over Twomey, O'Hagan and Mallon. There was some hesitation at first but when the prison officers saw the armed man was in earnest the three leading Republicans were released.

Drinking by candlelight in a Cork bar during an ESB powercut.

The EEC – What it will mean for Ireland

Monday, January 1

The most disconcerting feature of Ireland's entry into Europe was the impossibility of obtaining really detailed and precise projections of our prospects. The conflicting findings of economists deepened the dilemma.

The Government was committed to entry but nonetheless it was the inviting picture they painted of Irish life in the EEC which influenced a resounding 'Yes' vote. It is interesting at this point to record their answers to some of the more pressing questions.

What are the military commitments of membership?

There are no military or defence commitments in the treaties setting up the communities and no such commitments were involved in Ireland's entry to the communities.

Will EEC membership mean more or less employment?

There will, it is estimated, be 50,000 more jobs in Irish industry by 1978 as compared with 1970.

What are the prospects for our main farm products?

Cattle, beef and dairy products will be the main source of benefit. Barley will also attract higher prices.

How much will the food bill go up?

The weekly food bill, which accounts for about one third of the average household budget, will increase annually by 2p to 3p in the £1.

NEWS BRIEFS

Sept A submarine robot from the US Navy helps to rescue two men in a Vickers mini-submarine who had been trapped for three days 1,300 feet down on the sea bed off the south coast of Ireland. (1)

A *coup* in Chile deposes Salvador Allende, the world's first democratically elected Marxist head of state. Allende himself is reported to have committed suicide. (11)

Oct At a hearing concerning a dance licence at a hotel in Kill, Co Kildare, a Justice tells Naas District Court that discos are designed by the devil, that they are excruciatingly noisy and that the psychedelic lighting in them is driving people out of their minds. (3)

A record price of £115,000 is paid for nine tenths of an acre in Dublin at Sydney Parade Avenue, Sandymount, which is to be developed into luxury flats. (4)

The Cork Examiner

NO. 45,156 MONDAY MORNING, JANUARY 1, 1973 PRICE 4p (inc. V.A.T.)

HAPPY NEW EURO YEAR!

-and many happy returns ?

By VAL DORGAN

AT MIDNIGHT last night, Ireland, in company with Britain, officially joined the European Communities. The third new member of the Nine, Denmark, keeps continental time and qualified for membership one hour earlier. The giant step into Europe is as meaningful an occasion as any in Irish history. But we will take it unobstrusively and Euro Year 1973 begins as an anti-climax.

The British Government, which dispensed with a plebiscite, will spend hundreds of thousands of pounds in civic celebrations glamourising the advent of the new European adventure. The Irish Government, reassured by an overwhelmingly favourable referendum al'ow the new Euro Year to arrive virtually unnoticed. But wittingly or otherwise the Government's low key welcome will probably strike a responsive public chord here.

Our first entry into the European arena is filled as much with apprehension as appreciation of the historical importance of the moment. The Community ideal of an United Europe may come later. At this point, farmer, industrialist, worker and housewife alike are far more concerned with the economic implications of the E.E.C. — they want to know precisely "what's in it for us."

As yet there is no immediate answer. Only time and experience will define our prospects in Europe. The first effects, however, will be negligible.

TRANSITION PERIODS

We are cushioned against the full impact of free trade by transitional periods. The prices which Irish farmers get for their main products will be raised to the higher Community level in six stages beginning next month and finishing in 1977.

Tariffs on industrial goods in and out of Ireland will go in five instalments starting in April and ending in July 1977.

The first rise for Irish farmers will be equal to one sixth of the difference between Irish and E.E.C. prices and the duty on goods from E.E.C. countries into Ireland will be reduced by twenty per cent. of the existing duty.

Theoretically the increase in some food items, primarily beef, lamb, butter, cheese and milk will be marginal in 1973 but eventually prices will be 40 per cent. higher.

This is how the Government economists see it. But it is admitted that a completely ac-

TURN TO BACK PAGE COL. 1

Early sign of change

ONE of the first signs of change as we go into Europe was seen yesterday—a giant juggernaut lorry loaded with herrings direct from Irish fishing boats at Dunmore East, Co. Waterford.

The lorry, travelling overland and by ferry, is taking 20 tons of fresh fish to Boulogne, France, for distribution on the European markets.

Up to now herrings caught off the South East coast would have been sold to factory ships.

Pompidou: you never had it so good

President Pompidou, in a frankly [illegible] New Year's message, told his countrymen yesterday they never had it so good, but warned them they could have more prosperity and stability only through "continuity."

"No one can deny that economic expansion in France is now the first in Europe," he declared.

Italian President Giovanni Leone last night welcomed the enlargement of the Common Market.

In his New Year message to the nation, he said: "January 1, 1973, coincides with the entry into the Common Market of three nations with glorious traditions—Britain, Denmark and Ireland.

"The European Community will benefit from the contributions of these nations. But we look, in the long run to a political European community."

SALUTE TO EUROPE

At the National Press Ball in the Burlington Hotel, Dublin, last night the band of the Curragh Training Corps, under Comndt. Mellerick, provided a salute to Europe.

The band played tunes appropriate to the nine member countries of the E.E.C. Eight hundred patrons joined in the dancing.

The rostrum was draped in the flags of member states of the enlarged E.E.C.

The band concluded their selection half an hour into the New Year with the Anthem of Europe.

FUNERAL PROTEST

With heads bowed and wearing arm bands villagers at Hullbridge, Essex, staged a mock funeral procession yesterday to mourn Britain's entry into the Common Market.

Protest organiser Mr. Ron Leighton, a 42-year-old printer, who is also director of the Common Market Safeguards campaign, told marchers it was "a travesty of democracy" to carry Britain into the E.E.C. without giving the nation a say.

Senator Eoin Ryan, Chairman of the Executive Committee of the Irish Council of the European Movement, planted nine trees to mark Ireland's accession to the European Communities today Picture shows the Senator planting the Irish tree, a willow, on the bank of the canal.

Taoiseach's plea for peace, reconciliation

Each individual must play his part in helping to achieve in practice the theory and ideal of a true peace.

This is the Taoiseach's New Year appeal for peace and reconciliation which, he states, "is so earnestly wished for by all people of goodwill throughout the whole of Ireland."

Mr. Lynch, on behalf of the Government, issued the appeal in response to the message of His Holiness, Pope Paul VI for the celebration of New Year's Day as the Day of Peace

"The Government of Ireland is resolved to do all in its power, in the political and in other spheres, to make peace a dynamic reality and to create a more hopeful prospect for coming generations in Ireland and in the world at large."

The Taoiseach added: "In that spirit we look to the future of this Day of Peace 1973 with the reassurance of His Holiness that peace is possible. We echo the Pope's call for the renewal of the desire for peace in men's hearts, at all levels, and we pledge ourselves afresh to play our due part in achieving the peace and reconciliation which is so earnestly wished for by all people of goodwill throughout the whole of Ireland."

The Taoiseach continued: "My colleagues in the Government of Ireland and I warmly welcome this opportunity of associating ourselves with the noble and inspiring message of reassurance and hope from His Holiness Pope Paul VI on the occasion of World Day of Peace 1973, which we are confident, will evoke a profound and wholehearted response in Ireland.

"We believe that peace established on the foundation of justice is attainable."

History showed, stated the Taoiseach, that peace was not the product of chance and that it was necessary to work positively and constructively for its realisation. Each individual must play his part in helping to achieve in practice the theory and ideal of a true peace. The peace-makers must be vocal and active so that their cause might prevail.

VIOLENCE GREATEST PROBLEM FACING US —Cosgrave

The greatest problem facing the Irish people in 1973 was the continuing violence and bloodshed in Northern Ireland, the leader of Fine Gael Mr. Liam Cosgrave, T.D., stated in his New Year message.

Mr. Cosgrave's statement went on:-

"Latterly this violence seems to have developed into a succession of sectarian murders. The sooner that those involved on both sides realise the harm they are doing to their country, the better. It is already patently clear that the vast majority of the Irish people are horrified by the barbarities that have taken place and wish to see peace restored as an essential preliminary to a political solution of our country's problems. I shall do all I can to influence events in that direction.

SERIOUS PROBLEMS

"Our country has many serious political, social and economic (including price inflation) problems to solve. Firm purposeful leadership is necessary. All the resources of the State must be so used that the people's rights will be guaranteed and preserved. Everyone has an interest in the security of our democratic system and our Parliament must ensure that the Army and the Garda are adequate in strength to discharge this assignment on behalf of the people."

Mr. Cosgrave concluded: "The people will respond and the country will surmount these problems if the Nation is given decisive leadership to face the challenges of the coming year. If we resolve to make a united effort and trust in God, peace will come again to Ireland."

Pope Paul intervened in Vietnam

POPE PAUL yesterday welcomed the suspension of U.S. bombing raids over North Vietnam, and disclosed that he had personally intervened with the interested parties to restart the peace talks.

The Pope, addressing pilgrims gathered in St. Peter's Square for his Sunday blessing, told them of President Nixon's decision to resume the Paris peace talks and suspend bombing North of the 20th Parallel of latitude in Vietnam.

He had never ceased to call for them in public statements, in his prayers and "with urgency in our contacts with the interested parties" he said.

The 75-year-old Pontiff, obviously delighted with the news, braved a blustery, rainy day to appear at his study window although suffering from a slight attack of flu, which has forced him to cancel all private audiences until Thursday.

STABLE PEACE

He told the pilgrims, in a strong if slightly hoarse voice, that he hoped the latest developments would finally lead to a just and stable peace in Vietnam.

Soviet Premier Alexei Kosygin said that the Soviet people

TURN TO BACK PAGE COL 3

McGuinness arrested near border

Martin McGuinness, the young Derry Republican, was arrested yesterday by Gardai 14 miles from the Border.

He was seized with another man named Joseph McCallion after a car packed with explosives and ammunition was found abandoned near a Garda checkpoint.

In the boot were 50lbs. of gelignite and thousands of rounds of ammunition.

Then, near the spot at Ballybofey, Co. Donegal, two young men were stopped by Gardai as they walked away from the scene.

McGuinness and McCallion are being held under the Offences Against the State Act, which allows Gardai to detain suspects for up to 48 hours without making a charge.

Gardai said last night that McGuinness was "safely bedded down" in a Dublin Garda Station.

Four hurt as bus is sprayed with bullets

A BUS carrying passengers through a Belfast estate was sprayed with bullets yesterday, injuring four people. The Corporation double decker bus was travelling through the Protestant Highfield Estate when a man at a bus stop waved it down. As it pulled up, three men stepped out and fired up to 20 shots.

Police said there were about 12 passengers on the bus which was working a route between Belfast City centre and the Catholic Turf Lodge district.

Mr. Paddy Devlin, leader of the S.D.L.P. said last night that all the passengers were Catholics. "The bus rarely stops on this Protestant estate and Catholics have often been beaten up and even shot dead on this estate," said Mr. Devlin.

The passengers dived to the floor as the men opened up. After the attack the bus made off to the joint army and police post at the Henry Taggart Hall in the Catholic Ballymurphy area from where the injured passengers were taken to hospital.

NOT SERIOUS

Two women and two men were injured in the shooting. A man and a woman were still detained in hospital last night but were not seriously ill.

Earlier, four shots were fired through the front window of a house in the Old Park area of Belfast but no one was hurt.

Two soldiers were injured in separate shooting in-

TURN TO BACK PAGE COL. 6

Euro babies-and they're twins

The New Year was only one minute old when the first of twin boys were born at the Bedford Row Hospital, Limerick, to Mrs. Ann Keating, Mount Anglesby, Clogheen, Co. Tipperary. She is wife of Mr. Richard Keating, farmer.

The first boy weighed eight pounds and eight minutes later, his brother, who weighed $8\frac{1}{4}$ pounds, arrived.

Dr. Dermot Moloney and Nurses Frances O'Connor, Highfield, Limerick, and Anne Maria Dillon, Listowel, attended at the birth.

The first birth reported in Cork—a boy—to herald in the New Year of 1973 was born to Mrs. Marjorie Buttimer, St. Rita's, Georges Street, Mitchelstown, at the Bon Secours Maternity Hospital in Cork last night.

The boy, weighing $8\frac{1}{2}$ lbs., Mrs. Buttimer's first child, was born at two minutes past midnight.

Ireland's first Eurobabies born on New Year's Day will be presented with a silver Europa medallion to mark our entry to the E.E.C. as announced by the Irish Council of the European Movement on Friday.

The meadallion designed by Mr. Bill Watson carries a shamrock design and onthe reverse side the date and name of the child will be inscribed.

The New Ireland Assurance Company Limited is granting free fully paid up educational endowment policies of £1,000 each to ten babies born since midnight in Ireland to mark Ireland's entry to membership of the E.E.C.

The ten policies will provide the payment of £200 on the sixteenth, seventeenth, eighteenth, nineteenth and twentieth birthdays of the babies nominated.

The New Ireland it was stated, was asking the Chief Executive Officers of each of the eight Regional Health Boards to co-operate with them by nominating babies deemed to have been the first born within the area covered by the Regional Health Boards.

Three policies will be awarded in the area covered by the Eastern Regional Health Board which includes Dublin— and one each in the areas covered by the seven other health boards.

The 'promised land' of Europe —page 5

First class marriages!

Some wives might be able to save their marriages by teaching their husbands to read.

Reading lessons have helped to save several marriages in Bristol, two psychiatrists from the Barrow Hospital, Dr. W. A. Saunders and Dr. M. G. Barker, report in the British Medical Journal.

The husbands were all dyslexic unable to read or write as well as normal people of their intelligence.

Having to get their wives to do such things as read the menu for them when they went out to dinner, or fill in the forms to do with their work made them moody and irritable. Reading lessons, when the husband agreed to take them meant their marriage relationships improved. Others, however, refused to go back to school. They had to be treated with drugs and psychotheraphy.

U.S. reserves right to alter tariffs

The United States yesterday reserved the right to revise tariff levels during the next three years, in a move to give more flexibility to negotiate with trading partners.

The U.S. Administration confirmed that it had notified members of the General Agreement on Tariffs and Trade (GATT) but said it did not necessarily mean that any re-negotiation of tariffs would take place in the next three years.

The U.S. move, which had been reported to informed sources on Saturday, followed a similar action by the European Common Market. It heralded the opening of an intensive period of jockeying for position in advance of world trade talks next September, the sources said.

Girl For "Kidney" Woman—A 25 year old Israeli woman, who has been living on a transplanted kidney in Tel Aviv for the past two years, has given birth to a girl weighing four lb. three oz. Both were doing well, the hospital said

Dancing in the New Year at Jurys Hotel New Year's Eve celebrations, one of the many dances and functions held in Cork to welcome 1973. —("Examiner")

1974

The bombs in Dublin and Monaghan which killed 33 people made May 17, 1974 the bloodiest day in the history of the Troubles. That it happened in the Republic, which up until now had been relatively unscathed, brought the reality of the violence home to Southerners in a new way. The bombs were believed to be the work of loyalist paramilitaries, but nobody has ever been charged in connection with the attacks and the families of those killed are still seeking justice.

Among several bombs in Britain that year, 24 people were killed when the IRA targeted pubs in Birmingham and Guildford. The police soon arrested a number of people in connection with the bombings. Convictions were achieved on the basis of 'confessions' and forensic evidence and, the following year, those who become known as the Guildford Four and Birmingham Six were sentenced to long prison terms.

Pill Bill defeated

Wednesday, July 17

The Coalition Government was dealt a heavy blow in the Dáil last night with the sensational defeat of the controversial Contraceptives Bill. It was not the failure of the Bill itself to get through, so much as the action of the Taoiseach, Mr Cosgrave, and the Minister for Education, Mr Burke, in voting against it that shocked Government and Opposition members alike.

So surprised in fact were Fianna Fáil at the Taoiseach's action that they forgot to do what Oppositions normally do in circumstances - applaud and cheer - and the only reaction of this kind came from Mr Oliver J Flanagan, one of the other seven Fine Gael deputies who voted against the Bill.

'Avoid a backlash' pleas in Britain

Monday, November 25

As renewed appeals were made in Britain yesterday to keep the peace following the Birmingham bombings, it was learned that car industry troublemakers may be sent home if there are more anti-Irish incidents at the giant British Leyland factory at Longbridge, Birmingham, today.

Management and supervisory staff have been asked to be on the alert for shop floor scuffles of the type which led 1,500 car-workers to walk out of the Austin Morris factory on Friday. Irish workers were kicked and punched.

About 10 to 15% of the 25,000 strong workforce at Austin-Morris are Irish. Local Irish community leaders have appealed for restraint during the weekend and said that the vast majority of Irish people did not have pro-Provisional IRA sympathies.

In a phone call from Birmingham yesterday, an East Cork woman living in the city said that while the British and the vast bulk of the Irish people deplored the atrocities, the Irish in England were now living in fear of reprisals.

President Erskine Childers on one of his final official engagements before he died of a heart attack.

Nixon decides to resign

Friday, August 9

Richard Nixon.

President Nixon has decided to resign rather than be impeached over the Watergate scandal, and went on nationwide television at 2am this morning to announce his decision. The timing of the speech was announced to reporters by White House press secretary Ronald Ziegler, looking haggard and choked with emotion, yesterday afternoon.

Mr Ziegler, who has been with Mr Nixon since his election in 1968, was visibly tense and gloomy as he made what could well be his last announcement for the President.

Mr Nixon's fall from power came with astonishing speed after a two-year fight to clear himself of involvement in the Watergate scandals. Although his impeachment had appeared certain after the House of Representatives Judiciary Committee recommended it, it was only on Monday that evidence linking him with the Watergate cover-up emerged - and it was produced by the President himself.

He shocked his most ardent supporters when he disclosed he had discussed the political advantages of a cover-up as early as June 25, 1972.

NEWS BRIEFS

May James Hill MP, chairman of the EEC Transport Committee, states that Irish roads "are almost as bad as Sicily". (11)

Nov Erskine Childers, 69, becomes the first Irish president to die in office. An estimated 100,000 people throng the streets of Dublin for his funeral. (22)

Nov Richard Bingham, the seventh Earl of Lucan, goes missing after the discovery of the body of his child's nanny, Sandra Rivett, in London. He has never been found. (12)

Dec Seán MacBride, former Minister for Foreign Affairs and President of Amnesty International, becomes the first Irish person to win the Nobel Peace Prize. (11)

The Cork Examiner

NO. 48,584 SATURDAY MORNING, MAY 18, 1974 PRICE 5p

Bombs horror

Talbot Street, Dublin, shortly after the explosion there.

23 die in Dublin's Bloody Friday

By TONY RING and VIVION KILFEATHER

TERRORISM, Northern Ireland style, came to Dublin last evening when, as thousands of people were leaving shops and offices three car bombs exploded in the centre city area killing 23 people, wounding 83 seriously and over a hundred others superficially. The dead were 16 women, five men and two baby boys.

At least five people were killed and at least 20 injured when a massive car bomb exploded in Monaghan's town centre. A number of people were reported to be unaccounted for.

In an RTE broadcast, the Taoiseach, Mr. Cosgrave expressed "revulsion and condemnation" at the bomb outrages and said that everyone who had practised, preached or condoned violence must bear a share of responsibility.

The horror came to Dublin at about 5.30 p.m. when the centre city area was rocked by three explosions in quick succession.

One was in Parnell St., one in Talbot Street at the Junction of Gardiner St. and the third was in South Leinster Street, near the junction of Kildare Street and within three hundred yards of Leinster House.

No warnings had been given and unsuspecting pedestrians—there were more on the pavements than usual because of the bus strike — were blown into eternity by the explosions. Mutilated bodies were strewn around the blood-spattered streets as others more fortunate, panic stricken for a moment, ran in terror.

As the city centre, stunned by the blasts, regained its senses the calls to the fire, police and ambulances services flooded the telephone exchanges.

TRAFFIC JAMS

Ambulances, police cars, fire engines, Army bomb squads in landrovers struggled to get through the evening traffic jams to the scenes of horror and devastation which awaited them. The Fire Briade put its major disaster plan into operation.

The biggest car bomb seemed to be that at Talbot Street, outside Guiney's drapery shop. Here at least seven people died and about 30 were badly injured.

At Parnell Street, outside the "Welcome Inn" another large car bomb exploded killing at least five people and injuring several more.

At South Leinster Street, outside the old Kildare Street Club building, now occupied by the Phoenix Insurance company a bomb placed in a sports car killed three people and injured several more.

But as the night wore on the grim news came of even more fatalities.

Several millions of pounds worth of property damage was caused.

There was no indication up to late last night as to who had caused the bombings, whether they were the work of agents provocateurs, Northern Ireland extremists or I.R.A. or dissident republican groups, but Special branch detectives, acting on even the slightest tip-off were last night conducting feverish investigaions.

In one case less than two hours after the bombings a car load of detectives swooped on a centre city public house after a call had been made that some youths were acting suspiciously.

All available ambulances in the city were pushed into service to rush the dead and injured to hospital.

The blood transfusion service appealed for and got thousands of volunteers of "O" group donations.

And even after the three lethal explosions occurred the city was rife with rumours of more bombs and Army bomb squads set off several controlled explostions on packages and cases in and outside buildings which were suspect.

Some streets were blocked off as more suspect cars were kept under observation. Garda radio frequencies buzzed with urgent calls to squads to move in on suspect areas.

Even some veteran reporters who have covered many horrific tragedies in the North said it was the worst carnage they had ever seen. Two visibly shaken Gardai could not hold back the tears as they endeavoured to do everything possible for the maimed and horribly injured victims.

In Jervis Street Hospital, Middle Abbey Street, about thirty relatives and friends waited anxiously to receive news from doctors and nurses.

Some broke down as Surgeon Anthony Walsh told them it would take some considerable time before he could give them details as many of the victims were unrecognisable. Many, he said had only minor injuries, but others, besides those fatally injured, would require operations.

O'BRIEN ON SCENE

The Minister for Posts and Telegraphs, Dr. Conor Cruise O'Brien, arrived at the P. and T. building in Parnell Street shortly after the explosion adjacent to it.

Asked did he attach any significance to the car bomb being planted outside a building with such a large number employed in it, he said: "I suppose the people who do this kind of thing want to kill as many people as possible."

The explosions, he said, were a hideous outrage, and all feeling and sympathy must go out to those people injured and the relatives of the dead.

He hoped that the horror of what had occurred would finally bring home to anyone who had a leaning or sympathy with those who favoured violence — that there was no political reason that could justify what had occurred.

Large crowds foolishly converged on Talbot Street within minutes of the explosion there which wrecked shop windows within two hundred yards. Despite persistent appeals from the Gardai many people insisted on walking towards the centre of the tragedy. Ambulances found

TURN TO BACK PAGE, COL. 6

Mr. Michael Fitzpatrick, a native of Charleville, Co. Cork, and his wife Margaret with some of the staff of their wrecked public house, The Welcome Inn in Parnell Street.

Evil deeds strengthen resolve for peace

—TAOISEACH

EXPRESSING revulsion and condemnation of the bomb outrages, the Taoiseach, Mr. Cosgrave, said last night that these evil deeds would only "serve to strengthen the resolve of those, North and South, who have been working for peace."

Speaking on RTE Television, Mr Cosgrave said: "The Government and I wish to express our profound sympathy to the relatives of the victims of today's outrages and to those who have been injured and maimed. To the evil men who have perpetrated these deeds we express the revulsion and condemnation which every decent person in this island feels at their unforgiveable acts.

"The Government are as yet unaware of the identity of those responsible for these crimes. But everyone who has practised violence or preached violence or condoned violence must bear a share of responsibility for today's outrage.

UNSELFISH

"It is in moments of great tragedy like today's that we see and appreciate the dedication and unselfish service of members of the Gardai, Army, ambulance and fire services, doctors, nurses, and others engaged in rescue and humanitarian work. To all who have given and, as I am speaking are still giving of their services, including hundreds of ordinary men and women who responded so readily and magnificently to donate their blood, I offer on behalf of the whole community our sincerest thanks.

"While our society is menaced by men who perpetrate cowardly acts of violence, the Gardai and the Army will give the citizens all the protection they can. Their ability to protect you, will, however, depend to a large extent upon your vigilance and co-operation.

"I would, therefore, request you to report immediately to the gardai any suspicious or unusual movements, objects or motor vehicles. Occupants of buildings should take care to search and keep a watch upon their premises.

"What has happened today will help to underline the criminal folly and utter futility of violent action as a means for furthering political ends. It will also help to bring home to us here in this part of our island what the people in Northern Ireland have been suffering for five long years. Today's evil deeds will only serve to

TURN TO BACK PAGE, COL. 1

Cars were hijacked in Belfast

POLICE in Belfast confirmed last night that the three cars which blew-up in Dublin had been hijacked in Belfast. A Hillman Avenger was hijacked in Torrens Road in the Old Park area at 10 a.m. yesterday by three men. One of the men stayed with the driver who was not released until 4 p.m.

An Austin 1800 was hijacked at 8.30 a.m. in Richmond St., Shankill Road. Again the driver was held until 1.20 when the theft was reported.

The third car, a Hillman Imp was also hijacked in Belfast but the police had no details last night.

Bombers could strike again

GARDAI issued a dramatic warning to Irish people that the bombers could strike at any place and at any time.

Their warning said: "Any repetition is likely to take place in any town or village in the country and we exhort people to be extra-vigilant and to report anything of a suspicious nature to the police."

The gardai said there were no warnings of yesterday's bombs.

"They were acts of outright war. These people had no chance whatsoever."

FAULKNER CONDEMNS OUTRAGES

The North's Chief Minister, Mr Brian Faulkner, last night sent a message to Mr. Cosgrave.

It said: "It is with the deepest distress that my colleagues in the Northern Ireland Executive and I have heard of the atrocious outrages in Dublin.

"We in Northern Ireland, who have had to endure so much suffering and death in recent years, can appreciate fully the tragedy of those who have been struck down and the grief of those who have been bereaved or injured in your own capital.

"For far too long those of us in Ireland who believe in the democratic process have had to suffer the onslaughts of vicious and violent men.

"Whatever the differences of opinion which may exist on other matters, I believe the responsible people in Northern Ireland and the Republic alike want to see this island rid for ever of the evil forces which are guilty of such acts."

Mr. Faulkner also had a personal telephone conversation with Mr. Cosgrave.

NOT US, SAY UDA AND PROVOS

The Provisional IRA last night issued a statement in Dublin disclaiming responsibility for the bombs.

"The Irish Republican Army utterly condemns the vile **murders and bombings in Dublin and Monaghan this afternoon. Needless to say no branch of the Republican Movement was involved,**" it said.

"The events of this afternoon highlight the farcical security situations in this part of the country, which is orientated towards assisting this SAS-type operation."

At the headquarters of the UDA in East Belfast a spokesman strenuously denied that his organisation was involved in the Dublin bombings.

"We had absolutely nothing whatsoever to do with the bombings down South," he stressed.

Dr. Conor Cruise O'Brien, Minister for Posts and Telegraphs, arrives at the scene of the bomb blast outside the new international telephone exchange with Sgt. Michael Brennan, Fitzgibbon Street, Garda Station.

THE DEAD

AMONG those killed in Dublin were:

Maria Phelan (20), 209 Philipsburg Ave., Fairview, Dublin;
Breda Turner, 3 Mitchel Street, Thurles, Co. Tipperary;
Anton Molori, 81 Parnell Street, Dublin;
Anna Massey, (21), of 43 Pearse Villas, Sallynoggin, Co. Dublin;
Edmund O'Neill, 49 Lower Dominick Street, Dublin.

A French woman was also killed, but garda authorities would not release her name.

Two telephones in Dublin have been made available for personal calls concerning the identities of the victims. They are: Dublin 754763 and Dublin 781122.

MONAGHAN VICTIMS

Those killed in the Monaghan bomb blast included:
John Travers, Park Street, Monaghan;
Thomas Campbell, Silver Street, Monaghan;
Mrs. **White**, Belgium Park, Monaghan.

Car blast kills five in Monaghan

FIVE people are now known to have died and more than 20 were injured when a car bomb exploded without warning in the centre of Monaghan Town at about 7 o'clock last evening.

The explosion occurred at a bus stop on North Road and extensive damage was caused to adjoining property.

A number of people have not yet been accounted for.

A second car in an adjoining street, Park Street, was suspected of containing a bomb and a large portion of the town was evacuated. The second car was later cleared by Army bomb disposal experts.

A bus driver had a remarkable escape from injury. He had just parked his bus beside the car carrying the bomb. He walked away about 30 yards when the bomb went off.

The names of the victims have not yet been announced, but one of the dead is known to be a married woman.

Troops and Gardai from adjoining counties were rushed to the town for emergency duty and there was a general alert in other border towns last night.

For a time, Monaghan Post Office, which is near the scene of the bomb, was evacuated and communication with the town was disrupted for almost an hour.

Check points were set up by the security forces along the border.

King Baudouin's sympathy

The King of the Belgians, whose guest the President and Mrs Childers have been over the past three days last night personally telephoned his condolences to Mr Childers on the tragedy. Mr and Mrs Childers had returned from Belgium only a few hours earlier.

THE BIGGEST BLOODBATH

The death toll in the explosions was the biggest single bloodbath since the troubles in Northern Ireland began and the biggest in Dublin since 45 people died as a result of a German land mine exploding during World War II in the North Strand area.

The carnage in pictures
—page 9

Editorial
—page 6

1975

By the mid-1970s the word 'terrorist' was in wide usage across Europe as a number of armed groups grabbed the headlines with bombings, shootings, hijackings and hostage-taking.

In Ireland, the big story of the year would come from the kidnapping of Dutch industrialist Tiede Herrema and the 19-day siege of a house in Monasterevin, Co Kildare, where he was held. The kidnappers turned out to be Eddie Gallagher and Marion Coyle, republican dissidents who demanded the release of three prisoners, including Gallagher's lover, Dr Rose Dugdale.

The year would also see the loss of two of Europe's elder statesmen: Éamon de Valera, 92, in Ireland and Francisco Franco in Spain.

In popular music, Queen had a huge international hit with 'Bohemian Rhapsody', while Philomena Begley went to the top of the charts in Ireland with her version of 'Blanket On The Ground'.

NEWS BRIEFS

Apr Saigon falls to North Vietnamese forces. Amid chaotic scenes at the US embassy, the last of the Americans and their allies are evacuated by helicopter. In nearby Cambodia, Year Zero begins as Pol Pot's Khmer Rouge take power. (31)

Aug A survey in the Republic shows that 91% of Catholics attend Mass at least once a week. (20)

Dec Austria allows 'Carlos the Jackal' and his armed group to fly to freedom from Vienna to Algeria after they seized 70 hostages, including 11 oil ministers from nations in the Organisation of Petroleum Exporting Countries (OPEC). (22)

Dev's final journey

Saturday, August 30

Éamon de Valera wept softly when he privately visited his childhood haunts along the Cork-Limerick border for the last time three years ago. It happened in Charleville where he was warmly welcomed by a group of onlookers. As he stretched out his soft white hand in greeting, it accidentally touched and then patted a little girl's head. The old man's eyes filled with tears, for his youthful memories were also of this town and the countryside spreading across the county boundary to Bruree.

A visit from the 'Boy from Bruree' was always a nostalgic occasion for there was much to laugh and to chat about. Like the time he jumped in and out a neighbour's window and got a hammering from his uncle as a result. Or the day he fell asleep in a donkey and cart and rolled off and was still asleep when found lying on the roadway a short time later.

Some of the more treasured mementoes of his childhood were presented to the school museum in Bruree which he opened on a wintry October Sunday three years ago.

This was his last official visit and as he waved from the State Coach waiting at Charleville Railway Station that evening to take him back to Dublin, the significance was not lost on the cluster of people on the misty platform: Dev was bidding a final farewell. – Ray Ryan

How the mighty had fallen: George Best enters the pitch at Flower Lodge for his first match with Cork Celtic.

Miami – 'Murder Gang' theory

Friday, August 1

Police in the North believe that the two UVF men who blew themselves up during their bomb and gun attacks on the Miami Showband may have been members of a vicious sectarian murder squad which has been operating from and in the Dunganon-Portadown area.

The band had left the Castle Ballroom in the main street of Banbridge shortly before 2 o'clock. They travelled six miles along the dual carriageway towards Newry before being flagged down at about 2.08 by a man waving a red light and dressed as a soldier. The van pulled in to the side of the road and the five occupants were taken out at gunpoint by two UVF men and made to stand at the side of the road facing the hedge. As the other two UVF men were placing the charge inside the van, it exploded, killing them instantly.

Des McAlea was thrown by the blast into the hedge as the other two UVF men opened fire. Chief Supt McAtamney said the three dead musicians and the seriously injured Stephen Travers had been found in the field beside the carriageway. His impression was that they had tried to make a run for it but had been gunned down.

The Cork Examiner

NO. 49,041 SATURDAY MORNING, NOVEMBER 8, 1975 Price 7p (inc. VAT)

Herrema is free at last

KIDNAP COUPLE Eddie Gallagher and Marion Coyle were last night being questioned in the Bridewell Garda Station, Dublin after a dramatic surrender in the marathon 18-day Monasterevan siege. Their captive, Dr. Tiede Herrema, was said to be in the Curragh Military Hospital recovering from his 36-day ordeal at the hands of the pair. But later this was denied and his whereabouts were unknown.

The end came shortly before 10 o'clock last night when Gallagher and Coyle threw down their firearms from the top-floor front bedroom and, with Dr. Herrema walked down the stairs to give themselves up to Chief Supt. Laurence Wrenn and armed Special Branch detectives.

Twenty minutes later, the bearded Gallagher, looking gaunt after his lengthy hold-out, was led out of the house into a waiting police car surrounded by newsmen and photographers.

His accomplice, 19-year-old Marion Coyle, looking radiant in the bright lights of the spotlights and television crews, smiled and waved at journalists when asked if she was feeling alright.

Earlier Dr. Herrema (53), the Dutch Ferenka executive, was smuggled out of the St. Evin's Park Council Estate in a Garda car and taken to the Curragh Military Hospital. The specially-chartered cardiac ambulance was not required, as Dr. Herrema, looking "healthy" to Gardai, walked unaided from the house.

Dr. Herrema spurned a hospital visit. He asked the garda car taking him to the Curragh Military Hospital to drive instead to the Dublin residence of the Dutch Ambassador, Mr. Felix van Raalte, for a reunion with his wife, who was on her way back from Holland. Later this morning the Ambassador confirmed that Dr. Herrema was at his home.

"He is very well and just wants to sleep," the Ambassador said.

HELPED TO CAR

News of the end of the hold-out came suddenly when Garda Press Oficer, Supt. Tom Kelly, broke off a meal he was having in the town and dashed the half mile to the siege scene.

Journlaists were carried from their compound to within 20 yards of the floodlit house and watched as Gallagher, wearing a double-breasted black coat and dark blue trousers, was escorted along the garden path and into the back of a garda squad car. Two senior garda officers supported him on the short journey to the car.

Dr. Herrema.

Coyle, looking none the worse for the ordeal, and accompanied by Special Branch Chief, Supt. John Fleming, was led into the second police car.

CARRIED HANDBAG

She was dresed in a three-quarter length coat and blue jeans and her long black hair was swept back. She carried a handbag.

"Are you O.K. Marion?", reporters called out, to which she smiled and nodded.

The two squad cars then sped from the scene and road blocks throughout the whole area were immediately lifted. Press men were not allowed into the house and at a hurriedly convened press conference, Supt. Tom Kelly made the following statement:

At 9.50 p.m. Edward Gallagher and Marion Coyle, following a day in which there was extensive dialogue between them and Supt. Wrenn, discarded firearms and surrendered to the gardai on duty on the ground floor of house Number 1410.

"The aforementioned and Dr. Herrema came downstairs and Dr. Herrema left the scene immediately, apparently in good health.

"Edward Gallagher and Marion Coyle have been taken into custody and conveyed to the Bridewell in Dublin. The house, No. 1410, is still in the possession of the gardai and will remain so until the completion of technical examination".

DEAL DENIED

Neighbours living in the vicinity of No. 1410 told reporters that the first they knew of the surrender was when they heard breaking glass which w[illegible] caused by the

Continued on Back Page, Col. 6

Page One Comment

Safe and well

By THE EDITOR

THERE will be unconcealed relief throughout the country today at the news that Dr. Herrema is free, safe and well. The long nightmare is over; the great ordeal has ended. What could have ended in tragedy has now finished happily for the man who was forced to become the centre-point of this long-drawn-out drama. Legal considerations —there are certainly serious charges to follow—prevent us from commenting on Gallagher and Coyle, and in any event there is little to be said, except perhaps to point to the utter futility of it all.

But on another and very important aspect of the affair there is this to be said: the successful conclusion of this gruesomely spectacular affair is a tribute to the Government for its steadfastness in refusing to make any concessions; to the gardai and the army for their patience and endurance, and perhaps especially to the people in direct charge who had to make difficult decisions on the spot. The pressures must have been enormous; the temptations to compromise must have been equally great. There must have been times when nerves were frayed, when frustration was almost overwhelming. But the temptation to seek an easy solution was submerged and wildcat schemes were wisely ruled out.

Overall, this has been a tremendous moral victory for the security forces and a crushing defeat for the people of violence. It has put an end to the theory that all such kidnappings must necessarily succeed or else end in disaster. In the wider sense, it may mean that a successful psychological formula has been found to deal with them. But above all, it means that today everybody feels a little safer than they did yesterday.

PRAISE FROM DUTCH MINISTER

Dutch foreign minister May Van der Stoel last night praised Dr. Herrema for his endurance.

Mr. Van der Stoel said in a brief statement that he also admired the way in which the Irish Government had handled the 36-day kidnapping.

Referring to Dr. Herrema, Mr. Van der Stoel said: "Through his courage and endurance it was possible for a solution to be found for this affair without bloodshed and the flag did not have to be struck in the face of terrorism."

POLICE TACTICS SUCCEED

The two most dramatic sieges of recent weeks have both ended exactly the way police believed — both in England and the Republic—without injury.

At the end of the week-long London "Spaghetti House" siege, senior police officers — including Metropolitan Police Commissioner Sir Robert Mark — claimed that they were convinced that the kidnap would end in surrender.

The Herrema kidnap came just four hours after the London siege ended and both sieges were conducted with the same low profile, wait-and-see policy by police.

Big boost for Fine Gael candidate

The peaceful end to the kidnap siege at Monasterevan may provide a big boost to the chances of the Fine Gael candidate, Mr Enda Kenny, in the West Mayo by-election, writes our Political Correspondent.

The public by and large, have been very impressed by, and have fully supported the Government's firm stand in the Herrema affair. It was the one example of really strong government that they have had in recent times.

Now that this firmness has paid off at Monasterevan, the electors in West Mayo, may be in the mood to show its appreciation of strong government by giving the vacant seat to the Government candidate with something more to spare than might be expected.

On the international scene, too, the Government will have won many plaudits for its handling of the case and gain useful prestige for itself and the country.

Potential foreign investors will see that stability and the right climate for investment still exists in the Republic.

Chief Supt. Laurence Wrenn (left) watches Gallagher being escorted from the house.

'Absolutely thrilled' in Limerick

By Tony Purcell

THE news that Dr. Herrema had been released after five weeks of captivity was widely welcomed in the Limerick area last night.

Dr. Herrema, managing director of the £20 million Ferenka plant in Limerick, was kidnapped from near his home at Monaleen, Castleroy, on the morning of October 3 last when he set out for work. The following day the people of Limerick turned out in their thousands to express their utter revulsion and condemnation of the outrageous act.

The Mayor of Limerick, Cllr. Thady Coughlan, last night expressed delight at Dr. Herrema's release and said that he could be assured of a tremendous homecoming when he returns back to Limerick as soon as he has recovered from his horrifying ordeal.

FIRM STAND

Mayor Coughlan paid a tribute to the Government for their firm stand from the outset in refusing to give in to the kidnappers demands and to the gardai and army for their heroic efforts in tracking down the abductors and securing Dr. Herrema's eventual release.

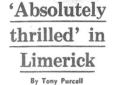

Mr. Nicholas McGrath, the spokesman for the 1,200 workers at the Ferenka plant which was forced to close down for two weeks on October 9 in response to one of the kidnappers' demands, last night said that the workers were "absolutely thrilled" with the news that Dr. Herrema had been released unharmed. Dr. Herrema, he said, could look forward to a most heartwarming welcome from the workers on his eventual return to Limerick.

"As far as we are concerned Ferenka would not be the same without him. Since he came to Limerick over two years ago he has won the respect and admiration from the workforce for his fairmindedness and honourable way he has dealt with the problems confronted by the factory during the current economic recession," stated Mr. McGrath.

It is ironic to note that Dr. Herrema's release coincides with the news that the Ferenka plant, which had been going through a most difficult period due to the recession, this week received a most timely boost with the announcement to the workers by management that the production schedules are being increased next year because of the increased demand for the company's top quality goods on the American market.

The workers said, Mr. McGrath, were indebted to the gardai and army as well as to the Government of this country for the wonderful job in securing with patience and great endurance Dr. Herrema's safe release.

TELEGRAM

The chairman of Limerick County Council, Cllr. Pat Ryan, last night sent the following telegram to the Dutch Ambassador, in Dublin:

"People in Co. Limerick rejoice at the ending of Dr. Herrema's ordeal and look forward to his early return among us."

Mr. Liam O'Connor, president of the Mid-West Regional Executive of the Federated Union of Employers, too expressed delight at Dr. Herrema's safe return and declared: "This is great news for industry and employment generally."

WIFE FLIES TO DUBLIN

MRS. ELIZABETH HERREMA left Nijmegen, Holland, for Ireland last night in a specially chartered plane after celebrating her husband's release.

She was accompanied by Mr. Gerald Krayenhoff, chairman of the multi-national chemical concern AKZO which owns the Ferrenka steel cord company in Limerick, of which Dr. Herrema is managing director.

Mr. Krayenhoff said he hoped Dr. Herrema, who was taken to a military hospital after his release, would be able to return to Holland with him soon.

Dutch backed Irish Govt's policy

Dutch Prime Minister Joop Den Uyl said in The Hague last night that the Dutch government respected the policy of the Irish government over the kidnapped industrialist.

He said after the weekly Cabinet meeting there had never been any question of a assault on the house in Monasterevan.

And recent reports saying that Mrs. Elizabeth Herrema had had a collapse were "definitely incorrect."

He added that Dr. Herrema's physical and mental condition was "admirable."

Gas dispute may spread to Cork

As about 150 manual workers employed by Calor Kosangas continue their unofficial strike which began in Dublin last Monday, a spokesman for the Irish Transport and General Workers Union said yesterday that their members in Cork had not been approached to take similar action.

The dispute concerns the appointment of a fitter which the union members say should have been filled by a senior man instead of a worker who had been with the company for a short time.

A spokesman for the I.T.G.W.U. said last night that a formula had been put to the workers by management on Thursday in an attempt to resolve the strike, but this had been "unanimously" refused by the workers.

Unofficial sources say that the threat of the dispute spreading to Cork is a very real possibility.

Marian Coyle.

Great joy and relief —Lynch

In a comment last night the leader of the Opposition, Mr. Jack Lynch, T.D., speaking from Westport, where he has been campaigning, said: "My first feelings are those that I know are shared by all Irish people—feelings of great joy and relief.

My first thoughts go to Dr. Herrema himself who must surely be a man of steel, physically and mentally, in the manner in which he endured his terrible ordeal and for his wife and family for whom I hope the sympathy and understanding of the Irish people were of some comfort during their agony.

"I congratulate the gardai for their efficient and successful investigation of the kidnapping and for the manner in which they conducted the affair at Monasterevan. I congratulate also the Defence Forces for the great assistance they gave.

"The Government are to be commended for their stand in which they received the complete and unstinting support of the Fianna Fail Party."

CARDINAL 'DELIGHTED'

Commenting on the release of Dr. Herrema, Cardinal Conway said: "I am delighted at this good news. Thank God, no-one has been injured."

Cosgrave says: 'we rejoice'

grave, sent the following message to Dr. Herrema: "I have just heard the news of your release."

"The people of Ireland will rejoice in the knowledge that after the horror of your 36 days in captivity you have escaped the threat of murder and that you are now free to be united with your wife and your family, who have suffered and waited with such noble courage.

"I convey to you the admiration of the Government who know of the strength of will and patient endurance with which you have borne the great physical and mental torture of your cruel captivity.

"Your safety brings great relief and joy to us all.

"I hope that the concern and respect which the people of Ireland have for you and your family will in some small way in the years to come compensate for the prolonged agony to which you and your family have been subjected."

COONEY PLEASED

The Minister for Justice, Mr. Cooney, said in Athlone last night, "My reaction is one of intense pleasure that Dr. Herrema's ordeal has ended and that he has been returned unharmed to his family. He is now in the Curragh Military Hospital for a preliminary check.

"I am sure I am speaking for everybody in the country when I say how much we regret how much he and his family has had to endure by this ordeal. It is a matter of some shame to us that a man like him who came to Ireland on our invitation to assist in the development of our country should have had to suffer so much, and I congratulate him on his fortitude and I congratulate his wife for her bravery and her understanding, of the Government's stand. I would like to pay tribute to the understanding and help received from the Dutch Government and their representative in Ireland, Ambassador Van Raante."

Mr. Cooney also expressed his thanks to the gardai for first locating the kidnappers and for pressing this matter to a successful and peaceful conclusion.

CHARGED WITH MURDER

Michael Bernard Rea (27), a farmer, Sraharla, Knockanevin, Mitchelstown, Co. Cork, was charged at a special court at Mitchelstown Garda Station, last evening, with the murder of David Rea at Sraharla, yesterday.

Mr. James Skinner, P.C., remanded the accused in custody to Fermoy District Court next Monday.

Supt. P. Whelan, Fermoy, represented the Director of Public Prosecutions and Mr. E. P. Finn, solicitor, appeared for the accused

1976

Jumping on a boat and leaving the country was an option many people took in 1977 as Ireland suffered from the worst unemployment and the highest inflation in the EEC. However, one group of men left Ireland's green shores with adventure on their mind rather than the quest for a better life overseas. Some historians had speculated that Irish monks could have been the first Europeans to travel to America, a feat that would have preceded Columbus by eight centuries. Tim Severin and his brave crew aimed to prove it.

A rare job vacancy in Ireland came to the fore in October when Cearbhall Ó Dálaigh became the first president to resign. Ó Dálaigh had taken exception to insulting remarks made by Paddy Donegan, Minister for Defence.

By now sex was obviously well-established in Irish popular culture with film-goers at mainstream cinemas having the choice of such titles as *The Graduate, Forbidden Photos of a Lady Above Suspicion* and *The Landlord*, which was advertised with a lady's stocking-clad leg and the phrase "The landlord's getting just about everything but the rent."

Rescue at Entebbe

Monday, July 5

Israel's defence Minister, Mr Shimon Peres, last night launched a strong verbal attack on Ugandan President Idi Amin, after Israeli commandos struck deep into Africa to rescue about 100 people held hostage by pro-Palestinian guerrillas at Entebbe Airport. Mr Peres charged the Ugandan president with personal responsibility for aiding the guerrillas killed in the "unprecedented and brilliant" Israeli rescue.

The Ugandan leader, he said, had allowed other guerrillas to join the original four hijackers of the Air France plane after it landed at Entebbe last Monday and Amin had also allowed Ugandan soldiers to help guard the hostages.

The Israeli force roared out of the darkness in three big C-130 Hercules transports at Entebbe shortly before midnight and stormed across the tarmac, blazing away at Ugandan troops who tried to resist.

"Come on, we've got planes for you," the troops shouted as they reached the hostages, most of them Israelis.

Tears flowed freely when the hostages arrived at Tel Aviv's Ben Gurion international Airport to be reunited with their families and greeted by near-hysterical crowds of well wishers.

Wexford full-back Willie Murphy is sandwiched by brothers Ray and Brendan Cummins in the All-Ireland hurling final. In the background is Jimmy Barry Murphy. Cork won the match in what would be the first of a three-in-a-row of titles.

NEWS BRIEFS

Jan Ten Protestant workmen are taken off a bus and shot dead by republican paramilitaries at Kingsmills, Co Antrim. (5)

July New houses for sale in Cork: Model Farm Road, three-bed detached, £14,500; Dundanion Court, Blackrock, four-bed semi-detached, £12,500; Carrigaline, three-bed semi-detached, £10,750.

Sept The European Commission on Human Rights finds Britain guilty of torturing republican prisoners in Northern Ireland. (2)

Oct A pint of stout in Mallow now costs 36p after publicans increase prices by a penny.

Overweight row may aid phone girls' claim

Wednesday, August 11

The current work to rule being operated by women telephonists in Dublin, Cork and Drogheda, in support of equal pay may be supported next week by the men telephonists who are angry over the threatened dismissal of one of them because he is overweight.

It is understood that a move might be made to have the dispute made official when the National Executive of the Irish Congress of Trade Unions returns from holidays.

The 500 men telephonists in Dublin plan to hold a meeting tomorrow over what action they should take to support the women operators.

At this meeting the matter of the threatened dismissal of what has become known as "the fat man" issue will also be discussed. The man in question is a 30-year-old bachelor and six footer. He weighs about 15 stone and his colleagues say he carries his weight well.

City Edition

The Cork Examiner

No. 48,201 TUESDAY MORNING, MAY 18, 1976 Price 9p (inc. VAT)

SHOWDOWN NEAR IN PAY TALKS

THE TAOISEACH, Mr. Liam Cosgrave, and a number of his senior ministers, met for over an hour at Leinster House yesterday to discuss the impasse that has developed in the National Wage Agreement negotiations. The unions yesterday gave the employers an ultimatum: delete the inability to pay clause by tomorrow or there will be no new National Wage Agreement.

The employers are expected to discuss this development either today or tomorrow. The government issued no statement after its meeting yesterday, but it is believed that the Minister for Labour, Mr. Michael O'Leary, has been instructed to make a further attempt to bring about a compromise between the employers and the unions.

Mr. Michael O'Leary, had been making strenuous efforts behind the scenes to secure a compromise between the sides, but so far appears to have made little headway.

The crisis began last Thursday when the sides broke up without setting a date for a further meeting. The talks had been running into difficulties for some time before that over the inability-to-pay clause, but few people predicted that the talks might break up because of it.

The unions have been pressing hard for the "escape hatch" as it is popularly called, to be left out of the agreement, but the employers' side has remained adamant that it must be written in.

It is argued by the unions that large numbers of their members have not even received the full benefits of the 1975 Agreement because of this "escape" clause. If it is included again this year, they hold it would mean these people would lose out on increases over a two year period.

The employers counter this by saying bluntly that if the clause is deleted there will be hundreds of workers made redundant and many companies forced to close.

The pay provisions of the agreement have been drawn up since April 16. They provide for two phased increases over 13½ months. Initially, there would be a pause of two months, and five months would elapse between the first and second increases.

The pay increases in the draft proposals already agreed upon would mean a minimum increase of £6 during the 13½ months, and a maximum increase of just over £10.

Brendan sails out into history

Report:Donal Hickey Picture:Michael Olney

FIVE MEN set sail from Brandon Creek on the Dingle Peninsula last night on an epic 4,000 mile voyage designed to convince a doubting world that St. Brendan could have beaten Columbus to America by 800 years.

Having waited all day for the right conditions, the craft was pushed into the sea by a group of men, including former Kerry footballer, Michael O Se, at 7.25, when the evening tide had ebbed by about 10 feet.

Up to 200 sightseers, photographers and television crewmen took up vantage points on the tiny pier and overhanging cliffs. Wives' goodbye kisses, the handshakes of well wishers and a loud cheer marked the start of a venture first thought of four years ago.

Three local fishermen, Tom Kennedy, Maurice Leahy, and Tom Leahy, guided the Brendan out to sea in a currach and extrovert Arthur "Boots" Magan uncorked a bottle of stout, of which the boat has an abundant store to complement a barrel of whiskey.

NEEDED HELP

The crew sought the help of journalists in a hired boat to raise the anchor. Then the wood and leather craft hoisted sail and disappeared into Tralee Bay to test the awesome Atlantic.

The Brendan was supported by a force four to five westerly wind (25 m.p.h.) and mission leader Timothy Severin was confident of reaching the Arran Islands in a day or two.

While shrewd Kerry fishermen admired the courage of the five, many more hopeful than confident about the Brendan's chances of reaching the final destination, Boston.

But not Severin. "We are very confident of achieving our aim and are anxious to get on with the job. I hope to be back in Dingle very soon after the trip."

TRIBUTE

He paid special tribute to John Goodwin (80) of the Maharees for his help with the medieval design of the craft and added that the crew had enough dehydrated tinned food and fresh water for 40 days.

Crew member Peter Mullet is from Goleen in West Cork. His English-born wife, Jill, said: "I've no apprehensions about my husband's safety. They are all very capable and I think they'll make it. Peter always liked the sea and I think it an incredible venture."

"Boots" Mangan's father, Francis, of Straffan, Co. Kildare, his mother and sister were also there. "If this is what he wants to do let him do it," said Francis. The Magans have a holiday home on Valentia Island.

ADVENTURER

Crewman George Malony was seen off by his mother, Pam, of Blackrock, Co. Dublin. She praised her son's adventurous spirit and added, "he was always like this. I could never see him as a 9—5 office worker."

Tim Severin's wife, Dorothy, did not, after all, join the crew. He explained that the conditions were not promising and she preferred not to go.

The fifth crew member is Rolf Hansen, a Norwegian.

Basically, the Brendan boasts only the kind of gear that the saint and the monks who travelled with him took on their voyage. But just in case of trouble, their modern counterparts have taken along a few up-to-date aids, including a radio transmitter.

Esso will quit 'oil show' well

By Pat Barry

ESSO EXPLORATION is to abandon its well in the Celtic Sea off the Cork coast where oil was discovered two years ago. Yesterday a company spokesman revealed that the Saipem Due drillship, shortly to return to Irish waters, will first of all seal this well in block 48/28-1.

Oil was discovered at a flow rate of 1,550 barrels per day from thin sand in this well, sited about 48 miles from Cork, and speculation was rife about its commercial potential.

Consequently, it was anticipated that Esso would re-enter this well last year but instead they concentrated on testing the geological formation to the south and west of this find.

They drilled two wells to depths of almost 9,000 feet in blocks 56/12-1 and 47/30-1, which they then plugged and abandoned.

Esso will now commence drilling an exploratory well in block 48/23-1, sited about 27 miles offshore, and directly north of their well in 48/28-1.

SHARE COSTS

According to the spokesman, the Saipem Due is expected to commence operations later this month on a joint basis for Esso and Marathon.

Under a farm out agreement between the two companies, both share in the drilling and development costs on a 50/50 basis after the seventh well drilled by Esso, a stage they reached at the end of last season.

Additionally the spokesman said that they planned to drill a well in block 57/6-1 later this season. This will test a structure in the central portion of the farm-in block in an area

TURN TO BACK PAGE, COL. 4

Ehrlichman's conviction upheld

The American Court of appeals yesterday upheld the convictions of former White House aides John Ehrlichman and Gordon Liddy in the so-called "plumbers" case, an offshoot of the Watergate scandal that ended Richard Nixon's presidency.

But the court reversed the convictions of the other two men convicted in the plumbers affair, Bernard Barker and Eugenio Martinzez—who were also convicted in the original Watergate case.

The plumber case involved a 1971 break-in at the office of a California psychiatrist treating Daniel Ellsberg, who had incurred the Nixon administrations's anger by releasing the Pentagon papers, a previously secret report on the roots of American involvement in Vietnam.

STUDENTS DIE

Two Turkish students died in hospital in Ankara, yesterday, from injuries received in clashes between left and right wingers, bringing to 46 the number of people killed in political violence over the past six months.

B.B.C. SEEK £27 COLOUR TV LICENCE

The B.B.C. is to ask the Government to give the go-ahead for a £27 colour television licence when talks aimed at a new increase start in midsummer.

Only a year ago the colour licence went up 50 per cent from £12 to £18. Now the B.B.C. is seeking another 50 per cent rise which if it gets Government approval — could be brought in next spring.

Although the B.B.C. has made no official statement about a licence increase, a spokesman said today: "It is no secret that we want an increase next year — and it must be a substantial one if the B.B.C. is to keep its head above water financially."

CHILDREN DIE IN BEIRUT "BLOOD LAKE"

A mortar attack on a Palestinian refugee camp yesterday left 10 children dead and raised fears of a repetition of the artillery duels which killed at least 150 people and wounded 400 on Sunday.

According to left-wing and Palestinian sources, the children were killed when a mortar shell smashed into the kindergarten of the Tel Al-Zatarr camp on the southeastern fringes of the Lebanese capital. About 30 children were injured.

The densely-populated "shanty-town" camp has been involved regularly in mortar exchanges with surrounding suburbs held by right-wing forces.

The victims of Sunday's artillery duels included 34 people killed and 100 wounded when a shell smashed into a crowded cinema in leftist-controlled western Beirut.

A left-wing newspaper yesterday accused the right of having turned Beirut into "A lake of blood" on Sunday. But the right charged that many people had been killed by indiscriminate left-wing shelling of hospitals in eastern Beirut.

PICTURE KEPT FROM DUCHESS

The Duchess of Windsor, nearing her 80th birthday in her Paris home, will not be shown a photograph of herself as an apparent invalid which appeared across five columns on page one of "France-Soir." France's largest newspaper, yesterday, friends said.

The duchess has recovered from the illness that brought her to the American Hospital in Paris last year for treatment.

Inside today

NEW CALL ON R.T.E. 2

Cork Multi-Channel TV Committee have renewed their call to the Minister for Posts and Telegraphs to reconsider his decision to award a second channel to R.T.E. which the committee calls "this national non broadcasting service". Page 7

CORK CITY BY-PASSED

A major international tour firm is by-passing Cork city as an overnight stop over. Dick Brazil reports on Page 7

NURSES SEEK ACTION

The Irish Nurses Organisation have asked the Department of Labour to intervene in their pay dispute with the Minister for Health Page 10

£10,000 PRO-AM

Details of the £10,000 Musgrave—Christy O'Connor Golf Pro-Am have been announced Page 11

Man dies after bus shooting

One man died in hospital in Derry last night after a shooting incident on a bus. Two other people who were injured were reported later to be seriously ill.

Mrs. Lemass is F.F. choice

Mrs. Eileen Lemass widow of the late Noel Lemass has been selected as the Fianna Fail candidate in the forthcoming Dublin South County by-election.

Examinations ban lifted by teachers

THE TEACHERS Union of Ireland meeting in Dublin last night decided to lift its ban on the preparation and correction of examination papers for students in the regional colleges of technology.

The executive ordered its members to co-operate with the holding of the tests before the summer holidays in order to allow students appropriate time for study.

Mr. Kevin McCarthy, acting general secretary of the union, said that there would probably be some delay, but he hoped the examinations would get under way from June 1.

The meeting accepted eight assurances from the Department of Education on the referral of the claims to the teachers' conciliation and arbitration scheme. The T.U.I. President, Mr. William Webb, and the Department Secretary, Mr. Dominic O Laoghaire, will sign the agreement today.

CASH ISSUE

The claim for examination money will be dealt with within three weeks and there will be an independent chairman of the Conciliation Council.

If disagreement is registered at conciliation level, the official side has promised that it will submit a rebuttal statement early and it will agree to have Mr. Rory O'Hanlon, Senior Counsel, as Chairman of the Arbitration Board. If the award is agreed then payment will be made as soon as possible to the teachers.

The Executive Committee of the National Council for Education Awards will hold an emergency session this morning to discuss the re-scheduling of the examination dates.

IN CORK

Six hundred and forty seven students of the Cork Regional Technical College had planned to vacate the College if the dispute was not settled.

Complaints about overflying

In the 12 months up to end of last month, the British Government had received compaints from the Republic of Ireland about 22 accidental acts of overflying by military aircraft, including helicopters.

The Defence Under Secretary, Mr. James Wellbeloved, stated this in a Commons written reply yesterday to Mr. Cyril Townsend (C).

Corresponding figures for years ending April 1975, and April 1974, were 19 and 28, he added.

German charter flights

The first of a series of German charter flights being run by the Deutsches Reiseburo Travel Organisation (D.E.R.)—one of the largest Tour Wholesalers in Germany featuring Ireland for 1976, is now operating.

The charter series comprises some 40 flights in all and runs from mid-May to end October 1976 to Shannon. This all jet charter series is with two charter airlines from Germany; Condor will operate ex-Dusseldorf each Saturday also.

The D.E.R. Agency has appointed Limerick Travel to handle their clients in Ireland in 1976, and the owner, Mr. Tony Brazil, stated that the response to the first-ever Irish Charter series and marketing programme was excellent.

APPOINTMENT FOR McFLYNN

Mr. Paddy McFlynn (Down), who was defeated by Mr. Con Murphy in the election for the G.A.A. Presidency, has been appointed by the Management Committee as Chairman of the Activities Committee. He succeeds Mr. Noel Drumgoole, the Dublin-born Bord na gCon executive in Limerick, who was also a Presidential candidate this year.

Fr. Seamus Gardiner, a son of a former G.A.A. President, and trainer of the winning St. Flannan's team which won the All-Ireland colleges hurling title on Sunday last, is the new Chairman of the Communications Committee. He succeeds Mr. Michael O'Callaghan of Roscommon.

28 remanded after jail demo

Twenty-eight people were remanded on bail until May 25 when they appeared before Birmingham magistrates yesterday charged in connection with a demonstration outside Winson Green Prison on Saturday.

They were charged with a variety of offences including breach of the peace, assaulting police officers and possessing offensive weapons.

The demonstration was staged by National Front supporters in protest at the imprisonment of Robert Relf for contempt of court for refusing to remove a "for sale to English family" notice outside his Leamingtom Spa house.

RTE anxious for talks as soon as possible

RTE MANAGEMENT in a statement last night said they were anxious that talks should begin at the earliest possible moment to secure a return to work of the 1,800 employees at the station.

But last night a spokesman for the five craft unions that initiated the dispute said no approach had been made to them for a meeting which they were prepared to attend at very short notice.

In their statement R.T.E. management said they had considered the circumstances in which the all-out picket was sanctioned by the Irish Congress of Trade Unions. They were also endeavouring to establish the views of Congress on how the present impasse might be ended.

"We are examining our own position to identify a basis on which negotiations might be reopened," said an R.T.E. spokesman.

DIRECT TALKS URGED

A spokesman for the craft unions said yesterday that they felt it would be much more advantageous for R.T.E. managament to have direct negotiations with them, instead of approaching Congress, who had already ratified the strike through their Industrial Relations Committee.

The R.T.E. dispute is over an higher grading claim by 30 craftsmen, manly carpenters and electricians, which would involve higher salaries.

1977

Elvis Presley, the king of rock 'n' roll, died on August 16, 1977. While the news of his death did make the front page, the same *Examiner* actually led with a story about fishermen defying restrictions on herring fishing.

A few weeks prior to Presley's death, Rory Gallagher, our own king of home-grown rock, was granted impressive coverage when he made a triumphant return to his home county at the Mountain Dew festival in Macroom.

Another local son in the news that year was Jack Lynch. The Fianna Fáil leader had led his party to a surprise landslide general election victory. Among the three government ministers who lost their seats was Conor Cruise O'Brien who had been dubbed 'Mr Prices' by an inflation-resenting public. The *Examiner* opined that O'Brien's "pro-British" attitudes and his "growing arrogance and disdain" for the electorate may have been factors in his ousting.

Ireland was to get another Nobel prize when the 'Peace Women' were awarded the Peace Prize for their work to end the violence in the North. Ultimately the prize was to lead to the unravelling of the peace movement in the province over a row when one of them, Mairéad Corrigan, kept her £38,000 share of the prize-money for herself.

Among the most memorable sporting contests of the decade were the battles between Dublin and Kerry in football. The finest of these came in the 1977 semi-final, when Dublin came back with two late goals to defeat their old foes.

The success of *Saturday Night Fever* spilled over from cinemas to the discos where big collars and fancy moves were all the rage.

It's a toast to the king

Saturday, June 16

In the pubs of Blackpool last night they were preparing to crown Jack Lynch as King of Ireland. And with more than double the quota to his credit, so well they might.

They would tell you triumphantly between sips: "Now they know who the REAL Taoiseach is." Few would blame them. They were savouring their moment of triumph and had every right to do so. For by any political standards, this was an extraordinary performance, even allowing for the personal charisma of the man. Let there be no mistake about it, the Fianna Fáil victory, the amazing political turnabout, was entirely due to one man.

Against all the odds this former Cork hurler, this former Taoiseach, this man of many battles, this son of Cork, this man of charm and distinction, had managed to prove once again the validity of the old saying about the old dog for the hard road.

So last night in Blackpool they were gathering the makings of the bonfires, and they were out hunting for tar barrels. When Jack Lynch comes home to his native city, he will receive a welcome that Parnell himself, the 'uncrowned king of Ireland', would have envied.

The difference, they will tell you in Blackpool, is that Jack is already crowned.

Kerry's Mike Sheehy is held back by Kevin Moran of Dublin in their sides' classic All-Ireland semi-final encounter.

Presley fans quietly go home

Saturday, August 20

The thousands who went to mourn Elvis Presley headed home yesterday. But first they went to the singer's tomb and many took a flower for a keepsake. They filed by the majestic marble mausoleum where the 42-year-old singer, who died of an apparent heart attack, was buried. Volunteers handed them flowers from the 3,000 bouquets and most paused only a moment to look at the tomb which is still closed to the public.

The mood was subdued and the crowd orderly, in contrast with wild scenes at the cemetery on Thursday and round Presley's Graceland mansion the day before. Twenty thousand strong, the pilgrims came from all over the United States, Europe, Asia and South America.

NEWS BRIEFS

Feb Seán Ó Ríordáin is described as the greatest poet of our time at his funeral in Ballingeary, Co Cork. He was buried a few yards from composer Seán O'Riada. "Now O'Riada is singing a requiem to Ó Ríordáin," said former president Cearbhall Ó Dálaigh at the graveside. (24)

June Tim Severin and his crew on the *St Brendan* reach Newfoundland, thus proving that Irish people could have made it to America long before Christopher Columbus. (26)

July Israel gives the go ahead for the first Jewish settlements in the West Bank, an area captured from Jordan in 1967. (26)

The Cork Examiner

No. 48,544 MONDAY MORNING, JUNE 27, 1977 Price 10p (inc. VAT)

Corish quits as Labour leader

MR. BRENDAN CORISH will not be accepting nomination for the leadership of the Labour Party when deputies meet on Friday next to elect their party leader.

He made this announcement yesterday and thus severed 17 years of spearheading the party into what many consider to be a major force in Irish politics. However his decision was not entirely unexpected and had been forecast earlier in the week.

Later yesterday Mr. Frank Cluskey T.D., the person tipped as the man most likely to succeed in the leadership stakes, confirmed that he would be a candidate for the post.

In his statement Mr. Corish said he believed this was the most opportune time to place the leadership in new hands, and indicated that his announcement had been timed so that Labour deputies might have time to deliberate on their choice of successor.

He stressed that he had decided, no matter what the outcome of the election, to vacate the leadership which he had held since March 1960.

The Labour Party, he said, had now emerged as a national party with clearly defined socialist policies and a national organisation. "The foundations have been laid on which to build a socialist party capable of facing all the social and economic challenges of the future".

He stressed that he was convinced that Labour's participation in the National Coalition Government had been beneficial for the party and vital for the country. "We got many of our most cherished policies implemented and helped the economy withstand the worst effects of the world

TURN TO BACK PAGE, COL. 6

Gave party a new image

From LIAM O'NEILL, Our Political Correspondent

MR. BRENDAN CORISH will be remembered as the leader who gave the Labour Party a new image in the 1960's by introducing new people and new policies.

He moved the party away from its old trade union base by encouraging people like Dr. Conor Cruise O'Brien, Mr. Justin Keating and Dr. David Thornley to take a more active part.

One of the most progressive things he did was to appoint a ney young dynamic general secretary Mr. Brendan Halligan.

Under Mr. Corish's patronage, Mr. Halligan has considerably reformed Labour. It is doubtful however, if Mr. Corish succeeded in making the party more socialistic. He himself can be accurately described perhaps as a social democrat and the Labour party under his leadership reflected a like image, particularly in Coalition with Fine Gael.

SETBACK

In the Irish context, a social democratic role is probably a better and more realistic one for Labour to adopt. It remains to be seen in terms of votes and seats in

TURN TO BACK PAGE, COL. 1

"Most loyal and honourable colleague"

THE TAOISEACH, Mr. Cosgrave issued the following statement yesterday afternoon.

"I wish Brendan Corish every happiness on his retirement as Leader of the Labour Party. He and I worked closely together on three occasions in Government.

"He was a most loyal and honourable colleague and rendered distinguished service as Tanaiste, Minister for Health, Minister for Social Welfare and Leader of the Labour Party. I hope that both Mrs. Corish and he will have many years to enjoy retirement."

REGRETS

Mr. Michael O'Leary, Minister for Labour and financial secretary of the Labour Party, issued the following statement:

"The announced departure of Brendan Corish as Leader of the Labour Party is a matter of regret to me as it is to all his other colleagues in the Parliamentary Labour Party and the members of the Labour Party constituency organisations throughout the country.

"Whether in Opposition or in Government the contribution of Brendan Corish towards the development of the modern Labour Party was immense. In the governments in which he served his concern for the underprivileged was always his prime motivation. I was privileged to work with him as a Cabinet colleague over the past four and a half years. It will be for his successor to emulate his example.

"It now falls to the members of the Parliamentary Labour Party to choose a new leader for the period of Opposition ahead of us. Our period in Opposition must be utilised to provide a reappraisal of existing Labour Party policies and the vigorous promulgation of those policies throughout our society.

"Outside the Dail our traditional alliance with the

TURN TO BACK PAGE, COL. 1

Cluskey favourite

Our political correspondent writes that Mr. Frank Cluskey will be firm favourite to succeed Mr. Corish as leader of the Labour Party when the election takes place on Friday next.

Roaring success for Rory

By Larry Lyons

Rory Gallagher performing for the huge crowd during the pop concert at the Macroom Mountain Dew Festival yesterday. ("Examiner)

"MACROOM," said the old man in the town square, "will never be the same again. Even the Redemptorists could not boast of anything like it during the General Mission in my boyhood days."

And one of the eight and a half thousand jean brigade looked at him and asked his companion, "is he for real?" "The generation gap," observed a journalist colleague. There was nothing else to say, except to correct him and say "generations, not generation."

Rory Gallagher, voted the world's top rock guitarist had come home to his native county to provide the star spot at the wistfully named Mountain Dew Festival on this fine June Sunday. The jean-clad brigade came from Cork, came from Dublin, from Galway and God knows where. They came by bus, they came by motor-bike, but mostly they came shanksmare and for many there were days in the coming and it looks if it will be longer in the going. They came with expectations and to a jean they swore that they were going homeward satisfied.

"NOT MY SCENE"

The occasion in the wooded Castle Grounds of Macroom was not my scene: I must have been the only person in the singing, dancing and gyrating crowd that wore a collar and tie. Talk about a fish out of water!

I do not pretend to be competent to give a verdict on the Gallagher performance but my own particular and very personal verdict was that it was a deafening success: and if anyone disagreed with me I can honestly plead that I cannot hear a word he says.

Rory took over and in a pound slimming performance he held the audience spellbound from the first shattering moment he went on the stage until two hours later when he left it. I found the music weird and wild and unwillingly I found it spellbinding. The audience was good humoured and during the concert there was no trace of viciousness. Whatever they did on Saturday night and what they did on Sunday night, they were a voraciusly enthusiastic audience who came to hear and see Rory and forget almost everything else. The result is etched in my mind like a scene from "Woodstock."

FANTASTIC

Pop is a phenenomon of the age and whether we like it or not the sound is expressive of the age: restless, loud, wild and "fantastic, man, fantastic."

But it also means big money. Yesterday's concert cost £23,500 to stage. Rory's fee was a cool £10,000, plus his expenses, plus a share of the profits if any. There was not a surplus. Denis Murphy, chairman of the festival, told me: "We just broke about even. Don't forget that the building of the stage alone cost £3,500."

"But look at the publicity for Macroom," said a loyal local man.

There were 114 professional security men augmented by about 50 local men; 50 uniformed gardai under a Chief Supt., a Supt., and an Inspector, plus detectives and dog patrols.

The security was good, make no mistake about it. You couldn't go behind a bush but somebody would pop from behind a tree, and Tony Long, who was in charge of the professional security men, told me that they confiscated daggers galore, sheath knives, hatchets, chains, blades and a quantity of drugs. One man who had a long carving knife caused a bit of bother when he refused to hand it over. "It is a family heirloom," he said. The confiscated articles were put into a guarded strong room and I am told that the hatchets would be handed back if claimed today but not the knives or the daggers. One man was arrested for being in possession of drugs.

PUB CLOSURE

Many of the pubs closed down but while the night scenes were sometimes wild the crowd generally was good humoured and the gardai said that overall the situation was well under control. None of the fears of some residents of orgies and mass fights were realised. And a good time was had by all, although after the Saturday night many were so broke that they had not the £2.50 for Rory's concert. But they lolled in the sun in the square and heard it if they did not see it. I am sure that if the wind was in the right direction you could have heard him 25 miles away in Cork.

For one day and two nights Rory Gallagher changed the life style of Macroom in a two-hour performance.

But if dat man idi Amin had come and the fat dictator and Rory, the Cork boy who became a world pop celebritiy, were in town together . . .

It boggles the imagination!

PEACEFUL

● Midnight call: The situation in Macroom was described by a garda as "peaceful. There were a few rows but nothing serious." There was a licensing extension until midnight. The town was heavily patrolled by gardai.

The Minstrel 'sweeps' home

CLAIM BY IRA PROVED A HOAX

A CLAIM that the Provisional IRA had executed a British soldier was proved false on Saturday when he was found alive and well in Dorset.

The Army in Northern Ireland was earlier investigating a claim that the Provos had murdered private Peter Wrightn (17), who vanished in London ten days ago.

A man who said he represented the Provos telephoned a Belfast newspaper and said that Wright was shot soon after he disappeared.

Using a recognised codeword he said the soldier was 'picked up' at Paddington Station and 'executed' two days later.

The caller said a Belfast active service unit carried out the killing in retaliation for the death of Majella O'Hare, a South Armagh schoolgirl, last August, who died in an accident involving the Army.

DISAPPEARED

Wright disappeared at Paddington as he was returning to the Parachute Regiment in Aldershot from an Easter visit to his mother in Wales.

Now he is in custody at Swanage, said a spokesman for Gwent police, and "will be dealth with as absent without leave by the military authorities."

★ A 36-year-old man was taken to hospital with gunshot wounds to his right knee yesterday after an incident in Lurgan, Co. Armagh. A spokesman at Craigavon Hospital said his condition was "fair."

Gardai search for murder weapon

GARDAI were last night searching the grounds of University College, Dublin at Belfield for the weapon used in the killing of an 18-year-old student during the regular Saturday night disco session on the campus.

A Garda spokesman confirmed that they were treating the killing of Patrick Coultry of St. Jarlath's Road, Cabra, Dublin, as murder.

The youth got two stab wounds during a flare-up at the dance and was rushed to St. Vincent's Hospital, Dublin by ambulance but was dead within an hour of admission.

FEARS

These dances are held in the disco every Saturday during academic term, and although there have been some minor incidents in the past, this stabbing is the first ever fatality. Fears now abound that this will call the whole business of running dances on the campus into question.

Half of the teenagers who attend the disco sessions come from outside the University, and in fact the dead youth was a student at St. Declan's Secondary School, Naphin Road, Dublin.

Although the area was immediately sealed off by Gardai when it was found that the youth's injuries were serious, it was difficult to find eye witnesses to the incident, and hopes of an early arrest faded.

A spokesman at Donnybrook Garda Station said last night: "I'm afraid no progress has been made so far."

Three Killed, Three Hurt In Road Accidents

THREE people were killed and three others injured in road accidents in Munster over the weekend.

A young Cork woman was killed and three others injured in a two-car crash at Sleeveen East, Macroom, early yesterday morning.

The dead woman, Helen Leahy (20), a clerk of 4, Church Avenue, Off Roman Street, Cork, was a back seat passenger in one of the cars. Injured were two men, who were the drivers of the cars, and a woman passenger.

The accident occurred about 200 yards on the Cork side of the town 45 minutes after midnight. The injured were brought to St. Finbarr's Hospital, Cork. A spokesman was unable to give their condition.

Four-year-old Jacqueline Walsh, 5, Harbour View, Cobh, Co. Cork, was dead on admission to Cobh Hospital following a traffic accident outside her home last evening. The tragedy happened while she was playing with some friends.

Jacqueline, who was one of five children of Mr. and Mrs. Richard Walsh, was struck by a passing car.

A 10 year old Co. Galway boy, Conor Slevin, Castlegar, died shortly after admission to Barrington's Hospital Limerick last night. He was injured when involved in an accident with a bus at Plassy where the All-Ireland B.L.O.E. athletic championships were held.

1978

Three different Popes in 1978 kept the Catholic Church on the front page for much of the year. The tumultuous changes began in August when 80-year-old Pope Paul passed away after a 15-year reign. Albino Luciani, an Italian of peasant stock, became Pope John Paul, the 'smiling Pope' who would reign for just 33 days before he also died. Thus Karol Wojtyla from Poland became John Paul II, the first non-Italian pontiff for 400 years.

In sports, it was a spectacular year for the southern counties, with Munster's shock defeat of New Zealand, Cork completing a three-in-a-row of hurling titles and Kerry taking a first step towards a four-in-a-row in football.

It was also a rich year for music in Ireland with Gloria topping the charts with 'One Day at a Time' and The Undertones having an international hit with 'Teenage Kicks'.

Fr Magee discovers dead pope

Saturday, September 30

Pope John Paul's out of character failure to turn up punctually for daily 5.30am Mass at a private chapel in the Vatican led to the discovery of his death by his Newry-born private secretary who has a brother living in Mallow.

Father John Magee, a 42-year-old Kiltegan Father, who was to have served the Holy Father's Mass, was surprised at his non-appearance and went to the Papal bedroom.

Vatican reports stated yesterday that Father Magee had knocked on the door, got no answer and then entered to find the pontiff dead in bed.

Father Magee, who was also personal secretary to Pope Paul for the past three years, immediately summoned a doctor and Jean Cardinal Villot, the French-born Vatican Secretary of State, who has again the responsibility of directing the 700 million members of the Catholic Church until a new pontiff is elected.

The Irish priest visited his brother, Mr Hugh Magee, at Lacknalocha, Mallow, shortly before Pope Paul's death and celebrated Sunday Mass at St Mary's Church. The brothers last met at a funeral of an aunt in England less than a month ago.

Gemma Craven is held aloft at the opening night of RTÉ 2.

Goodbye to *The Riordans*

Wednesday, December 20

It was a shock that would silence even Minnie Brennan. Leestown will never be the same again ... in fact it's being wiped off the screens by RTÉ. The station's longest running serial is being axed after 15 years from May next.

And the biggest shock of all for Tom, Minnie, Eamonn, Maggie, Murf, Julia Mac, and the other residents of Ireland's best-known village, was that they were told about it by the newspapers.

Hell's Angels flash into a quiet village

Monday, August 22

A large contingent of motorbike enthusiasts, apparently led by a Clonmel group, converged on Drangan in South Tipperary over the weekend, for what proved to be a nerve-wracking time for the villagers.

The group, numbering well over 100, were dressed in leather gear and driving powerful machines.

They camped in a field just outside the village and were supposed to stage various motor bike competitions on Sunday, but these did not take place. They frightened the locals with the noise of their bikes as they rode up and down the village street. They kicked doors and the public telephone was pulled from the box.

On Sunday the noise and rowdiness continued while the teenagers sat on the streets when people came to the village to attend Mass. Two of them 'streaked' through the village and one of the streakers made an obscene gesture to a passing woman, according to a local Garda. The Gardaí arrived, and the local parish priest went to plead with the Hell's Angels to mend their ways. On Sunday afternoon the thrill-seekers packed up and left the village which again returned to normal.

NEWS BRIEFS

Feb An IRA bomb at the Le Mon hotel in Belfast kills 14 people. (17)

Aug Around 6,000 people demonstrate at Carnsore Point, Co Wexford, against a proposed nuclear power plant. (19)

Nov Ireland got a second television channel when RTÉ 2 was officially launched from the Cork Opera House last night. Live entertainment was provided by Maureen Potter, Colm T Wilkinson, Gemma Craven and Terry Wogan. (3)

The Cork Examiner

No. 48,962 WEDNESDAY MORNING, NOVEMBER 1, 1978 Price 12p (inc. VAT)

Mighty Munster make rugby history

BY BARRY COUGHLAN

TOM KIERNAN'S MUNSTER created rugby history at a packed Thomond Park, Limerick, yesterday when they became the first ever Irish side to beat the mighty All-Blacks.

Over 12,000 people hailed the heroes in red shirts at the end of this action packed game. Their reaction was one of intense joy and even disbelief.

That they had beaten the New Zealanders was a surprise: that they had beaten them by 12 points even more so, and that the tourists had failed to register a score was almost incredible.

One would have to delve into the history books to find an occasion when the All Blacks were held scoreless on tour having been beaten 3-0 by Newport of Wales back in the '60's, but they never failed to score in Ireland and held their ground without defeat in this country since 1905.

They had a proud record to uphold against Munster, who had been written off as certain losers before this match. New Zealand had won four of the five games played between the sides, and drawn the other.

Way back in 1905 the tourists ran up 33 points without reply in Limerick and the visitors won again at the Mardyke ground in Cork on January 13, 1954 — but this time by only six points to three by virtue of a last minute try.

That was the shape of things to come in the battles between the teams, with Munster never again giving the All Blacks such scope as the early meeting.

The tourists learned to respect the province — possibly more so than any of the other sides they were to meet in the ensuing years.

At Thomond Park in 1963 the tourists again came out on top — and by the same scoreline as nine years earlier. Again they had to pull out all the stops to do so.

Ten years later they looked set to fall when a Barry McGann penalty goal gave Munster a 3 points to nil advantage which they held until the dying seconds. But then up came Trevor Morris to save the tourists from their first defeat as he kicked the equaliser. Three of yesterday's team, Seamus Dennison, Donal Canniffe and Moss Keane were in that side.

New Zealand and Munster met yet again the following year, to celebrate Ireland's centenary year. But this time, the traditional fire of the Munster side was missing, and they were lucky to escape with a 14-4 defeat. Five of the victorious team of yesterday, Larry Moloney, Donal Canniffe, Pat Whelan, Moss Keane and Colm Tucker, played that day.

But yesterday Munster lifted themselves to a peak never scaled before — they held the best the All Blacks could throw at them and then struck with venom.

Winger Jimmy Bowen lit the fuse with a searing 60 yard run in the 11th minute, shrugging off tackles before finding the support of Christy Cantillon who charged over to score near the posts to let Tony Ward convert.

Then enter Tony Ward, the "adopted" Dubliner in the side. He dug deeper eight minutes later with a drop goal and then applied the finishing touch 11 minutes from time with a similar effort.

And from that blow there was no way back for this ninth All-Blacks side. Munster had confounded all the critics after their poor early season performances in London against Middlesex and an Irish Exiles XV.

As Colm Tucker (left) breaks away from a loose ruck Donal Spring and Brendan Foley are in the thick of the action with Gary Knight and the rest of the All Blacks pack. Jimmy Bowen (11) and Donal Canniffe (9) look on anxiously

Inquiry call on sinking

IRISH trawlermen last night called for a public inquiry into the sinking of the Greek oil tanker Christos Bitas 250 miles closer to Ireland than had been decided earlier.

As the Christos Bitas lay at the bottom of the sea under three miles of water the Irish Fishermen's Organisation demanded an immediate inquiry into the change of plan and claimed the 1,000 tons of oil still in the ship could threaten Ireland's beaches.

The salvage company United Towing of Hull originally intended to sink the ship 580 miles off Ireland but changed its mind because of expected bad weather.

"We were told that extremely bad weather was expected, including force 10 gales, so it was decided to put her down," said a spokesman.

There was little trace of oil when she went down, according to a British Department of Trade spokesman.

The IFO said it was "gravely concerned" about the tanker's resting place. The vessel is now sunk in the path of strong westerly winds which will carry its oil on to Irish beaches, causing a serious threat to fish stocks and bird life," said an IFO spokesman.

But the Minister for Transport and Tourism, Mr Faulkner, who was involved in negotiations last week with British authorities about the sinking of the tanker, said: "I am satisfied that the decision to sink the ship was the right one.

"Consideration had already been given to this particular site. All the advice I had was that it would be satisfactory.

"It is most unlikely that any of the oil will come even near our coast. I don't think that anybody should be particularly worried."

A spokesman for Mr. Faulkner's Department said later that high seas were expected to break up any oil that might escape the wreck. The movement of any oil would be closely monitored by the Irish and British governments.

SINKING POINT

The exact sinking point is about 320 miles west of Fastnet Rock on the south-westerly tip of the country in water 1½ times deeper than the earlier chosen position.

The tanker had already started to sink before the scuttling was ordered.

The IFO said that last Thursday in the Dail Mr Faulkner announced that the vessel would be sunk 580 miles off Fastnet but it now transpired that the vessel had been sunk approximately 300 miles off the coast.

This meant that the vessel had been sunk right in the path of strong westerly winds which would carry the oil to Irish beaches.

"The Irish Fishermen's Organisation seriously questions the credibility of a Government Minister who can make such a blatantly misleading statement without acquainting himself with the facts. The Organisation cannot understand the reasoning behind the decision to sink the vessel half way towards the original sinking point and is asking for a public inquiry to be held into the matter."

The Department said that following reports earlier yesterday of imminent force 8-10 gales there was apprehension about the difficulty that would be encountered in transferring the salvage crew from the tanker in such weather, with the possibility of loss of life.

Furthermore, the vessel was reported to be losing buoyancy. It was considered also that if the tow-line were to part it would be extremely difficult to re-connect it, thus setting the vessel adrift in the open sea.

In these circumstances the salvage master recommended with the full support of the captains of the two escort vessels that the tanker should sink in her present position 320 miles west of Fastnet. In view of the worsening conditions and the threat to the safety of the crew members the Irish and British authorities had accepted this recommendation.

Triumph-and tragedy

While Donal Canniffe was captaining the Munster team to its historic victory at Thomond Park, Limerick, yesterday his father collapsed and died in Cork.

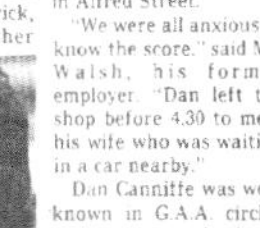

Donal Canniffe

Mr. Dan Canniffe collapsed 20 yards from where he had worked with Mr. W. D. Walsh, a wholesale fish merchant, in Alfred Street.

"We were all anxious to know the score," said Mr. Walsh, his former employer. "Dan left the shop before 4.30 to meet his wife who was waiting in a car nearby."

Dan Canniffe was well-known in G.A.A. circles and in his youth played for Cork.

He was interested in all sports and followed his son's career in rugby with great interest.

Mr. Canniffe is survived by his wife Kay, sons Brian, Kieran, Donal, and daughters Brenda, Marie, Cora and Deirdre.

Date set for Cork's cattle disease battle

By JIM MORAHAN

NEXT August is the date when Co. Cork joins in the big drive to wipe out the scourge of brucellosis in the country's animal herd. Announcing the date in Dublin yesterday, the Minister for Agriculture, Mr. Jim Gibbons, urged farmers in the county to start preparing now for the full-scale compulsory eradication programme.

Cork's dominant position in the dairying sector is widely appreciated. Largest of the 32 counties, it alone accounts for 22 per cent of the national cow herd and produces 25 per cent of the country's milk. But the indicators also point to a worrying brucellosis problem — which Mr. Gibbons seems determined to tackle in his accelerated disease plan first announced in detail last July.

According to date on the brucellosis milk ring survey carried out in the Southern dairying counties during the month of May this year, 26.9 per cent of the herds tested were infected. In Co. Cork 80.7 per cent of the 11,746 herds tested passed the test, giving 19.3 per cent herds failing.

The Minister decided that full-scale compulsory eradication for brucellosis would operate in Co. Kerry from July last and the actual level of incidence emerging in Kerry — now in the "clearance area" — under the State testing is 20 per cent of herds.

The Minister's accelerated plan is aimed, in the case of brucellosis, at declaring herds officially free of the disease in all parts of the country by 1986. Between 1965 and the end of last year, the State spent some £29 million on eradication measures but it is conceded that the disease incidence still remains at a high and unacceptable level.

But improvement has taken place over recent months. At the end of the full 1977 round of testing, disease incidence in herds stood at 4.16 per cent. During the 1978 round there was a reduction in herd incidence to 3.73 per cent.

Just two weeks ago, in his bid to tackle brucellosis and bovine TB, the Minister's package relating to the movement of animals — including the need to have cattle given a 30-day test prior to movement — came into effect.

How is the extension of the accelerated programme on brucellosis likely to affect Co. Cork?. Speaking recently in Dublin Dr. Jerome O'Shea told the Agricultural Economics Society annual conference that herd development and production could be "seriously affected, but, I might add, not in a fashion half so serious as would ensue if EEC markets were to close to infected produce while disease is still at a high level".

In his announcement yesterday, the Minister, Mr. Gibbons, urged farmers to get ready for the eradication programme.

In the coming weeks, the Department will be arranging a series of talks throughout Co. Cork on brucellosis and on what the eradication scheme will mean to farmers. These meetings will be attended by Department veterinary officers.

Under the compulsory scheme, all eligible animals — female cattle of 12 months and over and bulls of nine months and over — in Co. Cork will be blood tested annually for brucellosis. Where a reactor is disclosed in a herd the movement of animals into and out of the herd is restricted.

Identified reactors, marked by punching in the left ear, can only move off the farm for slaughter at a registered meat plant — and a grant is payable where the reactor is slaughtered within 30 days of identification. The herd is re-tested after reactor removal until such time as it has the necessary clear tests and the restrictions on movement are then lifted.

Raiders grab £11,000

TWO MEN believed to have been armed with a sawn-off shotgun yesterday seized over £11,000 in cash and cheques from members of the P.M.P.A. staff in Cork who were taking it to a bank night safe.

The robbery occurred at 5.50 p.m. shortly after six members of the staff had left the offices in Mary Street and were walking in the direction of Parliament Bridge. Two were carrying six night safe bags to the Bank of Ireland.

Threequarters way down Mary Street two men jumped out brandishing what appeared to be a sawn-off shotgun and ordered them to hand over the money.

After a scuffle, the bags were handed over and the robbers ran into Margaret Street from where they made their getaway on a motor-cycle.

Gardai said it was a red Honda GCI 771 or 774.

One of the raiders was described as being small, wearing a black helmet, coffee brown corduroy trousers and zipped anorack. The second man was about six feet tall and was wearing a helmet and motorcycle gear.

Gardai are following a definite line of inquiry.

Elsewhere yesterday armed raiders snatched £10,000 at Shannon and £12,000 in two Dublin bank robberies.

Beautiful start on RTE 2

Roisin Harkin

The stage is now set for the launching of RTE 2 from the Opera House in Cork tomorrow night.

The new channel has already chosen two attractive continuity announcers—Roisin Harkin and Bernadette Ni Ghallachoir—for its inaugural transmission.

The President, Dr. Hillery, will broadcast a message to mark the channel's opening. This will be followed by a gala variety performance from the Opera House, which will be attended by the Taoiseach, the Lord Mayor of Cork, members of the Government and Opposition, and of the diplomatic corps.

Bernadette ni Ghallachoir

Jury may be found guilty

How the Law's demands may cause honest citizens to break the law was demonstrated in the Cork Circuit Court yesterday.

When a trial was adjourned for the lunch break, the jurors were told they would be brought to a city hotel for lunch, and would be transported back to the court for the resumption of the case.

Up spoke the jury foreman to point out that he and other jurors had parked their cars in disc controlled areas. If they did not move the vehicles, or at least change the discs, they were liable to be fined.

Judge Fawsitt expressed his regret at their dilemma but, he said, he could do nothing to help them.

Round 1 to ex-chief Garvey: page 3

1979

The Troubles managed to dominate the rest of the world's view of Ireland when, on August 28, Louis Mountbatten, former viceroy of India, his grandson Nicholas and local teenager Paul Maxwell were blown up by the IRA in Co Sligo. Later that day, the British Army suffered their biggest loss of life in the Troubles when 18 soldiers were killed in Warrenpoint, Co Down.

The conflict in the North was also a major theme of the Pope's visit, an occasion which rivalled the Eucharistic Congress in 1932 as the biggest public event in the history of the state. Pope John Paul II's visit was deemed worthy of a colour Sunday edition by the *Examiner*.

In West Cork, it was a year of disasters with 50 people killed at Whiddy Island and another 17 dying when the Fastnet yacht race hit severe weather.

Forty feared dead in Whiddy inferno

Monday, January 8

A full-scale disaster alert was declared in Bantry early today after 40 seamen were feared lost in a massive tanker explosion at Whiddy Island. As the bodies of the tanker crew floated in the ocean, frantic efforts were made to get the oil depot staff off the island.

The first explosion, at 00.55am, cut the tanker in two, and minutes later a second almighty blast shook the whole area. The oily sea around the island was alight and rescuers were fighting a desperate battle to get through. Within a short time the blaze had spread to the jetty, which began to crumble and there were fears that the entire terminal might be destroyed as the flames began to spread towards the huge oil tanks.

Every house in Bantry was rocked by two explosions aboard the 120,000-ton *Betelgeuse* which was sailing under the French flag.

An eye-witness of the two explosions said it was "like looking into the flames of Hell".

The **Betelgeuse** *in flames in Bantry Bay.*

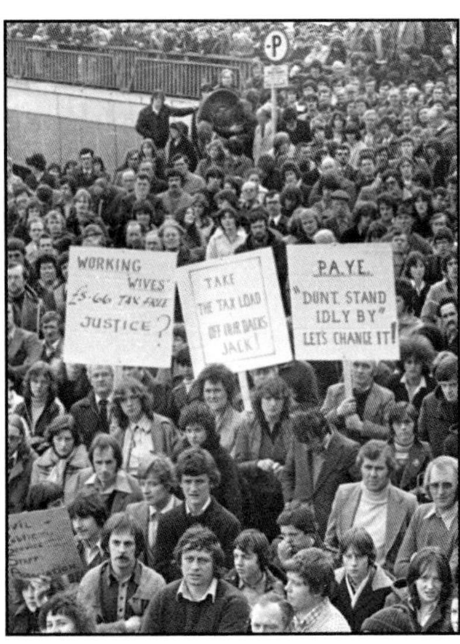

PAYE demonstrators in Cork.

A hero's farewell for the maestro

Monday, March 5

Christy Ring, the Wizard of Cloyne, was buried yesterday in a field where as a boy he developed the skills that made him the most spectacular hurler in history.

Cloyne Cemetery, where he was laid to rest after the biggest funeral through Cork since those of MacCurtain and MacSwiney in 1920, was once a commonage where Ring and his young friends played the game that later gave him a place of glory in the annals of the sport.

An estimated 50,000 to 60,000 people came to pay their respects. Ironically, that figure resembles the Munster final attendances for some of his epic clashes with the men from Tipperary.

At the graveside, the Taoiseach, Mr Lynch, his voice quivering with emotion, said of the maestro: "As long as young men will match their hurling skills against each other on Ireland's green fields, as long as young boys swing their camáns for the sheer thrill of the tingle in their fingers of the impact of ash with leather, as long as hurling is played, the story of Christy Ring will be told – and that will be forever."

NEWS BRIEFS

Feb The Ayatollah Khomeini takes power in Iran after the ousting of the Shah. Later in the year his followers would storm the American embassy and hold the occupants as hostages. (1)

May In Britain, the Conservative party win the election and Margaret Thatcher becomes Prime Minister. (4)

The Cork Examiner

No. 49,245 SUNDAY MORNING, SEPTEMBER 30, 1979 Price 14p (inc. VAT)

Pope's dramatic plea to gunmen

In the name of God, I beg you..

First greeting—Pope John Paul II greets the Irish people on arrival at Dublin Airport.

An ill-timed gust of wind cloaks the great moment when the Pope kisses the ground at the airport.

IT was the first of three days that will never be forgotten.

The Irish came together as never before to hail the Pope from Poland who looks so much like one of our own.

After all the pageantry, and the incredible scenes of mass emotion in Dublin, the Pilgrim of Peace went to Drogheda where, in the fading light, he issued a dramatic challenge to the men of violence to put away their bombs and guns.

"On my knees I beg you to turn away from the paths of violence and to return to the ways of peace. You may claim to seek justice. I, too, believe in justice and seek justice. But violence only delays the day of justice.

"Further violence in Ireland will only drag down to ruin the land you claim to love and the values you claim to cherish. In the name of God I beg you: return to Christ, who died so that men might live in forgiveness and peace."

The Pope, speaking on the banks of the Boyne, also stressed the obligations on politicians to ensure the conditions for peace, and he rejected the thesis that the Northern tragedy had its roots in religion.

The address was much more forceful and politically direct than most observers had anticipated, and it also revealed a man who doesn't mince words, whether spiritual or political.

Last evening, Pope John Paul — the man in a million — returned in triumph for a second time to the capital.

For him also it was a day to remember — unmatched even by his fellow countrymen a few weeks ago.

Drogheda address: Page Two. Reaction: Page Seven.

Onward, Christian soldier

AS the jumbo jet St. Patrick taxied on the runway at Dublin Airport yesterday morning I wondered how I could effectively convey to readers of this unique Sunday edition of the Cork Examiner how deep an impression the Polish Pope John Paul II had made on me during the trip from Rome. A few hours later a million voices from the Phoenix Park gave me the complete answer when they sang "He's Got the Whole World in His Hands." It was the summation of all that this great man had meant to me during the few hours in his company on the plane.

Young and old, rich and poor, religiously fervent and not-so-fervent, said in song to a billion others, through the modern miracle of television, what they felt about the visit of the Pope.

The figure in white, who in such a short time had made such a universal impact, had not alone by his mere presence healed divisions, softened the rancours of class distinction and the modern bitterness of industrial strife, but had, in the footsteps of the late Pope Paul VI, broken the tradition of the Pope being a "a prisoner of the Vatican."

By LARRY LYONS

A man of the people but set apart from the people in the gilded surroundings of the Vatican state palace.

John Paul II had come to the people to give them leadership and they had embraced him with their hearts. For a short while at any rate they had listened. The Phoenix Park ceremonies provided an extraordinary and heartwarming occasion in which this charismatic Pope had mixed the serious and the light, theology and pertinent comment on the current condition of humanity. He had shown us the perfect and the imperfect in what could be described as a fun sermon. And there is no hint of irreverence in that remark — rather the contrary.

Even the impact of the saintly and happy Pope John XXIII could not rival that of the Polish Pope who governs the Catholic Church today. He is not only a man of great personal charm, but one on whom God has bestowed extraordinary intellectual endowments as well as being a gifted allrounder in sport. In short, Pope John Paul II is to a great extent representative of the best in all men in both the fields of spiritual and human endeavour.

Truly out of the voices of the multitudes the tremendous chorus of voices joined in unison in the old pop standard "He's Got the Whole World in His Hands," was the ultimate verdict on the people to the visit of Pope John Paul II to Ireland.

In a word the verdict was 'a triumph'.

In the intimate surrounds of the Papal plane we had seen and spoken to the Pope as he moved amongst us and

TURN TO PAGE 7

A Cèad Míle Fáilte from President Hillery.

Pope John Paul in the secure company of the Army chiefs at the Airport.

1980

The killing of John Lennon caused major shock around the world in December. His music and celebrity status obviously prompted much of the interest in the former-Beatle's death, but people were also quite affected by the fact that he seemed to have been shot for no other reason than that he was famous.

In August, the County Cork village of Buttevant was the scene of Ireland's worst ever rail disaster when the train from Dublin to Cork was derailed due to a signalling fault. Eighteen people were killed and over 40 injured. Among the dead were two nuns from Gortner Abbey in Co Mayo, Sr Mary Lourdes O'Brien, 68, and Sr Mary Stanislaus Kelleher, 65, lifelong friends from Cork city. As teenagers they both joined the Order of Jesus and Mary on the same day.

The blameless driver later described how he had driven the Cork to Dublin train past the accident site the next day: "I was nervous, but it was like the jockey who has a fall and has to get back on the horse."

Larry Hagman as JR Ewing.

Irish soldiers slain

Saturday, April 19

Two Irish soldiers serving with the UN peace-keeping force in Lebanon were slain yesterday in a revenge attack by Christian Militia men. Another Irish soldier was wounded. The dead men were last night named as Private Thomas Barrett, a native of Macroom, who was a driver stationed at Collins Barracks, Cork, and Private Derek Smallhorne (31), Bluebell, Dublin, who was attached to the 5th Battalion. The wounded soldier is Private John O'Mahony (27), Scaraglen, Co Kerry. The cold-blooded murder was reported to be a revenge killing for the death of a Christian Militia man last week in a clash with the Irish forces. It was suggested, too, that relatives of that dead man took an active part in yesterday's ambush and slaughter.

The soldiers were driving to a forward observation post with an American photographer and two reporters about two miles north of Ras when they were stopped by seven or eight young Christian militia men led by an adult.

The three drivers were taken from their vehicle and brought to a ruined building. In a room there Private O'Mahony was shot in the back, thigh and foot, but the other two made their escape only to be recaptured. At that stage, according to the Army spokesman, the Christian Militia men appear to have arranged the transfer of the wounded soldier to Bint Jubail in a wounded car. From there he was flown to hospital. The other soldiers were then executed.

Mr Frank Cluskey, leader of the Labour Party, said: "The Israeli government must bear full responsibility for the activities of the Christian Militia forces who have carried out today's dastardly killings. They act under direct Israeli instructions within Southern Lebanon."

Neighbours phoned the news of the shootings to Pte Barrett's parents, Thomas and Eileen Barrett, at Barrett's Place, Macroom. The grief-stricken couple were so shocked that they were taken to the Regional Hospital for treatment.

JR: we know who

Saturday, November 22

At a time of international crisis of every description, of war in the Middle East, of the terrible troubles of the Third World, of the American hostage horror, of tottering economies and shaky currencies, of violence and unemployment, the only question on two hundred million lips all over the world this morning is: Who shot JR?

We may worry about world priorities, about manipulation of the human mind by the media, about the total lunacy of it all. But if there is one person who has no worries today, he must surely be Larry Hagman, the world anti-hero, the international super-badman, whose fantasy world has rivalled the greatest of man's achievements in terms of publicity.

The assailant's identity was made known early today but, not wishing to spoil tonight's episode for the viewers who are prepared to stick it out, we reveal the culprit's name on page 10, column 9, for those who cannot bear the suspense (Kristin).

Michelle Rocca is crowned Miss Ireland.

NEWS BRIEFS

Mar Bishop Eamonn Casey is among those in attendance in El Salvador at the funeral of assassinated Archbishop Oscar Romero when the church comes under attack and 39 people are killed. (30)

April The *Examiner* carries a story that former Taoiseach Jack Lynch is seeking political asylum in China. (1)

July Irish banks announce reductions in interest rates. A rate of over 17% now applies to most term loans. (1)

The Cork Examiner

No. 49,617 WEDNESDAY MORNING, DECEMBER 10, 1980 Price 15p (inc. VAT)

World rocked by superstar's murder

He came on a mission of death, say police

Mark Chapman shown in a 1973 High School picture. He was yesterday charged with Lennon's murder.

A SHOCKED world yesterday mourned the death of ex-Beatle and world famous song-writer John Lennon at the hands of a mad assassin.

He was gunned down in New York, the city he loved and died in the arms of his wife, Yoko Ono, as he was rushed in a police car to a city hospital.

His alleged killer, identified by police as Mark David Chapman, 25, a freelance photographer from Honolulu, Hawaii, dropped a .38-calibre revolver after the shooting and stood motionless, waiting for arrest.

Chapman came to New York from Hawaii with the deliberate intention of murdering him. "He accumulated a large amount of money to come to New York to do what he has done" assistant district attorney Kim Hogrefe said during the formal arraignment of Chapman, on a charge of second degree murder.

Lennon, born in Liverpool in 1940 idolised Elvis Presley and got actively interested in rock n' roll after his Aunt Mimi bought him a secondhand guitar for £10. "You will never make a living with it", she told him. A mutual friend introduced him to Paul McCartney and the incredible saga of the Beatles began.

Former Beatles Paul McCartney, George Harrison and Ringo Starr reacted with shock and grief yesterday to the slaying.

"I can't take it in at the moment," a pale and obviously shaken McCartney said when first informed of Lennon's death. "John was a great guy. He is going to be missed by the whole world."

Together Lennon and McCartney wrote the music that changed the sound of 20th century popular music and influenced an entire generation in the 1960s.

A spokesman for Ringo Starr said he left a vacation spot for New York to be with Lennon's wife. The spokesman said Star "is extremely shocked. He doesn't want to say more."

A spokesman for George Harrison, said the former Beatle was "deeply shocked," "after all we went through together I had and still have great respect for him", Harrison said.

Cynthia Lennon, who married again after her divorce from John, was informed of the death while on a trip to London. She has custody of their 17-year-old son, Julian.

Mick Jagger of the Rolling Stones was "shattered" by the news of Lennon's death. Speaking from Paris where the band is recording, he said: "I knew and liked John Lennon for 18 years".

Sir Harold Wilson said: "It's still a great tragedy. "He gave the kids something to think about, he kept them off the streets and did more than all the forces of law and order could have done put together".

U.S. President-elect, Ronald Reagan said John Lennon's death was tragic and "we have to find an answer" to stop such violence.

President Carter said last night: "John Lennon helped create the music and the mood of our time. "His spirit, the spirit of the Beatles — brash and earnest, ironic and idealistic all at once — became the spirit of a whole generation.

Wreaths, candles and photographs of John Lennon lay heaped in an impromptu shrine outside the apartment block. Mourning crowds mostly ignored a request from Yoko Ono to disperse. "John loved and prayed for the human race", she told them. "I suggest you go home and do the same".

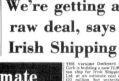

John Lennon during an interview with BBC Radio 1 disc jockey Andy Pebbles in New York at the weekend — his first radio interview for many years and, tragically, his last.

British are talking to hunger strikers

THE BRITISH government is negotiating by proxy with the hunger strikers at Long Kesh by using portable radios to communicate government policy and attitudes.

The radios were supplied to the seven hunger strikers when they entered the prison hospital several weeks ago.

Mr. Michael Alison, government minister responsible for prisons was interviewed on the B.B.C. at length last night about the hunger strike.

He was almost certain that the prisoners were listening, tuned in on the radios given to them by the government for that purpose.

Mr. Alison said in his broadcast that he hoped the hunger strikers would realise that many of their demands are already granted to prisoners who conform to general prison regulations.

He made a direct plea to the men in the prison hospital to come off their hunger strike so they could see for themselves what rights they would have under what he called "liberal rules and regulations".

Mr. Alison knows he can expect a communication from the prisoners which will be smuggled out of the jail in what has become a normal fashion if the prisoners decide to respond to his statements.

This unique form of negotiations with the prisoners by the use of radios makes it possible for the government to avoid being accused of dealing with the hunger strikers.

Exclusive by Peter Martin

The seven men at Long Kesh were moved to the prison hospital, earlier than expected and it's now believed that move was ordered so that the government could supply the prisoners with radios and allow them to watch television, knowing that the men would be anxious to hear all the latest developments about their hunger strike.

But, the government knew as well that the men would be hearing the government's repeated determination not to give in on political status. At the same time the men would be made immediately aware of any new moves by the government.

If the hunger strikers had remained in their prison cells they would not have the privilege of radios and the right to watch TV during leisure hours. But, once moved to the prison hospital the prisoners on hunger strike automatically qualified for special privileges.

Earlier yesterday, the N.I.O. said: "Steps will be taken to ensure that if any of those who are refusing to take food do not fully understand the Northern Ireland Office position, they will be informed of it."

The government spokesman said at the time he could not reveal how or when the seven hunger strikers would be informed.

On Monday night, after the summit in Dublin, Mrs. Thatcher said she wanted to make sure that the hunger strikers were aware of the "detailed and exhaustive" report issued by her secretary of state for the North, Mr. Humphrey Atkins.

Last night, Mr. Atkins' report, referred to by Mrs. Thatcher, was the basis of the entire interview by the B.B.C. with Mr. Alison, which Government officials then knew would be listened to inside the prison hospital by the hunger strikers.

Among the many points made by Mr. Alison was the major assessment of the rights granted to prisoners who conform.

Mr. Alison said he could go no further on clothing and association but, he said: "We don't want to see these lads die, but so far as a mediator is concerned, we are not looking for a mediator.

The Government Minister, knowing the prisoners were listening to him, was firm in saying that he would not give in on political status.

Lennon: the voice of a generation

By FRANK COUGHLAN

A MENTALLY deranged lunatic yesterday robbed the world of one of its greatest exponents of popular music. John Lennon, who along with Paul McCartney made up the most successful composing team of the modern era died in a senseless shooting, aged only 40 and with so much still to give.

Lennon's contribution to rock 'n' roll and popular music in general, cannot be over-emphasised. Not only was he the driving force behind the Beatles during their long reign at the top, he was also the conscience of a generation and the voice for millions in the turbulent sixties.

Ironically, Lennon did not die as many suspected he would. In his younger, wilder days he treated life with total disrespect; he was a hell-raiser who flirted with drugs and made outlandish outbursts to an amazed and unprepared world.

If he had died then, like Hendrix, Joplin and many more, smothered by his wealth and success, it would have been vaguely predictable, but to meet death the way he did was truly tragic.

As a writer/composer he must be especially remembered as a maker of great rock 'n' roll which was both energetic and catchy. His lyrics, often spiced with cynicism, turned their attention to a world he felt was diseased with corruption and deceit.

But there was a more mellow side to his nature. He wrote and co-wrote some of the most beautiful love songs of our time. These were not just 'formula' songs, churned out for greedy record moguls, but songs with a depth and tenderness usually lacking in contemporary music.

However, it was often in the over-sensitive pages of the British press that Lennon grabbed attention. He spent a week in bed for peace, he returned his MBE to the Queen — the 'papers even alleged he said the Beatles were more popular than Jesus — a story he always refuted.

But that was all in the sixties, a decade of unprecedented change and turmoil . . . the decade of Vietnam, hippies and student riots. In the more sedate seventies, with the break-up of the Beatles just behind him, he recorded some marvellous material before disappearing from the public eye into self-imposed exile.

Then this year, after seven silent years, Lennon returned with an album and single both of which are doing well. In interviews he appeared to be happier and more content than ever before. Lennon seemed like a man reborn, fresh and eager with a new sense of urgency and hope in his music.

Early yesterday morning, however, a crazed assassin emerged from the shadows in a New York street to shoot and kill this giant of modern music.

John Lennon is dead and for many rock 'n' roll will die with him.

Debate may end 'conflict'

By Liam O'Neill, Political Correspondent

A DAIL debate on the outcome of the Dublin Castle summit meeting on Northern Ireland between the Taoiseach and the British Prime Minister, Mrs. Thatcher, is to take place tomorrow.

The Government last night agreed to allow three hours for a discussion on the communique issued after the meeting in which the decision to launch joint studies by the British and Irish Governments into a range of subjects including possible new institutional structures for the two islands was announced.

The decision came after Fine Gael had surprisingly withdrawn a question on the Dublin Castle meeting from the Dail order paper yesterday afternoon and sought instead to have the Taoiseach make a statement on the meeting today or tomorrow.

Earlier yesterday, the Government issued a statement denying that there was any conflict between what the Taoiseach said and what Mrs. Thatcher said about the decisions at Monday's meeting.

Earlier in the afternoon, in a brief Dail exchange, the Taoiseach had said that the communique between himself and the prime minister was "crystal clear".

But there certainly remained a conflict over the interpretation of the decision to launch joint Irish and British studies. After Monday's meeting the Taoiseach said there was no limit to what new institutionsl arrangements might be conceived and brought forward from the study, including proposals for a federal or confederal solution.

But at a later press conference in London, Mrs. Thatcher ruled out the possibility of a federal or confederal plan to solve the Northern Ireland problem and said it was not intended to discuss constitutional changes as had been implied by Mr. Haughey.

We're getting a raw deal, says Irish Shipping

THE Verolme Dockyard in Cork is building a new 72,000 ton ship for Irish Shipping Ltd. at an estimate cost of £22 million, but yesterday Irish Shipping Company executives revealed that they could have bought the same type of vessel abroad for £11½ million.

The Oireachtas inquiry into semi-State sponsored bodies in Dublin was told that the reason it would cost so much in the Cork dockyard was because Verolme refused to give a fixed price contract.

Instead, the cost would be subject to an escalation clause which, with inflation, could hike the price up to £22 million. The dockyard also wanted some of the money in foreign currency, according to Irish Shipping chairman Mr. Percy Greer, but this was not generally known.

Mr. Greer said that his company had turned their face against buying a new ship at this particular time but the Government had requested them to help Verolme.

In this case Irish Shipping would get the ship for £12 million and the Government would subsidise the difference.

British soldiers 'legitimate targets' says rebel FF man

By TONY PURCELL

A ROW blew up within Fianna Fail in Limerick last night after a claim by City Councillor Jack Bourke that he believes British soldiers in the North of Ireland are "legitimate targets."

Cllr. Bourke made the statement at a meeting of the Limerick H-Block Committee. His remarks come at a time when Mr. Haughey and Mrs. Thatcher are discussing the Northern problem on a new political level.

Mr. Pat Cox, secretary of the Fianna Fail Limerick City Comhairle Ceanntair, said: "Cllr. Bourke does not support the men of violence in bombing and killing innocent people, but does accept that the military are legitimate targets."

"To justify any targets implicitly justifies the act of seeking them out for death or injury and furthermore seeks to legitimatise the perpetrators of such acts."

"This callous double think is extraordinary when one considers that those same elements have shown no less willingness and capacity to subvert the institutions of this State, through armed thuggery, bank raids, garda slaying and the assassination of diplomats."

Mr. Cox thought Cllr. Bourke's remarks did the Fianna Fail a great disservice.

Cllr. Bourke's attitude has deeply disturbed many Fianna Fail members in the city.

Mr. Cox pointed out that Cllr. Bourke's views are contrary to the policy of his party. Fianna Fail policy was spelt out at the Ard Fheis in which they support the case for a British withdrawal from Northern Ireland — but through democratic, constitutional and diplomatic means.

Cllr. Jack Bourke said last night that the men of violence in the North of Ireland were not all Catholics, nationalists and republicans. "As far as I'm concerned like any sensible person I would love the problem of the North to be settled by peaceful means.

"In my opinion as long as the British soldiers remain in that tiny part of this small island there will never be peace. When the British military were in the South prior to 1922 they were then accepted as legitimate targets. If they were still here the same thing would pertain."

Cllr. Bourke claimed that the vast majority of the people he spoke to in the Party agreed with what he said. "I am exhosting the British government to make a statement of intent to take the British soldiers from our soil."

1981

Events surrounding the hunger-strikes in the North dominated the news for much of the year. Ten IRA and INLA prisoners starved themselves to death in pursuit of political status in the H-blocks of the Maze prison. The first to die was Bobby Sands, who had also been elected as an MP during the campaign. In Dublin, a violent riot occurred during a march to support the hunger-strikers.

By then, the country had already experienced a major tragedy when 48 people died in a Valentine's Night inferno at the Stardust nightclub. A later enquiry found that at least one exit was locked and two others were obstructed.

In international music, Bob Marley passed away, while at home Davey Arthur and the Furey Brothers had a major hit with 'Sweet Sixteen'.

Disaster stuns Dublin

Monday, February 16

The Stardust fire began as 800 young people, mostly between the ages of 17 and 23, were enjoying an exhibition of a disco dancing competition in the popular disco club in Artane when the finalists were giving a demonstration.

It was just 2am when the flames shot from a partitioned-off section of the ballroom to the left of the bandstand. Within minutes it was a blazing inferno. Panic-stricken dancers rushed for the exits, ignoring appeals for calm from a disc jockey.

Some young men literally threw their girlfriends through the flames out the front door and saved their lives. It is believed that most of those who died were trapped in the toilet area and in the passages leading to them.

Hundreds of people ran around in uncontrollable hysteria shouting for friends, wives, husbands, brothers and sisters. Some of the crowd outside attacked the gardaí because they were being prevented from rushing inside the flames again to try to find their missing friends.

Dancers told stories of steel sheeting and padlocked doors blocking their exits from the club but this was denied by Jack Walsh, assistant manager of the Stardust, who said that all seven exit doors were open and none of them had chains securing them.

World prays for Pope

Thursday, May 14

Pope John Paul II was shot and wounded in five places, including in the intestines, yesterday, as he rode in his open car in St Peter's Square, by a man who identified himself as a Turkish citizen, police said.

The Pope was rushed to the Gemelli Policlinico, Rome's most modern hospital. The director of the hospital surgery unit, Prof Giancarlo Castilioni, said the operation was "successful". He did not give details of the Pope's condition, but he said the Pope would be transferred after the operation to the hospital's emergency care unit.

Witnesses said the alleged attacker, Mehmet Ali Agca, was reportedly standing on the steps of one of the two large mobile trailers located in the piazza which function as the Vatican post office during summer months.

The attack coincided with the anniversary of the appearance on May 13, 1977, near Fatima, Portugal, of an apparition of the Virgin Mary.

The coincidence in the date and the attack on the Pope revived interest in the "third secret" of Fatima, which recently was in the news when the Aer Lingus plane hijacker demanded that it be published.

NEWS BRIEFS

Mar Ronald Reagan, president of the United States, is wounded in an assassination attempt. (30)

July Prince Charles and Lady Diana are married in London. The wedding creates huge interest in Ireland. (29)

Sept Celebrated left-footed author Christy Brown dies, aged 51. (14)

Hunger strike riot

Monday, July 20

Garda representatives strenuously denied that excessive muscle had been used by the force to quell the riot in its biggest ever security operation of this kind. Both garda organisations repeatedly claimed they accepted "punishment" from the H-block mob for 25 minutes before retaliating.

Anyone still on the scene when the gardaí baton charged on Saturday afternoon should have known what to expect, the Taoiseach Garrett FitzGerald said. The baton-wielding gardaí had used the minimum force necessary, he said.

In St Vincent's hospital Andreas Oswald, who worked with the Berlin newspaper *Der Abend*, told how he ran when the baton charge started. He found himself in a narrow lane pursued by screaming gardaí. While he pleaded that he had not done anything, he said a group of gardaí pounded him with batons. They told him to go, but his glasses were broken in the confrontation and he could not see. Another group of gardaí arrived and systematically beat him up again.

The Cork Examiner

No. 49,732 MONDAY MORNING, APRIL 27, 1981 Price 17p (inc. VAT)

It's Mitterrand and Giscard

INCUMBENT Valery Giscard d'Estaing and Socialist leader Francois Mitterrand easily gained presidential run-off places in yesterday's first round voting that gave France's Communists a major setback.

President Giscard casts his vote

Giscard (55), seeking his second seven-year term, and Mitterrand (64) came in first and second, respectively, in the first round election, which narrowed the field from 10 to two candidates for next Sunday's vote.

The first round results were a blow for Communist Party leader George Marchais (60). He fell several points short of his goal of 20 p.c. in the worst Communist showing since 1936, putting his stature as a major political force in jeopardy.

Gaullist Paris mayor Jacques Chirac (48) passed Marchais to secure third place, giving his party added clout in bargaining that will be necessary for Giscard to have a guarantee of its support in the run-off.

Party returns with about 70 p.c. of the vote in showed Giscard with 28.8 p.c., Mitterrand with 26.2 p.c. (hailed by his party as "the highest score in the history of socialism in France"), Chirac 17.6 p.c. and Marchais 15.1 p.c. in a disappointing voter turnout.

Giscard aides said they were happy with his results, about 1 p.c. above poll predictions. But it was about 2 p.c. less than he scored in the first round of the 1974 election that sent him to the Elysee Palace, and aides admitted they were concerned about Mitterrand's high first-round showing.

Marchais later said he would not support Mitterrand in the May 10 run-off unless he agreed to include Communists in any eventual government.

Chirac, grinning but looking weary, declined to say how he would ask his supporters to vote. It was all but certain, however, that he will urge them to support Giscard, the man he helped elect in 1974 and under whom he was Prime Minister until 1976.

But among his campaign workers, there was little enthusiasm for the incumbent president. "Giscard au placard (Giscard to the closet)," they chanted.

Israelis pound Lebanese villages

Israeli warplanes yesterday pounded at least 14 villages around the southern Lebanese towns of Sidon and Nabatiyeh as Syrian helicopters and troops fought further north to wrest control of a Phalangist-held 8,500 ft. high strategic peak.

Palestinian officials said the Israeli air strikes were the worst recorded since the March, 1978, Israeli raid into south Lebanon.

Hospital sources said at least 12 civilians were killed and 20 injured, three of them seriously, in the bombing which lasted 45 minutes. Six Israeli jets continued flying over the area drawing Palestinian anti-aircraft fire, until late afternoon, witnesses said.

Palestinian radio said, "there were reports that one Zionist warplane was shot down," challenging a Tel Aviv statement that all aircraft returned to base. No other report mentioned the incident.

The Israeli jets flew at least nine sorties, Beirut radio said, quoting its correspondent in Sidon. They struck nine villages in the initial raids, then raided another five, the radio said.

The radio said the raids were aimed particularly at areas inhabited by people evicted from other southern villages hit by recent battles between the Israeli and Palestinian forces.

The towns of Sidon and Nabatiyeh lie 15 miles apart. Sidon is only 27 miles away from Beirut, while Nabatiyeh is 47 miles to the south of the capital.

Lebanese health minister Nazih Bizri visited the villages after the Israeli attack. He ordered a blood bank to be opened, and appealed to residents to donate blood to treat the injured.

Meanwhile, Palestinian Liberation Organisation (PLO) chief Yasser Arafat arrived in Tripoli early yesterday and immediately began talks with Libyan leader Col. Gadhaffi on ways of strengthening the Arab confrontation against Israel, Palestinian sources said.

The state-run Libyan radio reported the meeting, but gave no details about the discussions.

The broadcast quoted Arafat as saying that his visit to Libya "comes at a time when the imperialist, zionist and reactionary offensive against the Arab nation was escalating."

20,000 march as Sands on brink

By Peter Martin

I.R.A. hunger striker Bobby Sands lay on the brink of death in jail yesterday as 20,000 demonstrators marched in support of him in Belfast's biggest republican rally in a decade.

Doctors keeping a watch at Sands' bedside said he "almost died" on Saturday evening and told his family who visited him yesterday "to be by a telephone at all times" Sands supporters said.

Anxiety is mounting in the North over what could happen should Sands die, now that the Human Rights Commission has failed in its efforts to mediate in the confrontation between the hunger striker and the British government.

The Commissioners left Belfast yesterday morning with their mission in shambles and leaving in their wake an angry Catholic community, fearful of the consequences of Sands' death.

The government refuses to state if it is contemplating moving Sands to an outside hospital, which it did in the case of Sean McKenna, the hunger striker who was near death before Christmas.

The protest march in Belfast yesterday was led by Sands' sister, Marcella, and the mothers of hundreds of convicted I.R.A. prisoners.

Bernadette Devlin-McAliskey called for a general strike in the Republic and massive civil disturbance in the North to back Sands' campaign.

She also attacked the Taoiseach: "Mr. Haughey says he may have to postpone the election . . . Charlie" she said, speaking in a low voice, "if Bobby Sands dies, Fianna Fail will never see power again."

She warned the British prime minister, Mrs. Thatcher, that if Bobby Sands died his followers would unite and force Britain from the six counties of the North.

Later, Sands' supporters called for an emergency meeting with the Taoiseach. Mr. Haughey has rejected previous requests for meetings, but the Committee said the "gravity" of the situation might make him change his mind.

There seems little likelihood that Mr. Haughey will agree to a meeting.

Mr. Neil Blaney, T.D., yesterday on the *This Week* radio programme called for further intervention by the Government. Mr. Blaney said that the Taoiseach was "the person" to approach Mrs. Thatcher, either openly or secretly, and impress on her the gravity of the situation.

Nine young people claiming to be members of Fianna Eireann and supporting the H-Block protest, pirated the airways of a Cork city local radio station yesterday. A prepared tape and speech was transmitted. Listeners alerted the gardai and the group were later detained for questioning.

Similar demonstrations were made through other Cork local radio stations on Saturday.

There were H-Block protests in many centres over the weekend.

In Tralee about 20 people paraded outside the Mt. Brandon Hotel, Tralee, where President Hillery presented prizes at the end of Siogadh '81.

There was a demonstration in Cork city centre on Saturday by a group calling themselves Cork Youth in Support of H-Block. A spokesman for the group said their protest was a peaceful one and they were totally non-political.

Marcella Sands (left) sister of the hunger-striker, and Mrs. Bernadette McAliskey during yesterday's demonstration in Dublin.

3 hurt in freak accident

Three people were burned in a freak accident in a house at 76 Churchfield Avenue, Cork, last night. Part of the firegrate was defective and a shock absorber of a car was pushed in to prop it up. The absorber blew up and smashed practically every room in the house.

The three occupants, a mother and her two children, were burned in a flash fire which followed the explosion. They were rushed by the Cork Fire Brigade ambulance to the North Infirmary, where they were treated for minor burns.

A spokesman for the hospital said the three people — Mrs. Sandra Dunne and her children Tony (8) and Daniel (9) — were discharged after treatment.

Medical supplies valued at several thousand pounds were destroyed in a fire which broke out in a stockroom in the grounds of the South Infirmary yesterday morning.

In all, the Cork Fire Brigade received 17 calls yesterday.

Falling tree kills Co. Cork girl

A 2½-years-old girl was crushed to death on Saturday when part of an old tree fell on her in the avenue of her home near Midleton, Co. Cork. She was Georgina Horgan, youngest of the four children of Mr. and Mrs. Liam Horgan, Ballynona Cottage, Ballynona. She was walking with other family members when the lower half of an old fir tree, about 30 feet, came crashing down. The tree was weakened by recent storms.

Fr. Denis O'Connor C.C., Midleton; Dr. Liam Motherway and Garda M. Bolger were at the scene.

Mr. Horgan is an accountant at the oil refinery at Whitegate.

With a moderation in the gale along the south east coast yesterday, the Irish Continental Line St. Killian, with 500 passengers on board, was able to dock at Rosslare from Le Havre 15 hours late. The storm had compelled the ship to shelter near Lands End, Cornwall all day Saturday. The Sealink ferry from Fishguard and the B + I Line from Pembroke, which also had been held up on Saturday, docked at Rosslare yesterday also.

Later all three ferries sailed normally from Rosslare and schedules are expected to be fully restored today.

The Brittany Ferries Cork-Roscoff service had to head for the shelter of Plymouth after the raging seas began to break a number of port holes in the vessel and flood the main restaurant area.

Brittany service travellers into Cork had to spend the night in Plymouth before travelling to Fishguard and onwards to Ireland on the Sealink service into Rosslare.

Some 400 people and 70 cars were on board the ferry Penn-ar-Bed when she turned back to Plymouth. Amongst the groups on board was a school party from Colaiste Spioraid Naoimh in Cork and a group who had been involved in establishing a twinning relationship between Cork and Rennes in Brittany.

Brittany Ferries laid on coaches to bring foot passengers from Rosslare to Cork. On Saturday the coaches were used to transfer passengers from Cork to Rosslare to link up with the Irish Continental Lines service — the Cork-Roscoff service having been cancelled.

Some 120 passengers and 30 cars were due to be carried on the outward journey. But a number of intending travellers cancelled their plans when notified of the forced change in arrangements.

At Dun Laoghaire, a Dutch cargo vessel was severely damaged when blown against a quay wall. Ten yachts, including the former Admiral Cup yacht 'Golden Leigh,' were wrecked.

Fourteen Spanish fishermen, who abandoned their trawler when it sank about 100 miles off the Kerry coast yesterday, were rescued and taken to one of the oil rigs in the area of the Porcupine Bank. The men were taken from three life rafts to the rig where they received medical attention.

Police arrest 43 after UK demos

IN LONDON yesterday, police arrested 43 people who demonstrated at a rally and outside No. 10 Downing Street in support of Sands. Most were charged with threatening behaviour, a Scotland Yard spokesman said.

Fighting broke out between police and 500 Sands supporters outside Kilburn tube station in a rally organised by the H-Block Armagh National Committee.

Police had said before the rally they would not attempt to stop it as long as it remained in one place. It would not then be in defiance of the 28-day ban imposed on marches at the weekend by Home Secretary Mr. William Whitelaw.

But, speaking from the back of a lorry, veteran pacifist campaigner Pat Arrowsmith said that the rally would march to join a picket at Downing Street.

And immediately a mass of demonstrators dodged the police cordon by racing through the forefront of a garage into Kilburn High Street.

Traffic was brought to a standstill as hundreds of the demonstrators ran down the High Street followed by around 100 policemen.

Other police dashed from coaches parked in side-streets. But the demonstrators had run around 500 yards before the police could contain them. Violent scuffles and struggles followed and several people were arrested.

Three convictd I.R.A. men climbed onto the roof of Wormwood Scrubs jail during an exercise period yesterday and began yelling slogans about Sands.

Meanwhile, police last night warned M.P.s and public figures of a possible letter-bomb campaign by Sands supporters. The alert came after a Tory M.P. was sent a letter bomb in the post. It did not explode — even though he started to open it.

Mr. Barry Porter (41), Conservative M.P. for Bebington and Ellesmere Port on Merseyside, believes the incendiary device was sent by supporters of the Northern hunger striker.

Customs strike threat

Five hundred members of the Indoor Staffs Association of the Customs and Excise will strike on Friday next, unless there is a satisfactory response from the Revenue Commissioners.

The strike concerns a dispute between the Commissioners and the indoor staffs about the operation of a system to speed up process of entry of goods, and if it is not solved there is a danger of disruption of commercial traffic.

As well as the question of imports, on which many industries are so dependent, there are many other matters of both customs and excise duty which would be affected by the threatened strike.

Mr. Patrick Leahy, of the Cork branch of the union, which has about 50 members, said that the strike was official. Their members had no objection to the process, but they had made a number of suggestions which had been ignored by the Commissioners.

TUCKER OUT OF TOUR?

Colm Tucker, the Shannon wing forward, is almost certain to miss the planned Irish rugby tour to South Africa on Saturday week, writes Barry Coughlan.

Tucker injured his back in the Munster Senior Cup final against UCC nine days ago and last week entered the Cork Regional Hospital for treatment.

It is believed that he will remain there for a few more days and will be unable to train for at least two weeks. In those circumstances he is unlikely to travel with the touring party.

The player is expected to make a decision on the matter today, following medical advice.

Jewellery worth £100,000 taken in Dublin raid

About £100,000 worth of jewellery was stolen from McDowell's, O'Connell Street shop in Dublin over the weekend.

Election plans overshadowed by N.I. events

THE Fianna Fail cabinet's pre-election think-in at Barretstown Castle, Co. Kildare yesterday, supervised by An Taoiseach, Mr. Haughey, was overshadowed by the refusal on Saturday of Bobby Sands to meet the two European Human Rights Commissioners.

Though no statement was issued after the meeting it is believed that the election package to be put to the voters dominated proceedings.

But the almost inevitable death of Bobby Sands has posed a real problem for Mr. Haughey who has been expected to seek his first mandate from the Irish people within the next few weeks. It was also expected that Mr. Haughey would let his cabinet colleagues into the secret election date which he has so far kept to himself.

Should Sands die and Northern Ireland erupt into sectarian violence it would leave a serious vacuum in the Republic if the Dail was disbanded and the parties were embroiled in an election campaign. So the election may have been postponed.

Ross jobs could be saved if . . .

Mr. Paddy Shortall, the Receiver at Ross Shipyard in New Ross, Co. Wexford, said yesterday the 80 remaining jobs in the company could be saved provided the unofficial picket being maintained by redundant workers on the plant was called off.

Mr. Shortall, of Coopers and Lybrand, said he had also received a firm offer to purchase the plant as a going concern.

Strike affects Irish flights

BECAUSE of industrial action by British air traffic controllers today, delays on some flights to and from Ireland can be expected. However, Aer Lingus are confident that all its passengers booked to travel today will reach their destinations.

Many transatlantic flights are expected to be diverted to Shannon today.

Extra staff are standing by and at least some 2,000 passengers will have to be accommodated at Shannon. Some American airlines have indicated that their flights will remain in the US until the strike ends.

British Airways have cancelled nine flights from Heathrow today including one scheduled to operate to Dublin.

Airlines using Heathrow fear that there could be a complete shutdown at 7.30 a.m. when the action begins.

Pan American said: "It all hinges on the number of controllers who decide to turn up for duty for the early shift. If there is severe disruption we will use other airspace and overfly our services from America and take them into Frankfurt".

The controllers voted by a narrow majority to back industrial action.

Immigration men are expected to back up the action by skeleton staffing.

Union leaders have not revealed their targets for the rest of the week but they will include Gatwick, Belfast, Birmingham, Manchester, Liverpool, Stansted and Aberdeen.

Many of the controllers are unhappy about the half-day strike. And some may turn up for work as usual. British Airways will set up a special flight information Centre from 9 a.m. tomorrow to deal with enquiries. The number is 01-759 2525.

1982

It was a year of war, with Britain and Argentina fighting over the Falkland Islands and Israel invading Lebanon in an effort to crush the PLO. In Ireland, corporal punishment was outlawed in schools, while the national rugby team had their first Triple Crown win since 1949. There was no presidential salute before the home games as President Hillery had not attended internationals since the 1981 IRFU tour of apartheid South Africa.

It was the year that GUBU entered the Irish lexicon. Charles Haughey termed events surrounding the resignation of the Attorney General, Patrick Connolly, as Grotesque, Unbelievable, Bizarre and Unprecedented. Connolly's apartment was used, unbeknownst to him, by a man wanted for murder.

The tapping of journalists' phones by the government during the year would come back to haunt Haughey a decade later.

Michael Jackson's *Thriller* album achieved record sales, *E.T.* was the film of the year and the quiz boardgame *Trivial Pursuit* was top of the Christmas list in many households.

NEWS BRIEFS

Feb Fianna Fáil leader Charles Haughey becomes Taoiseach of a minority government. He also survives an attempt to replace him with Des O'Malley as leader of the party. The government didn't last the year and was replaced by a coalition led by Garret FitzGerald.

Oct In the midst of Israel's invasion of Lebanon, Christian militia forces in Beirut enter the Palestinian refugee camps of Sabra and Chatila and massacre around 3,000 people. An Israeli government enquiry would find then defence minister Ariel Sharon "personally responsible". (18)

Ireland celebrate Triple Crown glory

Monday, February 22

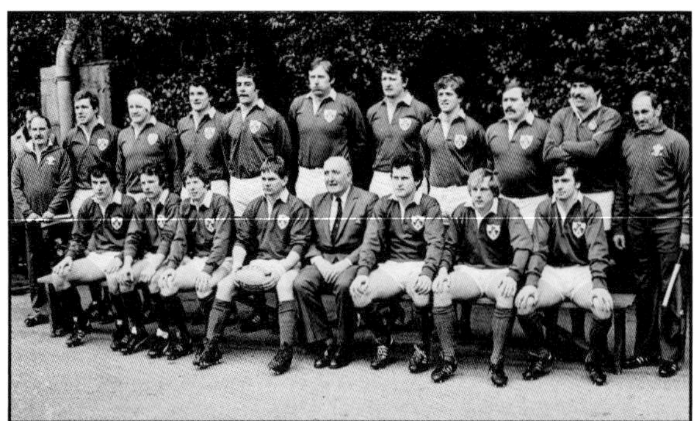

Ireland, 1982 Triple Crown winners. Front row (L to R): Michael Kiernan, Paul Dean, Ollie Campbell, Ciaran Fitzgerald, JJ Moore (President IRFU), Moss Finn, Robbie McGrath, Keith Crossan. Back row: A Richards (touch judge), Fergus Slattery, Gerry McLoughlin, John O'Driscoll, Donal Lenihan, Moss Keane, Willie Duggan, Hugo McNeill, Phil Orr, Clive Norling (referee), K Rowlands (touch judge).

There was a fascinating instance of motivation in the second half of Saturday's rugby match with Scotland, when Ireland won the Triple Crown (21-12) for the first time in 33 years.

The 17-stone Irish second-row forward Moss Keane was grimacing in pain at a back injury and being encouraged by team captain Ciaran Fitzgerald. Suddenly the dwarfed Fitzgerald pulled down Keane's head until their foreheads were touching.

The brief tableau had an intense quality, as though suddenly reflecting all Ireland's hopes and fears for the long sought after Crown. What, I asked Keane, were his captain's words at that dramatic moment in time, which came before Jim Renwick's penalty cut Ireland's lead to 18-9? Keane looked seriously into his pint, possibly reliving the trauma. He said: "My back hurt a bit, but I wanted to get on with the game. Fitzgerald said 'Hang on out of that. Duggan is b-------d, let him get his wind back'."

Within minutes, real rugby types in O'Donoghue's upstairs lounge in Merrion Row were relaying the Duggan interlude and a very tall, good-looking woman said in an affected tone: "Oh my God, what a darling man."

The story is already part of Triple Crown trivia, to be retold whenever they speak of Saturday's famous victory and inevitably of the massive, modest man from Currow.
- Val Dorgan.

Corporal punishment ends on Monday

Wednesday, January 26

Corporal punishment is to be outlawed in all schools from next Monday. The Government is imposing the ban immediately despite strong representation from the two biggest teachers' unions to delay its implementation until June 1, it was learned last night.

Britain and Ireland are the only two EEC countries where corporal punishment still exists. Britain is in the process of abolishing it also.

Mr Frank Cunningham, President of the 22,000-member INTO last night charged the Minister (John Boland) with getting the cart before the horse. An alternative strategy should be worked out before corporal punishment is banned, he said. The two unions had urged the Minister to set up a working party to formulate alternative strategies to maintain school discipline and in particular to bring forward proposals for dealing with disruptive pupils.

The use of corporal punishment was in most cases counter-productive, the Minister stated, and in many instances harmful. Many disciplinary problems had their origin outside the school. The home and family carried the primary responsibility in establishing correct behaviour patterns in children and "parents must not shirk this responsibility".

The Cork Examiner

No. 50,063 SATURDAY MORNING, MAY 22, 1982 Price 25p (inc. VAT)

Fierce battles rage for Falkland Islands

An aerial view of San Carlos where British forces staged amphibious landing yesterday.

BRITISH TROOPS STORM ASHORE

British Royal Marine commandos hoist the Union Jack over the Falklands yesterday

A 1,000-STRONG British assault force was last night digging in on East Falkland after storming ashore exactly seven weeks after the Islands were occupied by Argentine marines.

In a fierce four-hour battle, wave after wave of Argentine fighter bombers launched "near suicidal" attacks on supporting British destroyers and frigates manoeuvring in Falkland Sound and the narrow inlet leading to the landing beaches.

Latest reports from the British Defence Ministry claim a total of nine Argentine Mirage aircraft shot down together with five Sky Hawks and three Pucara ground attack aircraft.

One further Mirage was reported seriously damaged. But the Royal Navy seems to have taken a severe mauling too.

Five frigates or destroyers have been damaged, two of them seriously, by the air attacks launched from mainland bases.

Of the two seriously hit, one was said to be very badly damaged indeed by an Italian-built Aer Macchi MB339 jet armed with 500lb bombs and a 20mm gatling gun.

It was understood last night that no ships have been sunk and none of the civilian ships chartered or requisitioned damaged.

No details of British casualties have been released by the Defence Ministry yet, though it is believed that these were "moderate".

Each frigate and destroyer has a crew of between 200 and 400. A Task Force Harrier jet supporting the land forces is missing.

On land, the assault was on Port San Carlos, 50 miles west of Port Stanley, where there is a grass airstrip.

A crack force of Royal Marines and the Third Battalion Parachute Regiment rushed the beaches from landing craft and were initially unopposed.

They moved inland behind the protection of Scorpion light tanks, armed with 76mm guns.

Helicopters from the battle fleet ferried in 105mm light artillery, Rapier anti-aircraft missiles and ammunition, food and water.

A protective enclave was quickly set up with a helicopter landing pad erected by Royal Engineers.

If the bridgehead is held, work will soon begin on improving the airstrip possibly to take Phantom Interceptors and ground attack jets.

While the landing was made, 35 navy and RAF Harriers waged a fierce air battle described by one source as "the second battle of Midway".

As they fought desperately to break up the wave of aircraft, fighter controllers on the carriers *Hermes* and *Invincible*, 100 miles away, alerted the battle fleet's anti-aircraft defences as the hostile aircraft swept in at low level, seeking to hide from their radar among the hills of West Falkland.

Missile salvoes were firing bringing down more Argentine aircraft over the Sound.

But some got close enough to dive-bomb the frigates and destroyers bombarding shore targets with their 4.5 inch rapid-fire guns.

On land, two scouting helicopters — probably Marine Gazelles — were reported lost.

About 2,500 British commandos were last night ashore on East Falkland, according to a reliable military source.

This represented the "vast majority" of the Marines with the Task Force.

The source said it appeared there had been landings on four beaches, which went on throughout the night in "very fine" weather.

Naval gunfire support seemed to have been "incredibly successful," he said.

A Royal Marine spokesman at Plymouth said: "There are no casualties reported at this stage concerning members of Commando Forces, Royal Marines, or the Third Commando Brigade, Royal Marines.

"That is the force that makes up the land force. However, other Royal Marines are serving on board ships and we don't yet know if any of them have been injured."

According to the military source, during the landing diversionary tactics were put into operation to make the Argentinians reinforce the wrong area.

This gave the landing force the best opportunity of getting ashore.

A "substantial reserve" was late last night said to be still on shore in Falkland Sound. The intention was to consolidate the beachhead and to off-load stores as well as to deny air space to the Argentinians.

BBC reporter Robert Fox, who joined a Parachute Regiment unit as it made for the beaches, said only one of the Parachute Regiment units met opposition. Otherwise, surprise was "total and dramatic."

"There were Argentinian casualties and prisoners," he said. On board a British hospital ship doctors "struggled with basic Spanish" to reassure the wounded.

ITN reporter Michael Nicholson, who has been on board HMS *Hermes*, said: "At one of the unopposed landings near a small village — really just a cluster of white stone buildings — troops found 31 Falklanders in their own kind of makeshift shelter, including 14 children.

"They're all safe and they are all uninjured."

On the Argentinian side, two helicopters, a troop-carrying Chinook and a Puma, were destroyed on the ground.

The assault came after six commando-style raids by 300 special forces hit military targets around the Falklands.

The Ministry said all hit-and-run raids achieved their objectives.

But before this latest phase in the Falklands campaign began, a Royal Navy Sea King helicopter with 27 soldiers and three crewmen on board ditched in the sea due to a mechanical fault.

Nine men were picked up, one body was found and 20 more are listed missing, presumed dead.

This accident brought the total of British dead before yesterday's operations to 45.

Last night, the Falklands bridgehead was being consolidated with a protective perimeter of Rapier anti-aircraft missiles stationed on high ground and Scorpion light tanks ranging deep into the interior scouting for Argentine forces.

These vehicles, armed with 76 mm guns, will be used to destroy any thrusts by Argentine armoured personnel carriers pushing out from their 6,000-strong garrison at Port Darwin and Port Stanley.

British Defence Secretary John Nott said last night: "Seven weeks after the Argentine aggression, British forces are tonight firmly established back on the Falkland Islands."

Today, the full cost of that assault in terms of casualties and human suffering will begin to be known.

Somebody must shout 'stop'

IRELAND urged an emergency session of the U.N. Security council yesterday to give Secretary-General Xavier Perez de Cuellar a new and strengthened mandate to revive his peace efforts in the Falklands conflict.

"Someone must shout 'stop' before the present conflict becomes uncontrollable", Irish ambassador Noel Dorr said.

He suggested that the peace-keeping body ask Perez de Cuellar "formally to renew his efforts — this time with the added strength which a formal mandate from this council would give him".

Japan, another member of the 15-nation council, told the meeting it supported such a proposal.

Well-placed council sources said they expected a resolution to be drafted along the lines of the Irish proposal.

As the Falklands conflict worsened, a spokesman for the Government in Dublin said last night that the Minister for Foreign Affairs, Mr. Gerry Collins, had earlier yesterday instructed Mr. Dorr, to "re-activate" the call for a meeting of the Security Council, writes Liam O'Neill.

The spokesman said that the idea in calling for a Security Council meeting was to provide an opportunity for the Secretary-General to report on his negotiations with Britain and Argentina and to indicate what steps might now be taken to stop the conflict.

It appeared that the Irish Government would not be putting down any resolution on a ceasefire because such a move would almost certainly be vetoed by Britain, with the support of the United States.

The decision to re-activate the request for a meeting of the Security Council was taken yesterday morning before the Government held its usual Friday Cabinet meeting at which the latest developments in the Falklands crisis were discussed.

Britain told the Council that its delay in mounting military operations against Argentina's takeover of the Falkland Islands should not be seen as a sign of weakness.

"The British people are neither militaristic nor bellicose", Ambassador Sir Anthony Parsons told the council.

"Over the centuries, many nations have made the mistake of interpreting our slowness to be aroused with weakness. This has always proved a profound mistake.

"We are not carried away by slogans or rhetoric, but we are implacably stubborn in defence of principles and the rights of peoples".

The British delegate addressed the council at its first public session on the Falklands crisis since April 3, when the 15-nation body adopted a resolution that demanded an end to hostilities, Argentine withdrawal and a negotiated settlement.

Yesterday's meeting took place following U.N. Secretary-General Xavier Perez de Cuellar's public admission of the failure of his private efforts to resolve the dispute through separate negotiations with Argentina and Britain.

He told the Council yesterday that he was still personally committed to help in every way towards a lasting solution.

"The prospect which faces us is one of destruction, continuing conflict and, above all, the loss of many, many young lives", he said.

"Efforts must continue to find the means of avoiding this and restoring peace. There is no other course".

Argentine Deputy Foreign Minister Enrique Ros told the council that justice demanded recognition of Argentine sovereignty over the islands.

Mr. Ros said Argentina was prepared to negotiate, but it was up to the Security Council to assume its full responsibilities. "Any negotiations must involve recognition of Argentine sovereignty over the islands", he said.

He condemned Britain, saying it had demonstrated an aggressor's arrogance and disdain and said Argentina would defend its rights to the islands to the bitter end.

The debate will continue today, when Foreign Minister Nicanor Costa Mendez of Argentina is due to speak.

Irish travellers now at 'high risk'

By DAN COLLINS

BECAUSE of the Falklands conflict, travellers to and from Ireland, by either air or sea, are at 'high risk'.

This statement was made last night by a leading international aviation and marine disaster inspector, who said that the majority of British air/sea rescue helicopters and long-distance aircraft have been sent to the Falklands by the British Ministry of Defence.

"As is well known, Ireland and Britain have long-standing agreements whereby they work together on air/sea rescue missions. However, at the moment most if not all of the British rescue division's Nimrod aircraft, and a large amount of the Sea King helicopters have been sent to the Falklands", said Mr. Leo Sheridan, who added that because of this the RAF air/sea rescue resources were severely depleted.

He also said that in major rescue missions in the past, Ireland had always depended on the superior aircraft of the RAF. "It's absolutely ludicrous that in a country where deep sea fishing is one of the primary industries, there are no aircraft which can take part in night-time rescues".

At the moment Mr. Sheridan is based in Cornwall carrying out an independent investigation into the Penlee lifeboat. Just four miles from where he is staying is situated one of the major RAF air/sea rescue stations, Brawdy, Haverford West.

"Normally there are five squadrons of Sea King helicopters on the base in Haverford West, but now it reminds me of a post-Second World War scene, with its deserted ghost-like airstrips", said Mr. Sheridan, who added that to the best of his knowledge only four Sea Kings are left in Haverford.

Mr. Sheridan also stated that it has come to his notice that most, if not the entire fleet, of RAF Nimrod aircraft, which are invaluable in rescue missions because of their highly sophisticated electronic gadgetry and longevity in the air, have been recalled by the Ministry of Defence.

Three weeks ago the Nimrods were taken off the air/sea rescue fleet, and were fitted out with specially adapted fuel tanks, which would enable them to fly to the Falklands, where some are now being used as 'sub-hunters', Mr. Sheridan added.

The seriousness of this move by the Ministry of Defence was felt the very weekend the Nimrods were recalled from Cornwall, when three youths went missing in a dinghy. "Under normal circumstances a Nimrod would have been sent out immediately. None was, and sometime later the boat was found drifting, empty, 300 yards off the Cornwall coast", said Mr. Sheridan, who added that the bodies have not yet been found.

Mr. Sheridan told the *Examiner* that for some time now he has been calling on officials, both in Ireland and Britain, to press for a revamping of the air/sea rescue facilities, and to make them totally independent from the military. He said that if there is any major air or sea disaster, while the Falklands conflict is going on, then we could quite easily see the importance of having a civilian rescue service.

He concluded by saying that travellers entering or leaving Ireland by air or sea, and deepsea fishermen are now in a 'high-risk-ratio' should any disasters occur.

Hot line bombarded

British servicemen's wives and girlfriends in Plymouth bombarded a navy hotline last night in a frantic bid to find out more information.

Tey wanted to know if their loved ones were on the five British ships said to be hit.

But a spokesman had no information on which vessels were involved.

The Defence Ministry said it would take several hours to obtain information on survivors or casualties from today's fighting.

Trade embargo may not be renewed

BY VAL DORGAN

THE majority of EEC member States are likely to follow the lead of Ireland and Italy by dropping their trade sanctions against Argentina in Brussels on Monday.

A Council of Ministers meeting will be considering whether to renew the trade embargo. But, in view of the escalating war situation in the South Atlantic, it seems highly unlikely Britain can persuade its partners to continue their morale boosting economic support measures.

The reaction of Dutch Govreanment sources may be typical. They said that if there was a total invasion, there was no way the Netherlands could go along on Monday with the continuation of the sanctions.

The reason the country had extended the sanctions for a week was in the hope of helping a peaceful solution. The Netherlands' Government had been deeply concerned by the invasion of South Georgia and the sinking of the General Belgrano.

The invasion of the Falklands would be one step too much for the Dutch, and sources there thought other EEC countries would feel the same way.

It was a point of view shared in Belgian Government circles, to which even Britain's larger allies, West Germany and France, may also subscribe.

Any major shrinkage of the circle of states subscribing to the sanctions will be seen as justification for the action of the Irish Government which dropped the Community-wide trade measures last week.

Ireland felt the EEC move was designed to encourage a peaceful solution and not military action. Yet it infringed our neutral policy. Italy opted out because of internal political pressures.

One UK view is that Britain will salvage something from the Brussels meeting. It is felt in London that, because of faltering support for the sanctions and the over-riding of Britain's veto against the farm price package, its partners will be more generous on the contentious issue of British budget rebates, which is also on the agenda.

Decision day for Pope

POPE JOHN PAUL is expected to announce whether he will go ahead with his British visit at Mass in Rome's St. Peter's Square this morning.

The Pope, with full knowledge of Britain's attack on the Falklands, will have already made up his mind.

Catholic sources in Rome last night said they expected it would be quite clear in the Pope's message today whether or not he was going.

But they refused to speculate on how yesterday's landings may affect his decision.

The Archbishop of Westminster, Cardinal Basil Hume, and Cardinal Gordon Gray of Scotland met the Pope with two Argentine cardinals at the Vatican yesterday. Later, the two British cardinals met the two Argentine cardinals again.

After yesterday's first meeting, Cardinal Hume said: "My message to English Catholics is to keep praying and keep working.

"I believe that if hostilities don't escalate, then you can be reasonably sure that the visit will take place."

He was "reasonably optimistic that things are going to work out all right."

But it appeared that a full-scale invasion would still be enough to halt the visit.

Cardinal Hume said: "If there is an escalation of hostilities and a great deal of loss of life, then the judgement will have to be made that it will be improper for the visit to go ahead."

Both the British Cardinals know quite well their Argentine counterparts, Cardinal Raul Francisco Primatesta, Archbishop of Cordoba, and Cardinal Juan Carlos Aramburu, Archbishop of Buenos Aires. They described their meeting as "warm".

Also present at yesterday's meeting were Archbishop Derek Worlock, of Liverpool, Archbishop Thomas Winning, of Glasgow, Argentine Cardinal Pironio, who lives in Rome, and Archbishop Lopez Trujillo, the Colombian President of the Latin American Bishops' Conference.

Cardinal Hume said both he and Cardinal Gray had been anxious to see the problems of the visit through the eyes of the Argentine Cardinals.

At the same time they were anxious to protect the interests of all the British people who had worked so hard for the papal visit.

He added: "We are trying to work towards a unity of mind."

The Pope was in an extremely delicate situation, he said, but added: "He has been absolutely superb."

1983

The closure of the Dunlop factory in Cork was one of the watermarks of a terrible recession that gripped Ireland for much of the 1980s.

Unemployment and emigration rates climbed steadily through the decade and the 'brain drain' saw entire classes of college graduates leave the country.

In September, after an acrimonious debate, the electorate voted by two to one to place a ban on abortion in the constitution. This didn't stop thousands of Irish women travelling to Britain each year for the procedure.

The IRA took a new departure in fundraising with the theft of champion stud horse, Shergar. The former Irish Derby winner was never found, and it was reported in later years that the horse had been shot when he became difficult to handle.

Ronald Reagan, the US President, sparked a combination of welcomes and protests when he visited Ireland and his ancestral home in Ballyporeen in June.

Huge hunt for Shergar

Thursday, February 10

Cross-channel media who jetted in yesterday to join local journalists working on the Shergar kidnapping story at Newbridge, Co Kildare, found themselves scraping the barrel for facts. The truth was that Garda officers were wrestling with a baffling mystery with little to go on, and up to late last night there were no significant developments. Local newspaper offices were inundated with telephone inquiries from various parts of the world, including Australia and the Continent, so keen was the interest in the wonder horse heist.

The Ballymany Stud's kidnapped and later released stud groom, Mr John Fitzgerald, was closeted throughout the day, as top Garda officers and detectives heard his version of events over and over again. Chief Supt Murphy said last night that Mr Fitzgerald had been released between 30 and 40 miles from Newbridge in an adjoining county. His captors told him they would be demanding a ransom for the horse, that he was to go back and ring his boss, and that they would be making contact the next day (today). The Co Clare born Chief Supt told an *Examiner* reporter that a group of about five men were involved.

Not surprisingly last night, racing journalists and bloodstock personalities were expressing concern about the horse's welfare. Mr John McCririck of the *Sporting Life* said: "There is no need for anyone to be cruel to such an animal, one of the greatest horses in the world. He has had a wonderful life, enjoying the finest food. This is not like a human kidnapping. He can never tell who the kidnappers are."

The Aga Khan, who owns the Ballymany Stud, was informed of the kidnapping at his home in Geneva. A spokesman said last night: "It was an appalling and dastardly act. To do this to an innocent animal which does not even know its own value."

King Puck kicks recession away!

Thursday, August 11

King Puck is crowned in Killorglin, Co Kerry.

There were no signs of recession in Killorglin, Co Kerry, last night as thousands celebrated the coronation of a shaggy mountain goat as King Puck 1983. The town's 20 pubs, which were opened until 3am, did a roaring trade as carefree travellers satisfied their thirst.

Tourists from many corners of the world were among the estimated 7,000 crowd which witnessed the crowning of the goat after a colourful parade through the town in brilliant sunshine. Queen of the Fair, Liz O'Connor (11), granddaughter of former veteran TD Tim 'Chub' O'Connor, placed the copper crown around his treacherous horns, said to have a 28-inch span.

The goat's cage was then hoisted onto a 52-ft high platform by Pa Houlihan and family who have done the job for countless years. And it was expertly carried out, with the use of bare muscle and a strong rope.

The new King Puck was described by MC Declan Mangan as "a magnificent specimen from the vastness of Carrantuohill, who has seen only a couple of humans in his whole life". And so a pagan ritual which has been carried on unbroken through plagues, famines and wars, was religiously re-enacted last night, without a hitch.

NEWS BRIEFS

July The Supreme Court awards costs to David Norris, 37, who was unsuccessful in his High Court action and subsequent appeal to the Supreme Court to have the law making homosexual acts a criminal offence declared unconstitutional. (9)

Aug "Now I want to fulfil my dream and win an Olympic gold next year," said an elated Eamonn Coghlan when he easily won the world 5,000 metres title at Helsinki yesterday, capturing Ireland's first gold medal at a major track and field championship for 27 years. (15)

Dec Sixteen people – 11 soldiers and five civilians – are killed when an INLA bomb explodes at a pub in Ballykelly, Co Derry. (6)

The Cork Examiner

No. 50,397 FRIDAY MORNING, SEPTEMBER 30, 1983 Price 35p (inc. 6.54p VAT)

NI Minister fights on as escape details revealed

NORTHERN Ireland Prisons Minister Mr. Nicholas Scott moved swiftly last night to head off the growing demands for his resignation in the wake of the mass IRA Maze prison breakout.

He called in two Tory backbenchers and is understood to have given them a thorough briefing.

This confirmed a succession of apparently government-inspired leaks through the day which blamed a catalogue of human errors for the escape.

His message was that no resignations would be offered. The escape resulted from human, rather than organisational failings and the flow of rumours about inside collaboration were wrong.

The two MPs Mr. Michael Mates and Mr. Fred Sylvester are understood to have emerged satisfied from the meeting at the Northern Ireland Office in London and ready to stem the growing rumblings of discontent among their backbench colleagues.

The details of the escape appear to match those in the leaks.

But further details have come out, plus confirmation of three crucial security lapses which allowed the kitchen van containing the 38 escapees to reach the main gate.

It has been confirmed that the escaped prisoners had total control of the H-Block involved for almost two hours.

Between 2.30 and 3 p.m. on Sunday a prisoner in H-Block, which contained 130 inmates, and was guarded by more than 20 officers, approached the principal officer. The prisoner pulled a gun on the officer, then a second armed prisoner told him "this is for real."

Two officers who were guarding the central control circle were also overpowered by prisoners, both of whom are also believed to have been armed.

By that stage the IRA had successfully gained control of the entire H-Block.

One prisoner approached the first of the double gates and asked the officer guarding them if he could sweep the space between them. Once inside this prisoner also produced a gun and forced the officer back into the block.

When the canteen van arrived at about 3.40 it had already completed a journey from the kitchens through the two main sets of double gates.

The driver of this van was forced into the block and 37 other prisoners clambered inside the van and drove toward the main gates.

The van was waved through three checkpoints and continued unsearched until it arrived at the front gate.

When the vehicle reached the main gates five nearby prison officers were attacked by the prisoners who had been in the van. The prisoners then managed to pull the hydraulic lever which opened the main gate.

One prison officer, realising what had happened, attempted to block the entrance with his car. A fight then ensued during which time one prison officer was shot and four others stabbed.

Contrary to reports soldiers were present in the prison watchtowers, but with many of the prisoners dressed in officers' clothing they could not shoot in case they would hit genuine prison officers.

Once at the main gate the prisoners lost no time in hijacking vehicles from a nearby housing estate.

The RUC have meanwhile dismissed allegations that they plan to phase out plastic bullets in riot situations.

Mid-Ulster Assemblyman Alan Kane has claimed that blank plastic bullets have been used in selected areas of West Belfast as a first step towards phasing out live baton rounds.

A police spokesman said there was absolutely no question of the force giving up the option of using live plastic baton rounds to deal with rioters.

"We have always made it clear that we have no wish to use plastic baton rounds but they must and will be used in circumstances which require their use."

Plastic bullets have over the past few years accounted for no less than 14 deaths, mostly of women and children in riot situations.

● The IRA's Maze jailbreak plans have been found, it was disclosed last night.

They were dropped in the scramble to escape and according to sources close to the jail, only about six men were involved in the actual planning.

Twink weds in style

By Padraig Naughton

In untraditional fashion, showbiz star Twink — real name, Adele King — had to wait a quarter of an hour outside the Church of the Annunciation, Rathfarnham, Co. Dublin, yesterday for the arrival of her husband-to-be, David Agnew, a member of the RTE Orchestra.

But cheerful Twink, known to television viewers for her singing versatility waited in a horse-drawn carriage with her father, Mr. Leo Condron King of Anne Devlin Road, Templeogue, Dublin.

Radiant and without panic, she did admit to "butterflies in my tummy" — even worse than an opening night. "This is the kind of excitement you could only go through once", she confessed as the groom arrived at last.

The church was packed to capacity and outside the gardai had to clear a way through the excited crowd who had gathered from early morning to get a glimpse of the popular entertainer and her musician husband.

Pink and white was the theme of Twink's wedding dress of satin with a hand embroidered lace overlay, pearl encrusted bodice, puffed sleeves, and crinoline effect.

The Nuptial Mass was concelebrated by Fr. Hubert Condron a cousin of Twink, journalist priest, Fr Brian D'Arcy and Very Rev. Fr. Toohey, P.P., Rathfarnham.

The Young Dublin Singers of which Twink was a former member, joined with soprano Eileen Donlon and the groom's father, tenor Arthur Agnew in singing during the Mass. Instrumental music on the trumpet was provided by Earl Gill.

Turn to back page, col. 4

Sit-in feared as Dunlop shuts

By DONAL MUSGRAVE

WORKERS are expected to occupy the Dunlop factory in Cork today when it closes down for the last time with the loss of 680 jobs.

Up to last night the company had not announced a decision on whether or not to involve a Rights Commissioner in a bid to resolve the dispute with the staff over severance pay terms.

The Commissioner, Mr. T. J. Cahill, said he was still reasonably hopeful that the dispute would either be put before him or go to the Labour Court. It centres on a union demand for a £12 million severance pay deal as against a company offer of £5 million above the statutory terms.

"As long as I haven't got a definite 'no' from the company I believe there is still hope," said Mr. Cahill last night. He was formerly chairman of the Labour Court for 16 years and is a highly experienced negotiator.

"I am not setting any deadlines", he added. "I never like to rush people in these situations."

Observers feel, however the company will reject the mediation move which was called for in a substantial majority vote of the work force. Even if mediation is accepted today's closure will go ahead as planned bringing to an end a 48-year presence of Dunlop in Cork.

Anticipating a negative response the workers have formed a 20-man action group to organise a series of protests at the factory.

Among moves already planned are a sit-in beginning after a general meeting of the workforce at 9 a.m. this morning.

If the occupation goes ahead it will bring to a head the confrontation brewing between the workers and the company in recent weeks. However, Irish Dunlop has issued a warning that it will withdraw the £5 million offer completely if the workers take any industrial action.

Four Cork Fianna Fail TDs, Gene Fitzgerald, Pearse Wyse, Denis Lyons and Dan Wallace, in a statement yesterday, said "Today will always be remembered as the darkest day in Cork's industrial history."

"The closure of the Dunlop factory, and the loss of nearly 700 jobs, is a blow to the city from which it will take time to recover.

"We bitterly regret the closure and its devastating effect on the lives of so many people in the city."

Following a meeting with Fianna Fail Leader, Mr C. J. Haughey, and Front Bench spokesmen, the four TDs sought a meeting with Dunlop management in England to discuss the seriousness of the situation. "But our request was refused. We were told such a meeting 'would serve no useful purpose'."

The statement continued: "The coalition has shown an incredible lack of commitment to the Cork region. They have stood idly by while unemployment in the region has passed the national average and factory after factory has closed. Repressive Government budgetary policies have been the main contributory factor in the loss of jobs.

The TDs called on the Taoiseach and his ministers to ensure the continuance of tyre making in Cork by allowing the IDA to improve their package of incentives to potential purchasers of the plant.

"At this eleventh hour, we appeal to the Dunlop parent company to negotiate a reasonable settlement in the dispute over the level of redundancy payments. Failing that, we call on the Minister for Labour to intervene personally to work towards an amicable solution in the interests of industrial relations in the whole Cork area," the statement concludes.

● See also Back Page.

Farm fund cuts

STRINGENT cuts in Department of Agriculture funding next year were announced by the Minister, Mr. Deasy, yesterday.

First, the 1984 budget is being cut by 6% to £244 million. But agriculture must also accept its share of the £500 million Government cutback announced recently by the Taoiseach.

Mr. Deasy said he was hopeful the cuts made would not be harmful to the industry. He expressed a personal dislike of global cuts. He did not think it wise to make cuts in schemes which were designed to increase productivity.

He pointed out that taxation had reached its maximum levels and in some cases the levels were counter productive.

Funds under the reintroduced Farm Modernisation Scheme would be concentrated to provide grants for the housing of livestock, he said.

Staffing levels in the Department are falling. By the year end there will be an estimated 500 fewer in the 5,000 total.

A stern warning to the Government against any cutbacks in productive agricultural expenditure came last night from IFA Deputy President Hugh Ryan. He said that farmers will expect the Minister to

Turn to back page, col. 8

Deasy is confident about levy

By JIM MORAHAN,
Agriculture Correspondent

THE MINISTER for Agriculture, Mr. Deasy, said in Dublin yesterday he was confident this country would not be "lambered" with the proposed dairy super-levy. There was a realisation among other EEC countries that we would not accept it, he observed.

Mr. Deasy, who was speaking to agricultural journalists, said the Government was opposed to the principle of a super-levy. But a levy was needed for the countries which caused the problem.

"We utterly reject the idea that it should be applied to Ireland. We did not cause the problem", he said at a briefing at Agriculture House.

He blamed the EEC Commission for negligence in failing to take action to stop abuses of the price support system. He said he was referring to the importation of cereal substitutes, which in turn had led to intensive dairy production.

The Government, in advance of the real negotiations, has proposed to Brussels restrictions on cereal substitutes coming into the EEC and on concessionary imports, and a tax on intensive producers.

He said the Government was urging a higher tax than the four per cent suggested on intensive producers who use imported cereal substitutes. "These people have abused the price support system", said Mr. Deasy.

Britain might not want a super-levy because her own dairy production had been increasing at a high rate in recent years, he pointed out.

The Minister felt it would be interesting to see at the next Farm Council meeting on October 10 if any of the countries changed their view on the super levy.

"I suspect that many countries are waiting for us to make the running. I feel they are not in favour of a super-levy and want us to do their dirty work for them", said Mr. Deasy.

Britain claimed vital national interest to seek a rebate on her contributions equivalent to 0.25 per cent of GNP. Yet the super-levy would affect Ireland by up to five per cent of GNP, 20 times greater.

The Treaty of Rome concept of comparative advantage was being thrown out the window by those countries engaged in intensive production. The concept of policies aimed at "convergence" was being ignored. The richer countries were getting a higher price in relative terms.

Mr. Deasy, back from the Teheran International Fair, lamented the backward nature of Irish marketing in the face of opportunity. Technique needed to be improved, though the expense would be be quite minimal.

New Zealanders virtually threw their whole diplomatic effort into marketing their agriculture. "We tend to think of ourselves as diplomats and ambassadors. As a country I think we should have a very hard look at that", he suggested.

The Minister said that because of our neutrality and independent stance we could get contracts and markets where other countries would not be even entertained. We should capitalise on that. Of the Teheran experience, he said: "It's obvious there are

Turn to back page, col. 2

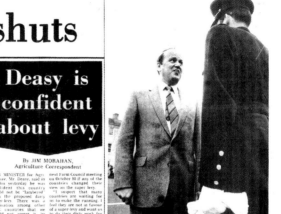

A tall order — Minister for Justice, Michael Noonan, T.D. facing up to the long arm of the law when the garda recruits reached new heights at the passing out parade at Templemore, yesterday. Report and pictures Page 11. —(Camera: Denis Minihane)

Man's arrest worries Woods

Dr. Michael Woods, Fianna Fail spokesman on Justice, said in a statement yesterday that following the arrest, detention and interrogation of Mr. Rory Buckley under the Offences Against the State Act and the subsequent press release from the Garda Press Office, information he had received had grave implications about the manner and purpose of this arrest and interrogation.

"It would appear that Mr. Buckley was arrested for interrogation purposes only, under the emergency legislation, and the purpose of his arrest and interrogation was stated by the Gardai concerned to be in connection with an alleged offence of malicious damage amounting to £15."

The employment of the emergency powers in these circumstances raised serious questions as to the use to which these powers were being put. The parties concerned, said Dr. Woods, had submitted full details of these events to the Garda Authority and he did not propose to comment further at this stage.

"However, I am concerned that certain matters are not covered in the garda statement. It fails to answer the allegations of personal abuse and harassment and political bias by the interrogating gardai concerned.

"I call on the Minister for Justice to say whether or not he condones the abuse to which the emergency powers appear to have been put in this case."

Bombers blast NI targets

Bombers attacked five targets in the North late last night. The devices all went off in Co. Tyrone — four of them in and around Dungannon.

Two filling stations, a warehouse and a building in the town centre were all hit. Fire started after the explosions but nobody was hurt.

Meanwhile at Strabane, a bomb damaged the Crown Buildings and again nobody was hurt. Early today a second device was being checked.

President decides today

PRESIDENT PATRICK HILLERY is expected to announce today whether or not he intends to stand down or accept a second term of office, according to reliable sources in Dublin last night.

Dr. Hillery has until next Tuesday to announce his decision, but he is probably bringing forward the announcement in response to the three main Dail party leaders who this week urged him to serve another seven years at Arus an Uachtarain.

From Tuesday begins the 60-day period in which a Presidential election must be contested, if necessary.

If President Hillery decides to serve on, the Taoiseach, the Tanaiste and the Opposition leader, Mr Haughey, will be happy.

There have been three Dail elections and a constitutional referendum within three years, and none of the parties is anxious for a high-powered campaign so soon after the referendum, and during a State expenditure crisis.

Should the President decide to leave office, the parties will have difficulty in securing an agreed candidate as both former Taoisigh, Mr. Jack Lynch and Mr. Liam Cosgrave, have indicated that they do not wish to stand.

A Cabinet meeting today will consider any announcement by the President and make plans accordingly.

1984

Two events in 1984 caused a lot of soul-searching in Ireland about the way women were treated and the apparent conflict that it created between the nation's espousal of 'Christian' values. Both incidents involved the birth of babies out of wedlock, which at the time was still a source of shame for many families.

First was the death of Anne Lovett while giving birth in secrecy near a grotto, and then in April a bizarre sequence of events began with the discovery of two bodies of recently-born children in Kerry.

The Kerry Babies affair saw Joanne Hayes – whose baby had been stillborn – accused of murder. These charges were subsequently dropped and a tribunal was set up to investigate claims that she and members of her family had made false confessions under pressure from gardaí. The origins of the other baby, who had been found on a beach at Caherciveen, never became known.

The south of the country lost another 1,000 jobs in July when Fords closed its factory in Cork. One worker summed up the general feeling on that Friday the 13th: "I'll miss my friends, the crack and fun but more than that I'll miss the steady money every week. It was good while it lasted but it's over now."

Probe urged into school mum death

Monday, February 6

The minister of State for women's affairs, Mrs Nuala Fennell, has called for a full enquiry into the death of a 15-year-old Co Longford schoolgirl who died giving birth to a child in a field last week. The child also died.

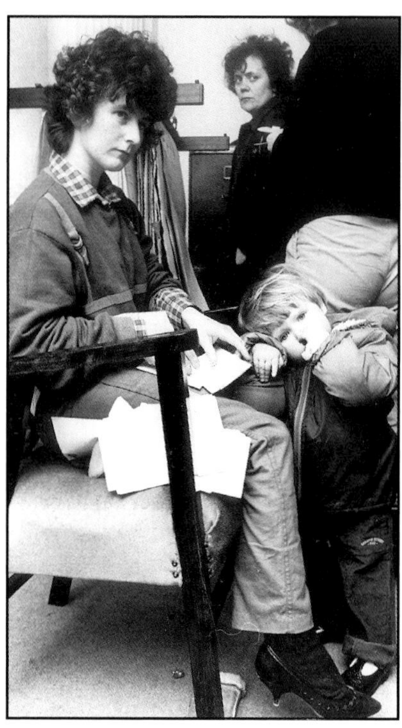

Joanne Hayes and her daughter Yvonne.

Anne Lovett of Main Street, Granard, died on Tuesday after giving birth to a son in a field. She had concealed her pregnancy and had attended school on the day she died.

In a radio interview yesterday, Mrs Fennell described the incident as a "national tragedy deserving of a full enquiry regardless of whose sensitivities are hurt".

"The girl must have been living in the most appalling fear and sense of guilt and shame. She must have been made feel like this to go into a field. That there was no door open to her that she could be felt welcome in and that she would not be blamed is appalling."

Deputy Mary Harney said that it was sad and strange that a minor was going through an obvious agonising ordeal on her own while the country was going through a pro-life amendment debate.

The Council for the Status of Women said that the fact that such a tragedy should occur in Ireland today was a shocking indictment of our society and its Christian principles.

Jack Lynch on Ford's closure

Saturday, July 14

This is truly the end of an era and for me the closure of Fords has a special nostalgia. Fords came to Cork in 1917, the year I was born, when they set down a major engineering facility for the manufacture of tractors for the European market. The closure is saddest for the workers (especially those of middle age and over) whose fathers and grandfathers worked there, and for whom Fords was a way of life. From the earliest days of assembly, tariff protection was necessary to maintain the viability of the Ford and other assembly plants. The inescapable advent of free trade meant the end of protection and in our negotiations for entry to the EEC, we procured a protocol for the continued assembly in Ireland for a period ending next year.

NEWS BRIEFS

Jan Luke Kelly, singer and former member of The Dubliners, dies. (30)

July Irish human rights campaigner Fr Niall O'Brien is released from prison in the Philippines after being held on a murder charge. Amnesty International had declared O'Brien a prisoner of conscience. (14)

Aug John Treacy from Villierstown, Co Waterford, wins a silver medal in the Olympic marathon in Los Angeles; Ireland's first track medal at the Games since 1956. The Soviet Union and its allies boycotted the event, Carl Lewis won three gold medals and barefooted South African runner Zola Budd, competing for Great Britain, collided spectacularly with local favourite Mary Decker in the 3,000m. (11)

Sept Trade union officials complain about the fact that none of the 90,000 Irish farmers brought into the tax net in April 1983 have yet been assessed for tax. (11)

Dec Band-Aid, formed by Bob Geldof and Midge Ure, are top of the pop charts with 'Do They Know it's Christmas', in aid of famine-ravaged Ethiopia.

The Cork Examiner

No. 50,719 SATURDAY MORNING, OCTOBER 13, 1984 Price 40p (inc. 7.48p VAT)

Provos warn: You will have to be lucky always after . . .

Thatcher survives murder attempt

Mrs. Thatcher and her husband Denis, in defiant mood at the Conservative Party conference yesterday

FOUR people were feared dead last night after IRA bombers devastated Brighton's Grand Hotel - but narrowly failed to assassinate Mrs. Thatcher. Senior Tory M.P. Sir Anthony Berry, whose four children are cousins of the Princess of Wales, is one of two people known to have been killed by the IRA bidding to wipe out the Cabinet.

Also among the dead are Mrs. Roberta Wakeham, wife of present Government Chief Whip Mr. John Wakeham, and Mrs. Jeanne Shattock wife of President of S.W. Conservative Association Mr. Gordon Shattock.

Sussex police said one other is missing, feared dead among the rubble - but the IRA just missed their main target, the Prime Minister herself.

Twenty pounds of gelignite, with a timed detonator, had been placed in a 5th floor room designed to send hundreds of tons of masonry collapsing onto the Prime Minister's first floor Napoleon Suite.

The huge blast, shortly after 2.45 a.m. ripped open the front of the hotel and wrecked the bathroom she had visited just two minutes earlier.

Firemen were last night frantically digging in the ruins of the Grand Hotel for up to three people still believed to be buried.

Earlier thev had dug out Cabinet Minister Mr. Norman Tebbit and Government Chief Whip Mr. John Wakeham, among 15 of the 34 injured detained in the Royal Sussex Hospital.

Sir Anthony Berry, Conservative M.P. for Enfield Southgate for 20 years, was deputy chief whip until asked to resign after last year's general election.

Amid the chaos, the Iron Lady, shaken but unhurt, showed steely calm as she and other Cabinet members, many still in pyjamas, were led to safety.

A few hours later, it was back to business as usual for the Prime Minister as she insisted that the party conference go on as scheduled and she told the bombers, you cannot win.

Emotional but grimly resolute, she bravely went before her shocked supporters and said of the outrage: "It was an attempt to cripple Her Majesty's democratically-elected Government".

The fact that they had gathered again in the conference centre, "shocked but composed and determined", was a sign that "not only has this attack failed, but that all attempts to destroy democracy by terrorism will fail."

But the IRA, who admitted responsibility for the blast in a statement to the Press Association in Dublin, warned Mrs. Thatcher: "Today we were unlucky, but remember, we have only to be lucky once, you will have to be lucky always".

The attack on the Tory conference base came only hours after the party had been celebrating at their traditional ball. Many were still chatting over drinks when the bomb exploded, turning the light-hearted atmosphere to terror.

Some guests plunged seven floors as the blast caused floors to collapse, leaving a gaping hole through the heart of the hotel.

Trade and Industry Secretary Mr. Tebbit and his wife Margaret plunged 30 feet as the floor of her room, no. 228, gave way.

Firemen quickly rescued Mrs. Tebbit as the couple held hands and she was last night "serious but stable", with back injuries in the Royal Sussex County Hospital.

But Mr. Tebbit (53) was buried alive for four hours under tons of rubble, masonry, beds and mattresses.

As TV flood lamps lit up the shattered foyer, only Mr. Tebbit's bare feet could be seen as firemen frantically dug him out.

Despite the pain of broken ribs and chest and hand injuries, he was able to joke with rescuers, telling one fireman: "Get off my bloody feet, Fred." Finally they got him out. Last night he was recovering well in the same hospital as his wife.

Mr. Wakeham, MP for Maldon, Essex, who was buried for six hours after falling to the ceiling of the ground floor, underwent surgery for serious leg injuries and was last night described by a hospital spokesman as "conscious and stable."

Fifteen people were still being detained in hospital last night as the

Turn to back page, col. 5

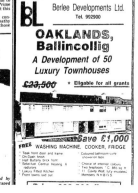

A view of the devastated front of Brighton's Grand Hotel after the explosion

Aimed to wreck any initiative

IN the Irish Government's view the aim of the IRA in carrying out the Brighton bombing was to damage the efforts of the Irish and British Governments to produce a new initiative for Northern Ireland based on the report of the New Ireland Forum, writes **Liam O'Neill.**

But the Taoiseach, Dr. FitzGerald, and other Ministers were said to be convinced that they would not succeed. They believed that the attack could, in fact, prove counter-productive for the IRA.

As far as an initiative by Britain was concerned, the belief was that if Mrs. Thatcher had already decided to respond to the Forum in a particular way, the Brighton outrage would not be likely to bring about any significant change in the decision.

The Taoiseach, Dr. FitzGerald, who had earlier sent a message to Mrs. Thatcher, expressing the Government's outrage at the bombing and offering sympathy to the relatives of those killed and injured, spoke at length about the Government's feelings in a speech to the annual conference of the Irish Association for Cultural, Economic and Social Relations in Dun Laoghaire last night.

The Opposition leader, Mr. Haughey, also condemned the bombing. He telephoned the British Ambassador in Dublin, Mr. Alan Goodison, yesterday morning and asked him to convey to the British Prime Minister his "dismay at this outrage."

Mr. Haughey also conveyed his deepest sympathy to the relatives of those killed and injured.

In his speech last night, the Taoiseach said the IRA sought to divide the Irish and British people but they had only succeeded by their attempted massacre in Brighton in creating "a fresh impulse of solidarity between us and in reinforcing our common will to defeat their own evil."

Those of the Irish nationalist tradition were deeply angry at the arrogance of the Provisional IRA in doing these things "in the name of our tradition, in the name of our aspiration, in the name of our legitimacy," he said.

Dr. FitzGerald said the IRA were also determined to prevent the British and Irish Governments creating new structures in which the condition of the Northern nationalist minority could be transformed in such a way as to give hope to that community for the very first time ever.

He held a strong conviction that the carnage in Brighton served only to reinforce the growing determination of the people of Britain and Ireland that "we are in this together, and that the will of the people - not that of the evil bombers - will prevail and endure."

The Workers Party in a statement condemned the bomb attack.

"While we are absolutely opposed to the political philosophy of the Conservative Party, there can be no justification whatsoever for this bomb attack," it said.

The Catholic Press office in Dublin in a statement from the Auxiliary Bishop of Armagh, Most Rev. James Lennon, on behalf of Cardinal O Fiach who is attending a meeting abroad, said:

"The bomb outrage in Brighton was a brutal assault on innocent human life. This cowardly and evil deed, claimed by the IRA, is a crime against God and humanity to be condemned unreservedly and without qualification."

The Lord Mayor of Cork, Ald. Liam Burke, said the perpetrators of the "dastardly deed" must be brought to justice. He sent a telegram of sympathy to the Mayor of Brighton.

The Lord Mayor said all decent citizens of this country would be disgusted and horrified at the outrage.

The Lord Mayor sent this telegram to the Mayor of Brighton, Cllr. John Blackman: "I am outraged and disgusted at the foul deed perpetrated in your city. On behalf of the people of Cork and on my own behalf, please accept our deepest sympathy."

SUMMIT ON

Foreign Affairs Minister Peter Barry said the Anglo-Irish Summit planned for next month will go ahead despite the bombing. Neither the Taoiseach or Mrs. Thatcher would be put off by the attack, he said.

RUC asked for suspects' list

IN Northern Ireland, the RUC chief constable Sir John Hermon held a top level meeting of senior officers to discuss the bombing. Special branch officers were ordered to supply a list of suspects.

Mr. James Prior, who has just stepped down as Northern Ireland Secretary, thought an IRA cell dormant for some time in Britain might now have been activated.

A man described as short and stocky was seen running away after the blast. Bomb disposal expert Nick Collins, who said the man had an Afro hair style, was sure he was not part of the general confusion.

"I have had certain training. The guy was getting out of the situation."

The Rev. Ian Paisley, leader of the Democratic Unionist Party, sent a telegram to Mrs. Thatcher in which he expressed sorrow for the relatives of those killed and injured.

"Northern Ireland people during the past 10 years know exactly what these bombings are like and the sorrow and pain they inflict," read the text of the telegram. Mr. Paisley added: "We look to you prime minister, to rid our country of the terrorist scourge."

Unionist Party leader James Molyneaux described the bombing as a dastardly outrage

Mr. John Cushnahan newly elected leader of the Alliance Party said the people of the province were horrified and outraged

Mr. Seamus Mallin, deputy leader of the SDLP also condemned the attack and warned those who had perpetrated it that terrorists would never bomb their way to a united Ireland.

Kelly's disbelief at positive dope test

IT WAS with a heavy heart that Sean Kelly spoke to the journalists in Milan yesterday evening. The news of a positive drugs control test was in the air and the Irish cyclist was at the centre of a storm which he will forever want to forget.

Early yesterday morning Kelly was informed that a second examination of the urine sample he gave after finishing third in the Paris to Brussels race on September 18 showed traces of a prohibited substance Stimul.

For the first time in his eight year professional career, it is alleged that Sean Kelly used more than his natural talents but the facts of the case are far from clearcut. Primarily, it must be stated that Kelly swears that he did not take any illegal product. Because of his 31 victories this season he has been tested more than any rider on the continent and in over 20 tests prior to the Paris— Brussels race, he was negative each time.

His performance in Paris-Brussels was not one of his better efforts as, having escaped in the break of four near the finish, he could only finish third.

If there was a prohibited substance in Kelly's system, it certainly was not evident from the performance. Since turning professional Kelly has been tested over 200 times and, as this is the first occasion he has been declared positive, his punishment is nothing more than a £500 fine and the loss of that Paris-Brussels third placing.

Kelly was first informed of the positive result of his test last Tuesday week. His reaction was one of disbelief and he immediately sought to have a second verdict with the assistance of the Irish cycling official Karl McCarthy and Irish witnesses present to oversee yesterday's second test.

Kelly proposes two possible reasons for the positive finding. "Either something was put into my bottle before the race or the jar which should have contained my urine contained somebody elses."

It is normal at all tests for each rider to go into a room and give his sample to a doctor on an individual basis but in Paris-Brussels we were all in a room together. There were a lot of people walking around and it was all very much against regulations."

Defiant as ever, Kelly said he will fight this judgement and will not relent until he has proven his innocence. Yet his defiance was tinged with sadness for he knows that a great deal of damage has already been done. "I know what some people will think and this is what makes this one of the greatest disappointments of my career."

Tidey escapes death

SUPERMARKET chief Don Tidey yesterday escaped death for the second time in less than 12 months when an anti-personnel bomb contained in a parcel delivered to the Dun Laoghaire headquarters of Quinnsworth was blown up by army explosive experts.

The parcel bomb, delivered in the post, was taken by suspicious staff to the roof top car park and placed in a car belonging to one of the store's managers.

Comdt. Patrick Trears, head of the Army bomb disposal team which blew up the package, said the parcel contained a small device which would have killed anybody who had tried to open it.

Members of the public and shop staff in the multi-storey complex were evacuated from the building and a fleet of ambulances stood by in case of injuries. The car in which the bomb was placed was completely wrecked.

... Mr. Don Tidey," immediately attracted the attention of Quinnsworth office staff. When it triggered off a security screening device, they alerted the gardai.

Mr. Tidey was at his desk at the Dun Laoghaire store when the mystery parcel arrived and told colleagues he was not expecting delivery of such an item.

Earlier this week he gave evidence in the Special Criminal Court about his kidnapping in November and December of last year. A Kerryman, William Kelly, of Caherina, Tralee, was jailed for three years for his part in the abduction.

Since Mr. Tidey's release last Christmas, gardai have maintained a security check on his Rathfarnham, Co. Dublin home.

The 50-year-old Brighton-born executive is both Chairman and Chief Executive of the Quinnsworth chain which controls 20% of the Republic's

Don Tidey, kidnapped by the I.R.A. last year, escaped

1985

The *Examiner* found itself at the centre of the news world for a few days in June when an Air India jet was blown up off the south-west coast of Ireland. The city's airport and main hospital became the centre of operations for the recovery of the bodies and the wreckage of the plane.

The year also saw major famine in Africa and disasters at stadiums in Brussels and Bradford. Given the terrible stories in the news, perhaps it's not surprising that there was a certain amount of religious fervour in the air and thousands flocked to Ballinspittle, Co Cork, following reports that a statue of the Blessed Virgin was moving.

A move away from Catholic teaching was seen in the fact that contraception was made available without a prescription to those over the age of 18.

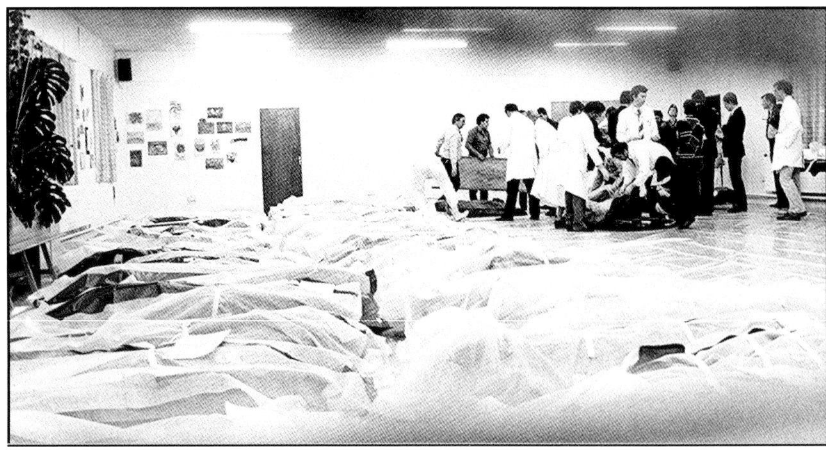

The scene at the gymnasium of the Regional Hospital, Cork, after the recovery of some of the bodies from the Air India plane. Denis Minihane's picture became the defining image of the disaster. While access to the area was blocked to the media, Minihane got the picture by climbing up to the window of the makeshift morgue and waiting for a gust of wind to blow the curtain up so he could get his shot.

Denis Minihane's picture of the ordination, as Bishop of Kerry, of Dr Diarmaid Ó' Suilleabháin, in Killarney won a prize at the Press Photographers' Association of Ireland Awards.

Our man sees statue 'move'

Saturday, July 27

It certainly seemed to move from the shoulders up. It could have been one of the greatest optical illusions of all time. The halo of lights around the head of the statue of Our Lady in the grotto at Ballinspittle glared from the recess in the rock at the multitude below. Gardaí estimated that in excess of 3,000 people from all around Munster had made their way to the small village which has suddenly hit the headlines.

An elderly lady was already drawing a comparison between the fallen Italian dam and the grotto in Ballinspittle. Our Lady was giving us a message.

"What is wrong with the world at all?" asked another in desperation. "It must be terribly wrong."

Yesterday local Garda Sergeant John Murray confirmed that he had again seen the statue move on Thursday night.

He said he had not seen the hands move as previously reported but had seen the statue "move to and fro" as though it would topple. However, his concentration was broken by the hysterical reaction of some of those present.

'Barrytown' awaits McGuigan champ

Monday, June 10

Barry McGuigan, the new featherweight boxing champion of the world, will get a no-holds-barred civic reception when he returns tonight to his home at 'Barrytown', County Monaghan.

The unofficial change of name for Clones was signalled yesterday by a white banner strung across the main street within minutes of McGuigan's title fight victory in London on Saturday night.

While almost everyone in the town sat glued to their TV sets, there was one important exception - the boxer's mother, Mrs Katie McGuigan. Almost overcome by nerves she stayed on duty behind the counter of her grocery shop home - later damaged in an early hours fire - and listened to the tones of an opera record rather than the strains of her husband Pat singing 'Danny Boy' at the ringside.

NEWS BRIEFS

May A terrible month for soccer. Forty people were killed in a fire at Bradford City's stadium. A couple of weeks later, 41 people died at the Heysel Stadium in Brussels when a wall collapsed during a riot by Liverpool fans at the European Cup final.

July *Live Aid* concerts in London and Philadelphia organised by Bob Geldof raise over £50 million for famine relief in Ethiopia and Sudan. (13)

Nov The Anglo-Irish Agreement is signed, setting up a framework for regular conferences between the governments of Ireland and the UK to talk about affairs in Northern Ireland. Unionists object strongly. (15)

The Cork Examiner

No. 50,934 MONDAY MORNING, JUNE 24, 1985 Price 43p (inc. VAT)

JET CRASH A MASSACRE

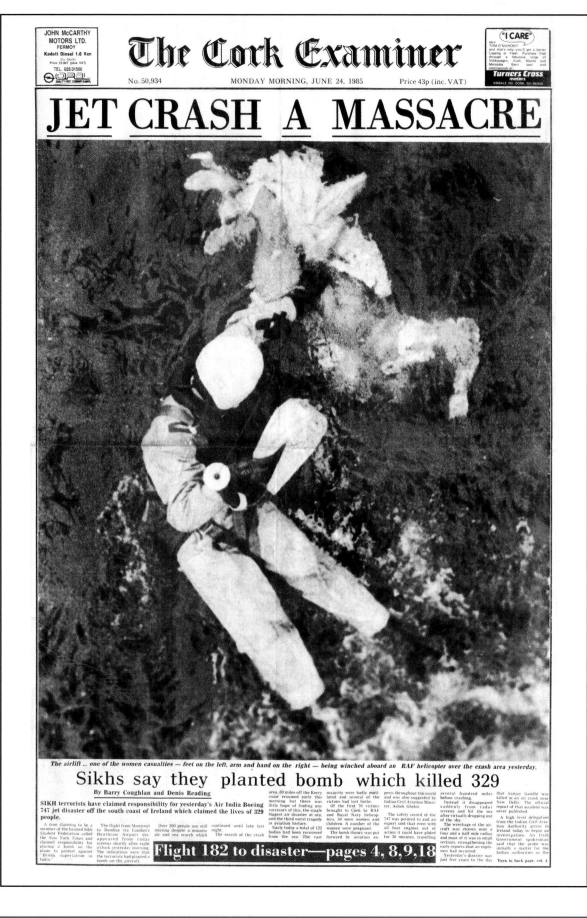

The airlift ... one of the women casualties — feet on the left, arm and hand on the right — being winched aboard an RAF helicopter over the crash area yesterday.

Sikhs say they planted bomb which killed 329

By Barry Coughlan and Denis Reading

SIKH terrorists have claimed responsibility for yesterday's Air India Boeing 747 jet disaster off the south coast of Ireland which claimed the lives of 329 people.

A man claiming to be a member of the banned Sikh Student Federation called the *New York Times* and claimed responsibility for placing a bomb on the plane to protest against "Hindu imperialism in India."

The flight from Montreal to Bombay via London's Heathrow Airport disappeared from radar screens shortly after eight o'clock yesterday morning. The indications were that the terrorists had planted a bomb on the aircraft.

Over 200 people are still missing despite a massive air and sea search which continued until late last night.

The search of the crash area, 80 miles off the Kerry coast resumed early this morning but there was little hope of finding any survivors of this, the single biggest air disaster at sea, and the third worst tragedy in aviation history.

Early today a total of 123 bodies had been recovered from the sea. The vast majority were badly mutilated and several of the victims had lost limbs.

Of the first 70 victims brought to Cork by RAF and Royal Navy helicopters, 54 were women and children. A number of the women were pregnant.

The bomb theory was put forward by aviation experts throughout the world and was also suggested by Indian Civil Aviation Minister, Ashok Ghelot.

The safety record of the 747 was pointed to and an expert said that even with all four engines out of action it could have glided for 30 minutes, travelling several hundred miles before crashing.

Instead it disappeared suddenly from radar screens and hit the sea after virtually dropping out of the sky.

The wreckage of the aircraft was strewn over a four and a half mile radius and most of it was in small sections, strengthening the early reports that an explosion had occurred.

Yesterday's disaster was just five years to the day that Sanjay Gandhi was killed in an air crash near New Delhi. The official report of that accident was never published.

A high level delegation from the Indian Civil Aviation Authority arrive in Ireland today to begin an investigation. An Irish Government spokesman said that the probe was initially a matter for the Indian authorities as the

Turn to back page, col. 4

Flight 182 to disaster—pages 4, 8,9,18

1986

In April, as radiation readings in Europe began to reach abnormally high levels, the Soviet Union was slow to release details about the fire in the Chernobyl nuclear reactor. Several people were killed in the accident, and long-term affects of the radiation leak have included birth deformities among many children from the region.
In Ireland, Hurricane Charlie swept across the country causing at least four deaths and widespread floods and destruction. It was the second lashing by the elements that the south of the country received that month, and the difference in the government's response when Dublin was affected prompted an outraged comment by the *Examiner*, an excerpt from which is printed below.
In June, a referendum to allow divorce was rejected by 61% of those who voted.

A tragic loss to the world of rock

Monday, January 6

An air of stunned disbelief hung over the usually raucous world of rock and roll this weekend following news of Phil Lynott's death after an 11-day fight for life in a Wiltshire hospital.
The shock was even greater as colleagues from the music business, fans, family and friends had just been told that the Dublin-born singer's condition was "slightly improved". Word had also gone out that Phil had been planning to re-form his band, Thin Lizzy, and this would probably happen with his return to health.
Thin Lizzy first broke in the international charts with a unique version of the old traditional ballad 'Whiskey in the Jar' back in 1973. That it took them three years to find a suitable follow-up with 'The Boys are Back in Town' is of no consequence; from then on they had a steady stream of record successes until they finally disbanded in 1983.

Phil Lynott during his last concert tour with Thin Lizzy.

Priests exorcise shrine of 'Devil's shadow'

Saturday, August 23

Two priests carried out an approved exorcism this week at a Marian shrine near Inchigeela, Co Cork, after a local girl praying there claimed to have seen a sign of the Devil.
Last Wednesday, as the faithful were gathered in prayer at the grotto, the girl became very distressed and claimed she had seen the Devil, whose appearance there, according to locals, was not the first.
Her 'vision' was described as a huge black shadow over the grotto. Two priests visiting the shrine were so distressed by the girl's 'experience' that they performed an exorcism without the bishop's approval.
"The little I have heard about the happenings makes me very sceptical," Bishop Murphy said last night. "How do you recognise the presence of the Devil?"
Numerous apparitions and cures have been reported at the shrine since it was built and dedicated to Our Lady of Lourdes in 1989. According to a recent circular on the Inchigeela phenomenon: "apparitions occur whenever a visionary attends, but Wednesday is the best day to come."

When it happens in Dublin, they really get the wind up

Wednesday, August 27

Out of evil may yet come some good. It is very regrettable that our neighbours in Dublin and on the east coast have had to suffer, like the rest of us, the effects of the tail end of Hurricane Charlie.
But while we will probably be accused of cynicism for making the suggestion, the fact that the capital has been hit by the storm means that at least the Government is sitting up and taking notice.
Only a few short weeks ago, it will be remembered, the Munster region among others in the provinces, was severely battered by a gale of equal proportions, with consequent flooding, damage and destruction. Following on that experience and despite many calls for special assistance, nothing was done and it seemed to those affected that the central authorities simply did not care what happened to them.
Now, because the gales have struck at the very heart of bureaucracy, we have all the flutterings of concern and good intent. The Taoiseach is cutting short his holidays to lead the mopping-up operation. The Cabinet is holding a special meeting tomorrow. There is much talk of disaster areas.
Against this background, is it any wonder that people in Munster are now asking if dire natural phenomena are only taken into account when they strike at the capital?

NEWS BRIEFS

Jan The *Challenger* space shuttle explodes just after take off in the United States. (28)

June Dawn Run, the greatest National Hunt racing mare of all time, is dead. Yesterday, in the French Champion Hurdle at Auteuil she fell at the fifth flight from home, landed on her neck and died instantly. (28)

Diego Maradona scores two goals – one with his hand, the other after a sublime run from his own half – as Argentina beat England 2-1 in the quarter-final of the World Cup before going on to win the tournament in Mexico. (29)

Aug John Stalker is cleared of accusations which had seen him removed from an investigation into an alleged shoot to kill policy by the RUC. (22)

The Cork Examiner

No. 51,198 WEDNESDAY MORNING, APRIL 30, 1986 Price 45p (inc. VAT)

A nuclear nightmare

EXPERTS worldwide were united yesterday in predicting that thousands may have died and 10,000 more been fatally contaminated due to the nuclear explosion in Russia over the weekend.

Although the Soviets yesterday announced that only two people were killed in the Chernobyl nuclear power plant disaster, several top scientists around the globe claimed the disaster was of far greater magnitude.

In a television interview in Stockholm, Swedish nuclear expert Gunnar Bengtssen said thousands could have died if all the radiation leaked out, while Professor Jens Scheer, of Bremen University, West Germany's leading expert on the Soviet nuclear programme, said it was conceivable the disaster could cause 10,000 deaths through lung cancer over the next 10 years.

And in Washington, a U.S. official said the explosion could cause severe air and water contamination. U.S. Arms Control and Disarmament Agency head Kenneth Adelman said the area near the plant was lethal and had been evacuated within an 18-mile radius.

U.S. intelligence were reporting that smoke was still billowing from the plant and threatening another reactor at the same site. Intelligence agencies had concluded that there was definitely a nuclear meltdown at the plant, probably touched off by an internal chemical explosion.

A high-ranking U.S. government source said: "Smoke was still billowing from the site. The roof had been blown off and large portions of the walls (of the reactor) had caved in."

The source added that the U.S. government was convinced there had been a huge release of radiation and that the most serious radioactive fallout on the ground occurred within 10 miles of the Ukrainian plant.

American experts called the accident "100 times worse than a meltdown." They said the tragedy was compounded by an outmoded Soviet technology that relied on graphite, a form of lead, instead of water to moderate nuclear reactions.

And they said Soviet refusal or inability until recent years to house reactors in protective concrete containment buildings — as is routine in the United States — had contributed mightily to the accident.

As a result, they said, uncontrolled radiation was spewing into the air and a fire was raging out of control.

Dr. Helen Caldicott, a longtime campaigner against nuclear weapons and an expert on the effects of radiation, told Reuters that the next few days could see thousands of people killed or afflicted with killer diseases.

Reports from the Soviet Union have been sketchy. The official death toll so far has been given as two and a Soviet official in Washington said western news reports that thousands had been killed and injured were grossly exaggerated.

Citing rumours of thousands of casualites, Dr. Caldicott said: "If 2,000 people have already died from this accident, then 3,300 could die within the next couple of days."

Dr. Herman Cember, a nuclear accident expert at Northwestern University, near Chicago, compared the Soviet accident with Hiroshima and Nagasaki. He said that as in those Japanese cities devastated by atomic bombs the effects of radiation would be seen for generations to come.

Another American expert said those most endangered were the 2,000 people living in a village for workers at the nuclear facility and their families. And he warned that a shift in the winds could also endanger Kiev, 60 miles away, and its 2.5 million residents.

Reports from foreign workers in the area said an area 20 miles round the plant had been declared a security zone. At least 30,000 people live in the zone, mainly in the town of Pripyat.

A meteorologist in Kiev told Reuters by telephone that the wind there had now changed from southerly to westerly.

The southerly wind on Sunday carried a radioactive cloud 1,000 miles north to Scandinavia where it was detected by Finnish and Swedish scientists and experts in Denmark.

There were also reports of high radioactivity in Poland and in West Germany, near the Danish border.

West German technicians in Kiev reported to their embassy that officials had told them a zone 19 miles around the four-reactor station had been sealed off.

In Finland, tourists returning from the city said that 25,000 people had been evacuated.

Meanwhile, the European Commission is "carefully" considering the Irish Government's request for a special force to supervise safety at nuclear plants in the Community.

Experts are now examining the suggestion and will be giving their verdict shortly, according to Mr. Stanley Clinton Davis, European Commissioner with responsibility for nuclear safety policy.

This library picture shows operators preparing one of the four nuclear power plants at the Chernobyl site.

No reason for alarm says Energy Board

THE Irish Nuclear Energy Board and Junior Energy Minister Eddie Collins said yesterday there was no reason for the Irish public to be alarmed at the prospect of any nuclear contamination falling here following the Soviet disaster.

The Board's been told by the Meteorological Service here that prevailing weather conditions are unlikely to carry contamination in the direction of Ireland in the "immediate future."

The water cooled graphite moderated reactor involved in the Ukraine accident is only used in the USSR and, according to reports, has no secondary containment.

If this is the case, says the Irish Board, it would have "contributed significantly" to the magnitude of the release.

Air-borne radioactive contamination is routinely measured by the Board on a daily basis in collaboration with the Meteorological Service at two monitoring stations, in Dublin and Valentia, Co. Kerry.

The board says these monitoring programmes will be continued and it plans to keep in touch with developments concerning the Russian reactor accident.

Meanwhile, the Green Alliance political party pointed out that nuclear accidents were transnational catastrophies and put at risk people living thousands of miles from the source of the contamination.

Nuclear power, it said, was inherently unsafe and accidents would continue to happen. Ireland was within 100 miles of British nuclear plants at which there was a continuing risk of similar accidents.

The Irish environmental group Earthwatch has called on the Government to commission a full independent assessment of the potential for a major accident at Sellafield and the implications for Ireland.

"Although the consequences of the Russian accident may prove to be horrific when the full damage is known, it must be remembered that this only involved a release from a nuclear reactor. By contrast, the accident potential at a nuclear reprocessing plant such as Sellafield is many times greater", it says.

(See also page 8)

Limerick girl safe in Kiev

By DECLAN COLLEY

A CO. LIMERICK girl who was in the Russian city of Kiev when Monday's nuclear disaster happened north of the city, was last night reported to be alive and well.

The Irish Embassy in Moscow confirmed last night that they had been in contact with Fidelma O'Leary and they said she had not been affected by the accident at the Chernobyl nuclear power plant complex.

The Embassy was unable to give any details of where Fidelma comes from in Co. Limerick, but they said that their consular section in Dublin had been in contact with her parents to give them the good news.

Fidelma is staying in Kiev for 12 weeks with a group from the University of Guildford in Surrey, England, studying at the city's Institute of Foreign Languages.

An attache at the Embassy said last night that they are "happy she is safe and well and has not been affected by the accident." No other Irish people are known to be in the vicinity of the Ukrainian capital, Kiev.

He added that the situation in Kiev itself seemed to be normal and there had been no indications to the contrary. Local transport, phone lines, electricity supplies and other essential services were all continuing as usual. "Kiev does not appear to us to be a dramatic area."

The attache said that the Embassy was not aware of any other Irish nationals in the area, and commented that the small Irish community in Russia was almost entirely situated in Moscow.

"We are nonetheless pleased to be able to say that from the information at hand Fidelma O'Leary's health has been confirmed and she is in no danger," he commented.

"The Embassy left their number with her just in case she needs us, but she has not been in contact and we presume she is relaxed about the situation locally."

Europe not in danger: page 7

Members of the Rodna Pesen Choir from Bulgaria pictured after their 14-hour, non-stop trip to Cork for the International Choral and Folk Dance Festival which opens today. —(Examiner)

Thatcher talks with Unionists next week?

THE first meeting to agree a framework for negotiations between Unionist leaders and British Prime Minister Mrs. Margaret Thatcher could take place next week, according to the Rev. Ian Paisley.

Mr. Paisley said yesterday that he and Unionist leader Jim Molyneaux had been carrying out a "reconnaisance" by going through agreed channels, including the Whip's office at Westminster, and expected progress soon towards "real dialogue."

The last meeting of the Anglo-Irish inter-governmental conference was seven weeks ago, and the British government had refused to discuss any plans for a further ministerial meeting.

Unionist leaders have insisted that there should be no further implementation of the Accord while negotiations with Mrs Thatcher are taking place.

Quizzed about the progress over talks with the British government, Mr. Paisley said he expected the initial meeting to be with high ranking officials.

Its purpose would be to explore a framework within which real negotiations on the Province's future could take place.

He said "the suggestions we have put so far have been received favourably and are almost finalised for the first meeting."

Mr. Paisley said his hope was that constitutional parties would end up around the negotiating table and that whatever came out of any such talks would be put to the electorate for approval.

But the DUP leader criticised Mr. John Hume for the "strange way" in which he had recently

Thatc[illegible] to press Rea[illegible] for help

suggested talks - through radio interviews - while in the past he had chosen to ignore letters from Unionists seeking dialogue.

Mr. Paisley said Mr. Hume had said he was offering talks without pre-conditions. That was false, he said, as the SDLP leader was insisting that talks should take place within the Anglo-Irish framework.

He insisted that Mr.

Paisley hoping for real dialogue

Hume should support the suspension of the Agreement to allow negotiations to take place.

DUP Deputy leader Mr. Peter Robinson claimed that pressure from the Unionist campaign against the Agreement had meant that the inter-governmental conference and its secretariat had been able to produce "virtually nothing" so far.

Issues, such as disbanding the UDR, setting up joint courts and repealing the Flags and Emblems Act, had all been forecast for change.

Meanwhile, Mr. Paisley said he expects to be charged with helping to organise an illegal march in Portadown on Easter Monday.

"I have been told by the authorities that I am going to be in court because of it," he said.

Mrs. Thatcher yesterday pledged to press President Reagan for more help against Northern Ireland terrorism when she attends this week's Tokyo summit.

She said that she would make the point to the President that she hoped the Senate would pass the extradition treaty that would enable suspected terrorists to be extradited from the US.

Barry: Fine Gael's campaign director

Barry heads divorce team

FINE GAEL yesterday gave Mr. Michael O'Leary, TD, his first major job since he joined the party over three years ago, when they appointed him deputy director of the divorce referendum campaign, under the Minister for Foreign Affairs, Mr. Peter Barry.

They also named four other campaign leaders — Mr. Alan Dukes, Minister for Justice, director for Leinster; Mr. Michael Noonan, Minister for Industry & Commerce, director for Munster; Mr. Paddy O'Toole, Minister for Defence, director for Connacht/Ulster; and Mr. Jim Mitchell, Minister for Communications, director for Dublin.

All six will act as a campaign committee, meeting at regular intervals to assess the situation and plan future stragegy.

So far the party has been getting a rather adverse reaction to the Government's proposal to delete the constitutional ban on divorce.

Telephone calls to the Fine Gael office were running three to one against the referendum proposal, party sources revealed.

Teachers stick to pay demand

By Richard Murphy

VITAL peace talks were continuing late last night in an effort to resolve the teachers dispute and remove the boycott that threatens the state exams next June.

Following last week's adjournment, discussions were resumed under the direction of the Employers Labour Conference at the offices of the Federated Union of Employers in Dublin, but signs of a breakthrough were not good from early on.

It is believed that the Government was prepared to pay over to the teachers the money that it saved in wages as a result of the three-day strikes.

The unions, on the other hand, are thought to have demanded full retrospection of the arbitrator's 10% award on a phased basis over a few years. They rejected the Government's new offer as being only a fraction, or around one-tenth, of this £120m requirement.

Already the TUI and the ASTI have voted massively in favour of blacking the Leaving, Inter and Group Certificate exams, which will effect around 135,000 students, and of holding further waves of strikes.

Desmond: oil sell-out not on

THOSE who urged the Government to make life easier for private speculators who had been adversely affected by falls in oil prices would not succeed in stampeding the Labour Party in Government to "sell out" to those interests, the Minister for Health and deputy leader of the Labour Party, Mr. Barry Desmond, said yesterday.

Quite contrary to all the hype of some Irish shareholders in oil exploration companies and their associated political supporters, i.e. the Progressive Democrats, this was not the time to expect much activity in oil exploration, he said during an address delivered in Cabinteeley, Co. Dublin.

At present, as an oil importer, we could take full advantage of all the benefits of low oil prices while not suffering the problems faced by the oil producers.

"Our own oil reserves can safely wait to be exploited until a rational commercial view would justify this, that is when oil prices have increased sufficiently to provide a decent return for both private investor and the State," Mr. Desmond said.

Cheeky cheetah arrives at Fota

GROANAH, the four-year-old cheetah whoate his way out of his box on board a flight from South Africa to London, arrived at the Fota Wildlife Park in Cork last night.

Groanah startled workers at London airport when it was discovered he had got out of his crate in the hold of the aircraft. He was sedated and was held over for a few days because he was ill.

Valued at £750, he was well secured when he arrived at Shannon where veterinary inspector Thomas J. Bracken conducted his inspection before allowing him to be removed to Fota to undergo six months quarantine.

He was collected by Mr. Sean McKeown and after quarantine will be released into the Fota Sanctury.

On the cowboy trail

COMMUNICATIONS Minister Jim Mitchell last night declared there were too many cowboys in the Irish road haulage business, cowboys who have got away with shoddy standards for far too long.

But the Government was now on their trail and, with the help of new roadside inspectors who will have power to stop and examine all goods vehicles, will either put them off the road or force them to get their act together.

1987

The nation was gripped by a countrywide hunt for INLA 'renegade' Dessie O'Hare, aka the Border Fox, in the latter half of the year. At times the dramatic events could have been taken straight from a black comedy, with embarrassing bungles by O'Hare's gang and the Gardaí alike.

It all began on October 13, when O'Hare and his gang arrived at a house in Dublin to kidnap millionaire professor Austin Darragh. However, their intended target no longer lived at the house so they instead took his son-in-law, dentist John O'Grady.

During his 23-day ordeal, O'Grady had parts of two of his fingers cut off which were then left in Carlow Cathedral with a note demanding a £1 million ransom. In early November O'Grady was finally released by Gardaí after a shoot-out in Dublin.

Around the same time, two suspected members of the kidnap gang escaped from Garda custody in Tipperary amidst farcical circumstances.

As the men were being led from a police car to the station, one of them ran off. The other prisioner was brought into the station but, according to a local superintendent, when Gardaí were searching him "he just bolted and escaped".

The Border Fox himself remained at large, but soon showed up in Dunleer, Co Louth, and chased his distressed wife into a crowded pub, firing several shotgun blasts at her. Nobody was injured in an incident headlined by the *Examiner* as 'Border Fox goes ape' and O'Hare sped off with his seven-year-old daughter.

The eventual 'Outfoxed' headline came on November 28 when O'Hare was wounded and captured in an ambush by armed detectives in north Kilkenny, in which accomplice Martin O'Brien was shot dead. O'Hare was sentenced to 40 years in prison for his offences and was reported to be doing an anger management course as part of his reform programme.

Provo bloodbath

Monday, November 9

Eleven civilians were killed yesterday in one of the North's worst atrocities in many years. Men, women and children were among those killed or injured when a massive bomb, believed to be the work of the Provisional IRA, was set off in a community hall during a war memorial service in Enniskillen, Co Fermanagh.

The blast ripped through the quiet market town without warning as crowds gathered for the Remembrance Sunday wreath-laying ceremony.

Eyewitnesses spoke of indescribable scenes of devastation following the blast which also left over 50 people injured.

The father of a young nurse who died after five hours on a life support machine said last night he forgave her killers. Mr Gordon Wilson (60) was slightly injured in the explosion.

At his home he said: "We were only there about 15 seconds when the bomb went off. It wasn't a loud explosion. I was pushed forward on my face. The rubble and the wall and the railings fell on top of us and I thought I wasn't badly hurt. I then felt somebody holding my hand. It was Marie. She said, 'Are you all right daddy?' and I said 'yes'. I asked her if she was all right and she said yes. I asked her this question four or five times. She was crying all the time. When I asked her the fifth time if she was all right she said, 'Daddy I love you very much.' I knew then there was something wrong."

Bono and Shane MacGowan onstage at the Siamsa Cois Laoi, Páirc Uí Chaoimh, Cork.

Lottery fever hits nation

Tuesday, March 24

The State-sponsored National Lottery began yesterday, and emptied many a pocket. £1 million was spent on tickets – the target for Lottery Week 1 – in just one day! Some you win, but more you lose. By today, most of the country knows someone who 'won' in the National Lottery. But the biggest winner of them all is the State, which is laughing all the way to the bank.

That Ireland is a nation of gamblers was confirmed yesterday – as if confirmation were needed. Money poured into the national coffers – threatening to wipe out the national debt in no time at all, as mattresses were slit open to reveal dormant, hidden hoards, prime for a little flutter.

Huge national advertising lured the guarded shekels to the 3,000 outlets around the country, all of which reported a massive level of interest and business. Cork's GPO was sold out of a fortnight's supply of tickets by lunchtime, and a national spokesperson for the lottery company told the *Examiner* that extra tickets were being dispatched to hundreds of outlets overnight.

The Cork Examiner

No. 51,583 MONDAY MORNING, JULY 27, 1987 Price 50p (inc. VAT)

Special Offer
IN CLASSIFIED
ring
TELE ADS 274455

Our CHAMP Élysées

Tour de Roche as Irish revel in victory

By BRENDAN MOONEY in Paris

STEPHEN ROCHE rode himself into cycling history yesterday by winning the Tour de France. The Taoiseach, Mr. Charles Haughey, was amongst the estimated 1,000 Irish who watched the stage finish from Cretiel on the Champs Elysees in Paris.

Roche (27), the first Irishman to win the Tour, also joined the elite group of cyclists who have won the Tour de France and the Tour of Italy in the same year — Fausto Coppi of Italy, Belgian Eddy Merckx and Frenchmen Jaques Anquetil and Bernard Hinault, the only other riders to achieve the double.

Mr. Haughey travelled the Champs Elysees circuit with the French Prime Minister, Jacques Chirac, behind the peloton and described it afterwards as one of the most memorable experiences of his life.

He was on the podium alongside Mr. Chirac when the yellow jersey of the Tour winner was presented to the Dubliner, and posed for photographs from the battery of cameramen from across the world who have been covering the event for the past 26 days.

Mr. Haughey said the victory was significant for Ireland for several reasons. "From the point of view of national morale it is important, and it will also help boost our export trade, our tourism industry and Aer Lingus.

"This victory will provide the country with just the kind of lift it needs at the moment," he said. "Today I had the privilege of travelling behind the peloton at the invitation of the French Prime Minister and it was an unbelievable experience.

"Paris is one of my favourite cities, and to watch Stephen Roche win here today, and to savour the atmosphere and the excitement of the occasion, was a tremendous experience and something I will always remember.

"Our Ambassador to France paid a tribute to Stephen last night when he said that he had done more for Ireland abroad than all the ambassadors together. I think that was a very generous tribute, and a deserving one," he said.

It was an emotional ceremony on the podium on the Champs Elysees as Roche was presented with the yellow jersey and bouquets that go with winning the Tour de France. When the band played *Amhrán na bhFiann* the tears trickled down Roche's face.

"It is a long time since I heard the national anthem played. We don't hear it over here. It was a very emotional occasion for me," he said afterwards.

"It was very moving to see so many Irish people on the course. I think the crowd must have been half Irish and half French. It was a moving experience. I have to pay tribute to the people at home for their support throughout the tour, and particularly today.

"I am looking forward to going back to Dublin tomorrow. I would like to shake all their hands but that just would not be possible. I will only be there for a short time, but I will have the opportunity to thank them personally."

The race was decided in the individual time trial in Dijon on Saturday when Roche beat the Spaniard, Pedro Delgado, by 61 seconds to go 40 seconds clear at the top of the general clasification sheet.

Roche arrives back in Dublin today for a parade through O'Connell Street. He is due in Dublin Airport at noon. tonight he will be accorded a civic reception by the Lord Mayor of Dublin, Carmencita Hederman, at the Mansion House. Tomorrow he will be back on the continent for a criterium race.

He confirmed yesterday that he will ride both Kellogg's races in Cork and Dublin next month, and it is virtually certain that he will take part in the Kellogg's professional Tour of Britain in two weeks time.

Roche's triumph, Page 3; Editorial, Page 4; Final road to victory, Page 16; colour picture, Page 18.

Victorious: Stephen Roche shows his delight after yesterday's Tour de France triumph.

Over 700 die as Greece sizzles

Temperature soars to 111° F in Athens

By Michael Moloney

HEATWAVE has caused more than 700 deaths in Greece following eight days of oven-like temperatures. But there are no reports of any Irish casualties.

The Greek Government has declared a state of national emergency in the country, which has proved a popular destination for young Irish holidaymakers.

The Department of Foreign Affairs said last night that they had received no information yesterday of any Irish nationals being among those stricken by the intense temperatures in Greece.

"We have been in touch with the Irish Embassy and, so far, there have been no reports of any Irish people being involved," a spokesman for the Department said.

The dead were mainly elderly people with heart and breathing complaints and, in all, more than 1,500 people were admitted to hospital with heat-related problems.

Hundreds of deaths caused by searing heat have also been reported in Turkey and Italy.

In Greece temperatures went as high as 44 degrees C (111° F). Most of the dead were elderly heart and respiratory cases. However, the heat wave has also proved fatal for those in the 10 to 40 years age bracket.

In Athens — where cemeteries remained open for weekend burials — an estimated one million inhabitants fled for the countryside, leaving the city almost deserted.

A Cork GP has given a number of safety guidelines for people travelling to hot climates.

He warned that a sudden rise in temperature to a very high level could cause death in a matter of two to three hours.

People who fell victim to this kind of situation were generally unaware of how ill they actually were. Many went to bed and died in their sleep, he said.

Anyone with a heart or respiratory condition should, he advised, consult with their family doctor before heading for warmer climes during the summer months.

Ideally, when temperatures soared, holiday-makers should stay out of the midday sun; take frequent cold showers; drink plenty of fluids and have a supply of medicine that keeps temperature down, such as aspirin or its equivalent, he said.

Hundreds miss final

Report by Liam Heylin

CROWD control problems prevented hundreds of people from seeing yesterday's thrilling Munster Final between Cork and Kerry, when Kerry grabbed the lead with a final minute goal only for Cork to snatch a quick point a draw. The replay will be in Killarney next Sunday.

Just minutes before the match started the turnstyles were locked and 600 people were left shouting to be let in at the Blackrock end of the stadium. There were similar scenes at the other entrance points, according to Gardai on duty.

"It didn't get out of hand, but there were angry scenes when people couldn't get in," a garda spokesman said after the match.

The people in the tunnels found that they were both unable to get into the match, or out of the stadium during the first half. Some people who asked for their money back were told that they should have got to the grounds in time, one caller to the *Examiner* claimed last night.

The crowd difficulties were further compounded at half time as those on the terraces tried to get out to the toilets.

Residents of Rockcliff Villas in Blackrock complained angrily that their entrances had been blocked by fans' parked cars. Although the matter was reported to the gardai, no action was taken, they said.

Match report, pages 18 and 19.

1988

While many people have clearer memories of Italia '90, the party was already well under way for soccer supporters by the time Ireland took on England in the 1988 European Championships. Entry to the team's first ever major tournament was long overdue and most of the credit went to Jack Charlton and his tactics of "put 'em under pressure" when opponents had the ball and quickly pumping it forward when Ireland had it.

For the *Examiner*, the match against England was a particularly big occasion as the front page report of the match featured the first colour wire photo published in an Irish newspaper.

Even by the standards of the Troubles in Northern Ireland, March was a terrible month with a horrific sequence of interlinked killings by the three main sides in the conflict. It began when three members of an IRA active service unit were killed by British forces in Gibraltar. Mairéad Farrell and her two companions appear to have been planning attacks on British targets in the area, but were unarmed when they were shot.

At the funeral of the 'Gibraltar Three' at Milltown cemetery in Belfast, loyalist Michael Stone began throwing grenades and shooting into the crowd of mourners. Three people were killed before Stone was arrested.

Three days later at the funeral of IRA man Kevin McCracken, one of those killed in the cemetery attack, a car reversed towards the funeral procession. A group of mourners, fearing they were again under attack, jumped on the car and attacked the two male occupants, who turned out to be members of the British Army. It has never been fully explained what the out-of-uniform soldiers were doing near the funeral, but they too joined the list of casualties of that awful month.

The publishing phenomenon of the year was Alice Taylor's *To School Through the Fields*, a hugely successful account of the author's rural childhood.

Thank you Ireland

Monday, August 1

This is the message to fans today from Michael Jackson – the Peter Pan of pop – who delivered the Greatest Show on Earth and turned Cork into Hollywood.

I became the only Irish journalist to be granted an exclusive audience with the song and dance king at the end of a magical holiday weekend by the Lee. I met a polite 29-year-old American who exudes charm and kindness. He leaves you awestruck – almost as if you have met royalty or a head of state.

The truth is that so-called Wacko Jacko, a horribly unfair description of the man, strikes you as a shy and gentle individual, ill at ease with strangers off the stage. When Frank (Dileo – Jackson's manager) introduced me as an Irish friend, Michael shook my hand and said: "How are you doin' Vince." So simple was the gesture that it could have been any chance encounter with someone of my own age.

Dressed in his trademark black jacket and tight trousers, studded with buckles and belts, he emerged from behind a veil as Frank and I entered the dressing room.

As we posed side-by-side, it was obvious that his facial features looked good close-up with few signs of those much publicised surgical treatments.

– Vincent Power

Michael Jackson and guitarist Sheryl Crowe on stage in Páirc Uí Chaoimh.

NEWS BRIEFS

Aug A conference in Dublin warns that the size of the average family could drop to Continental levels by 1990. Apparently, the average family has dropped from four to three children in the past 10 years, "one of the sharpest falls in the world". The amount of Irish housewives going to work has trebled since 1960, from five % to 15%. (4)

Dec The Irish government refuses to extradite suspected IRA member and former priest Paddy Ryan on the grounds that he wouldn't receive a fair trial in Britain. Mrs Thatcher considers the decision a "great insult". (13)

At least 273 people were feared dead last night after a Pan-Am jet crashed on a small Scottish town in Britain's worst ever air disaster. The jumbo hit a hill at Lockerbie and started to break up before crashing on to a petrol station and destroying dozens of homes. (22)

Woodchester for Leasing
Tel. MARGO 021/506555

The Cork Examiner

No. 51,659 MONDAY MORNING, JUNE 13, 1988 Price 55p (inc. VAT)

Ireland 1 England 0

HERE WE GO

Examiner 1 The Rest 0

The first colour wire photo published in an Irish newspaper.

■*Gotcha...Ray Houghton (right), being congratulated by teammates Ronnie Whelan and John Aldridge (left), after he scored Ireland's winning goal against England.* *(Exclusive wire colour photo from Associated Press)*

Sting Ray clinches it

IT'S always nice to score – and scoring against your neighbour England is extra special, says man of the moment Ray Houghton, the Glasgow-born Ireland goal-scorer.

It was his first goal in 18 internationals, he noted yesterday – and at six minutes into the first half of the all-important match in Stuttgart, it couldn't have come at a better time.

The 26-year old, who plays midfield for Liverpool, yesterday afternoon took the "nod" from fellow Liverpool team player John Aldridge, and putting his head to good use, buried the ball in English keeper Peter Shilton's

His goal gave Ireland the psychological boost needed to fend English challenges off, despite several heart-stoppiong attacks on the Irish goal right up until the final whistle

Jack the giant killer

FOR Jack Charlton, dubbed a 'traitor' by the UK tabloid press, the victory in Stuttgart was 'the longest 84 minutes I have ever sat through in a match'.

"Having scored the goal we had to sit back and hope we could break out," he said after a match which had sent Irish hearts 'a racing' on a sunny afternoon.

"Although we had been saying we could beat England, I was a bit doubtful when I saw how hot it was and I though we would be under pressure.

Now, the man now more 'Irish than the Irish themselves', is assured of a royal welcome in Ireland after the Championships, regardless of what happens from here on.

Irish on the town, English on the rampage

From MARK WOODS in STUTTGART

IRISH soccer fans celebrated into the early hours here this morning following Ireland's heroic 1-0 victory yesterday over 'the auld enemy'.

Some 15,000 jubilant Irish fans brought in the dawn good humouredly, toasting Jack Charlton 'and the boys in green' as the city centre of Stuttgart was taken over by the Emerald Isle.

Ireland's ecstatic supporters, dubbed the best behaved followers in Europe, lived up to their reputation: "We had no problems with the Irish, as was expected," said German police chiefs.

Fans began to arrive at the 79,000-capacity Necker Stadium shortly after 11 a.m., as thousands of police threw a cordon around the ground.

Rival followers were segregated and carefully searched going into the stadium and some under the influence were turned away after being breathalysed.

A police helicopter circled the stadium and nearby roads while video cameras were in constant use to prevent troublemakers making any headway.

After the game, however, 11 youths, three English and the remainder German, were arrested after the Germans charged into a group near Stuttgart's railway station.

Last night, UK Sport Minister Colin Moynihan, reacted angrily to the behaviour of his countrymen: "This is a cancer on the back of English football."

However, in the end the police were understandably proud of the end result. So, too, were the Irish followers.

The sixth minute header from Ray Houghton, which followed a pass from John Aldridge that left the English at sixes and sevens, sent the country into raptures.

However, the thousands of Irish there, and the millions at home, had to endure agonising moments near the end as England struggled to pull out of a crushing defeat.

■ **Match reports 16; Fleet Street boys get a 'wapping' 17; Irish celebrate North and South 18.**

The tension was unbelievable as Donegal-born goalkeeper Packie Bonner pulled off a series of breath-taking saves to keep Ireland on course for victory.

"The final whistle produced a scene which will be savoured by everyone fortunate enough to have been there," said one thrilled onlooker.

Inhibitions were brushed aside as players and officials hugged one another, with Bonner, the hero of the moment, dropping to his knees and blessing himself.

Others, especially Paul McGrath and Ronnie Whelan, danced with joy — for Charlton, the man who made it all possible, his smile told a multitude.

"There will be one big party here tonight. The Irish know how to party and I reckon they will drink the place dry, but they will not cause trouble," said Charlton later.

On the terraces and the stands the Irish had already begun, roaring themsleves hoarse as the players applauded them.

Meanwhile, the English quarter was quiet, scarcely believing what had happened.

●In the other Group 2 match, Russia beat Holland 1-0 last night.

Chair-raising spectacle

Seán Dunne was one of millions who watched the match on television.

THERE I was, plonked before the television calm as a Buddha. By the time Ray Houghton got the goal with a ball that ricocheted from his head with the force of a deflected Exocet, I was up from the chair and roaring at the screen.

Sometimes this can make you look an awful eejit, especially if someone sees you through the window, but I didn't give a hoot.

I switched from RTE to HTV with the tension of a man stuck under a searchlight on the Berlin Wall. Liam Brady spoke to HTV at half-time. He held a microphone which looked like an orange impaled on a pool-cue. Huge headphones and wires surrounded his head as if he had just rushed out from a brain operation. He stuck up for his own and he patted Brian Clough into place for criticising Mick McCarthy.

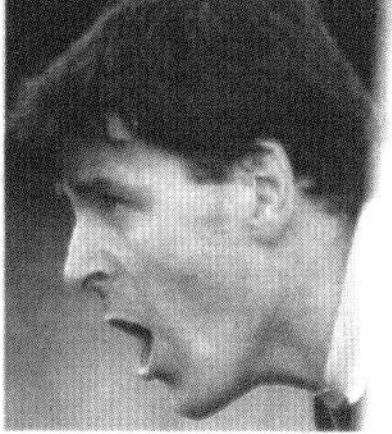

■ *BONNER: brilliant.*

Back at the match, the crowd were singing *Molly Malone* in a sea of green broken by the odd hairy chest bared to the blistering sun. It looked as hot as the desert. And the mayor of Stuttgart, where the game was played, is actually the son of Rommel, the Desert Fox. I'm sure he was secretly pleased at the result as well, after what they did to his poor father, as they might say in Cork.

Bits of the commentary drove me bonkers. On HTV, when the English came near to scoring again and again, it was called the luck of the Irish when the ball barely went wide. When the same thing happened to the Irish, it was said to be due to the skill of the English backs.

Every now and then, the camera panned the crowd as if expecting a good scrap to break out. No such thing happened. Not even Gary Lineker could make the ball blitz into the net. Packie Bonner, the Irish goalkeeper, stopped balls with the never-failing

Turn to back page, col. 7

Flying high on Ireland's win

By Fergus O'Callaghan

THERE were two heroes on the holiday flight from Salou to Cork yesterday.

Suntanned but far from relaxed, holidaymakers were in transit and a long way from the drama unfolding in Stuttgart.

The atmosphere was electric aboard the plane, rumours were rife, the hostesses were polite but could not help. Relief and jubilation were simultaneous. One passenger who had the foresight to bring a Walkman on board picked up a faint broadcast and he thought the commentator said Ireland were ahead. We were all ears.

The news flashed from seat to seat and was greeted with thunderous applause, tears of joy and the inevitable- how much time is left?

More fiddling on the Walkman brought a stronger signal.There were only six minutes left and it was then the nail biting began in earnest. News filtered through that it was Ray Houghton who scored from an Aldridge knock-on and we had our second hero of the afternoon.

Fulltime came to a crescendo of cheers and clapping, even the hostesses were caught up in the euphoria.The rest is history.

TODAY

Health shake-up

■ FG Deputy Bernard Allen has produced a document proposing a major shake-up of the health services: Page 5.

Setback for Mitterrand

■ PRESIDENT Francois Mitterrand fails to win majority for the Socialist Party in the French general elections: Page 9.

Bishop's warning

■ BISHOP Murphy yesterday warned parents on their rôle in teaching religion to their children: Page 7.

Salmon scheme

■ A UNIQUE scheme is being launched on Sherkin Island to corner a portion of the lucrative salmon farming industry: Page 4.

Index

Haughey backs talks move by Unionists

THE Taoiseach, Mr. Haughey, tonight throws his weight behind an All-Ireland constitutional conference to end the political deadlock in the North.

Mr. Haughey is interviewed during a special BBC *Panorama* programme entitled "Ireland - The Long Peace"

SDLP leader John Hume, the Rev. Ian Paisley and Sinn Fein President Gerry Adams are all interviewed on the same programme.

The Taoiseach told reporter BBC Peter Taylor of the conference proposed by Unionists: "I would be hopeful that if the British Government thought such a conference feasible and that such a conference would bring progress then they would certainly support such a concept.

"I'm quite certain that if they could see it as offering any prospect of bringing peace and stability or indeed even improving the situation that there would be no great reluctance on their part."

DUP Leader, Mr. Paisley, also reveals that he and his colleagues are seeking "urgent talks" — even if it means cancelling holiday arrangements.

He believes that a roundtable conference must take place quickly. "It's too late to leave to the autumn," he states.

And he adds: "We would be prepared to start talking tomorrow. He also admits: "I think Ulstermen can do business with anyone including Charles Haughey."

The programme examines the Unionist proposals which were forwarded to Secretary of State Tom King six weeks ago and also examines the ongoing talks between Sinn Féin and the SDLP.

Mr. King, for once, is remarkably blunt about his views on the long-running anti-Irish stance by Protestant Leaders.

On the effects of the Agreement, Mr. King states: "There is no doubt that the Anglo-Irish Agreement provided the shock to the system that has made a lot of Unionists think more fundamentally than probably many did before.

"They thought they could live permanently behind the protection of the veto and somehow preserve a Unionist Orange card that was always trumps — the ace of trumps — that would always be delivered and they did not really have to consider the position.

"I think they now recognise they do have to consider seriously a fair basis on which the Government can continue."

The programme is a sequel to a Panorama investigation 'The Long War' which was screened earlier this year.

Pact faces court test

THE Anglo-Irish Ulster Agreement, due to reach its third anniversary in November, faces a major test on constitutional grounds in the High Court this week.

The challenge is being mounted by two prominent members of the Unionist party — brothers Christopher and Michael McGimpsey — utilising sections of the Irish constitution that stake claim to the whole island of Ireland.

The brothers, one of whom holds a degree from Dublin's Trinity College, believe the intergovernmental pact runs counter to the terms of the 51-year-old constitution.

They have so far raised half of the £85,000 estimated costs fo the action, and engaged a team of top Dublin lawyers to fight their corner.

The case, which begins on Tuesday, is expected to last up to five days and end with a reserved judgement. The issue could be taken on to the Supreme Court.

Legal opinion is split over the prospects of success for this first legal challenge to the pact.

1989

On the international front, 1989 will be remembered as the year that marked the end of communism in Europe. People power reigned across the continent as uprisings hastened the end of the one-party system that had been in place since the end of World War II. The most symbolic event of the time was the demolition of the wall in Berlin that had separated the two sides of that city. When events in East Germany were hotting up in early November, *Examiner* reporter Des O'Sullivan suggested it might be worth sending him out there. How right he was - on the day that he arrived in Berlin, the dismantling of the wall began. The Iron Curtain was torn down, brick by brick.

The Communist Party in China was one of the old regimes that did manage to survive a popular uprising when it sent in tanks against the student demonstrators in Tiananmen Square, Beijing. Ayatollah Khomeni of Iran issued a fatwah against Salman Rushdie for his 'blasphemy' after the publication of his novel *The Satanic Verses*. The writer's chances of having the call to killing rescinded dwindled when Khomeni died soon afterwards.

The man who keeps faith with communism

Monday, June 19

Michael O'Riordan was only 11 years old when he made his first stand against establishment thinking. "I refused to learn Irish going to school," he said. "It was identified with the formation of the new Irish Free State." He saw the folly of that particular protest later on. He has believed for nigh on 50 years that the two most important languages in the world today are Russian and Irish.

Brenda Fricker and Daniel Day Lewis both won Academy Awards for their roles in **My Left Foot.**

He is National Chairman of the Communist Party of Ireland. Five years ago, when he retired from full-time work with the party, he had the distinction of being the longest serving general secretary of any Communist Party in the world.

"We are becoming more acceptable, people no longer cross to the other side of the street when they see me coming and bless themselves," he said with a smile.

The fact that Michael O'Riordan was born five days after the October Revolution in Russia in 1917 continues to give him satisfaction.

He wondered why he hadn't been asked about Cork during the interview. "I like the Cork sense of humour and the feeling of 'we are all together,' but what I don't like about Cork is the merchant princes. They are terrible bloody snobs."

Thanks a million, says delighted Rita

Friday, May 12

Lotto millionaire Rita Power from Co Galway yesterday travelled to the National Lottery headquarters in Dublin to pick up her cheque for £1.2 million.

The 45-year-old farmer's wife from Portumna hopes that her new-found wealth will bring her family back together again – three of her four children have had to go to England to find work. The Power family were accompanied by their relatives, friends, parish priest, bank manager, solicitor and Billy Salmon, the owner of the newsagent in Portumna where Rita purchased her ticket.

Rita and her family and friends drank champagne and enjoyed a sing-song at the National Lottery headquarters. She plans to have a big 'hooley' in Portumna, but as yet has not decided on a date.

A shy retiring woman, Rita said she had no plans to leave her home in Portumna: "Why should I? I have a nice home and great neighbours and friends," she said.

Ireland's first Lotto millionaire, Rita Power.

NEWS BRIEFS

Oct Three of the Guildford Four, wrongly imprisoned in Britain since 1975 for being involved with an IRA bombing campaign, are released. (19)

Dec Reclusive Irish playwright Samuel Beckett was buried in strict secrecy in a Paris cemetery yesterday, four days after he died at the age of 83. The Nobel Prize winning writer lies next to his wife, Suzanne, whom he had met after she helped him to hospital when he was mugged in 1938. (27)

The Cork Examiner

No. 52,070 SATURDAY MORNING, NOVEMBER 11, 1989 Price 60p (inc. VAT)

BERLIN REUNITED

Troops begin to demolish the Wall

EAST GERMANY'S RULERS last night sent their troops to tear down part of the hated Berlin Wall, and promised their rebellious people free elections and sweeping reforms. The longed-for demolition started quietly.

Just two soldiers began taking down a section of barrier in a side street to be used as a new crossing point from today and later a bulldozer arrived to clear away part of the concrete structure.

Meanwhile a government minister said all travel restrictions had been scrapped — and would remain scrapped.

INSIDE

News that the Wall was at last tumbling was broken to 20,000 wildly cheering people in the West of the divided city by West German Foreign Minister, Hans-Dietrich Genscher.

He said on Friday that East Germany will start knocking down portions of the Wall at the Potsdamer Platz and that 18 new border crossings would be opened.

As the most solid symbol of the Cold War divide in Europe at last began to crumble West German Chancellor Helmut Kohl said he wants to meet East German leader Egon Krenz straightaway — either today or tomorrow.

Mr Kohl told thousands of cheering Berliners that West and East Germany belonged together and had to work for a common future.

"We are and will remain one nation and we belong together," he said at a rally outside West Berlin's town hall last night.

East German leader Egon Krenz: Due to have urgent talks with West German Chancellor Helmut Kohl.

Changes striking at the very heart of communist domination in the East were announced by the policy-making Central Committee and the end of an astonishing three-day session.

"East Germany is awakening," said the official ADN news agency.

An "action programme" to be implemented a new government to replace the one that resigned on Tuesday calls for new laws on freedom to assemble and freedom of association as well as new media and election laws.

The judiciary should be able to work independently from the communist party, it said, and parliament should have control over the defence and state security ministries.

Police said more than 100,000 people from all over East Germany crossed into West Berlin yesterday after a night of celebrating the opening of the Berlin Wall and other borders for the first time in 28 years.

"Last night the Germans were the happiest people in the world," West Berlin Mayor Walter Momper said.

The party continued yesterday as revelers popped champagne corks, lit sparklers and embraced on both sides of the border.

"The Berlin Wall will come down, and Berlin will live," said former

Continued on page 8, column 5.

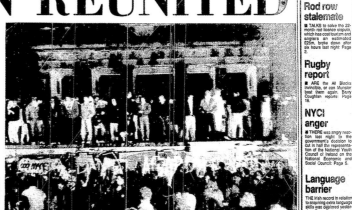

CROWDS ON THE WALL: Berliners from the East and the West crowd in front of the Brandenburg gates yesterday, celebrating after the announcement by the East German authorities that they were to dismantle the Berlin Wall and to open more border crossing within the next few days.

Krenz fights for time as East Germans taste freedom

***CORK EXAMINER* reporter DES O'SULLIVAN (right) was in Berlin yesterday where he met East Germans on their first visit to the West. He watched the celebrations after it was announced that the Berlin Wall was to be dismantled. It had divided the city for nearly three decades. Our reporter also spoke to East Germans who visited the West, looked in the shop windows, and decided to return to the East. This is his report.**

AS THOUSANDS of celebrating East Berliners brought central areas of West Berlin to a virtual standstill last night Egon Krenz was desperately buying time with their fellow citizens on the Eastern side of the hated Wall.

Without saying when they would be held the East German leader identified free elections and radical social reform as the two main planks of his action programme.

His first initiative, Krenz told a 10,000 strong party rally Marx-Engels Plaz, had been to open the Border. This was done to renew the confidence of the people in the party.

The Border is to be kept open as the East German authorities are now anxious to build up trust amongst the people.

But as Krenz adressed a rally of party faithful in East Berlin far greater numbers were celebrating their new found freedom in the West. The scenes in West Berlin last night were in stark contrast to the sombre communist party rally on the other side of the Berlin Wall.

There was wild jubilation with crowds thronging the streets. From midnight the previous night when the first wave of an estimated 20,000 East Berliners crossed into the West Border checkpoints had been thronged with travellers coming West, many having their first glimpse of West Berlin.

They spent the day sightseeing, looking in amazement at the shop windows with their wide range of consumer goods, and visiting friends and relatives.

They were quite obviously delighted to be in the West. One East Berliner, who I spoke to on the Western side, said it was a very special day for Germans. This sentiment was echoed enthusiastically by West Berliners.

The people mixed very easily and happily on the streets. There was spontaneous handclapping, dancing, cheering as crowds spilled over from the pavements onto the streets.

Gradually city centre traffic came to a complete standstill, the buses stopped running, diversions went into operation and an atmosphere of carnival high spiritedness prevailed.

There was evidence that many of the East Berliners were happy just to come and look and then go home again. On the Eastern side of the Wall a young man who had just got back told me he had been delighted to see West Berlin but that he was not prepared to give up his flat and his family to go and live there.

Berliner kneels on top of the wall near the Brandenburger Gate yesterday morning, and uses a hammer and chisel to demolish the Berlin Wall which has divided the city for nearly three decades.

In East Berlin there were long queues of people at the checkpoints. Many seemed unable to believe that they were to be allowed to travel to the West and to come back again. Though most East Berliners have been willing to talk to foreign journalists and to air their many grievances those in the queues were decidedly reluctant to become involved in discussions.

Mr. Krenz highlighted the importance of building up the trust of the people and it is quite obvious that many of his citizens need to have this trust proven. They are not taking too much for granted just yet.

From about midday yesterday there were large queues of East Berliners at passport control points leading into their country. They were the ones who were going back. Thousands and thousands of visits took place yesterday and though many stayed to keep on celebrating large numbers returned home.

Col. Gerhard Lauter, head of the passport and registration office for East Germany said on television that the measures had been adopted by the Government on the initiative of the SED (The Socialist Party of the German Democratic Republic).

The new regulations had gone into force with immediate affect and thousands of people had gone to the Border crossing points spontaneously. To prevent a situation developing action was taken to abandon red tape and to allow people without valid visas to cross the Border.

Col. Lauter appealed to people to go to their local police stations and apply for a visa for private trips or permanent exit. It was important, he insisted, that trust in the new policy was fully established. He expressed the hope that the new measures would reduce the numbers who were leaving for good.

A the lifting of the travel restrictions was widely welcomed in the West the central committee of the SED, on the last day of their three-day meeting, made further personnell changes in the Politburo and announced an investigation into corruption.

The East German prosecuter suggested that a paliamentary committee be established to investigate charges of corruption and power abuse by state and party officials

Continued on Page 8, Column 1.

Clashes in Soviet Moldavia

NATIONALISTS in Soviet Moldavia fought police and troops in the republic's capital late last night and unofficial reports said dozens of people were injured, some seriously.

Eyewitnesses said the clashes erupted after a crowd of several thousand demonstrators ringed Interior Ministry headquarters in Kishinyov.

They protested against the detention of around 20 fellow nationalists who disrupted a parade last Tuesday marking the anniversary of the 1917 Bolshevik revolution.

TODAY

Rod row stalemate

TALKS to solve the 22-month rod licence dispute, which has cost tourism and anglers an estimated £25m, broke down after six hours last night: Page 2.

Rugby report

ARE the All Blacks invincible, or can Munster beat them again. Barry Coughlan reports: Page 16.

NYCI anger

THERE was angry reaction last night to the government's decision to cut in half the representation of the National Youth Council of Ireland on the National Economic and Social Council: Page 5.

Language barrier

THE Irish record in relation to acquiring extra language skills was deplored yesterday: Page 7.

Acid test

THE organiser of an acid house party in Britain was jailed for ten years: Page 8.

Cot deaths

PROFESSOR Gerald Cussen of UCC, head of the Irish Sudden Infant Death Association, focused yesterday on cot deaths, the most common cause of death in infants between the age of one month and one year: Page 9.

Index

1990

The Republic of Ireland's performances at Italia '90 sparked the greatest outpouring of joy and public euphoria ever seen in the state. The team's first World Cup transcended anything resembling a sports event as the nation happily partied for three weeks until the foot of Italian striker Toto Schillaci brought it all to an end in the quarter final.

An estimated one million people welcomed the boys in green back to Dublin, an event that helped limit the impact of recently-released Nelson Mandela's visit to the capital.

In politics, Mary Robinson, a 33-1 outsider, became the first woman president of Ireland. Hot favourite Brian Lenihan's campaign faltered over untruths he told on television and an attempt by his colleague Pádraig Flynn to discredit Robinson backfired when a deeply personal attack against her on radio aroused much public sympathy.

Nelson Mandela and his wife Winnie salute the crowd on their first visit to Dublin.

Italia '90 celebrations

Tuesday, June 26

They were very late bringing in the cows across the fertile dairying lands of Munster last night. But it had more to do with a super save by Packie Bonner and super goals by the Genoa Five than with the super levy.

For the World Cup had even disrupted the peak of the milk production season as farmers and their families sat glued to their television sets. It was like the time the little North Koreans attracted men from the bogs on the Cork Kerry border during the 1966 finals in England.

But this World Cup penalty shoot-out will go down in folklore alongside the night of the big wind, the deeds of Master McGrath and the bouts of boxer Jack Doyle. For it embraced all of the human emotions and provided material galore for the ballad-makers who are now likely to elevate Packie from the Rosses and Darling Dave O'Leary to the same tuneful status of Bould Thady Quill. - Ray Ryan

Team medic Charles O'Leary, and the rest of the Irish entourage, chat with the Pope during their visit to the Vatican.

Mandela gets a rousing welcome

Monday, July 2

The deputy leader of the African National Congress, Mr Nelson Mandela, received a rousing welcome when he arrived in Dublin yesterday on his state visit to Ireland.

Although the visit was overshadowed by the homecoming of Ireland's soccer heroes, about 2,000 people cheered the South African civil rights leader from the balconies of Dublin Airport and waved ANC black, green and yellow flags.

He told his Irish supporters of his interest in Ireland which he said attracted him by its history of fighting for human rights and self determination. He thanked the Irish Congress of Trade Unions for opposing apartheid over many years and he paid a special tribute to the workers in Dunnes Stores who had carried on their strike against apartheid for almost three years up to April 1987 when they lost their jobs.

Majestic Mary

Saturday, November 10

A new phase in Irish history began last night when constitutional lawyer Mary Robinson swept into power as Ireland's first woman president. The result showed her with a whopping 86,557 votes over her nearest rival, the Fianna Fáil presidential nominee Brian Lenihan.

Mrs Robinson's acceptance speech was joyful and enthusiastic as she praised those who had stepped out from the faded flags of the Civil War and voted for a new Ireland.

"It's a great day for Irishwomen," a jubilant Mary Robinson said. "The women of Ireland went out to vote because they had a sense of purpose. This is a great day for them and for their children."

NEWS BRIEFS

Feb The Soviet Union's top Communists yesterday voted to ask parliament to end the Party's monopoly on power in a dramatic move that should clear the way for a multi-party system. (8)

July Steps to stop the spread of mad cow disease in Ireland were taken with an order banning the feeding of meat and bonemeal to cattle, sheep, goats and deer. (26)

Aug Belfast man Brian Keenan has been released by Islamic Jihad after spending more than four years in captivity in Beirut. (24)

Nov The Thatcher era came to a dramatic end yesterday as Britain's Prime Minister swallowed the bitter pill of resignation. Europe turned out to be Margaret Thatcher's graveyard. She fought so hard to keep it at bay that she ultimately rendered her trenchant views irrelevant. (23)

Better than '66 says Big Jack: Page 17

The Cork Examiner

No. 52,258 TUESDAY MORNING, JUNE 26, 1990 Price 60p (inc. VAT)

THE SAVIOUR

Rome awaits the Green army

THE CARDIAC KIDS ride on! Ireland's death-defying heroes climbed to astonishing new heights last night — and sent a nation into unprecedented rapture.

TONY LEEN writes from GENOA

A nerve-tingling 5-4 penalty shoot-out victory over Rumania has won its eternal place in soccer folklore.

It sends us to Rome to take on hosts, Italy.

It will undoubtedly be the greatest moment in our brief soccer heritage.

And at this stage, who is going to bet against the impossible dream continuing?

"Winning the World Cup in 1966 was wonderful, but I think this was even more wonderful," reckoned the-man-who-can-do-no-wrong, Jack Charlton.

But the magnificent eleven are not thinking that far ahead yet.

"We'll think of them when we sober up," said Big Jack after the game.

The 20,000 strong Irish support at the game was an undoubted tonic for the troops.

Said team boss Charlton: "Where did they all come from?".

It was the biggest travelling army of soccer fans in living memory.

Heroes of the hour were Packie Bonner and the iceman, David O'Leary.

After Bonner had saved the Rumanians fifth spot kick, O'Leary strode forward and planted the winner with the eyes of the world fixed squarely on him.

It was an unbelievable climax — pure melodrama.

And what a moment for O'Leary in his first, and probably last World Cup.

"I had made up my mind before I hit it. I was determined to take that fifth penalty.

"I wasn't that nervous really, but I was glad to see it hit the back of the net."

Said Bonner: "I was able to judge by the way he walked up to the ball which way it was going".

The Irish backroom staff had secretly ordered champagne before the game. It was cracked open with a vengeance once the on-field celebrations finally died down.

An enormous exodus from Genoa commenced last night, and will continue today.

But already, Rome is bracing itself for the battle of the two largest followings in the competition.

The Irish fans proved they have surpassed the famed Brazilian support for dedication and manners.

The FAI is smiling too from ear to ear.

Qualification for the last eight entitles them to a greater share of the £50 million profits than heretofore.

It will set them up for years to come.

For the first time since the adventure began on June 11, the Irish who remained in Genoa last night were able to have a monumental celebration.

Bars ignored the alcohol ban — a testimony to the superb Irish support.

Some of the players were overcome afterwards. Captain, Mick McCarthy, close to tears, repeatedly spoke of the huge Irish support.

"I just can't believe them," he kept on saying.

TODAY

Summit accord

■ THE EC summit in Dublin yesterday agreed to have negotiations on political union: Page 4, 24.

Takeover bid denied

■ SPECULATION that Larry Goodman is set to move on a massive £230m takeover bid for Golden Vale in Tipperary has been discounted by both sides: Page 3.

Rushdie sends aid

■ AUTHOR Salman Rushdie, sentenced to death by the late Ayatollah Khomeini, yesterday contributed £5,000 to the Iran earthquake appeal: Page 8.

Bush on violence

■ PRESIDENT Bush yesterday urged ANC leader Nelson Mandela to renounce violence: Page 9.

Index

■ *SAVE OF A LIFETIME: Ireland's Pakie Bonner saves the penalty, struck by Romania's Timofte. Bonner's save allowed David O'Leary to score Ireland's fifth penalty and qualify to meet Italy in the World Cup quarter finals, in Rome, on Saturday.* *(Picture: EDDIE O'HARE)*

Then the nation went wild

Report: T. P. O'MAHONY

THE nation went to the brink, the nation gambled, the nation won — and then the nation went wild.

It was the soccer equivalent of the shoot-out at the OK Corral, and Ireland's nerve held when it counted most.

Bonnar in goal was the secondary cause of victory in the most extreme of circumstances.

He saved the vital last penalty from Romania.

But it was David O'Leary who signed the tickets for Rome by putting the ball in the back of the net.

It was nerve-racking stuff. But the gods of soccer were with us — and it is on now to the Eternal City.

After this, who knows?

In the centre of Cork lines of trucks, cars and taxis led by delighted, flag-carrying fans held the city to ransom. Or so it seemed.

But nobody minded.

It was that kind of night.

And it was repeated in villages, towns and cities all over the country in a collective celebration of national spirit, determination, courage and character.

In pubs, clubs and hotels all over the town and the nation, people who were strangers at the kick-off behaved like lovers at the end of the penalty shoot-out.

Embracing has suddenly become a national pastime. And long may it last.

Romance was in the air last night. Barriers of shyness, propriety, and decorum came down when that last vital ball rattled the back of the Romanian net.

It was a victory whose ramifications deserved to be celebrated *urbe et orbi* — not just nationwide, but worldwide.

Rome is another day and another chapter. And we wait in vibrant anticipation the outcome of the next stage in what has been an unforgettable World Cup for the boys in green.

But the glory will not be diminished if this gallant run comes to an end on the banks of the Tiber.

When Barry Healy made a pronouncement in a Cork pub last night, he little thought that he was speaking for a nation on edge.

"My heart will never be the same again," he said, to loud cheers.

His and the nation's hearts will settle back, of course, to something approximating to normality.

But the great festival of endeavour and pride will start all over again on Saturday.

And if the gods are kind we shall witness again scenes which boggle the imagination.

Standing amid screaming fans in a pub off Cork's central thoroughfare, Maurice Brennan made one of the most salient comments of all.

"It all goes to show that we can go beyond this narrow preoccupation with this island on the edge of Europe.

"In the aftermath of victory, it seems like collective madness, but what our performance as a team and as supporters really show is that we are much bigger than this island on which we live — we are part of a universal community, and we bring to it qualities which nobody else can match!"

To which we can only say — *Olé!*

As for Rome, we will leave it to those strange deities who have looked after us so far, and in whose hands our destiny now rests.

■ *CELEBRATION: Frank O'Brien from Tallow, Co. Waterford, celebrating Ireland's penalty-shoot-out win over Romania last night.* *(Picture: PADDY BARKER)*

Streets erupt in explosion of joy

THE streets of this soccer-mad nation were empty at 4 o'clock yesterday afternoon. It was as if a nation-wide bomb alert has been issued.

But it took two-and-a-half hours for the explosion to erupt — when Dave O'Leary detonated a penalty in the Romanian net, clinching Ireland's place in the World Cup quarter finals.

Seconds later, the country erupted in a state of frenzied excitement. The boys in green did it — and we were given a reason to party. Oh what a party!

Every corner of the island was a riot of colour and excitement, with massive crowds taking to the streets to revel in our World Cup achievement.

Folks went wild in Dublin, Cork, Waterford, Limerick, Galway and Donegal. (Oh God bless Donegal!) And every hamlet and crossroads throughout the Republic also held its own impromptu street hooley.

But it was all good clean fun, and the gardai gave the good-humoured fans their vote of approval.

Never in Ireland's history has so much joy been given to so many — by so few. Within seconds of O'Leary's decisive penalty kick, the country took on the chaotic splendour of Rio in carnival time. In Cork, it was Mardi Gras on 'Pana'.

Thousands of ebullient citizens rushed headlong into the street to give vent to their unbridled passion.

Cars, bedecked in green, white and orange made their way joyously through the city centre, horns blaring in unison, adults and children clinging to doors, windows and sun-roofs.

Three enterprising fans were given a roller coaster ride up and down Cork's Patrick Street in a speeding shoping trolley. Next to beer, it was the fastest moving thing in Cork.

An elated Taoiseach, Charles Haughey, though preoccupied with the EC summit in Dublin, found time to relay his congraultations to the players and to Jack Charlton. He danced for joy in the courtyard of Dublin Castle as our proud soccer men wrote World Cup history.

"We are absolutley over the moon", he enthused. He lived the pulsating final moments of the Genoa shoot-out watching a TV set, the very success of the EC summit depending, it seemed, on a kick of the ball.

Mrs Thatcher, also at the talks, said she was "enthralled" at the televised shoot-out and relayed her delight to Mr Haughey immediately.

In fact, all 120 TV sets at Dublin Castle — officially there to provide information on delegation briefings — were instead tuned into the big match.

Meanwhile, bar owners all over the country came in for a welcome windfall.

Many publicans estimated that the previous success netted them tens of thousand of pounds.

INSIDE

■ FIVE pages of World Cup coverage: Pages 13, 14, 15, 16 & 17.

Now, the team's holy preparation

THE Republic of Ireland soccer heroes are set for a surprise audience with his holiness, Pope John Paul II, this week, it was learned last night.

Sources said the meeting had been provisionally planned for tomorrow — depending on the papal schedule.

The audience is not a direct consequence of last night's Genoa heroics.

Donegal-born Monsignor Liam O'Boyle has been working behind the scenes to arrange the Vatican visit for some weeks.

He is believed to have got positive news yesterday to co-incide with his 60th birthday.

1991

Iraq's invasion of its neighbour Kuwait in 1990 had prompted UN resolutions and threats of military intervention. When a UN deadline for withdrawal passed on January 16, the bombing of Iraq by US and British planes marked the start of the Gulf War.

It only took six weeks for Saddam Hussein's forces to be comprehensively defeated, but the Iraqi dictator did hold on to power. Ireland's involvement in the war came through the use of Shannon Airport by US forces.

Dublin was European City of Culture, and *The Commitments*, a film adaptation of Roddy Doyle's story of a blues band in the capital, was an international success.

Free at last

Friday, March 16

After 16 years they are free. Just before 4 o'clock yesterday afternoon Gerry Hunter, Paddy Hill, Billy Power, Hugh Callaghan, Johnny Walker and Richard McIlkenny were free men for the first time since 1974.

The long years of waiting came to an end for the Six when they were asked to stand by Chief Justice Lloyd, immediately after the defence had rebutted allegations from the Crown that they were guilty men.

In the light of fresh evidence, he said that their appeal was allowed and that they were free men – to scenes of initial disbelief, and then spontaneous applause throughout the courtroom. Shortly afterwards, outside the Old Bailey, the Six voiced their condemnation of the British judiciary.

Mr Paddy Hill said the British judiciary were not fit to try and judge cases involving Irish people.

One of the Guildford Four, Mr Paul Hill, released in 1989, said: "What needs to be exposed is not the fact that they've been found innocent, but the fact that they've been waiting for 17 years to be proved innocent."

Quickly afterwards, the men were whisked away for a reunion with friends and family in the Irish Centre – the first of many to come.

The Birmingham Six celebrate their release with Chris Mullan, a Labour MP who had campaigned on their behalf. In the background is Paul Hill of the Guildford Four.

NEWS BRIEFS

Feb Rock group U2 offer to pay the £500 fine imposed on the Irish Family Planning Association for selling condoms in the Virgin Megastore in Dublin. The law dictates that condoms may only be sold to those over 18 at chemists or outlets approved by the Department of Health. (28)

Apr Writer Seán O'Faoláin dies in a Dublin nursing home, aged 91. He had fought in the War of Independence and won acclaim for his portrayal of Irish life after the creation of the Free State. (21)

May The Goodman Group reject claims made in an ITV World in Action documentary on the Irish meat industry. Allegations of political connections with Fianna Fáil, the use of bogus stamps and the re-boxing of meat were described as "outrageous" by the company. Fall-out from the programme would lead to a lengthy tribunal into the beef industry. (14)

Sept New York's Metropolitan Taxicab Board of Trade offers to provide 1,500 work opportunity letters to Irish people applying for the Morrison visas. The visas will be distributed on a lottery basis and 48,000 of them have been earmarked for Irish people over three years. (2)

Drugs seized at rave party

Monday, June 17

Gardaí seized quantities of ecstasy – now the most popular drug after cannabis on the Cork drug scene – during a swoop on teenagers who attended a disco party night at the City Hall on Saturday.

A team of 30 uniformed and plain-clothes Gardaí mounted a successful operation outside the venue. They made on-the-spot searches of dozens of partygoers throughout the city centre and in streets near the City Hall. Various quantities of ecstasy, amphetamines and cannabis were seized and taken away for analysis.

The disco – billed as the 'Banba Rave' party and hyped as the gig of the year – attracted a crowd of over 1,500 young people. The revellers were generally well behaved and little trouble was reported. The event showcased DJs from Ireland and Britain on stage. Special lighting effects and smoke were featured on the dance floor.

The seizures brought further confirmation that ecstasy is not only widely available in Cork but has become the most sought-after drug after cannabis. It has a street value of about £30 to £35 per tab. It causes euphoric feelings and heightens sexual activity.

Gardaí are concerned that it could promote promiscuity among young people and spread AIDS.

The Cork Examiner

No. 52,432 THURSDAY MORNING, JANUARY 17, 1991 Price 65p (inc. VAT)

BAGHDAD POUNDED AS WAR RAGES

Allies blast key targets

WAR ERUPTED in the Gulf late last night as President Bush hurled the world's mightiest airforce against Iraq.

Waves of US and British fighter planes and bombers roared low over the desert sands and across the Saudi Arabian border to strike military targets deep within Iraq.

Anti-aircraft fire lit up the night sky and air raid sirens screamed across Baghdad as bombs pounded the Iraqi capital.

The order to launch Operation Desert Storm at 11pm GMT came from the White House.

"The liberation of Kuwait has begun," presidential spokesman Marlin Fitzwater said.

President Bush, who addressed the American people at 2am GMT, consulted British Prime Minister John Major before the offensive got under way.

The aerial bombardment of Baghdad continued through the night with waves of three or four planes coming every 15 minutes to attack the city.

Eyewitness reports from America's Cable News Network said the planes were flying high above the anti-aircraft fire flaring over the city.

"They are just unloading their hardware and they are heading off. The planes are flying through a lot of flak but they seem intent on hitting specific targets and getting on their way," one CNN reporter said in a live report.

As the reporters crawled across the floor of their hotel room, a massive explosion some distance away rocked the building.

"If you look out you see bright flashes of light on the ground. Due west there's more fire going up," one reporter said.

And as the sound of huge explosion ripped across the broadcast, he added: "That was a big blast. I could feel it through the window. I'm going to back away from the window now."

An RAF spokesman in Bahrain confirmed that Tornado ground attack aircraft took off at 0215 local time (1115 GMT) to mount attacks in Kuwait and Iraq.

Two Victor refuelling aircraft also took off to keep the Tornados in the air for the maximum possible time.

Reuter reported that British troops in Bahrain donned chemical war protection suits and gas masks.

Telephone links to Baghdad from Britain were cut after the attack was launched.

In Saudi Arabia, reporters were being shepherded into air raid shelters as sirens went off amid fears that the Iraqis would retaliate.

ITN's Jeremy Thompson was in the middle of telling viewers there had been no Iraqi reaction when he was hurried off the air down to his hotel's air raid shelter as yet another warning went off.

"So far it's reported the Iraqis have not reacted, though we've had a number of air raid warnings in the last hour and have been sent to the air raid shelter," he said before cutting short his report.

As the news flashed across the world that a war had begun:

- NATO called an emergency meeting of ambassadors from the 16 allied nations, scheduled to take place in Brussels at 2.30am GMT.
- Israel ordered its citizens to stay at home and prepare for a possible Iraqi chemical weapons attack.
- Oil prices shot up more than five dollars in early Far East trading.

In Saudi Arabia, Sky News reporter Aernout van Lynden said shortly before 1.45am that he had been ordered to the air raid shelter as he had been told missiles were heading for Dhahran.

President Bush followed the progress of the war from the Oval Office in the White House, but Baghdad remained silent on the hostilities.

There was no word of the whereabouts of Saddam, who on Wednesday took personal command of his one-million strong armed forces.

Saudi jets were also involved in the attack, a spokesman at the Saudi Embassy in Washington said.

He said he did not know how many American and British planes were involved, but that the Saudis alone had 150 F-15s and Tornados taking part.

The United States received Saudi agreement before launching the strike.

NBC television reported that the White House learned the attack in Baghdad had actually begun from a live US television report on the scene and not from the Pentagon.

It also reported that the attack in Baghdad started with Tomahawk cruise missiles, followed up by F-15s.

The bomb attacks seemed to be aimed at the top Iraqi command centre as well as the communication sites in the city, the report said.

Iraqi missiles aimed at Israel were also bombed, the Israeli Army said.

Asked whether missile sites on Iraq's western border had been attacked, Brigadier-General Zeev Livneh told Israel Television: "Yes, we know that area has been under attack from the start of the American air attack and we very much hope that the missile system ... took a serious hit."

■ *President Bush: This will not be another Vietnam.*

Bush tells world 'we won't fail'

AMERICAN president George Bush this morning told the world that Allied forces were attacking military targets in Iraq and Kuwait in a conflict begun by Iraqi leader Saddam Hussein.

In a solemn address from the White House in Washington, President Bush said: "Saddam Hussein started this cruel war against Kuwait. Tonight the battle has been joined."

Opening his address, Mr Bush said the Allied attack had begun just two hours earlier on military targets in Iraq and Kuwait.

"These attacks continue as I speak," the American president said.

Ground forces were not engaged in the conflict, he told Americans.

In his televised address the President said that the allied forces would crush Iraq's chemical and nuclear weapons capability in the drive to liberate Kuwait.

Mr Bush blamed the Iraqi leader for the conflict which had begun five months earlier with the invasion of Kuwait.

"This conflict started August 2 when the dictator of Iraq invaded a small and helpless neighbour," said the President.

"Kuwait, a member of the Arab League and United Nations was crushed. Its people brutalised."

He said military action had been taken in accord with United Nations resolutions and with the consent of the US Congress.

The strike had followed "months of constant and virtually endless diplomatic activity" on the part of the UN, the US and many other countries, he said.

"This will not be another Vietnam and I repeat this here today — our troops will have the best possible support in the entire world and they will not be asked to fight with one hand tied behind their backs," said a solemn President Bush.

He said America together with the UN "exhausted every means at our disposal to bring this crisis to a peaceful end".

"However, Saddam clearly felt that by stalling, threatening and defying the United Nations he could undermine the forces arraigned against him. He met our overtures of peace with open contempt."

The President said the objectives of war were to force Saddam out of Kuwait, restore a legitimate government and restore peace.

He said the allies had no other alternative but to "drive Saddam Hussein from Kuwait by force ... we will not fail".

Mr Bush reiterated the allies determination to target Iraq's vast military arsenals and chemical weapons capabilities.

"As I report to you, air attacks are under way against military targets in Iraq. We are determined to knock out Saddam Hussein's nuclear bomb potential. We will also destroy his chemical weapons facilities."

In the 12-minute address he said: "Saddam was warned over and over again to comply with the will of the United Nations; leave Kuwait or be driven out.

"Instead he tried to make this dispute between Iraq and the United States of America. Well, he failed.

"Tonight, 28 countries have forces in the Gulf area standing shoulder to shoulder against Saddam Hussein.

"These countries had hoped the use of force could be avoided. Regrettably, we now believe that only force will make him leave."

Mr Bush said he prayed for the safety of innocent people caught up in the war which he referred to as "not the conquest of Iraq but the liberation of Kuwait".

And he urged the Iraqi people to "convince their dictator that he must lay down his arms and let Iraq join the family of peace loving nations".

He said that "out of the horror of combat will come the recognition that no nation can stand against a world united" or "brutalise" a nation.

■ **Gulf special: Pages 14 and 15.**

We'll drive Saddam out, says Allied chief

ALLIED commander Major-General Norman Schwarzkopf told his men in the Gulf today that Operation Desert Storm would drive Iraq's occupation armies from Kuwait.

Soon after wave upon wave of allied bombers pounded strategic targets in Iraq and occupied Kuwait, the general said:

"This morning ... we launched Operation Desert Storm, an offensive campaign that will enforce UN resolutions that Iraq must cease its rape and pillage of its weaker neighbour and withdraw its forces from Kuwait."

Gen Schwarzkopf told troops in a statement: "My confidence in you is total. Our cause is just."

Said Schwarzkopf: "Soldiers, sailors, airmen and Marines of United States Central Command. This morning at 0300 hours (0000 GMT) we launched operation "Desert Storm," an offensive campaign that will enforce United Nations resolutions that Iraq must cease its rape and pillage of its weaker neighbour and withdraw its forces from Kuwait.

"The President, the Congress, the American people and indeed the world stand united in their support for your actions.

"You are a member of the most powerful force, our country, in coalition with our allies, has ever assembled in a single theatre to face such an aggressor. You have trained hard for this battle and you are ready.

"During my visits with you, I have seen in your eyes a fire of determination to get this job done quickly so that we may all return to the shores of our great nation.

"My confidence in you is total. Our cause is just. Now you must be the thunder and lightning of Desert Storm. May God be with you, your loved ones at home and our country," he concluded.

■ *President Saddam: Bush blamed him for starting cruel war.*

LUXEMBOURG early yesterday called an emergency meeting of European Community foreign and defence ministers in Paris, after US-led military forces launched an attack on Iraqi forces.

A government spokesman in Luxembourg, which currently holds the rotating EC presidency, said the meeting would take place at 1600 GMT.

Jean-Pierr Kasel, political director of Luxembourg's foreign ministry, told Reuters the talks would take place during an already planned meeting of the Western European Union (WEU).

The WEU, which groups nine European countries that are members of the EC and Nato, had been due to hold a meeting of foreign and defence ministers in Paris.

A largely consultative body on defence matters, the WEU has been co-ordinating much of the European naval contribution to the UN-imposed blockade of Iraq.

Oil prices soar

OIL prices shot up more than five dollars in early Far East trading last night after news of the outbreak of war.

Cargoes of West Texas Intermediate crude oil were bid at 37 dollars and offered at 38 dollars against 32 dollars at the New York close yesterday, oil traders in Tokyo said.

Crude oil almost instantly hit 35 dollars a barrel in cash trading in New Orleans and Houston and soared to 40 dollars, after closing at 32 dollars on Wednesday, on the New York Mercantile Exchange.

1992

The abortion issue was prominent for much of the year when the High Court granted an injunction preventing a 14-year-old rape victim from travelling to England to terminate her pregnancy.
The Supreme Court subsequently overturned the decision, taking the view that the life of a possibly suicidal mother takes precedence over that of her unborn child.
Two of Ireland's most prominent personas bowed out of public life in shame with the resignation of Bishop Eamonn Casey and Taoiseach Charles Haughey.
Casey's fathering of a child many years previously was the first of a number of major scandals during the decade that would undermine the Catholic Church's exalted position in Irish society.
He was an outspoken campaigner for social justice with a cheery, affable personality and messages of tribute and support came from many sections of Irish society. Poet and academic Brendan Kennelly referred to Casey as "the least hypocritical man in Ireland" while the *Examiner* headlined its editorial on his resignation, "Bishop will be sorely missed."
The Kerry-born Bishop of Galway did lose more public support when details of the rejection of his son emerged.
Past deeds also came back to haunt Haughey who was forced to resign when it was revealed he knew about the phone tapping of journalists' phones for which the then Minister for Justice Seán Doherty had taken the rap a decade earlier.
Ireland won two medals at the Barcelona Olympics courtesy of boxers from very big families; Belfast's Wayne McCullough was one of seven children, while Michael Carruth from Dublin was one of nine.

Bishop wanted baby adopted

Saturday, May 9

The woman at the centre of the Bishop Casey resignation storm, Ms Annie Murphy, claimed yesterday that he tried to "brainwash" her and force her into giving up the baby for adoption.
Ms Murphy denied that she initiated the affair with the bishop when she came to Ireland after a bad divorce in 1973. She spoke too of four years of "haggling" before Dr Casey agreed to increase maintenance payments to her.
The relationship broke down, she said, due to the pregnancy and the fact that it could ruin Dr Casey's career as Bishop of Kerry. She alleged: "He led me into brainwashing, that I was an immoral person, that I had to be cleansed and give up the baby because that was God's will and then I would be reborn as a good Christian Catholic person. He gave me many books to read and laboured the subject many times."
She hoped that something good would come out of her story, saying: "I hope people will realise this is 1992 and these things happen. Why should Peter be called a mistake? Why should Peter not be allowed talk to his father? Why should his father dare call my house and not address his son out of fear of the Catholic Church?"

Bishop Eamonn Casey's past misdeeds caught up with him in May.

Olympic medals in Barcelona

Monday, August 14

The UDA commander was in a philosophical mood. He wanted the *Cork Examiner* to know there was no problem about Wayne McCullough boxing for Ireland.
"Alright, a few of the lads don't like the tricolour bit, but he's a Highfield lad who done us all proud. And, for the record, we are just as delighted Michael Carruth won the gold medal," said Billy Courtenay, a man who does not pull punches himself.
Surrounded by a group of lads who had obviously a deep knowledge of combat, unarmed or otherwise, the UDA man insisted there would have been no problem with the Irish national anthem had Wayne won the gold.
"You can always turn the sound down, and you can be bloody certain Wayne doesn't know the words," quipped Mr Courtenay.

NEWS BRIEFS

Oct Ireland's biggest seizure of poitín was made by Gardaí yesterday in a swoop on farmland in West Cork. They discovered a massive haul of 300 gallons of finished poitín hidden in an underground cellar in a remote townland some five miles from Ballineen. (30)

Nov A referendum enshrines in the constitution the right to travel and the right to abortion information, but rejects the right to have an abortion in the state. The referendum had been necessitated by a European Court of Human Rights ruling against Ireland's ban on abortion information. (25)

The Cork Examiner

No. 52,907 THURSDAY MORNING, MAY 7, 1992 Price 70p (inc. VAT)

Weather

■ RAIN, drizzle and fog patches will extend southeastwards this morning. Clearer, dry weather with periods of sunshine will follow. Strong , mild southwest winds. Afternoon temperatures 16 or 17° C. Outlook: Showers in the north will become more widespread during tomorrow.

Priest held in crime probe

Report: VINCENT KELLY

REPUBLICAN priest Patrick Ryan, who was arrested yesterday, was still being held early today at Clonmel Garda station where he is being questioned about serious crime.

A woman, believed to be a friend of the ex-Pallotine priest, was detained earlier in Dublin and is also being held in Clonmel.

The dual arrest came a week after Fr Ryan, a former British extradition target, claimed in a *Cork Examiner* interview that gardaí suspected him of involvement in the £2.8 million Waterford bank robbery last January.

The 62-year-old priest, who was detained last night under Section 30 of the Offences Against the State Act, claimed he had been offered a substantial sum of money for information about the raid, an allegation strongly denied by gardaí.

He was arrested yesterday afternoon by armed Special Branch detectives at Leixlip, Co. Kildare, and taken by high speed convoy to Clonmel.

The Garda Press Office said last night he was being questioned about "serious crime"

Fr Ryan has been under intense security surveillance for some time and last week claimed he had been stopped by gardaí about 40 times in the past three months.

A week ago gardaí arrested the occupants of a house at Mockler's Hill, near Cashel, Co. Tipperary, where Fr Ryan was an overnight guest.

Among items seized from vehicles parked at the back of the house were clothing resembling uniforms, according to garda sources.

The highly controversial cleric was at the centre of a major extradition case in November 1988 in Belgium. But the authorities refused to hand him over to Britain where he was wanted to face charges of conspiracy to

Turn to back page, col. 2

Bishop Casey resigns

Report: VINCENT KELLY

THE KERRY-born Bishop of Galway, Dr. Eamonn Casey (65), has resigned for "personal reasons," the Catholic Press and Information Office confirmed last night.

The bombshell announcement has rocked the Irish Hierarchy, Church sources confirmed.

Bishop Casey, who was born in Firies on April 24, 1927, had been a member of the Irish Episcopal Conference for almost 23 years. He has been chairman of Trocaire, the Hierarchy's agency for Third World Development, since 1973.

The news was conveyed in an after-midnight statement to the media, a move which caused great surprise amongst Church observers.

Said one: "It is unusual for announcements to be made in this manner".

In a statement early this morning, Bishop Casey said he would now be devoting the rest of his active life to working on the Missions.

"In this way, and with the help of God, I will continue my life-long commitment to the Church and his people," he added.

Dr. Casey was Bishop of Kerry from November 1969 to September 1976 when he was installed as Bishop of Galway.

Bishop Casey: resigning for personal reasons

He gave no details of the personal reasons which had prompted him to retire.

But he paid tribute to the people of his diocese, and said that it had been a great privilege to serve them.

The diocese will now be "run" by Msgr. James McLoughlin, the Vicar General, until a replacement is appointed.

In December 1986 Dr. Casey, who at 42 was the youngest Bishop when appointed to Kerry in 1969, was banned from driving for a year and fined £200 by a London Court for drink driving in London.

The court heard that he was more than twice over the drink drive limit when police stopped him for speeding along Bayswater road near Marble Arch.

He later apologised to the people of his diocese, saying that he very much regretted the "embarrassment and hurt" he had caused them by the widely publicised incident.

"I know you will forgive me. Pray for me as I continue to pray for you".

Bishop Casey made his name for his work on behalf of emigrants in the UK

His work with the Catholic Housing Aid Society made headlines all over the world.

A flamboyant clergyman with a love for fast cars, he was a stern critic on occasions of the Government.

He once urged it to break off diplomatic relations with the US over El Salvador, and frequently urged an increase in State aid to the Third World.

UN envoy is hopeful of averting famine

A UNITED Nations envoy in Somalia said yesterday he was encouraged about prospects for averting famine after talks with leaders of warring factions who have reduced the capital Mogadishu to rubble.

Millions of people throughout Somalia face starvation, but an international effort to feed the hungry in Mogadishu is underway.

"I have been encouraged that I found a good response from both sides," said Ambassador Mohammed Sahnoun, who has spent two days in what was recently described as the most terrifying city on earth.

He met self-declared President Ali Mahdi Mohammed and representatives of rival warlord Mohammed Farah Aideed.

Civil war has killed at least 5,000 people since November and left countless others mutilated.

This week a ship arrived in Mogadishu and was for the first time allowed by the several armed bands which control the city to unload its cargo of 5,000 tonnes of food.

A vessel which arrived earlier was turned away without unloading, despite what aid agencies say is the worst famine in Africa today.

In Kenya the UN High Commissioner for Refugees said he would provide relief supplies for the 32,000 Somalian refugees who crossed into eastern Kenya in the last week after new fighting erupted in Somalia's northwest.

■ **A young victim (pictured above) of the Somalian tragedy clings to life, but for how long?**

TODAY

San Francisco is something special

■ TOP spot in our travel page this week is San Francisco, where Tim Vaughan found that in spite of its "tourist-trap" image, the Californian city really has something special: Page 14.

Agri shows at risk

■ FINE GAEL Deputy Jim O'Keeffe (right) said last night that a country-wide bovine T.B. test dispute between the veterinary profession and the Dept. of Agriculture has put agricultural shows at risk. Page 7.

Death of Dietrich

■ MARLENE Dietrich, the legendary femme fatale of the silver screen, died yesterday afternoon in Paris. She was aged 90: Page 4.

Index

Lotto: 12, 18, 17, 11, 7, 29

Postal peace talks

BOTH sides in the postal dispute have agreed to unconditional peace talks, but no date has been set.

Small Firms Association chairman, Peter Faulkner, has called on both sides to meet urgently because the dispute was causing considerable problems for many firms, not only in the capital but in rural areas.

He said despatch of letters by courier costs betweeen £6 and £10 per item compared to the normal 32p.

In additon, overseas contracts in the post were held up, resulting in our international trading reputation being damaged.

An Post management confirmed yesteray that because of the suspension of postal workers in the Dublin payments office, up to 2,600 company employees may not be paid this week.

Communication Managers' Union general secretry Pat Nolan said he had informed Minister Maura Geoghegan Quinn of the union's concern at An Post's refusal to pay its non-suspended Dublin staff.

Communications Workers Union president, Eugene Keenan, told his union's annual conference yesterday that they were realists and were willing to do a deal on the future of An Post, but it would require mutual trust between management and themselves.

Speculation on Apple job losses 'premature'

Report: MICHAEL MOLONEY

APPLE'S director of European operations, Corkman Dan Byrne, last night described speculation on possible job losses at the computer giant's Hollyhill plant as premature.

While a decision about relocating the Cork plant's printed circuit board (PCB) division is not expected until July, the IDA plans to send senior officials to the US for talks with Apple executives.

Speaking from Apple headquarters in Cupertino, California, where he will shortly take up a new senior post, Mr. Byrne said he understood the anxiety and concern in Cork, but stressed that current analysis in respect of their Hollyhill operation was "very much in the investigative stage."

The results of the analysis would not be ready for another couple of months, and at that stage they would be submitted to the corporation for approval or otherwise.

Such analysis was constantly going on in Apple. "In an industry like ours, where competition is always snapping at our heals, we have to look at all scenarios."

A former Apple managing director in Cork, Mr. Byrne added that never a week or a month went by when this was not being done, and "I think it's premature for people to be jumping to conclusions."

Due to take over as vice-President of Customer Support Products Services for Apple USA next month, Mr. Byrne said he could not predict what the outcome would be, or whether there would be job losses.

He said it would be premature to discuss possible alternatives for Holyhill if the PCB division was transfered to the Far East. "There are many possibilities — some have more merit than others."

He said Apple would look at all opportunities and alternatives, and "no stone would be left unturned" depending on the outcome of the analysis currently in progress.

Mr. Byrne said any decision on PCB strategy would be based on a total cost perspective, not just on labour costs alone; other factors such as duties, freights and services were involved. "This is why it is a very complex analysis, which is why it is premature to comment."

The director of the CII's Federation of Electronic and Informatic Industries, Mr. Ed Johnston, said that from contacts in recent days with Apple executives in California and Paris, he had received no negative suggestions about any downgrading of the Cork plant.

■ Further report: Page 3.

"If they are to decide that PCB assembly would cease, the objective then would be to move something of greater added value into the plant. I actually do not feel that the decision, if made, would have any dramatic impact either on the plant or surrounding support

Turn to page 2, col. 4

Abortion demo on ferry

ABOUT 200 Irish women returned from the "abortion trail" to Britain last evening to demonstrate their outrage at the Constitutional ban on abortion.

And the man at the centre of the latest abortion controversy is believed to be having second thoughts about taking legal action.

When the Dun Laoghaire/Holyhead car ferry returned to Dublin the Women's Coaliton Group released hundreds of balloons with the names of abortion agencies and information outlets attached to them.

While in Holyhead they met leaders of the British Pregnancy Advisory Council and brought information leaflets back to Dublin for distribution. They also declared their intention to continue their protests until such time as Irish women secured the right to abortion.

About 100 Irish women travel every week to England to have their pregnancies terminated.

Meanwhile, gardaí refused to comment on whether a Derry man's complaint that his pregnant ex-girlfriend is intending to travel to Britain for an abortion is an elaborate hoax or a genuine grievance.

According to some sources the amount of publicity in the case may have put the man off taking legal action.

The man is understood to be a casual building worker living in a flat on the southside of the city and returns to Derry each week.

He split up with his girlfriend about two months ago after a row, but when he heard she was pregnant and intended to travel to England for an abortion he attempted to stop her leaving their flat.

The woman, however, said she intended terminating the pregnancy, and warned that she would climb down the drain pipe on the outer wall of the building if she had to in order to go ahead with a termination of the pregnancy.

1993

Sonia O'Sullivan began to stake her claim as the nation's greatest ever female athlete when her silver at the World Championships was the first medal won by an Irish woman at a major athletics event.
While there were some horrific killings in the North, as well as revelations that the British government had been having secret talks with republicans, increased links between the SDLP and Sinn Féin raised hopes for the beginnings of a peace process.
Meanwhile, the Beef Tribunal trudged along, giving journalists plenty of opportunities to use the pun about there being something rotten in the Irish meat industry.

Gay law passed

Friday, June 25

The Bill to legalise homosexual acts was passed by the Dáil without a vote yesterday evening, after a debate that lasted for just over five hours on two days. The age of consent in the Bill is 17 years.
Champagne corks popped as gay rights activists celebrated outside the Leinster House gates and there was clapping among a small group in the public gallery as Ceann Comhairle Seán Treacy declared that the Bill had passed all stages and would be sent to the Senate.
Meanwhile, gay groups yesterday applauded Minister Geoghegan-Quinn for her "great courage" in legalising homosexual acts.

Roy Keane with Nottingham Forest manager Brian Clough during the 21-year-old midfielder's last months with the club.

Condoms to go on sale in supermarkets

Friday, February 12

Condoms are expected to be on sale in supermarkets and big stores by the summer, according to the main distributor for Durex in this country. Up to now condoms were purchased in chemist shops.
Yesterday, Durex announced the results of a survey. Key findings include:

* 60% of condoms are bought by men
* 26% of people use no form of contraception
* 2% have sex every day

The condom is particularly popular among 25-29 year olds, upper social class groups and those who live in urban areas. By contrast, natural methods of birth control are practised almost exclusively by married couples aged over 30, and those who live in country areas. Many people are still embarrassed when it comes to buying condoms.

Roddy Doyle, ha ha ha!

Wednesday, October 27

Irishman Roddy Doyle last night won the 25th Booker Prize, making him the first Irish writer to do so. He collected the £20,000 prize for his novel *Paddy Clarke Ha Ha Ha*, in London's Guildhall.
A former teacher, Doyle (35) had international success with his first novel, *The Commitments,* which was turned into an award-winning film by Alan Parker.
While Doyle has created his own fictional world that has provided pleasure to hundreds of thousands of readers, there is still an unease about him in some literary circles. In an era of top-heavy literary novels, he manages to be very funny and very stylish at once.
In *Paddy Clarke Ha Ha Ha*, his style is honed and shaped with a mastery that belies the sneers cast at him in the past. In a way that's rare nowadays, he has combined popularity with quality and this has been especially true of *Paddy Clarke Ha Ha Ha*.
This is his finest book yet and while the history of the Booker Prize is hard to take seriously, the victory confirmed what was obvious – that his work has literary merit as well as popular appeal. – Seán Dunne

NEWS BRIEFS

Feb Seven people were killed and up to 500 injured yesterday as a huge explosion and fire rocked New York's World Trade Centre. Local television stations reported that it was caused by an explosive device and Police Commissioner Raymond Kelly said he did not rule out a car bomb in an underground multi-storey car park. (27)

July Roy Keane is set to begin his Manchester United career in South Africa later this week. The 21-year-old midfield genius, signed from Nottingham Forest for an English record £3.75m over the weekend, travels to Johannesburg tomorrow for a pre-season tour. (19)

Aug An *Examiner* editorial on the 70th anniversary commemoration of the death of Michael Collins states that the current unemployment figure of 300,000 makes a mockery of all that Collins and the people of his generation set out to achieve. (23)

The Cork Examiner

No. 53,279 | MONDAY MORNING, AUGUST 23, 1993 | Price 80p (inc. VAT)

ROSES

Tralee's delight

■ TANAISTE Dick Spring opened the huge Rose of Tralee Festival on Saturday night:

PAGE 12

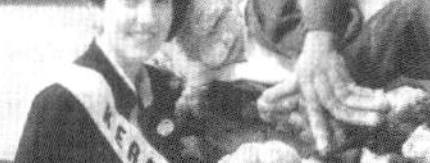

■ *Kerry Rose Trudie O'Sullivan*

CONCERT

Ready for U2

■ WORK has started at Pairc Ui Chaoimh in preparation for the U2 concert tomorrow:

PAGE 7

■ *U2 promoter Oliver Barry*

MILLSTREET

Charles on top

■ PETER Charles won the Heineken Irish Derby at Millstreet International Horse Show:

PAGE 13

■ *Peter Charles big winner*

Slimmer FG plan to revive fortunes

By TONY LEEN, Political Reporter

BELEAGURED Fine Gael is set to axe ineffective party structures and beef up the organisation with a new centralised executive council.

The commission on the renewal of the party will recommend in its first draft that the national executive, national and regional councils be abolished.

But it has steered clear of the continuing uncertainty over the leadership of the party.

The three existing national bodies would be replaced by a new central council with a high profile chairperson, likely to be from outside party ranks.

It is likely to have up to 20 members, with half elected at the Ard Fheis and a number nominated by the party leader. The remainder would probably come from the ranks of the parliamentary party.

The recommendations come as front bencher, Michael Noonan, continues to insist that leader, John Bruton has his full support.

Speaking in Cork yesterday, Mr Noonan said that all elected leaders of Fine Gael enjoyed his full backing, and Mr Bruton was no different.

However, Mr Noonan felt that the self-analysis of Fine Gael had run its course.

"We have gone through the phase of self analysis. You have to stop looking under the bonnet and drive the car."

The Commission move towards a "slimmer" and more co-ordinated party may face resistance from some grassroot branches who will interpret the proposal as a further step towards centralising power.

The FG think-tank will avoid any recommendation on individuals within the party, and is only expected to comment on the leadership in the context of the support services required for the position.

Sources stressed that the final report would not be brought forward, and was still on course for release towards the end of October.

"There is a clear view on the Commission that the national council, national executive and regional councils should be abolished," said one party figure.

The plan for an executive council is one of a number of sweeping changes and proposals mooted by the Commission, which gathered for its penultimate meeting at the weekend.

Among other proposals is a separate party committee for Dublin, where Fine Gael only has nine of 41 seats, and the sale of the party's Mount Street headquarters to facilitate a move closer to Leinster House.

Greater scrutiny of TDs and senators is proposed, both in terms of their parliamentary performance and discipline, by a new group which would consist of people from outside the parliamentary party.

This move is likely to irk some Fine Gael Oireachtais members. "Some TDs mightn't be the best orators on the floor of the House, but they are effective in their own constituencies," remarked one senior party deputy.

Commission members were left in no doubt that the leadership of John Bruton was not their issue. Chairperson Ms. Gary Joyce said yesterday that some party TDs were dragging the work of the Commission into the leadership struggle.

"It is irritating to have the work of the Commission devalued. To even associate the Commission and the leadership in the same breath is making a football out of our work," she commented on RTE radio.

Ambulance men hitch lift to dying woman

By TONY LEEN

SOUTHERN Health Board chiefs are to probe the weekend breakdown of an ambulance less than a mile from a bar where a Cork woman lay dying of a suspected heart attack.

Mrs Eucharia Harte, a 61-year-old mother-of-four, died in Ballygarvan, Co. Cork, despite the best efforts of ambulance crew members, who had been forced to hitch a ride to the bar from passing motorists.

A spokesperson for the Health Board confirmed last night that the matter was being investigated, but stressed in advance of any findings that such delays and breakdowns are extremely rare.

"All vehicles are maintained in strict accordance with regulations," the Board said.

A second ambulance was answering a call elsewhere in Cork, it is understood.

The SHB ambulance stranded in Ballygarvan

A back-up ambulance was called to Paddo's Bar in Ballygarvan, but did not arrive for nearly 45 minutes, according to three witnesses who wish to remain anonymous.

One witness told the *Cork Examiner*: "In this particular instance the delay may not have made a difference, but it could be the difference between life and death on another day".

"It made the situation even worse than it was," he said.

One witness described how ambulance staff were pushing the vehicle in an attempt to restart it after the breakdown. The crew brought cardiac equipment with them to the bar, where a local doctor had arrived in the meantime.

"People in the bar were extremely upset, and there was a feeling of utter frustration and helplessness," said one local person.

Mrs Harte lived in Hillside, Ballygarvan.

Three injured

THREE people were taken by SHB ambulance to the Cork Regional Hospital last night following a traffic accident in Skibbereen. There were no serious injuries, a hospital spokesperson said.

SONIA'S SILVER LINING

THE SILVER LADY: Sonia O'Sullivan acknowledges the adulation from the Stuttgart crowd after she had been presented with a silver medal in the 1,500m final yesterday. Picture: ALLSPORT

Long wait ends in glory

By BRENDAN MOONEY in Stuttgart

SONIA O'Sullivan has won the heart of a nation with her exploits on the track over the past couple of years.

And the nation celebrated yesterday when she won a world championship medal that testified to her high standing on the fiercely competitive athletics stage.

Messages of congratulations poured into the Irish team quarters, where team members and officials were left in no doubt about who would have been queen of the championships if she had beaten the Chinese women who won many medals but very little favour

Dong Liu of China won the 1,500m title in 4:00.50 from Sonia in 4:03.48, and Hassiba Boulmerka, the reigning world and Olympic champion.

INSIDE: Editorial - Page 4; Pride of Ireland - Sports section, Pages 1 and 6.

The 23-year-old Cobh girl's disappointment in last Monday's 3,000m final had turned to anger by Friday morning's heats of the 1,500m, and yesterday morning she was just hyper.

"I went for a 15 minute run and I just talked to myself all the way. By the end of it I was sprinting," she said.

A banana sandwich for lunch and she was ready for what turned out to be the greatest moment of her life. The winner of the race was never going to be caught after she exploded from the field with 700m to go, but the race for the silver medal was a spellbinding contest.

At the end of it Sonia O'Sullivan was handed the Irish flag by Sean Calnan, paid her tributes to the huge Irish following at that end of the Gottlieb-Daimler Stadium, and set out on her lap of honour along with Hassiba Boulmerka.

She stopped for a moment to wave to her parents, John and Mary, who watched the race from alongside the startline although her mother admitted afterwards that she had seen very little of it. "I just kept looking down. I will watch it all on television," he said.

And the ovation the Irish girl received from the 48,000 fans who thronged the stadium surpassed that accorded the gold medallist.

"It felt great on the podium and watching the Irish flag being raised. It was unbelieveable really. I knew everybody was behind me going out there from hearing the vibes all day long. Down at the far end of the stadium where there were no Irish flags at all the roar was just unbelievable. I want to do it all again.

"The disappointment on Monday, and then

Turn to Page 2, Col. 7

O'Sullivan's achievement praised by delighted nation

SONIA O'Sullivan can look forward to unparalleled scenes of joy when she returns home tomorrow. And the Lord Mayor of Cork has promised a civic reception in her honour.

President Mary Robinson praised the Cork woman's courage and determination. Sonia, she said, had succeeded in the face of formidable competition, and established beyond doubt her place among the foremost athletes of the world today.

Taoiseach Albert Reynolds offered his congratulation for for a "brilliant performance".

Tanaiste Dick Spring said Sonia had achieved a magnificent silver medal through tenacity and hard work. Her performance was a source of great national pride, and would prove a shining example to young athletes here.

Crork Lord Mayor, Cllr John Murray, said he would be arranging a civic reception for Sonya. "The city is very proud of her indeed."

"I sent Sonia a message before the 3,000 metres and said that regardless of whether she won gold, silver or bronze she would do us proud. She did that coming in fourth. Yesterday she excelled in winning silver."

Sonia's mother and father were in Stuggart for the race, while the rest of her immediate family spent a nail-biting four minutes in front of the television in Cobh.

Her brother, Tony, admitted they were "not really expecting much" because there were so many favourites in the race. But "in the last two laps we thought - she's really in with a chance."

He uncle, Terry Shealy, commented: "We knew it was in her. It was just whether she could pick herself up after the 3,000 metres."

Local TD John Mulvihill said it was "a great day for Cobh, for Cork and for Ireland." Sonia was a fantastic role-model for young people and a great ambassador for Ireland.

Fine Gael spokesman on Youth and Sport, Deputy Micheal Creed, said Sonia's performance was "a triumph of innate ability, conviction and courage. It had lifted the nation."

Junior Sports Minister, Liam Alyward, in a telephone message of congratulations praised Sonia

WELL DONE: Sonia's grandfather, Mick Shealy, aunt Francis, Uncle Terry and his two children, Fiona and Eamon, share in a wonderful moment. (Picture: DAN LINEHAN)

1994

A watershed year in Northern Ireland saw the IRA declare a ceasefire. Though it didn't bring total peace to the province, the move did lead to a huge reduction in the amount of violence and a return to 'normal' life that hadn't been experienced since the 1960s.

In the Republic, issues surrounding paedophile priest Brendan Smyth led to the resignation of Fianna Fáil leader and Taoiseach Albert Reynolds and former Attorney General Harry Whelehan, as well as further damaging the reputation of the Catholic Church. Throughout his career Smyth had sexually abused children and when complaints were made against him, the Church hierarchy had usually sought to defuse the situation by moving him elsewhere.

When charges against him in the North had been pending, an extradition warrant was 'buried' in the Attorney General's office in the Republic for seven months. When Reynolds appointed Whelehan as President of the High Court, the Labour members of the coalition objected, provoking a political crisis that ultimately led to the Taoiseach's resignation.

In international news, early reports from Rwanda mentioned that thousands were feared dead in tribal bloodletting. It took several weeks for the full extent of the killings to become known. 800,000 people - mostly from the country's minority Tutsi tribe - had been killed by rival Hutus.

Examiner journalist Eamon Timmins went to the region in the wake of the slaughter, and his reports from the squalid refugee camps in Zaire set up for fleeing Tutsis made for harrowing reading.

Terrible scenes in Goma

Thursday, July 28

It was like a scene from the Holocaust, but the truckloads of bodies being dumped into the large pit were Rwandans, not Jews. Truck after truck pulled up, the limp bodies being thrown from the high back of the military vehicles onto the ever-growing pile on the floor of the pit.

The English language does not contain words to describe the sight. It was overwhelming, shocking, heart-breaking. The lump grew in my throat, the feelings of repulsion and shame were overpowering.

The number of bodies arriving was mind-numbing. As we were leaving two more trucks arrived along with a GOAL truck. All were full with bodies. Aid agencies believe official estimates that 13,000 people a day are dying of cholera are dramatically understated.

Limerick soldier Tom Boyce, who is one of three soldiers seconded to GOAL from the Irish Army, has the gruesome task of running GOAL's death trucks.

It was his first day on the job and he was bearing up well. "I tell myself I should not look at their faces, but I can't help it - they are human," he said. "You know you have had a hard day when you find the babies easier because they are lighter." - Eamon Timmins

Dolores O'Riordan of The Cranberries on her way to her wedding.

Rock star weds

Tuesday, July 19

It was truly a unique wedding to remember for 22-year-old Dolores O'Riordan, lead singer of The Cranberries, as she arrived yesterday on an old horse-drawn cart to marry Canadian Don Burton at the 12th Century Holy Cross Abbey in Thurles, Co Tipperary.

The big talking point was undoubtedly her ivory lace and chiffon outfit designed by well-known New York designer Cynthia Rowley. Beneath an almost transparent shimmering ivory chiffon dress, the bride wore a pair of lace hipster-hugging trousers with knee-high beige boots. On her head was a delightful crown.

NEWS BRIEFS

Jan The Irish government lifts Section 31 of the Broadcast Act, which had prevented members of Sinn Féin or the IRA being interviewed on television or radio. (11)

Apr Kurt Cobain, lead singer of the hugely popular rock band Nirvana, was found shot dead at his Seattle home yesterday. A suicide note was found near his body.(9)

Sept A 550-cow dairy herd faces destruction following a mad cow disease outbreak in Passage West, Co Cork. It brings to 91 the total number of outbreaks of the deadly disease in Ireland since 1989. (15)

WEATHER

■ MOST of the country staying dry today. Just some light rain near the south coast. A mixture of sunshine and cloud. Light to moderate easterly winds. Mainly dry this evening with fog patches forming after dark. Full report: Page 14

The Cork Examiner

No. 53,596 WEDNESDAY MORNING, AUGUST 31, 1994 Price 80p (inc. VAT)

BUILDING

Boost for Dungarvan

■ THREE projects with an investment potential of £18m are in the pipeline for Dungarvan.

PAGE 7

■ *The Town Square, Dungarvan.*

Howdy Partner

■ FASHION goes to the Wild West.

■ *Wild West influence.*

MOTORING

Sporty Subaru

■ THE Subaru Impreza Sportswagon's individuality is one of its most appealing features.

PAGE 13

■ *The Subaru Impreza Sportswagon.*

■ *SIGN OF PEACE: A message for the men of violence as a child plays against a wall in north Belfast yesterday.*

Peace process won't be halted

By DICK BRAZIL, Special Correspondent

THE Irish and British governments accept there will be occasional and possibly serious acts of republican-linked terrorism in the wake of the IRA ending their military campaign.

■ Editorial: Page 4; Fears of bloody backlash: Page 5; 25 years of violence in North: Page 10.

But last night sources close to the Irish government stressed, "wild men" will not be allowed to destroy the peace process.

Government sources admitted the proposed end to the IRA campaign, expected within hours, will be, "viewed in a similar light to the agreement which Yasser Arafat reached with the Israeli authorities on Palestine. You must allow for those who will simply not go along with the majority."

However, it is clear there is an "understanding" that the IRA will actively support the peace movement on the ground.

In the coming days both governments will continue to insist that the status of Northern Ireland will remain in the hands of a majority of the people of Northern Ireland.

The IRA are said to be relatively happy with the proposals, particularly the promise that the British government will amend their claims of authority on Northern Ireland in the Government of Ireland Act and leave it to a majority decision of the people.

They believe there is a commitment from both governments to facilitate a coming together of opinions in the North.

The IRA are said to have offered their own evidence of a willingness to make concessions — a significant cutback in the bombing of commercial targets in central Belfast was one.

It is said that loyalist groups have responded favourably also to approaches from both governments but will probably wait a period before confirming their halt to terrorist acts.

At least two Church figures, Church of Ireland Primate Dr Robert Eames and Rev Roy Magee are said to have played a crucial role in reassuring loyalists in recent days that their position is not undermined in any arrangement to encourage the positive IRA response.

Sources in Belfast say Mr Reynolds in particular has built up a good working relationship, even trust, with both republican and loyalist groups and that only history will show the extent to which both governments have gone to find a settlement which can be seen as acceptable to both groups.

The process will move significantly from here and a summit of the Irish and British leaders within weeks will likely come up with a "model" for the Ireland of the future.

It will probably first allow Sinn Féin "access" to the conference table through the Forum for Reconciliation and Peace and within a specific period at round table talks on new structures of government

Amongst the early initiatives will be greater cross-border co-operation. The establishment of an All Ireland Forum to enable the island as a whole to promote tourism, agriculture and industrial investment internationally is seen as important.

In the North itself, there will be significant positive initiatives by the security forces, with the police taking over the public management of security from the army and demilitarisation possibly being introduced initially on a zoned basis.

IRA set to lay down weapons

By LIAM O'NEILL, Political Editor

THE Government expects a full cessation of IRA violence to be announced from midnight.

It will end a 25-year reign of the bomb and bullet and open the way for Sinn Féin to become involved in all-party talks on Northern Ireland's future at the end of three-month cooling off period.

The ending of violence will be unconditional, sources in Dublin predicted last night. "No deals have been done, the Downing Street Declaration is the only basis for participation in democratic politics," said one source.

Clearly anticipating not just a short-term ceasefire but a complete ending of violence, Taoiseach Albert Reynolds last night said he believed we were now poised for peace and that, in a very short time, we would be able to make a new beginning on this island.

In an obvious move to reassure Unionists, the Taoiseach urged that nobody should be afraid of peace and the vista of opportunity which could now open up for the benefit and economic prosperity of all the people of Ireland.

"A complete cessation of violence and the principles of the Downing Street Declaration are our new starting point," he said in a statement.

Tánaiste and Foreign Affairs Minister Dick Spring said last night the Government was interested in one thing only, a permanent cessation of violence and the removal of the bomb and the bullet from politics on this island.

Like the Taoiseach, he also set out to reassure the Unionists when he said they had nothing to fear from the ending of violence.

Last night, the Government were preparing their response to what they now expect to be an announcement today from the IRA that there will be a complete cessation of violence, after the Cabinet had earlier considered the prospects for peace.

A report to Cabinet by the Taoiseach followed a flurry of activity over the previous three days, involving Mr Reynolds and Mr Spring having contacts with their British counterparts and with Northern

Turn to Page 2, Col. 6

£14,000 more for Taoiseach as top people get pay hikes

By MARK HENNESSY, Political Correspondent

THE Government last night approved pay rises — including £14,000 more for the Taoiseach — for 650 top State employees. Altogether, the increases will cost the taxpayer £3 million a year.

Finance Minister Bertie Ahern defended the pay rises, saying "I don't think the increases are in any way excessive."

Cabinet Ministers will see their pay packets grow by 17.1% to £76,300 annually. Ministers of State will get 5.6% more (£52,320), while Ceann Comhairle Seán Treacy will get an extra £11,000 (£76,300).

The salary of Taoiseach Albert Reynolds will move from £82,020 to £95,920, while that of Tánaiste and Foreign Affairs Minister Dick Spring rises from £69,991 to £82,295.

Mr Ahern said the decision by the Gleeson Review Group to award just 3.8% to TDs, taking them to £32,700, was a major source of disappointment to them.

"This has been a major disappointment. I do not believe that pay rates of £32,000 for active TDs — and I contend that the majority of politicians, from all parties, are active — are excessive," he said.

The difficulties created by this relatively low compensation for politicians was illustrated by the problems political parties faced when they went looking for new, capable candidates, he said.

The Chief Justice will be paid £95,920, up 16.9%; the President of the High Court will get £86,110, up 17%, while other senior members of the judiciary will get approximately 17% more.

Half of the increases proposed by Gleeson will be backdated to April last, and can be accommodated in this year's Public Pay Bill, while the remainder will be paid from May 1 next year.

The Government refused to implement Gleeson's findings in 1992 because of its ban then on special pay awards, but it has now felt able to go ahead in the aftermath of the agreement on the Programme for Competitiveness and Work.

Mr Ahern emphasised that greater use of bonuses would be made to properly motivate senior management in semi-State companies; and to ensure that the companies' boards supervised their work properly.

The boards will be able to award up to 30% in special payments to high performing executives; and bonuses for "outstanding performance" by civil servants will also be made available.

But, a 30·2% rise listed for the chief executive of Aer Lingus, and a 12·9% rise for the counterpart in Telecom Éireann, will not be implemented, since the holders of these posts have individual contracts which pay them the above the Department of Finance's recommended rate.

EDITORIAL — Page 4

Examiner leaves its rivals well behind

■ *Titles of distinction.*

THE *Cork Examiner*, with 214,000 readers, commands a lead of 64% over its nearest morning rival, according to new statistics.

The Joint National Readership Research survey shows a dramatic increase in readership figures over the past year.

Significant gains have also been made in key social groups by sister paper the *Evening Echo*.

More women, business people and young people are now reading both papers, which combined have 35% of the Munster readership, at 264,000.

Last night, Alan Crosbie, chief executive of Cork Examiner Publications Ltd, said the figures consolidated the papers' dominance of the Munster market.

When it comes to Cork city and county, the *Cork Examiner* and the *Evening Echo* combined reach 224,000, or 72% of the population, increasing their dominance of the Cork market over all other media.

According to the survey, the number of *Cork Examiner* readers increased from 199,000 to 214,000 between 1993 and 1994.

The figure represents an increase of 7·5% over the last 12 months.

■ Full report: Page 24.

1995

When the Republic of Ireland went 1-0 up against England in a friendly match at Lansdowne Road, it provided the signal for visiting supporters to begin ripping up their seats and firing them onto the pitch.

The match was abandoned and an hour later English fans were still resisting police attempts to clear the stadium. An inquiry into the riot proved an embarrassment for the FAI and the Gardaí alike and revealed that the Garda riot squad were actually outside when the trouble started. The Gardaí then had trouble entering the stadium because of locked doors.

Later in the year, a far more welcome visitor was Bill Clinton. The US president received a rapturous reception in Northern Ireland and Dublin, not least because of his efforts in the peace process.

Divorce was legalised in the Republic after a Dublin 'yes' vote in the referendum helped shade the result by 50.3% to 49.7%. The Dáil also voted through a £60 million fund to pay compensation to victims of the Hepatitis C affair.

Scandals continued to engulf the Catholic Church, with lately-deceased celebrity priest Michael Cleary revealed as the father of two children.

In sport, the exuberant celebrations which greeted Clare's victory in the All-Ireland hurling final spilled over to the rest of the country with almost everybody – except the losers, Offaly – glad to see the Banner County win its first championship since 1914.

Overseas, Bosnian Serb forces massacred up to 8,000 Muslims in Srebrenica in the worst atrocity of the war in the former Yugoslavia.

Welcome, Mr President

Friday, December 1

The man from Hope, Arkansas sat and listened to the real thing in West Belfast yesterday in the guise of two young children blighted by the Northern Troubles.

When tiny nine-year-old Catherine Hamill and her new-found friend, David Sterrit (10), finished their poignant introduction at Mackies' textile factory, the US President had his keynote address to the North written to perfection.

"What I wanted to say has been said," said President Clinton, with open hands and an air of submission.

"My name is Catherine Hamill. My Daddy works as an assistant in Stuarts warehouse. I live in Belfast and I love where I live. My first Daddy died in the Troubles. It was the saddest day of my life and I still think of him. Now it is nice and peaceful. I like having peace and quiet for a change instead of people shooting and killing."

"My Christmas wish is that peace and love will last forever in Northern Ireland. Please have a safe journey back to America. I hope you enjoyed your visit to Ireland."

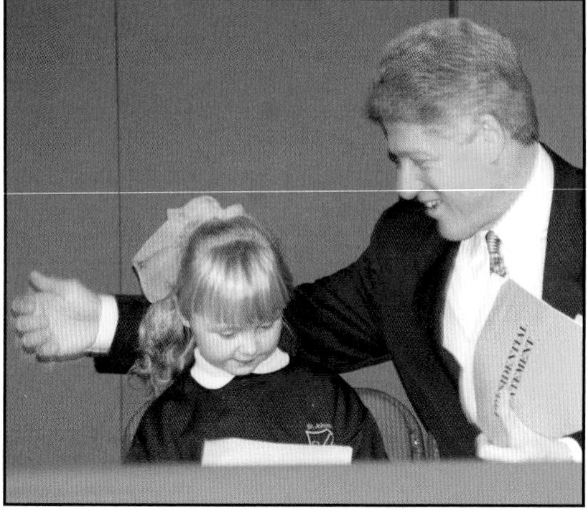

US President Bill Clinton embraces local girl Catherine Hamill during his visit to Belfast.

NEWS BRIEFS

Mar At the Green Glens Arena in Millstreet, Co Cork, Steve Collins became WBO super-middleweight champion after he knocked out title holder Chris Eubank before a crowd of 8,000. (19)

June Bishop Thomas Flynn, spokesperson for the Catholic Hierarchy, said he did not believe allegations that the late Fr Michael Cleary had a lover and had fathered two sons. The Bishop was reacting to a claim by a Dublin woman, Phylis Hamilton, 45, that Fr Cleary had been her lover for 25 years and that he was the father of her two sons. (26)

Aug The country was warned to brace itself for a major influx of New Age Travellers from abroad over the next few years. Fianna Fáil TD Ned O'Keeffe predicted that as many as 350,000 people seeking alternative lifestyles could arrive here from Britain and other parts of Europe. (26)

Plans were unveiled in Dublin detailing how Irish rugby players would benefit financially from the historic weekend decision to abandon 125 years of amateurism in the sport. (28)

Sept Five Waterford men have been infected with AIDS by a woman, hundreds of mass-goers were told yesterday by their local priest. Up to 80 more are awaiting HIV test results as a consequence of sexual relations with the woman, who is said to be angry at having been infected herself. The priest, Fr Michael Kennedy, is a third cousin of the late President John F Kennedy. (11)

Oct Ireland's best-known poet, Seamus Heaney, is the toast of the literary world after winning the prestigious 1995 Nobel Prize for Literature. (6)

Dec The Dayton Peace accords bring an official end to the war in Yugoslavia. (14)

The Cork Examiner

No. 53,740 THURSDAY MORNING, FEBRUARY 16, 1995 Price 80p (inc. VAT)

England's disgrace

■ Three English fans viciously attack an Irish supporter on the pitch at Lansdowne Road last night.

Officials knew thugs were at game

By DECLAN KELLY and SEAN O'RIORDAN

BRITISH and Irish authorities knew English neo-Nazi football hooligans were in Lansdowne Road for last night's soccer international.

The game was abandoned after 27 minutes, with Ireland a goal in front, when a section of English fans in the upper tier of the West Stand ripped out seats and hurled them at spectators below.

Dublin hoteliers confirmed last night they were warned by gardaí that convicted football thugs were travelling to Dublin with tickets for the game.

Fianna Fáil leader Bertie Ahern also revealed that English football officials had identified members of the banned National Front organisation before the kick-off.

The dramatic revelations came as investigations began into the riots which forced the abandonment of last night's international match and left many injured and in hospital.

Early today there were unconfirmed reports that one of those arrested was an official of the England Travel Club — the organisation established to ensure screening of fans travelling abroad for England games.

Garda sources said the midnight estimate was of 60 arrests and up to 40 injured.

Last night, English football was in disgrace and a major question mark hung over the European Championships being held there next year.

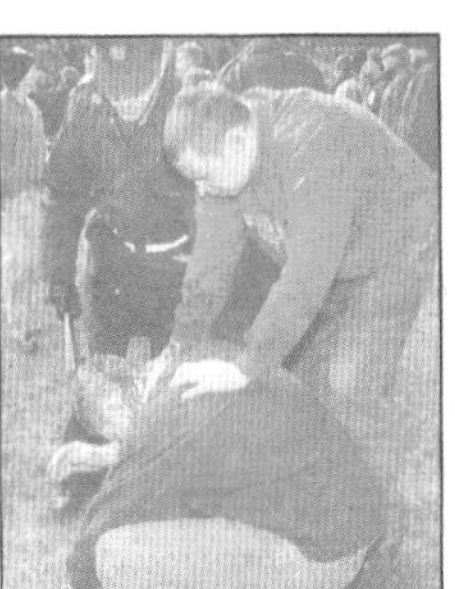

■ A blood-spattered fan at Lansdowne Road last night. (Picture: Eddie O'Hare).

Thousands of English fans — detained for some hours in Lansdowne Road — were escorted directly to Dun Laoghaire and put on ferries home.

Others, however, were still in Dublin and not all were waiting for court appearances.

A huge security operation continued into the early hours in the city centre with a reported 1,000 English fans under heavy garda surveillance.

The FAI admitted last night that serious mistakes had been made as calls rang out for the resignation of senior officials in the organisation.

Sports Minister Bernard Allen has ordered an immediate investigation into how match tickets got into the hands of known football criminals through official English FA channels.

He will contact his British counterpart today to seek a full explanation for the tickets fiasco.

Senior English and Irish soccer officials will meet in emergency session today to pinpoint the mistakes which led to last night's debacle.

Gardaí refused to confirm last night they had contacted several hotels in the capital yesterday to warn them that known football hooligans would be attending the game.

However, Pat Fox, the manager of the Regency Hotel on Dublin's Swords Road, confirmed gardaí had contacted his hotel early yesterday morning to warn that about eight convicted hooligans would be amongst a group of English soccer fans staying with them last night.

FAI boss Sean Connolly claimed their security was well prepared. The fact that they were able to clear the stadium so easily was a tribute to the Irish fans as well.

Meanwhile, an Irish soccer fan collapsed and died while leaving Lansdowne Road when the match was abandoned.

Gardaí said the man, in his 60s, suffered chest pains as he was leaving.

■ Inside: Pages 12-13.

Sunbeam jobs at risk

By DECLAN KELLY, Industrial Correspondent

MORE than 100 jobs are at risk at the Sunbeam factory in Cork because of serious cash flow problems.

Crisis talks between unions and management got underway yesterday, amid fears for the company's future.

It is understood the problems stem from a failure to meet a deadline for a large order just before Christmas.

The company was left with a large amount of stock because of the delay, and began experiencing cash flow problems soon after.

The problems are believed to be in the knitwear division which has 108 production employees, all members of SIPTU.

Branch secretary Gerry Mullins confirmed last night the situation was now "extremely serious."

He also confirmed the workers had been made aware of the situation and were now very concerned about their jobs.

"It is a cash flow problem which has arisen because of the fact that the deadlines were not achieved, and now we are faced with a very difficult and delicate situation," he said.

Negotiations between unions and management will resume early today. It is also understood the IDA may be approached to try to solve the difficulties.

Talks are also expected to take place between the firm and a company in Dublin.

Sunbeam management were not available for comment last night.

1996

The 1996 Olympics was one of the most extraordinary events in the history of Irish sport. Sonia O'Sullivan, the nation's sure thing for at least one medal, failed miserably to make an impact when she was hit with a stomach upset. Conversely, 26-year-old swimmer Michelle Smith won three golds and a bronze, among them the first ever medal to be won by an Irish woman at the Games.

Innuendo about Smith's "barely-believable" performances were dismissed in Ireland as sour grapes and the feel-good factor helped blind people to the questionable sudden improvements in Smith's times.

Some of Ireland's new breed of gun-toting drug-financed criminals ensured their own demise with the killing of *Sunday Independent* journalist Veronica Guerin. Guerin had made enemies of some of the major players in the underworld by writing about their activities. Her killing was to spark a massive clampdown by the state against these criminals.

The death of Brigid McCole in October appeared to be a blow to the hopes of 1,600 women who had been infected with Hepatitis C through infected blood from the Blood Transfusion Service Board. The Board's tactics of initially refusing to accept responsibility for the débâcle and warning that it would fight any claims brought against it were widely criticised. The government was forced into setting up a Tribunal of Inquiry into the matter.

The IRA showed it hadn't gone away, with huge bomb explosions at Canary Wharf in London and in Manchester city centre, while nationalists in Drumcree, Portadown, were outraged at the reversal of a decision not to let an Orange Order parade through their area.

For the *Examiner*, the expansion from its traditional base was signalled with the dropping of the word 'Cork' from the masthead.

Veronica Guerin shot dead

Thursday, June 27

The hitman who gunned down award-winning crime reporter Veronica Guerin in Dublin yesterday was brought in from Britain by a notorious Dublin underworld figure, senior Garda sources believe.

Her assassination stunned the country, and provoked statements of condemnation and outrage. Less than 18 months ago, she was shot and seriously injured in the thigh after answering the door of her north Co Dublin home to a masked gunman. Yesterday, the reporter who had vowed "I won't back off" paid the ultimate price. Her husband and six-year-old son Cathal were being comforted by family and close friends.

Ms Guerin died in a hail of bullets at about 1pm, moments after stopping her car at traffic lights on the Naas dual-carriageway, at the junction with Boot Road, Clondalkin. She was travelling alone from Naas Court, where she was charged with speeding.

A high-powered motorbike, apparently following her red Opel Calibra car, drew up and the pillion passenger shot her five times with a handgun. She was hit twice in the head and three times in the upper body and died instantly.

Sunday Independent editor Aengus Fanning said: "This is one of the darkest days in the history of Irish journalism."

Liam Neeson and wife Natasha Richardson next to a picture advertising the biopic about Michael Collins that he starred in.

Blood board climb down after Hep C Death

Thursday, October 3

It has emerged that the Blood Transfusion Service Board (BTSB) dramatically climbed down and accepted, just days before a woman died of liver failure, that plasma given to her in the 1970s was infected with Hepatitis C.

The Dongeal mother-of-12, Mrs Brigid Ellen McCole, passed away surrounded by her grieving family on Tuesday night, a week before her High Court action for compensation was due to open.

In return for an estimated £350,000 in damages, Mrs McCole agreed to withdraw all charges against State agencies and the State itself.

Her death has come as a serious blow to many of the 1,600 left infected with Hepatitis C, who believed she could prove the Board stood to be blamed for the crisis.

NEWS BRIEFS

June The massive Garda hunt continues across the country today for a military-style gang that executed 52-year-old Det Garda Jerry McCabe and wounded Det Garda Ben O'Sullivan, in Adare, Co Limerick. (7)

Nov Fine Gael Minister Michael Lowry was last night fighting for his political life, following allegations that Dunnes Stores paid the £200,000 restoration bill for his Tipperary home. (30)

The Examiner

Established 1841
No. 54,110
SATURDAY
July 27, 1996
85p (inc. VAT)

Reporting the real world

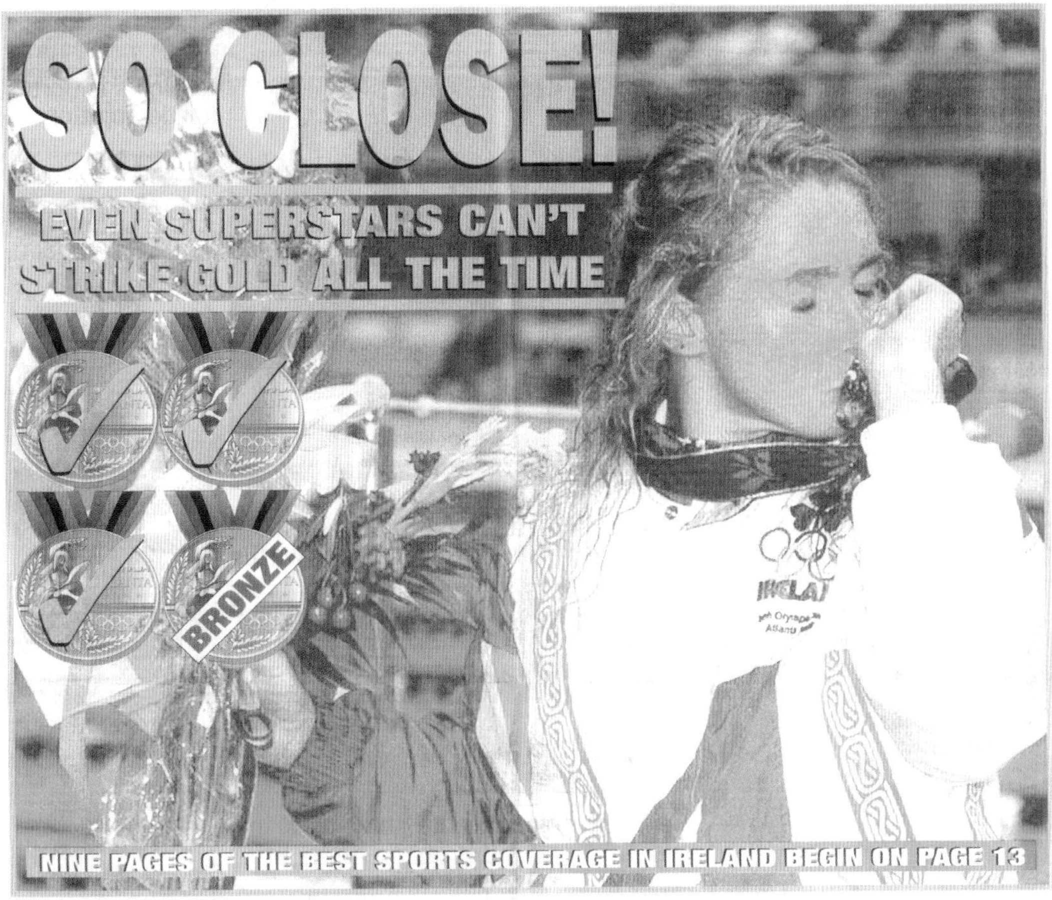

SO CLOSE!

EVEN SUPERSTARS CAN'T STRIKE GOLD ALL THE TIME

BRONZE

NINE PAGES OF THE BEST SPORTS COVERAGE IN IRELAND BEGIN ON PAGE 13

Bronze medal but it's still glittering finale

by Billy George and Brendan Mooney in Atlanta

MICHELLE SMITH'S stunning sequence of Olympic gold medal performances ended last night — but couldn't halt her elevation into Irish sporting immortality.

Ireland's swimming sensation has still achieved in six days what it took Ireland a lifetime to achieve in terms of Olympic gold medallists.

"I don't know how long it will take for this all to sink in, but it hasn't yet. I am proud for myself, but also for Ireland. That's all I know at the moment," Michelle said.

The Irish superstar said she held no bitterness towards the US over the ill-mannered comments of some officials and representatives. The American people, had been wonderful, she said – "but not as wonderful as the Irish here and at home." Michelle finally succumbed to fatigue in the 200m butterfly final as she was beaten into third place, giving her a bronze medal to go with three golden Atlanta successes.

Already the country's most lavish homecoming for a sporting superstar is in the pipeline.

"I will relax now with Erik. He has been with me for everything, and we will enjoy the rest of the games together."

Olympics chiefs, meanwhile, warned last night they were ready to take strong action against rumour-mongers commenting on Michelle's success.

President Clinton meets Michelle in a bid to repair Irish American relations after the drugs claims.

The International Olympic Committee said the matter had gone far enough, calling for an immediate end to the poolside gossip which threatened to tarnish Michelle's week of glory.

IOC spokeswoman Michele Verdier commented: "I warn people not to use the name of an athlete along with unsubstantiated allegations and rumours. Besides being an athlete, they are a human being and they have the rights of a human being. Simply throwing a name around when nothing is proved is very wrong and very unfair on the athlete. President Clinton met Michelle in an apparent bid to restore Irish-American relations battered by rowing over the swimmer's success.

The get-together — organised at Mr Clinton's request — was seen as a bid by him to put links with Ireland back on line after anger generated in the American and Irish Olympic camps over Michelle's medal success.

Michelle's father, Brian hit out at the American media's reaction to his daughter's success, and an insinuation from American swimming star Janet Evans that Michelle could have been taking steroids.

Speaking on BBC Radio, he said: "They are insular. They do not see anything but themselves. Their conduct has been less than good. It has been despicable — Janet Evans in particular. This criticism does not apply to the American people, nor to the other American swimmers, who have expressed regret and anger at Janet Evans and the American Swimming Association." He joked at reports that Michelle had been taking steroids: "Obviously, they did not work. She is only 5ft 3in, and we are going to get our money back."

Almost one half of the Republic's population watched early hours television coverage of Michelle's fourth Olympic gold medal bid of the week. The figures have been compiled by Ireland's Media Bureau, which reports on viewing statistics for advertisers.

The Irish pub trade is using Michelle's Olympic victories to back a campaign for longer opening hours. VFI chief Paul O'Grady said: "The fact that Irish people cannot watch Michelle winning in their local pubs is just another example of how ridiculous our law is

1997

The death of Princess Diana in late July rivals the death of John F Kennedy as the biggest news story of the latter half of the century. And while the passing of Mother Teresa of Calcutta less than a week after Diana was a major story, it still didn't occupy the space afforded to 'the people's princess'.

For politicians and the clergy it was another year of shame, with corruption at the highest levels being exposed by the McCracken report and Brendan Smyth at last being sent to prison in the Republic when he received a 12-year sentence for offences dating back to 1958.

The Irish economy was growing at such a rate that the situation was being compared to earlier booms in Asia, and the country was being tagged with the 'Celtic Tiger' nickname.

The literary honours for Ireland continued when Frank McCourt won the Pulitzer prize for *Angela's Ashes*, his tale of deprivation in Limerick in the 1940s.

For the *Examiner*, it was a momentous year with the publication of the newspaper's first ever internet edition.

Ireland mourns Diana's death

Monday, September 1

Deep distress was expressed by President Mary Robinson at the tragic death of Princess Di. "In particular, I remember her work with the National Aids Trust and her recent campaign on land mines – issues she worked on with huge personal courage and commitment," said the President.

Throughout yesterday in Dublin there was a constant stream of people pulling up in cars outside the British Embassy on the Merrion Road to pay tribute to the late Princess.

Meanwhile, in Northern Ireland many people who have no love for the British royal family put aside age-old rivalries to grieve for Princess Diana.

In a staunchly republican district a supporter of Sinn Féin said she cried over the news of the death of the princess. "I was in tears this morning when I heard the news. I could cry now," said the smartly dressed Catholic mother after attending morning Mass. "I am a republican, I support Sinn Féin and I am absolutely devastated by Princess Diana's death."

Haughey could be jailed

Tuesday, August 26

Charles Haughey could be jailed following the damning findings by Judge Brian McCracken in his Tribunal report on payments to politicians, which also called for serious sanctions against Michael Lowry for tax evasion.

Judge McCracken described former Taoiseach Haughey's evidence to the Tribunal as unbelievable, and said ex-Minister Lowry's offshore accounts and the funding of the £395,00 renovations to his Tipperary home were designed to evade tax.

Judge McCracken found Mr Haughey had failed consistently to answer questions from the Tribunal about his receipt of £1.3 million from Ben Dunne and said he was asking the DPP to consider whether the former leader should be prosecuted. If found guilty of obstructing the work of the Tribunal, he could face a £10,000 fine or two years in prison.

From poverty to Pulitzer Prize

Tuesday, April 7

It is deeply ironic that the destitution of Limerick in the 1940s which Frank McCourt has earned international fame describing almost cost him his life. McCourt was just ten-years-old when he contracted typhoid as he lived among the lice, fleas and rats of tenement life in Limerick.

Author Frank McCourt and his wife Ellen at the conferring of the Pulitzer Prize-winning author's honorary degree at the University of Limerick.

A drunken doctor diagnosed a bad cold, and he was just hours from death when he was brought to the local fever hospital where he was nursed back to health. A blind man, Mr Timoney, whom he met at the time began his love affair with the works of Jonathan Swift.

The seeds were sewn which over 50 years later resulted in Frank writing the Pulitzer winning *Angela's Ashes, A Memoir Of A Childhood*. These days Frank is hot property. Foreign language rights for the best-selling book have already been sold and a film is also in the pipeline.

NEWS BRIEFS

July Whatever about rotting in prison, 12 years behind bars for pervert priest Brendan Smyth wasn't enough in the eyes of one of dozens of people he terrorised recently. "Rot in hell, Smyth" came the angry shout from one of Smyth's male victims as the priest was led away. (26)

Oct Ray Burke, Minister for Foreign Affairs, resigns from the Dáil amidst allegations that he had received a payment of £30,000 from a property developer. (7)

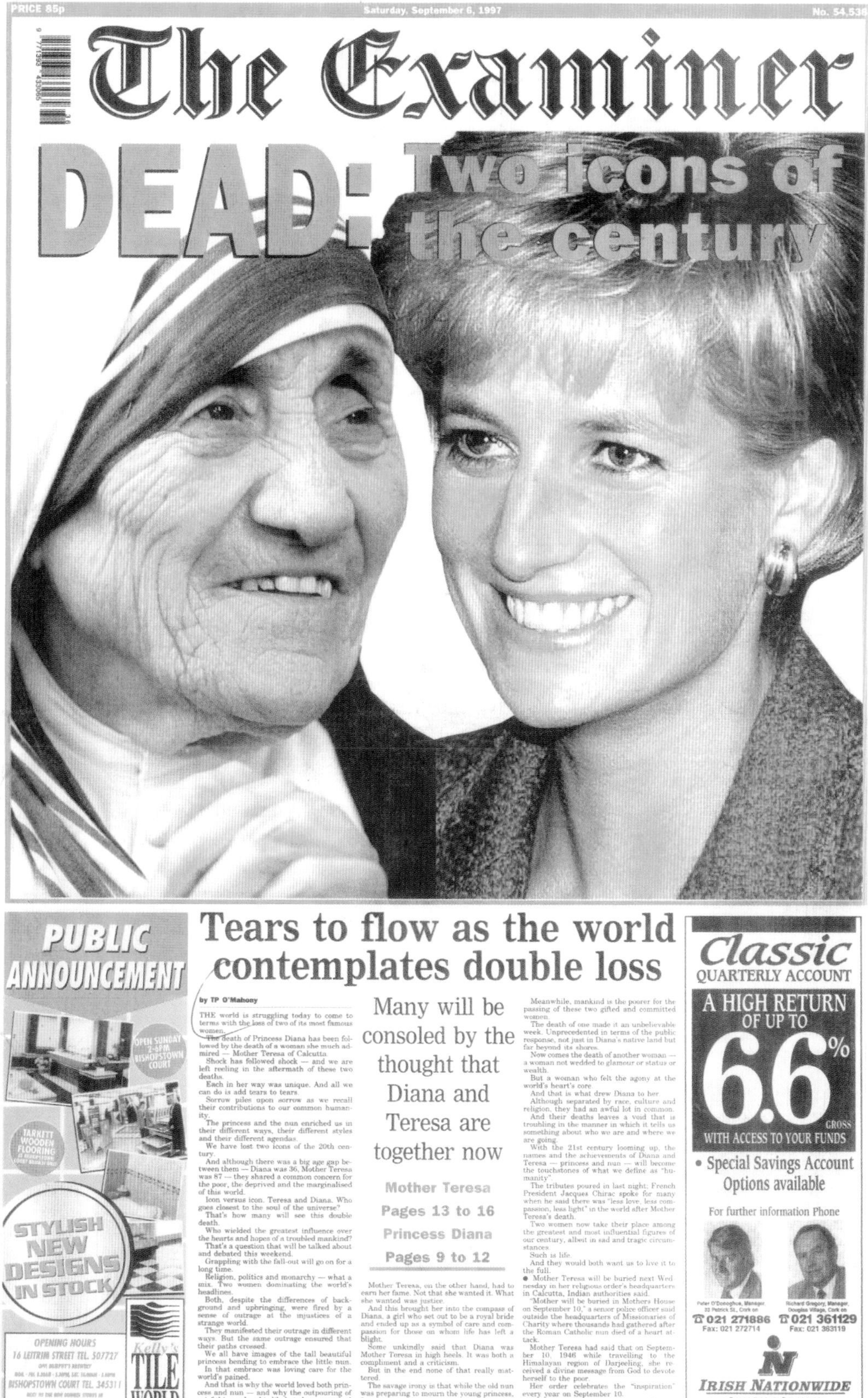

PRICE 85p Saturday, September 6, 1997 No. 54,538

The Examiner

DEAD: Two icons of the century

Tears to flow as the world contemplates double loss

by TP O'Mahony

THE world is struggling today to come to terms with the loss of two of its most famous women.

The death of Princess Diana has been followed by the death of a woman she much admired — Mother Teresa of Calcutta.

Shock has followed shock — and we are left reeling in the aftermath of these two deaths.

Each in her way was unique. And all we can do is add tears to tears.

Sorrow piles upon sorrow as we recall their contributions to our common humanity.

The princess and the nun enriched us in their different ways, their different styles and their different agendas.

We have lost two icons of the 20th century.

And although there was a big age gap between them — Diana was 36, Mother Teresa was 87 — they shared a common concern for the poor, the deprived and the marginalised of this world.

Icon versus icon. Teresa and Diana. Who goes closest to the soul of the universe?

That's how many will see this double death.

Who wielded the greatest influence over the hearts and hopes of a troubled mankind?

That's a question that will be talked about and debated this weekend.

Grappling with the fall-out will go on for a long time.

Religion, politics and monarchy — what a mix. Two women dominating the world's headlines.

Both, despite the differences of background and upbringing, were fired by a sense of outrage at the injustices of a strange world.

They manifested their outrage in different ways. But the same outrage ensured that their paths crossed.

We all have images of the tall beautiful princess bending to embrace the little nun.

In that embrace was loving care for the world's pained.

And that is why the world loved both princess and nun — and why the outpouring of grief this weekend is likely to be unmatched in our lifetime.

Diana was famous from the moment she married the man who seemed destined for the Throne of England.

Many will be consoled by the thought that Diana and Teresa are together now

Mother Teresa Pages 13 to 16
Princess Diana Pages 9 to 12

Mother Teresa, on the other hand, had to earn her fame. Not that she wanted it. What she wanted was justice.

And this brought her into the compass of Diana, a girl who set out to be a royal bride and ended up as a symbol of care and compassion for those on whom life has left a blight.

Some unkindly said that Diana was Mother Teresa in high heels. It was both a compliment and a criticism.

But in the end none of that really mattered.

The savage irony is that while the old nun was preparing to mourn the young princess, fate intervened.

Both are now dead. And those for whom belief in an afterlife is unshakeable will console themselves with the thought that Diana and Teresa are together now — and forever.

Meanwhile, mankind is the poorer for the passing of these two gifted and committed women.

The death of one made it an unbelievable week. Unprecedented in terms of the public response, not just in Diana's native land but far beyond its shores.

Now comes the death of another woman — a woman not wedded to glamour or status or wealth.

But a woman who felt the agony at the world's heart's core.

And that is what drew Diana to her.

Although separated by race, culture and religion, they had an awful lot in common.

And their deaths leaves a void that is troubling in the manner in which it tells us something about who we are and where we are going.

With the 21st century looming up, the names and the achievements of Diana and Teresa — princess and nun — will become the touchstones of what we define as "humanity".

The tributes poured in last night; French President Jacques Chirac spoke for many when he said there was "less love, less compassion, less light" in the world after Mother Teresa's death.

Two women now take their place among the greatest and most influential figures of our century, albeit in sad and tragic circumstances.

Such is life.

And they would both want us to live it to the full.

● Mother Teresa will be buried next Wednesday in her religious order's headquarters in Calcutta, Indian authorities said.

"Mother will be buried in Mothers House on September 10," a senior police officer said outside the headquarters of Missionaries of Charity where thousands had gathered after the Roman Catholic nun died of a heart attack.

Mother Teresa had said that on September 10, 1946 while travelling to the Himalayan region of Darjeeling, she received a divine message from God to devote herself to the poor.

Her order celebrates the "inspiration" every year on September 10.

Her body will kept at St Thomas Church of Loreto Day School in Middleton Row in south Calcutta from tomorrow to September 10 for public viewing, City Police Commissioner Dinesh Bajpai told reporters.

1998

Again in the North, it was a case of two steps forward, one step back. The positive moves came in August when simultaneous referenda north and south of the border passed the Good Friday Agreement.

Among the main provisions of the agreement were a removal from the constitution of the Republic's territorial claim to the North, the release of paramilitary prisoners belonging to organisations observing a ceasefire and the entitlement of anybody born on the island of Ireland to Irish citizenship.

Ironically, the overwhelming support for the agreement was overshadowed a few months later by the North's bloodiest day since the beginning of the Troubles when a bomb planted by republican splinter group, the Real IRA, killed 30 people in Omagh, Co Tyrone.

Viagra goes on sale

Tuesday, September 29

September 28, 1998 will go down in Irish history as V-Day – the day the wonder-drug, Viagra, became available on prescription after an unprecedented hype for the launch of a new medical treatment.

Thousands of Irish males are expected to be liberated from the problem of impotence with the availability of the little blue tablet as doctors anticipate the doors of their waiting rooms being stormed by men eager to get their hands on the Pfizer Riser.

Estimates that as many as 120,000 Irish males may be experiencing erectile dysfunction are generally viewed as being conservative.

The story of sildenafil citrate – to give Viagra its proper medical term – has also put the small Cork town of Ringaskiddy on the international map. As the sole manufacturer of the bulk raw material for Viagra worldwide, Pfizer's Ringaskiddy plant is set to increase its production capacity to cater for increased demand as the drug is licensed for new markets.

Gay Byrne and John Hume on **The Late Late Show.** *The longest-running TV talk show in the world was to lose its popular presenter to retirement during the year, while the SDLP leader received the Nobel Peace Prize with David Trimble for their efforts in the Northern Ireland peace process.*

Car-free capital

Monday, July 13

Courtesy of the Tour de France, the planners who favour banning traffic from Dublin city centre caught a vision of a brave new world over the weekend.

The world's greatest cycling race achieved the seemingly impossible where countless politicians and even the proposed Luas system have failed. An unreal air of calm hung over the city as pedal power allowed Dubliners reclaim their city back from the constant gridlock of cars under which it seems ever more likely to sink.

Dublin can certainly be heaven with coffee at 11 and a stroll down Stephen's Green and the presence of the Tour helped citizens of the capital to realise the words of the Dublin Saunter for the first time in the modern age.

But if a car-free Stephen's Green helped the square to recapture some of its old-world charm, O'Connell Street, the official start for yesterday's stage, became a willing slave to the two-wheeled monster.

The main thoroughfare was home to the colourful array of bikes and their lycra-clad riders as large crowds lined the street, watching in fascination the huge cavalcade and circus attendant on the 189 cyclists.

NEWS BRIEFS

Jan Bill Clinton yesterday made a dramatic bid to defuse the sex scandals surrounding his presidency, by angrily denying he had sex with Monica Lewinsky, and asking his lawyers to speed up the Paula Jones case. The President made an unexpected appearance at the White House at the launch of a new after-school care scheme to try to scotch reports of sexual encounters with the former trainee White House Worker. "I need to say this to the American people. I did not have sexual relations with that woman, Miss Lewinsky." (27)

Aug Michelle de Bruin (formerly Smith) had her swimming career ended by FINA, the sport's governing body, when she was suspended for four years after being found guilty of interfering with a urine sample requested by drugs testers. (7)

Dec Political rivals David Trimble and John Hume stood shoulder-to-shoulder as peacemakers last night, symbolising the hopes of shattered Northern Irish communities as they accepted the Nobel Peace Prize. (11)

The Examiner

Monday, August 17, 1998 · www.examiner.ie · No. 54,829 85p

BUTCHERS

INSIDE

Joe Oliver has reported on carnage for 30 years but nothing prepared him for Omagh

Page 7

One of the staff in the hospital saw their child brought in for treatment

Page 8

Sinn Féin has condemned the massacre

Page 9

Internment could play into the hands of the terrorists

Page 10

Pages 7 to 12

Police know the killer and fear he will strike again

by Dan Collins and Joe Oliver

THE TERRORIST leader suspected of orchestrating the massacre of the innocents in Omagh, Co Tyrone, in which 28 people were butchered, including nine children and 13 women, is known to the security forces on both sides of the Border.

Believed to be the former IRA quartermaster, who founded the self-styled Real IRA, is still at large. Furthermore, he is regarded by both the Gardai and the RUC as somebody capable of masterminding further acts of terrorism.

It emerged yesterday that three generations of one family - including a pregnant mother carrying twins - were among the 28 innocent people blown to pieces by the 500lb carnival day car bomb.

The majority of the fatalities were women and children, including three school children from Buncranna, County Donegal, and a total of 220 people were injured in Saturday's blast which destroyed the town centre.

A major crackdown on splinter terrorist groups was promised by Taoiseach Bertie Ahern, yesterday, as the Government moved to review the security threat posed by organisations which are opposed to the Northern Ireland peace agreement.

Mr Ahern voiced his determination to take whatever action necessary to crush the threat posed by paramilitary groups, after yesterday's meeting of the cabinet's security sub-committee.

Yesterday, the Taoiseach met with Minister of State at Foreign Affairs Liz O'Donnell, Garda Commissioner Pat Byrne and the head of the Garda security and crime division, Assistant Commissioner Pat O'Toole, as well as officials from several Government departments.

Following the meeting, Mr Ahern said nothing – including the possibility of re-introducing internment – could be ruled out.

Mr Ahern said he had no doubt that the dissidents styling themselves the 32 County Sovereignty Movement, the political wing of the Real IRA were behind the Omagh bomb. "Whatever resources are necessary to crush this organisation will be given," he pledged.

President Mary McAleese, who visited the scene of the blast yesterday, said she was "deeply shocked. "The bombing has obliterated the hopes and dreams of so many families in one cruel afternoon of purposeless terrorism," said President McAleese. She said everything had to be done to ensure that the people responsible for the atrocity would face the full rigour of the law.

Relatives react to the carnage of the Omagh car bomb while awaiting information on the fates of their loved ones at the Omagh Leisure Centre, on Saturday. The casualty toll of 28 dead also included 220 injured.

Minister for Justice John O'Donoghue arrived back in Dublin Airport last night after cutting short his holiday and pledged that no group of terrorists would be allowed to subvert the Northern Ireland peace initiative.

"The people who have perpetrated this heinous and most awful crime will be brought to justice," the Minister promised.

US President Bill Clinton condemned the "butchery" of the Omagh bombing and said he did not intend to let it interfere with his visit to Northern Ireland next month.

British Prime Minister Tony Blair broke off his holiday in France to fly to the North to meet political leaders and pledged the killers would not be allowed to wreck the Northern Ireland peace process: "We will not let these people wreck the future. The future belongs to the decent people of Northern Ireland. It doesn't belong to the criminals and psychopaths," he told reporters. "They are a small group of people, a tiny fanatical group of people. They have no political base, they have no votes, they have no support in Northern Ireland. They have just this capacity for evil."

Yesterday, the Taoiseach and the British Prime Minister met at Stormont House after which both men said the Irish and British governments would work closely to "crush" the individuals responsible for the Omagh atrocity.

Sinn Féin President Gerry Adams was jostled and jeered yesterday by people waiting at the emergency centre in Omagh for news of missing friends and relatives. Mr Adams condemned the bombing "without any equivocation whatsoever."

Last night, the 32 County Sovereignty Movement issued the following statement: "We are deeply saddened and devastated by the terrible tragedy in Omagh. We share the grief and sorrow of everyone on the island of Ireland and we offer our sincere sympathy to the injured, the bereaved, their families and friends at this time. The killing of innocent people cannot be justified . . . We reject categorically any suggestion that has been publicly made that our movement was responsible in any way." However, the first rumblings from those connected to RIRA's political wing, the 32 County Sovereignty Committee, hinted that the phone warning of the bomb had been accurate and explicit about the stolen car's location.

But police were in no doubt they had deliberately provided the wrong information in order to maximise casualties. Forensic experts were still examining the remains of the devastated car. Its number plates were vaporised in the explosion but police have suggested the vehicle was hijacked in the Republic some days ago.

Two Spaniards became the first tourists to be killed in Northern Ireland's troubles. A woman teacher and pupil, who were visiting Omagh as part of an exchange group from Madrid staying in Buncranna, County Donegal, were caught in the terrorist maelstrom.

Three months ago, an overwhelming majority of the 20,000 people of Omagh voted in favour of the Good Friday peace agreement.

Omagh's heart ripped out as bodies were identified

by Niall Murray

FAMILIES and communities on both sides of the border were united in grief in the wake of the horrific bomb attack which ripped through Omagh on Saturday afternoon, claiming 28 innocent lives.

Most of the victims who had been identified last night — 14 women, five men, four boys and three girls — were from the Omagh area.

Three boys from Co Donegal, a woman originally from Co Cork, and two young Spanish people were also killed.

The grim list slowly lengthened yesterday, as distressed family members visited the temporary morgue in the town's army barracks to identify bodies.

The incident centre set up in Omagh's sports complex was busy all day, with people seeking information of friends and relatives who were unaccounted for.

People flocked to churches of all denominations throughout the day, remembering those who were killed and injured, and uniting in prayer.

Mary Grimes (left) and her daughter Avril Monaghan, who were among the 28 murdered in Omagh. They are two of three members of their family who were murdered on Saturday. Avril was expecting twins.

RUC expect to publish full list of victims today

THE RUC expect to release full details of all the deceased at lunch-time today. These are some of the unofficial identifications which were available last night:

Lorraine Wilson, 15, from Omagh
Samantha McFarland, 17, from Omagh
Brian McCrorry, in his 40s, from Omagh
Gareth Conway, 19, from Carrickmore
Julie Hughes, 21, from Omagh
Brenda Logue, 17, from Carrickmore
Elizabeth Rush, 57, from Omagh
Geraldine Breslan, 35, from Omagh
Sean McLaughlin, 12, from Buncrana
Oran Doherty, 8, from Buncrana
James Barker, 12, from Buncrana
Mary Grimes, 65, from Beragh
Avril Monaghan, 30, from Augher
Maura Monaghan, 18 months, from Augher
Fernando Blasco, 12, Madrid
Rosio Abad, 24, Madrid
Philomena Skelton, 39, Drumquin
Esther Gibson, late 20s, from Beragh

Members of the emergency services spent the day carrying out the arduous task of identifying limbs and other body parts which were ripped from the victims.

The extent of the injuries to dozens of people required hospital staff to amputate arms and legs. Many of the victims had taken advantage of Saturday's fine weather to shop for school uniforms, while others were looking forward to the festival parade later in the evening.

Last night, the people of Omagh were still trying to come to terms with the gruesome consequences of the bomb, which has devastated their lives and their town, while church and political leaders united in condemnation of the brutal terrorist attack.

The Donegal town of Buncrana was also in mourning for three young boys and two Spanish visitors who were killed in the blast that claimed 28 lives. The boys, aged between 8 and 12, were on a day-trip with a group of Spanish students visiting their town to learn English.

They were unofficially named last night as eight-year-old Oran Doherty, 12-year-old Seán McLaughlin, and James Barker, also 12.

A 12-year-old boy, Fernando Blasco, and his 24-year-old teacher, Rosio Abad, both from Madrid, were also among the victims of the bomb.

Spain's Foreign Minister and Deputy Prime Minister are expected to arrive in Northern Ireland today, along with families of the dead and injured Spanish visitors.

The town was suffering from complete shock and disbelief at the tragic news yesterday, as the families and friends of the young victims were being comforted by neighbours.

It emerged yesterday that the 65-year-old woman who died along with her daughter and 18-month-old grand-daughter was a native of North Cork.

Mary Grimes, a retired nurse moved to Co Tyrone 35 years ago, but originally hailed from Lismire, near Kanturk, Co Cork. Her husband, James, is a native of Omagh, and the couple kept a farm at Beragh, near the town.

Saturday's blast killed the mother-of-12, along with her 30-year-old daughter, Avril Monaghan, who was heavily pregnant with twins, and her infant daughter, Maura.

News of Mrs Grimes' tragic death brought shock to the parish of Lismire, where she was a regular visitor, most recently just two weeks ago. Many of her immediate family still live in the area, including three brothers and three sisters.

They were last night preparing to make the 200-mile journey to Omagh.

A further tragedy hit the Tyrone town yesterday morning, when a motorist died after colliding with an ambulance transferring victims of the bomb between hospitals.

1999

The international community had been widely criticised for its unwillingness to get involved in the war in Yugoslavia during the earlier part of the decade. When similar ethnic cleansing began against ethnic Albanians in the province of Kosovo, NATO led a war against the Serbs in an attempt to stop another escalation of the war in the Balkans. It would eventually lead to a removal of Serb control over the province and the beginning of the end of Slobodan Milosevic's reign.

In Ireland, the privatisation of Telecom Éireann seemed to come at the perfect time for the government. Even though the initial share-price was surprisingly high, it still managed to climb another 20% in the first week of trading. For many people, it was their first encounter with the stock market.

Years of revelations about sexual and other abuse of children in state and religious institutions finally came to a head with an RTÉ documentary which showed how such treatment was systematic and widespread. The government had to act. Taoiseach Bertie Ahern apologised on behalf of the state and steps were taken to provide compensation and counselling to victims.

The end of the millennium brought worries that computer clocks might malfunction as many of them hadn't been designed to deal with the number 2000, and fears were expressed that the Y2K bug could cause accidents at nuclear power plants and on planes.

Millennial sky's the limit for fatcats

Wednesday, February 3

British Airways executives have been ordered to make the ultimate sacrifice on New Year's Eve – put your life on the line for the airline. With computer geeks, religious gurus and doomsday analysts predicting global chaos when the clock strikes midnight on December 31, company fatcats will take to the skies in a determined, if somewhat sweaty, show of faith.

The bold BA move follows the publication of a poll showing that at least 40% of computer operators will refuse to fly over the New Year.

A similar plan for top dogs in Aer Lingus failed to take off, with directors unanimous in their belief that the best way to serve the two-wings-and-a-prayer travelling public was to remain 35,000 feet below the average flight path.

Ray MacSharry and Mary O'Rourke in a happy mood as they announce the details of the privatisation of semi-state company, Telecom Éireann.

Victims back government plans to address child abuse

Wednesday, May 12

The announcement yesterday by the Taoiseach of a package of measures relating to child abuse has been enthusiastically but cautiously welcomed by the abuse victims featured in the RTÉ States of Fear series.

The details of the package include the establishment of a 'Commission to Inquire into Childhood Abuse'. In response to this measure, Mary Phil Drennan, who spent her childhood in the orphanage run by the Sisters of Mercy at Cobh and Rushbrooke, County Cork, believes this measure will help to bring some of her tormentors to justice.

"I cannot rest until I get an apology from those who hit me and even worse, forced me to hit other children in the orphanage. There was systematic violence, though we never knew where or when it would occur, and the head nun did her best to pit us against each other."

NEWS BRIEFS

Jan Economic history was created yesterday with the much-heralded arrival of the euro on the international currency market.

July Over 574,000 Irish people and 700 financial institutions became shareholders in Telecom Éireann yesterday in the biggest ever public flotation in the State's history. Speculation about the long-awaited share price ended at 8pm yesterday when Minister for Public Enterprise, Mary O'Rourke, announced a price of £3.07 in Dublin. (6)

Nov Anti-globalisation protestors in the United States city of Seattle battled with police at the World Trade Organisation's meeting, forcing a cancellation of some events. (30)

The Examiner

www.examiner.ie

thursday

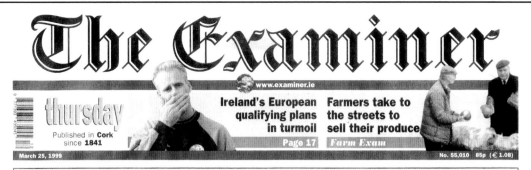

Published in Cork since 1841

March 25, 1999

No. 55,010 85p (€ 1.08)

Ireland's European qualifying plans in turmoil

Page 17

Farmers take to the streets to sell their produce

Farm Exam

NATO forces unleash blitz on targets across Yugoslavia

Two jets may have been lost during air strikes

NATO forces launched a barrage of long-threatened attacks on targets in Yugoslavia last night, and threaten to continue to hit up to 300 key areas over the next few days.

The atten Yugoslav pple Yugoslavia's military capability comes after months of diplomacy failed to bring an end to fighting in the province of Kosovo where the mainly Albanian population want autonomy.

NATO confirmed last night that one of their jet's was shot down north of Kosova and the pilot catapulted ont. A second plane is also believed to have been shot down while at least one Yugoslav Mig was hit.

Yugoslav authorities said women and children who lived in an army base where killed during the raid and a number of civilians were wounded in the seven towns hit by cruise missiles and bombs.

While European leaders and the US President issued statements justifying the attack on the soverign state, furious Yugoslav politicians likened the action to them becoming involved in the war in Northern Ireland.

The attack, announced by NATO Secretary-General Javier Solana at alliance headquarters in Brussels, was its first against a sovereign country in NATO's 50-year history and was carried out without reference to the UN.

Explosions resounded in Kosovo's capital Pristina just before 7pm, according to residents reached by telephone, and the city of 280,000 was plunged into darkness when the electricity failed.

In Belgrade, witnesses reported seeing eight explosions, some near a military airport and at least one near a power plant.

In neighbouring Montenegro, which with Serbia forms Yugoslavia, three areas were hit, including an army military barracks in Danilovgrad which was in flames.

Explosions were also heard in the area of Novi Sad in northern Serbia, northwest of Belgrade.

In Macedonia, villagers piled into cars and headed away from the border after hearing explosions in neighbouring Kosovo.

British Prime Minister Tony Blair said the attacking forces included US B-52 bombers which took off from Britain, B-2 bombers from the US and the British submarine HMS Splendid, armed with Tomahawk cruise missiles.

RAF armourers check a 1,000lb Paveway laser-guided bomb fitted to a Harrier GR7 aircraft at the Gioia del Colle airbase in Southern Italy prior to making a strike on Yugoslavia.

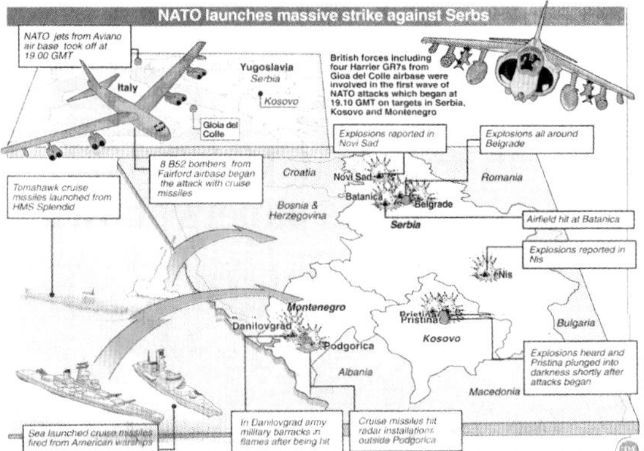

NATO launches massive strike against Serbs
NATO jets from Aviano air base took off at 19.00 GMT
Italy
Yugoslavia
Serbia
Kosovo
Gioia del Colle
British forces including four Harrier GR7s from Gioa del Colle airbase were involved in the first wave of NATO attacks which began at 19.10 GMT on targets in Serbia, Kosovo and Montenegro
Explosions reported in Novi Sad
Explosions all around Belgrade
8 B52 bombers from Fairford airbase began the attack with cruise missiles
Tomahawk cruise missiles launched from HMS Splendid
Croatia
Novi Sad
Batanica
Belgrade
Romania
Bosnia & Herzegovina
Serbia
Airfield hit at Batanica
Explosions reported in Nis
Nis
Montenegro
Danilovgrad
Podgorica
Pristina
Kosovo
Bulgaria
Albania
Macedonia
Explosions heard and Pristina plunged into darkness shortly after attacks began
Sea launched cruise missiles fired from American warships
In Danilovgrad army military barracks in flames after being hit
Cruise missiles hit radar installations outside Podgorica

British Harrier GR7 bombers based in Italy also took part alongside forces from the United States, France, Spain, Canada, Germany and Italy in a first wave of attacks on Yugoslav air defence systems.

Yugoslavia last night declared a state of war after the NATO attacks, the state-run Tanjug news agency announced.

The Minister for Foreign Affairs David Andrews last night accepted the NATO-sanctioned air strikes on Slobodan Milosevic's military forces in Kosovo – despite the decision of two fellow EU neutral member states to question the legality of the attacks.

Speaking during a break in meetings at the Berlin EU Summit, Mr Andrews said Ireland had repeatedly called for a peaceful resolution.

"However the position adopted by other neutrals was far stronger. Austria closed its airspace to the NATO strike force, while the Swedish Foreign Minister warned the attacks were not in compliance with international law, since they were without official United Nations approval.

Accepting that the situation had become extremely dangerous, Mr Andrews declared: "It is a consequence of the inability of President Milosevic to see reason. It is a consequence of him sending in his army to ethnically cleanse the people of Kosovo, the Albanians.

"It appears that he may see reason after two, or three days of bombing. Naturally, from my point of my view, from my country's point of view, we would wish that not to happen," he said after the EU Council had agreed a statement on the crisis.

Three members of the UN Security Council, the United States, France and the UK believed NATO had a mandate to attack because of the Serbian military attacks on Kosovo's civilian population.

The decision by the Austrians – who are sharply split over whether, or not to join NATO in future – to close their air space was forced by a constitutional requirement to display the country's neutrality in the face of an international crises.

The EU leaders' declaration expressed deep concern about the failure of the efforts led by the United States' Richard Holbrooke to persuade Milosevic to accept a ceasefire to stop a humanitarian catastrophe: "On the threshold of the 21st Century, Europe cannot tolerate a humanitarian catastrophe in its midst."

SEE: Pages 11, 15

Bombing is act of revenge, says hero

by Niall O'Connor

HERO of the Bosnian conflict, Dr Mary McLaughlin, last night described the bombing as a high profile act of revenge, but said NATO could not back down on their threats.

Recently returned from the region where she has been working with the aid agency Goal, she described the Serbian people as a fanatically nationalistic.

"They look constantly to the past and are at this moment completely behind their government." She believes the bombing raids will strengthen the Serbian government.

Having lived through some of the worst acts of terrorism during the Bosnian war when her nightly faxes to the world forced the UN to take action to save the so-called safe area of Gorazda, she said some military action was needed in Serbia.

Recalling her experiences while working for the UN when she described Gorazda as a place where only the dead were lucky, she said.

"People in these areas when under attack normally get on with their business and hope that the bombs won't hit them."

Ahern under pressure to name several Commission contenders

by Katherine Butler and Mark Hennessy

TAOISEACH Bertie Ahern will have to put forward more than one candidate as successor to outgoing European commissioner Padraig Flynn.

The appointment yesterday of a President of the European Commission has increased pressure on all 15 governments to nominate successors to the discredited Commission.

EU leaders meeting in Berlin agreed with unexpected speed, to name Romano Prodi, the former Italian premier to lead the EU executive into the next century. Barring legal obstacles he will become President designate from next month. He will be formally ratified by Strasbourg in April although he will not take up the appointment until after European Parliament elections in June.

This leaves the Government just eight weeks to draw up a list of acceptable candidates. Under the terms of the Amsterdam Treaty the new President will have the right to reject individuals.

By the end of June or early July Commissioner Flynn along with the other outgoing commissioners will be expected to have cleared their desks.

Taoiseach Bertie Ahern is under pressure to select an Irish candidate who has the political experience and authority to command a senior portfolio in the Commission. But Dáil arithmethic and the government's reliance on independent support, means he would want to avoid nominating a sitting Fianna Fail TD a move which would prompt a by-election.

Speaking in Berlin yesterday Mr Ahern played down the dilemma. "We have not put any thought into who would be the next commissioner, or otherwise. We will do so now in line with the programme laid out. It creates no difficulty for us"

Sources close to the Taoiseach hinted he may choose a member of his cabinet for Brussels. "People should not get too hung up about by elections. We either have the independents supporting us or we don't".

So far the names speculated on include Máire Geoghegan-Quinn, Euro MP Gerry Collins; and the attorney general David Byrne.

However the possible selection of either former Tánaiste and Labour leader Dick Spring or independent MEP Pat Cox has been completely discounted.

Whatever else is clear about the succession race it seems certain that Mr Ahern will not venture outside of the ranks of Fianna Fail. One source said he could see no circumstances under which Mr Ahern would give the Brussels job to a non-Fianna Fail person.

The other certainty is that an unknown appointee will end up with a junior job in the new Brussels hierarchy. "It has to be a solid candidate with experience of Europe at a senior level. Otherwise you are looking at paper clips" said one Brussels source.

SEE: Page 4

Gerry Collins and Máire Geoghegan-Quinn: possible nominees to succeed Padraig Flynn.

Faulty equipment keeps patients waiting

by Caroline O'Doherty

SERIOUSLY-ILL patients have to wait long periods to discover the extent of their illness because a vital EEG machine is out of order in the one of the country's biggest hospitals.

Managers at Cork University Hospital are waiting for a replacement part for the machine, which measures brain activity in patients suffering a range of illnesses and injuries, including meningitis. But a senior medical practitioner said the breakdown was indicative of a service that was falling asunder due to lack of planning and investment. According to the medic, neurologists in the region were being referred twice as many patients as they could see and waiting lists were now running into thousands.

Those put to the back of the queue while emergency accident and cancer cases were handled included people with strokes, epilepsy, multiple sclerosis, Alzheimer's and Parkinson's Disease. Neurological facilities at CUH serve a population of 1.2 million people in Cork, Kerry, Limerick, Waterford, south Tipperary and Clare. There are just three neurologists covering the region, one for every 400,000 people. Most European countries have 10 times that number, and Britain is considered poorly-served with a ratio of one to 100,000.

There is anger that the Government has failed to implement the recommendations of a 1991 report by Comhairle na nOspideal, which said CUH should have double its complement of neurologists. The new appointments were to have included a specialised child neurologist and a neurophysiologist expert in interpreting tests in EEG departments.

But the medical source said along with lack of manpower, CUH had been deprived of the equipment needed to meet its responsibilities as one of only two specialist neurological centres in the country.

The Southern Health Board said every effort was being made to have the EEG machine back in operation as soon as possible.

2000

The new millennium was marked with ceremonies and celebrations all over Ireland, though concerns about crowds and increased prices had meant fewer people than usual at New Year' s Eve celebrations in some centres.

The Y2K computer scare passed without event, causing speculation that either everybody had prepared very well for the changeover or that the media and companies involved in profiting from correcting the glitch had exaggerated the danger.

The continuing boom in the economy was reflected in the 28% jump in house prices during the year.

Major music events during the year included the dance-orientated Homelands festival which drew 30,000 revellers to see such acts as Leftfield and Paul Oakenfold, while Bryan Adams and Moby played at Slane Castle.

In the United States, a bizarre post-election battle saw George Bush emerge as victorious after the Supreme Court ruled in his favour. The problem had been caused by confusion over votes cast in a crucial Florida county by use of a machinated system of 'punching' the ballot paper.

In the Middle East, the second Intifada uprising against Israeli rule was sparked by a visit by Ariel Sharon to a disputed part of Jerusalem.

For the *Examiner*, a change of title saw the newspaper renamed as the *Irish Examiner*.

George Bush is president

Thursday, December 14

George W Bush finally emerged triumphant from the United States' epic presidential battle yesterday. Thirty-six days after a historically close election, Mr Bush was at last given the all-clear to become the 43rd American president after his Democratic rival Al Gore admitted defeat and wound up his efforts to contest the result. The dramatic end came in the shape of a ruling from the US Supreme Court which ended Mr Gore's hopes of restarting manual recounts of ballots in Florida.

George Bush.

The Gore camp accepted the Supreme Court ruling only reluctantly and yesterday many Democrats attacked the court – traditionally seen as above politics – in fiercely partisan terms.

Mr Bush now faces an uphill battle to establish his presidency as legitimate. Mr Gore actually won 337,000 more votes across the US out of 103 million cast.

Monday, September 12: The Cats got their claws into Offaly yesterday by singing altered words to Robbie Williams' latest hit single after winning the Guinness All-Ireland hurling final. Victorious Kilkenny fans made his chart hit their new anthem and chanted the words "You're never going to rock DJ" throughout the city last night as they toasted the first All-Ireland winning hurling team of the new millennium.

NEWS BRIEFS

Feb British doctor Harold Shipman got 15 life sentences after being found guilty of murdering 15 of his patients, including Marie Quinn from Tipperary. Shipman, Britain's most prolific serial killer, was estimated to have killed over 200 people by injecting them with lethal drugs. (1)

Apr Westlife continue Ireland's reputation as a major contributor to the boy-band phenomenon in pop music when they achieve their fifth consecutive number one hit in the UK singles charts with 'Fool Again'.

Sept Dublin bus driver Gerry O'Grady became the first person in Ireland to be convicted under incitement to hatred legislation. O'Grady had made racist remarks against a Gambian man getting on the bus he was driving. (22)

Nov Eddie Ryan, 41, was gunned down in a gangland-style shooting in the Moose bar in Limerick. The killing was to be a taste of things to come in the city as rival families continued a vicious feud. (12)

The Examiner

01.01.2000

The dawn of a new millennium

Let an age of great hope begin

THE dawning of a new Millennium is a time for reflection, a time for assessing the defining moments and the social, political, cultural and economic issues, which shape Ireland 2000.

It is also a time for looking forward, a time for dreaming new dreams and for creating new visions to inspire future generations.

In the Ireland of this truly historic day, contradictions abound and change is happening at bewildering pace. The economy tops the EU league and 20 years from now we will be among Europe's richest people.

But a major dilemma yet to be addressed is how we will include people who are excluded from the nation's wealth in an unequal and divided society scarred by poverty, loneliness and alienation manifested in the soaring rate of suicide among young people.

At the same time we are witnessing unprecedented economic growth and the creation of an elite super-rich.

But this brings its own price and lifestyles will change dramatically. Already, life has become more stressful and pressurised. People are struggling to come to terms with change as old certainties are swept away, and traditional family life is sacrificed in the rush for higher incomes and wealth.

To meet soaring mortgage payments, couples are double jobbing, with worrying consequences for a generation of children reared largely by non-family minders.

Traffic gridlock is a high-stress ingredient of daily life in Dublin and its hinterland on the East coast. As property costs soar, people are forced to look for homes at prices they can afford in outlying counties, effectively generating a new breed of commuters — and that unwelcome phenomenon, road rage.

Few local authorities have grappled with problems of traffic congestion or created an environment where people can live, work and play without having to spend half their lives commuting. Developers turn scenic rural areas into holiday reservations, peopled by outsiders in summer and emptied of life in winter.

Growing competition in a market place plagued by manpower and skills shortages will have profound implications. The notion of a job for life has become a relic of a more certain age.

Controversy surrounds the genetic revolution with protests against trials on Irish farms. Pollution of rivers and waterways grows worse by the day. Global warming and changing weather patterns threaten coastal regions.

Forty years ago the 60s ushered in a sense of promise following the dark days of the 50s. Symbolically President John F Kennedy became a beacon of youth and vitality for a nation emerging after decades of economic stagnation, a period in which Ireland's ability to cope with independence was severely tested.

As farm prices fell, imports increased, foreign borrowing grew, unemployment soared, and young people left in droves for America, England and Australia, a telling barometer of the nation's economic health.

If Independence was the cornerstone of modern Ireland, joining the European Economic Community in 1973 was a major landmark in our development. The expansion of the Irish consciousness to embrace the European ideal was truly remarkable. Across the diaspora, from San Francisco to Sydney, Irish people are discovering a new sense of identity, a cultural revival visible in a confident resurgence of dance and an outflow of Irish poetry, literature and dance.

For generations, perennial concerns had focused on emigration, the cultural and political identity of the Irish people, and relations with Northern Ireland. Crucially, under the guiding hands of Seán Lemass and Ken Whitacker, the foundations of a fledgling economy laid in the 60s, paved the way for today's undreamed of growth levels. By the early 90s, spending cuts, hair-shirt policies, falling oil prices, and a stream of cash from Brussels, economic prosperity and confidence in the country's future had revived. With affluence came profound social and cultural change. As curtains were drawn in the valley of the squinting windows, people increasingly questioned fundamental tenets of religious and social teaching.

The Examiner

Established 1841

IN RECENT times the ethos of society has been transformed. Battles against contraception and divorce were lost by the Catholic church and a bitter abortion debate is looming. Rocked to the core by scandals over sex and child abuse, vocations dwindle and the authority of the institution of the church diminishes apace.

In contrast with the idealism and integrity which had characterised the founding fathers of the State, today's crop of politicians are held in low esteem by a jaundiced electorate. Epitomising their fall from grace, ex-Taoiseach Charles Haughey stands humiliated, a "kept man" whose Charvet shirts and princely lifestyle were bank-rolled by wealthy businessmen and unsuspecting taxpayers. Restoring public confidence is a major challenge facing politicians.

As the new century opens, tribunals will continue to probe allegations of bribery and fraud at the highest level. Major banks and their customers have been found guilty of tax evasion on a massive scale. Against this bleak background, a ray of hope for a better future is shining in the North. After 30 years of bloody warfare and mayhem, radical new concepts of rapprochement, partnership, equality and mutual respect are the building blocks of a new and durable peace. As the Republic's relationship with Britain changes, the challenge facing Belfast, Dublin and London will be to steer the peace train through minefields planted by lunatic fringe republican and loyalist terrorists. We pray there will be no more Omaghs or Warringtons, Bloody Sundays, Enniskillens or Greysteeles.

As the new Millennium begins, we ask what has been achieved in the North? Was it worth the deaths of 3,637 men, women and children? The answer is a resounding NO.

And yet, hopefully, with the IRA poised to decommission weapons, a new and lasting peace is tantalisingly within our grasp, a phenomenal development which few believed would happen in their lifetime.

In the pages of time, the names of peacemakers are etched — former Taoiseach Albert Reynolds, Sinn Féin leader Gerry Adams, Unionist leader David Trimble, Taoiseach Bertie Ahern, British Prime Minister Tony Blair, US President Bill Clinton and former Senator George Mitchell. But when historians look back, the influence of Nobel Peace prize winner John Hume will stand out.

If the Lemass era was the springboard for our new-found prosperity, how we manage our thriving economy will be the biggest challenge of the Millennium. What we do with our new wealth will have a decisive influence on the shape of the new Ireland.

Information technology is transforming the face of industry. We are moving from traditional manufacturing to new home-grown products making Ireland the world's second largest exporter of computer software.

Inevitably, the demands for skills means many low-wage workers, poorly-educated and unemployable, will be trapped on the margins. The risk is that companies and not people will reap the benefits. Arguably, too much of Ireland's industry is foreign-owned and increasingly mobile. If America sneezes, we will catch the 'flu.

WILL the bubble burst? Some economists predict a stock market crash on Wall Street would send shock waves through an economy heavily based on US companies. Inexorably, as Brussels turns off the tap and EU grant aid dries up, farming as a way of life will also change utterly. Traditional communities are dying. Farmers will depend on off-farm activities for survival.

Around the world, a legacy of failed leadership and lack of vision have caused enormous imbalances. Side-by-side with vast economic wealth, starvation and illiteracy are spreading.

Globalisation dominates world trade. With the cohesiveness of society threatened by monopolies wielding power greater than nations, protests like the wrecking of the world trade organisation summit in Seattle will become commonplace.

Across the Millennium will fall the cloned shadow of Dolly the sheep. Advances in medicine will prolong life. Computers will rule our lives.

As we cross the threshold it is moot whether the Irish people will remain inward-looking and insular or adopt the role of keeper of the moral conscience in a materialistic world.

Hopefully, we will be less enthralled by the trappings of history which have haunted our past and more concerned with making choices, realising unprecedented opportunities for progress and fulfilling the promise which will shape the future Ireland.

2001

On September 11, 2001, two hijacked planes crashed into the twin towers of the World Trade Centre in New York, causing both buildings to collapse. Another plane ploughed into the Pentagon in Washington, while a fourth crashed in Pennsylvania. Approximately 3,000 people died in the attacks, including at least four Irish citizens.

September 11 was widely believed to be the work of Al-Qaida, an Islamic fundamentalist group headed by Osama Bin Laden. US president George Bush promised that a new 'war on terror' would be undertaken. US and British forces attacked Afghanistan in October in an attempt to get Bin Laden and topple the Taliban government which had sheltered him. By the end of the year, the US, with the help of local militias, had removed the Taliban in a war that also claimed thousands of civilian lives. Bin Laden escaped and was believed to be hiding in Pakistan.

Chaos in New York

Wednesday, September 12

New Yorkers stood and cried. A cloud of choking black ash and smoke smothered lower Manhattan and left unsuspecting early morning workers devastated. Workers, reporters and camera men ran for their lives as the first of the 120-storey towers crashed to the ground.

Thousands of emergency workers were trapped trying to save the lives of others. Over 20,000 people ran terrified for safety. "I just can't explain what happened. I saw people hanging from railings hundreds of feet up in the sky. Then, amazingly some took their own lives and jumped," Ed Risdeol from Staten Island said. He was smothered in volcanic-like ash as he spoke to reporters. "Why do this to innocent people?" he said, tears filling his eyes.

Distraught parents and children, on their way to the Holycross school in the Ardoyne area of Belfast, flee after a blast bomb thrown by loyalist paramilitaries exploded near them.

Cruel twist leaves family reeling

Thursday, September 13

Ronnie Clifford ran for his life from the World Trade Centre as it was hit by a hijacked plane, but the Irishman's relief was shortlived – his sister and niece were on board the stricken plane.

Yesterday the Cliffords were devastated as they tried to come to terms with the death of Ruth McCourt and her four-year-old daughter Juliana.

John and Mark Clifford reached out to comfort each other as they spoke of their beloved sister and her daughter, killed when their plane from Boston to LA was hijacked by terrorists on Tuesday. Their brother, Ronnie, had just walked through the doors of the Twin Towers for a meeting when the plane carrying his sister and niece slammed into the building. Although the woman behind him was killed, Ronnie, 47, escaped unscathed but traumatised.

"It just seems so terribly ironic that someone could leave one part of the States and the other could be in a completely different part, and they could both get caught in the same awful tragedy," Mark Clifford said yesterday.

"Ronnie had just walked into the building when the explosion happened. The woman who was just behind him got caught and was horribly burned. Ronnie went to help her and then there was a second explosion. Some people came along and ran with him and her and got them out of the building, but she subsequently died," John said.

Muslims under seige as Irish backlash begins

Saturday, September 15

Irish Muslims are being bombarded with racist insults and in some cases physically assaulted in a backlash over the slaughter in America. In Northern Ireland, a mosque in Belfast came under attack yesterday when youths threw stones at the building, but no-one was injured.

Islamic leaders say the attackers do not seem to realise that hundreds of Muslims may have died in the World Trade Centre. Fazel Ryklief of the Islamic Foundation of Ireland said that since the tragedy on Tuesday the Islamic centre has been inundated with racist and abusive phone calls. He has also had reports of assaults of Muslims: "In one case an 11-year-old boy was beaten up by kids over what happened in the US."

NEWS BRIEFS

Jan Fianna Fáil TD Liam Lawlor was sentenced to three months in prison for contempt, when he defied court orders to provide details of his financial affairs to the Flood Tribunal into corruption in land planning in Dublin. The same tribunal would later find that former government minister Ray Burke had received corrupt payments from property developers. (16)

Dec The bodies of eight refugees, including three children, were found in a container in Wexford. Originally from Turkey, they had been smuggled to Ireland from Belgium. (8)

The Fellowship of the Ring, the first part of a film adaptation of JRR Tolkien's book *The Lord of the Rings*, was released. (19)

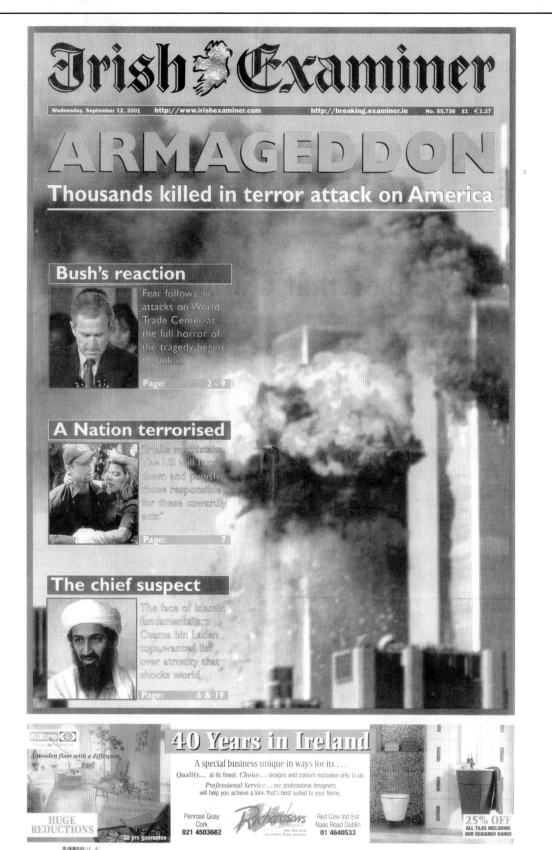

Irish Examiner

Wednesday, September 12, 2001 http://www.irishexaminer.com http://breaking.examiner.ie No. 55,736 £1 €1.27

ARMAGEDDON

2

Thousands killed in terror attack on America

Bush's reaction

Fear follows air attacks on World Trade Center as the full horror of the tragedy begins to sink in

Page: 2 - 9

A Nation terrorised

"Make no mistake. The US will hunt down and punish those responsible for these cowardly acts"

Page: 7

The chief suspect

The face of Islamic fundamentalism Osama bin Laden tops wanted list over atrocity that shocks world

Page: 6 & 19

2002

When the story began to break that Republic of Ireland soccer captain Roy Keane was leaving the team just before the World Cup, the initial reaction amongst the public was one of disbelief. Keane's performances in a qualifying campaign had been magnificent and any hopes of Irish success in Japan/South Korea seemed to rest on his shoulders.

Unfortunately, poor organisation at the team's Saipan training base and a bitter row with manager Mick McCarthy ensured that Ireland's star player flew back to his family in Manchester. While opinions differed as to who was to blame for the crisis, frantic attempts at mediation between Keane and McCarthy got nowhere.

The team did surprisingly well without Keane, being narrowly put out after a penalty shoot-out against Spain in the second round. However, in a tournament where several of the fancied nations failed to perform, Irish soccer fans were left to eternally wonder 'what if?'. A series of poor results at the end of the year forced McCarthy to retire as manager, and an independent report into the FAI would vindicate most of Keane's criticisms of the organisation.

NEWS BRIEFS

Jan Pounds and pennies are no longer in use as the euro is introduced as Ireland's currency. (1)

May The interim report of the Irish Government's task force on alcohol reported that consumption had gone up by 50% in the past six years. Assaults and public order offences doubled over the same period. (29)

Oct Seven Irish tourists were injured in a bomb detonated by Islamic fundamentalists on the Indonesian island of Bali which also killed 202 people. (12)

Limerick-born actor and rugby supporter Richard Harris died, aged 72. (25)

Protest marchers back Roy

Wednesday, May 29

As the Saipan One was circulating his final statement to the world media, 2,000 men, women and children marched through the streets of Cork city last night chanting "We want Roy!".

In a staggering display of support for the embattled sporting hero, the citizens of Cork turned out in surprising force, not knowing that as they marched through Patrick Street, Roy Keane had already made his decision not to rejoin the World Cup squad.

As the march wound its way from the top of Patrick Street to Bishop Lucey Park, car horns blared and pedestrians stood, watched and clapped their hands in support for the gathering.

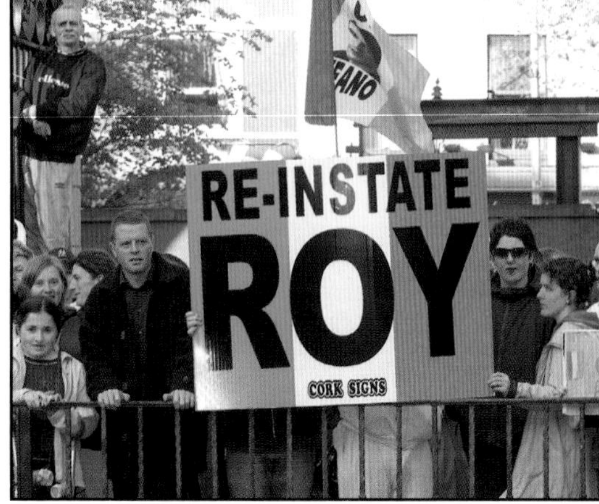

Protestors in Cork make it clear whose side they are on in the row between Roy Keane and Mick McCarthy.

The passing of John B Keane

Friday, May 31

John B Keane was one of Ireland's major and most prolific literary figures in the second half of the 20th century, a playwright, poet, novelist, essayist and ballad-maker.

It has often been said there isn't a home in the country without a Keane book and there's scarcely a parish hall that hasn't staged at least one of his plays.

John B Keane.

Keane had the gift of touching ordinary people, who greatly loved him and his work. He had a quick temper but he also had the ability to make up just as quickly and could be amazingly tender and generous.

"I started writing out of a sense of desperation," he revealed on one occasion. "And if I hadn't become a writer, I'd be in jail somewhere. I'd have gone stone, stone mad. Or rather, if I hadn't met my wife I'd have gone mad. I'd be up to every mischief."

A controversial man who despised pomp and hypocrisy, he had the courage to tackle taboo subjects such as sexuality and clerical power, as well as greed and violence.

Since 1994, he suffered from prostate cancer but, typically, battled against the disease. During his painful illness, his thoughts sometimes turned to death, but he said his attitude towards death had not changed.

"I always felt I would be able to cope when it came. I'm a religious person and I have lived a very happy and contented life," he noted.

World Cup Crisis

News: 6, 7, 8, 9, 16 & 17 Sport: 19, 20, 21 & 22

Irish Examiner

Friday, May 24, 2002 http://www.irishexaminer.com http://breaking.examiner.ie No. 55,949 €1.30

They think it's all over ... it is now

"I love playing for my country but my sanity's more important"

Down and out: Roy Keane training in Saipan before his final bust-up with Mick McCarthy. His international career came to an end as it had endured: with drama, intrigue and suspense. Picture: Inpho

by **Bill George**
Saipan

ROY KEANE was scheduled to fly out of Saipan in the early hours of this morning, leaving Ireland's World Cup dreams in tatters and the country asking: who was right — Mick McCarthy or the Irish captain?

Keane's international career came to an end as it had endured: with drama, intrigue and suspense.

His club, Manchester United, is understood to have chartered a private plane from Tokyo to collect Keane and take him to an unknown destination to be reunited with his family.

The Football Association of Ireland, new Irish captain Steve Staunton and all the Irish squad backed the Ireland manager, while several former Irish footballers, including the Irish captain in the 1994 World Cup, Andy Townsend, backed Roy Keane.

Almost 10,000 people phoned the Marian Finucane show in one hour — even before Keane's shock departure from Saipan. An overwhelming 86% sided with Keane, who less than an hour later was sent home.

Prior to his axing by Mick McCarthy, Keane spoke to reporters about his decision to retire from international football after the World Cup: "I love playing for my country but my sanity's more important.

"I had no intentions of quitting. I do love the 90 minutes, it's the rest of the crap.

"I travel a lot, I have four kids. I miss them. Everyone is different. All I can do is look after me and my family. The European Championships would have been my swansong. It's just come early.

"You've seen the training pitch and I'm not being a prima donna. Training pitch, travel arrangements, getting through the bloody airport when we were leaving, it's the combination of things ... enough is enough.

"You wonder why players get injured? Well, playing on a surface like that. One or two of the lads have picked up injuries. I'm amazed there hasn't been more, but give it time. But you know, we're the Irish team, it's a laugh and a joke."

McCarthy called a clear-the-air meeting with the players, where Keane — asked for his opinion as captain — launched into foul-mouthed abuse of the manager.

McCarthy, himself an uncompromising, emotive character who has had a difficult relationship with Keane from the outset, had enough. Describing Keane as a "disruptive influence" he said: "I have made the right decision not only for the benefit of me but for the squad. I cannot and will not tolerate being spoken to with that level of abuse being thrown at me so I sent him home.

"There has been an uneasy feeling around the place for a few days. I was asked today for my comments about remarks he made in a newspaper article and I don't want to be doing that throughout the World Cup because doing tit-for-tat in the media is not my way.

"I called a meeting at 7.30pm (10.30am Irish time). I got everyone together because I felt it was important to air any grievances among the players or staff.

"I asked anybody to make their comments and unfortunately it became a slanging match. We all know his ability but when he makes a public and open show of his opinions and makes such public criticisms everybody starts talking about it.

"He is one of the best players in the world but he is a disruptive influence. I asked him as captain to give his opinions and I was prepared to be reasonable and rational. I know this is one of the biggest stories of the World Cup and it is my decision and I stand by it 100%.

"You don't see too many complaints from anyone else here. But sometimes Roy sees the world through his eyes only.

"I did it with the best interests of the team at heart when I said he should go home.

"I am tired of it. When he wanted to go home the other day he said it was for personal reasons. I said 'Is it me? Is it the training ground? Is it the flight? Is it the media circus at the airport?'

"But he just said 'It's none of these, it's personal, it's me, it's me'."

"All the players here have had a great time relaxing but maybe Roy has missed the point.

"This is a weight off my mind. I came here to enjoy the World Cup and I was stopping enjoying it. But from tomorrow I am going to start enjoying it again.

"As a player, a coach, and a person I will not tolerate the things he said to me. This is a huge decision but I am happy to go to the World Cup one man down rather than with a man who shows utter disregard and disrespect for me."

Former players were as divided as people throughout the country.

"If Roy was beginning to criticise everything he (McCarthy) did then he had to do something," Frank Stapleton said. "The good of the team is more important than one individual. I think it will be a major disappointment to Roy when he looks back."

Tony Cascarino said the FAI had taken the right decision but added that problems with organisation and facilities had occurred before.

"The problem seems to be that there's been some opinions between Mick and Roy. They're both stubborn men. It's probably the best solution. It's not good having an unhappy camp this close to the tournament. Unfortunately, Roy's our best player."

Ray Houghton said Keane was within his rights as the team's captain to demand the best for his team-mates.

"Roy was standing up for the whole side. This was about the lads and their preparations for the World Cup.

"If the facilities — the pitch, buildings, equipment — are not up to scratch, he has a right to complain about them. The quality of the facilities during my career did bother me in some respects. We would not necessarily go by the cheapest method but, if you like, the easiest way."

Football commentator Eamon Dunphy, who is Keane's official biographer, said McCarthy had made "a monumental blunder".

ForRoy

"Let's get this straight — Roy was right in every single thing he said about facilities. The FAI is an embarrassment, it is not acceptable that can happen."

Andy Townsend — 19

AgainstRoy

"When Roy sits down and thinks about what he's done he will have a few regrets. It upsets me that this should have happened but we'll have to get through it."

Jack Charlton — 21

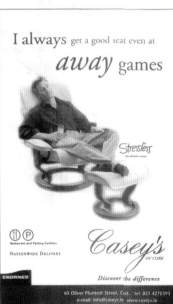

2003

For the first few months of the year, the news was dominated by the build-up to the war in Iraq. The United States and Britain pushed their case for the war, quoting intelligence reports that Iraq was planning to use weapons of mass destruction, and also hinting at links between Saddam Hussein's regime and Al-Qaida.

Many opponents of the war believed it was motivated by a desire to gain control of Iraq's huge oil reserves. In one of the biggest demonstrations in living memory in Ireland, 100,000 people in Dublin marched in protest against US plans.

While the Irish government claimed it was opposed to the war, US forces were allowed to use facilities at Shannon airport.

In Limerick, a simmering feud between two gangs escalated into a series of armed attacks and several murders. One of the most mysterious events occurred with the disappearance of Kieran and Eddie Ryan. Presumed kidnapped, a huge search got underway for the brothers. When they showed up, they refused to divulge details of what had happened to them.

Miss World, Rosanna Davison.

Limerick gang feuds escalate

Wednesday, January 29

Crime gangs in Limerick battling each other to gain control of the drugs trade in the mid-west region are among the most organised and well armed criminals in the country.

Gardaí have seized dozens of sawn-off shotguns and rounds of ammunition as part of their investigations into the gangs. The criminals also have powerful handguns and machine guns. The feud primarily involves four families from the city's north side and has resulted in a spate of shootings over the past three years.

The latest phase of the dispute was sparked two years ago when two teenage girls fought in a disco. The girls were part of two families that had been involved in the feud for decades. Another fight between the girls in a field the following day culminated in one of them biting the other's ear off.

It is believed that some days later the injured girl's family captured the other girl's mother and marked the letter 'S' on her face with a knife. The families started wearing bullet proof vests that were ordered over the internet.

Kieran Ryan (white top) celebrates his release with his friends and cousins at home in Killeely, Limerick.

Dolly's demise sparks fears over cloning

Saturday, February 15

The death of Dolly the sheep, the first animal to be cloned from an adult cell, sparked renewed fears over the safety of cloning techniques last night.

The Roslin Institute announced the decision was taken to 'put down' six-year-old Dolly after a veterinary examination showed she had a progressive lung disease.

Dolly was cloned from the breast cell of a six-year-old adult ewe and born on July 5, 1996, at the Roslin Institute in Scotland. Her birth was only announced seven months later and was heralded as one of the most significant scientific breakthroughs of the decade.

Religious sect Clonaid has claimed to have cloned three human babies in the last six weeks but the scientific world remains unconvinced.

Expert on the ethics of human cloning, Dr Patrick Dixon, said: "The greatest worry many scientists have is that human clones will need hip replacements in their teenage years and perhaps develop senile dementia by their 20th birthday."

NEWS BRIEFS

Feb An outbreak of Severe Acute Respiratory Syndrome (SARS), a form of pneumonia which kills 10% of infected people, spread from China to Singapore and several other countries around the world, causing 775 deaths and restrictions on travel from affected areas.

June The Special Olympics for people with a learning disability opened in Croke Park, Dublin, before a crowd of 75,000 people. Around 7,000 athletes competed in the event. (20)

Dec Rosanna Davison, daughter of pop singer Chris de Burgh, became Ireland's first winner of the Miss World competition. (7)

Former Iraqi leader Saddam Hussein was captured near his home town of Tikrit. (15)

Irish Examiner

Biting criticism
Time to review the powerful influence of negative press

Weekend

Celtic Xena
Documentary set to tackle Irish pirate queen

News: 4

Fully focused
Ireland taking nothing for granted

Sport: 19-21

Saturday, March 22, 2003 | http://www.irishexaminer.com | No. 56,206 €1.45

Death and destruction

Mass destruction: Smoke covers the presidential palace in Baghdad yesterday during a US-led air raid on the Iraqi capital. Smoke billowed from a number of targeted sites, including one of Saddam Hussein's palaces. Picture: Ramzi Haidar

Baghdad ablaze as 'shock and awe' begins

by Brian Carroll

MUSHROOM clouds plumed into the skies over Baghdad last night as hundreds of cruise missiles and bombs rained down upon Iraq's capital.

In a night of mass destruction, the US and allied forces pummelled Baghdad with a deadly array of weaponry.

Ground troops could storm Baghdad in a matter of days after the US 3rd Infantry Division advanced within 200 miles of the Iraqi capital.

Late last night leading elements of a coalition armoured column were at the gates of Basra, Iraq's second city. There were sporadic reports of the city having fallen, but none of these were confirmed.

Big explosions were also heard around the city of Kirkuk in the north, and anti-aircraft guns peppered the skies over Mosul.

In a day of swift developments, US and British marines captured the Iraqi port of Umm Qasr while troops also seized two airfields in the Iraqi desert 140 and 180 miles (225km and 290km) west of the capital, part of a move to encircle Baghdad.

Fires raged across the Iraqi capital, with President Saddam Hussein's "Old Palace" compound, the main seat of government, among the targets hit at the start of "A-Day" — marking the beginning of the air war. There were reports that the Old Palace was hit by a dozen bombs.

As a huge fire raged in the south of the city, the US military said last night up to 1,000 targets would be attacked during the course of the night.

During the bombing in Baghdad, the district housing and information ministries and Iraqi television stations were among those hit, but state television remained on air.

In a lull after the first blitz, the station broadcast footage showing Saddam and his son Qusay, but it was unclear when the footage was shot. There were persistent reports that Saddam was injured or killed in Wednesday night's raid on Iraq.

The US Navy launched some 320 Tomahawk cruise missiles — each one costing US$1m — from ships in the Gulf and the Red Sea into Baghdad, senior US officials said.

RAF fighters and Royal Navy submarines firing cruise missiles were also involved alongside US warships and warplanes.

The bombing began shortly after 1700GMT and reached a first dramatic crescendo in Baghdad around an hour later when strike after strike was caught by live television lighting up the capital's skyline. The assault raged as the US said coalition forces had pushed 100 miles into Iraq, one-third of the way toward the Iraqi capital.

America unleashed its promised war of "shock and awe" with a massive aerial bombardment into Iraq that aimed to destroy 1,000 sites.

There were no indications last night of the amount of deaths caused but in a city with a population of five million, hundreds of casualties were expected.

Baghdad was bombarded in an assault intended to paralyse the Iraqi military and force Saddam into submission.

US Defence Secretary Donald Rumsfeld said the air attacks would be of a "scope and scale which made it clear to Iraqis that Saddam and his regime were finished".

"They are beginning to realise, I suspect, that the regime is history and as that realisation sets in their behaviour is likely to begin to tip and to change.

"Those close to Saddam Hussein will likely begin searching for a way to save themselves," Mr Rumsfeld said.

Iraqi troops were reported to be surrendering across the country in "significant numbers" as US and British armoured columns punched deep into Iraq.

Reports that senior Iraqi military officials were in talks about surrender were dismissed last night by Iraqi officials. A spokesman defiantly rejected talks of surrender and called US President George W Bush and British Prime Minister Tony Blair "criminals".

War in Iraq: Pages 7 to 11
Opinion: Page 16. Analysis: Page 17

2004

When reports first began filtering through of an earthquake and resultant tsunami waves causing a large amount of deaths in Asia, people in Ireland were shocked to read of over 11,000 casualties. Over the next few weeks, the official death toll would rise to over 280,000, making it the worst natural disaster in living memory. The waves mostly claimed the lives of coastal dwellers in countries such as Indonesia and Sri Lanka, but a number of Irish tourists were also killed.

When bombs exploded in Madrid in March, killing 191 people, the Spanish government was quick to point the finger at ETA, the Basque nationalist group. The *Examiner* stuck its neck out with a headline blaming Al-Qaida, but was shown to be correct as more details about the attacks began to emerge.

In Ireland, a constitutional referendum to remove the automatic right of citizenship for people born in the country was carried by a huge majority. The government had said it was trying to remove 'citizenship tourism' where pregnant female asylum seekers from outside the EU targeted Ireland. Opponents accused the government of exaggerating the amount of non-national births in the country.

Martin wins clash of the ash

Tuesday, March 30

March 29, 2004, was by any measure a momentous day for Irish society when the country's most radical social experiment forced hundreds of thousands of people to smoke on the street. But they gathered in the open not to protest or to march on Leinster House but to meekly accept – with surprising good humour in most cases – the tough medicine meted out to them by Health Minister Micheál Martin. And in doing so we witnessed the landscape of Ireland changing forever within the space of 24 hours.

Health Minister Micheál Martin at Maguires Pub in Baggot Street, Dublin with publican Ted O'Sullivan and Maureen Mulvihill, Irish Heart Foundation.

Walking through Dublin was a strange experience yesterday. The streets bustled like the overcrowded cities of India with people standing in smoky huddles that grew larger as the evening wore on. What they were doing (smoking) was what they were talking about. For once, descriptions of the capital as the Big Smoke achieved a literal accuracy.

There was the carping you would expect from first-day stuff. Pubs reported drops in business. There were a couple of isolated reports of rebellions in smaller country pubs. Militant smokers mumbled about the 'nanny state'.

But, anecdotally at least, the widespread public backing predicted by Health Minister Micheál Martin materialised. Even hardened smokers were largely positive, perhaps temporarily beguiled by the novelty aspect of it. How long that will last is anyone's guess. – Harry McGee

The best country to live in

Wednesday, November 17

It might not be the cheapest, but Ireland is the best place in the world to live, according to a life satisfaction survey by *The Economist* magazine. We beat the Americans, the Swiss and the British, among others, in the study of living conditions in 111 countries.

The factors used to decide a country's score were: income, health, freedom, employment, family life, climate, political stability and security, gender equality, and family and community life.

The survey tracked the Celtic Tiger, showing that in 1987 Irish GDP per person was 69% of the EU average, and by 2003 it was 136%. Unemployment fell from 17% in 1987 to 4% in 2003 and Government debt shrank from 112% of GDP to 33%.

NEWS BRIEFS

Apr The trial of Circuit Court judge Brian Curtin on charges of possessing child pornography collapsed in Tralee when the court found that Gardaí had used an out-of-date warrant to search Curtin's house. (23)

Sept Chechen separatists seized hundreds of hostages at a school in Beslan, Russia. As police tried to free the hostages, at least 334 people – most of them children – were killed.

Nov Yasser Arafat, the guerrilla icon turned Nobel Peace Prize winner who ended up isolated and locked in renewed conflict with Israel, died yesterday, his dream of a Palestinian state unfulfilled. He was 75. (12)

Amidst growing insurrection against foreign forces and the US-installed government in Iraq, Irish aid worker Margaret Hassan became the latest Western kidnap victim to be executed.

Dec Police believe the IRA are behind the £22 million robbery from Northern Bank Headquarters in Belfast. (20)

Irish Examiner
2004 Year in review – January to March
From Ian Bailey's libel case to the Madrid bombings
News Review: 12-15
Fergie fury
United boss brands Fulham star Haim a disgrace
Sport: 20
Tuesday, December 28, 2004
www.irishexaminer.com
No. 56,752 €1.50 / Stg £1.00

God, God, God... why, why, why?

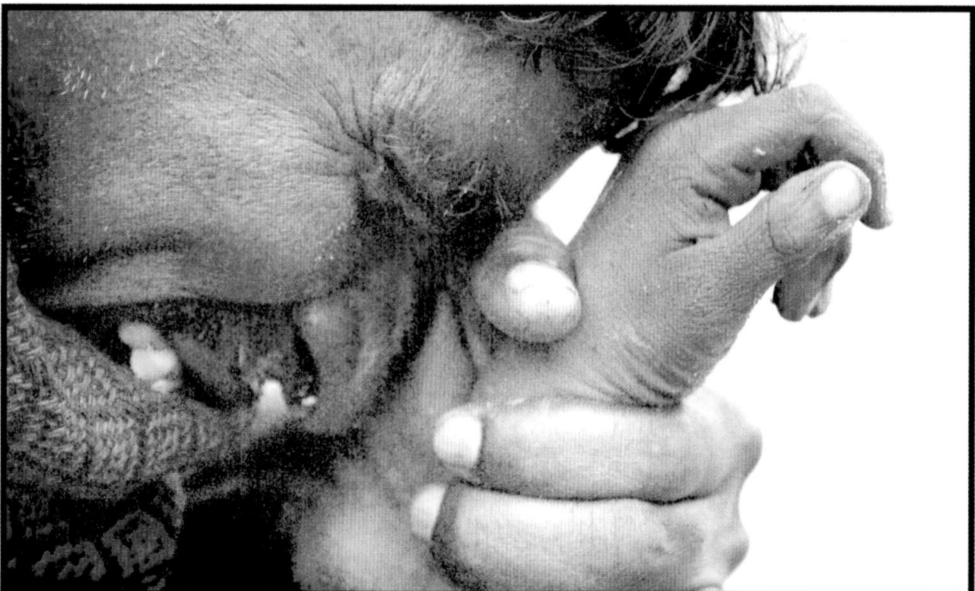

An Indian man cries as he holds the hand of his eight-year-old son killed in a tsunami in Cuddalore, 180km south of the Indian city of Madras. About half the 400 dead in the town were children.

Picture: Reuters

by S Srinivasan
Cuddalore, India

AFTER the couple had laid the body of their daughter in a deep pit, a bulldozer poured sand and the little girl disappeared from their view forever.

Then they were asked to move aside and make way for the others who had their own loved ones to bury, denied any chance for a service or private mourning.

In a scene repeated dozens of times, weeping and red-eyed parents held a mass burial yesterday for more than 150 children who died in the killer tidal wave that battered India's south-eastern coast.

About half of the nearly 400 people who perished in Cuddalore in Tamil Nadu state were children, leaving the town of 100,000 people in stunned bereavement.

According to Hindu tradition, children are not cremated like adults but buried. For the grim task, two pits, together the size of half a basketball court, were dug near the banks of Pennai river on the edge of this coconut palm-fringed town.

Most of the children, who were aged between five and 12, were buried as they were found — in their Sunday clothes without even the luxury of a shroud. The district administration was eager to get the burial — and the cremation of adults — over quickly so that they could turn their attention to providing relief for the survivors.

"There will be a time for crying, but that will come later. Now the priority is to shelter those who survived," said fisherman Akilan, 28, who lost two nephews when the waves struck their seaside house. Akilan uses only one name.

A mile away at the town morgue, bodies of young and old lay unclaimed, awaiting identification by relatives. They were called in one by one by doctors on a public address system.

Many people came out of the morgue shaking their heads in silence. Once in a while, a heart-rending cry would pierce the buzz of conversation.

As a small body was lowered from a morgue van to a bed, a man cried out: "My son, my king."

Venkatesh, 37, wept inconsolably as he identified 11-year-old Suman.

Venkatesh was in Dubai when he got a call from his wife in Cuddalore that their boy was missing in the tsunami.

He flew out of Dubai immediately and reached Cuddalore yesterday morning, heading straight to the morgue where he was united with his wife and daughter minutes before Suman's body was brought in. A few moments later an identification tag was tied to the boy's hand and the body taken inside the morgue for paper work before being handed over to the parents.

Venkatesh's cries were drowned out as more parents surged forward.

Similar scenes of grief and despair were unfolding all round the devastated continent.

In Galle, Sri Lanka, where the earthquake has claimed 12,000 lives, the corridors of the hospital were lined with bloated bodies.

"We have had over 950 bodies here so far and they are still coming in," said hospital administrator Dr Jayaratne.

Desperately anxious Sri Lankans tip-toed around the dead, looking for their loved ones.

One woman collapsed as she found the body of her five-year-old daughter, her tiny body bruised all over and her face locked in a grimace.

"God! God! God! Why? Why? Why?" she wailed, tearing at her hair.

QUAKE DISASTER

THE streets of Banda Aceh are filled with overturned cars and the rotting corpses of adults and children.
World: 6

WAILING relatives scrambled over hundreds of bodies piled in a Sri Lankan hospital yesterday, searching for loved ones.
World: 7

INDIANS scattered flower petals at sea and sacrificed chickens to pray for the safe return of those carried away in a tsunami.
World: 8/9

AS the death toll in South East Asia continued to rise yesterday, the international community began to absorb the extent of what may be the worst natural disaster in recent history and began reacting accordingly.
Editorial: 16

THE colossal scale of the earthquake which devastated much of southern Asia was more powerful than all the world's earthquakes of the past five years put together.
Analysis: 17

Battered nations struggle as tsunami death toll continues to rise

by Dilip Ganguly
Colombo, Sri Lanka

RELIEF workers are continuing to pile up bodies along Asian coastlines, devastated by the giant waves that obliterated seaside towns and killed more than 23,700 people in nine countries.

Aid officials believe the tally will rise higher, with thousands still missing.

Foreign Affairs Minister Dermot Ahern said there were no reports of Irish fatalities. His department officials are still liaising with Asian embassies to establish the safety of about 500 Irish people resident in the disaster zones.

The scale of the devastation became a little clearer yesterday. More than 3,000 died on islands in the Bay of Bengal but the final death toll there may be 10 times higher. Sweden said 2,000 of its citizens were unaccounted for.

Hundreds of children were buried in mass graves in India as morgues and hospitals struggled to cope with the catastrophe.

Chaos erupted at airports in Thailand as tourists, many wounded and weeping, tried to board flights.

Scores died in Somalia, 2,880 miles away from the earthquake's epicentre.

Walls of water crashed into Asian shorelines, sweeping people out to sea, including a grandson of Thailand's king.

The torrents swept a six-month-old Australian baby to her death from her father's arms in the Thai island resort of Phuket.

The international Red Cross said it was concerned about waterborne diseases like malaria and cholera.

Rescuers converged on beaches and islands to search for survivors as offers of aid poured in from around the globe.

Officials in Indonesia and Thailand conceded that public warnings that could have saved lives in places further from the quake site were never issued or were too little, too late.

The true danger, officials insisted, was not known due to the absence of any international system to track tidal waves in the Indian Ocean.

In Sri Lanka, the death toll reached 13,000. Indonesia and India also each reported thousands dead, and Thailand said 1,000 were dead there. Deaths also were reported in Malaysia, Maldives, Burma, Bangladesh and in Somalia.

IRISH EXAMINER
28.12.04
Recommended retail price in Ireland €1.50
9 771393 956427 01

2005

While the true devastation of the Asian tsunami continued to be revealed, the disaster was pushed off the pages for a while in January with the disappearance of Robert Holohan. Thousands of volunteers searched for the 11-year-old from Midleton, Co Cork, until his body was found in scrubland a few miles from his home. A local youth was subsequently charged with manslaughter.

In other news, Cork began its reign as European Capital of Culture, disgraced politician Ray Burke was sent to prison and the fall-out from the previous year's Belfast bank robbery resulted in much criticism for Sinn Féin from other political parties.

Capital of Culture uncorked

Monday, January 10

Fireworks explode over Cork.

Luck shone upon Cork on Saturday as a one-day window in the weather opened up to allow the city celebrate the start of its reign as European Capital of Culture.

Cork 2005 director John Kennedy credited the divine intervention of St Finbarr, Cork's patron saint, in bringing good weather for the 85,000 who had turned out to watch the opening spectacular along the River Lee.

The day before the fireworks and outdoor carnival in the city had seen gale force winds and driving rain. And only a few hours after the ceremony the rain and wind returned. To say lucky is an understatement.

The three and a half tons of fireworks were the highlight of the evening, exploding high above the river and throwing their red, white and green lights over the entire city.

Heartbreak after the tsunami

Monday, January 3

As dawn breaks over Sri Lanka's shores, dozens of parents come to the beach where huge waves seized their children a week ago. "They believe their kids are alive and the sea will return them - one day," UNICEF chief Carol Bellamy said yesterday after touring the island's tsunami-devastated shore.

Children account for 40%, or 12,000, of Sri Lanka's total death toll of 30,000, officials say. Numerous parents have scoured some of the 800 refugee or relief centres for their missing children. Many have no evidence that they are dead. Some children were buried in mass graves without their parents' knowledge.

Day after day since the tsunami struck, parents come after daybreak and wander the beach in the devastated districts of Ampara and Batticaloa. "They don't talk to anyone. They stay for an hour or two and then go back," said N Wijewickrema, the Batticaloa police superintendent. "They return the next day," he told the UN official.

At Navalady yesterday, a few couples walked along the beach. Other people walked alone. Sometimes they knelt down, checked a slipper or shoe to make sure it didn't belong to their own children. "I have never seen a tragedy like this," Ms Bellamy said, as surviving parents waited for a miracle. "They don't want to accept their children are dead."

NEWS BRIEFS

Jan Ireland has exported over €26 billion in military-related products, documentation released to the *Examiner* reveals. (5)

The country's roads will go metric from midnight tonight. The old 33,000 speed signs are being replaced by 59,000 signs, at a cost of €9 million. (19)

ACS, a cosmetic surgery company, reported that breast augmentation was the most popular operation among the huge increase in demand for their services in Ireland over the past year. (26)

Burke sent to jail

Tuesday, January 25

Ray Burke stood up and the prison officers moved in. Judge Desmond Hogan had already handed out the six-month sentence on two counts of tax evasion, derived from legislation that he as a minister had voted for in the Dáil.

Now they started the strange procession out of the cocoon of the court and into the open, to be trapped by the searchlights of flashing cameras and the walk of shame to the prison van. This was the moment of final humiliation. The confirmation to the world that Ray Burke was no longer a citizen, a former TD, a former minister, but was now Prisoner 33791.

Irish Examiner

Friday, January 14, 2005 | www.irishexaminer.com | No. 56,768 €1.50 / Stg £1.00

The hearse carrying the remains of 11-year-old Robert Holohan arriving at Cork University Hospital. Picture: Denis Minihane

30 suspects, 1,000 queries, 100 gardaí: on a killer's trail

by Niall Murray, Sean O'Riordan, Catherine Shanahan and John Breslin

GARDAÍ hunting the killer of schoolboy Robert Houlihan are concentrating their investigations on 30 people, several of whom are known sex offenders.

The post-mortem examination on Robert's body was carried out last night by State pathologist Dr Marie Cassidy.

Gardai were unable to confirm if the schoolboy had sustained any sexual injuries or if DNA evidence had been recovered from the scene.

Neither were they able to say precisely when or how he died.

They confirmed he was fully clothed and that his mobile phone was recovered where his body was found.

They revealed the upper half of his body was covered in a plastic bag.

With earlier confirmation that he had been murdered, after being missing for nine days, investigating officers appealed to the public for specific information:

- Two men who had not signed in but had paid green fees at East Cork Golf Club on Tuesday, January 4, at about 11am.
- Two men who visited East Cork driving range on January 4 had not yet made contact with gardai.
- A well-dressed man who was spotted at Egan's Field, near Robert's home on January 4 looking out of place.
- A number of white vans, particularly one with a red stripe down the side, a black jeep and a silver/grey jeep in the area between Ballyedmond and East Cork Golf Club on January 4 between 1pm and 6pm.
- A red van or car spotted near the carpark area at the entrance to Curragh Woods on January 4.
- Anyone who had visited or walked the Inch Beach area between January 4 and when the body was found.
- They asked anyone who had a holiday home or mobile home in the area to check to see if the properties had been occupied.

In total, the garda investigation team are following 1,000 lines of inquiry.

Garda search teams, backed by troops, will this morning continue to search specific areas for clues that may lead to the identity of the killer. The searches involving 100 gardaí will be concentrated on three areas, close to where the body was found, a wider area around Whitegate and the Water Rock Golf Club near Midleton. Gardaí confirmed they had questioned a number of convicted sex offenders with what they called a "track record" since the disappearance of the 11-year-old schoolboy.

It is understood detectives spoke to more than 50 people with sex offence convictions and it is expected that officers will revisit many of these over the coming days after receiving post-mortem details.

They also confirmed they had been in contact with police forces across Europe in relation to a possible link to a international sex ring.

Assistant garda commissioner Tony Hickey admitted people in the local community were concerned at the prospect of a killer on the loose.

"Naturally there is concern. People have to be sensible at all times with children. It is important we get the perpetrator of this crime to allay that concern."

However, Mr Hickey said the murder of a child was extremely rare. In 40 years, there had only been three such cases — Mary Boyle from Donegal, Bernadette Connolly from Sligo and Phillip Cairns from Dublin.

He said it was possible Robert's killer wanted to admit his guilt and appealed for him to come forward.

The eight day search for Robert involved thousands of volunteers.

Mr Hickey said there had been grave concern for the fate of the boy because of his age, family circumstances and the fact he had not gone missing before.

He acknowledged there had been criticism of the force for publicly treating the disappearance of Robert as a missing person's inquiry for eight days.

However, he said, from day one, a parallel investigation had been set up which treated the disappearance as a homicide.

"It would be foolish, it would be idiotic for us not to strongly suspect he'd been abducted or come to his death by some type of misadventure."

He added the sensitivities of the Holohan family, who had been hoping for their son's safe return, had also been taken into account.

The family were informed of the latest developments last night by Midleton District Superintendent Liam Hayes. He said it had been very traumatic for the boy's parents, Majella and Mark.

"They're coping well, they've been advised by their doctors.

"They're going to get through it," he said.

Parents hold children close as fear grips

by Niall Murray

WORRIED parents shepparded their children to school in Midleton yesterday in the wake of Robert Holohan's murder.

Instead of dropping them near the school, as they would usually do, they instead walked them, often in silence with their arms around their shoulders, right up to the school gates, as fear spread that the killer might strike again.

The principal of Midleton CBS boys secondary school, Denis Ring, called for increased security measures for pupils as the reality of the brutal murder struck forecfully home.

"We're not too far from the day when schools are going to have to look at providing security. In other countries, security checks are the normal course for getting past school doors and gates," he said.

"Parents are going to take stock of how they allow their kids travel to and from school and social events. It's something schools are going to have to do as well, and not just in Midleton," said Mr Ring.

Earlier, Midleton CBS primary school issued a statement expressing the shock and sadness felt by pupils, staff and management at Robert's tragic death.

"He was a happy, friendly, bubbly and energetic boy who was well liked by all who knew him. He had many interests, was a keen hurler and he loved to be in the presence of animals, especially horses," the statement said.

Parents collect their children from Midleton CBS primary school yesterday. The school issued a statement expressing shock and sadness at Robert's death. Picture: Dan Linehan

Denis Ring: a depressing reality for society.

School board chairperson Canon Bertie Troy and principal Seán Ó Floinn asked for time and space to allow pupils and staff grieve and re-establish routines as quickly as possible.

"This is a very difficult time for the entire school community. A long-term plan is in place and support will be available for as long as is necessary. The school will be a support system for Robert's young friends and will ensure the pupils get all the help they need," they said. At lunchtime, groups of parents waited eagerly for younger pupils at the school to emerge from what was probably the toughest day in their lives so far.

Fr Jim Moore, chair of the CBS secondary school board of management, said there was a feeling that students genuinely wanted to pray.

"There's a sense that evil visited the place and it manifested itself in an appalling way. When something like this happens, people want to be together, talk and support each other," he said.

"But there is that fear in people, asking the greater question about how it could happen" said Fr Moore.

As a curate in the Aghada parish in which the body was found on Wednesday, he said there was a sense of unreality in the rural but close community, which is feeling very pained by what has happened.

At a packed morning Mass in the Church of the Holy Rosary in Midleton, local curate Fr Billy O'Donovan prayed for parents and children everywhere.

Last night, he said that Robert's parents, Majella and Mark, have shown remarkable strength since he had disappeared.

"They are still strong, distraught, upset, but strong. They're doing well," he said.

"Majella was down in town visiting her parents, visiting the local church this afternoon. They're aware of the enormous support and goodwill and solidarity," Fr O'Donovan added.

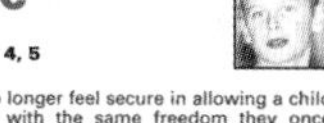

Inside

News: 2, 3, 4, 5

FAMILIES no longer feel secure in allowing a child out to play with the same freedom they once enjoyed. That sense of liberty has been callously eroded. Parents have become fearful and protective of their children. **Editorial: 16**

A SYSTEM to tag minor offenders could also track paedophiles and save children. However, the Government is slow to use it for sexual predators. **Analysis: 17**

IRISH EXAMINER

14.01.05

Recommended retail price in Ireland €1.50

9 771393 956458 03

Index